Sensor Systems for Gesture Recognition

Sensor Systems for Gesture Recognition

Editors

Giovanni Saggio
Marco E. Benalcázar

Basel • Beijing • Wuhan • Barcelona • Belgrade • Novi Sad • Cluj • Manchester

Editors
Giovanni Saggio
University of Rome "Tor Vergata"
Rome, Italy

Marco E. Benalcázar
Escuela Politécnica Nacional
Quito, Ecuador

Editorial Office
MDPI
St. Alban-Anlage 66
4052 Basel, Switzerland

This is a reprint of articles from the Special Issue published online in the open access journal *Sensors* (ISSN 1424-8220) (available at: https://www.mdpi.com/journal/sensors/special_issues/Sens_Gesture_Recognition).

For citation purposes, cite each article independently as indicated on the article page online and as indicated below:

Lastname, A.A.; Lastname, B.B. Article Title. *Journal Name* **Year**, *Volume Number*, Page Range.

ISBN 978-3-0365-8694-6 (Hbk)
ISBN 978-3-0365-8695-3 (PDF)
doi.org/10.3390/books978-3-0365-8695-3

Cover image courtesy of Giovanni Saggio

© 2023 by the authors. Articles in this book are Open Access and distributed under the Creative Commons Attribution (CC BY) license. The book as a whole is distributed by MDPI under the terms and conditions of the Creative Commons Attribution-NonCommercial-NoDerivs (CC BY-NC-ND) license.

Contents

About the Editors vii

Jorge-Luis Pérez-Medina, Santiago Villarreal and Jean Vanderdonckt
A Gesture Elicitation Study of Nose-Based Gestures
Reprinted from: *Sensors* **2020**, *20*, 7118, doi:10.3390/s20247118 1

Arman Savran and Chiara Bartolozzi
Face Pose Alignment with Event Cameras
Reprinted from: *Sensors* **2020**, *20*, 7079, doi:10.3390/s20247079 23

Imad Afyouni, Abdullah Murad and Anas Einea
Adaptive Rehabilitation Bots in Serious Games [†]
Reprinted from: *Sensors* **2020**, *20*, 7037, doi:10.3390/s20247037 47

Xin Zhang and Yang Xue
A Novel GAN-Based Synthesis Method for In-Air Handwritten Words
Reprinted from: *Sensors* **2020**, *20*, 6548, doi:10.3390/s20226548 77

Aldo-Francisco Contreras-González, Manuel Ferre, Miguel Ángel Sánchez-Urán, Francisco Javier Sáez-Sáez and Fernando Blaya Haro
Efficient Upper Limb Position Estimation Based on Angular Displacement Sensors for Wearable Devices
Reprinted from: *Sensors* **2020**, *20*, 6452, doi:10.3390/s20226452 95

Jordan J. Bird, Anikó Ekárt and Diego R. Faria
British Sign Language Recognition via Late Fusion of Computer Vision and Leap Motion with Transfer Learning to American Sign Language
Reprinted from: *Sensors* **2020**, *20*, 5151, doi:10.3390/s20185151 115

Jinkue Lee and Hoeryong Jung
TUHAD: Taekwondo Unit Technique Human Action Dataset with Key Frame-Based CNN Action Recognition
Reprinted from: *Sensors* **2020**, *20*, 4871, doi:10.3390/s20174871 135

Bruna Salles Moreira, Angelo Perkusich and Saulo O. D. Luiz
An Acoustic Sensing Gesture Recognition System Design Based on a Hidden Markov Model
Reprinted from: *Sensors* **2020**, *20*, 4803, doi:10.3390/s20174803 155

Chanhwi Lee, Jaehan Kim, Seoungbae Cho, Jinwoong Kim, Jisang Yoo and Soonchul Kwon
Development of Real-Time Hand Gesture Recognition for Tabletop Holographic Display Interaction Using Azure Kinect
Reprinted from: *Sensors* **2020**, *20*, 4566, doi:10.3390/s20164566 169

Alimed Celecia, Karla Figueiredo, Marley Vellasco and René González
A Portable Fuzzy Driver Drowsiness Estimation System
Reprinted from: *Sensors* **2020**, *20*, 4093, doi:10.3390/s20154093 183

Giovanni Saggio, Pietro Cavallo, Mariachiara Ricci, Vito Errico, Jonathan Zea and Marco E. Benalcázar
Sign Language Recognition Using Wearable Electronics: Implementing k-Nearest Neighbors with Dynamic Time Warping and Convolutional Neural Network Algorithms
Reprinted from: *Sensors* **2020**, *20*, 3879, doi:10.3390/s20143879 199

Wookhyun Park, Woong Choi, Hanjin Jo, Geonhui Lee and Jaehyo Kim
Analysis of Control Characteristics between Dominant and Non-Dominant Hands by Transient Responses of Circular Tracking Movements in 3D Virtual Reality Space
Reprinted from: *Sensors* **2020**, *20*, 3477, doi:10.3390/s20123477 213

Hwayoung Park, Changhong Youm, Myeounggon Lee, Byungjoo Noh and Sang-Myung Cheon
Turning Characteristics of the More-Affected Side in Parkinson's Disease Patients with Freezing of Gait
Reprinted from: *Sensors* **2020**, *20*, 3098, doi:10.3390/s20113098 229

Qinghua Gao, Shuo Jiang and Peter B. Shull
Simultaneous Hand Gesture Classification and Finger Angle Estimation via a Novel Dual-Output Deep Learning Model
Reprinted from: *Sensors* **2020**, *20*, 2972, doi:10.3390/s20102972 245

Myoungseok Yu, Narae Kim, Yunho Jung and Seongjoo Lee
A Frame Detection Method for Real-Time Hand Gesture Recognition Systems Using CW-Radar
Reprinted from: *Sensors* **2020**, *20*, 2321, doi:10.3390/s20082321 265

Jiuk Jang, Yoon Sun Jun, Hunkyu Seo, Moohyun Kim and Jang-Ung Park
Motion Detection Using Tactile Sensors Based on Pressure-Sensitive Transistor Arrays
Reprinted from: *Sensors* **2020**, *20*, 3624, doi:10.3390/s20133624 283

Nicolas Lemieux and Rita Noumeir
A Hierarchical Learning Approach for Human Action Recognition
Reprinted from: *Sensors* **2020**, *20*, 4946, doi:10.3390/s20174946 313

About the Editors

Giovanni Saggio

Giovanni Saggio (GS) graduated with an M.Sc. degree in Electronic Engineering from the University of Rome "Tor Vergata" in 1991, and a Ph.D. degree in Microelectronic and Telecommunication Engineering in 1996. GS is an Associate Professor with tenure at the Electronic Engineering Department of the University of Rome "Tor Vergata" and is a coordinator of the Hiteg (Health Involved Technical Engineering Group) Lab. GS participated in 15 scientific projects, being the coordinator in 10 projects, and founded 3 Spinoffs (Captiks Srl, Seeti Srl, Voicewise Srl). To date, GS has authored 9 books, authored/co-authored 255 scientific publications, and was Guest Editor for 3 Special Issues related to electronics.

Marco E. Benalcázar

Marco E. Benalcázar earned a Ph.D. in electronic engineering from the Universidad Nacional de Mar del Plata in Argentina. Currently, he is an associate professor and researcher in the Department of Informatics and Computer Science at the Escuela Politécnica Nacional of Quito, Ecuador. He is also the director of the Artificial Intelligence and Computer Vision Research Lab at the Escuela Politécnica Nacional. He has directed several research projects on the fundamentals and applications of artificial intelligence for medical image processing and hand gesture recognition. He has published more than 30 articles in scientific conferences and journals on topics related to the theory and applications of artificial intelligence and machine learning. He has 10 years of experience working in these areas. He is also a scientific disseminator and a consultant on artificial intelligence.

Article
A Gesture Elicitation Study of Nose-Based Gestures

Jorge-Luis Pérez-Medina [1,*], Santiago Villarreal [2] and Jean Vanderdonckt [2]

1. Intelligent and Interactive Systems Lab (SI^2 Lab), Universidad de Las Américas, Quito 170504, Ecuador
2. LouRIM Institute, Université Catholique de Louvain, B-1348 Louvain-la-Neuve, Belgium; santiago.villarreal@uclouvain.be (S.V.); jean.vanderdonckt@uclouvain.be (J.V.)
* Correspondence: jorge.perez.medina@udla.edu.ec; Tel.: +593-2-398-1000 (ext. 2701)

Received: 6 November 2020; Accepted: 27 November 2020; Published: 11 December 2020

Abstract: Presently, miniaturized sensors can be embedded in any small-size wearable to recognize movements on some parts of the human body. For example, an electrooculography-based sensor in smart glasses recognizes finger movements on the nose. To explore the interaction capabilities, this paper conducts a gesture elicitation study as a between-subjects experiment involving one group of 12 females and one group of 12 males, expressing their preferred nose-based gestures on 19 Internet-of-Things tasks. Based on classification criteria, the 912 elicited gestures are clustered into 53 unique gestures resulting in 23 categories, to form a taxonomy and a consensus set of 38 final gestures, providing researchers and practitioners with a larger base with six design guidelines. To test whether the measurement method impacts these results, the agreement scores and rates, computed for determining the most agreed gestures upon participants, are compared with the Condorcet and the de Borda count methods to observe that the results remain consistent, sometimes with a slightly different order. To test whether the results are sensitive to gender, inferential statistics suggest that no significant difference exists between males and females for agreement scores and rates.

Keywords: agreement rate and score; gesture elicitation study; gestural interaction; wearable sensor

1. Introduction

Sensors have become so miniaturized that they can be integrated into virtually any wearable device or everyday object, such as smart watches and glasses, thus offering new forms of interaction [1]: a sensor is able to recognize human movements performed on some dedicated parts of the human body [2–4].

One primary form of gestural interaction has recently been linked to a new source of input with myography [5]: electrooculography (EOG) sensing [6]. An electrooculogram allows the measurement of the corneo-retinal standing potential difference between the front and the back of the human eye. Electrodes are placed by pair "left/right of the eye" or "above/below the eye". When the eye moves from its central position toward one electrode, it senses the positive side of the retina while the other electrode perceives the negative side of the retina. A movement is obtained by calculating the change in position for a short duration of time.

The Itchy Nose [6] is another representative example. It embeds, in the bridge of a pair of eyeglasses, an electrooculography-based sensor. The J!NS MEME, is a wearable computer solution that detects eye and head movements. The Itchy Nose recognizes five nose-based gestures [7]: left/right flick (Figure 1a), left/right push (Figure 1b), and rub (Figure 1c). Beyond these five system-defined gestures, the vocabulary of nose-based gestures can be largely expanded by user-defined gestures [8], which has not been done so far. Since the Itchy Nose is the first system of its kind, more experimental implementations can be expected in the future.

Nose-based gestures are original as they offer unique opportunities: they are intended to be discreet, being performed without attracting the attention of the user in public [6,7], they replace gestures when all other parts of the human body are either occupied or covered, such as in cold circumstances [9] or when no device is imposed for touchless interaction [10], they serve for authentication [11], they convey emotional states [9], they operate for nose-pointing [12]. Overall, these kinds of gestures are envisioned for two interaction families:

1. Dual task interaction: a primary task is ongoing (e.g., a conversation during a meeting) and a secondary task (e.g., a phone call) occurs, potentially interrupting the primary one, and requires some discreet interaction to minimize interference with the primary task. For example, a Rubbing gesture discreetly ignores a phone call without disturbing the conversation too much. This is inspired by the dual task performance, a test for assessing the cognitive workload in psychology [13]
2. Eyes-free and/or touch-free interaction [14]: a task should be carried out by interacting with a system without requiring any visual attention and physical touch. Gestures are discreetly performed on the face, an always-accessible area in principle.

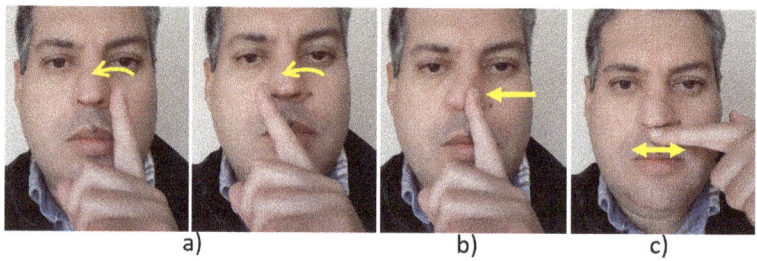

Figure 1. Examples of the ItchyNose [6,7] gestures: Flick (**a**), Push (**b**), and Rub (**c**).

This paper aims at addressing a main research question: what is the vocabulary of nose-based gestures preferred by end users for executing various actions? This main question includes two sub-questions: (1) Does the method used to measure preference impact the results or, in other words, would the vocabulary of user-defined gestures change if another measurement is performed? (2) Are these results sensitive to gender or, in other words, would male and female participants prefer nose-based gestures differently or consistently since their respective preference is subject to social acceptance? To address these questions, this paper makes the following contributions:

1. A gesture elicitation study conducted with two groups of participants, one composed of 12 females and another one with 12 males, to determine their user-defined, preferred nose-based gestures, as detected by a sensor [7], for executing Internet-of-Things (IoT) actions.
2. Based on criteria for classifying the elicited gestures, a taxonomy of gestures and a consensus set of final gestures are formed based on agreement scores and rates computed for all actions.
3. A set of design guidelines which provide researchers and practitioners with some guidance on how to design a user interface exploiting nose-based gestures.
4. A comparison of the results obtained by agreement scores and rates with respect to those obtained with two other measurement methods, i.e., the Condorcet [15] and the de Borda [16] methods.
5. An inferential statistical analysis testing the gender effect on preferred gestures.

To this end, this paper is organized as follows: Section 2 discusses the work related to nose-based interaction and gesture elicitation studies. Section 3 details the research method used in the experiment conducted. Section 4 discusses the results of this experiment by classification criteria, by agreement score and rate, and by gender. Section 6 compares the results obtained in Section 4 for preferred gestures with those obtained by two other measurement methods. Section 5 suggests a set of six design guidelines. Section 7 concludes the paper and presents some avenues to this work.

2. Related Work

This section defines some terms for facial anatomy, reviews prior works on nose-based interaction are presented, and summarizes the outcome of a GES.

Facial Anatomy. The external appearance of the nose is made up of a surface and a series of skeletal structures [17]: the root is the part located between the eyebrows, the root is connected to the rest of the nose by means of a bridge. The tip of the nose is known as the apex, the ala is a cartilaginous structure that covers the lateral side of each naris, or nostril opening, one on each side of the apex. The nostrils are surrounded by the nasal septum and the cartilaginous wings of nose. The philtrum consists of a concave surface. This connects the apex to the upper tip, a very protruding and stable point [18], and the dorsum nasi is the length of the nose.

Nose-based Interaction. Nose-based interaction appears in 1991 as a joke, it was introduced by using the pointed nose on a surface to move objects [19]. Two decades later, this hoax becomes a reality, something that was never thought by its authors. In reality, NoseDialSee https://buhmann-marketing.de/nosedial/index.html is an iOS application enabling end users to dial contacts by pointing the nose on contact targets. The software allows end users to customize the format, size and position of the contacts according to the nose anatomy. This application, unique in its style, is useful in contexts of use where there is no other pointing mechanism available, i.e., in extreme hand-busy conditions. For example, a user could avoid removing gloves to dial a person in a freezing environment. Swiping left/right scrolls among contacts, holding the nose 0.2 sec dials a contact, and double tapping returns to the initial application that was suspended after a call was answered. Similarly, the Finger-Nose stylus See https://variationsonnormal.com/2011/04/28/finger-nose-stylus-for-touchscreens/. is a funny prototypical device replacing finger touch-based gestures by nose-based gestures on a surface.

The review of the literature allows us to observe that the social acceptability of facial gestures has been the object of studies. Rico and Brewster [20] investigated the social acceptability of nose-based gestures. They found that some facial gestures are more perceived in public than others. Freeman et al. [21] reports that most preferred regions are: cheek (34%), forehead (16%), jaw (8%), apex of the nose and others like chin, ear, and temple having more or less 7%. Although the cheek received the largest percentage (34%) due to its maximal surface, the alae and philtrum were not tested, thus leaving the potential of the nose full surface unexplored. SNOUT [22] conducted a non-standard study of touch interaction using mobile devices. The study had 13 participants who performed various nose interactions. Subsequently, these interactions were compared. As a result of the survey carried out, the authors found five design guidelines for nose-based interaction. NoseTapping [9], allows end users to tap or swipe a touchscreen with their nose. With this application, a great need to use these input modalities in contextual situations was revealed. For instance, restricted user contexts, short use cases. Likewise, its impossibility was revealed in more complex functions, such as writing a message or editing content. Nose-based gestures remain an underexplored area in the field of on-skin gesture interaction, like in SkinWatch [23], Serendipity [24], and SensIR [25].

Gesture Elicitation Studies. Capturing, analyzing, and understanding end-user needs, preferences and behavior in relation to the new interactive technology from the initial stages of a design process allows the work team to have valuable information to design the characteristics of a more effective and efficient product. This process is known as guessability studies [26] or Gesture Elicitation Studies (GES) [8] to understand users' preferences for gesture input in a wide variety of user contexts [27]. For example, Wobbrock et al. [8] revealed users' preferences for multi-touch gestures in a context based on interactive tabletops. Vatavu [28] addressed mid-air gestures to control a smart television. Ruiz et al. [29] investigated users' preferences for motion gestures by using smartphones. The outcome of a GES characterizes users' gestural behavior with valuable information for practitioners, such as designers and developers, as well as for end users regarding the consensus level between participants, the most frequent gesture proposals for executing a given action with a particular device, and insights into users' mental models.

GES have been primarily conducted along the three dimensions of the context of use [27]: users and their interactive tasks [30], their platforms, devices, and associated sensors [8,31], and the environments in which they are working [32]. Since their inception, GES initially focused on some particular platform, device, or sensor, ranging from the most popular and widespread ones to the most recent and original ones: tabletops [8,31], mobile interaction [29], smart television [33], virtual hologram [34], and radar-based sensors [10]. GES then focused on gestures performed on particular physical component, such as the trackpad [35] or on the bezels of a smartphone [36]. The advent of cross-platform interaction resulted in GES for Multi-Display Environments (MDE) [37] and between any platform combination, such as for migrating contents across mobile phones, public displays, and tabletops [38].

Villarreal et al. [39] reported that GES were performed on almost all human limbs: the most frequent cover hand gestures [40] and their fingers [2,41], on-skin freehand gestures [42], arms gestures [43], head gestures[44,45], while the least frequent investigate limbs with less mobility, such as the mouth [33], the head and shoulders [46], the torso [47], and the belly [48]. GES can be the object of study in contexts where it is required to understand any particular physical capacity or human ability or the deficiency thereof. It turns out that the existence and the frequency of GES is correlated with the mobility level of the studied limb.

In conclusion, this paper motivates a GES for exploring nose-based gestures: this region has never been subject to any GES [39] although it is extensively used for face recognition since the tip of the nose is the most prominent and stable part of the human face [18], the gesture vocabulary is unknown, apart from the Flick, Rub and Tap gestures [7], no analysis, either qualitative or quantitative, has been reported in the literature, about the gestures preferred by users when exploring nose-based gestures. Studying nose-based gestures and natural expressions represents a great challenge. Most of the available video corpus and gesture sets do not have one or more factors that are crucial for our analysis. These datasets and corpora did not capture any nose interactions. Seipp & Verbert [49] identified "null" gestures as having no particular meaning, but that could be recognized and mapped onto a command. Among them are: Rub chin, Tap finger on face, Scratch head. The nose is common to all human. Therefore, male and female should in principle elicit the same gestures, except if these people experience social acceptance differently [20]. Whether the gender influences the gestures elicited remains untouched, knowing that human face is subject to social acceptation before preference [21]. Inspiration could also come from the field of communication, where body language expresses a wide range of knowledge about the use and interpretation of gestures [50]. Morris [50] conducted a study of 20 gestures in 40 European countries. As a result, the author found that the meanings of nasal puncture vary, yet they all share the metaphor of "sniffing out problems".

3. Experiment

A Gesture Elicitation Study (GES) following as reference a well-known methodology was carried out. The initial methodology is defined in [8,26,41,51,52] to collect users' preferences for nose gestures. Kendon [53] defines a gesture as any particular type of body movement performed in any amount of dimensions (e.g., linear to spatial), which falls into two categories: involuntary movements and actions, which can be practical actions (e.g., a manipulation gesture) or gestural actions (gesticulation and autonomous gestures). To distinguish a nose gesture from others, a *nose gesture* is defined as any movement involving the nose as an intentional movement of the nose itself (called *nose movement*, e.g., holding the nostrils open, moving the bridge) or any hand, respectively device, movement on the nose (*hand-to-nose gesture*, e.g., pushing, flicking, and rubbing the apex, swiping the dorsum nasi, respectively *device-to-nose gesture*, e.g., nose-pointing [9]). Any combination or repetition of these movements is a compound gesture.

3.1. Participants

Twenty-four people took part in the experiment voluntarily (12 Males, 12 Females; aged from 12 to 68 years, $M = 30.2$, $SD = 12.2$). The participants were recruited for the experiment through a list of contacts in various organizations. The recruitment process was carried out following the convenience sampling guidelines to participate in the experiment [54].

All the participants declared to be right-handed. Their occupations of the participants included director, teacher, psychologist, secretary, employee, retirees, and students in domains such as transportation, nutrition, law, history, chemistry, and economics. Usage frequencies were captured for various devices, in which they are: smartphones, tablets, computers, game console and depth cameras such as Kinect. All participants reported that they make frequent use of smartphones and computers in daily life.

The age groups are distributed as follows: 2 people below 18 years (8%), 8 people between 18 years and 24 (33%), 9 people between 25 and 34 (38%), 4 people between 45 and 54 (17%), and only one person above 55 years (4%). The age group was chosen for our participants to be as representative as possible for adopters of wearable technology. The percentage of individuals who use wearable is the highest for the age group 25–34 years old (30.8%), followed by the 18–25 y group (29.1%), and the 35–44 y. group (25.3%). All participants reported unaware of the existence and use of the nose interaction. All participants reported previously unaware of the existence and use of the nose interaction.

3.2. Apparatus

The experiment took place in a usability laboratory to guarantee complete control over all stages of the experiment. A computer screen was provided to the participants so that they could visualize the referents used by the experiment. All the gestures made by the participants were recorded by a camera. The camera allowed to capture the faces of the participants, in this way the region of the nose could be covered as well as their hands. To keep the study focused on the topic, the participants were asked to limit their movements to their hands and fingers without any other instrumentation.

3.3. Procedure

The procedure consists of three sequential phases conducted individually for each participant.

3.3.1. Pre-Test Phase

Prior to the experimentation phase, the participants were welcomed by the researchers. They were then asked to sign an informed consent document, compatible with the GDPR regulation. Then they were given detailed information about the study, the experimentation setting, and the entire experiment process. They were also invited to complete a sociodemographic questionnaire followed by a creativity test and a motor-skill test.

The researchers collected the sociodemographic data (e.g., age, gender, handedness) about each participant to use some of these parameters in the study. The questionnaire also asked a series of questions about the use of technologies. All questions in the questionnaire were based on a seven-point Likert scale [55] ranging from 1 = strongly disagree to 7 = strongly agree. The participants' creativity was studied through http://www.testmycreativity.com/: the instrument consists of a series of questions that allowed us to obtain the levels of creativity of each participant. Finally, the Motor-skill test, described in [56], was applied to check the participants' dexterity.

3.3.2. Test Phase

In this phase, the participants were informed about the meaning and use of the nose interaction. Each participant had the opportunity to ask questions about their concerns. The participants were informed about the following tasks that they had to perform. The researchers also reported on the types of gestures allowed, consistent with our definition. The participants worked bearing in mind that no restriction was imposed on them, neither technological nor on the recognition of gestures. This had allowed to preserve the natural and intuitive character of elicitation.

Each session implemented the original GES defined in [8]. The participants were presented with a series of *referents*. They consisted of actions to control various objects in IoT. From them, the participants made two gestures to execute those references. The condition was to perform those gestures that fit well with the referents, apart from being easy to produce and above all to remember. Participants were instructed to remain as natural at all times as possible. The referents are assigned randomly. Each participant received a list of random numbers generated with the link: www.random.org.

The *thinking time* was timed in seconds. This time allowed to capture the duration between the first sample of the referent and the moment in which the participant knew what gesture she would make. Each gesture produced by the participant was valued between a range of 1 to 10. The evaluation allowed the participant to express how appropriate the gesture was for the referent. Each session took approximately 45 min per participant. The number of experimenters present in the experiment was 3. Only one of the participants had the responsibility of presenting the referent from the random list of numbers. The remaining experimenters supported the logistics of the experimental process at all times.

3.3.3. Post-Test Phase

The participants' sessions culminated with an invitation to answer the IBM Post-study System Usability Questionnaire (IBM PSSUQ) [57]. This questionnaire allows participants to express their level of satisfaction with the usability of the scenario and the testing process. This instrument was used because it is effective and empirically validated, its effectiveness has been demonstrated with large numbers of participants bearing in mind a significant set of stimuli [58]. The IBM PSSUQ is widely applicable to any interactive system, its reliability coefficient is $\alpha = 0.89$ in relation to its results and the appraisals of perceived usability of the system [57]. The questions in the IBM PSSUQ questionnaire are measured using a 7-point Likert scale, a value of 1 represents a strongly disagree while a value of 7 shows a strongly agree appreciation. In the IBM PSSUQ four measures are computed: items from 1 to 5 correspond to the system usefulness (SysUse), the quality of the information or (InfoQual) is represented by items from 6 to 11, quality of the interaction or (InterQual) consists of the items from 12 to 15, and finally the system quality or (Overall) is represented by the item 16.

3.4. Design

Our study was within-subjects with two groups (female vs. male) and with one independent variable: REFERENT, a nominal variable with 10 conditions, representing common actions executed in IoT: Turn On the TV, Turn Off the TV, Start Player, Turn the Volume up, Turn the volume down, Go to the next item in a list, Go to the previous item in a list, Turn Air Conditioning On, Turn Air Conditioning Off, Turn Lights On, Turn Lights Off, Brighten Light, Dim Light, Turn Heat On, Turn Heat Off, Turn Alarm On, Turn Alarm Off, Answer a phone call, End Phone Call.

3.5. Quantitative and Qualitative Measures

Five measures were captured to understand the preferences as well as the performance of the participants nose gestures:

1. AGREEMENT SCORES—"$A(r)$" [8] and CO-AGREEMENT RATES—"$AR(r)$" [51] were obtained for each REFERENT "r" condition by using the equation:

$$A(r) = \sum_{P_i \subseteq P} \left(\frac{|P_i|}{|P|}\right)^2 \geq AR(r) = \frac{|P|}{|P|-1} \sum_{P_i \subseteq P} \left(\frac{|P_i|}{|P|}\right)^2 - \frac{1}{|P|-1} \quad (1)$$

where r means the referent for which a gesture is elicited, $|P|$ refers to the number of elicited gestures, and $|P_i|$ means the number of gestures for the i-th which is subgroup of P.

2. Participants' CREATIVITY was evaluated using an online creativity instrument. The test returns a result between the values 0 and 100 where higher scores denote more creativity. The results are calculated from a set of responses grouped into categories: (1) abstraction of concepts from the presentation of ideas; (2) connection between things/elements or objects without an apparent link; (3) perspective shift in terms of space, time, and other people; (4) curiosity to change and improve things/elements and situations accepted as the norm; (5) boldness to push boundaries beyond the normally accepted conventions; (6) paradox the ability to accept and work with concepts that are contradictory; (7) complexity the ability to operate with a large amount of information; and (8) persistence to derive stronger solutions even when good ones exist.
3. Participants' fine motor skills was measured with a standard motor test of the NEPSY (a developmental NEuroPSYchological assessment) test batteries [56]. The test consists of touching each fingertip with the thumb of the same hand for eight times in a row. Higher motor skills are reflected in less time to perform this task.
4. THINKING-TIME measures the time, in seconds, elapsed to elicit any gesture for a referent.
5. GOODNESS-OF-FIT represents participants' subjective assessment, as a rating between 1 and 10, of their confidence about how well the proposed gestures fit the referents. Participants could elicit their two gestures in any order with a different Goodness-of-Fit.

4. Results and Discussion

A total amount of nine hundred 12 (912) gestures were elicited from 2 groups × 12 participants × 19 referents × 2 gestures. The groups were formed bearing in mind the following criteria

1. Dimension: the cardinality of the gesture space: 0D (point), 1D (line), 2D (plane), 3D (space).
2. Laterality: which side(s) have been used to issue the gesture, unilateral (when a gesture is elicited only on one side of the dorsum nasi) or central (if the gesture is issued on the edge).
3. Gesture motion: which is the intensity of the movement stroke (as a snap or a hit), static (if performed on a single location) or dynamic (if the speed or movement is changing over time).
4. Nature: describes the meaning of a gesture with four values adapted from [8]: symbolic gestures depict commonly accepted symbols conveying information, such as emblems and cultural gestures, e.g., the CALL ME gesture performed with the thumb and little finger stretched out, or swiping the index finger from left to right; metaphorical gestures give shape to an idea or concept, such as using the thumb to press a button on an imaginary remote control to turn on/off the TV set; abstract gestures have no symbolic or metaphorical connections to their referents; physical gestures refer to the real world physics.
5. Number of fingers: how many fingers were involved.
6. Finger type: type of finger involved in the elicited gesture.
7. Path type: direct, flexible, without any particular path.
8. Movement axis: stationary, horizontal, vertical, or composed.
9. Area: above the nose, under the nose, left part of the dorsum nasi, right part, center, multiple areas.

4.1. Gesture Classification

The 912 elicited gestures are classified into 23 categories, with a sub-category when relevant to finely distinguish the nose area involved in the gesture, thus producing 53 individual gestures. The sub-categories below are defined so that they can be used consistently throughout the categories (Figure 2). For instance, *0.5, respectively *0.6 sub-categories, indicate that the gesture was issued on the right part of the dorsum nasi, resp. the left part:

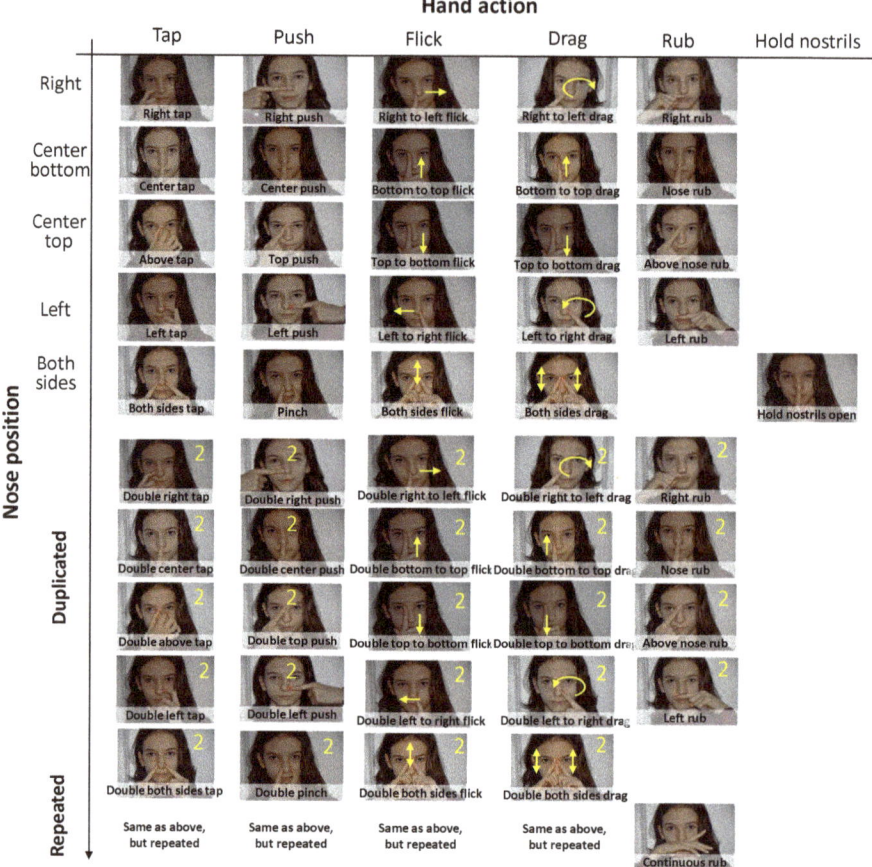

Figure 2. Taxonomy of nose-based gestures: by hand action, nose position, and factor of repetition.

1. Tap: tap any side of the dorsum nasi with the back or the top of one or several fingers with one hand (1.0), on the center (1.1), with two hands on both sides of the nose (1.2), repeated center tap (1.3), right tap (1.5), left tap (1.6).
2. Double tap: tap two times on the center (2.1), both sides of the nose (2.2), right (2.5), left (2.6), above the nose (2.7).
3. Triple tap: tap three times in a row on the center (3.1), right (3.5), left (3.6), above (3.7).
4. Flicking: from right to left (4.5), from left to right (4.6), from the top of the dorsum nasi to the bottom (4.7).
5. Pushing: center push (5.1), right push (5.5), left push (5.6).
6. Rubbing: rub once on right/left side (6.5/6.6), above the nose (6.7), continuous rub on the right/left (8.8/8.9).
7. Double rubbing: repeat rubbing two times in a row.
8. Triple rubbing: repeat rubbing three times in a row.
9. Drag: stays pressed from the initial point to the final one with the right (9.1) or left hand (9.2), from bottom to top (9.3) or vice versa (9.4), from right to left (9.5) or inverse (9.6).
10. Double drag: on the right (10.5), on the left (10.6), bottom to top (10.7), from top to bottom (10.8).
11. Triple drag: drag repeated three times in a row.
12. Quadruple drag: drag repeated four times in a row.
13. Pinch: when two fingers come far from each other.

14. Double pinch: when two fingers come far, close to each other.
15. Circle: draw a circle on a facet.
16. Double flicking: rapid unilinear movement repeated twice.
17. Hold nostrils open: as defined.
18. Push nose up: push on the nose with a finger up
19. Wrinkle: pulling up the nose without hands.
20. Double wrinkle: repeat the wrinkle two times.
21. Pull on nose: pull the nose with a finger.
22. Finger in nose: in the right/left nostril (22.5/22.6).
23. Sniffing: right part (23.5), left part (23.6).

Some nose gestures have never been elicited, because of their underlying connotation or social acceptance [21]. For example, the Snook gesture where the thumb is put on the apex and the rest of the hand is extended in space to mean defiance, disrespect, or derision; the waggling gesture is avoided for the same reason; the Wiggle nose, which moves a nostril up and down or left to right, is physically uncomfortable to produce; the slapping gesture because it could be painful, it communicates forgetfulness [50]; and gestures with a strong connotation: (a) putting the full hand on the nose, (b) rubbing the whole hand, (c) the "shut up" gesture, and (d) the Smell gesture. On the other hand, some gestures were not discarded although initially it was thought that they would be, such as the rub gesture, a sign of deception or nervousness [50].

4.2. Agreement Scores and Co-Agreement Rates

Figure 3 shows the agreement scores (bottom) and co-agreement rates (top) obtained for each REFERENT conditions sorted in decreasing order of the co-agreement rate. The values are decomposed into the female group (purple), the male group (blue), and the global sampling (green). For each referent, the first and the second most frequently elicited gestures, classified according to the above list, are reported. The ordering of agreement scores and co-agreement rates remains consistent from one computation to another, except for two pairs of referents (depicted by red arrows): Dim light was ranked higher according to its rate than for its score and Hang up call was ranked lower according to its rate than for its score and comes just a little bit before Dim light. The same phenomenon occurs with the pair of Turn AC On and Turn Heat Off referents.

Categories of the first most frequently elicited gestures are: Tap (7), Push (5), Flick (3), Rub (3), Pinch (1). Categories of the second most frequently elicited gestures are: Tap (4), Drag (6), Rub (3), Push (2), Flick (1), Pinch (1), Finger on nose (1), and Hold nostrils open (1). The Tap gesture is the most preferred for both ranks. Although Push and Flick often occur for the first choice, participants tend to rely on other types of gestures for their second choice, like Drag, Finger in the nose and Hold nostrils open, which never appears as a first choice. Rub is common to both categories with a medium frequency.

Overall, agreement rates are small in magnitude, between 0.123 and 0.319 for the global sampling ($M = 0.179$, $SD = 0.048$), between 0.109 and 0.509 for the female group ($M = 0.211$, $SD = 0.104$), and between 0.77 and 0.244 for the male group ($M = 0.164$, $SD = 0.049$). Regarding the female group, $17/19 = 89\%$ rates belong to the medium range and $2/19 = 11\%$ rates are high according to Vatavu and Wobbrock's method [51] to interpret the magnitudes of agreement rates. It turns out that most of these rates are superior to those given for the male group: $1/19 = 5\%$ belongs to low value, $18/19 = 95\%$ belong to medium value. These results are very similar to the other rates reported in the GES literature ([51], (p. 1332)) that summarizes agreement rates of 18 studies, for which the smallest value (0.108) was reached by Liang et al. [59] and Seyed et al. [37] for motion+surface and multi-display gestures, respectively. According to the recommendations [51], our results fall inside medium consensus (<0.3) category.

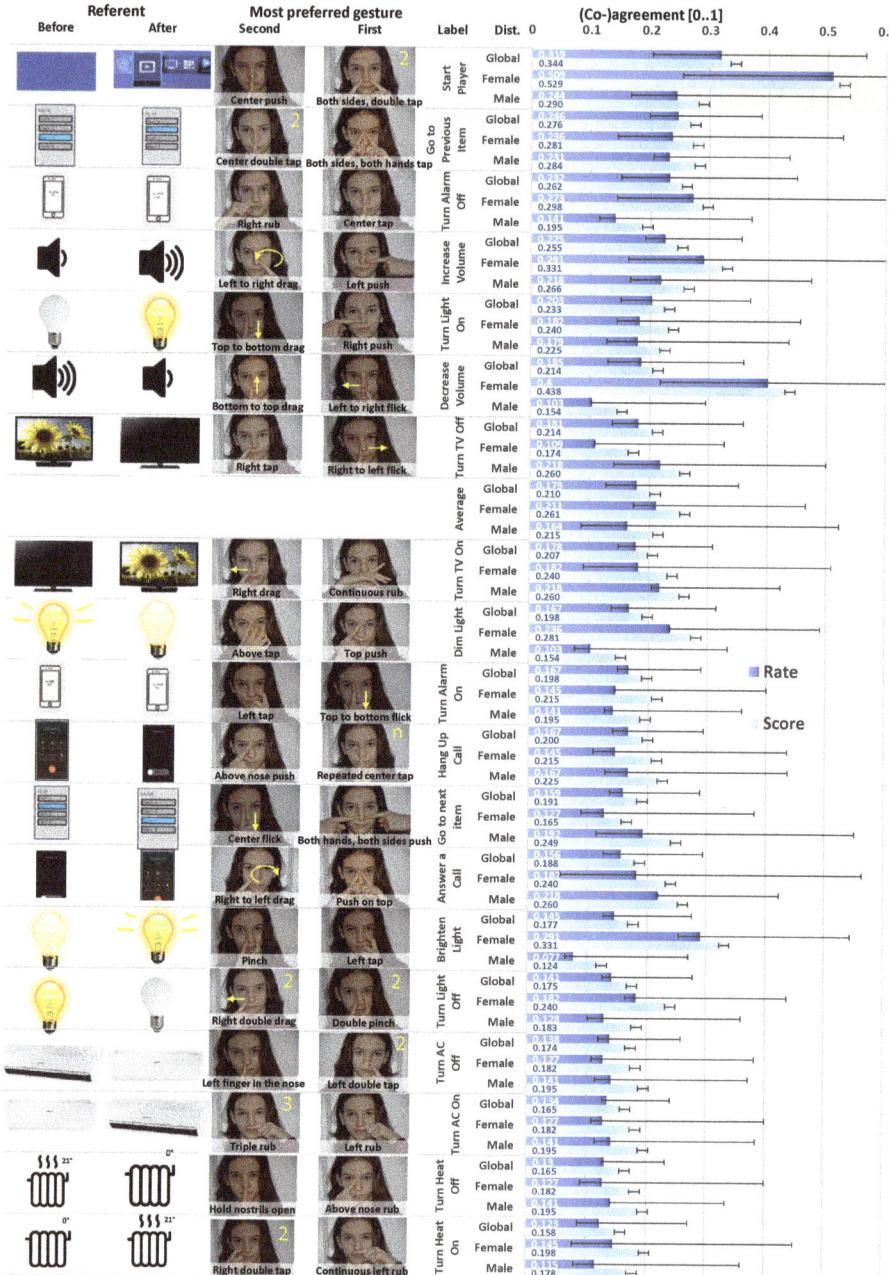

Figure 3. Co-agreement rates [51] agreement scores [8] by gender (global, male, and female) with the two most preferred gestures by referent, sorted in decreasing order of their co-agreement rate. Error bars show 95% confidence intervals ($\alpha = 0.05$) for the rates and standard errors for the scores.

Beyond agreement scores and rates, it was also necessary to know whether female and male would elicit different gestures for the same set of referents, which can be expressed as:

H_0 = both groups of female and male have equal agreement rates,
H_1 = there is a difference among the agreement rates of the $k=2$ groups.

Vatavu and Wobbrock [51] introduced a statistical test for comparing agreement rates of $k \geq 2$ independent groups and a measure to compute agreement shared between these independent groups. Each individual agreement rate captures how much consensus there is within its female or male but, considered alone, cannot describe the consensus between groups.

Therefore the freely accessible AGATe [51] software was used to compute C_{Rb}, the co-agreement rates between our two independent groups and V_{bg}, the variation in agreement for repeated-design experiments. Out of the 19 referents, only two cases were identified with a low p-value. For the Turn down volume, the following results are obtained: $V_{bg}(2, n = 24) = 144.500$, $p = 0.009$, Male: $AR = 0.091$, CI 95% = $[0.091, 0.288]$, Female: $AR = 0.348$, $CI95\% = [0.227, 0.697]$, C_{Rb}(Male, Female) = 0.153, a value for which the post-hoc tests gave: $V_{bg}(2, n = 24) = 144.500$, $p = 0.009$. For the Turn alarm off: $V_{bg}(2, n = 24) = 60.500$, $p = 0.064$, Male: $AR = 0.167$, CI 95% = $[0.152, 0.409]$, Female: $AR = 0.333$, $CI95\% = [0.182, 0.697]$, C_{Rb} (Male, Female) = 0.215, a value for which the post-hoc tests gave: $V_{bg}(2, n = 24) = 60.500$, $p = 0.064$. AGAte returned non-significant results with two exceptions: 0.161 for Answer phone call and 0.217 for Brighten lights.

4.3. Further Analysis and Gender Effect

4.3.1. Gender

An independent-samples t-test was conducted to compare agreement scores and agreement rates conditions. First of all, when examining the groups respectively (Figure 4), there was a highly significant difference in agreement for scores and rates conditions within the female group (A: $M = 0.260$, $SD = 0.094$, AR: $M = 0.211$, $SD = 0.104$; $t_{(18)} = -15.696$, $p \leq 0.001$ ***), within the male group (A: $M = 0.220$, $SD = 0.047$, AR: $M = 0.0164$, $SD = 0.049$; $t_{(18)} = -39.174$, $p < 0.001$ ***), and for the global sampling (A: $M = 0.210$, $SD = 0.048$, AR: $M = 0.179$, $SD = 0.048$; $t_{(18)} = -51.994$, $p \leq 0.001$ ***). These results are aligned with Equation (1) stating that $AR(r) \leq A(r)$. There was a significant difference ($t_{(18)} = -3.639$, $p \leq 0.01$ **) in the values for the male score ($M = 0.220$, $SD = 0.047$) and the global rate ($M = 0.179$, $SD = 0.048$). There was also a highly significant difference ($t_{(18)} = -4.653$, $p \leq 0.001$ ***) in the values for the male rate ($M = 0.164$, $SD = 0.049$) and the global score ($M = 0.210$, $SD = 0.048$). At first glance, female agreement values seem to be higher than for male and for the global sampling (which would suggest that female come to a better agreement than male): the respective averages for female are always higher than their male and global counterparts, but their standard deviations are also the widest with respect to male and global. After a closer look, there was a significant difference only in some very specific cases. The only significant difference ($t_{(18)} = -4.116$, $p \leq 0.001$ ***) found between female and male was found in the values for the female score and the male rate. Since these two metrics vary only by two corrective terms, this may suggest that the correction is welcome. With respect to the global sampling, there was a significant difference ($t_{(18)} = -3.212$, $p \leq 0.01$ **) in the values for the female score ($M = 0.260$, $SD = 0.094$) and the global score, as well as a highly significant one ($t_{(18)} = -5.286$, $p \leq 0.001$ ***) for the female score and the global rate. All others seven t-tests out of the 15 conducted did not reveal any significant difference. No significant difference was found between female vs. male agreement scores and rates ($t_{(18)} = 1.799$, $p > 0.05$, n.s.).

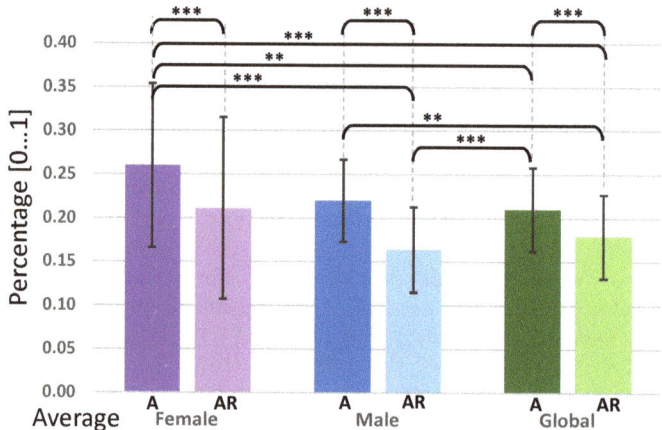

Figure 4. Agreement scores (A) and co-agreement rates (AR) by gender.

4.3.2. Type and Dimension

Figure 5a depicts how gestures are distributed by type. All gestures elicited less than 5 times (<1% of the sampling) fall in the Others category (4% in total). The most frequently elicited gesture is the Tap, a 0D gesture involving only one point, with one third (27%) of the total sampling. Five other gestures similarly represent one tenth of the total sampling: Flick (2D-16%), Push (0D-15%), Drag (1D-14%), Rub (1D-12%), and Pinch (0D-10%). The Circle (1%) was the only 2D symbol gesture and Hold nostrils, the only 3D gesture. The preference goes to the gestures with less dimensions: 0D (52%), 1D (26%), 2D (17%), and 3D (5%).

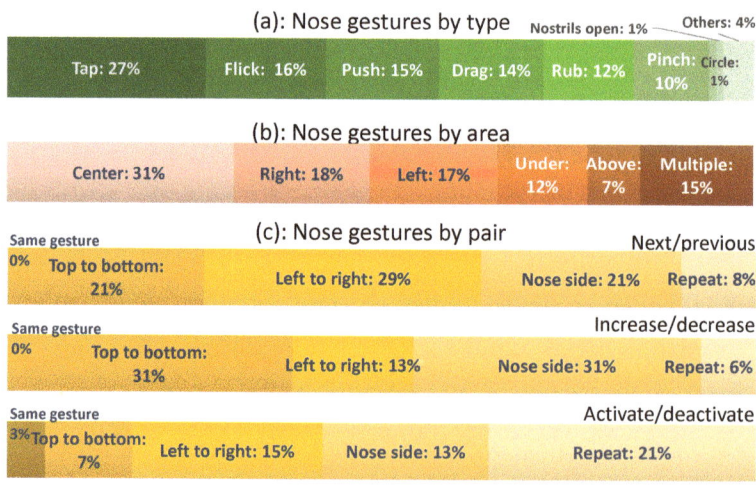

Figure 5. Distribution: (a) by type, (b) by area, (c) by pairs.

4.3.3. Area

Figure 5b depicts how gestures are physically distributed over the areas of the human face: participants largely prefer centered gestures (31%) because they do not need to distinguish laterality. Left (17%) and right (18%) faces are considered equal when chosen. Under the nose was selected in 12% of cases, and above in 7% of cases. Although single areas represent a total amount of 85%, multiple areas were selected in 15% of cases. These results refine suitable areas [21].

4.3.4. Pairs of Commands

The set of referents actually contains nine pairs of semantically related referents, such as opposite, complementary or mutually exclusive. Activate/deactivate pairs cover two-state actions: turn TV/AC/light/ heat/alarm on/off, and Answer/end phone call. Increase/decrease pairs cover a range of values: Increase/decrease volume, Next/previous, Brighten/dim lights, pair only covers: Go to next/previous item in a list. Since referents were presented randomly, participants sometimes complained that they did not remember the gesture they elicited for a previous referent linked to the current one.

Figure 5c depicts which reasoning has been used by participants for these various pairs of referents. Participants hope to observe some logic and/or some reasoning when they elicited gestures coming in pairs. However, it was observed that 30% of elicited gestures did not follow any such logic or reasoning. For Activate/deactivate pairs, Repeat was the most frequent pattern (21%), followed by changing the face of the dorsum nasi (13%), gesture direction (15% left/right and 7% top/bottom). Only one gesture category was used for the same pair (3%). To address the question of which variables influence participants to elicit gestures without any apparent logic or reasoning (see Table 1), some test was performed, but no such correlation was found with creativity (Pearson's $\rho = 0.117$), with age (Person's $\rho = 0.065$), with familiarity of devices (Pearson's $\rho = -0.321$), and thinking time (Pearson's $\rho = 0.215$) ($n = 24$). After checking Levene's test for equality of variances and t-test for equality of means, an independent-samples t-test was conducted to compare creativity, age, items, familiarity with devices, and thinking time. Only one correlation was found between creativity and familiarity with devices ($\rho = 0.410$ significant with $\alpha = 0.05$: 2-tailed) among all possible combinations (See Tables 2 and 3).

Table 1. Descriptive statistics of variables by genre.

Variable	Gender	Mean	Standard Deviation	Standard Error M.
Creativity	Female	64.503	7.780	2.345
	Male	57.825	10.274	2.849
Unlogical items	Female	3.36	2.157	0.650
	Male	2.08	1.977	0.548
Device familiarity	Female	4.000	0.721	0.217
	Male	3.754	1.042	0.289
Thinking time	Female	7.406	4.825	1.455
	Male	6.891	3.118	0.864
Age	Female	30.82	9.888	2.981
	Male	29.69	14.620	4.055

Table 2. Correlations between variables. (*) represents the correlation value between creativity and familiarity with devices among all possible combinations.

		Creativity	Age	Unlogic Items	Familiarity	Think Time
Creativity	Pearson c.	1	0.080	0.117	0.410 *	0.071
	Sig. (2-tld.)		0.712	0.587	0.047	0.742
Age	Pearson c.	0.080	1	0.065	−0.307	−0.259
	Sig. (2-tld.)	0.712		0.761	0.144	0.222
Unlogic items	Pearson c.	0.117	0.065	1	−0.321	−0.215
	Sig. (2-tld.)	0.587	0.761		0.126	0.313
Familiarity	Pearson c.	0.410 *	−0.307	−0.321	1	−0.302
	Sig. (2-tld.)	0.047	0.144	0.126		0.151
Thinking time	Pearson c.	0.071	0.259	0.215	−0.302	1
	Sig. (2-tld.)	0.742	0.222	0.313	0.151	

Table 3. Independent Samples Test.

		Levene's Test for Equality of Variances		t-Test for Equality of Means					95% Confidence Interval of the Difference	
		F	Sig.	t	df	Sig. (2-Tailed)	Mean Difference	Std. Error Difference	Lower	Upper
Creativity	Equal variances assumed	0.577	0.456	1.767	22	0.091	6.67825	3.77911	−1.15914	14.51564
	Equal variances not assumed			1.809	21.775	0.084	6.67825	3.69096	−0.98092	14.33742
Unlogic items	Equal variances assumed	0.534	0.473	1.524	22	0.142	1.287	0.844	−0.465	3.038
	Equal variances not assumed			1.512	20.597	0.146	1.287	0.851	−0.485	3.058
Familiarity device	Equal variances assumed	0.207	0.654	0.660	22	0.516	0.2462	0.3732	−0.5277	1.0200
	Equal variances not assumed			0.680	21.250	0.504	0.2462	0.3619	−0.5058	0.9981
Thinking time	Equal variances assumed	3.577	0.072	0.315	22	0.756	0.51483	1.63311	−2.87205	3.90170
	Equal variances not assumed			0.304	16.590	0.765	0.51483	1.69274	−3.06329	4.09294
Age	Equal variances assumed	2.099	0.161	0.217	22	0.831	1.126	5.198	−9.655	11.907
	Equal variances not assumed			0.224	21.086	0.825	1.126	5.033	−9.338	11.589

4.3.5. User Satisfaction with Nose Interaction

Figure 6 reports the results from the IBM PSSUQ questionnaire. The results express the subjective satisfaction of the participants with respect to the interaction of the nose according to the experiment presented in this document. Error bars allow observing a confidence interval of 95%. The four measures of the PSSUQ questionnaire are considered valid to support the correlation with perceived usability, as long as their value is greater than or equal to 5 on a scale of ranges from 1 to 7.

Participants were very reliable in their answers to this questionnaire (Guttman' $\lambda-2$ gives a score of 0.9701, which is usually wished for high-stakes decisions). Only Information quality (InfoQual: $M = 5.00$, $SD = 1.48$) reaches this threshold with a wide standard deviation for this type of measure, though. System usefulness (SysUse: $M = 4.43$, $SD = 1.72$), Interaction quality (InterQual: $M = 4.23$, $SD = 1.65$), and Overall satisfaction (Overall: $M = 4.00$, $SD = 1.50$) all share a value below 5, which suggests that participants were not quite subjectively satisfied with nose interaction. Two reasons may explain this: the nose is an area that is sensible to suitability in public spaces (the body language is quite related to some gestures [50]).

It was found that the nose gestures are not easy to reproduce, but it is even difficult to perform them consistently and above all, It was found that there is no guidance, there are no immediate user comments on how the gestures should be emitted. Also, there are no immediate comments on how they could be recognized and then trigger an action. Some of the participants stated that they were divided between two aspects: (1) the desire for some guidance or feedback and (2) the guarantee that only the resulting action that is being executed should be the only feedback due to the discretion. These statements are also partially contrasted with the individual questions reported by the participants. The group of questions contained in the category InfoQual were considered "not appropriate" by the participants, consequently, fewer values are reported in Figure 6). However, the reality related to the quality of the information is that this group of questions are considered positive because of the discretion goal. It was also observed that all the remaining questions corresponding to the other measures of the instrument received disagreeing ratings. However, these appreciations never exceeded $5/24 = 20\%$) of participants. Finally, it was observed that the participants expressed a satisfactory trend towards efficiency in carrying out the tasks, where questions Q3 and Q6 obtained the highest results.

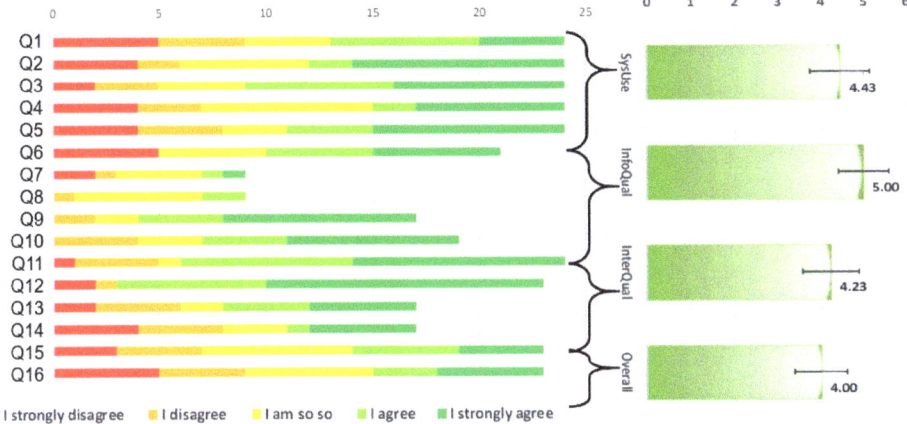

Figure 6. Results of the IBM PSSUQ.

4.3.6. Nose-Based Gesture Recognition

This section discusses some mechanisms useful for recognizing nose-based gestures as we devised them. The context of use, which is made up of the end-user and the tasks, the device(s), and the environment, of course determines appropriate mechanisms to recognize nose-based gestures.

The gesture capture and recognition process with Itchy Nose is ensured by a sensing technique for detecting finger movements on the nose. Itchy Nose is based on electrooculography (EOG) sensing and on-body interaction [60]. Three EOG sensors embedded in the J!NS Meme are located around the nose [60]: two on the nose pads and one on the nose bridge. Five EOG signals with a probability (i.e., Left/right Push, Left/right Swipe, and Rub) captured by these sensors are sent via Bluetooth to a remote computer where the signals are processedAn open-source GUI gesture toolkit for J!NS Meme is available at https://github.com/sebaram/jins-gesture-toolkit. and the gestures are subsequently classified by the Random Decision Forest method [61]. This configuration is intended to recognize nose-based gestures only. Thus, gestures based on the smart glasses themselves, such as spectacle-based gestures or holding glasses, were not tested although they could be recognized by the sensors as they are close to the sensors. Face-based gestures, such as cheek touching or pushing, tongue moving, cannot be recognized with this method since they are located too far away or in an inaccessible area.

When the end-user does not possess smart glasses, computer vision offers multiple methods for automatic analysis of facial actions [62]. In [63], several face detection and recognition methods were evaluated in order to provide a complete image-based face detection and recognition with high recognition rate, even from the initial step, such as in video surveillance. Methods are proposed based on performed tests on face databases with variations in terms of subjects, poses, emotions, races, and light conditions. Despite these studies, self- expression of these facial expressions is not sufficient to recognize nose-based gestures: finger movement recognition [64] should be involved. Facial expression recognition combined with finger movement recognition should enable us to recognize more nose-based gestures being inspired by our taxonomy (Figure 2).

Facial expression and finger movement recognition methods for nose-based gestures will have their primary resource the use of an effective face detection [65,66] and hands recognition [67]. Consequently, techniques largely vary depending on their source input (e.g., still images, pictures, videos, and real-time streams) and their scientific approach. Support Vector Machines (SVMs) [68], k-Nearest Neighbor (k-NN) [69,70] and other classification methods could solve this classification problem.

5. Design Guidelines

Based on our results on preferred gestures, some design guidelines were devised:

1. Match the gesture dimension to task dimension. Used referents cover 0D and 1D tasks. Participants prefer gestures whose dimension is consistent with the task dimension, such as tap for activate/deactivate, tap to select, swipe to scroll. pinch and reverse pinch to shrink or enlarge an object. There is no need to add any extra dimension to the task dimension.
2. Prefer gestures with low dimension. From all elicited gestures, the amount of preferred gestures dramatically decreases with their dimension to the point that probably only 0D and 1D gestures are required as the minimum. Higher dimension gestures were always coming afterwards.
3. Prefer larger areas over small ones. Larger areas (e.g., the dorsum nasi) are adequate for 1D gestures such as scrolling, swiping gestures while small areas (e.g., the ala, the apex or the philtrum) are available for 0D gestures.
4. Favor repetition as a pattern over location. When a gesture is repeated, the repetition factor replaces the fine-grained distinction between individual gestures belonging to the same category. Participants tend to rely less frequently on the physical areas, such as changing the face of the dorsum nasi or preferring the apex.
5. Favor centrality instead of laterality. Gestures that are independent of any laterality are easier to produce and remember than asymmetric ones. For instance, swiping on the dorsum nasi is easier than on any face.
6. Use location only as a last factor. Location could distinguish between gestures, but only as the last refining factor.

6. Other Measures for Elicited Gestures

Agreement captures whether some consensus emerges from participants who elicited gestures for the same referent. An agreement measure is computed globally for each referent and is based on their frequency of selection, as reported in Figure 3. To adopt a complementary view on agreements and to identify any particular variation in the agreements, two other methods for consolidating votes from participants on candidates were performed: the Condorcet method [15] and the de Borda method [16], which is used when the first one is unable to identify a *Condorcet winner*. Each method ranks candidates (here, rank elicited gestures) for a selection based on votes (here, based on elicitation and goodness-of-fit). To choose a winner, the Condorcet method is based on the rule: for each referent, select the elicited gesture (if one exists) that beats each other elicited gesture in exhaustive pairwise comparison. The de Borda method is based on the rule: for each referent, select the elicited gesture that on average stands highest in the participants' rankings. To rank the elicited gestures, Condorcet's rule is: rank the elicited gestures in descending order of their number of victories in exhaustive pairwise comparison with all the other gestures. Borda's rule is: rank the elicited gestures in descending order of their standing in the participants' rankings. In this method, it is common to give the lowest score to the last preferred candidate and to increase the score with the ranking: a score of 1, resp. 2, is assigned to for the second, resp. first, most frequently elicited gesture. Condorcet's and de Borda's winners are two methods that must choose an elicited gesture with a claim to democratic legitimacy. The GOODNESS-OF-FIT could introduce an additional weight to moderate the confidence with which participants elicited gestures. This explains why two gestures were captured per participant and per referent.

The de Borda method with weights based on Goodness-of-Fit returns the following list: Both side double tap, Both sides-both hands, Center tap, Center push, Right tap, Left push, Left to right drag, Right push, Top to bottom drag, Left to right flick, Repeated center tap, Right rub, Continuous rubbing, Right drag, Top push, Pinch, Above tap, Top to bottom flick, Double pinch, One hand tap, Above nose push, Center flick, Left tap, Two hands push, Right double drag, Wrinkle, Left double tap, Left finger, Left rubbing, Triple rubbing, Circle, Hold nostrils open, Right double tap. More or less, this list confirms most of the initially selected gestures, but in a different order of preference, apart for the most preferred gestures such as Tap, Push, Drag, and Flick. Some gesture appeared in a more favorable position, such as pinch. Some gestures disappeared, such as some individual rubbing, probably replaced by other gestures which were considered insignificant up to now, like wrinkle and circle. The circle was the only real 2D gesture operated and considered to be the simplest drawing possible that could be produced consistently. The de Borda method without weight, but with a score 1 or 2 and defined above, give more or less a similar list with little variations.

7. Conclusions and Future Work

A gesture elicitation study with two samples of equal size (12 females and 12 males) was conducted. The study elicited a series of 912 nose-based gestures (a few nose movements and a large set of hand-to-nose gestures) for 19 referents associated with frequent IoT tasks. These initially elicited gestures are then classified according to several criteria to come up with a classification of 53 individual (unique) gestures falling into 23 categories of gestures, each category potentially having sub-categories. The final consensus set consists of 38 gestures for nose-based interaction (Figure 3 gives the two most frequently elicited gestures per referent). Beyond classification, no significant difference between female and male in the gestures elicited was found. The only significant difference was found between the female score and the corresponding global score. However, no significant difference was found between male and female for the same agreement score and rate. There were some significant differences, though, across the measures (e.g., between female scores and male rates). The analysis confirmed that there is indeed always a significant difference between agreement scores and rates, the last being always inferior or equal to scores. Based on the analysis of the elicited gestures, some design guidelines are suggested for designing nose-based gestures, which could be applicable to wearable devices, sensors, and mobile applications.

Due to the discussion on agreement scores and rates, Scores were also calculated with the Condorcet and the de Borda methods, with a weight based on the goodness-of-fit provided by each participant or without. This analysis suggests that the resulting consensus set remains more or less constant in its selection, but that the order of most preferred gestures within the set could change, with local variations. For instance, two pairs of gestures are swapped when comparing agreement scores and rates (Figure 3). Although participants were asked to express their overall preference through the goodness-of-fit, they were not asked to provide a separate score for social acceptance, like in [21]. From the informal comments gathered during the session, participants also reported that they would never elicit some gestures for different reasons, such as those expressing negative feelings of the body language [50]. This may suggest that a future elicitation study should incorporate not only the most preferred gestures, but also discard the most unwanted gestures. Some participants reported in this case of interaction that they could accommodate different nose gestures taken from the consensus set, but they absolutely want to avoid producing unwanted gestures. Therefore, it is possible to discard the least preferred gestures with a negative filter while keeping the most preferred ones with a positive filter.

Automatic gesture identification for nose interactions represents one of the next steps in our research. The results found from the gesture elicitation study presented in this document will provide a valuable input to start the experiments.

Author Contributions: Conceptualization, J.-L.P.-M. and J.V.; methodology, J.V.; validation, J.V.; formal analysis, J.V.; investigation, J.-L.P.-M. and J.V.; resources, J.V.; data curation, S.V. and J.V.; writing—original draft preparation, J.-L.P.-M., S.V. and J.V.; writing—review and editing, J.-L.P.-M., S.V. and J.V.; visualization, J.-L.P.-M. and J.V.; supervision, J.V.; project administration, J.-L.P.-M.; funding acquisition, J.-L.P.-M. All authors have read and agreed to the published version of the manuscript.

Funding: This research was funded by the Universidad de Las Américas. Quito-Ecuador grant number SIS.JPM.20.02.

Acknowledgments: The authors acknowledge the support from the project Emerald Casting Assistant (ECA), under contract no. 7901 awarded by SPW, DGO6 Walloon Region and the competivity pole MecaTech. The authors are also grateful to the participants, the anonymous reviewers, and Amy Yan for contributing to this version of the manuscript. Special thanks to Marina Vanderdonckt for the pictures collected in the taxonomy of nose-based gestures.

Conflicts of Interest: The authors declare no conflict of interest.

Abbreviations

The following abbreviations are used in this manuscript:

A(r)	Agreement score
AR(r)	Agreement rate
GES	Gesture Elicitation Study
EOG	electrooculography
IoT	Internet-of-Things

References

1. Aliofkhazraei, M.; Ali, N. Recent Developments in Miniaturization of Sensor Technologies and Their Applications. In *Comprehensive Materials Processing*; Hashmi, S., Batalha, G.F., Van Tyne, C.J., Yilbas, B., Eds.; Elsevier: Oxford, UK, 2014; pp. 245–306. [CrossRef]
2. Benitez-Garcia, G.; Haris, M.; Tsuda, Y.; Ukita, N. Finger Gesture Spotting from Long Sequences Based on Multi-Stream Recurrent Neural Networks. *Sensors* **2020**, *20*, 528. [CrossRef] [PubMed]
3. Abraham, L.; Urru, A.; Norman, N.; Wilk, M.P.; Walsh, M.J.; O'Flynn, B. Hand Tracking and Gesture Recognition Using Lensless Smart Sensors. *Sensors* **2018**, *18*, 2834. [CrossRef] [PubMed]
4. Zengeler, N.; Kopinski, T.; Handmann, U. Hand Gesture Recognition in Automotive Human-Machine Interaction Using Depth Cameras. *Sensors* **2019**, *19*, 59. [CrossRef] [PubMed]
5. Luo, X.; Wu, X.; Chen, L.; Zhao, Y.; Zhang, L.; Li, G.; Hou, W. Synergistic Myoelectrical Activities of Forearm Muscles Improving Robust Recognition of Multi-Fingered Gestures. *Sensors* **2019**, *19*, 610. [CrossRef]
6. Lee, D.; Oakley, I.R.; Lee, Y. Bodily Input for Wearables: An Elicitation Study. In Proceedings of the International Conference on HCI Korea 2016 (HCI Korea '16), Jeongseon, Korea, 27–29 January 2016; pp. 283–285.
7. Lee, J.; Yeo, H.S.; Starner, T.; Quigley, A.; Kunze, K.; Woo, W. Automated Data Gathering and Training Tool for Personalized Itchy Nose. In Proceedings of the 9th Augmented HCI (AH '18), Seoul, Korea, 7–9 February 2018; pp. 43:1–43:3.
8. Wobbrock, J.O.; Morris, M.R.; Wilson, A.D. User-defined gestures for surface computing. In Proceedings of the Conference on Human Factors in CS (CHI'09), Boston, MA, USA, 4–9 April 2009; pp. 1083–1092.
9. Polacek, O.; Grill, T.; Tscheligi, M. NoseTapping: What else can you do with your nose? In Proceedings of the 12th International Conference on Mobile and Ubiquitous Multimedia (MUM'13), Lulea, Sweden, 2–5 December 2013; pp. 32:1–32:9.
10. Magrofuoco, N.; Pérez-Medina, J.L.; Roselli, P.; Vanderdonckt, J.; Villarreal, S. Eliciting Contact-Based and Contactless Gestures With Radar-Based Sensors. *IEEE Access* **2019**, *7*, 176982–176997. [CrossRef]
11. Horcher, A.M. Hitting Authentication on the Nose: Using the Nose for Input to Smartphone security. In Proceedings of the Usenix Symposium on Usable Privacy and Security (SOUPS '14), Menlo Park, Canada, 9–11 July 2014.
12. Cooperrider, K.; Núñez, R. Nose-pointing: Notes on a facial gesture of Papua New Guinea. *Gesture* **2012**, *12*, 103–129. [CrossRef]
13. Sanders, A. Dual Task Performance. In *International Encyclopedia of the Social & Behavioral Sciences*; Smelser, N.J., Baltes, P.B., Eds.; Pergamon: Oxford, UK, 2001; pp. 3888–3892. [CrossRef]
14. Oakley, I.; Park, J.S. Designing Eyes-Free Interaction. In *Haptic and Audio Interaction Design*; Oakley, I., Brewster, S., Eds.; Springer: Berlin/Heidelberg, Germnay, 2007; pp. 121–132.
15. Pivato, M. Condorcet meets Bentham. *J. Math. Econ.* **2015**, *59*, 58–65. [CrossRef]
16. Emerson, P. The original Borda count and partial voting. *Soc. Choice Welfare* **2013**, *40*, 353–358. [CrossRef]

17. Eston, P. Anatomy and Physiology. Chapter 22.1 Organs and Structures of the Respiratory System. 2010. Available Online: https://open.oregonstate.education/aandp/chapter/22-1-organs-and-structures-of-the-respiratory-system/ (accessed on 1 October 2020)
18. Harshith, C.; Shastry, K.R.; Ravindran, M.; Srikanth, M.V.V.N.S.; Lakshmikhanth, N. Survey on Various Gesture Recognition Techniques for Interfacing Machines Based on Ambient Intelligence. *Int. J. Comput. Sci. Eng. Surv.* **2010**, *1*, 31–42. [CrossRef]
19. Henry, T.R.; Hudson, S.E.; Yeatts, A.K.; Myers, B.A.; Feiner, S. A Nose Gesture Interface Device: Extending Virtual Realities. In Proceedings of the 4th Annual ACM Symposium on User Interface Software and Technology, UIST '91, Hilton Head Island, SC, USA, 11–13 November 1991; pp. 65–68. [CrossRef]
20. Rico, J.; Brewster, S. Usable gestures for mobile interfaces: Evaluating social acceptability. In Proceedings of the SIGCHI Conference on Human Factors in CS (CHI'10), Atlanta, GA, USA, 10–15 April 2010; pp. 887–896.
21. Freeman, E.; Griffiths, G.; Brewster, S.A. Rhythmic micro-gestures: Discreet interaction on-the-go. In Proceedings of the 19th ACM International Conference on Multimodal Interaction (ICMI'17), Glasgow, UK, 13–17 November 2017; pp. 115–119.
22. Zarek, A.; Wigdor, D.; Singh, K. SNOUT: One-handed use of capacitive touch devices. In Proceedings of the International Working Conference on Advanced Visual Interfaces (AVI'12), Capri Island, Italy, 22–25 May 2012; pp. 140–147.
23. Ogata, M.; Imai, M. SkinWatch: Skin Gesture Interaction for Smart Watch. In Proceedings of the 6th Augmented Human International Conference, AH '15, Marina Bay Sands, Singapore, 9–11 March 2015; pp. 21–24. [CrossRef]
24. Wen, H.; Ramos Rojas, J.; Dey, A.K. Serendipity: Finger Gesture Recognition Using an Off-the-Shelf Smartwatch. In Proceedings of the 2016 CHI Conference on Human Factors in Computing Systems, CHI '16, San Jose, CA, USA, 7–12 May 2016; pp. 3847–3851, [CrossRef]
25. McIntosh, J.; Marzo, A.; Fraser, M. SensIR: Detecting Hand Gestures with a Wearable Bracelet Using Infrared Transmission and Reflection. In Proceedings of the 30th Annual ACM Symposium on User Interface Software and Technology, UIST '17, Quebec, QC, Canada, 22–25 October 2017; pp. 593–597. [CrossRef]
26. Wobbrock, J.O.; Aung, H.H.; Rothrock, B.; Myers, B.A. Maximizing the guessability of symbolic input. In Proceedings of CHI'05 EA on Human Factors in CS, CHI'05, Portland, OR, USA, 2–7 April 2005; pp. 1869–1872.
27. Calvary, G.; Coutaz, J.; Thevenin, D.; Limbourg, Q.; Bouillon, L.; Vanderdonckt, J. A unifying reference framework for multi-target user interfaces. *Interact. Comput.* **2003**, *15*, 289–308. [CrossRef]
28. Vatavu, R.D. User-defined gestures for free-hand TV control. In Proceedings of the 10th European Conference on Interactive tv and Video EuroITV '12, Berlin, Germany, 4–6 July 2012; pp. 45–48.
29. Ruiz, J.; Li, Y.; Lank, E. User-defined motion gestures for mobile interaction. In Proceedings of the SIGCHI Conference on Human Factors in Computing Systems (CHI '11), Vancouver, BC, Canada, 7–12 May 2011; pp. 197–206.
30. Mauney, D.; Howarth, J.; Wirtanen, A.; Capra, M. Cultural similarities and differences in user-defined gestures for touchscreen user interfaces. In Proceedings of the 28th International Conference on Human Factors in Computing Systems (CHI '10), Atlanta, GA, USA, 10–15 April 2010; pp. 4015–4020.
31. Morris, M.R.; Wobbrock, J.O.; Wilson, A.D. Understanding Users' Preferences for Surface Gestures. In Proceedings of the Graphics Interface 2010, Canadian Information Processing Society (GI '10), Toronto, ON, Canada, 31–2 June 2010; , pp. 261–268.
32. Akpan, I.; Marshall, P.; Bird, J.; Harrison, D. Exploring the effects of space and place on engagement with an interactive installation. In Proceedings of the 28th International Conference on Human Factors in Computing Systems (CHI '13), Paris, France, 27 May–2 June 2013; pp. 2213–2222.
33. Dong, H.; Danesh, A.; Figueroa, N.; El Saddik, A. An elicitation study on gesture preferences and memorability toward a practical hand-gesture vocabulary for smart televisions. *IEEE Access* **2015**, *3*, 543–555. [CrossRef]
34. Yim, D.; Loison, G.N.; Fard, F.H.; Chan, E.; McAllister, A.; Maurer, F. Gesture-Driven Interactions on a Virtual Hologram in Mixed Reality. In *Proceedings of the 2016 ACM Companion on Interactive Surfaces and Spaces*; ISS'16 Companion; Association for Computing Machinery: New York, NY, USA, 2016; pp. 55–61. [CrossRef]

35. Berthellemy, M.; Cayez, E.; Ajem, M.; Bailly, G.; Malacria, S.; Lecolinet, E. SpotPad, LociPad, ChordPad and InOutPad: Investigating gesture-based input on touchpad. In Proceedings of the 27th Conference on L'Interaction Homme-Machine IHM '15, Toulouse, France, 27–30 October 2015; ACM: New York, NY, USA, 2015; pp. 4:1–4:8.

36. Serrano, M.; Lecolinet, E.; Guiard, Y. Bezel-Tap gestures: Quick activation of commands from sleep mode on tablets. In Proceedings of the SIGCHI Conference on Human Factors in Computing Systems, CHI '13, Paris, France, 27 April–2 May 2013; ACM: New York, NY, USA, 2013; pp. 3027–3036.

37. Seyed, T.; Burns, C.; Costa Sousa, M.; Maurer, F.; Tang, A. Eliciting usable gestures for multi-display environments. In *Proceedings of the 2012 ACM International Conference on Interactive Tabletops and Surfaces*; ACM: New York, NY, USA, 2012; pp. 41–50.

38. Kray, C.; Nesbitt, D.; Dawson, J.; Rohs, M. User-defined gestures for connecting mobile phones, public displays, and tabletops. In Proceedings of the 12th International Conference on Human Computer Interaction with Mobile Devices and Services, MobileHCI '10, Lisbon, Portugal, 7–10 September 2010; ACM: New York, NY, USA, 2010; pp. 239–248.

39. Villarreal-Narvaez, S.; Vanderdonckt, J.; Vatavu, R.D.; Wobbrock, J.O. A Systematic Review of Gesture Elicitation Studies: What Can We Learn from 216 Studies? In *Proceedings of the 2020 ACM Designing Interactive Systems Conference*; DIS '20; Association for Computing Machinery: New York, NY, USA, 2020; pp. 855–872. [CrossRef]

40. Bostan, I.; Buruk, O.T.; Canat, M.; Tezcan, M.O.; Yurdakul, C.; Göksun, T.; Özcan, O. Hands as a controller: User preferences for hand specific on-skin gestures. In Proceedings of the 2017 Conference on Designing Interactive Systems, Edinburgh, UK, 10–14 June 2017; pp. 1123–1134.

41. Chan, E.; Seyed, T.; Stuerzlinger, W.; Yang, X.D.; Maurer, F. User elicitation on single-hand microgestures. In Proceedings of the 2016 Conference on Human Factors in Computing Systems, San Jose, CA, USA, 7–12 May 2016; pp. 3403–3414.

42. Havlucu, H.; Ergin, M.Y.; Bostan, İ.; Buruk, O.T.; Göksun, T.; Özcan, O. It made more sense: Comparison of user-elicited on-skin touch and freehand gesture sets. In *International Conference on Distributed, Ambient, and Pervasive Interactions*; Springer International Publishing: Cham, Switzerland, 2017; pp. 159–171.

43. Liu, M.; Nancel, M.; Vogel, D. Gunslinger: Subtle arms-down mid-air interaction. In Proceedings of the 28th Annual ACM Symposium on User Interface Software & Technology, Charlotte, NC, USA, 8–11 November 2015; pp. 63–71.

44. Mardanbegi, D.; Hansen, D.W.; Pederson, T. Eye-based head gestures. In Proceedings of the Symposium on Eye Tracking Research and Applications, ETRA '12, Santa Barbara, CA, USA, 28–30 March 2012; ACM: New York, NY, USA, 2012; pp. 139–146.

45. Rodriguez, I.B.; Marquardt, N. Gesture Elicitation Study on How to Opt-in & Opt-out from Interactions with Public Displays. In Proceedings of the 2017 ACM International Conference on Interactive Surfaces and Spaces, ISS '17, Brighton, UK, 17–20 October 2017; ACM: New York, NY, USA, 2017; pp. 32–41.

46. Vanderdonckt, J.; Magrofuoco, N.; Kieffer, S.; Pérez, J.; Rase, Y.; Roselli, P.; Villarreal, S. Head and Shoulders Gestures: Exploring User-Defined Gestures with Upper Body. In *Design, User Experience, and Usability. User Experience in Advanced Technological Environments*; Marcus, A., Wang, W., Eds.; Springer International Publishing: Cham, Switzerland, 2019; pp. 192–213.

47. Silpasuwanchai, C.; Ren, X. Designing concurrent full-body gestures for intense gameplay. *Int. J. Hum. Comput. Stud.* **2015**, *80*, 1–13. [CrossRef]

48. Vo, D.B.; Lecolinet, E.; Guiard, Y. Belly gestures: body centric gestures on the abdomen. In Proceedings of the 8th Nordic Conference on Human-Computer Interaction: Fun, Fast, Foundational, Helsinki, Finland, 26–30 October 2014; pp. 687–696.

49. Seipp, K.; Verbert, K. From Inaction to Interaction: Concept and Application of the Null Gesture. In *Proceedings of the 2016 CHI Conference Extended Abstracts on Human Factors in Computing Systems*; CHI EA '16; Association for Computing Machinery: New York, NY, USA, 2016; pp. 525–540. [CrossRef]

50. Morris, D.; Collett, P.; Marsh, P.; O'Shaughnessay, M. *Gestures: Their Origins and Distribution*; Cape London: London, UK, 1979.

51. Vatavu, R.D.; Wobbrock, J.O. Formalizing agreement analysis for elicitation studies: New measures, significance test, and toolkit. In Proceedings of the 33rd ACM Conference on Human Factors in Computing Systems, CHI '15, Seoul, Korea, 18–23 April 2015; ACM: New York, NY, USA, 2015; pp. 1325–1334.

52. Gheran, B.F.; Vanderdonckt, J.; Vatavu, R.D. Gestures for Smart Rings: Empirical Results, Insights, and Design Implications. In *Proceedings of the 2018 Designing Interactive Systems Conference*; DIS '18; Association for Computing Machinery: New York, NY, USA, 2018; pp. 623–635. [CrossRef]
53. Kendon, A. *Gesture: Visible Action as Utterance*; Cambridge University Press: Cambridge, UK, 2004.
54. Dornyei, Z. *Research Methods in Applied Linguistics*; Oxford University Press: Oxford, UK, 2007.
55. Likert, R. A technique for the measurement of attitudes. *Arch. Psychol.* **1932**, *22*, 5–55.
56. Korkman, M. NEPSY: A Developmental Neuropsychological Assessment. *Test Mater. Man.* **1998**, *2*, 375–392. [CrossRef]
57. Lewis, J.R. IBM computer usability satisfaction questionnaires: Psychometric evaluation and instructions for use. *Int. J. Hum. Comput. Interact.* **1995**, *7*, 57–78. [CrossRef]
58. Lewis, J.R. Sample sizes for usability tests: Mostly math, not magic, interactions, v. 13 n. 6. *November + December* **2006**, *13*, 29–33.
59. Liang, H.N.; Williams, C.; Semegen, M.; Stuerzlinger, W.; Irani, P. User-defined surface+ motion gestures for 3d manipulation of objects at a distance through a mobile device. In Proceedings of the 10th Asia Pacific Conference on Computer Human Interaction, APCHI '12, Matsue-City, Shimane, Japan, 28–31 August 2020; ACM: New York, NY, USA, 2012; pp. 299–308.
60. Lee, J.; Yeo, H.S.; Dhuliawala, M.; Akano, J.; Shimizu, J.; Starner, T.; Quigley, A.; Woo, W.; Kunze, K. Itchy nose: Discreet gesture interaction using EOG sensors in smart eyewear. In Proceedings of the 2017 ACM International Symposium on Wearable Computers, Maui, HI, USA, 13–15 September 2017; pp. 94–97.
61. Ho, T.K. Random decision forests. In Proceedings of 3rd International Conference on Document Analysis and Recognition, Montreal, QC, Canada, 14–16 August 1995; Volume 1, pp. 278–282, [CrossRef]
62. Martinez, B.; Valstar, M.F.; Jiang, B.; Pantic, M. Automatic Analysis of Facial Actions: A Survey. *IEEE Trans. Affect. Comput.* **2019**, *10*, 325–347. [CrossRef]
63. Ahmad, F.; Najam, A.; Ahmed, Z. Image-based face detection and recognition: "State of the art". *arXiv* **2013**, arXiv:1302.6379.
64. N. Shah, M.; R. Rathod, M.; J. Agravat, M. A survey on Human Computer Interaction Mechanism Using Finger Tracking. *Int. J. Comput. Trends Technol.* **2014**, *7*, 174–177. [CrossRef]
65. Guo, G.; Wang, H.; Yan, Y.; Zheng, J.; Li, B. A fast face detection method via convolutional neural network. *Neurocomputing* **2020**, *395*, 128–137. [CrossRef]
66. Zhang, S.; Chi, C.; Lei, Z.; Li, S.Z. Refineface: Refinement neural network for high performance face detection. *IEEE Trans. Pattern Anal. Mach. Intell.* **2020**, *1*. [CrossRef] [PubMed]
67. Bandini, A.; Zariffa, J. Analysis of the hands in egocentric vision: A survey. *IEEE Trans. Pattern Anal. Mach. Intell.* **2020**. [CrossRef] [PubMed]
68. Schölkopf, B.; Smola, A.J.; Williamson, R.C.; Bartlett, P.L. New support vector algorithms. *Neural Comput.* **2000**, *12*, 1207–1245. [CrossRef] [PubMed]
69. Silverman, B.W.; Jones, M.C. E. fix and jl hodges (1951): An important contribution to nonparametric discriminant analysis and density estimation: Commentary on fix and hodges (1951). *Int. Stat. Rev. Int. Stat.* **1989**, *57*, 233–238. [CrossRef]
70. Cover, T.; Hart, P. Nearest neighbor pattern classification. *IEEE Trans. Inf. Theory* **1967**, *13*, 21–27. [CrossRef]

Publisher's Note: MDPI stays neutral with regard to jurisdictional claims in published maps and institutional affiliations.

© 2020 by the authors. Licensee MDPI, Basel, Switzerland. This article is an open access article distributed under the terms and conditions of the Creative Commons Attribution (CC BY) license (http://creativecommons.org/licenses/by/4.0/).

Article

Face Pose Alignment with Event Cameras

Arman Savran [1,*] and Chiara Bartolozzi [2]

1. Department of Computer Engineering, Yasar University, 35100 Izmir, Turkey
2. Event-Driven Perception for Robotics, Istituto Italiano di Tecnologia, 16163 Genova, Italy; chiara.bartolozzi@iit.it
* Correspondence: arman.savran@yasar.edu.tr

Received: 30 September 2020; Accepted: 5 November 2020; Published: 10 December 2020

Abstract: Event camera (EC) emerges as a bio-inspired sensor which can be an alternative or complementary vision modality with the benefits of energy efficiency, high dynamic range, and high temporal resolution coupled with activity dependent sparse sensing. In this study we investigate with ECs the problem of face pose alignment, which is an essential pre-processing stage for facial processing pipelines. EC-based alignment can unlock all these benefits in facial applications, especially where motion and dynamics carry the most relevant information due to the temporal change event sensing. We specifically aim at efficient processing by developing a coarse alignment method to handle large pose variations in facial applications. For this purpose, we have prepared by multiple human annotations a dataset of extreme head rotations with varying motion intensity. We propose a motion detection based alignment approach in order to generate activity dependent pose-events that prevents unnecessary computations in the absence of pose change. The alignment is realized by cascaded regression of extremely randomized trees. Since EC sensors perform temporal differentiation, we characterize the performance of the alignment in terms of different levels of head movement speeds and face localization uncertainty ranges as well as face resolution and predictor complexity. Our method obtained 2.7% alignment failure on average, whereas annotator disagreement was 1%. The promising coarse alignment performance on EC sensor data together with a comprehensive analysis demonstrate the potential of ECs in facial applications.

Keywords: event camera; dynamic vision sensor; low power; event-driven; face dataset; motion detection; face alignment; pose estimation; cascaded regression; extremely randomized trees

---

1. Introduction

Event cameras (ECs) are an emerging type of visual sensor that captures contrast changes at individual pixels. These changes are quantized into a stream of pixel-events each of which carries the time, coordinates and sign of the change. This approach leads to unprecedented capabilities as very high temporal resolution (in the order of μs), low latency, low power consumption (in the order of tens of mW [1]), and very high dynamic range (in the order of 140 dB [2]). ECs capture high frequency information free of motion blur in scenes with very bright, very dark, or uneven, illumination and can work on a low power budget, both at the sensor level, both thanks to the extremely compressed data representation, which allows for light weight computation, especially in scenarios with relatively low motion. These characteristics make ECs suitable for embedded applications in unconstrained environments, and where the information is mostly in the dynamic content of the scene, such as automotive, autonomous robotics and mobile. In this work we focus on coarse, but efficient, estimation of head pose, which can be used as pre-processing step for many face-related application, such as tracking, recognition and visually aided speech applications, needed for smooth human-device interaction.

The last decade witnessed a great progress in the face alignment field, thanks to the creation of comprehensive databases and advances in machine learning [3–5], however, to the author's knowledge, this is the first time an EC is used for this task, also for the lack of adequate EC datasets. To fill this gap, we recorded an EC dataset with human subjects, characterized by large head rotations, varying movement speeds and repetitions, speaking intervals, and multi-human annotations, available upon request, and developed a coarse and efficient face pose alignment technique. A wide range of facial applications can benefit from our method even though we do not align very precisely for fine facial details. Existing EC-based voice activity detection [6], visual speech [7] or face recognition [8] can be implemented in a robust way against large head pose variations. However, our method does not aim at applications where fine detail alignment is necessary, as in 3D face reconstruction, facial performance capture or face transfer, unless it is used as a bootstrap initialisation technique in hybrid EC/frames systems.

The proposed method aims at a coarse but extremely efficient face alignment. At first, the detection of pose change activates the alignment, preventing unnecessary processing when the head doesn't move. Alignment is then performed by regression cascade of tree ensembles, exploiting their superior computational efficiency [9,10] with respect to (possibly more accurate) state-of-the-art alignment methods based on deep neural networks (DNNs) [5,11–31]. In a scenario where energy efficiency is a matter of the utmost importance, a DNN-based alignment pre-processor might eclipse the energy efficiency advantage of ECs. Tree ensembles have also been suggested in a very recent study [32] instead of DNNs for the similar efficiency reasons, though for a different vision problem. Although DNNs have also been applied with ECs for different vision problems [33–35], those studies aim at benefits of ECs other than the energy efficiency, thus are computationally very demanding. The comparison of our method to human performance in facial landmark placement on the same dataset shows that extremely randomized trees (ERT) cascade applied directly on pixel-events—i.e., without facial image reconstruction and training on image datasets—has good accuracy. The method proposed in this manuscript implements a good trade-off between power efficiency and accuracy for different levels of head movement speeds, alignment with different initial localization uncertainty ranges, different resolution and different complexity levels of the predictor.

2. Related Work

2.1. Face Alignment

Face alignment, or facial landmark detection, is usually performed after face detection. It was studied for robust detection of key facial points and high precision alignment under highly varying conditions over many frame-based databases. These methods can be grouped into holistic, constrained local and regression-based methods [3,4]. Holistic methods explicitly model the whole face appearance and landmark-based face shape/pose patterns. Constrained local methods, instead, explicitly model local appearance patterns around landmarks. In both categories alignment can be realized by model fitting, or by regression-methods, that learn to predict landmark coordinates by implicitly imposing shape/pose constraints. Although considerable progress has been made with the two direct model fitting approaches, in general, regression methods offer better alignment and computation efficiency; more specifically, when realized in a cascade [3,4].

Cascaded regression is a gradient boosting machine [36], however, for improved alignment, pose/shape invariance is integrated by re-generating feature coordinates in accordance with the pose/shape prediction at the current stage. Dollár et al. [37] used cascaded random ferns to predict 2D affine pose transformations over three landmarks on the eye and mouth centers. Later their method was extended using more landmarks [38] to cope with occlusions. Non-linear least-squares fitting can be realized also as cascaded regression, leading to the supervised descent method for alignment [39]. Cao et al. [40] proposed shape regression with two-levels gradient boosting by efficient computation of shape-indexed feature coordinates. Extremely fast cascaded regressions with ensemble of regression trees were introduced in Kazemi and Sullivan [9] and in Ren et al. [10] using local binary features, reaching up to 3000 frames per second. Joint cascades of face detection and alignment improve the performance of both [41]. Robustness against large head pose variations or occlusions and self-occlusions due to large out-of-plane rotations have become a major objective to following studies with this approach [42–44]. By training on large face databases, DNNs improved regression performances, especially for large head rotations and 3D alignment [5,11–31], at the cost of much heavier computation than ensemble methods.

For video alignment, the performance of run face detection and image alignment run at every frame can be improved by exploiting spatio-temporal dependencies and temporal continuity. However, tracking without detection often suffers the drifting problem. A comprehensive comparison of detection versus tracking versus tracker-detector hybrids with failure detection, re-initialization and smoothness components are available in Cheysos et al. [45]. Cascaded regression methods require different sets of regression functions for detection and for tracking, since the level of initialization imprecision with detection is considerably higher. A spatio-temporal cascade is proposed with a time-series regression model in Yang et al. [46], and a cascade for incremental tracking is developed in Sanchez-Lozano et al. [47]. A joint optimization of alignment and tracking over a cascade with DNN-based features was proposed in Khan et al. [48]. Finally, end-to-end learning via DNNs was also applied to video, e.g., using recurrent neural networks [20,27] and two-stream transformer networks [24].

2.2. Event-Camera-Based Vision

Early EC studies focused on efficient low-level vision algorithms such as optical flow estimation, feature detection/tracking and motion segmentation [49]. They explored data representations and new frameworks for event-driven computing, needed to handle the unconventional event-stream and information encoding. More recent work focused on higher-level vision applications such as motion estimation and object recognition, using deep learning techniques. Due to the lack of large datasets, the proposed methods use pre-training on state-of-the-art networks of conventional image data and transfer learning using smaller EC datasets [50]. The collection of larger EC datasets shows improved performance of the proposed deep learning techniques over conventional sensing, mostly thanks to their robustness to challenging illumination conditions and fast motion [35].

An alternative approach to overcome the dataset handicap may be to perform video reconstruction [34].

A limited number of prior work is available on EC-based face processing tasks; no face alignment study exists to the best of our knowledge. For face detection, Barua et al. [51] applied a patched-based model via dictionary learning. Face tracking can work with a mass-spring system over parts of the face [52], or using eye blinks [53]. In Lagorce et al. [8], face recognition was tested with hierarchical time-surface representation of event-streams. Recovery of facial motion field and brightness while the camera is in motion were shown in several studies [34,54], where conventional cameras suffer from dynamic range limitations and motion blur. Finally, Savran et al. [6] applied spatio-temporal event-based convolution to locate and detect lip activity, and Li et al. [7] proposed a DNN on audio-visual events for speech recognition.

3. Face Pose Alignment Dataset

The absence of EC face databases is a major obstacle that hinders EC-based face alignment studies. While for alignment with conventional cameras huge databases were collected by downloading from the internet, the same approach is not possible with ECs. A temporary solution to the generation of large EC datasets is the use of video to events simulators [55,56], that interpolate the videos and simulate realistic noise conditions. This technique can be then supported by transfer learning techniques on real datasets. For this reason, we prepared a face pose alignment dataset, which is also included as a subset of an EC-based visual speech dataset [6]. The acquisition setup is presented in Section 3.1. We carefully prepared the content not only to include different subjects to increase appearance variability, but also to have a high degree of motion variability, as explained in Section 3.2. While EC datasets do not suffer from motion blur, this is true if the data visualisation adapts to the motion of the input. Long temporal windows create motion blur for fast moving targets, but short temporal windows can lack important information for slowly moving targets, as only a few events are generated and the full profile of the target can be incomplete. This poses a challenge for the manual annotation of datasets, required for the ground truth. To facilitate the annotation task, we developed an annotation tool described in Section 3.3 with which an annotator can aggregate temporal information through visualization to locate the facial features.

3.1. Acquisition

The database was acquired with the "ATIS" [2]. Since our goal was facial analysis, we aimed at close-up face shots, without background, that can be nevertheless added with data augmentation tools. Based on sensor resolution (304 × 240 pixels) and lens (f = 8 mm), subjects sit at about 70 cm away from the camera so that the face is covering a big part of the image plane. This setup results in 67 pixels frontal view eye-to-eye distance on average with 9.6 pixels standard deviation. As the average eye-to-eye distance is roughly 60 mm, 1 pixel corresponds to roughly 0.9 mm on average. The recording has standard illumination.

3.2. Content

In the dataset there are 108 clips of 10.2 min in total, from 18 subjects (9 males and 9 females). All of the subjects gave their informed consent before they participated in the study. The study was conducted in accordance with the Declaration of Helsinki, and the protocol was approved by the Ligurian Ethics Committee with identification CER_IIT_ECOMODE_01. Subjects were selected to include as many as visual variations as possible, comprising long hairs (which can partly occlude the face), different beard and moustache types. A different subset of eight subjects wear eyeglasses.

Clips were collected during continuous head motion, and while subjects were talking and performing guided head movements. Since with EC datasets motion variability is a critical factor, we captured different motion types at varying speeds. We divide the clips into two categories, as intense and moderate head motion clips. The former category contains continuous roll, pitch and yaw rotations ranging from slow to very high speed. Clip duration, movement speed and number of head rotation repetitions vary arbitrarily from clip to clip. In the latter category, each subject turns his/her head in different directions starting from a neutral frontal face pose, then says a short sentence, and finally turns back to the starting pose. This category contains moderate head motion in terms of speed and angle. For each category, three clips were captured for each subject. The content of the clips is listed in Table 1, and various snapshots are shown in Figures 1, 2 and 4.

Table 1. Pose-annotated clip category contents. Intense category includes faster, longer range and more frequent movements with multiple repetitions within a clip compared to moderate category.

Category	Actions	Clips	Length (min)
Intense head motion	rotations (roll, pitch, yaw), eye-blinks	54	4.3
Moderate head motion	rotations (roll, pitch, yaw), talking lips, eye-blinks	54	5.9
Total		108	10.2

3.3. Pose Annotation on Event-Sensor Data

All the clips were annotated in a semi-automated way by human annotators marking eyes and mouth centers on pixel-event data. Figure 1 shows the visualization with the annotation tool developed for this task. The tool shows an image generated by accumulating events for 10 ms centered at a selected time-point. The pixel intensity is proportional to the event-rate, and the hue is proportional to the ratio of positive and negative pixel-events to gradually change the color. The tool also shows the event rate time profiles for the regions around eyes and mouth as well as for the whole image. The annotator can select a time-point where there is high event-count, i.e., when the face is visible thanks to relative movement with respect to the camera, then can visualize the corresponding image and click on the three reference landmarks (center of mouth, left and right eye) to generate the ground truth position. Event-rate profiles throughout the clip are estimated over the rectangular regions centered at the landmarks.

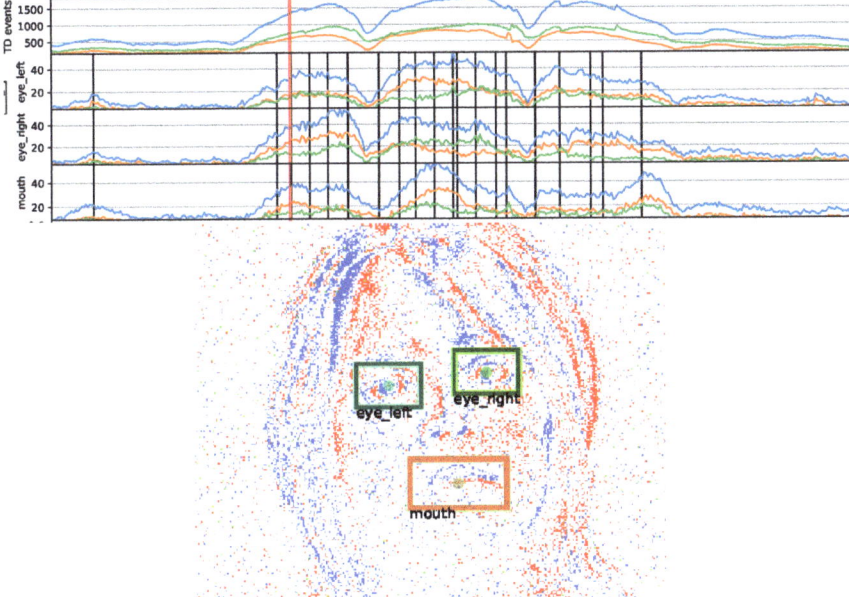

Figure 1. Snapshot of spatio-temporal eyes-mouth annotation of a rotating face, with a frame length and step size of 10 ms. Annotation times are shown with event rate sequences of rectangular areas displayed in the frame image (red thick line designates the frame image). Also the polarity events are plotted as time-series, and are colored differently in the frame image.

For all the time-points where there is no annotation, linear interpolation is applied to find the landmark coordinates. As soon as a landmark point is updated, the temporal plots are re-drawn by calculating event-rate for the interpolated landmark points as well. Since the peaks and high value regions in the event-rate plots correspond to significant motion, the annotator quickly finds where to annotate on the event-data, usually at the peak, onset and offset moments, and sometimes also at several in-between places if interpolated landmark points are clearly away from observed facial feature locations. Annotations usually start at high event-rate occurrences, then gradually more time-points are added and coordinates are refined by several passes over a clip.

Due to the ambiguity on landmark positions, annotation precision level is expected to be much lower compared to conventional image annotations. To evaluate annotation precision, we prepared two sets of annotations on the whole dataset with four annotators. In the first set, all the clips were annotated by the same person, and in the second, the dataset subjects were grouped into three and each was annotated by a different annotator. By calculating the disagreements between these two sets, using the standardized distance in Equation (10) at regularly re-sampled time-points as explained in Section 5.1, we found that the average disagreement error is 0.125 pixels with a standard deviation of 0.061. In all the experiments, we use the first set for training and testing, then compare the results with the second set, i.e., with inter-human annotation disagreements as a strong human-baseline.

4. Event-Based Face Pose Alignment via Cascaded Regression

In the proposed event-based method, face pose alignment is conveyed via a sequence of pose-events over a given temporal window. The input and output event sequences up to time t

are $E_t = \{e^i \mid t^i \leq t\}$ where e^i represents the pixel-event tuple indexed by i, and $\hat{P}_t = \{\hat{P}^j, \hat{t}^j, \mid \hat{t}^j \leq t\}$ where the predicted pose vector ($\hat{P}^j$) and time-stamp ($\hat{t}^j$) are indexed by j. A pose-event is generated when facial motion is detected, then alignment is performed by regression. In this study, we align for 2D affine pose, i.e., the relative pose of the face is an affine transformation of the template landmarks. Affine transformation has six degrees of freedom corresponding to 2D translation, scale, rotation, aspect ratio and shear, and is considered an approximation of rigid 3D pose on the image plane. Since motion of three non-collinear 2D points induces an affine transformation, we employ three landmarks to estimate the affine pose transformation of the face. Face pose is represented by the landmark coordinates vector $\mathbf{P} = [x_1, y_1, x_2, y_2, x_3, y_3]^T \in \mathbb{R}^6$. We use the eye and mouth center landmarks as in Dollár et al. [37]. As for the template, a mean shape in a standardized coordinate system, $\tilde{\mathbf{P}}$, is estimated over a training set by Generalized Procrustes Analysis (GPA) [57].

4.1. Event Sensor Data Representation in Space-Time

We convert the sensor's pixel-events stream into a space-time representation to efficiently perform detection and alignment. EC sensors generate events asynchronously when logarithmic intensity changes at pixels are detected by adjustable thresholds [49]. Each pixel-event is represented by a tuple of values indexed with i, $e^i = (x^i, y^i, t^i, p^i)$, where x, y is the location of the pixel in the image plane, t is the time at which the change has been detected, and p is a binary polarity value which represents the direction of the intensity change.

For down-scaling and efficient processing, events are down-sampled on regular space-time grids at multiple spatial scales. Cells in the grid are space-time volumes with square shape; for each location, there is a pair of cells of positive and negative polarities. Pixel-events falling in a cell at time t within the temporal window of length τ, $E_{t-\tau:t}$, are accumulated onto the cells of the multi-layered grid, $\mathcal{G}$, where each cell is addressed by a multi-index tuple (p, s, i, j), which are of polarity (p), spatial scale (s), vertical (i) and horizontal (j) discrete coordinates. The set of the index tuples of $\mathcal{G}$ is the domain of the discrete function, $\mathcal{C}_t$, which maps onto an event count, C:

$$\mathcal{C}_t \triangleq \text{Accumulate}(E_{t-\tau:t}; \mathcal{G}) \tag{1}$$
$$C = \mathcal{C}_t[p, s, i, j], \; C \in \mathbb{Z}^*.$$

$\mathcal{C}_t$ can be imagined as spatial pyramids of positive and negative polarity of event-cell masses over the image plane, for a given temporal window at t. The resulting *event-mass* is an unnormalized down-scaled representation of an event sequence in multiple spatial scales. We set $\tau = 40$ ms as it obtains the best average alignment performance over various values from 10 ms to 160 ms. The step size of the time-frames is set to 20 ms for smooth transition.

4.2. Pose Motion Detector

We developed a motion detector to generate a *pose-event*, irrespective of the location of the face; i.e., the detector does not find where the face motion is but only when. Motion detection is based on pixel-event density over the face region, assuming big and frequent illumination change is very unlikely. We estimate local event-densities at different spatial scales separately and then average at each scale. This multi-scale density estimate is more informative than a single global estimate, since sizes of dense event regions depend both on the speed of motion as well as the scale. For this purpose, a multi-scale grid is created on the alignment template (in an offline phase). Then the density for each grid cell is obtained by re-sampling from the event-cell mass representation of the sensor output, $\mathcal{C}_t$, defined in Equation (1), dividing event-masses by their cell areas. We perform nearest neighbor interpolation for scale-space re-sampling, as it is the simplest interpolation and finer details are not required for the detection. Density estimate is invariant to rotation and shape due to averaging over cells. Moreover, for invariance against motion polarity, we pick the maximum of the event polarities at each spatial cell coordinate, since an opposite motion direction inverts the event polarities.

The grid is generated by extending the square bounding box of an eyes-mouth template. To be able to cover the whole face region, its width is set to $3.5 s_{rms}$ where s_{rms} is the scale of the eyes-mouth triangle defined by Equation (10). Square grid cells are placed by overlapping half of their width and height. For a multi-scale grid with L levels, grid width for the scale l is

$$w_l = w_{min} \left(\frac{w_{max}}{w_{min}} \right)^{\frac{l}{L-1}} \quad (2)$$

where $[w_{min}, w_{max}]$ is the scale range. This provides L density estimates, hence features to be classified for detection. Spatial pyramids of event-cells are constructed in an octave range of $\{sz.2^{-s}\}_{s=1}^{3}$ where sz represent sensor width and height. We empirically set $L = 5$ scales in the range $w_{min} = 0.2$ and $w_{max} = 1.0$. This multi-scale grid is superimposed on an initial pose prediction, $\mathbf{P}^0$, to re-sample the event-densities. Superposition aligns only for the translation and scale due to invariance to rotation and shape. This alignment is done by finding the center and scale of the points in $\mathbf{P}^0$. Scale is two times the radius which is given as the root mean square deviation from center. Two example detection grids (cell centers) at different scales with the superimposed reference triangular GPA shapes are shown in Figure 2.

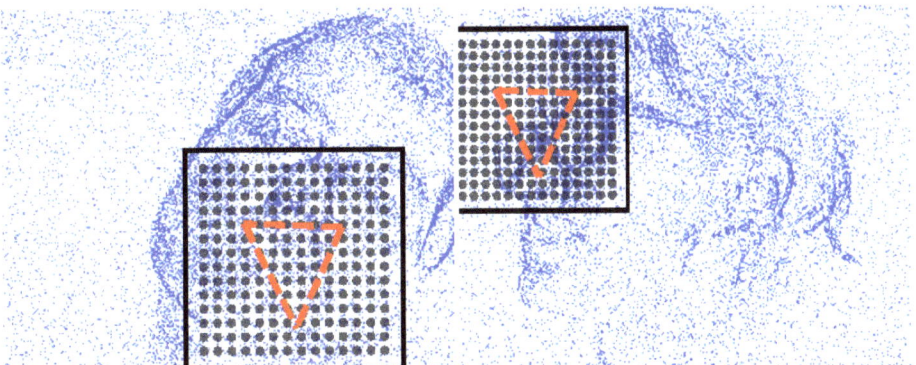

Figure 2. Two example superimpositions of motion detection grid (square domain and cell centers) as well as the reference eyes-mouth triangle according to the initial translations and scales.

Detection target (class label for presence of motion), $y(t)$, for a time t and duration τ is calculated from the distance between two ground-truth pose vectors at the start and end of its time-frame as

$$y(t) = \mathbb{I}(\| \mathbf{P}_{(t+\tau/2)} - \mathbf{P}_{(t-\tau/2)} \|_2 > 0) \quad (3)$$

where $\mathbb{I}$ is the indicator function (returning 1 if the logical proposition holds, or 0 otherwise). $\mathbf{P}_{(t)}$ is estimated by linear interpolation on ground-truth labels which are assigned to key frames over a clip via manual annotation. To predict we use logistic regression with L_2 regularization and by class weighting to balance the unbalanced positive and negative sample sizes. Detector threshold is determined on a validation set to meet a certain false negative rate (FNR) as explained in Section 5.1.

4.3. Pose-Invariant Cascaded Regression

The key factor that leads to high performance alignment with the cascaded regression framework is the pose/shape invariance integration to gradient boosting machines (reviewed in Section 2.1). With a cascade of length K, pose prediction is recursively performed by

$$\hat{\mathbf{P}}^k = r^k(\hat{\mathbf{P}}^0) \quad (4)$$
$$= r^{k-1}(\hat{\mathbf{P}}^0) + (\mathbf{M}_S^{k-1})^{-1} \circ g^k(\hat{\mathbf{P}}^{k-1})$$

where $k \in 1, ..., K$, $r^k(.)$ is the partial cascade regressor of length k, $\hat{\mathbf{P}}^K = r^K(\hat{\mathbf{P}}^0)$ being the output of the complete cascade given a starting point, $\hat{\mathbf{P}}^0$, and with $\hat{\mathbf{P}}^0 = r^0(\hat{\mathbf{P}}^0)$ as the initial prediction. $g^k(.)$ is the stage regressor at stage k which predicts a displacement vector to approach the true pose coordinates, however, in a normalized coordinate system. Please note that the regressor operates on pixel-event cell representation (Equation (1)), though we omit here for brevity. $(\mathbf{M}_S^{k-1})^{-1}$ is the similarity transformation which maps the displacements predicted by $g^k(.)$ in a normalized coordinate system back onto the observation domain (here, ∘ denotes rotation and scale only transformation since translation has no effect on displacement). Normalization is realized by mapping onto a template, which here is the mean shape obtained by GPA. Training targets of $g^k(.)$ are the normalized residual displacements,

$$\Delta_S \mathbf{P}^k = \mathbf{M}_S^{k-1} \circ (\mathbf{P} - \mathbf{P}^{k-1}), \tag{5}$$

where S denotes the similarity normalization by $\mathbf{M}_S^{k-1}$ which is estimated via linear least square minimization

$$\mathbf{M}_S^{k-1} = \arg\min_{\mathbf{M}_S} \|\bar{\mathbf{P}} - \mathbf{M}_S \cdot \hat{\mathbf{P}}^{k-1}\|^2. \tag{6}$$

The same minimization is also used in prediction to directly estimate $(\mathbf{M}_S^{k-1})^{-1}$ for the opposite mapping. Thus, the training set for $g^k(.)$ is composed of triplets $\{(E_i, \mathbf{P}_i^{k-1}, \Delta_S \mathbf{P}_i^k)\}_{i=1}^N$, where E_i represents the pixel-event observations for the ith sample.

Pose/shape invariance is gained by re-sampling the features at each stage k relative to the last pose/shape estimate $\hat{\mathbf{P}}^{k-1}$, through a map $\mathbf{M}_P^{k-1}$ such that $\bar{\mathbf{P}} = \mathbf{M}_P^{k-1} \circ \hat{\mathbf{P}}^{k-1}$. Though the attained invariance is approximate as shown in Dollár et al. [37], in practice it works well since the prediction at each stage becomes more aligned with the true landmark coordinates. Within the cascaded regression framework, instead of warping the observations with $\mathbf{M}_P^{k-1}$ to extract pose-invariant features, feature coordinates in the standardized template coordinate system are mapped onto the observation domain via the inverse warp $(\mathbf{M}_P^{k-1})^{-1}$ for re-sampling. This is because transforming only a few coordinates is computationally much simpler, as a sparse feature coordinate set is sufficient for good prediction in this framework. Thus, given a set of standardized feature locations, $\{x_i\}$, the re-sampling coordinates are obtained via

$$\mathbf{x}' = (\mathbf{M}_P^{k-1})^{-1} \circ \mathbf{x}. \tag{7}$$

We apply Equation (7) by the computationally lightweight approximation suggested in Cao et al. [40], which avoids direct estimation of $(\mathbf{M}_P^{k-1})^{-1}$ to simplify calculations.

Except the initial work by Dollár et al. [37] where weak regression is performed at each cascade stage using random ferns, strong regression is commonly employed for the stages. Similar to Cao et al. [40], we found that boosting of strong regressors provides faster convergence in training and higher performance in testing, confirming their conjecture also with an EC, i.e., weak learners cause unstable pose-aligned feature coordinates. We apply bottom-level gradient boosting without pose/shape invariance updates as the strong stage regressor of the top-level, as in Kazemi and Sullivan [9], Cao et al. [40] and Lee et al. [44]. Also we use regression trees instead of ferns [40] as they offer high performance when applied as random forest or extremely randomized tree (ERT) ensembles. More specifically, we apply ERT similar to Kazemi and Sullivan [9], however, with a model for pixel-event masses as explained in Section 4.4.

4.4. Extremely Randomized Trees over Event Masses

We use extremely randomized trees [58] with event-cell mass pair difference features to predict normalized residual pose displacements. These features are similar to pixel difference features which are commonly preferred due to very lightweight computations while providing high capacity with regression trees [9] or ferns [37,40]. As the leaves of trees or ferns constitute some linear combination of training samples, face shape constraint is satisfied intrinsically for alignment. In order to have invariance to motion direction when aligning over pixel-event data, we take the maximum over polarity masses at each cell location. ERT fitting is completely stochastic including feature selection, i.e., by randomly sampling features as well as decision functions. Due to the infeasibly high dimension of all possible location pairs, candidate features are randomly sampled but computed only when needed for a random test that is performed for each split node of each tree. Binary test for a decision function with a pair difference feature is defined as

$$b(C; \hat{\mathbf{P}}^{k-1}) = \begin{cases} 1 & C_{max}(y'_1, x'_1) - C_{max}(y'_0, x'_0) > c_{th} \\ 0 & \text{otherwise} \end{cases}$$

$$C_{max}(y, x) = \max_{p}(C(y, x, p)) \tag{8}$$

which uses the threshold, c_{th}, while testing the difference of a maximum polarity cell mass pair, i.e., a pair of C_{max}. If the evaluation result is one, the left child, otherwise the right child node is selected. Here, $\mathbf{x}'_n = [x'_n, y'_n]^T$ are the coordinates on the input domain which are obtained by mapping the pose-indexed feature coordinates from the template domain onto the input via Equation (7). We perform nearest neighbor re-sampling on the base level of the event-cell mass pyramid (see Equation (1)). By sampling many random pairs and decision thresholds, a set of candidate decision functions are created for a node, and evaluated with the total square error loss over the training set which is assigned to that node. Feature coordinates are initially sampled in the template domain with a uniform distribution over a square region encapsulating the template (to speed up training a sufficiently large random pool of coordinates is sampled together with the event-masses at the beginning of each pose-invariant stage). However, to focus on the local patterns of facial features, we re-sample using the prior proposed in Kazemi and Sullivan [9]

$$p(\mathbf{x}_0, \mathbf{x}_1) \propto e^{-\lambda \|\mathbf{x}_1 - \mathbf{x}_0\|_2} \tag{9}$$

setting λ to match local feature scales in the standardized domain. The decision thresholds are sampled with a bounded uniform distribution where the boundaries are set according to the typical range of pixel-event masses. Then learning at a split-node is realized by selecting the candidate combination which yields the minimum training error.

4.5. Clustering-Based Multiple Initialization

We apply clustering-based multiple initialization, to improve learning as well as prediction. In training, it simply serves as a data augmentation technique to increase the generalization capability. In prediction, each different initial pose leads regression to a different alignment, which helps to improve robustness by reducing the risk of misalignment, as commonly employed in the regression framework. It is especially crucial in our study due to highly varied and ambiguous differential EC observations as well as due to big head rotations.

In the training phase, we aim at finding a diverse set of pose perturbations to be added to a given initial pose, $\mathbf{P}^0$, which also have a high occurrence probability given a training set. For this purpose, we apply the k-means algorithm on the set of normalized displacements $\{\Delta_S \mathbf{P}_i\}_{i=1}^N$. Having C cluster centers of normalized translations, $\{\Delta_S \mathbf{P}_c\}_{c=1}^C$, multiple initialization are calculated by $\mathbf{P}_c^0 = \mathbf{P}^0 + \mathbf{M}_S^{0^{-1}} \circ \Delta_S \mathbf{P}_c$.

As the resulting pose vectors after multiple regression can be widely distributed, mean estimate over them usually causes inaccurate alignments. Therefore several methods were applied in the literature. Among them are pose clustering to get the mode of the most dense region [37], component median [40], and optimizing via replicator dynamics [42]. In this work we use the component median since its computation is extremely simpler, while being satisfactorily accurate for the task.

5. Experimental Results

We first describe various components of our evaluation methodology in Section 5.1. Then in section 5.2, we compare the prediction performance of our method with a second set of human annotations, i.e., against a human-baseline. Finally, we analyze the effects of face resolution in Section 5.3 and model complexity in Section 5.4.

5.1. Evaluation Methodology

Pose-event rate: We measure the output pose-event rate in Hz as $f_{det} = \hat{P}/T_{total}$, where $|\hat{P}|$ and T_{total} are the total number of predicted pose events and total duration, respectively.

Error metric: Alignment quality is evaluated via scale-invariant landmark localization error, as average Euclidean distance divided by a scale estimate. To account for large pose variations, scale estimates are based on bounding boxes of landmarks, either calculating the box diagonal [45] or the geometric mean of width and height [5], since the commonly used inter-ocular distance underestimates the scale with yaw. For more accurate scale estimates under large poses, we calculate the root mean square (RMS) of the three landmark deviations from center. Thus, the pose alignment error is

$$E_P = \frac{1}{3} \frac{\sum_{k=1}^{3} \|\hat{\mathbf{p}}_k - \mathbf{p}_k\|_2}{s_{rms}}, \quad s_{rms} = \sqrt{\frac{\sum_{k=1}^{3} \|\mathbf{p}_k - \bar{\mathbf{p}}\|_2^2}{3}} \qquad (10)$$

where $\bar{\mathbf{p}}$ is the center of the ground-truth landmarks, and $\mathbf{p}_k$ and $\hat{\mathbf{p}}_k$ are the ground-truth and predicted coordinates for the kth landmark, respectively.

Accuracy and precision: We evaluate accuracy and precision using the error metric in Equation (10). Accuracy is measured by a failure percentage. We assume that, within a maximum error allowed for successful alignment, human annotations of the same pose should agree with 99% probability. Therefore the failure threshold is set to the 99th percentile of the annotator disagreement error, which is 0.308. As a consequence, precision is calculated as the average error of the predictions that are deemed as successful.

Regular temporal re-sampling: Due to sparse prediction, we perform regular re-sampling via bounded nearest neighbor (BNN) interpolation since each event has a finite time-support. This is realized by assigning the index of the predicted pose-change event at t according to

$$j_{BNN}(t) = \underset{j \in \{d_j(t) \leq \frac{\tau}{2}\}}{\arg\min} [d_j(t)], \quad d_j(t) = t - \hat{t}_j. \qquad (11)$$

Thus, if the normalized distance is $d_j(t) > \tau/2$, then $j_{BNN}(t) = \emptyset$, meaning time-point t is not supported by any pose-event, i.e., alignment is not activated. For those time-points, we take the given initial pose as the prediction not to cause a misleading bias on error statistics. The re-sampling step size is 1 ms. For the regular re-sampling of the ground-truth that is available only at key-frames, linear interpolation is applied.

Speed-balanced evaluation: With ECs, motion is a major source of variation unlike in the conventional camera observations. Especially head movement speed is a crucial variable that can affect performance. Highly imbalanced speed distribution of a test dataset can be misleading when generalized for dissimilar speed distributions. Therefore it is essential to assess speed dependent alignment performance. For this evaluation, we do speed quantization by partitioning the regularly re-sampled test samples according to their ground-truth speed levels. Moreover, we can practically estimate expectations over any distribution of the speed levels. Particularly in this study, we take expectation on the uniform speed distribution to be able to evaluate with a more generalized average performance score, i.e., to suppress the speed bias of the test set. We calculate the observed speed on the image plane by estimating RMS speed of the pose vector (concatenated landmark coordinates) at time-point t by differentiation

$$v_t = \frac{d_t}{\Delta t} = \frac{\|\mathbf{P}_{(t+\Delta t/2)} - \mathbf{P}_{(t-\Delta t/2)}\|_2}{\Delta t \sqrt{3}} \qquad (12)$$

where d_t is the RMS distance between successive ground-truth pose vectors. Then we compose six speed levels with the upper interval boundaries: $\{1, 75, 150, 225, 300, 375, 450\}$ pix/s (pixels per second). The range of $[0, 1]$ pix/s is evaluated separately, by labeling them as still head poses. We chose six speed levels; because, while it allows us to observe sufficiently different levels of movement speeds, it is also small enough to concisely report the evaluations. The upper limit is chosen to exclude very high speed outliers; after a statistical outlier analysis and then rounding to 450 for convenience as it is divisible by six.

Dual cross validation: We evaluate by cross validation and by separating training and test subjects, since the subject variation is limited by 18 subjects in our dataset. As we have two different predictors running in a cascade, their training and testing are performed by two different cross validation. For the detector, we apply 3-fold cross validation providing $(12, 6)$ splits of the subjects; and for the pose regression, 6-fold cross validation is applied providing splits of $(15, 3)$. We opted for a smaller training set for the former to considerably reduce the training and testing times as the method requires multiple passes over the whole EC database. Because the model complexity of the detector is very low, i.e., there are only a few parameters to estimate, smaller training sets do not deteriorate the detection performance. Also, the training set of the detector is further divided as $(8, 4)$ to adjust the FNRs on four subjects within each training fold while fitting on the eight. We set the FNR goal to 0.05 as it provides a good compromise between detection and pose-event rates, and observed that by this method resulting FNR values on the test sets met the goal closely.

Initialization: In a complete face analysis system, a face template is initially aligned via a coarse similarity transformation estimate. Commonly the face detection bounding box is used to obtain coarse location and scale estimates. A better initialization can be made in a tracking framework based on temporal continuity of pose/shape vectors [45], with joint detection and alignment [41], or using a coarse pose estimation [46]. Good initialization simplifies the alignment task. However, regression-based methods can be sensitive to the face detector as well as the bounding box configuration, since a model of mapping learned in the training stage may not correspond well to the mappings due to initialization with a different detector applied in testing in Sagonas et al. [59]. For experimentation, we simulate face detectors of different quality regarding the position and scale uncertainty, with the expectation that a typical detector predicts the face position within the size of the eyes-mouth triangle. We assume rotation and the rest of the affine pose components are totally unknown, therefore we fix them to identity transformations. For this reason, in-plane and out-of-plane rotations can cause very high errors even when translation and scale initialization is good. Translation is sampled using a uniform density over a circular region of radius r_{trl}, and scale is sampled within a uniform density at logarithmic scale of the range $[1/r_{scl}, r_{scl}]$. Since s_{rms} in Equation (10) is the statistical size measure, we parameterize the translation range in the units of s_{rms}. We experiment with three levels of scale-space localization uncertainty settings given in Table 2. While the low simulation setting can be considered to be a state-of-the-art face detector with conventional cameras or a tracker with significant jitter noise, the medium and higher cases correspond to less precise detectors. We simulate also by high localization imprecision since EC-only face detectors may be much less precise than the conventional face detectors due to differential observations and motion induced uncertainty.

Table 2. Pose initialization uncertainty ranges.

Uncertainty	Low	Medium	High
r_{trl} (translation)	0.25	0.5	1.0
r_{scl} (scale)	0.1	0.2	0.4

5.2. Comparison against Human Performance

Since there is no prior work on pose alignment with ECs, we evaluate our method by comparing against a second set of human annotators who annotate the landmarks on the EC observations as described in Section 3.3. Thus, the errors due to the disagreement between the two sets of annotators serve as a very strong EC baseline.

For feature search and selection in the training for regression, we sample event-cell pairs over a square area of width $8s_{rms}$ centered at the input pose center; because, relatively large sampling domain is helpful to capture patterns that can occur far away due to motion or due to poor initialization. We apply down-sampling to lower the spatial input resolution as explained in Section 5.3. We empirically found good parameter values of feature selection that help to complete training in a reasonable amount of time without degrading the performance significantly as follows. The prior on the coordinate pairs is modeled by $\lambda = 0.5$ with the $1/s_{rms}$ unit (Equation (9)). The random feature selection pool size is set to 1000. We sample cell-mass difference thresholds of the node splits, i.e., c_{th} in Equation (8), in the range of $[-0.01, 0.01] \cdot \tau \cdot \Delta x^s \cdot \Delta y^s$ events, i.e., within the centered density interval of 0.02 events/(ms · pix^2). 40 trials are performed to find an optimal pair of features and decision thresholds at each tree node.

We adjust the predictor model with an optimal complexity as follows, which is comparatively evaluated in Section 5.4. A forest of 40 trees at each stage of gradient boosting is used, as it is sufficiently big to regularize while small enough not to degrade the accuracy. Tree depth is set to four. 16 initialization clusters are estimated to fit the model as well as to be used in prediction. Both the bottom-level and top-level cascade lengths are set to 10, hence feature sampling for pose-invariance is done at every 10 stages and the total cascade length is 100.

Table 3 compares our predictor performance and inter-human annotation disagreements by average accuracy and precision in terms of failure percentages and precision errors, separately for intense and moderate head motion clips as well. The averages are taken excluding the still frames that are in RMS speed range of [0,1) pix/s. Here the predictor runs under low initial localization uncertainty setting (see Table 2). We see that inter-human disagreements in terms of average accuracy and precision are smaller than prediction errors, as expected. However, for moderate head motion clips, average prediction errors are very close to inter-human disagreements.

Human superiority is seen for almost all the head movement speed levels in Table 4 as well. The only exceptions are the second fastest level ([300, 375) pix/s) and the speed levels above 75 pix/s in the moderate motion category where the results are comparable. In general, at the fastest and slowest movements alignment mismatches are getting worse. While inter-human disagreements are slightly increasing, predictor performance worsens strikingly, especially at the highest speed level. These degradations can possibly be due to higher degrees of ambiguity, as in a fixed temporal window significant motion blur can occur at the fastest speeds and observations can become very weak at the slowest speeds.

We also see the resulting pose-event rates in Table 3. EC skips still head pose moments by means of motion detection, thus avoids unnecessary processing for alignment. The resulting average pose-event rate is 32.2 Hz as seen in Table 3. The processing rate with conventional video frames corresponds to the fixed rate of 50 Hz due to 20 ms time-steps. Please note that pose-event rate is even less with moderate motion clips.

Face detectors or trackers provide face position and scale with some degree of uncertainty to initialize the alignment. To characterize with respect to scale-space localization uncertainty, and thus to be able to determine required precision levels of EC-based face detectors and trackers, we evaluate under three uncertainty ranges given in Table 2. Figure 3 compares the accuracy and precision of our predictor and human annotators (using an optimal model complexity configuration for each uncertainty level according to Section 5.4). Please note that the resulting average pose-event rates for the three uncertainty levels are almost the same; as 32.2 Hz, 32.0 Hz, 32.7 Hz from low to high uncertainty, respectively. On the left of Figure 3, the heat map shows the failure percentages of the individual speed levels as well as the averages over all excluding the still head labels. As expected, failures escalate with increasing uncertainty range for all the speed levels. The worsening effect at the fastest and slowest motion levels as explained above are much more prominent with increasing localization uncertainty. Moreover, the two slowest speed levels cause more severe degradations, which can be explained by undetected motion not activating the alignment, since in the absence of activity EC sensors only emit pixel-events due to noise.

Table 3. Comparison of average prediction errors under low localization uncertainty with inter-human annotation disagreement errors for all, intense and moderate head motion clips (E-rate: average pose-event rate in Hz., Fail %: alignment failure percentage and P. Err.: alignment precision error).

Category	Prediction			Human Annotation	
	E-Rate (Hz)	Fail %	P. Err.	Fail %	P. Err.
All	32.2	2.73	0.13	1.02	0.12
Intense motion	36.3	3.15	0.13	1.10	0.12
Moderate motion	29.1	0.42	0.11	0.36	0.11

Table 4. Speed level comparison of prediction and human annotation in terms of failure percentages under low localization uncertainty for all, intense and moderate head motion clips. Each column displays prediction (Pr.) and human annotation (Hu.) failures for a RMS speed range in pix/s.

Category	[0,1)	[1,75)	[75,150)	[150,225)	[225,300)	[300,375)	[375,450)	avg.
	Pr. – Hu.	Pr. – Hu.	Pr. – Hu.	Pr. – Hu.	Pr. – Hu.	Pr. – Hu.	Pr. – Hu.	Pr. – Hu.
All	2.1 – 1.0	2.6 – 1.0	1.2 – 0.8	1.3 – 0.4	1.1 – 0.7	1.5 – 1.8	8.8 – 1.6	2.7 – 1.0
Intense motion	4.1 – 1.7	4.5 – 1.3	1.7 – 0.8	1.4 – 0.4	1.1 – 0.7	1.5 – 1.8	8.8 – 1.6	3.2 – 1.1
Moderate motion	1.1 – 0.7	1.7 – 0.8	0.0 – 0.6	0.0 – 0.0	0.0 – 0.0	–	–	0.4 – 0.4

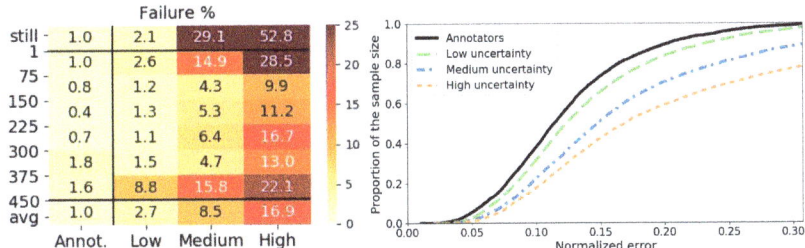

Figure 3. Comparison of prediction and human annotation under low, medium and high localization uncertainty ranges. Failure percentages are shown on the heat map where rows are the speed levels (still: no head motion label [0,1) pix/s, avg: average over levels excluding [0,1) pix/s). Cumulative distribution curves of the precision error are shown on the right where speed balancing is realized by sub-sampling without replacement equally from each speed interval.

On the right of Figure 3, cumulative distributions of the precision error are shown, after speed level balancing by sub-sampling without replacement from each speed interval with the size of the smallest speed partition. For all the uncertainty levels, the curves start from similarly low error values, but with increasing error, higher uncertainty in localization makes the error distribution more dissimilar to the annotators curve worsening the precision.

Figure 4 shows example snapshots of alignments (orange triangular shapes) at the high initial localization uncertainty setting (initialized by blue dashed triangular shapes) compared to the two sets of human annotators (ground-truth: red dots, second set: green circles). We see accurate prediction of landmarks (below the failure threshold 0.308) for various poses involving talking lips and eye blinks as well as roll, yaw and pitch rotations. An example of alignment by eye blinks are at the cell "6b", and by talking lips are at "1c", "2b", "2d", and "6d". Alignment can accurately be done also when the mouth is cropped as seen at "7d". Precision of the detector, in general, slightly worse than the human annotators. However, occasionally there are opposite cases as well. For instance, due to the hair occlusion on the left eye at the cell "4c", human disagreement is higher than the prediction error whereas prediction could locate the left eye similarly to the ground-truth. Small annotator disagreements are observed also due the talking lips in "2d" and on the eyes due to a fast movement at "7b".

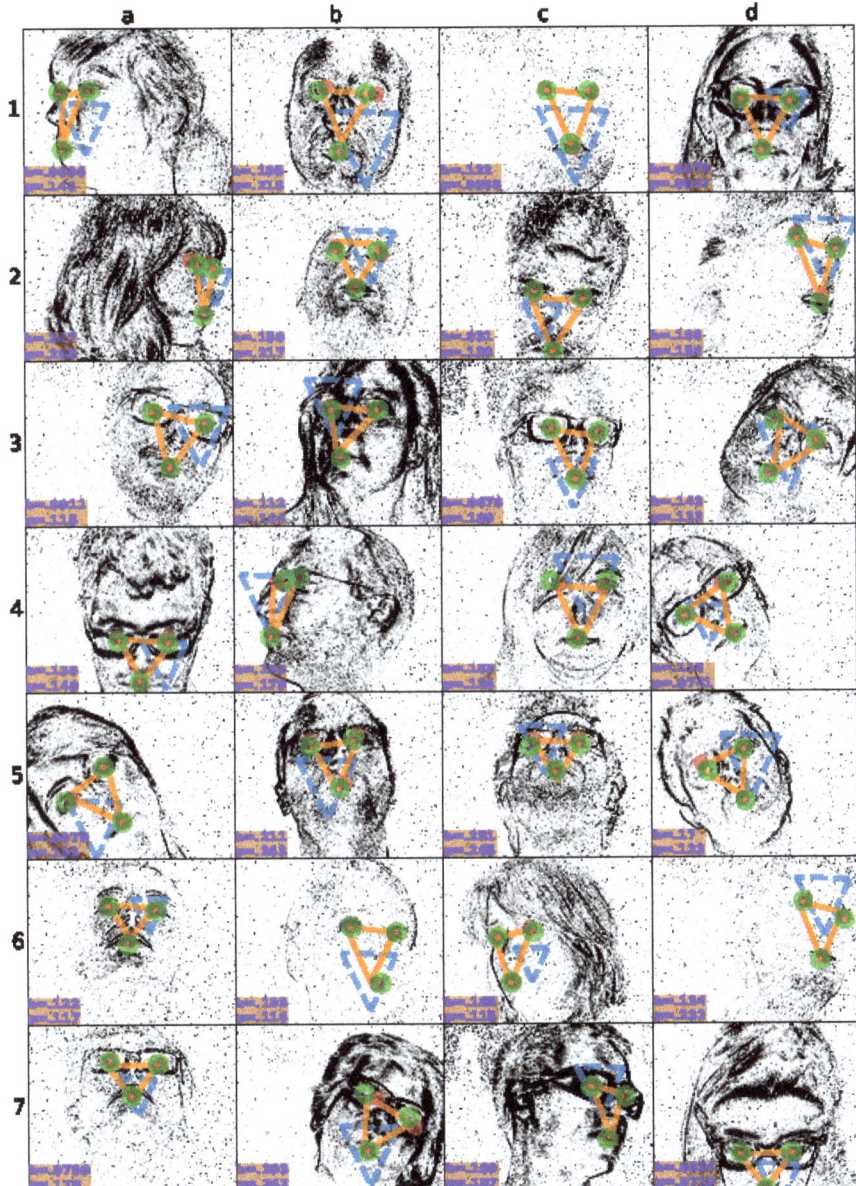

Figure 4. Snapshots of alignments at the high localization uncertainty setting. Each plot (**a–d, 1–7**) shows a different snapshot from a different subject, or head pose. At each snapshot ground-truth annotation (red dots), second human annotation (green circles), initialization (blue dashed triangular shape), and prediction (orange triangular shape) are overlaid. Inter-human disagreement (h) and prediction (p) errors are written at the left-bottom corners.

5.3. Evaluation of Face Resolution

In our dataset, face resolution is quite high, as eye-to-eye distance frontal view is 67 pixels on average. Depending on the sensor, lens, and distance to camera, acquired face resolution can be much lower in different applications. Lower resolutions might have an unexpected negative impact on the performance, since event sensor data has the complexity of high degree of variations due to motion dependence which may complicate the alignment if some necessary details are lost. Conversely it may also lead to improvements, since learning is facilitated due to reduced feature search space which originally contains too much redundancy for the alignment task. To clarify these possible cases, we investigate the effects of lower resolutions on the performance.

We experiment by applying spatial down-sampling via pixel-event cells, with the down-scaling ratios of 2^{-1}, 2^{-2} and 2^{-3}, and using odd cell sizes. Example snapshots of the resulting spatial-scales are shown in Figure 5. Table 5 shows the corresponding event-cell sizes, resolutions and alignment failure percentages for the three levels of uncertainty depending on the down-sampling ratio. Failures increase one octave below 2^{-3} for all the uncertainty levels. In this experiment, to reduce the experimentation time, we use four initialization clusters and tree depth of four. It is seen that optimal down-sampling ratio also greatly depends on the localization uncertainty. The optimal ratios are 2^{-2} for the low level, and 2^{-3} for the medium and high level uncertainties. These results indicate the benefit of eliminating redundancy and fine details for the coarse pose alignment task with ECs, especially for the more challenging cases of higher localization uncertainties, as well as demonstrate the pose alignment capability for wider range of applications and with cheaper lower resolution sensors.

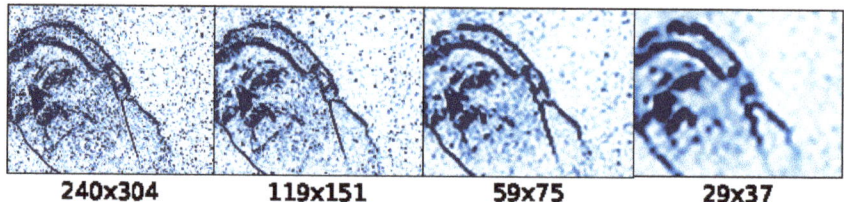

Figure 5. Pixel-event snapshots of 40 ms frame at different spatial scales while head is rotating (71.2 pix/s RMS speed). The scales from left to right are 1, 2^{-1}, 2^{-2} and 2^{-3}, with pixel sizes written below.

Table 5. Alignment failure percentages for varying down-scales at the three levels of localization uncertainties. In bold, the optimal performance for a given uncertainty level.

Spatial down-sampling	2^{-1}	2^{-2}	2^{-3}
Event-cell size	3×3	5×5	9×9
Resolution	119×151	59×75	29×37
Low Uncertainty	3.1	**2.7**	4.0
Medium Uncertainty	14.6	13.7	**12.6**
High Uncertainty	26.9	25.6	**24.0**

5.4. Evaluation of Model Complexity

Complexity of a predictor alters the trade-off between computation requirements and performance. Also, higher complexity models can cause over-learning which degrades the generalization on the test set. For these reasons, we analyze the performance of EC-based pose alignment by varying the complexity of our predictor, for different levels of localization uncertainty ranges. The main parameters that change the model complexity are tree depth, cascade length and number of initialization clusters. We observed significant improvements up to 16 initialization clusters. For instance, more than 3% of failures are recovered by increasing the clusters from four to 16 for the high uncertainty level case, and about 1% for the other ranges. Higher number of clusters improves the performance by reducing the chance of getting stuck at poorly initialized predictions and by enabling a richer data augmentation in training. However, from 16 to 32 the improvements were negligible with the expense of doubling the computations. Therefore we set the number of clusters to 16.

Second, we investigate the effects of tree depth. Table 6 shows that increasing the tree depth improves the learning capacity, up to a certain level after which over-fitting starts to cause significant degradation. While depth of six is the best for the high and medium uncertainty cases, four levels obtains the lowest rate for the low case.

Table 6. Alignment failure percentages for varying tree depths at the three levels of localization uncertainties. In bold, the optimal value for each uncertainty level.

Tree Depth	2	4	6	8
Low Uncertainty	4.2	**2.7**	3.0	3.2
Medium Uncertainty	14.7	10.3	**8.5**	9.7
High Uncertainty	26.4	18.9	**16.9**	17.3

Finally, we evaluate the cascade length in Figure 6 which shows the failure percentage versus top-level cascade length, for each localization uncertainty level using the best tree depths according to Table 6. The majority of the improvements are rapidly achieved in the first few stages, and then failure percentages slowly decrease. We picked the length of 10 for all the comparative evaluations in this paper, though some small amount of improvement is still possible with longer cascades. Similarly, the length of the bottom-level cascade is also fixed at 10 (hence total number of stages is 100), due to insignificant changes on the results. The results with the selected optimal parameters are reported in Table 7.

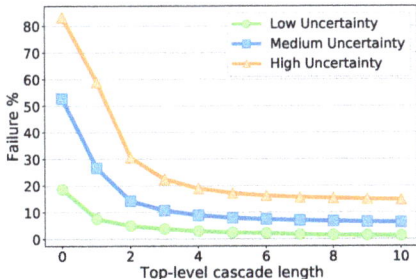

Figure 6. Failure percentages with varying cascade length for the three initialization uncertainty ranges.

Table 7. Optimal settings and resulting failure percentages at the three levels of localization uncertainty ranges.

Method	Prediction Low	Prediction Medium	Prediction High	Human Annotators
Spatial down-sampling	1/4	1/8	1/8	–
Tree depth	4	6	6	–
Failure %	2.7	8.5	16.9	1.0

6. Time Complexity Analysis

We estimate time-complexity of the proposed face pose alignment as a measure of its efficiency. It depends on pose-event rate and on the time-complexity of the cascaded regression. Compared to regression, time-complexity of pixel-event accumulation (integer increments) and of the detector are negligible. While pixel-events are accumulated at a rate depending on scene activity and sensor configuration, the motion detector has a fixed rate determined by the time-step, and each detection activates the pose regression, thus generates a pose-event.

The time-complexity of the detector is $O(N_{det})$ where N_{det} is the total number of cells in the multi-scale grid of L levels. For each cell, superimposition (a multiplication and an addition) and nearest neighbor re-sampling operations are performed. As operations per second, i.e., in Hz, time-complexity is measured by the product of the detector sampling rate and complexity, $O_{Hz}(fN_{det})$, where f is the sampling rate. Since 20 ms time-steps correspond to 50Hz rate and $N_{det} = 1886$ (for multi-scale grid of $L = 5$ levels), scalar multiplication operations per second is expressed as $O_{Hz}(50 \times 1886) =$

$O_{Hz}(94,300)$. It is much lower than of the matrix operations for alignment which is given in the sequel. Therefore, the complexity of the detector becomes dominant only for the rare or no activity cases. It can also be reduced by tuning for the spatial grid resolution and detection trade-off (being already lightweight, we did not tune in the experiments).

Time-complexity of a single pose-invariant cascaded regression is determined by the alignment refinement performed at each top-level cascade stage since it involves matrix multiplication of feature coordinates, as the most expensive operation. The maximum number of matrix multiplications is twice the total number of split nodes, since there is a feature point pair at each. However, since we sample from a random coordinate pool at each top-level stage (see Section 4.4) which has a total point size less than of the number of the feature points in the ensemble due to the parameter configuration in Section 5.2, the upper bound in our study is lower. Given N_{pool} pool feature points per stage and N_{mult} multiple regressions, the complexity is $O(N_{align}) = O(N_{mult} \cdot K \cdot N_{pool})$. The sum over six dimensional pose displacement vectors of the tree leaves is relatively insignificant. On the other hand, the overall detection-based pose alignment complexity depends on the detection frequency, f_{det}, which in turn changes depending on the input, i.e., scene activity. The upper bound on the operations per second is $O_{Hz}(f_{det}N_{align})$.

Since the average detection rate on the whole dataset is $f_{det} = 32.2$ Hz (see Section 5.2), applying the alignment complexity based on upper bound on the matrix multiplications with $N_{mult} = 16$, $K = 10$, $N_{pool} = 1000$, the operation rate is obtained as $O_{Hz}(32.2 \cdot 16 \cdot 10 \cdot 1000) = O_{Hz}(5,152,000)$. Also, after reducing by $N_{mult} = 4$ for the low uncertainty setting with the expense of less then 1% drop on performance, we obtain $O_{Hz}(1,288,000)$. In MFlops (mega floating point operations per second), these values translate to about 5 MFlops and 21 MFlops, as total scalar multiplications due to 2×2 matrices. The complexity of the detection is insignificant compared to the matrix multiplications performed in alignment. Moreover, we also observed that by reducing the pool size, N_{pool}, the regression computations can be greatly reduced with only small alignment performance loss. However, in the absence of significant activity, operation rate will be at the bottom levels of the motion detector. On the other hand, the same alignment with the same time-steps would be at a fixed video rate of 50 Hz, hence with about 1.6 times more operations.

Similar cascaded ensemble regression-based methods on video are the fastest methods in the literature (1k frame per second [9] and 3 kfps [10]). While computation speed is not a measure of efficiency, since speed depends on other factors and usually relies on power-hungry hardware acceleration, methods that perform at such high speed can trade off high efficiency with speed, similarly to implementations based on pose-event rate. Real-time DNN inference is a challenge, and faster DNNs can only be obtained by means of binarization [26]. Efficiency of DNNs is by no means comparable to the efficiency of cascaded ensemble based prediction as they require GPUs which have demanding power requirements. While our method only performs coarse alignment with three landmarks, prior methods perform detailed alignment with about 70 [10] or 200 landmarks [9]. Although there is no linear relationship between landmark count and efficiency, still low landmark count considerably improves efficiency. Combining with the efficiency of the sensor (we elaborate on it in Section 7), we can safely conclude that the proposed face pose alignment is an extremely efficient method to fulfill the coarse alignment task we aim at.

7. Discussion

Compared to frame-based image acquisition, bio-inspired, activity dependent, sparse encoding from ECs offers lower power consumption, higher temporal resolution, higher dynamic range, at the cost of lower spatial resolution and lack of full image intensity measurements. The continuous improvement of such sensors in terms of spatial resolution, quality and cost, thanks to the involvement of companies that are developing products for mass production, and the demonstration that their output is highly informative [60,61], support the development of algorithms such as the one proposed in this work. Below we discuss all these pros and cons in the context of EC-based face pose alignment.

Low power consumption. EC power consumption inversely depends on scene activity, and power requirements stay at minimal levels in the absence of motion. For instance, ATIS sensor [2] that is used in this work consumes 50 mW in the idle state while 175 mW with intense scene activity. The values for some other well known ECs changes as follows: 27–50 mW for Samsung-DVS-Gen2 [62], 10–170 mW for DAVIS346, 5–14 mW for DAVIS240 [1] and 23 mW for DVS128 [63]. Facial movements elicit a low number of events, as they are produced only during head motion, or blinks and speech production, maintaining the sensor's activity, and hence power, at a minimum. In comparison, power consumption of conventional cameras mounted in mobile phones are around 1 W and can go up to 1.5 W depending on the model [64]. Therefore ECs are highly suitable in battery critical scenarios. Such cases are specifically common in robotics and for some mobile device applications. For instance, as a mobile phone application, we can use our method either for pose-free or pose-dependent extension of voice activity detection which has shown to be power efficient and noise robust [6]. As the phone stays active for long durations, EC-based processing can save considerable energy, and with the advantage of using the visual channel to cope with noisy acoustic environments. Other types of facial actions, head/facial gestures and expressions, can also be implemented similarly for low-power scenarios by employing coarse pose alignment. Thanks to the adaptive sampling, ECs can considerably reduce computation as well, if the rate of processing is adapted to the pixel-event rate. In the pipeline proposed in this paper, the average processing rate ranges between 29.1 and 36.3 Hz (for clips with moderate and intense motion, respectively), roughly 40% less than in a frame-based implementation (Table 3).

High temporal resolution: ECs can provide up to MHz sampling resolution with high speed input motion, and with proportionally low latency. The stream of events from ECs does not suffer from motion blur [54], which is often observed in images of fast head rotations, on the mouth during speech, or due to camera motion, avoiding the need to implement costly de-blurring in face alignment [12]. ECs are therefore suitable in applications where motion provide the most relevant information, as in facial action recognition, voice activity detection and visual speech recognition, that must be robust to face pose variations.

High dynamic range: Although exploitation of the high intra-scene dynamic range feature of ECs is out of scope of our study, in general, it offers robustness to changing and uneven illumination conditions in all applications in uncontrolled environments, as shown for facial image reconstruction [54], for autonomous driving [35] and for drone vision [65].

Lack of full intensity measurements: Conventional methods work on whole static intensity images, and therefore their precision and detail level (number of landmarks) can be very high. Intensity reconstruction may be considered to be an alternative way for higher precision alignments but it requires expensive computation. For these reasons, certain kinds of applications are not suitable, at least currently, with ECs. For instance, facial performance capture for animation or 3D reconstruction of the whole facial surface and applications based on it (3D face recognition, face transfer, etc.) can be realized by using video cameras with much less effort and with higher fidelity.

Low spatial resolution: Most of the current ECs have lower spatial resolutions than video cameras. Nevertheless, in various applications where motion and dynamics information are the most relevant, high spatial resolution is not critical, unlike texture related processing, such as in 3D face surface reconstruction. Besides, depending on the specific requirements of the application, higher spatial resolution ECs can be used, at the cost of higher computational cost and higher power budget [66].

Hybrid pipelines: Hybrid of complementary event and image sensors can remove some of their shortcomings while enabling the benefits. There also exists compact hybrid sensor solutions [1] sharing the same lens, which can be employed, for instance, for motion de-blurring as shown recently [33]. Therefore, alternatively, for energy efficient higher precision and detailed alignment, the coarse face pose estimation can activate a more precise frame-based image acquisition and processing, after a first detection, implementing an approach similar to progressive initialization [43].

8. Conclusions and Future Work

We showed for the first time face pose alignment with an EC, validated on a challenging EC dataset featuring large head pose variations at different speeds and large differences in face appearance. We devised an evaluation methodology which also takes EC sensor related issues into account. We applied motion detection to drive a cascaded tree ensemble regression for alignment. The proposed coarse pose alignment is thought as a preliminary processing for pose-free EC-based facial processing applications. Specifically, the use of EC sensors coupled with the proposed face alignment, can favour the development of EC-based algorithms for applications that mostly rely on temporal information extraction, such as voice activity detection, speech recognition or dynamics-based identity recognition.

Since ECs are motion sensitive, we made speed-dependent assessments and performed speed-balanced quantitative characterisation, to suppress the speed bias on the test set for better generalization. Our work targeted extremely efficient coarse alignment exploiting the characteristics of EC. The algorithm implementation is therefore tuned to such data. A comparison with the state of the art would require the translation of the event stream into frames and vice versa. The results would depend on the method used to generate frames from events, making the comparison dependent not only on the algorithm used for regression. For an assessment of the proposed pose predictor we therefore compared to human performance, exploiting the ground truth data from human annotators. In parts of the dataset there is significant disagreement between human annotators, due to absence of static texture measurements with event sensors, in these points, the errors of the predictor are more pronounced than inter-human disagreements both in terms of accuracy and precision. When the human disagreement rate is about 1%, the average predictor failure rate is about 2.7%. The failure rate increases to 3.15% for intense motion clips while human disagreement rate slightly goes up to 1.1%. On the other hand, with moderate motion clips, failure and disagreement rates are 0.42% and 0.36%, respectively. In general, both predictor and human performance deteriorates in correspondence of the slowest and fastest movements.

We characterised the predictor performance under different levels of initial scale-space localization uncertainty, to simulate face detectors/trackers of different precision. With increasing uncertainty, the alignment errors significantly increase. In addition, we investigated the performance of different levels of predictor complexity. When the given face location is relatively closer to the true coordinates, i.e., at low localization uncertainty, a simpler predictor obtains performance close to the human-baseline, except for the fastest and the slowest speed levels. To improve robustness to increased localisation uncertainty, the predictor must rely on more complex models. Decreasing the spatial resolution to as low as 29×37 pixels degrades the performance of about 1%, showing that EC-based pose alignment can work at very low spatial resolution.

In addition to the alignment quality, we also evaluated the time-complexity of the predictor, which is extremely low thanks to the use of the most efficient alignment approach in the literature. Our analysis shows that the alignment operation is the computationally dominant part and the motion detector is extremely lightweight. Since the alignment is activated only when there is motion, our method also helps to keep power consumption at lower levels in the absence of significant motion and is extremely appealing for always-on embedded processing. The average alignment rate in our dataset, after combining intense motion and moderate motion clips, is 32.2 Hz, instead of 50 Hz for fixed video-rate processing. Consequently, average time-complexity performance changes from 5 MFLOPs to 21 MFLOPs, depending on the level of localization uncertainty conditions.

Using EC as a novel vision modality for face pose alignment opens up a new area of future study. We believe there is a big room for improvements. More informative or more invariant pixel-event features as well as different predictor models can be explored. To deal with high initial localization uncertainty, and allow for the use of imprecise, but efficient, EC-based face detectors, joint face motion localization and detection can be developed. To better handle the slowest and fastest motion levels, speed-dependent prediction can be studied. Another future work could focus on improvements to computation efficiency, especially taking advantage of the highly sparse nature of EC data.

Including tracking could be highly beneficial, though with additional challenges. While detection-based alignment is still needed at initialization and is crucial to prevent drifting [45,48], tracking can reduce alignment complexity by relying on previous predictions, and accuracy can be improved by exploiting temporal information and spatio-temporal continuity. Finally, higher precision alignment may be achieved by using more landmarks, if ground-truth of sufficient precision can be acquired, by incorporating intensity sensors or perhaps by the help of intensity reconstruction [34].

Author Contributions: Conceptualization, A.S.; methodology, A.S.; software, A.S.; validation, A.S.; formal analysis, A.S.; investigation, A.S.; resources, C.B.; data curation, A.S. and C.B.; writing—original draft preparation, A.S.; writing—review and editing, A.S. and C.B.; visualization, A.S.; supervision, C.B.; project administration, A.S. and C.B.; funding acquisition, C.B. All authors have read and agreed to the published version of the manuscript.

Funding: This work is supported by the European Union's Horizon2020 project ECOMODE (grant No 644096).

Conflicts of Interest: The authors declare no conflict of interest. The funders had no role in the design of the study; in the collection, analyses, or interpretation of data; in the writing of the manuscript, or in the decision to publish the results.

Abbreviations

The following abbreviations are used in this manuscript:

EC	Event camera
ERT	Extremely randomized trees
DNN	Deep neural network
GPA	Generalized Procrustes analysis
FNR	False negative rate
RMS	Root mean square

References

1. Brandli, C.; Berner, R.; Yang, M.; Liu, S.C.; Delbruck, T. A 240 × 180 130 dB 3 µs Latency Global Shutter Spatiotemporal Vision Sensor. *IEEE J. Solid-State Circuits* **2014**, *49*, 2333–2341. [CrossRef]
2. Posch, C.; Matolin, D.; Wohlgenannt, R. A QVGA 143 dB Dynamic Range Frame-Free PWM Image Sensor With Lossless Pixel-Level Video Compression and Time-Domain CDS. *IEEE J. Solid-State Circuits* **2010**, *46*, 259–275. [CrossRef]
3. Wu, Y.; Ji, Q. Facial Landmark Detection: A Literature Survey. *IJCV* **2018**, *127*, 115–142. [CrossRef]
4. Jin, X.; Tan, X. Face Alignment In-the-wild. *Comput. Vis. Image Underst.* **2017**, *162*, 1–22. [CrossRef]
5. Bulat, A.; Tzimiropoulos, G. How far are we from solving the 2D & 3D Face Alignment problem? (and a dataset of 230,000 3D facial landmarks). In Proceedings of the IEEE International Conference on Computer Vision (ICCV), Venice, Italy, 22–29 October 2017.
6. Savran, A.; Tavarone, R.; Higy, B.; Badino, L.; Bartolozzi, C. Energy and Computation Efficient Audio-Visual Voice Activity Detection Driven by Event-Cameras. In Proceedings of the 13th IEEE International Conference on Automatic Face & Gesture Recognition (FG 2018), Xi'an, China, 15–19 May 2018.
7. Li, X.; Neil, D.; Delbruck, T.; Liu, S. Lip Reading Deep Network Exploiting Multi-Modal Spiking Visual and Auditory Sensors. In Proceedings of the 2019 IEEE International Symposium on Circuits and Systems (ISCAS), Sapporo, Japan, 26–29 May 2019. [CrossRef]
8. Lagorce, X.; Orchard, G.; Gallupi, F.; Shi, B.E.; Benosman, R. HOTS: A Hierarchy Of event-based Time-Surfaces for pattern recognition. *IEEE Trans. Pattern Anal. Mach. Intell.* **2016**, *39*, 1346–1359. doi:10.1109/TPAMI.2016.2574707. [CrossRef]
9. Kazemi, V.; Sullivan, J. One Millisecond Face Alignment with an Ensemble of Regression Trees. In Proceedings of the IEEE Conference on Computer Vision and Pattern Recognition, Columbus, OH, USA, 23–28 June 2014. [CrossRef]
10. Ren, S.; Cao, X.; Wei, Y.; Sun, J. Face Alignment at 3000 FPS via Regressing Local Binary Features. In Proceedings of the IEEE Conference on Computer Vision and Pattern Recognition, Columbus, OH, USA, 23–28 June 2014. [CrossRef]

11. Zhu, X.; Liu, X.; Lei, Z.; Li, S.Z. Face Alignment in Full Pose Range: A 3D Total Solution. *IEEE Trans. Pattern Anal. Mach. Intell.* **2019**, *41*, 78–92. [CrossRef]
12. Sun, K.; Wu, W.; Liu, T.; Yang, S.; Wang, Q.; Zhou, Q.; Ye, Z.; Qian, C. FAB: A Robust Facial Landmark Detection Framework for Motion-Blurred Videos. In Proceedings of the IEEE/CVF International Conference on Computer Vision (ICCV), Seoul, Korea, 27 October–2 November 2019.
13. Miao, X.; Zhen, X.; Liu, X.; Deng, C.; Athitsos, V.; Huang, H. Direct Shape Regression Networks for End-to-End Face Alignment. In Proceedings of the IEEE Conference on Computer Vision and Pattern Recognition, Salt Lake City, UT, USA, 18–22 June 2018.
14. Wu, Y.; Hassner, T.; Kim, K.; Medioni, G.; Natarajan, P. Facial Landmark Detection with Tweaked Convolutional Neural Networks. *IEEE Trans. Pattern Anal. Mach. Intell.* **2018**, *40*, 3067–3074. [CrossRef]
15. Bulat, A.; Tzimiropoulos, G. Super-FAN: Integrated Facial Landmark Localization and Super-Resolution of Real-World Low Resolution Faces in Arbitrary Poses With GANs. In Proceedings of the IEEE Conference on Computer Vision and Pattern Recognition, Salt Lake City, UT, USA, 18–22 June 2018. [CrossRef]
16. Dong, X.; Yu, S.I.; Weng, X.; Wei, S.E.; Yang, Y.; Sheikh, Y. Supervision-by-Registration: An Unsupervised Approach to Improve the Precision of Facial Landmark Detectors. In Proceedings of the IEEE Conference on Computer Vision and Pattern Recognition, Salt Lake City, UT, USA, 18–22 June 2018.
17. Merget, D.; Rock, M.; Rigoll, G. Robust Facial Landmark Detection via a Fully-Convolutional Local-Global Context Network. In Proceedings of the IEEE Conference on Computer Vision and Pattern Recognition, Salt Lake City, UT, USA, 18–22 June 2018.
18. Honari, S.; Molchanov, P.; Tyree, S.; Vincent, P.; Pal, C.; Kautz, J. Improving Landmark Localization With Semi-Supervised Learning. In Proceedings of the IEEE Conference on Computer Vision and Pattern Recognition, Salt Lake City, UT, USA, 18–22 June 2018.
19. Feng, Z.H.; Kittler, J.; Awais, M.; Huber, P.; Wu, X.J. Wing Loss for Robust Facial Landmark Localisation With Convolutional Neural Networks. In Proceedings of the IEEE Conference on Computer Vision and Pattern Recognition, Salt Lake City, UT, USA, 18–22 June 2018.
20. Peng, X.; Feris, R.S.; Wang, X.; Metaxas, D.N. RED-Net: A Recurrent Encoder-Decoder Network for Video-Based Face Alignment. *IJCV* **2018**, *126*, 1103–1119. [CrossRef]
21. Xiao, S.; Feng, J.; Liu, L.; Nie, X.; Wang, W.; Yan, S.; Kassim, A.A. Recurrent 3D-2D Dual Learning for Large-Pose Facial Landmark Detection. In Proceedings of the IEEE Conference on Computer Vision and Pattern Recognition, Honolulu, HI, USA, 21–26 July 2017.
22. Jourabloo, A.; Liu, X.; Ye, M.; Ren, L. Pose-Invariant Face Alignment with a Single CNN. In Proceedings of the IEEE Conference on Computer Vision and Pattern Recognition, Honolulu, HI, USA, 21–26 July 2017.
23. Bhagavatula, C.; Zhu, C.; Luu, K.; Savvides, M. Faster than Real-Time Facial Alignment: A 3D Spatial Transformer Network Approach in Unconstrained Poses. In Proceedings of the IEEE Conference on Computer Vision and Pattern Recognition, Honolulu, HI, USA, 21–26 July 2017. [CrossRef]
24. Liu, H.; Lu, J.; Feng, J.; Zhou, J. Two-Stream Transformer Networks for Video-Based Face Alignment. *IEEE Trans. Pattern Anal. Mach. Intell.* **2018**, *40*, 2546–2554. [CrossRef]
25. Lv, J.; Shao, X.; Xing, J.; Cheng, C.; Zhou, X. A Deep Regression Architecture with Two-Stage Re-initialization for High Performance Facial Landmark Detection. In Proceedings of the IEEE Conference on Computer Vision and Pattern Recognition, Honolulu, HI, USA, 21–26 July 2017.
26. Bulat, A.; Tzimiropoulos, G. Binarized Convolutional Landmark Localizers for Human Pose Estimation and Face Alignment with Limited Resources. In Proceedings of the IEEE Conference on Computer Vision and Pattern Recognition, Honolulu, HI, USA, 21–26 July 2017. [CrossRef]
27. Gu, J.; Yang, X.; Mello, S.D.; Kautz, J. Dynamic Facial Analysis: From Bayesian Filtering to Recurrent Neural Network. In Proceedings of the IEEE Conference on Computer Vision and Pattern Recognition, Honolulu, HI, USA, 21–26 July 2017. [CrossRef]
28. Trigeorgis, G.; Snape, P.; Nicolaou, M.A.; Antonakos, E.; Zafeiriou, S. Mnemonic Descent Method: A Recurrent Process Applied for End-to-End Face Alignment. In Proceedings of the IEEE Conference on Computer Vision and Pattern Recognition, Las Vegas, NV, USA, 27–30 June 2016. doi:10.1109/CVPR.2016.453. [CrossRef]
29. Zhang, J.; Shan, S.; Kan, M.; Chen, X. Coarse-to-Fine Auto-Encoder Networks (CFAN) for Real-Time Face Alignment. In Proceedings of the 13th European Conference on Computer Vision (ECCV), Zurich, Switzerland, 6–12 September 2014.

30. Zhang, J.; Kan, M.; Shan, S.; Chen, X. Occlusion-Free Face Alignment: Deep Regression Networks Coupled with De-Corrupt AutoEncoders. In Proceedings of the IEEE Conference on Computer Vision and Pattern Recognition, Las Vegas, NV, USA, 27–30 June 2016.
31. Wu, Y.; Ji, Q. Robust Facial Landmark Detection Under Significant Head Poses and Occlusion. In Proceedings of the 2015 IEEE International Conference on Computer Vision (ICCV), Santiago, Chile, 7–13 December 2015. [CrossRef]
32. Manderscheid, J.; Sironi, A.; Bourdis, N.; Migliore, D.; Lepetit, V. Speed Invariant Time Surface for Learning to Detect Corner Points with Event-Based Cameras. In Proceedings of the 2019 Conference on Computer Vision and Pattern Recognition, Long Beach, CA, USA, 16–20 June 2019. [CrossRef]
33. Zhang, L.; Zhang, H.; Chen, J.; Wang, L. Hybrid Deblur Net: Deep Non-Uniform Deblurring with Event Camera. *IEEE Access* **2020**, *8*, 148075–148083. [CrossRef]
34. Rebecq, H.; Ranftl, R.; Koltun, V.; Scaramuzza, D. Events-To-Video: Bringing Modern Computer Vision to Event Cameras. In Proceedings of the 2019 Conference on Computer Vision and Pattern Recognition, Long Beach, CA, USA, 16–20 June 2019. [CrossRef]
35. Maqueda, A.I.; Loquercio, A.; Gallego, G.; García, N.; Scaramuzza, D. Event-Based Vision Meets Deep Learning on Steering Prediction for Self-Driving Cars. In Proceedings of the 2018 Conference on Computer Vision and Pattern Recognition, Salt Lake, UT, USA, 18–23 June 2018.
36. Friedman, J.H. Greedy Function Approximation: A Gradient Boosting Machine. *Ann. Stat.* **2001**, *29*, 1189–1232. [CrossRef]
37. Dollár, P.; Welinder, P. Cascaded pose regression. In Proceedings of the 2010 Conference on Computer Vision and Pattern Recognition, San Francisco, CA, USA, 13–18 June 2010. [CrossRef]
38. Burgos-Artizzu, X.; Perona, P.; Dollár, P. Robust Face Landmark Estimation Under Occlusion. In Proceedings of the IEEE International Conference on Computer Vision, Sydney, Australia, 1–8 December 2013.
39. Xiong, X.; la Torre, F.D. Supervised Descent Method and Its Applications to Face Alignment. In Proceedings of the 26th IEEE Conference on Computer Vision and Pattern Recognition, Portland, OR, USA, 23–28 June 2013. [CrossRef]
40. Cao, X.; Wei, Y.; Wen, F.; Sun, J. Face Alignment by Explicit Shape Regression. *IJCV* **2014**, *107*, 177–190. [CrossRef]
41. Chen, D.; Ren, S.; Wei, Y.; Cao, X.; Sun, J. Joint Cascade Face Detection and Alignment. In Proceedings of the 13th European Conference, Zurich, Switzerland, 6–12 September 2014. [CrossRef]
42. Zhu, S.; Li, C.; Loy, C.C.; Tang, X. Face alignment by coarse-to-fine shape searching. In Proceedings of the 28th IEEE Conference on Computer Vision and Pattern Recognition, Boston, MA, USA, 7–12 June 2015.
43. Xiao, S.; Yan, S.; Kassim, A.A. Facial Landmark Detection via Progressive Initialization. In Proceedings of the 2015 IEEE International Conference on Computer Vision Workshop, ICCV Workshops, Santiago, Chile, 7–13 December 2015.
44. Lee, D.; Park, H.; Yoo, C.D. Face alignment using cascade Gaussian process regression trees. In Proceedings of the 28th IEEE Conference on Computer Vision and Pattern Recognition, Boston, MA, USA, 7–12 June 2015. [CrossRef]
45. Chrysos, G.G.; Antonakos, E.; Snape, P.; Asthana, A.; Zafeiriou, S. A Comprehensive Performance Evaluation of Deformable Face Tracking "In-the-Wild". *IJCV* **2018**, *126*, 198–232. [CrossRef] [PubMed]
46. Yang, J.; Deng, J.; Zhang, K.; Liu, Q. Facial Shape Tracking via Spatio-Temporal Cascade Shape Regression. In Proceedings of the 2015 IEEE International Conference on Computer Vision Workshop, ICCV Workshops, Santiago, Chile, 7–13 December 2015. [CrossRef]
47. Sánchez-Lozano, E.; Martínez, B.; Tzimiropoulos, G.; Valstar, M.F. Cascaded Continuous Regression for Real-Time Incremental Face Tracking. In Proceedings of the 14th European Conference, Amsterdam, The Netherlands, 11–14 October 2016. [CrossRef]
48. Khan, M.H.; McDonagh, J.; Tzimiropoulos, G. Synergy between Face Alignment and Tracking via Discriminative Global Consensus Optimization. In Proceedings of the International Conference on Computer Vision, Venice, Italy, 22–29 October 2017. [CrossRef]
49. Gallego, G.; Delbrück, T.; Orchard, G.; Bartolozzi, C.; Taba, B.; Censi, A.; Leutenegger, S.; Davison, A.J.; Conradt, J.; Daniilidis, K.; et al. Event-based Vision: A Survey. *arXiv* **2019**, arXiv:1904.08405.

50. Gehrig, D.; Loquercio, A.; Derpanis, K.G.; Scaramuzza, D. End-to-End Learning of Representations for Asynchronous Event-Based Data. In Proceedings of the 2019 International Conference on Computer Vision, Seoul, Korea, 27 October–2 November 2019.
51. Barua, S.; Miyatani, Y.; Veeraraghavan, A. Direct face detection and video reconstruction from event cameras. In Proceedings of the EEE Winter Conference on Application of Computer Vision, Lake Placid, NY, USA, 7–9 March 2016. [CrossRef]
52. Valeiras, D.R.; Lagorce, X.; Clady, X.; Bartolozzi, C.; Ieng, S.; Benosman, R. An Asynchronous Neuromorphic Event-Driven Visual Part-Based Shape Tracking. *IEEE Trans. Neu. Netw. Learn. Syst.* **2015**, *26*, 3045–3059. [CrossRef]
53. Lenz, G.; Ieng, S.H.; Benosman, R. Event-Based Face Detection and Tracking Using the Dynamics of Eye Blinks. *Front. Neurosci.* **2020**, *14*, 587. [CrossRef]
54. Bardow, P.; Davison, A.J.; Leutenegger, S. Simultaneous Optical Flow and Intensity Estimation from an Event Camera. In Proceedings of the 2016 IEEE Conference on Computer Vision and Pattern Recognition (CVPR), Las Vegas, NV, USA, 27–30 June 2016. [CrossRef]
55. Delbruck, T.; Hu, Y.; He, Z. V2E: From video frames to realistic DVS event camera streams. *arXiv* **2020**, arXiv:2006.07722.
56. Mueggler, E.; Rebecq, H.; Gallego, G.; Delbruck, T.; Scaramuzza, D. The event-camera dataset and simulator: Event-based data for pose estimation, visual odometry, and SLAM. *Int. J. Robot. Res.* **2017**, *36*, 142–149. [CrossRef]
57. Gower, J. Generalized procrustes analysis. *Psychometrika* **1975**, *40*, 33–51. [CrossRef]
58. Geurts, P.; Ernst, D.; Wehenkel, L. Extremely Randomized Trees. *Mach. Learn.* **2006**, *63*, 3–42. [CrossRef]
59. Sagonas, C.; Antonakos, E.; Tzimiropoulos, G.; Zafeiriou, S.; Pantic, M. 300 Faces In-The-Wild Challenge. *Image Vis. Comput.* **2016**, *47*, 3–18. [CrossRef]
60. Akolkar, H.; Meyer, C.; Clady, X.; Marre, O.; Bartolozzi, C.; Panzeri, S.; Benosman, R. What can neuromorphic event-driven precise timing add to spike-based pattern recognition? *Neural Comput.* **2015**, *27*, 561–593. [CrossRef] [PubMed]
61. Scheerlinck, C.; Rebecq, H.; Gehrig, D.; Barnes, N.; Mahony, R.; Scaramuzza, D. Fast image reconstruction with an event camera. In Proceedings of the IEEE Winter Conference on Applications of Computer Vision, Snowmass Village, CO, USA, 1–5 March 2020; pp. 156–163.
62. Son, B.; Suh, Y.; Kim, S.; Jung, H.; Kim, J.S.; Shin, C.; Park, K.; Lee, K.; Park, J.; Woo, J.; et al. 4.1 A 640×480 dynamic vision sensor with a 9 µm pixel and 300Meps address-event representation. In Proceedings of the 2017 IEEE International Solid-State Circuits Conference (ISSCC), Francisco, CA, USA, 5–9 February 2017. [CrossRef]
63. Lichtsteiner, P.; Posch, C.; Delbruck, T. A 128×128 120 dB 15 µs Latency Asynchronous Temporal Contrast Vision Sensor. *IEEE J. Solid-State Circuits* **2008**, *43*, 566–576. [CrossRef]
64. Tarkoma, S.; Siekkinen, M.; Lagerspetz, E.; Xiao, Y. *Smartphone Energy Consumption: Modeling and Optimization*; Cambridge University Press: Cambdridge, UK, 2014; p. 460.
65. Vidal, A.R.; Rebecq, H.; Horstschaefer, T.; Scaramuzza, D. Ultimate SLAM? Combining Events, Images, and IMU for Robust Visual SLAM in HDR and High-Speed Scenarios. *IEEE Robot. Autom. Lett.* **2018**, *3*, 994–1001. [CrossRef]
66. Guo, M.; Huang, J.; Chen, S. Live demonstration: A 768 × 640 pixels 200Meps dynamic vision sensor. In Proceedings of the 2017 IEEE International Symposium on Circuits and Systems (ISCAS), Baltimore, MA, USA, 28–31 May 2017; p. 1.

Publisher's Note: MDPI stays neutral with regard to jurisdictional claims in published maps and institutional affiliations.

© 2020 by the authors. Licensee MDPI, Basel, Switzerland. This article is an open access article distributed under the terms and conditions of the Creative Commons Attribution (CC BY) license (http://creativecommons.org/licenses/by/4.0/).

Article

Adaptive Rehabilitation Bots in Serious Games [†]

Imad Afyouni [1,*], Abdullah Murad [2] and Anas Einea [3]

[1] Department of Computer Science, University of Sharjah, Sharjah P.O. Box 26666, UAE
[2] College of Computer and Information Systems, Umm Al-Qura University, Makkah 21421, Saudi Arabia; aamurad@uqu.edu.sa
[3] PROS Corporate, Houston, TX 77098 USA; anasainea@gmail.com
[*] Correspondence: iafyouni@sharjah.ac.ae
[†] This paper is an extended version of the papers "Towards an Adaptive Gaming Framework for TeleRehabilitation" written by I. Afyouni, A. Einea, A. Murad, published in the 12th ACM International Conference on PErvasive Technologies Related to Assistive Environments, Rhodes, Greece, 5–7 June 2019. and "Gamified virtual assistants to- wards adaptive telerehabilitation" written by Afyouni, I., Einea, A., Murad, A., published in the 27th Conference on User Modeling, Adaptation and Personalization, Larnaca, Cyprus, 9–12 June 2019.

Received: 1 October 2020; Accepted: 30 November 2020; Published: 9 December 2020

Abstract: In recent years, we have witnessed a growing adoption of serious games in telerehabilitation by taking advantage of advanced multimedia technologies such as motion capture and virtual reality devices. Current serious game solutions for telerehabilitation suffer form lack of personalization and adaptiveness to patients' needs and performance. This paper introduces "RehaBot", a framework for adaptive generation of personalized serious games in the context of remote rehabilitation, using 3D motion tracking and virtual reality environments. A personalized and versatile gaming platform with embedded virtual assistants, called "Rehab bots", is created. Utilizing these rehab bots, all workout session scenes will include a guide with various sets of motions to direct patients towards performing the prescribed exercises correctly. Furthermore, the rehab bots employ a robust technique to adjust the workout difficulty level in real-time to match the patients' performance. This technique correlates and matches the patterns of the precalculated motions with patients' motions to produce a highly engaging gamified workout experience. Moreover, multimodal insights are passed to the users pointing out the joints that did not perform as anticipated along with suggestions to improve the current performance. A clinical study was conducted on patients dealing with chronic neck pain to prove the usability and effectiveness of our adjunctive online physiotherapy solution. Ten participants used the serious gaming platform, while four participants performed the traditional procedure with an active program for neck pain relief, for two weeks (10 min, 10 sessions/2 weeks). Feasibility and user experience measures were collected, and the results of experiments show that patients found our game-based adaptive solution engaging and effective, and most of them could achieve high accuracy in performing the personalized prescribed therapies.

Keywords: serious games; motion capture; TeleRehabilitation; user adaptation; intelligent alerting; automatic correction

---

1. Introduction

As of late, the challenge of designing a highly engaging serious game has been a subject of interest to various fields including training, simulation, healthcare, and education, among others. Specifically, the direction towards creating a home-based individualized training plan for patients diagnosed with mental and/or physical disorders has attracted more interest due to the recent advances of technologies and techniques related to gamified telerehabilitation. Traditionally, physical therapy solutions present several challenges. First, the patient-to-therapist ratio for physical rehabilitation is generally unable to comply with the ideal guidelines for staffing assumptions [1]. This usually results in appointment delays and reduced treatment time. Second, patients are, in most cases, required to perform additional exercises at home, allow timely recovery, and reduce the recurrent expensive visits to hospitals or rehabilitation centers [2]. Third, traditional therapy methods require the supervision and monitoring of experienced professionals in order to assess patients' performance and improvement over time. However, home-based exercises are considered as non-attractive, and are kept unmonitored without advanced analytics that allow measuring the patient's key performance indicators [3].

We believe there are some unique features that can overcome the mentioned challenges, which are illustrated in Figure 1. Advanced 3D motion capture devices can lay the groundwork for developing noninvasive and home-based physiotherapy solutions, while maintaining highly accurate monitoring of patient's performance in real-time. On the other hand, a successful telerehabilitation platform should provide instantaneous and session-based therapy progress analytics. Moreover, using the power of AI and intelligent algorithms, a personalized set of exercises should be developed within an adaptive serious game framework, which we refer to as "adaptive exergames", so that patients can have an entertaining and immersive experience with clinically validated and personalized games that adapt to different levels of difficulty.

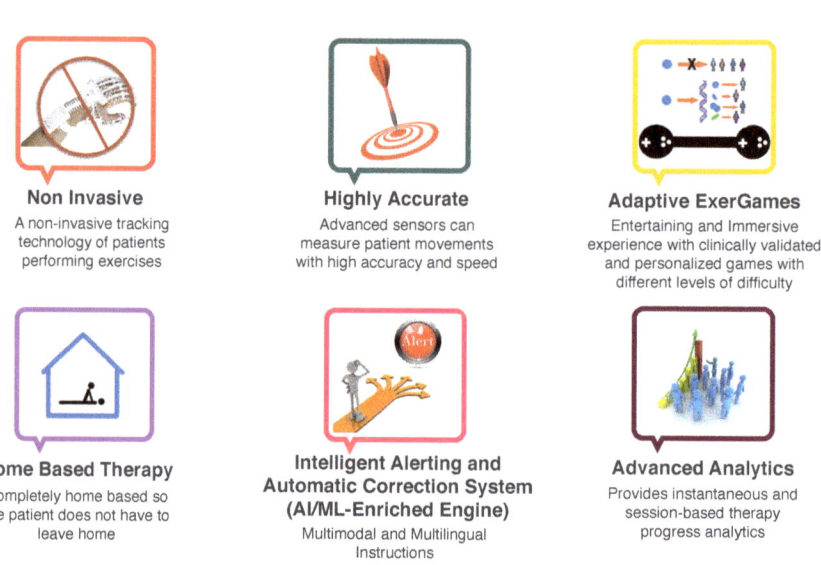

Figure 1. Required features for building adaptive serious games.

Consequently, we introduce the "RehaBot" system to overcome the challenges presented by the traditional therapy solutions, and it differs from existing work in many ways: (i) RehaBot is comprehensive in that it was not designed for rehabilitating specific body parts, but rather it accepts various therapies to cover the whole body; (ii) in addition, RehaBot embeds virtual assistants to direct patients to perform the exercises correctly through 3D illustrations, while in case of failure, it indicates the joints/gestures that need improvement; (iii) furthermore, RehaBot is intelligent in assessing patients' range of motions of various body parts and then adjust the game's level of difficulty in real-time tailored to the patients' abilities, so that they do not lose interest of the game due to unrealistic difficulty levels. A variety of upper limb and lower limb disabilities can be covered in this platform due to the use of motion caption sensors, such as the MS Kinect 2, which covers the body joints starting from head, neck, spine and upper body joints, to knees, foots, and ankles. However, in our evaluation we have focused on upper limb disabilities, including cervical spine diseases, and lower back pain, as they are very common among all ages and the access to patients dealing with such disorders is much easier than other types of disability.

This paper extends our previous work introduced in [4,5] by demonstrating all algorithmic details behind our posture matching, smoothing, and adaptation techniques in "RehaBot", and by conducting a clinical study to investigate the impact of this adaptive game-based physiotherapy solution on patients dealing with chronic neck pain as a case study. We believe, to the best of our knowledge, that there is no similar work in literature that integrates adaptive virtual assistants in real-time within serious games for rehabilitation. The main contributions in this paper are summarized as follows.

- RehaBot embeds real-time pattern and gesture recognition and different adaptation techniques to tailor to patients' preferences and needs.
- The game engine incorporates three levels of adaptation: (1) an embedded virtual assistance, a rehab bot, that shows the users how to perform the exercises correctly; (2) a module of intelligent notifications that reads and represents the patient postures/movements in 3D, then if needed, adjusts the game to the appropriate level that ensures a better outcome; and (3) a dynamic correction module that takes into consideration both the game level of difficulty and the virtual assistant readings to produce a tailored set of exercises that are more appropriate to the patients' abilities; thus, reducing the gaps between the current range of motions patients are able to perform and the ideal suggested ones.
- Advanced real-time and session-based analytics are also generated to allow for automatic learning of patient behavior over the different sessions.
- A fully-fledged system was developed with both therapist and patient dashboards. 3D motion capture and VR daemons will be running on patient's front-end with a possibility to adapt game configuration and controls in a seamless way based on performance.

It should be noted that while the system implements its functionality using the MS Kinect 2 and HTC VR headsets, these devices do not constitute an essential factor for the platform and can be replaced by other alternatives (such as Intel RealSense and Oculus Rift) if needed. Indeed, while motion sensors provide data about joint positions and vector orientations, VR devices report the position and orientation blueprints of the headset. Different case studies including upper or lower limb disorders can be considered to evaluate the performance of the proposed system, as our employed motion tracking device (i.e., Kinect) can track 25 joints covering the full body. The presented clinical trials focus on patients with chronic neck pain with the aim of having a homogeneous group of patients. However, this study can be easily covering other common cases in upper limb disorders, such as lower back pain and scoliosis.

The remainder of this paper is organized as follows. Section 2 discusses the related work in serious games for telerehabilitation. Section 3 first presents the smoothing filters employed in motion tracking, then introduces the different adaption techniques towards the generation of personalized and adaptive serious games. Section 4 presents the system development and usage, and describes the salient components of the system architecture. Section 5 presents the implementation details, while Section 6 describes the methodology of the clinical study and highlights the evaluation process towards proving the effectiveness and usability of our system. Finally, Section 9 concludes this paper with a discussion on future work.

2. Related Work

Recent studies explored the possibility of utilizing patient-centered telerehabilitation as an adjunctive therapy to overcome the challenges in conventional therapy solutions [6,7]. Within this context, serious games appeared to be a promising candidate in bridging that gap, by providing an engaging environment to perform the required exercises, while using 3D monitoring devices that allow tracking of patients' gestures and performance in real-time [2,8]. Remote rehabilitation of patients dealing with musculoskeletal disorders through serious games allows for close guidance and encourage patients towards performing online low-cost physiotherapy exercises that can help them live independently at home [9]. In its attempt to improve the physical therapy outcomes, the human–computer interaction (HCI) community has proposed using several new interactive tangible and intangible devices together with serious games [10,11]. The authors of [12] show that serious games are effective for the physical therapy of stroke patients. This is also resulting from the fact that the more time is spent in rehabilitation, the greater the extent of recovery. The authors of [13,14] designed a game-based system for detecting, tracking, and visualizing joint therapy data. Afyouni et al. [15] developed a game to be played with a Leap Motion controller for rehabilitation of the hand movement of upper extremity for the stroke patient. Jonsdottir et al. [16] designed a game framework for arm rehabilitation to motivate patients dealing with multiple sclerosis. The authors of [7,17] presented reviews on serious games for motivating body exercises in case of stroke and physical rehabilitation. Another approach for cognitive rehabilitation using a serious game platform was proposed in [18]. More specific serious games for physical rehabilitation of patients with chronic musculoskeletal back and neck pain were proposed in [19], by using the motion capture (MoCap) system and virtual reality.

Several challenges need to be addressed while designing serious game solutions in physical rehabilitation, as discussed in [20]. These challenges need to be considered for developing successful serious games in general and were adopted as guidelines in our framework design. They are categorized within different phases as follows.

1. The pre-design phase consists in analyzing the needs, audience, best technologies to be used, goals and outcomes, and assessment tools for measuring the performance.
2. The design phase covers the development of all necessary components in the serious game, while considering factors such as game interactivity, enjoyment, clarity, and user experience. We believe that adaptiveness of the serious game to patients' needs and performance should also be taken into account at this stage.
3. Finally, the evaluation phase, which consists in measuring the outcomes achievement and the user experience. With respect to physical rehabilitation, outcomes are related to skills acquired and range of motion improvement. Outcomes are considered as achieved when the patient performs the prescribed training correctly and with no side effect on his/her overall medical conditions. Measuring the user experience should also cover the satisfaction level and usability of the proposed serious game.

Additional challenges related to the development of evaluation guidelines were also discussed in [21]. The evaluation guidelines consist in defining several evaluation metrics, the process towards conducting the clinical trials, the analysis of results and feedbacks, and the improvement of the game design.

2.1. 3D Motion Capture and Virtual Reality

Several devices can be used to capture 3D motions and identify the physiological features from a rehabilitation session, such as Intel Realsense, Microsoft Kinect, StereoLabs Zed https://www.stereolabs.com/zed/, and Orbbec https://orbbec3d.com. When integrated with algorithms of skeleton pose tracking and point cloud, these sensors can assess various types of physical functions and anatomy [22,23]. Others have used Vicon cameras to recognize gestures with aids of markers and computer vision technology https://www.vicon.com/products/camera-systems. However, unlike Microsoft Kinects [24,25], Vicon cameras are not widely adopted in healthcare studies due to the high price and level of complexity to set them up at patients' homes. Kinect 2 is well known for its ability to track 25 joints simultaneously allowing it to capture the full human body gestures. However, Kinect 2 sometimes falls short when it comes to (1) capturing subtle hand motions with high accuracy, (2) recognizing short-range motions, (3) functioning in bright sun light, and (4) immunity to interference caused by other nearby sensors [26]. A recent work [27] demonstrates a superiority in pose tracking performance of the Azure Kinect over the Kinect 2, in which the Azure Kinect more accurately measured the spatial gate parameters. Improving joint position estimation of Kinect using various types of filters can greatly enhance the rehabilitation experience [28].

Virtual reality-based exergames for rehabilitation were proposed in several studies. The aim behind these studies is to identify the advantages and barriers perceived by experts to using an immersive Exergame as an adjunctive treatment to conventional therapy. VR-based serious games are designed using VR headsets, which are head-mounted displays (HMDs) integrating inertial measurement units (IMUs). The two branded VR headsets that are mostly used are Oculus Rift (in its three versions) and HTC Vive, in addition to other low-immersion solutions such as cardboards or Gear VR. The use of 3D motion tracking sensors and virtual reality headsets in rehabilitation has been investigated in [29–31], among others. A comprehensive review of developed serious games for learning and training purposes in immersive VR-environments was presented in [20]. The proposed studies discuss different types of exercises by which the patient can train or rehabilitate several aspects such as musculoskeletal or cognitive disorders. These studies commonly suggest that using virtual reality exergaming technology as an adjunct treatment to traditional therapy is engaging and safe for post-stroke rehabilitation and can be beneficial to upper extremity functional recovery. A recent work on designing rehabilitation exercises for chronic neck pain using serious games and virtual reality was also proposed in [19]. However, a few limitations have been highlighted on the use of immersive VR-based serious games. For instance, virtual reality devices might result in some sort of motion sickness, referred to as '1cybersickness", mostly resulting from conflicting signals about the body's orientation and motion [32]. Checa and Bustillo [20] suggest that this VR sickness syndrome might be diluted by considering new strategies for user interaction and the development of rich storytelling in the VR-based serious games. Maier et al. [33] also suggest to build neuro-scientifically grounded protocols for more effective VR-based interventions. Another important challenge is related to the evaluation of such VR-based serious games, and especially related to the number of subjects that are recruited for testing purposes [20]. Having a sufficient number of patients will increase the statistical significance of the study, but usually in physical rehabilitation, the size of the target group is very limited. Finally, existing works focus on better human interaction with mounted devices and generic games for all patients. Therefore, they lack the integration of patient-centered techniques that learn from user's current and past behavior and performance, thus adapting the gaming environment to their needs.

2.2. Adaptation in Serious Games

Games can be adapted in various ways to create a user experience that is both personalized and customized. In order to create an adaptive game, a dynamic process of adjustment of the game components, such as user interfaces and strategies, game mechanics, and difficulty levels, has to be embedded [31,34]. Some games assess the user's performance at the beginning and adjust the game upfront, while others continuously adjust the game during sessions [35]. There are two types of game difficulty level adaptation: static or dynamic. A static difficulty level implies that the parameters of the game are adjusted based on a predefined set of formula that increase/decrease the difficulty levels of the game as cited in [36]. A game-based exercising program in health sport, presented in [36], is an example of a game's static difficulty level, in which the workout settings and the individualized needs of the players are preset. By contrast, the dynamic difficulty levels require close monitoring of users' performance along with a wide range of parameters that can be dynamically adjusted [37]. Thus, the more parameters that can be adjusted, the better game adaptation can be achieved. Furthermore, the adaptation techniques that are fully dynamic make the performance of home-based therapy sessions much easier compared to the static ones [38].

Nonetheless, there is one drawback associated with adopting a fully dynamic gaming environment in that it may not leave enough room for therapists to test their therapeutic plan in a controlled environment aside from other factors. Thus, the semi-dynamic approach enables therapists to adjust non-related game parameters, while leaving the adjustment of the game-related parameters to the system based on the performance of the patients. An example of a game that was designed using a semi-dynamic approach is the game of catching falling fruits [39], in which the system controls the falling fruits' number, size, weight, fall frequency, and the number of baskets needed to collect them. On the other hand, the non-game-related parameters controlled by the therapist are the exercise type, session period, number of repetitions, and movement constraints. Another example is the serious game environment presented in [40], in which the therapist provides real-time guidance allowing for live interactions with the patients and thus better performance. A third example is the adaptive hand therapy game created in [41], in which the therapist's prescription is translated into a 3D path which the patient has to follow to complete the therapy exercise. A fourth example is an algorithm used in the education field to produce personalized learning lessons using a Kinect-based system [42]. A fifth example presented in [9] demonstrates a system that uses the user's interactions, previous performances, and preferences to recommend new game-based exercises.

Although the presented approaches consider adaptation techniques from different perspectives, none of them focused on automatically generating adaptive game configurations and embedding adaptive virtual characters from therapeutic instructions, which is a major concern in our work. Moreover, full body posture adaptive design and matching, as well as self-adaptivity of our rehab bots based on patient performance, were not previously discussed. In this work, we have also adopted a semi-automatic adaptation strategy whereby an expert can author a set of recorded postures along with a few non-game-related parameters (e.g., number of repetitions or exercise duration), while the system takes that input and thoroughly generate new game configurations specifically designed to fit that particular patient.

2.3. Existing 3D Motion Capture Systems from Market Perspectives

A market study demonstrates an increasing interest in remote physiotherapy solutions. A number of companies have implemented and presented various platforms for 3D motion capture with applications in different domains from sports, to entertainment, virtual reality, and physical rehabilitation. Figure 2 illustrates a list of relevant systems that are assessed with respect to a set of criteria we believe are important for an effective adaptive serious game platforms. Those systems, including Mira from Mira Rehab www.mirarehab.com/, JRS from Jintronix for Kinect-based rehabilitation www.jintronix.com, Vicon from the Oxford Instruments Group www.vicon.com/, MotionCare360 www.mobihealthnews.com/tag/motioncare360, and Doctor Kinetic doctorkinetic.com, are among remote physiotherapy solutions that employ relatively tangible and intangible sensors for tracking body joints and measuring therapy compliance. However, to the best of our knowledge, none of these systems embed dynamic techniques for designing personalized and self-adaptive serious games, such as the ones proposed in our Rehabot system.

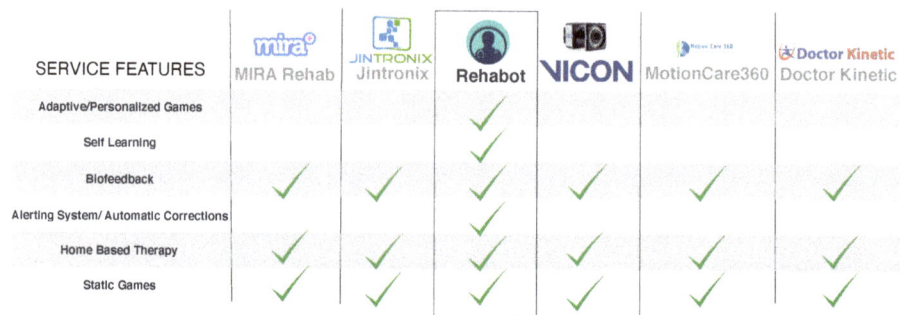

Figure 2. Evaluation of the closest related works in literature.

3. Adaptive Game Generation

The progression of creating adaptive serious games for therapeutic purposes, also called exergames, has been accelerated after the advance monitoring devices surfaced. Exergames allow patients to take part in a customized, enjoyable, and immersive sessions, while conducting clinically validated training exercises. Adaptive exergames assess patients needs and capabilities to automatically generate personalized sets of training exercises. The challenges in developing adaptive serious games include (1) transforming recommended postures by an expert into a series of virtual assistants exhibiting those postures in the right place, time, and number of occurrences within the game environment; (2) implementing an accurate real-time posture mechanism that allows guiding the patient towards performing the right exercises and detecting the imperfect gestures within and over sessions; and (3) redefining the rehab bots' behavior by adapting the game level of difficulty to suits patients needs and performance.

Rehabot embeds adaptation techniques at different levels to tailor to the patient' profile. The automatic adaptation requires integrating *"virtual coaching"* into the gaming environment to ensure that patients are performing the exercises correctly. Such an integration is associated with three levels of adaptation techniques as mentioned above and described in Sections 3.2–3.4, respectively.

3.1. Smoothing Filters for the Kinect Tracking System

3D motion capture sensors and virtual reality head-mounted displays (HMDs), namely, the Microsoft Kinect 2 and HTC Vive, are used in this platform, thus leveraging real-time monitoring of patients' gestures and activities. Nonetheless, the tracking system of body postures in Kinect presents noisy data and is sometimes unstable, especially when multiple joints appear in front of each other [28,43,44]. Consequently, the first objective in this work was to employ smoothing and noise reduction filters, so that joint position and orientation remain stable over time.

In this phase, the accuracy of the Kinect data has undergone several filtering stages in order to achieve the best performance. It is worth mentioning that the Kinect device might show inconsistent data, especially when two body joints appear on top of each other. In this case, the hidden joints' positions might be predicted in a wrong way. The filtering process aimed at smoothing these inconsistencies by removing unreliable data streams, or by applying extrapolation between previous positions of the same joint in order to predict the right next position. Different filtering algorithms for improving joint position estimation of Kinect have been proposed, such as, low-pass filtering, double exponential filtering, and Kalman filter [28,44]. Due to the dynamic nature of our tracking system, we propose to a two-stage filtering process: the first stage applies double exponential filtering using Holt's method to skeleton data as time-series data [45]. Then, in a second phase, the smoothing process uses a statistical analysis to create a moving average of joints data, thus reducing outliers from the generated frames. The double exponential filtering proves to be working well with joint movements that do not interfere with each other. However, the double exponential filtering does not consider the nature of the joint, its location within the body, and the occurring movement in real-time. Consequently, a second filtering stage was added, which evaluates the distances between each joint and its parent joint, and keeps track of the history of joint positions and orientations in order to predict the best new values considering the value input form phase 1. We believe this double-stage filtering can naturally understand human motion, thus providing us with smooth body tracking in highly dynamic situations when compared to other filtering approaches.

This process shows a better stability and reasonable results even in highly dynamic situations with multiple joint interference. Algorithm 1 describes our developed filtering process. The algorithm takes the Kinect frames, joints names and their distances to parents, and joint historical positions and orientations. Typically, we consider the last frames in a given temporal range for historical positions and orientations, so that we can detect the pattern and movement evolution for each joint. This algorithm uses the double exponential filter in its first phase, then performs extra calculations and validation to produce the updated frame as an output in the second phase. The detailed steps are highlighted as follows.

- In the first phase, each frame should undergo a double exponential smoothing to ensure the series of data for joint positions exhibit some form of trend without outliers (line 3). This smoothing filter takes the historical datasets for joint positions and orientations up to a certain instant t in order to estimate the best value for the joint position at the instant $t + m$. The filtering parameters include the 'data smoothing factor' that defines how much the predicted value should remain close to raw data, the 'trend smoothing factor' which takes the historical evolution of the data series over time, the 'jitter radius' for jitter reduction, and the 'maximum deviation radius' which depicts the distance that filtered positions are allowed to deviate from raw data. The output of this stage is an updated frame with smoothed series of values estimated according to the mentioned parameters.
- The second phase consists in evaluating the estimated values obtained from the double exponential filtering, by considering two main factors: the distance between each joint and its parent, and the maximum angular velocity for each joint. The set of distances between joints is determined statically, whereas the maximum rotation is calculated for each joint based on its motion nature and the historical records. Lines 5–10 highlight this process for each joint. First, the algorithm determines the joint parent and calculates the distance difference between the two joints in the current frame data; then, it evaluates the mismatch with the static distance between the joint and its parent ϵ_{j_k}. Similarly, the angle rotation is retrieved from the current frame, and compared to the maximum angular rotation estimated δ_{j_k}. The algorithm then estimates the percentage of error based on these two parameters, and decides based on a given threshold whether the current predicted value for each joint can be trusted.

The output of this algorithm is the new set of frames with updated predicted series of values. Only values of joint positions and orientations that are not trusted, are marked with a low confidence level, which is taken into account in posture matching as described in Section 3.2.

Algorithm 1: Kinect Data Smoothing Algorithm.

Data: $\mathcal{F} = \langle f_1, f_2, \ldots, f_n \rangle$: Kinect frames in $[t-1, t+1]$;
$\mathcal{J} = \langle (j_1, dist_{j_1}^{parent}), \ldots, (j_m, dist_{j_m}^{parent}) \rangle$: joints and distances to their parents; $HistorySet = \langle (j_1^{PSet}, j_1^{OS}), \ldots, (j_m^{PSet}, j_m^{OS}) \rangle$: historical positions and orientations for each joint

Result: $F' = \langle F' = \langle f'_1, f'_2, \ldots, f'_n \rangle$: updated frames

1 **begin**
2   **foreach** $f_i \in \mathcal{F}$ **do**
3         $f'_i = doubleExponentialFilter(f_i, HistorySet)$;
4   **foreach** $j_k \in \mathcal{J}$ **do**
5             $j_{parent} = getJointParent(j_k)$;
6             $\alpha_{j_k} = calculateQAngle(j_k, j_{parent})$;
7             $Max\alpha_{j_k} = getMaxRotation(j_k, j_k^{OS})$
            $\epsilon_{j_k} = getDistanceMismatch(dist(j_k, j_{parent}), dist_{j_k}^{parent})$;
8             $\delta_{j_k} = getOrientationMismatch(\alpha_{j_k}, Max\alpha_{j_k})$;
9             $pe_{j_k} = estimateError(\delta_k, \epsilon_{j_k})$;
            // pe_{j_k} is the percentage of error at the joint $j_k \in f_i$
10   **if** $(pe_{j_k} > \psi)$ $dropConfidence(j_k, f'_i)$;
11   **end**
12   **end**
13 **end**

3.2. Posture Matching

To start the exergame, a therapist inputs a set of correct postures for the corresponding patient to practice. The system then identifies a set of joints that are used with each inputted posture and starts monitoring them. In order to identify the joints, the system compares the correct posture with the human body in an idle position, and identified joints are given more weights as opposed to other unidentified body joints. *mathcalW* indicates the set of weights that is assigned to the identified body joints to be monitored. The significance of each joint with respect to a specific posture is represented by its assigned weight.

A posture matching technique is developed to calculate the closeness indicator with the ideal posture displayed by the virtual character, so that patients' joints are compared against their ideal counterparts following the specifications prescribed by the therapist. The posture matching technique is described in Algorithm 2. The algorithm takes, as inputs, the values of $\mathcal{F}$, BP, and $\mathcal{W}$, which depict the patient current frame, the correct bot posture, and the set of weights that indicate the significance of the identified joints, respectively. The algorithm returns, as an output, a series of 3D quaternion indicators calculating the differences for all body joints together with the error percentage for each joint compared to the correct gesture. Moreover, the system returns the overall percentage of matching. More details are presented next.

Algorithm 2: Posture Matching Algorithm

Data: $\mathcal{F} = \langle f_1, f_2, \ldots, f_n \rangle$: Kinect frames in $[t-1, t+1]$; $\mathcal{J} = \langle j_1, j_2, \ldots, j_m \rangle$: Joints of the body; $\mathcal{ROMS} = \langle ROM_{j1}, ROM_{j2}, \ldots, ROM_{jm} \rangle$: Set of Normal ROM ranges for all joints; BP: ideal posture of the virtual bot; $\mathcal{W} = \langle w_1, w_2, \ldots, w_m \rangle$: Set of weights that marks the significance of each joint for that particular posture; // m is equal to the number of joints // tracked by the Kinect device (25 in this case)

Result: $\mathcal{Q} = \langle \delta_0, \delta_1, \ldots, \delta_m \rangle$: Sequence of 3D unit quaternions indicating the differences for all body joints; $\mathcal{PE}$: Set of error percentages for all individual joints; and *successPercentage*: Overall matching percentage

1 **begin**
2   **foreach** $f_i \in \mathcal{F}$ **do**
3   **foreach** $j_k \in \mathcal{J}$ **do**
4           $j_{parent} = getJointParent(j_k)$;
5           $\alpha_{jk} = calculateQAngle(j_k, j_{parent})$;
6           $\alpha'_{bp} = calculateBotQAngle(BP, j_k, j_{parent})$;
7           $\delta_k = getAngleDifference(\alpha_{jk}, \alpha'_{bp})$;
8           $\mathcal{Q}.add(\delta_k)$;
9           $pe_{jk} = estimateError(\delta_k, ROM_{jk})$;
            // pe_{jk} is the percentage of error at the joint j_k
10          $\mathcal{PE}.add(pe_{jk})$;
11   **end**
12       $successPercentage_{fi} = (\sum_{n=1}^{m} w_n * pe_n) / m$;
         // success percentage for the frame f_i
13   **end**
14    $successPercentage = max(successPercentage_{fi \in \mathcal{F}})$;
15 **end**

- The matching process launches when the patient reaches the next virtual bot posture range. The matching process calculates all the frames that are recorded within the $[t-1, t+1]$ time frame, where t represents the appearance timestamp of the virtual bot (Line 2).

- The system returns all joint positions and their respective directions for each frame in the form of 3d vectors relative to each bone. As demonstrated in Figure 3, MS Kinect 2 tracks continuously 25 body joints. For each bone, the system computes the 3d axis-angle, such as the quaternions unit α_{jk} that links the parent bone, such as leg with hip, with the bone (Lines 3–5). The system also calculates the equivalent unit quaternion of correct posture as suggested by the virtual bot, such as α'_{bp} and then determines the 3d angel difference δ_k of that specific joint (Lines 6–7).
- The system also computes for each frame the overall matching percentage between all bones from the frame of the patient and their corresponding ones from the registered posture of the virtual assistant. The matching percentage is calculated by dividing the 3d ratio of rotational deviation over the interval of range of motion. For instance, Figure 4 shows the estimated neck lateral bending ROM is between ($-45°$ (left), $45°$ (right)). Thus, the estimated percentage of errors is 33% resulting from the 15% deviation of the neck lateral bending towards the right. In this manner, for each bone, the system starts the matching process at the local scale, then calculates the nearest indicator for every vector, after that produces an abstracted matching indicator of the whole body posture relative to the virtual bot (Lines 9–10).
- Finally, for each frame, the system calculates the final score and compares it with the score of the correct posture that comes from the virtual assistant (Line 12). Then, the best frame within range is selected and compared to the threshold value (i.e., 85% success rate) (Line 14). If the score is greater than the threshold value, it is considered a success; otherwise, the system will suggest guiding instructions to help the patients improve their performance.

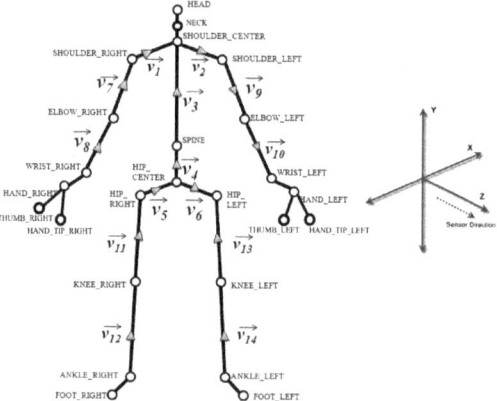

Figure 3. Body joints and vectors as detected by the Kinect sensor.

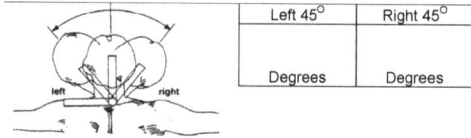

Figure 4. Neck lateral bending range of motion interval.

3.3. Intelligent Alerting

In order to provide the user with real-time guidance, Rehabot takes advantage of the closeness indicator computed previously and recommends multimodal instructions towards improving the patient performance while exercising. Computing such alerting instructions is done by analyzing the positions and orientations of the whole body joints. As a result, the system can determine the deviation from the ideal posture at a high level, but also can estimate detailed joint deviations, so that the patient can understand exactly if something goes wrong. Estimating the deviation in direction and 3D angular rotation of each joint with respect to the virtual bot in real-time is challenging. An example instruction that is expected would be "move your left wrist up/right by 45 degrees". Algorithm 3 highlights the different steps towards generating real-time guidance and feedback on current performance.

Algorithm 3: Intelligent Alerting Algorithm.

Data: f: Best selected Kinect frame from patient data for a particular posture; $Q = \langle \delta_0, \delta_1, \ldots, \delta_m \rangle$: Sequence of 3D unit quaternions indicating the differences for all body joints; $\mathcal{J} = \langle j_1, j_2, \ldots, j_m \rangle$: Joints of the body; BP: ideal posture of the virtual bot;
Result: $\mathcal{IS} = \langle inst_0, inst_1, \ldots, inst_m \rangle$: Set of instructions generated for the relevant joints

1 **begin**
2   **foreach** $j_k \in \mathcal{J}$ of frame f **do**
3         $removeOffset(j_k, BP)$;
4         $V_{jk} = getJointDirection(j_k, j_{parent})$;
5         $V'_{jk} = getBotJointDirection(BP, j_k, j_{parent})$;
6         $RectV = Slerp(V_{jk}, V'_{jk})$;
            // spherical linear interpolation applied to unit quaternions
7         $RectV = normalizeAndProjectOn3DAxis(RectV)$;
            // RectV includes values of x,y,z used in
            // instruction generation
8         $inst_k = generateInstructions(RectV)$;
9         $\mathcal{IS}.add(inst_k)$;
10   **end**
11 **end**

- We evaluate the posture matching between the virtual bot and the patient posture in real-time. If the closeness indicator representing the overall posture deviation is less than a specified threshold (e.g., 85%), then the system starts a detailed investigation and reports the least performing gestures.
- For each joint in the detected posture frame, the system determines the deviated angle on the 3D axis between the parent bone of the patient and the corresponding one from the virtual bot, then the 3D angle is adjusted by removing the generated offset from the rotation of the user bone, thus realigning joint directions between the user and the bot, and removing any initial offset of the parent bone (Lines 2–3).
- Lines 4–6 explain the process for computing the direction of movement vectors for both the patient and the virtual assistant. The system then spherically interpolates the rotation between both vectors, and calculates the straightest and shortest paths between its quaternion end points V_{jk} and V'_{jk} through the *Slerp* function.

This quaternion path is usually referred to as the "rectification" vector $RectV$. Normalization is then applied to $RectV$, in order to determine the axes used in the recitifcation process (i.e., estimating in which direction the user has to move his/her bone). For example, a positive value on x axis suggests moving the corresponding bone to the right, while a negative value would require moving it to the left (line 7).

There, we apply the same technique on up/down directions, so that we can generate relevant instructions in order to improve the patient's gestures for each exercise (Lines 8–9). Generally, to avoid an overwhelming information load, instructions are focused on the three least performing gestures when evaluating the posture in real-time. Displayed instructions include the joint description, desired direction (e.g., up | right), and angle in degrees.

3.4. Automatic Correction

Different groups of gestures are evaluated separately over several occurrences of gestures of the same type, and recommendations are generated by the system in real-time to improve the patient performance. However, in case the overall performance has been improving after several attempts, the virtual assistant acts as an adaptive character that can adjust itself to match to patient capabilities. This can be done in a reverse way to what has been described in Algorithm 3. Indeed, Rehabot takes advantage of the sequence of 3D angle differences for all body joints Q over the last attempts, as well as the calculated rectification vectors. The purpose is to minimize the gaps calculated in rectification vectors of the relevant joints (i.e., those with high precalculated weights) by reducing the rotational difference in the monitored joints by a threshold ε. As a result, an updated posture with a lesser difficulty level is generated and shown by the virtual assistant in the next attempts.

This automatic verification of patient performance is performed after a minimum of three attempts for each group of gestures. If the patient is unable to perform as expected after those attempts, the system decides to automatically decrease the difficulty level for the assessed posture or group of gestures to maintain a convenient level of difficulty. On the other hand, and upon the successful completion of a group of gestures, an upgraded level of difficulty is generated by creating a complementary set of gestures until reaching the best performance for a given exercise as prescribed by the therapist. Therefore, virtual bots are adapted by generating updated postures that are slightly superior or inferior with respect to the previous postures based on patient performance. This helps in keeping the gaming environment enjoyable, while pushing the patient towards a better performance.

4. System Development and Usage

This section demonstrates the system architecture overview and discusses how its two types of users—therapists and patients—can interact with it. The aim of this platform is to produce a serious game for physical rehabilitation that is proactive, adaptive and personalized. Figure 5 demonstrates the three essential components of the platform. These are (1) the frontend component, which includes dashboards for the patients and therapists as well as the adaptive game; (2) the processes component, which includes all the processes that run in the background and collect data from the therapists and patients; and (3) the backend components that comprise the intelligence of the game's engine, the three methods of analytics, and the storage residing at the cloud.

As shown in Figure 5, two dashboards are created to attend to the therapists' and patients' needs. The therapists use the dashboard to record gestures and input prescriptions. Then, the therapists assign the appropriate exercises to the patients based on their capabilities and needs (see Figure 6). In order to record gestures, therapists need to use a 3D motion capturing sensor such as Kinect XBOX. Moreover, therapists use the dashboard to manage and monitor patients' progress and performance over time. The therapists' panel includes the following.

- Create and manage exercises through groups of gestures.
- Select single or multiple joints.
- Record a set of postures to be performed by the patient
- Select categories of groups to be performed for therapy.
- Select number of reps for each movement in a set or select a recursive time-based set.
- Assign therapies to existing patients.
- Monitor session-based patient performance.
- Suggest updated gestures based on current performance.

After the completion of each session, the system generates a report to the therapists which includes the percentages of the success rate, improvement, and fail attempts compared to other previous sessions.

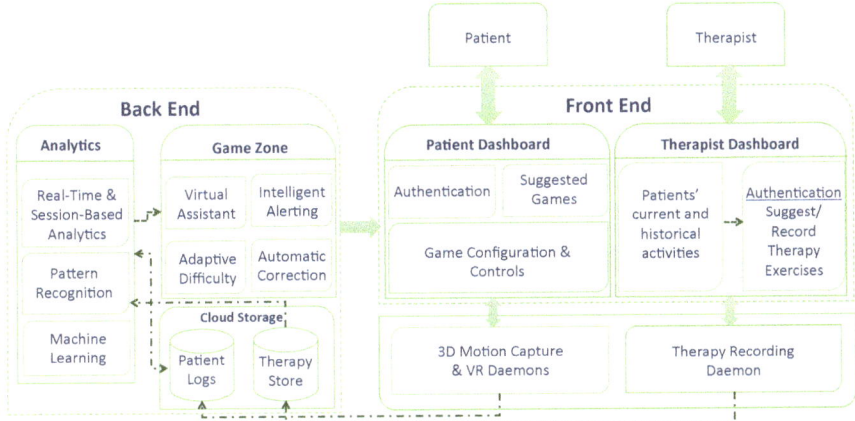

Figure 5. System architecture.

In order to access the patient's dashboard, users have to log in first. The system has a profile for each patient, which saves all the prescriptions and exercises assigned to each individual by the therapist. Upon successful log in, the selected game is generated automatically with all the embedded exercises for that particular patient (see Figure 7). To play the game, a MS Kinect Xbox One is used to control the game via capturing the patient's motions/gestures, together with an optional HTC VR headset which enhances the gaming experience. Using these devices eliminates the need for Joysticks and enables the penitents to move naturally while playing the games. At any moment, the patient is able to navigate to the dashboard in order to achieve the following.

- Receive notifications of newly assigned therapies
- Select and play several games after logging in
- Choose whether to use the VR headset (optional)
- Perform required exercises by matching postures from the virtual assistant, and by taking the multimodal instructions into consideration
- Notify the patient about the current status of successful or failed sets at a specific time or after each session
- Display incomplete therapy steps

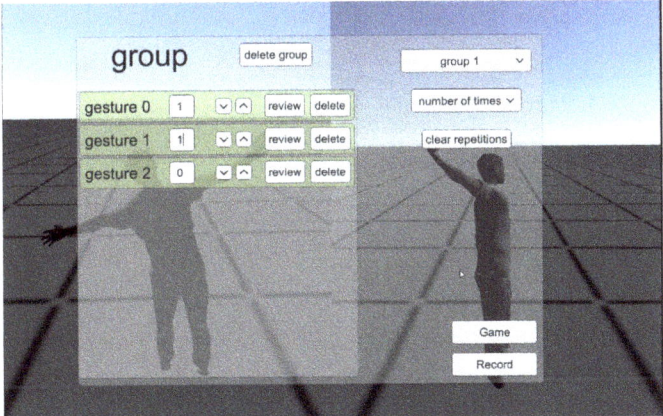

Figure 6. Dashboard for therapists to input groups of gestures.

It is worth noticing that the VR headset has been made discretionary to permit patients, who might feel discomforted when exposed to a completely virtual environment. A couple of side effects can be observed on a few patients, which are alluded to as "cyber sickness", which includes dizziness, headache, disorientation, and postural instability affecting the patient's overall performance [46]. Our system leverages the VR headset integration (HTC VIVE) with the Kinect in order to achieve a fully immersive experience. The position data and orientation tracking provided by the HTC Vive virtual reality device were combined with the body joint data captured by the MS Kinect, in order to generate a rich description of the human body motion. Nonetheless, the platform does not depend on the VR headset due to its complex control, particularly for patients who are diagnosed with disorder of upper limbs (i.e., cerebral paralysis or hand injuries). Thus, upper limb disorders involving the arms can be monitored, such as aches, pains, tension, and disorders involving any part of the arm from fingers to shoulders.

Figure 7. Screenshot of the gaming environment showing the patient character and the virtual assistant with different postures to be performed.

4.1. Intelligent Game Engine

When the game starts, various background processes/daemons start gathering Kinect frames on various body joints, direction data, and VR orientation. Data are continuously stored on the cloud to allow for expert monitoring, as well as real-time and sessions analytics. Different types of data are generated over time: (i) precalculated posture data that is generated based on the therapist inputs, including the defined parameters for each gesture and group of gestures, as well as the recorded postures for each therapeutic exercise, and (ii) the real-time patient data generated from both devices, which are saved with a high-frequency sensor producing up to 30 frames per second, following the specifications of the Kinect 2. Some of these frames can be dropped depending on the level of details required in the analysis.

RehaBot embeds a component for online game adaptations, which we call an intelligent game zone. These adaptation techniques are reflected in the algorithms described in Section 3. Adaptive configurations are progressively updated to the game profile in real-time based on patient's performance. The new rules are then circulated to the configuration manager, which translates them into new adaptive postures that are performed by the virtual assistant. The injected virtual characters will display the required personalized posture that should be performed by the patient during the session. RehaBot takes into account the different vector dimensions and 3D angle rotations for all human body joints from both the ideal posture and the user current posture, in order to generate an adapted posture that matches and improves the user posture as much as possible. The virtual character can also adapt to users with special sitting positions or those using wheelchairs.

Consequently, the game scene should be adapted with a matching character behavior and posture (i.e., sitting character). Therefore, RehaBot allows for capturing accurate posture data, and the results depend on the user context and experience.

Another sub-component of the game zone is the intelligent alerting responsible for generating instructions (i.e., voice and textual descriptions) for each matching process as illustrated in Figure 8. There is a high-level analysis (i.e., overall body posture) as well as a detailed performance assessment with the aim of guiding the patient to achieve a speedy recovery on each required exercise during the session.

Figure 8. Alert is triggered with information on the gesture accuracy and instructions on how to improve.

One extra step beyond the posture matching and intelligent alert is the assessment of the overall exercise and individual gestures during one session, or multiple. The objective of the automatic correction component is to analyze each group of gestures and suggest adaptations to the difficulty level of that group with the aim of reaching the targeted performance. For example, a failure to achieve the target for a given exercise over several attempts will result in gradually decreasing the exercise difficulty, so that the target can be met by the patient in the next occurrences. Once the right posture is successfully recorded over three attempts, the component suggests a new set of exercises within the same group with a higher difficulty level until accomplishing the full set. A successful record on the full set allows for an adapted game strategy and scene with a more advanced level of exercises to be integrated, thus escalating the challenge to be met.

4.2. Advanced Analytics

Because RehaBot is designed as an adjunctive treatment that helps physiotherapist follow the patient progress in real-time and over sessions, instantaneous and session-based analytics are considered as a core component in the system. A deeper understanding and assessment of a patient's performance can definitely help in drawing better conclusions and tailoring the game parameters to suit the patient's behavior over sessions. Among many factors, the system monitors the response time in each exercise, body posture correctness and joints' range of motion, thus maintaining an appropriate game difficulty level. Moreover, a modified or upgraded set of gestures will be proposed for the next sessions, while keeping a high standard of entertainment and personalization to achieve a rich and effective user experience. The mining techniques are used to search for consistent patterns as well as systematic relationships between the different input variables. For example, by knowing the user profile (e.g., age, gender, and preferences), and the physical challenges they are facing currently (e.g., upper/lower limb disorders, back pain, and hemiplegia), the therapist can define a few parameters on which our system can be based to enrich the game scenario with personalized configurations and adaptive exercises. The goal of the data mining is data prediction. For instance, we can use the mining techniques to predict improvement on a timeline by following a calculated schedule of exercises over sessions. Other measurements include (i) weekly- and monthly-based performance indicators; (ii) physical effort required and level of pain while performing the game-based exercise over a session, a week, or a month; (iii) effort vs. improvement analysis; (iv) VR vs. non-VR-based assessment; (v) reaction time and time to accomplish a given exercise; and (vi) number of practiced vs. cleared game levels, among others.

5. Implementation

We have developed an e-health platform that offers several advantages over traditional systems for therapy design and monitoring. Figure 9 demonstrates the setup environment with one user playing the game, by using the Kinect and VR devices. The user presented in this figure was a volunteer who does not specifically have a specific disability but, rather, deals with a mild lower back pain. Based on our discussion with experienced physiotherapists, we tested standard stretching postures and exercises that help in stretching and strengthening back muscles. As illustrated in the figure, the user is freely and naturally performing their required therapy without the need of any extra holders. Using the Kinect 3D motion capture sensor, the system is capable of tracking the movements of 25 joints in the body with up to 30 frames per second. This gives us the ability to record the motion of each joint over time as well as its Range Of Motion (ROM). Second, a Vive VR headset is coupled with the system to allow for a fully immersive environment, where users are engaged in a interactive 3D scene, and adaptive tasks are assigned to them according to their cumulative performance over time.

Figure 9. Screenshot of the setup environment showing one patient trying to replicate the virtual assistant posture.

Within the platform, two applications have been developed to address the needs of therapists and patients. Both store their data and analysis on the same cloud environment. To use the application at home, patients need a computer linked to the internet, a Kinect device, and, only if desired, a VR headset. The patient logs in, selects the game, and starts playing. The therapist, on the other hand, accesses the authoring interface using a similar equipment to design, record, and assign personalized exercises to each patient. Particularly, the authoring interface enables the therapist to select the joints that need to be focused on using a model of a human body anatomy and then utilizes the Kinect sensor to record the appropriate postures. Both therapists and patients can replay any session in a 3D representation. The patient mainly uses this feature to check the ideal therapy postures recorded by the therapist, while the therapist can view the complete motions performed by the patients during the session. Moreover, both therapists and patients are able to visualize current or previous session's performance improvement metrics plotted on a live graph.

Using the Unity 3D game engine, this adaptive game has been created. Although the algorithm has been developed to record data captured by the Kinect Xbox One and the HTC Vive headset, the game engine can be easily modified to support other 3D capturing devices of motion like the Intell Real Sense devices. The adaptation algorithm is continuously utilizing the JASON formatted precomputed data generated by the virtual assistant as well as the real-time data generated during the therapy session to create the next appropriate set of exercises/gestures based on the performance of the patient. The system gathers two types of real-time data: (1) the game data, and (2) the output of the 25 joints captured in each Kinect frame and the 3D angular rotation recorded by the Kinect devices. Kinect data consist of a sequence of frame IDs associated with time stamps. There are a number of properties for each frame, including the vector direction between any two adjacent joints (i.e., *ShoulderRight* $\longrightarrow$ *ElbowRight*), the confidence level (a floating number between 0 and 1), the position of the joints, and the 3D angular rotation, among others. The game data, on the other hand, store computed positions of game's objects, the collected coins, the repellent objects, and the virtual assistant's positions and postures. It is worth noting that these positions are continuously adjusted in real-time depending on the capability of the patients together with the game's level of difficulty. For instance, for a patient who uses a wheelchair, the height of the collected and repellent objects will be adapted to be attainable by that patient.

6. Evaluation

Different case studies can be considered to evaluate the performance of the proposed system, such as chronic neck pain, lower back pain, and scoliosis. With increasing medical costs, reduction in paid benefits, longer waiting periods, and a shortage of rehabilitation specialists, individuals with such diseases are in need of low-cost, quality, home-based sensorimotor rehabilitation. One of the main medical conditions which a lot of people encounter, and which requires a continuous monitoring in all periods and not only during therapy sessions, is non-specific chronic neck pain. Non-specific chronic neck pain is a disease of the neuromusculoskeletal system, which has postural or mechanical basis and affects between 30% to 50% of the general population in developed countries [47]. If it progresses, it can have serious consequences on the patient [48]. The following study will then focus on treatment of non-specific chronic neck pain due to its importance and the availability of patients. Our platform was also tested on a small number of lower back pain patients, and results were reported in our previous work [5].

Methodology for the Clinical Study

After a discussion with specialized physiotherapists on the requirements for developing a comprehensive evaluation study to assess our platform, a series of exercises for stretching and strengthening neck muscles was proposed. Ten patients (6 male and 4 female) diagnosed with non-specific mechanical neck pain were recruited (i.e., neck pain continued for at least the last 12 weeks) to evaluate the intrinsic properties of the adaptive gaming platform, while four more patients were recruited to perform the traditional procedure with an active program for neck pain relief. The duration of the training program was two weeks (10 min, 10 sessions/2 weeks) for all patients. Recruited patients, with an age ranging between 18 and 50 years, were all office workers (with an average of at least six hours sitting in front of a computer screen), as studies have demonstrated that the highest annual prevalence of neck pain is shown among office workers [49,50]. To determine eligibility of participation, patients referred for inclusion were evaluated by a physiotherapist. Exclusion criteria include neck pain associated with vertigo, osteoporosis, vertebral fractures, psychological disorders, tumors, metabolic diseases, and previous neck surgeries. The evaluation process was conducted over two weeks with 10 sessions of 10 min duration.

Stretching and strengthening exercises include lateral flexion of the upper part of the trapezius, ipsilateral flexion and rotation for the scalene, and flexion for the extensor muscles, holding each movement for 10 s (see Figure 10 for neck muscles). Furthermore, Figure 11a shows the co-contraction flexors, rotators, and inclines, where a patient performs cranial nerve flexion, while the physiotherapist asks him/her to tilt, rotate, and look toward the same side while he/she opposes a resistance with his hand. There are several possible movements in the normal range of motion of the cervical spine (see Figure 11b). These are highlighted as follows.

- Flexion: a movement by which the chin attempts to touch the chest. The normal cervical range of motion for flexion is 80 to 90 degrees.
- Extension: starts with both shoulders relaxed and the head in a neutral position, then by moving the head to look up towards the ceiling (ROM up to 70 degrees).
- Lateral Flexion: happens when moving your head from one side to another, while trying to bend your neck to bring your ear down towards your shoulder. This movement is equal on both sides. The ROM is between 20 to 45 degrees on both sides.
- Rotation: starts from the center by looking forward, then rotates to look over you shoulder, then returns back to the center (works equally on both sides, with a ROM of 90 degrees).

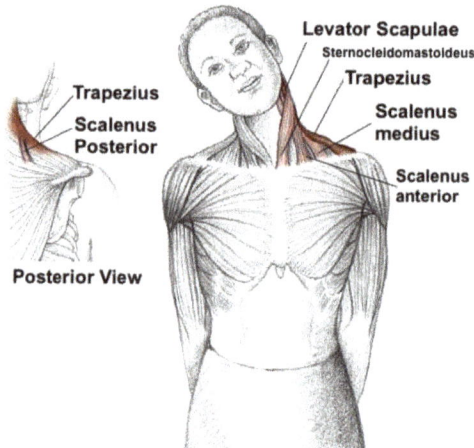

Figure 10. Lateral Neck Stretch: Main Neck and Shoulder Muscles.

Exercise sets 1 and 2 were assigned randomly to two groups of patients, and each group was evaluated based on the assigned set and by using the same evaluation criteria. Each exercise was automatically injected and repeated 5 times during a game session. Finally, a neck straightening exercise was performed by returning the head 5 times for 3–5 s. Patients were advised to perform the stretching program 5 times a week, with a single session taking about 8–10 min to perform.

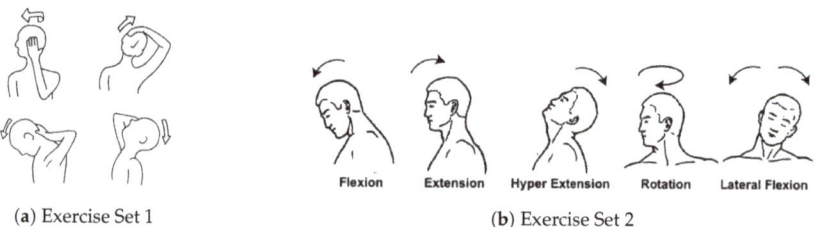

(a) Exercise Set 1   (b) Exercise Set 2

Figure 11. Two sets of exercises for stretching and strengthening of neck muscles.

7. Experimental Setup

The first phase is the experimental evaluation, which consisted in requesting the therapists to assess the effectiveness of the platform and to finalize the different metrics to monitor the patient performance in real-time and on session basis. Following on from the first phase, the platform was updated and made ready for a detailed evaluation of the platform.

The evaluation phase is designed to answer three main questions:

Q1. How efficient is the platform to perform its intended tasks?
Q2. How effective is the platform in fulfilling its intended use?
Q3. What is the user perceived value (satisfaction level) about the usability of the platform?

Both quantitative and qualitative methods are used to evaluate the effectiveness and usability of our system. In quantitative methods, different metrics were studied and monitored to analyze the quality of improvement of the patient, such as, the visual analogue scale (VAS) before and after exercising, and the range of motion, among others. The aim of these metrics is to assess the performance, reliability, correctness, and effectiveness of the system. Other metrics also include the following.

- Movement of the joints: it represents the therapy distribution impact over the body distinct joints. During the therapy session, the positions of each moving joint of the patient's body are recorded. In fact, the Kinect device generates up to 30 frames per second, each frame contains the joint position and orientation in 3D axes. By taking the sequence of frames into account, one can identify the joint motion, orientation, and speed, thus providing accurate measurements regarding the range of motion and improvement of motor controls.
- Incorrect Body Gestures: One example of the incorrect body gestures is moving the forearm to practice a gesture that is supposed to be performed using the wrist. The system records the number of times an incorrect gesture is performed associated with a time stamp.
- Reaction Time: it is the time period between the instruction appearance and its implementation.
- Range of Motion (ROM): the system records the minimum, maximum, and average ROM of each therapy gesture along with the full session of the therapy. Measuring the ROM is done by recording the minimum and maximum position for a given joint and for each performed gesture. For example, if the monitored exercise is the neck lateral flexion (moving the neck to the right and left), the ROM will be determined from the recorded frames, starting from the initial neck position to the most flexed position as performed by the user. Then, the difference between the two vectors is calculated to determine the maximum ROM.
- Speed: It is defined as the velocity of the patient's moving gestures during the game.
- Pattern Matching: it is defined as the accuracy of the matched patterns of each exercise and the full session.
- Success Rate: it is defined as ratio of the number of completed therapy sessions over the number of collected objects during the game.
- Error Rate: it is defined as the total number of therapy session that are not performed correctly over the number of total completed sessions.
- Hits: it is defined as the number of obstruction hits.
- Interest: it is defined as the engagement level in the game (how fast the patient gets bored of playing the game)
- Other Metrics: We are also calculating various other metrics that are needed by the therapist. These include the angular speed, angular rotation, and acceleration, which help in reporting the muscle power. The Visual Analog Scale (VAS) pain score is also determined before and after each session by filling a standard form by the patient for comparison purposes.

A qualitative evaluation has been conducted to measure the system's usability and users' satisfaction. Two separate sets of questions were prepared to be used appropriately with the therapists and patients. Each has questions about users' perceived value of usability, adaptiveness, efficiency, enjoyability, fatigue, efficiency, level of motivation, and mental effort needed to use the system. The next section demonstrates the results of the qualitative questionnaires and feedback of the users.

8. Results and Discussion

Our objective lies in enabling patients to achieve and maintain the correct cervical alignment and sagittal balance. This requires performing stretching and balance activities for a sufficient period of time, while maintaining an accurate level of difficulty created and carefully adjusted for each exercise.

8.1. Correctness and Efficiency

System efficiency is evaluated using several metrics including joint-to-joint vector analysis for a given gesture, posture matching accuracy, gesture duration (i.e., reaction time and accomplishment of each gesture), exercise completeness, and percentage of hits for attractive and repellent objects (i.e., obstructions). Some of the metrics can be collected and analyzed from raw motion sensor data (e.g., posture matching), while other metrics are developed with samples of patient data over a session or multiple sessions, such as the mean time, duration, and joint range of motion evolution.

Figure 12 demonstrates a close monitoring of the range of motion for a lateral flexion gesture performed by one patient during a small time interval. This measurement was meant to show the accuracy of the calculated data based on the raw Kinect data. As illustrated in this figure, one can see the ROM ranges between 0 to 35 degrees in this case, which is normal as the maximum ROM possible for this action is 45 degrees. However, some records show negative results, which are noises produced in the collected Kinect frames. Most of these outliers are filtered out in the filtering process as discussed in Section 3.1. Figure 13 shows the total time for reaching a given set of exercises was calculated. For clarity purpose, only the results of five patients is shown in this figure, where patients were required to perform the same set of gestures with ideal completion time of 4 min. The common behavior seen here is that the learning curve is quick and patients were quickly improving their time records over sessions.

Figure 12. One patient's Kinematic analysis over time of a lateral flexion exercise in different sessions.

Moreover, we designed an experiment to measure the accuracy of the posture matching algorithm by comparing its performance in detecting the right posture and detailed user gestures dynamically. For that purpose, we compared the original approach that uses the basic body tracking available in the Kinect 2 without filtering, against the approach that is based on the double-staged filter described in Algorithm 1. Figure 14 demonstrates our analysis based on two sets of exercises: (i) upper limb exercises and (ii) neck pain exercises. Upper limb exercises (e.g., for lower back pain, hand, and shoulder therapies) comprise more complex body gestures that can sometimes be challenging to detect due to overlapping joints from the Kinect perspective. The other factors that may affect the capturing performance are (1) the user going out of the field of view of the Kinect and (2) signal fluctuation. The results show a better performance by using the smoothing technique in both sets of exercises. The neck pain exercises are easier to detect due to no overlapping joints, and thus shows a high detection rate when using filtering because of the previously mentioned factors.

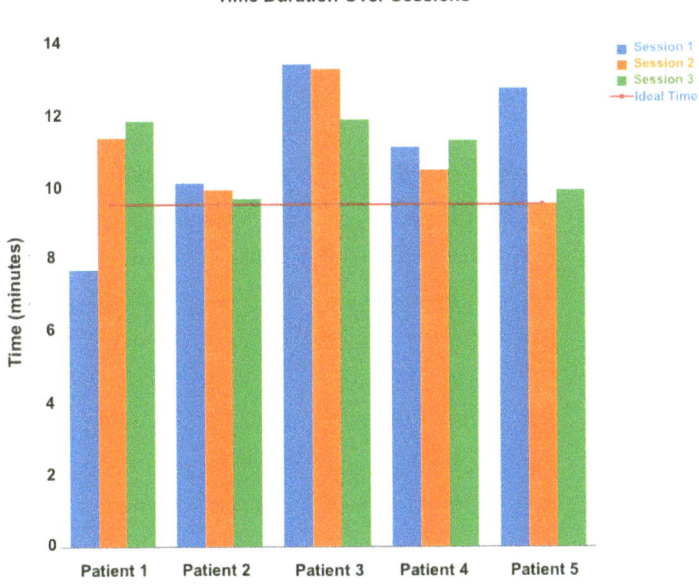

Figure 13. Total time required to finish the prescribed therapy in different sessions.

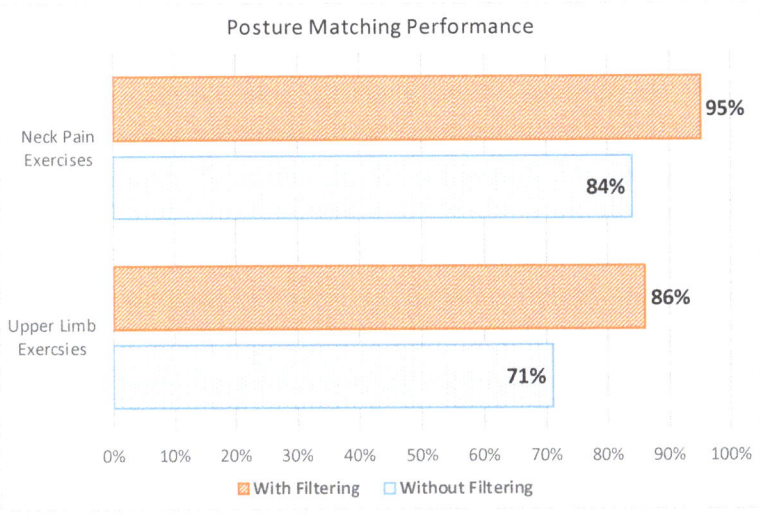

Figure 14. Posture matching accuracy performance before and after filtering.

On the other hand, we evaluated the average percentage of correct gestures performed by patients over different sessions. Figure 15 demonstrates the results of patient performance in each session. This result considers all the gestures required in a given prescribed therapy. The threshold adopted to consider a given gesture as correctly performed is 80%. Thus, gestures performed with a lower matching percentage are considered as being not acquired. The overall performance of the users shows a general increasing of correctness percentage, with some patients were performing better than others, mainly those who adhered to the gaming environment faster.

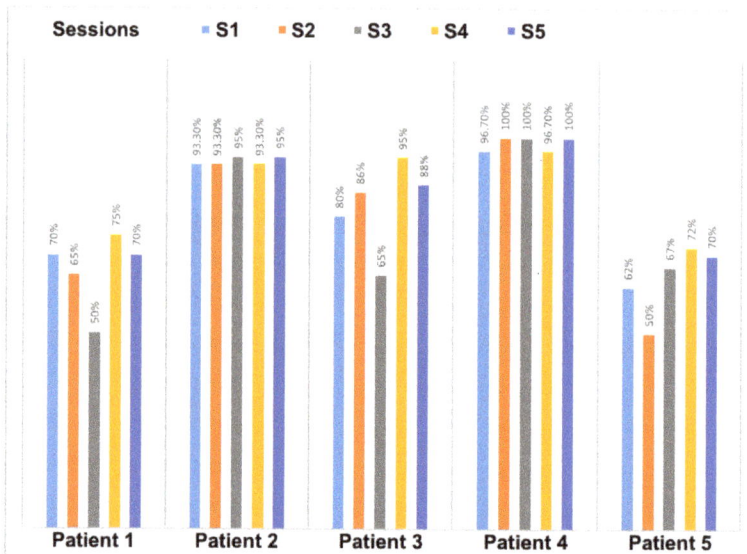

Figure 15. Percentage of achievement and correctness with respect the prescribed therapy.

8.2. Measures of Effectiveness

For comparison with the traditional procedure, we selected four patients out of ten from those who are testing the gaming platform, and which have the closest conditions to the patients performing the traditional program. Three males and one female were assigned the exercise set number 2 in both groups (see Figure 11b). Both groups had an age range between 27 and 42, and did not present any chronic disease or other types of disability. Measurements were conducted in the same order: flexion, extension, hyperextension, rotation, and lateral flexion. All the tests were performed in the department of physical rehabilitation of the University of Sharjah by an experienced physiotherapist. To measure the outcomes of this program on both groups, the Visual Analog Scale (VAS) for pain level and the Neck Disability Index (NDI) were collected at three different period of time: (i) before starting the training program, (ii) after five session, and (iii) after ten sessions. The subjects involved in the study will record their pain intensity according to a VAS score. They should estimate their pain on a scale from 0 to 10, where 0 indicated "no pain" and 10 would be "the worst conceivable pain". The NDI is an instrument that measures the functional status of subjects with neck pain within 10 categories, including pain, personal care, weight gain, reading, headache, concentration, work, driving, sleeping, and leisure. Each category is rated on a scale of 0 to 5, where 0 means "painless" and 5 means "the worst conceivable pain". The resulting scores are added to a total average. The questionnaire is computed as an average percentage. The disability categories for NDI are 0–8%, without disability; 10–28%, mild; 30–48%, moderate; 50–64%, serious; and 70–100%, for complete disability [51].

Figure 16 demonstrates the evolution of VAS score on patients of both groups, SG-P1 → SG-P4 for those who exercising using our serious games, and TT-P1 → TT-P4 for patients with traditional therapy. On the other hand, the NDI index for both groups is illustrated in Figure 17. The recruited subjects were having mild to moderate neck pain in the beginning, and they all showed a progress when exercising towards reducing their pain. We observed, however, that patients SG-P1 (male: 35) and SG-P3 (male: 27) were very engaged and performed their exercises more accurately, which resulted in having less pain and a decrease in their NDI index by the end of the ten sessions. It should be also noted that the group who performed the traditional program was closely monitored by an expert to ensure the correctness of gestures, which was not needed while using our platform.

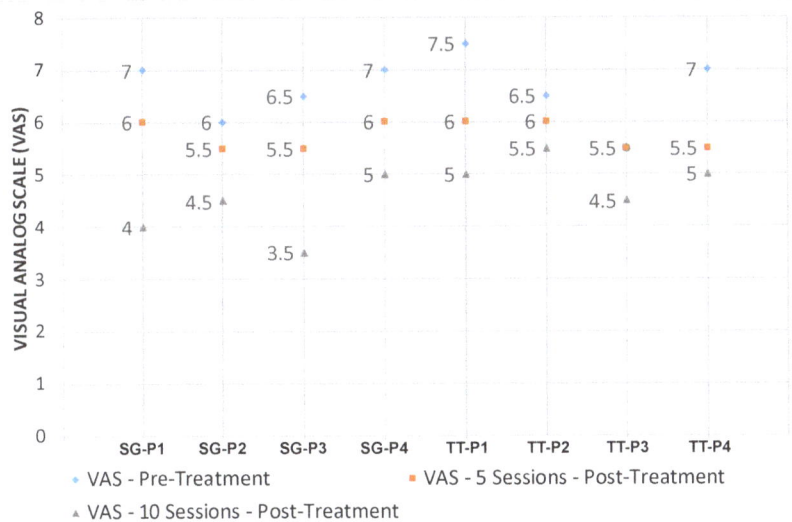

Figure 16. Evolution of Visual Analog Scale (VAS) score for patients using RehaBot vs. patients using traditional therapy.

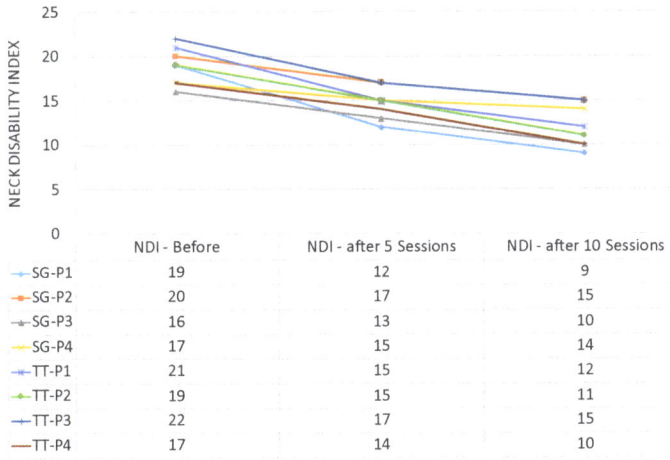

Figure 17. Neck Disability Index for patients using RehaBot (SG-P1 → SG-P4) vs. patients with traditional therapy (TT-P1 → TT-P4).

In order to measure the usability and adaptiveness of the system, the ten patients who used our platform were also requested to fill out different questionnaires. Three types of self-administered, close-ended questionnaires were designed and distributed to the users. All questionnaires were written in English and it was considered that all users were capable of understanding the language. System Usability Scale Questionnaire (SUS) standard criteria were considered in the first questionnaire, which aims at assessing the learning curve and confortability while using RehaBot. Another specialized questionnaire was designed to measure the effectiveness of the adaptive platform on users' performance. Results are highlighted in Figures 18–21. Other questionnaires are going to be considered in the full clinical test to evaluate the gamefulness of our system such as the one proposed in [52].

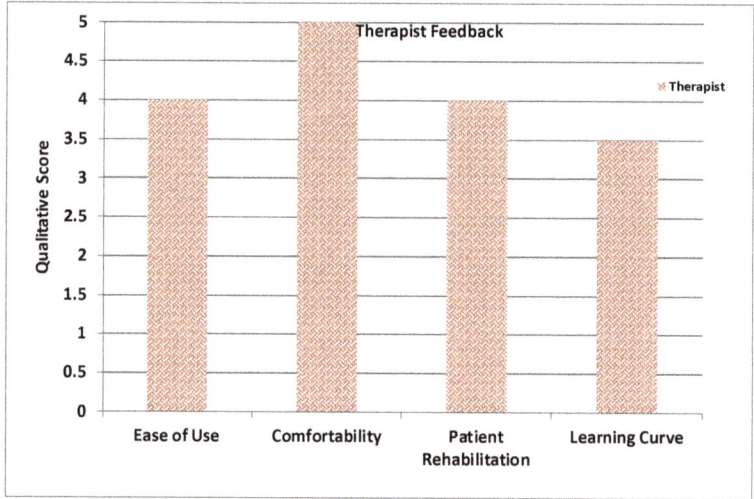

Figure 18. Average therapists' feedback.

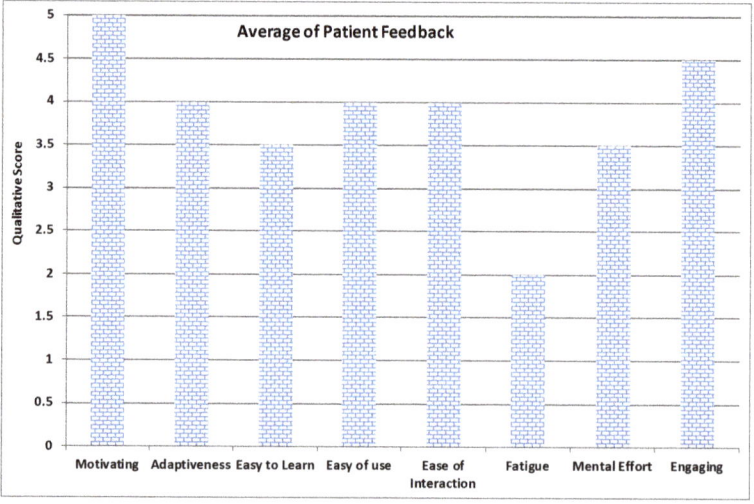

Figure 19. Average of patient feedback.

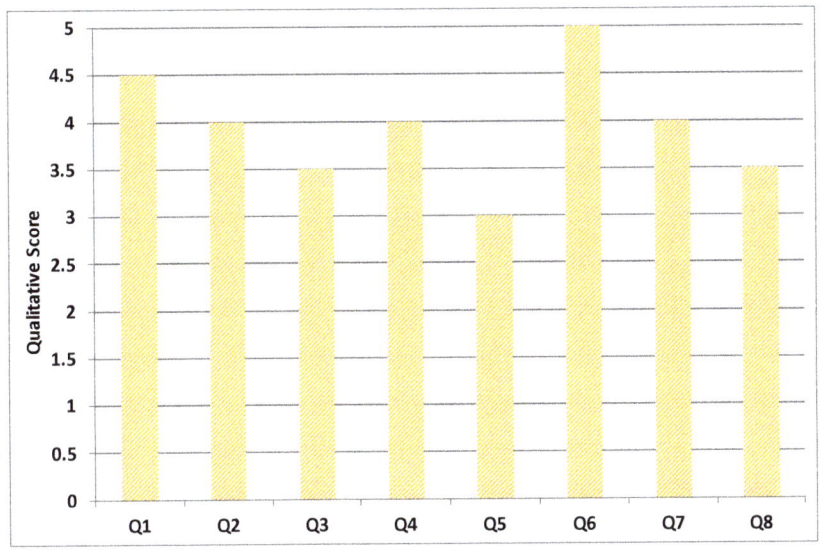

Figure 20. Average of patient feedback based on System Usability Scale Questionnaire (SUS) criteria.

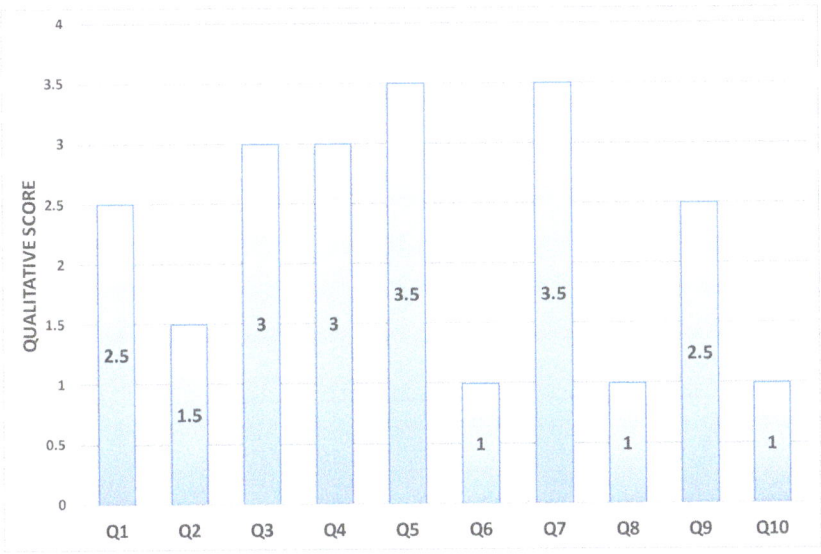

Figure 21. Average of patient feedback on adaptiveness.

Figure 18 illustrates the average feedback given by the therapists who devised the set of gestures and tested the features in the therapist dashboard including creating exercises with several groups of gestures, assigning therapies to patient, and monitoring patient performance. Figure 19 displays the average of patient feedback with respect to several usability measures such as enjoyability, learnability, ease of interaction, etc. Figure 20 illustrates the average patient feedback on the System Usability Scale Questionnaire (SUS) as a standard and reliable tool for measuring the usability of our platform. The questions of the SUS questionnaire are presented in Annex A. The questions are a mix between positive and negative questions, and the scale is between 0 for strongly disagree, and 4 for strongly agree.

Finally, Figure 21 demonstrates how patients have perceived the adaptiveness of our system with respect to several factors. The questions Q1–Q8 that are shown on the X-axis represent the eight-questions of the questionnaire as follows. Q1. *The virtual assistant guides me to do the right posture.* Q2. *The automatically generated set of exercises exactly reflect my needs.* Q3. *The system understands and adapts to my capabilities and performance.* Q4. *The multimodal instructions help me to understand my mistakes.* Q5. *The instructions provide me with clear suggestions on how to improve my gestures.* Q6. *The system helps me to be more effective.* Q7. *I can recover from mistakes quickly and easily.* Q8. *The adaptive virtual assistant adapts the posture difficulty, and this makes me feel more confident.*

All plots demonstrate satisfaction results on a scale from 0 to 5. In general, most metrics show satisfactory results, although the learning curve was mentioned as an important factor that could affect the initial sessions performance, and this can be improved by increasing the number of training sessions for both therapists and patients.

8.3. Discussion

Both types of users demonstrated a high level of confidence in utilizing RehaBot and believed it can play a significant role in remote rehabilitative therapies. The motivation and engagement of participants while using our serious games was significant, which allowed for longer periods of practice. As a result, improvements in alignment has been associated with improved outcome of the treated neck muscles. We also took into consideration the recommendations suggested by the therapists and participants with respect to the user interface and the admin dashboard, as well as the "how" alerts and instructions displayed on the patient's dashboard.

Furthermore, when comparing the results of efficiency and correctness between traditional therapy and using our system, both groups showed close performance. However, all patients agreed that performing such exercises at home using our platform would be much more convenient, as it is more engaging and ensures the correctness of performed gestures. Therefore, our findings support the feasibility and impact of using an adjunctive treatment with online adaptive rehabilitation, thus augmenting usual care for persons with chronic neck pain in a clinical context with potential similar role in continuity of other upper limb rehabilitation.

Limitations

This study investigated the feasibility and effectiveness of adaptive serious games developed for body rehabilitation for patients with musculoskeletal disorders. Although the results presented are promising and provide initial evidence on the impact of the approach in online rehabilitation, the experiments were limited to rather a small sample size and only on patients with chronic neck pain disease. Therefore, effectiveness and validity of the approach will have to be further tested on a larger-scale randomized controlled trial, and on other upper limb disorders, as well as for lower limb rehabilitation.

9. Conclusions

We present an adaptive serious game platform for patients with musculoskeletal disorders, referred to as "RehaBot". This platform allows experts to remotely prescribe personalized therapies by only recording a screenshot of posture required and the exercise duration. RehaBot digitizes those postures and creates virtual characters, called rehab bots, that are injected within the serious game environment. These bots dynamically act as an adaptive coach and adapt themselves gradually according to patient's performance. RehaBot presents an intelligent alerting and auto-correction system that adapts the level of game difficulty while controlling game configurations and objects in real-time. RehaBot embeds advanced AI and pattern matching techniques to build adaptive and personalized serious games, also referred as exergames. These exergames not only allow for an entertaining experience, but also pave the way for an effective training and rehabilitation. The prototype has been developed, and a clinical study was conducted with a number of patients and under the supervision of three physiotherapy consultants. To the best of our knowledge, RehaBot is the first fully-fledged, low-cost online platform for helping patients with physical disabilities, while naturally embedding fully adaptive assistant within the gaming framework for tracking and guiding patients' progress over therapy sessions. This platform can also be applied to fitness training domain, where athletes can perform personalized and adaptive training with the help of the embedded virtual coach.

Author Contributions: Conceptualization, I.A; methodology, I.A. and A.M.; software, A.E.; validation, I.A. and A.E.; formal analysis, I.A. and A.E.; writing–original draft preparation, I.A.; writing–review and editing, A.M.; funding acquisition, I.A and A.M. All authors have read and agreed to the published version of the manuscript.

Funding: This project was partially supported by the KACST Small Research Grants Program number MS-37-60 in Saudi Arabia. We would like to thank the researchers from the physiotherapy department at the University of Sharjah: Ibrahim AbuAmr, Fatma Hegazy, and Tamer Shousha, and an independent practitioner Rayane Afyouni for the fruitful discussions and recommendations.

Conflicts of Interest: The authors declare no conflict of interest.

References

1. Gimigliano, F.; Negrini, S. The World Health Organization "Rehabilitation 2030: A call for action". *Eur. J. Phys. Rehabil. Med.* **2017**, *53*, 155–168.
2. Aguilar-Lazcano, C.A.; Rechy-Ramirez, E.J.; Hu, H.; Rios-Figueroa, H.V.; Marin-Hernandez, A. Interaction Modalities Used on Serious Games for Upper Limb Rehabilitation: A Systematic Review. *Games Health J.* **2019**, *8*, 313–325. [CrossRef]
3. Lykke, S.; Handberg, C. Experienced Loneliness in Home-Based Rehabilitation: Perspectives of Older Adults With Disabilities and Their Health Care Professionals. *Glob. Qual. Nurs. Res.* **2019**, *6*, 1–12. [CrossRef]
4. Afyouni, I.; Einea, A.; Murad, A. Towards an Adaptive Gaming Framework for TeleRehabilitation. In Proceedings of the 12th ACM International Conference on PErvasive Technologies Related to Assistive Environments, Rhodes, Greece, 5–7 June 2019.
5. Afyouni, I.; Einea, A.; Murad, A. RehaBot: Gamified Virtual Assistants Towards Adaptive TeleRehabilitation. In Proceedings of the Adjunct Publication of the 27th Conference on User Modeling, Adaptation and Personalization, Larnaca, Cyprus, 9–12 June 2019.
6. Eichenberg, C.; Schott, M. Serious games for psychotherapy: A systematic review. *Games Health J.* **2017**, *6*, 127–135. [CrossRef]
7. Bonnechère, B. Serious games in rehabilitation. In *Serious Games in Physical Rehabilitation*; Springer: Cham, Switzerland 2018; pp. 41–109.
8. Yahya, M.; Shah, J.A.; Kadir, K.A.; Yusof, Z.M.; Khan, S.; Warsi, A. Motion capture sensing techniques used in human upper limb motion: A review. *Sens. Rev.* **2019**, *39*, 504–511. [CrossRef]
9. González-González, C.S.; Toledo-Delgado, P.A.; Muñoz-Cruz, V.; Torres-Carrion, P.V. Serious games for rehabilitation: Gestural interaction in personalized gamified exercises through a recommender system. *J. Biomed. Inform.* **2019**, *97*, 103266. [CrossRef]
10. Bachmann, D.; Weichert, F.; Rinkenauer, G. Review of three-dimensional human-computer interaction with focus on the leap motion controller. *Sensors* **2018**, *18*, 2194. [CrossRef]
11. Rechy-Ramirez, E.J.; Marin-Hernandez, A.; Rios-Figueroa, H.V. A human–computer interface for wrist rehabilitation: A pilot study using commercial sensors to detect wrist movements. *Vis. Comput.* **2019**, *35*, 41–55. [CrossRef]
12. Mubin, O.; Alnajjar, F.; Al Mahmud, A.; Jishtu, N.; Alsinglawi, B. Exploring serious games for stroke rehabilitation: A scoping review. *Disabil. Rehabil. Assist. Technol.* **2020**, *2020*, 1–7. [CrossRef] [PubMed]
13. Afyouni, I.; Rehman, F.U.; Qamar, A.; Ahmad, A.; Abdur, M.; Basalamah, S. A GIS-based Serious Game Recommender for Online Physical Therapy. In Proceedings of the Third International ACM SIGSPATIAL Workshop on HealthGIS (HealthGIS'14), Dallas, TX, USA, 4–7 November 2014.

14. Qamar, A.; Afyouni, I.; Hossain, D.; Ur Rehman, F.; Toonsi, A.; Abdur Rahman, M.; Basalamah, S. A Multimedia E-Health Framework Towards An Interactive And Non-Invasive Therapy Monitoring Environment. In Proceedings of the ACM International Conference on Multimedia, Orlando, FL, USA, 3–7 November 2014.
15. Afyouni, I.; Qamar, A.M.; Hussain, S.O.; Ur Rehman, F.; Sadiq, B.; Murad, A. Motion-based serious games for hand assistive rehabilitation. In Proceedings of the 22nd International Conference on Intelligent User Interfaces Companion, Limassol, Cyprus, 13–16 March 2017.
16. Jonsdottir, J.; Bertoni, R.; Lawo, M.; Montesano, A.; Bowman, T.; Gabrielli, S. Serious games for arm rehabilitation of persons with multiple sclerosis. A randomized controlled pilot study. *Mult. Scler. Relat. Disord.* **2018**, *19*, 25–29. [CrossRef]
17. Tamayo-Serrano, P.; Garbaya, S.; Blazevic, P. Gamified in-home rehabilitation for stroke survivors: Analytical review. *Int. J. Serious Games* **2018**, *5*, 2384–8766. [CrossRef]
18. Rego, P.A.; Rocha, R.; Faria, B.M.; Reis, L.P.; Moreira, P.M. A serious games platform for cognitive rehabilitation with preliminary evaluation. *J. Med Syst.* **2017**, *41*, 10. [CrossRef] [PubMed]
19. Mihajlovic, Z.; Popovic, S.; Brkic, K.; Cosic, K. A system for head-neck rehabilitation exercises based on serious gaming and virtual reality. *Multimed. Tools Appl.* **2018**, *77*, 19113–19137. [CrossRef]
20. Checa, D.; Bustillo, A. A review of immersive virtual reality serious games to enhance learning and training. *Multimed. Tools Appl.* **2020**, *79*, 5501–5527. [CrossRef]
21. Idriss, M.; Tannous, H.; Istrate, D.; Perrochon, A.; Salle, J.Y.; Tho, M.C.H.B.; Dao, T.T. Rehabilitation-oriented serious game development and evaluation guidelines for musculoskeletal disorders. *JMIR Serious Games* **2017**, *5*, e14. [CrossRef] [PubMed]
22. Latorre, J.; Llorens, R.; Colomer, C.; Alcañiz, M. Reliability and comparison of Kinect-based methods for estimating spatiotemporal gait parameters of healthy and post-stroke individuals. *J. Biomech.* **2018**, *72*, 268–273. [CrossRef]
23. Clark, R.A.; Mentiplay, B.F.; Hough, E.; Pua, Y.H. Three-dimensional cameras and skeleton pose tracking for physical function assessment: A review of uses, validity, current developments and Kinect alternatives. *Gait Posture* **2019**, *68*, 193–200. [CrossRef]
24. Lun, R.; Zhao, W. A Survey of Using Microsoft Kinect in Healthcare. In *Consumer-Driven Technologies in Healthcare: Breakthroughs in Research and Practice*; IGI Global: Hershey, PA, USA 2019; pp. 445–456.
25. Al-Jubouri, A.A.; Ali, I.H. A Survey On Movement Analysis (Hand, Eye, Body) And Facial Expressions-Based Diagnosis Autism Disorders Using Microsoft Kinect V2. *Compusoft Int. J. Adv. Comput. Technol.* **2020**, *9*, 3566–3577.
26. Zago, M.; Luzzago, M.; Marangoni, T.; De Cecco, M.; Tarabini, M.; Galli, M. 3D Tracking of Human Motion Using Visual Skeletonization and Stereoscopic Vision. *Front. Bioeng. Biotechnol.* **2020**, *8*, 181. [CrossRef]
27. Albert, J.A.; Owolabi, V.; Gebel, A.; Brahms, C.M.; Granacher, U.; Arnrich, B. Evaluation of the Pose Tracking Performance of the Azure Kinect and Kinect v2 for Gait Analysis in Comparison with a Gold Standard: A Pilot Study. *Sensors* **2020**, *20*, 5104. [CrossRef]
28. Das, P.; Chakravarty, K.; Chowdhury, A.; Chatterjee, D.; Sinha, A.; Pal, A. Improving joint position estimation of Kinect using anthropometric constraint based adaptive Kalman filter for rehabilitation. *Biomed. Phys. Eng. Express* **2018**, *4*, 035002. [CrossRef]
29. Lin, H.T.; Li, Y.I.; Hu, W.P.; Huang, C.C.; Du, Y.C. A scoping review of the efficacy of virtual reality and exergaming on patients of musculoskeletal system disorder. *J. Clin. Med.* **2019**, *8*, 791. [CrossRef] [PubMed]
30. Nguyen, A.V.; Ong, Y.L.A.; Luo, C.X.; Thuraisingam, T.; Rubino, M.; Levin, M.F.; Kaizer, F.; Archambault, P.S. Virtual reality exergaming as adjunctive therapy in a sub-acute stroke rehabilitation setting: Facilitators and barriers. *Disabil. Rehabil. Assist. Technol.* **2019**, *14*, 317–324. [CrossRef] [PubMed]
31. Ferreira, B.; Menezes, P. An Adaptive Virtual Reality-Based Serious Game for Therapeutic Rehabilitation. *Int. J. Online Biomed. Eng.* **2020**, *16*, 63–71. [CrossRef]
32. Gallagher, M.; Ferrè, E.R. Cybersickness: A multisensory integration perspective. *Multisensory Res.* **2018**, *31*, 645–674. [CrossRef] [PubMed]
33. Maier, M.; Rubio Ballester, B.; Duff, A.; Duarte Oller, E.; Verschure, P.F. Effect of specific over nonspecific VR-based rehabilitation on Poststroke motor recovery: A systematic meta-analysis. *Neurorehabil. Neural Repair* **2019**, *33*, 112–129. [CrossRef]

34. Streicher, A.; Smeddinck, J.D. Personalized and adaptive serious games. In *Entertainment Computing and Serious Games*; Springer: Cham, Switzerland, 2016; pp. 332–377.
35. Nyamsuren, E.; van der Maas, H.L.; Maurer, M. Set-theoretical and Combinatorial Instruments for Problem Space Analysis in Adaptive Serious Games. *Int. J. Serious Games* **2018**, *5*, 5–18. [CrossRef]
36. Hardy, S.; Dutz, T.; Wiemeyer, J.; Göbel, S.; Steinmetz, R. Framework for personalized and adaptive game-based training programs in health sport. *Multimed. Tools Appl.* **2015**, *74*, 5289–5311. [CrossRef]
37. Hocine, N.; Gouaïch, A.; Cerri, S.A.; Mottet, D.; Froger, J.; Laffont, I. Adaptation in serious games for upper-limb rehabilitation: An approach to improve training outcomes. *User Model. User-Adapt. Interact.* **2015**, *25*, 65–98. [CrossRef]
38. Pinto, J.F.; Carvalho, H.R.; Chambel, G.R.; Ramiro, J.; Goncalves, A. Adaptive gameplay and difficulty adjustment in a gamified upper-limb rehabilitation. In Proceedings of the 2018 IEEE 6th International Conference on Serious Games and Applications for Health (SeGAH), Vienna, Austria, 16–18 May 2018.
39. Miljanovic, M.A.; Bradbury, J.S. Making Serious Programming Games Adaptive. In Proceedings of the Joint International Conference on Serious Games, Darmstadt, Germany, 7–8 November 2018.
40. Herrlich, M.; Smeddinck, J.D.; Soliman, M.; Malaka, R. Grab-that-there: Live Direction for Motion-based Games for Health. In Proceedings of the 2017 CHI Conference Extended Abstracts on Human Factors in Computing Systems, Denver, CO, USA, 6–11 May 2017.
41. Afyouni, I.; Rehman, F.U.; Qamar, A.M.; Ghani, S.; Hussain, S.O.; Sadiq, B.; Rahman, M.A.; Murad, A.; Basalamah, S. A therapy-driven gamification framework for hand rehabilitation. *User Model. User Adapt. Interact.* **2017**, *27*, 215–265. [CrossRef]
42. Xu, M.; Zhai, Y.; Guo, Y.; Lv, P.; Li, Y.; Wang, M.; Zhou, B. Personalized training through Kinect-based games for physical education. *J. Vis. Commun. Image Represent.* **2019**, *62*, 394–401. [CrossRef]
43. Edwards, M.; Green, R. Low-latency filtering of kinect skeleton data for video game control. In Proceedings of the 29th International Conference on Image and Vision Computing New Zealand, Hamilton, New Zealand, 19–21 November 2014.
44. Tang, T.Y.; Wang, R.Y. A Comparative Study of Applying Low-Latency Smoothing Filters in a Multi-kinect Virtual Play Environment. In Proceedings of the International Conference on Human-Computer Interaction, Toronto, Canada, 17–22 July 2016.
45. Webb, J.; Ashley, J. *Beginning Kinect Programming with the Microsoft Kinect SDK*; Apress: New York, NY, USA, 2012.
46. Liu, C.L. A study of detecting and combating cybersickness with fuzzy control for the elderly within 3D virtual stores. *Int. J. Hum.-Comput. Stud.* **2014**, *72*, 796–804. [CrossRef]
47. Steilen, D.; Hauser, R.; Woldin, B.; Sawyer, S. Chronic neck pain: Making the connection between capsular ligament laxity and cervical instability. *Open Orthop. J.* **2014**, *8*, 326. [CrossRef] [PubMed]
48. Beltran-Alacreu, H.; López-de Uralde-Villanueva, I.; Calvo-Lobo, C.; Fernández-Carnero, J.; Touche, R.L. Clinical features of patients with chronic non-specific neck pain per disability level: A novel observational study. *Rev. Da Assoc. Méd. Bras.* **2018**, *64*, 700–709. [CrossRef] [PubMed]
49. Hush, J.M.; Maher, C.G.; Refshauge, K.M. Risk factors for neck pain in office workers: A prospective study. *BMC Musculoskelet. Disord.* **2006**, *7*, 81. [CrossRef]
50. Sterling, M.; de Zoete, R.M.; Coppieters, I.; Farrell, S.F. Best Evidence Rehabilitation for Chronic Pain Part 4: Neck Pain. *J. Clin. Med.* **2019**, *8*, 1219. [CrossRef]
51. Bernal-Utrera, C.; González-Gerez, J.J.; Saavedra-Hernandez, M.; Lérida-Ortega, M.Á.; Rodríguez-Blanco, C. Manual therapy versus therapeutic exercise in non-specific chronic neck pain: Study protocol for a randomized controlled trial. *Trials* **2019**, *20*, 487. [CrossRef]
52. Högberg, J.; Hamari, J.; Wästlund, E. Gameful Experience Questionnaire (GAMEFULQUEST): An instrument for measuring the perceived gamefulness of system use. *User Model. -User-Adapt. Interact.* **2019**, *29*, 1–42.

Publisher's Note: MDPI stays neutral with regard to jurisdictional claims in published maps and institutional affiliations.

© 2020 by the authors. Licensee MDPI, Basel, Switzerland. This article is an open access article distributed under the terms and conditions of the Creative Commons Attribution (CC BY) license (http://creativecommons.org/licenses/by/4.0/).

Article

A Novel GAN-Based Synthesis Method for In-Air Handwritten Words

Xin Zhang and Yang Xue *

School of Electronic and Information Engineering, South China University of Technology, Guangzhou 510641, China; 201821011494@mail.scut.edu.cn
* Correspondence: yxue@scut.edu.cn

Received: 30 September 2020; Accepted: 13 November 2020; Published: 16 November 2020

Abstract: In recent years, with the miniaturization and high energy efficiency of MEMS (micro-electro-mechanical systems), in-air handwriting technology based on inertial sensors has come to the fore. Most of the previous works have focused on character-level in-air handwriting recognition. In contrast, few works focus on word-level in-air handwriting tasks. In the field of word-level recognition, researchers have to face the problems of insufficient data and poor generalization performance of recognition methods. On one hand, the training of deep neural learning networks usually requires a particularly large dataset, but collecting data will take a lot of time and money. On the other hand, a deep recognition network trained on a small dataset can hardly recognize samples whose labels do not appear in the training set. To address these problems, we propose a two-stage synthesis method of in-air handwritten words. The proposed method includes a splicing module guided by an additional corpus and a generating module trained by adversarial learning. We carefully design the proposed network so that it can handle word sample inputs of arbitrary length and pay more attention to the details of the samples. We design multiple sets of experiments on a public dataset. The experimental results demonstrate the success of the proposed method. What is impressive is that with the help of the air-writing word synthesizer, the recognition model learns the context information (combination information of characters) of the word. In this way, it can recognize words that have never appeared in the training process. In this paper, the recognition model trained on synthetic data achieves a word-level recognition accuracy of 62.3% on the public dataset. Compared with the model trained using only the public dataset, the word-level accuracy is improved by 62%. Furthermore, the proposed method can synthesize realistic samples under the condition of limited of in-air handwritten character samples and word samples. It largely solves the problem of insufficient data. In the future, mathematically modeling the strokes between characters in words may help us find a better way to splice character samples. In addition, we will apply our method to various datasets and improve the splicing module and generating module for different tasks.

Keywords: in-air handwriting recognition based on inertial sensors; adversarial learning; corpus; splicing module; generating module

1. Introduction

Human–computer interaction (HCI) [1–3] is a new research hotspot. In the past, HCI methods were mostly limited to hardware devices, such as touch screens, keyboards, etc. With the continuous development of HCI systems, many promising solutions have emerged. The in-air handwriting system based on inertial sensors introduced in this work is one of them. In-air handwriting means writing characters or words freely in 3D space, which is a smarter way of HCI. In recent years, with the development of MEMS (micro-electro-mechanical systems), smartphones and wearable devices with built-in inertial sensors have become more and more popular. Therefore, in-air handwriting systems based on inertial sensors have attracted wide attention from many researchers.

In the field of in-air handwriting, most of the previous works focused on character-level in-air handwriting recognition (char.-IAHR) [4,5]. Few studies involve word-level in-air handwriting recognition (word-IAHR). There is a big difference between char-IAHR and word-IAHR. Char-IAHR is a classification task based on a single character. Usually, this is a relatively simple task and does not require much training data. Using thousands of samples, the char-IAHR model can usually achieve good generalization performance [6–8]. Unlike char-IAHR, word-IAHR not only needs to consider the characteristics of the current character, but also the influence of the characters before and after it. In other words, the word-IAHR model not only learns to classify characters, but also learns the combinations of characters. It is a more complicated task and usually requires a large amount of training data. In practice, for in-air handwriting system, outputting words has broader application prospects than outputting single characters. Therefore, the research on word-level in-air handwriting is more meaningful.

However, the word-IAHR task faces two difficulties. Firstly, the training of deep neural networks usually requires a particularly large data set. Adequate data collection is a solution, but it will take a lot of time and money. Furthermore, it is difficult to collect a well-distributed dataset. Secondly, a deep recognition network trained on a small data set can hardly recognize samples whose labels do not appear in the training set. In the word-IAHR task, the classification of the current character depends not only on its own characteristics, but also on characteristics of contextual characters. The recognition model is likely to fail to give the correct answer if the combination of characters is fresh to the model. Therefore, it is really important to introduce the corpus in the training process. For example, we use the dataset "economics" to represent a dataset whose vocabulary belongs to the field of economics. Generally, if training is performed on the dataset "medicine", the recognition model will perform poorly on the dataset "economics". This is because there are many professional words in the field of economics, and their character combinations are very rare in the field of medicine.

Therefore, it is of practical significance to apply a method to synthesize realistic word-level in-air handwritten samples. This will greatly solve the problem of insufficient data in the word-IAHR task.

In this work, we propose a novel synthesis method for in-air handwritten words, named the "air-writing word synthesizer". Figure 1 shows the pipeline of the air-writing word synthesizer. When the word synthesizer is well trained, the output of the generating module will be used to train a word-IAHR network.

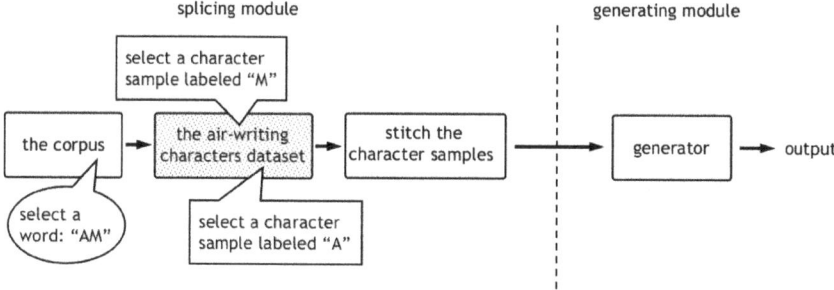

Figure 1. Pipeline of the air-writing word synthesizer. It can be divided into a spicing module and a generating module. The splicing module splices the character samples according to the corpus. The generating module takes in the spliced samples and generates realistic word samples.

The air-writing word synthesizer consists of two modules, namely the splicing module and the generating module. (1) The splicing module splices the character samples according to the corpus to get the spliced samples. Note that the corpus is a collection of words, which can provide a rich combination of characters for the proposed method. The splicing module is not trainable. It consists of a series of steps. The specific splicing steps will be introduced in Section 3.2. (2) The generating module takes in the spliced samples and generates realistic word samples. We regard the conversion from the spliced samples to realistic word samples as a domain-transferring task. The generating module is actually a generator in a generative adversarial network (GAN). This is a trainable network that is trained by adversarial learning. In order to enable the network to process time series, we redesigned the network structure and loss function. The details of the generating module, including training details, network architecture, etc., will be introduced in Section 3.3.

The air-writing word synthesizer proposed in this paper mainly includes the following characteristics:

- The air-writing word synthesizer is a two-stage synthesis method. It creatively combines the splicing module and the generating module to achieve the best performance. Due to its unique design, the air-writing word synthesizer can synthesize a large number of realistic word samples based on limited character samples and word samples.
- The splicing module introduces an additional word set, namely the corpus. The splicing module synthesizes word samples by splicing character samples according to words in the corpus. In our design, the corpus provides important guidance for the combination of characters.
- To make the spliced samples more real, adversarial learning is adopted in the training process of the generating module. In order to process word samples of arbitrary length, we use a fully convolutional U-Net [9] generator and a Markovian discriminator [10]. This design also makes our model pay more attention to the details of the generated samples.
- In the training process of the generating module, the distance loss is adopted to maintain semantic consistency.

In particular, we design a word recognition model to verify the effectiveness of the air-writing word synthesizer on a public dataset. Experiments show that the recognition model trained on synthetic data performs well on samples with fresh labels. To a certain extent, the proposed method solves the problem of insufficient data of in-air handwritten words.

We propose a novel and promising GAN-based synthesis method for in-air handwritten words. We believe that this work will provide some new inspiration for other researchers.

2. Related Work

2.1. In-Air Handwriting System

As a new hotspot in the field of human–computer interaction, many kinds of in-air handwriting systems based on different sensors have emerged. Most famous air-writing systems are mainly based on two types of sensors, namely optical and depth cameras [11–13] and inertial sensors. The former allows users to write virtual text directly on the desktop or in the air with their fingers and uses optical and depth cameras to record hand movement information. The latter allows users to write freely in the air using a handheld device with built-in inertial sensors and uses an accelerometer and gyroscope to capture motion information. Inertial-sensor-based systems are not affected by ambient light intensity or camera coverage, so they can be applied to more scenarios.

In this article, we mainly discuss an in-air handwriting system based on inertial sensors. As illustrated in Figure 2, inertial sensors are integrated into smartphones. The red, blue, and green arrows refer to the x-axis, y-axis, and z-axis of the inertial sensor (accelerometer and gyroscope), respectively. Figure 2a and Figure 2b respectively illustrate the process of writing the character sample and word sample in the air. Note that the writing process is completed in one stroke regardless of character sample or word sample.

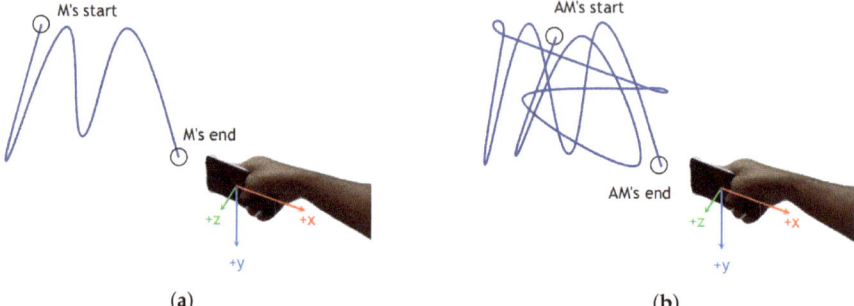

Figure 2. In-air handwriting system: (**a**) writing a character sample "M" in the air; (**b**) writing a word sample "AM" in the air. The red, blue, and green arrows refer to the x-axis, y-axis, and z-axis of the inertial sensor in the smartphone, respectively.

2.2. Generative Adversarial Networks

Generative adversarial networks (GANs) [14] were proposed by Ian Goodfellow. A GAN is composed of a generative module and a discriminative module. The discriminative module learns to determine whether a sample is from the model distribution or the data distribution. The generative module can be seen as a team of counterfeiters trying to produce fake currency. The discriminative module can be seen as the police trying to detect the fake currency. Competition in this game drives both teams to improve their methods until the fake currency is distinguishable from the genuine articles. The purpose of GAN is to narrow the gap between the model distribution and data distribution through sample-level adversarial training.

More importantly, compared to the previous loss in the pixel level or feature level, a GAN creates a domain-level loss, which provides a better solution to many problems. At present, GANs have been well applied in the fields of image generation, image super-resolution, text-to-image generation, image-to-image translation, and so on.

2.3. Unsupervised Image-to-Image Translation

Since GANs propose a novel loss from a domain perspective, unsupervised image-to-image translation work has achieved great success. CycleGAN [15], discoGAN [16], and dualGAN [17] separately applied an image converter for each domain to learn image translation through the proposed cycle consistency constraints. In order to further strengthen the constraints, DistanceGAN [18] proposed distance loss, forcing the distance between two pictures in domain A to be equal to the distance between the two translated pictures in domain B. Cycada [19] combined feature-level loss and pixel-level loss to achieve the alignment of the source domain image and the target domain image. TraVeLGAN [20] proposed a Siamese network that can be used to replace the cycle consistency loss, thereby reducing the complexity and training cost of the model. The Siamese network is used to learn the advanced semantic features of the image to ensure that the translated image is similar to the original domain image. In addition, PatchGAN [10] applied a Markovian discriminator to make the generator pay more attention to the details of the generated samples. What the Markovian discriminator does is cutting the image into patches and classifying whether each patch is real or fake.

In our design, the generating module takes in spliced samples and outputs realistic word samples, just like the unsupervised image-to-image translation. To some extent, our work can benefit a lot from the above literature.

2.4. Scene Text Recognition

In our work, we need to design an air-writing recognition network to demonstrate the effectiveness of the proposed method. The recognition task of air-written words is similar to the scene text recognition. In traditional text recognition methods [21,22], the task is generally divided into three steps: preprocessing, character segmentation, and character recognition. Character segmentation is considered to be the most challenging part due to the complex background and so on. It also greatly limits the performance of the whole recognition system.

In the era of deep learning, in order to avoid character segmentation, two main techniques are adopted, namely the Connectionist Temporal Classification (CTC) [23] and the Attention mechanism [24,25]. The first application of the CTC in text recognition can be traced to the handwriting recognition system of Graves et al. [26]. Now, this technique is widely adopted in scene text recognition[27–29].

In our work, we design a CRNN (Convolutional Recurrent Neural Network) [28] combined with CTC to verify the superiority of our method. Details about the network structure will be introduced in Section 4.1.

3. Methodology

We propose a novel two-stage synthesis method for in-air handwritten words. The proposed method can synthesize realistic samples under the condition of limited in-air handwritten character samples and word samples. The synthesis method proposed contains two modules. (1) Splicing module: The splicing module splices the air-written characters according to the order of characters in the specified word that comes from the corpus. The splicing module is not trainable. It consists of a couple of steps, which will be introduced in Section 3.2. (2) Generating module: The generating module takes the output of the splicing module as input and outputs the generated samples. A well-trained generating module generates realistic word samples, which could be used to train a recognition network. The details of the generating module will be introduced in Section 3.3.

For the convenience of the following description, we refer to the output samples of the splicing module as spliced samples and the output samples of the generating module as generated samples. The domain of spliced samples is called the spliced domain, and the domain of the real word samples is called the real word domain. The generating module mentioned above is actually a generator in a GAN. It takes in spliced samples and outputs realistic word samples. In other words, it learns the mapping from the spliced domain to the real word domain through adversarial training.

3.1. Motivations

The task of recognizing air-written words is similar to scene text recognition. In scene text recognition, a recognition network with good generalization performance not only learns to recognize a single character, but also learns a combination of characters (also called corpus information). Therefore, in the air-writing word synthesizer, we introduce a word set as a corpus to guide the splicing of character samples. The corpus can ensure that the synthetic dataset contains a variety of character combinations. Since the spliced samples are not realistic enough at the junctions, it is necessary to use adversarial training to modify the junctions of the spliced samples.

What the generating module does is somewhat similar to unsupervised image-to-image translation. However, when dealing with time series data, there are still several challenges to be solved.

Lack of paired training data: Usually, paired samples can provide a good guide for the model. However, in this synthesis task, a pairwise database requires the collector to record the start and end points of each character in the word while writing the words in the air. This is nearly impossible in practice. To solve this problem, cycle consistency is adopted.

Handling time series data. The in-air handwritten word samples based on inertial sensors are six-dimensional time series data. Due to the difference in the writing speed and the number of characters of different words, the duration of different word samples varies greatly. Interpolation or padding is usually used to normalize the length of time series data. However, when the duration varies greatly, interpolation or padding is not the best choice. In our work, we adopt U-Net as the backbone of the generator and a Markovian discriminator [10] as the discriminator of our proposed network to solve the above problem.

3.2. Splicing Module

The splicing module produces spliced samples through the process shown in Figure 3. In the splicing process, an air-writing character dataset and a word set (also called corpus) are needed. A word set is a collection of words. It can be a ".txt" file with many words in it. Through the splicing module, we can get a less real spliced sample.

The pipeline of the splicing module can be divided into three steps, as shown in Figure 3. For example, first, we randomly select the word "AM" from the corpus. Then, since "AM" is composed of "A" and "M", an inertial sample labeled "A" and an inertial sample labeled "M" are randomly selected from the character dataset. Finally, we stitch the two character samples together but leave a gap between them, and then fill the gap using linear interpolation. In our experimental setting, we set the length of the gap to 20.

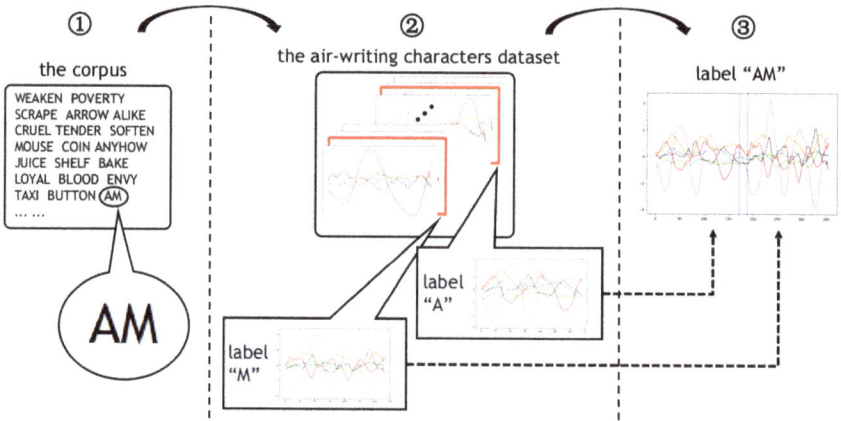

Figure 3. Pipeline of the splicing module. 1. The word "AM" is selected from the corpus. 2. A character sample labeled "A" and a character sample labeled "M" are picked from the air-writing character dataset. 3. The two character samples mentioned above are stitched together, but a gap is left between them. Then, the gap is filled using linear interpolation.

3.3. Generating Module

The generating module is actually a generator of the GAN. In order to better train the generating module, we specially designed an adversarial network, as shown in Figure 4. Note that the generating module in Figure 1 refers to generator G_{S2R}.

As shown in Figure 4, the network we designed consists of two generators (G_{S2R} and G_{R2S}) and two discriminators (D_S and D_R). Let S and R denote the spliced domain and the real word domain, respectively. G_{S2R} is used to learn the mapping from S domain to R domain, and G_{R2S} is used to learn the mapping from R domain to S domain. D_S and D_R represent the discriminators of S domain and R domain, respectively. They are used to distinguish whether the input sample is real or fake.

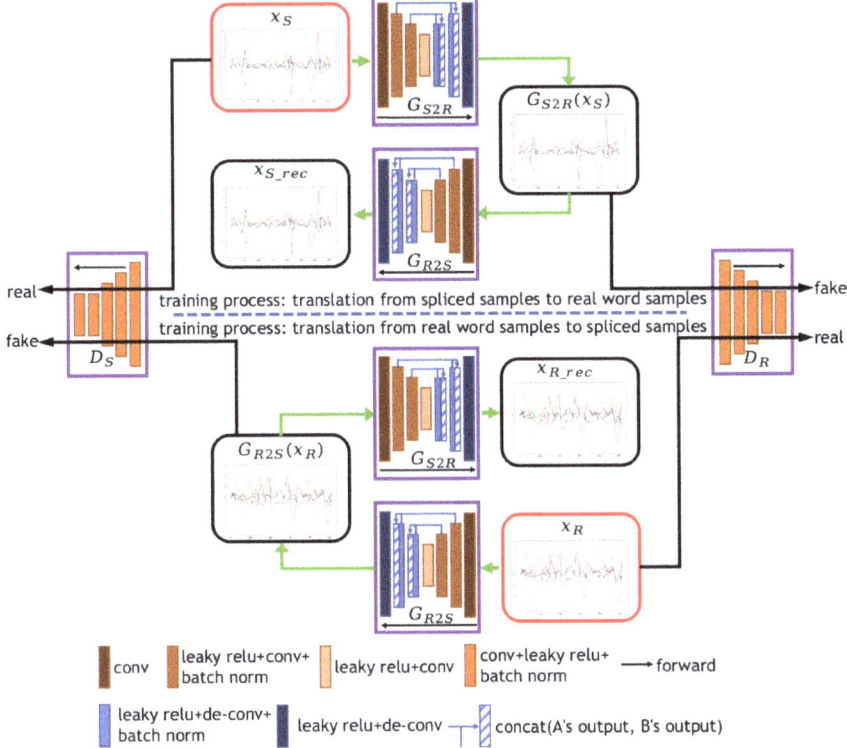

Figure 4. Training process of the generating module. The generating module refers to G_{S2R}. x_S and x_R in the red boxes denote input samples from the spliced domain and the real word domain. G_{S2R} denotes the generator that maps from S domain to R domain. G_{R2S} denotes the generator mapping from R domain to S domain. D_S and D_R denote discriminators in each domain.

For the conversion from S domain to R domain, given a labeled spliced sample x_S, G_{S2R} maps x_S into $G_{S2R}(x_S)$, which means the sample is translated into R domain. $G_{S2R}(x_S)$ is shared by two parts. Firstly, G_{R2S} uses it to produce a reconstructed sample $x_{S_{rec}} = G_{R2S}(G_{S2R}(x_S))$. Secondly, the discriminator D_R uses it to distinguish whether the sample is real. The conversion from R domain to S domain is similar to the above conversion.

3.3.1. Architecture Details

We assign a generator and a discriminator to each domain. Figure 4 illustrates the architecture of generators and discriminators. In our design, the two generators G_{S2R} and G_{R2S} adopt the U-Net as the backbone. Each generator consists of a contracting path for capturing context and a symmetric expanding path for generating samples. Among them, the contracting path contains eight convolutional layers and the expanding path contains eight de-convolutional layers. As shown in Figure 4, the input of each de-convolutional layer is a feature map that concatenates the output of the previous layer with the feature map of the same size in the contracting path. Both generators are fully convolutional networks, which are very suitable for handling variable-length input samples.

In Figure 4, the two discriminators D_R and D_R are Markovian discriminators. Each discriminator consists of five convolutional layers. The first four convolutional layers are used to downsample the input samples. The last convolutional layer compresses feature maps with multiple channels into feature maps with one channel. The average value of the last feature map is output as the final score.

There are two reasons for using the Markovian discriminator. Firstly, the length of the air-writing word samples varies greatly. In this case, padding or interpolation performs badly in the GAN. A fully convolutional network can solve this problem well. Secondly, since the splicing samples are not real enough at the junctions, we hope that the GAN model can pay more attention to the details of the generated samples. In the last feature map output by the Markovian discriminator, each point corresponds to a patch in the input sample. The Markovian discriminator tries to classify whether each patch is real or fake. In other words, the Markovian discriminator pays more attention to the details of the generated samples.

In addition, we have modified the structure of these models to handle time series input. We also adopt a strip-shaped convolutional kernel in all convolutional and de-convolutional layers. The kernel size of each layer in the generators and discriminators is 9×3.

In the last feature map output by the discriminator, each point corresponds to a patch of length 33 in the input sample. Therefore, in the splicing module, the gap between the two samples should not exceed the size of the discriminator's receptive field. In the experimental setting, we set the length of the gap to 20.

3.3.2. Loss Functions

In this section, we will only introduce the loss functions in the conversion from S domain to R domain. The conversion from R domain to S domain uses similar loss functions. Since the training of the generating module is based on the GAN, we introduce the loss functions of the discriminator and the generator.

The loss function of the discriminator is as follows.

$$L_{disc} = L_{adv/disc}, \tag{1}$$

where $L_{adv/disc}$ is the adversarial loss of the discriminator.

The loss function of the generator is mainly composed of three parts. In our attempt, $\lambda = 10$ and $\beta = 1$ perform best.

$$L_{gen} = L_{adv/gen} + \lambda * L_{cyc} + \beta * L_{dist}, \tag{2}$$

where $L_{adv/gen}$ is the adversarial loss of generator, L_{cyc} is the cycle loss, and L_{dist} is the distance loss.

(1) Adversarial loss: The G_{S2R} (generating module) learns a mapping from S domain to R domain by adversarial training. Unlike the original GAN, this proposed model uses a fully convolutional Markovian discriminator. As mentioned above, the Markovian discriminator tries to classify if each patch is real or fake across input samples and averages all responses to provide its final output.

The adversarial loss we used is as follows:

$$L_{adv/disc} = \mathbb{E}_{x_R \sim p_R}[(D_R(x_R) - 1)^2] + \mathbb{E}_{x_S \sim p_S}[D_R(G_{S2R}(x_S))^2] \tag{3}$$

$$L_{adv/gen} = \mathbb{E}_{x_S \sim p_S}[(D_R(G_{S2R}(x_S)) - 1)^2], \tag{4}$$

where x_R denotes real air-writing word samples, x_S denotes spliced air-writing word samples, D_R is the discriminator in the real word domain, and G_{S2R} is the generator that inputs spliced samples and outputs generated samples.

(2) Cycle consistency loss: The adversarial loss ensures that samples with the distribution of S are translated to samples with the distribution of R. However, there are many possible mappings. We apply cycle consistency loss to force the mapping from S to R to be the inverse process of the conversion from R to S, which reduces the number of admissible mappings. To a great extent, cycle consistency loss ensures stable training.

The following is the cycle consistency loss:

$$L_{cyc} = \mathbb{E}_{x_S \sim p_S}[(G_{R2S}(G_{S2R}(x_S)) - x_S)^2], \quad (5)$$

where x_S denotes spliced air-writing word samples, G_{S2R} is the generator that inputs spliced samples and outputs generated samples, and G_{R2S} is the generator that maps samples from R domain to S domain.

(3) Distance loss: To further maintain the semantic consistency between S domain and R domain, distance loss is adopted. The distance loss forces the distance between two samples in S domain to be preserved in the mapping to R domain.

The distance loss is as follows:

$$L_{dist} = \mathbb{E}_{x_i, x_j \sim p_S}[|||x_i - x_j||_1 - ||G_{S2R}(x_i) - G_{S2R}(x_j)||_1], \quad (6)$$

where x_i and x_j are spliced air-writing word samples, and G_{S2R} is the generator that inputs spliced samples and outputs generated samples.

3.3.3. Training Strategy

The air-writing word synthesizer is a two-stage synthesis strategy. Specifically, it includes a splicing module and a generating module. The splicing module is not trainable, while the generating module is end-to-end trainable. In this section, we introduce the specific training strategy of the generating module in detail.

Since the generating module is a part of the GAN, we adopt an alternate training strategy. We alternate between k steps of optimizing the two discriminators and one step of optimizing the two generators. When training D_S and D_R, the parameters of G_{R2S} and G_{S2R} remain fixed. When training G_{R2S} and G_{S2R}, the parameters of D_S and D_R remain fixed. Note that we set $k = 1$ to keep the balance of adversarial training. With the ADAM [30] optimization method, we set the learning rate to 2e-4 and batch size to 64. Finally, our model is trained on NVIDIA-1080Ti GPU, so it is GPU-accelerated.

4. Experiment

In this section, we aim to prove that the air-writing synthesizer can greatly improve the performance of the word recognition model. Therefore, we designed a word-IAHR model and conducted experiments on a public data set named 6DMG [31].

4.1. Word-IAHR Model

The word-IAHR model contains five convolutional layers for downsampling and two layers of bidirectional LSTM (Long-Short Term Memory) [32] for capturing long-distance information. Like the generating module in the air-writing word synthesizer, in order to better process the time series samples, we adopt a strip-shaped convolutional kernel in the convolutional layers. The kernel size of each layer is 9×3. Finally, the model is trained by CTC loss. We use an ADAM optimizer to update the network with a learning rate of 1×10^{-4} and a batch size of 256. Figure 5 illustrates the architecture of the word-IAHR model we used for experiments.

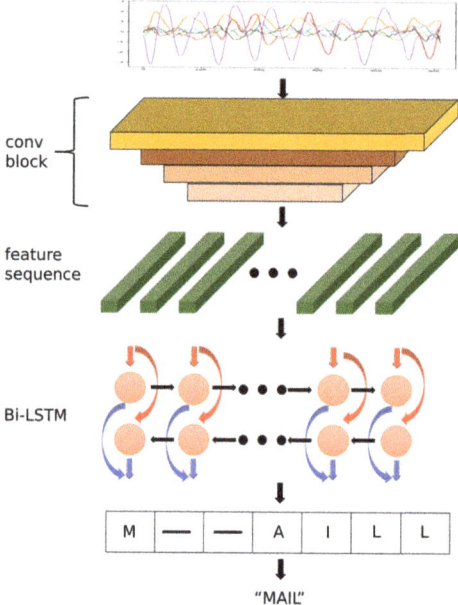

Figure 5. Architecture of the word-level in-air handwriting recognition (word-IAHR) model.

4.2. Dataset

The 6DMG dataset contains two subsets, namely the air-writing character dataset (char-6DMG) and the air-writing word dataset (word-6DMG). Both the character dataset and the word dataset are collected within a fixed range. A total of 25 volunteers participated in the collection of the dataset. Ten volunteers participated in the collection of both the char-6DMG dataset and the word-6DMG dataset, while the remaining 15 writers only participated in the char-6DMG dataset collection.

The char-6DMG is composed of 26 uppercase letter categories. It contains 6500 samples in total, with an average of 250 samples in each category. The number of samples in each category is approximately equal. In the char-6DMG dataset, most samples' lengths vary between 100 and 200. The maximum length of a character sample is 297, and the minimum is 89. Figure 6 shows some examples from the char-6DMG dataset. Samples of the same category or samples of different categories have different lengths.

The word-6DMG dataset contains 1230 samples in total, including 40 categories of words. The number of samples in each category is approximately equal. Figure 7 shows some examples in the word-6DMG dataset. As shown in Figure 7, the lengths of air-writing words vary greatly.

In the word-6DMG dataset, most samples' lengths vary between 300 and 700. The number of characters in most word samples is usually between three and seven, but the longest word sample contains nine characters and is 1512 in length. The shortest word sample contains only two characters and is 145 in length.

Word set: Due to the particularity of our method, we use a word set (corpus). The word set is a text file consisting of 2000 common words. In our proposed method, the words in the word set are used as labels for synthetic samples. It is worth noting that the corpus we used in the training process does not contain the 40 words in the word-6DMG dataset.

Synthetic dataset: According to the method proposed in this work, if we suppose we want to synthesize a sample labeled "CAT", we need to select the corresponding character samples from the char-6MDG dataset. Since each category in the char-6DMG dataset contains 250 samples, theoretically, in the synthetic dataset, there are a total of 250^3 different samples in the "CAT" category. It is a very large dataset, which will bring challenges in terms of data storage and data reading.

Therefore, we use an online synthesis strategy instead of synthesizing the dataset in advance. The pipeline of the air-writing word synthesizer can be seen in Figure 1. In the following part, the synthetic dataset refers to data synthesized by the proposed online synthesis method.

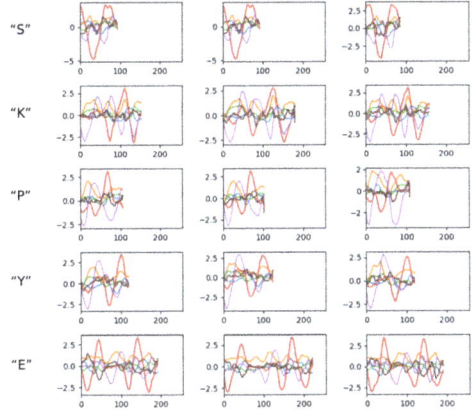

Figure 6. Samples in the air-writing character dataset (char-6DMG) dataset. Samples in each row belong to the same category.

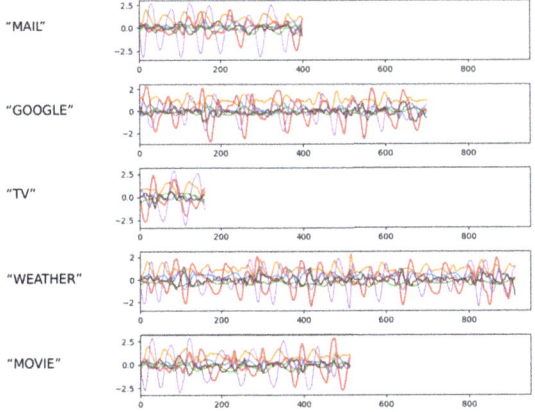

Figure 7. Samples in the air-writing word dataset (word-6DMG) dataset.

4.3. Dataset Pre-Processing

We apply a moving-average filter with a window length of 3 to filter out the noise in both the char-6DMG dataset and the word-6DMG dataset. For samples whose length exceeds 700 in the word-6DMG dataset and synthetic dataset, we resize their length to 700.

4.4. Experiments and Results

In order to demonstrate the superiority of our method, we conduct the following experiments under two principles. One is user-independent, which means that users in the test data will never appear in the training data. The other is user-mixed, which means that when the dataset is divided into folds, each fold is composed of samples recorded by each user.

4.4.1. Experiments on the Word-6DMG Dataset

In scene text recognition, a well-performed recognition network usually requires millions of samples for training. A recognition model can learn more corpus information from a larger dataset. Therefore, we design the following four experiments to verify whether a large dataset is necessary in the word-IAHR task.

- Non-cross-label experiments: As shown in the first two rows of Table 1, we take 80% of the word samples in 6DMG as the training set and the rest as the test set. When dividing the dataset, it is necessary to ensure that samples of the same categories can only appear in the same set and the labels of the training set cover all 26 capital letters. So, we call these non-cross-label experiments. For example, all samples labeled "AM" can only appear in either the training set or test set. That is, we take 32 categories out of 40 as the training set and the remaining eight categories as the test set. The training set contains 984 samples, and the test set contains 246 samples.
- Cross-label experiments: The last two rows of Table 1 show the settings of the cross-label experiments. We take 80% of the word samples in 6DMG as the training set and the rest as the test set. When dividing the dataset, we make sure both the training set and test set contain all 40 categories.

Table 1. Experimental settings for the word-6DMG dataset.

Experiments	Number of Categories in Training Set	Number of Categories in Test Set	Number of Categories in Both Training Set and Test Set
Non-cross-label (user-mixed)	32	8	0
Non-cross-label (user-independent)	32	8	0
Cross-label (user-mixed)	40	40	40
Cross-label (user-independent)	40	40	40

We report the results of these four experiments in Table 2. Whether it is user-independent or user-mixed, the accuracy of the non-cross-label experiment is close to 0.0%. For cross-label experiments, under user-mixed principle, the word-level accuracy is 98.8%. Under the user-independent principle, the word-level accuracy is 88.1%.

Table 2. Experimental results for the word-6DMG dataset.

Experiments	Word-Level Accuracy
Non-cross-label (user-mixed)	0.02
Non-cross-label (user-independent)	0.00
Cross-label (user-mixed)	0.988
Cross-label (user-independent)	0.881

Based on the experimental results, we can draw the following conclusions.

- A word-IAHR model trained on a small dataset performs badly. It is almost impossible to identify samples that do not appear in the training set even if the labels of the training set have covered

all 26 capital letters. A word-IAHR model with good generalization performance requires a large amount of data for training.
- Even trained on such a small dataset, the model can still recognize samples whose labels have already appeared in the training set, regardless of whether it follows the principle of being user-mixed or user-independent. This is because samples of the same word category have similar features.

4.4.2. Quality Testing

According to the results in Table 2, we can know that a recognition model can easily recognize a sample whose label is the same as that of the training sample.

In this section, we want to verify the quality of the synthetic dataset. Based on the experimental results of Table 2, we can infer that synthetic samples can be considered to be of high quality if they are correctly recognized by the word-IAHR model.

In terms of the synthetic dataset used in this section, we use the labels of the word-6DMG dataset (40 words) as a corpus to synthesize a dataset. We refer to this synthetic dataset as the "synthetic dataset of 40 words". It includes 40 categories and 1230 samples.

As shown in Table 3, we conducted quality testing based on the user-mixed and user-independent principles. For comparison, the well-trained models (rows 3 and 4 of Table 2) are adopted. In the quality testing based on the user-mixed principle, the training set is the same as the training set used in the third row of Table 1. In the quality testing based on the user-independent principle, the training set is the same as the training set used in the fourth row of Table 1. We take the "synthetic dataset of 40 words" as the test set. It is of great significance that the "synthetic dataset of 40 words" shares a label space with the word-6DMG dataset.

Table 3. Experiment setup for quality testing.

Experiments	Training Set	Number of Categories in Trainig Set	Test Set	Number of Categories in Test Set	Number of Categories in Both Training Set and Test Set
Quality testing (user-mixed)	word-6DMG	40	"synthetic dataset of 40 words"	40	40
Quality testing (user-independent)	word-6DMG	40	"synthetic dataset of 40 words"	40	40

We report the results in Table 4. In the quality testing based on the user-mixed principle, the word-level recognition accuracy is 86.7%. In the quality testing based on the user-independent principle, the word-level recognition accuracy is 72.3%. Compared with the results in the last two rows of Table 2, the accuracy is slightly lower, but this also shows that the synthetic samples are very similar to the real word samples. The results prove that synthetic samples are of high quality.

Table 4. Experimental results of quality testing.

Experiments	Word-Level Accuracy
Quality testing (user-mixed)	0.867
Quality testing (user-independent)	0.723

4.4.3. Verification of Generalization Performance

As shown in Table 5, we design generalization performance experiments based on the user-mixed and user-independent principles to verify the effectiveness of the proposed method. We use the synthetic dataset as the training set and the word-6DMG dataset as the test set. It is of great significance that not every category in the training set can appear in the test set.

Table 5. Experimental settings for generalization performance experiments.

Experiments	Training Set	Number of Categories in Trainig Set	Test Set	Number of Categories in Test Set	Number of Categories in Both Training Set and Test Set
Generalization performance experiment (user-mixed)	synthetic dataset	2000	word-6DMG	40	0
Generalization performance experiment (user-independent)	synthetic dataset	2000	word-6DMG	40	0

We report the results in Table 6. In the experiment under the user-mixed principle, the word-level recognition accuracy is 62.3%. In the experiment under the user-independent principle, the recognition accuracy is 44.6%. Compared with the non-cross-label results (the first two rows in Table 2), the deep model trained on the synthetic dataset improves performance by 62% and 44%, respectively. With the help of the air-writing word synthesizer, the recognition model can achieve an excellent performance improvement in samples whose labels are fresh to the model. These experimental results demonstrate the success of our method.

The air-writing word synthesizer can synthesize a large number of samples under the condition of limited character samples and word samples. In our design, we have greatly enriched the combination of characters by introducing a corpus. This makes the recognition model not only learn to recognize a single character, but also learn combinations of characters (also known as the corpus information of the dataset). Generally speaking, a word-IAHR model can benefit a lot from the corpus information of the dataset.

Table 6. Experimental results of generalization performance experiments.

Experiments	Word-Level Accuracy
Generalization performance experiment (user-mixed)	0.623
Generalization performance experiment (user-independent)	0.446

4.5. Discussion on the Splicing Module and Generating Module

The air-writing word synthesizer is a two-stage synthesis method. In this section, we intend to show the respective effects of the splicing module and the generating module.

In Figure 8, we illustrate several word sample outputs of the splicing module and the generating module (i.e., "JEW", "RUN", "HULK", and "READ"). For example, we take the word "JEW" as the target word. First, we pick character samples "J", "E", and "W" from the char-6DMG. Then, we splice them using the splicing module to obtain the spliced sample. Finally, the generating module takes in the spliced sample labeled "JEW" and outputs the synthetic sample.

In Figure 8, the dashed box represents the junctions between the characters in the spliced word sample. The characters in the spliced samples are connected by linear interpolation. We can see that, after processing by the generating module, the junctions become more natural. We believe that adversarial training helps a lot.

The main disadvantage of our model is the dependence on datasets. Our method requires that the character dataset and word dataset used for training must be collected under the same rules. For example, the users must write within a fixed range while collecting data. If the two datasets are collected under different rules, the air-writing word synthesizer will not perform so well. In addition, using linear interpolation to splice characters may not be the optimal solution. In the future, we will try to model the strokes between characters mathematically. In this way, we can figure out a better solution for splicing characters. In addition, we will try to apply the method to various datasets. For example, we can improve our method so that it can be used even if the data collection rules are different.

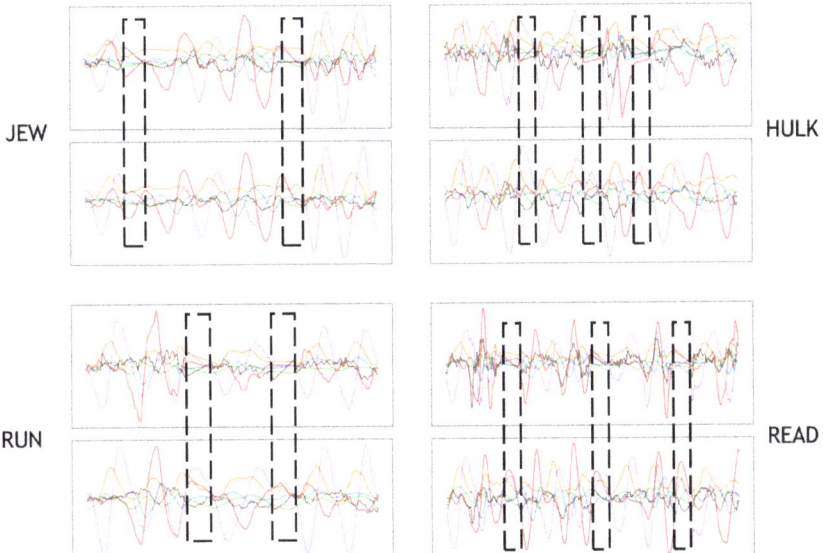

Figure 8. Outputs of the splicing module and generating module. There are two sample outputs for each word: The upper one is the wave of the spliced sample, and the lower one is the wave of the synthesized sample.

4.6. Evaluation of Computational Efficiency

In this section, we evaluate the computational efficiency of our proposed method. Note that the air-writing word synthesizer is a synthesis method that works in the training phase. This synthesis method can greatly improve the generalization performance of the recognition model, but it will not slow down the inference process.

In Table 7, we report the computational efficiency of our proposed method. The "synthesis (per sample)" refers to the average time taken to synthesize one sample by the air-writing word synthesizer. The "recognition (per sample)" refers to the average time taken to recognize one sample. We argue that our approach is conducive to devices with limited computing resources and has a wide range of application scenarios.

Table 7. Computational efficiency of our proposed method.

Item	Average Time (ms)
Synthesis (per sample)	1.96
Recognition (per sample)	19.09

5. Conclusions

In-air handwritten word recognition usually suffers from insufficient data. In this work, we propose a new two-stage synthesis method (named the air-writing word synthesizer) for in-air handwritten words to solve this problem. The proposed method includes two components: a splicing module and a generating module. In the splicing module, a corpus is introduced to provide guidance for word splicing. In the generating module, adversarial learning is introduced to guide word synthesis. In addition, the network architecture is carefully designed to handle time series.

Experiments on public datasets show that the proposed method can synthesize samples of high quality. Most air-writing recognition tasks can benefit from the air-writing word synthesizer.

The main disadvantage of our model is its dependence on datasets. Our method requires that the character dataset and the word dataset used for training are collected under the same rules. For example, the users must write within a fixed range while collecting. If the two datasets are collected under different rules, the air-writing word synthesizer will not perform so well. In addition, linear interpolation is adopted to splice characters, which may not be the optimal solution.

In the future, we will try to mathematically model the strokes between characters in a word. In this way, we may figure out a better plan for splicing characters. In addition, we will try to apply the method to multiple datasets. For example, we can improve our method so that it can be used even if the data collection rules are different.

Author Contributions: Conceptualization, X.Z. and Y.X.; methodology, X.Z. and Y.X.; software, X.Z.; validation, X.Z. and Y.X.; resources, Y.X.; writing—original draft preparation, X.Z.; writing—review and editing, Y.X.; supervision, Y.X. All authors have read and agreed to the published version of the manuscript.

Funding: This research was funded by NATIONAL NATURAL SCIENCE FUNDS, grant number 61771199.

Acknowledgments: We thank anonymous reviewers for their careful reading and insightful comments.

Conflicts of Interest: The authors declare no conflict of interest.

References

1. Ahmed, D.B.; Diaz, E.M.; Domínguez, J.J.G. Automatic Calibration of the Step Length Model of a Pocket INS by Means of a Foot Inertial Sensor. *Sensors* **2020**, *20*, 2083. [CrossRef] [PubMed]
2. Chang, W. Electrooculograms for Human-Computer Interaction: A Review. *Sensors* **2019**, *19*, 2690. [CrossRef] [PubMed]
3. Bachmann, D.; Weichert, F.; Rinkenauer, G. Review of Three-Dimensional Human-Computer Interaction with Focus on the Leap Motion Controller. *Sensors* **2018**, *18*, 2194. [CrossRef] [PubMed]
4. Elzobi, M.; Al-Hamadi, A. Generative vs. Discriminative Recognition Models for Off-Line Arabic Handwriting. *Sensors* **2018**, *18*, 2786. [CrossRef] [PubMed]
5. Alam, M.S.; Kwon, K.; Alam, M.A.; Abbass, M.Y.; Imtiaz, S.M.; Kim, N. Trajectory-Based Air-Writing Recognition Using Deep Neural Network and Depth Sensor. *Sensors* **2020**, *20*, 376. [CrossRef] [PubMed]
6. Xu, S.; Xue, Y. A long term memory recognition framework on multi-complexity motion gestures. In Proceedings of the 14th IAPR International Conference on Document Analysis and Recognition (ICDAR), Kyoto, Japan, 9–15 November 2017; pp. 201–205. [CrossRef]
7. Yang, C.; Ko, H.; Han, D.; Ku, B. Alpha-numeric hand gesture recognition based on fusion of spatial feature modelling and temporal feature modelling. *Electron. Lett.* **2016**, *52*, 1679–1681. [CrossRef]
8. Xu, S.; Xue, Y. Air-writing characters modelling and recognition on modified CHMM. In Proceedings of the IEEE International Conference on Systems, Man, and Cybernetics (SMC), Budapest, Hungary, 9–12 October 2016; pp. 001510–001513. [CrossRef]
9. Ronneberger, O.; Fischer, P.; Brox, T. U-net: Convolutional networks for biomedical image segmentation. In Proceedings of the International Conference on Medical image computing and computer-assisted intervention, Munich, Germany, 5–9 October 2015; pp. 234–241. [CrossRef]
10. Isola, P.; Zhu, J.Y.; Zhou, T.; Efros, A.A. Image-to-image translation with conditional adversarial networks. In Proceedings of the IEEE conference on computer vision and pattern recognition, Honolulu, HI, USA, 21–26 July 2017; pp. 1125–1134. [CrossRef]
11. Li, Y.; Chu, Z.; Xin, Y. Posture Recognition Technology Based on Kinect. *IEICE Trans. Inf. Syst.* **2020**, *103-D*, 621–630. [CrossRef]

12. Lu, X.; Qi, B.; Qian, H.; Gao, Y.; Sun, J.; Liu, J. Kinect-based human finger tracking method for natural haptic rendering. *Entertain. Comput.* **2020**, *33*, 100335. [CrossRef]
13. Wang, B.; Li, Y.; Lang, H.; Wang, Y. Hand Gesture Recognition and motion estimation using the Kinect Sensor. *Mechatron. Syst. Control.* **2020**, *48*. [CrossRef]
14. Goodfellow, I.; Pouget-Abadie, J.; Mirza, M.; Xu, B.; Warde-Farley, D.; Ozair, S.; Courville, A.; Bengio, Y. Generative adversarial nets. *Adv. Neural Inf. Process. Syst.* **2014**, 2672–2680.
15. Zhu, J.Y.; Park, T.; Isola, P.; Efros, A.A. Unpaired image-to-image translation using cycle-consistent adversarial networks. In Proceedings of the IEEE international conference on computer vision, Venice, Italy, 22–29 October 2017; pp. 2223–2232. [CrossRef]
16. Kim, T.; Cha, M.; Kim, H.; Lee, J.K.; Kim, J. Learning to discover cross-domain relations with generative adversarial networks. In Proceedings of the 34th International Conference on Machine Learning, Sydney, NSW, Australia, 6–11 August 2017; Volume 70, pp. 1857–1865.
17. Yi, Z.; Zhang, H.; Tan, P.; Gong, M. Dualgan: Unsupervised dual learning for image-to-image translation. In Proceedings of the IEEE international conference on computer vision, Venice, Italy, 22–29 October 2017; pp. 2849–2857.
18. Benaim, S.; Wolf, L. One-sided unsupervised domain mapping. In Proceedings of the Advances in Neural Information Processing Systems, Long Beach, CA, USA, 4–9 December 2017; pp. 752–762.
19. Hoffman, J.; Tzeng, E.; Park, T.; Zhu, J.Y.; Isola, P.; Saenko, K.; Efros, A.; Darrell, T. CyCADA: Cycle-Consistent Adversarial Domain Adaptation. In Proceedings of the 35th International Conference on Machine Learning, Stockholm, Sweden, 10–15 July 2018; Dy, J., Krause, A., Eds.; PMLR: Stockholm, Sweden, 2018; Volume 80, pp. 1989–1998.
20. Amodio, M.; Krishnaswamy, S. TraVeLGAN: Image-To-Image Translation by Transformation Vector Learning. In Proceedings of the IEEE Conference on Computer Vision and Pattern Recognition (CVPR), Long Beach, CA, USA, 16–20 June 2019; pp. 8983-8992.
21. Shivakumara, P.; Bhowmick, S.; Su, B.; Tan, C.L.; Pal, U. A New Gradient Based Character Segmentation Method for Video Text Recognition. In Proceedings of the 2011 International Conference on Document Analysis and Recognition (ICDAR 2011), Beijing, China, 18–21 September 2011; pp. 126–130. [CrossRef]
22. Bissacco, A.; Cummins, M.; Netzer, Y.; Neven, H. PhotoOCR: Reading Text in Uncontrolled Conditions. In Proceedings of the IEEE International Conference on Computer Vision (ICCV 2013), Sydney, Australia, 1–8 December 2013; pp. 785–792. [CrossRef]
23. Graves, A.; Fernández, S.; Gomez, F.; Schmidhuber, J. Connectionist temporal classification: labelling unsegmented sequence data with recurrent neural networks. In Proceedings of the 23rd international conference on Machine learning, Pittsburgh, PA, USA, 25–29 June 2006; pp. 369–376.
24. Ghosh, S.K.; Valveny, E.; Bagdanov, A.D. Visual attention models for scene text recognition. In Proceedings of the 2017 14th IAPR International Conference on Document Analysis and Recognition (ICDAR), Kyoto, Japan, 9–15 November 2017; pp. 943–948.
25. Cheng, Z.; Bai, F.; Xu, Y.; Zheng, G.; Pu, S.; Zhou, S. Focusing Attention: Towards Accurate Text Recognition in Natural Images. In Proceedings of the IEEE International Conference on Computer Vision (ICCV), Venice, Italy, 22–29 October 2017; pp. 5076–5084.
26. Graves, A.; Liwicki, M.; Bunke, H.; Schmidhuber, J.; Fernández, S. Unconstrained on-line handwriting recognition with recurrent neural networks. In Proceedings of the Advances in Neural Information Processing Systems, Vancouver, BC, Canada, 8–10 December 2008; pp. 577–584.
27. Su, B.; Lu, S. Accurate scene text recognition based on recurrent neural network. In Proceedings of the Asian Conference on Computer Vision, Singapore, 1–5 November 2014; Springer: Berlin/Heidelberg, Germany, 2014; pp. 35–48.
28. Shi, B.; Bai, X.; Yao, C. An end-to-end trainable neural network for image-based sequence recognition and its application to scene text recognition. *IEEE Trans. Pattern Anal. Mach. Intell.* **2016**, *39*, 2298–2304. [CrossRef] [PubMed]
29. Liu, W.; Chen, C.; Wong, K.Y.K.; Su, Z.; Han, J. STAR-Net: A SpaTial Attention Residue Network for Scene Text Recognition. In Proceedings of the British Machine Vision Conference (BMVC), York, UK, 19–22 September 2016.
30. Kingma, D.P.; Ba, J. Adam: A Method for Stochastic Optimization. In Proceedings of the 3rd International Conference on Learning Representations (ICLR 2015), San Diego, CA, USA, 7–9 May 2015.

31. Chen, M.; AlRegib, G.; Juang, B.H. Air-writing recognition Part I: Modeling and recognition of characters, words, and connecting motions. *IEEE Trans. Hum. Mach. Syst.* **2015**, *46*, 403–413. [CrossRef]
32. Hochreiter, S.; Schmidhuber, J. Long short-term memory. *Neural Comput.* **1997**, *9*, 1735–1780. [CrossRef] [PubMed]

Publisher's Note: MDPI stays neutral with regard to jurisdictional claims in published maps and institutional affiliations.

© 2020 by the authors. Licensee MDPI, Basel, Switzerland. This article is an open access article distributed under the terms and conditions of the Creative Commons Attribution (CC BY) license (http://creativecommons.org/licenses/by/4.0/).

Article

Efficient Upper Limb Position Estimation Based on Angular Displacement Sensors for Wearable Devices

Aldo-Francisco Contreras-González [1], Manuel Ferre [1], Miguel Ángel Sánchez-Urán [1,2,*], Francisco Javier Sáez-Sáez [1] and Fernando Blaya Haro [2]

[1] Centro de Automática y Robótica (CAR) UPM-CSIC, ETS Ingenieros Industriales, Universidad Politécnica de Madrid, Calle de José Gutiérrez Abascal, 2, 28006 Madrid, Spain; af.contreras@alumnos.upm.es (A.-F.C.-G.); m.ferre@upm.es (M.F.); franciscojavier.saezs@upm.es (F.J.S.-S.)
[2] ETS Ingeniería y Diseño Industrial, Universidad Politécnica de Madrid, Ronda de Valencia, 3, 28012 Madrid, Spain; fernando.blaya@upm.es
* Correspondence: miguelangel.sanchezuran@upm.es

Received: 9 October 2020; Accepted: 9 November 2020; Published: 12 November 2020

Abstract: Motion tracking techniques have been extensively studied in recent years. However, capturing movements of the upper limbs is a challenging task. This document presents the estimation of arm orientation and elbow and wrist position using wearable flexible sensors (WFSs). A study was developed to obtain the highest range of motion (ROM) of the shoulder with as few sensors as possible, and a method for estimating arm length and a calibration procedure was proposed. Performance was verified by comparing measurement of the shoulder joint angles obtained from commercial two-axis soft angular displacement sensors (sADS) from Bend Labs and from the ground truth system (GTS) OptiTrack. The global root-mean-square error (RMSE) for the shoulder angle is 2.93 degrees and 37.5 mm for the position estimation of the wrist in cyclical movements; this measure of RMSE was improved to 13.6 mm by implementing a gesture classifier.

Keywords: motion capture; soft angular displacement sensors; upper limb; motion tracking; wearable sensors

1. Introduction

In the fields of biomechanics, physiotherapy and kinesiology, motion capture plays a fundamental role in the study of the measurement of physical activity, either to know the performance of a device or the evolution of a therapy. Optical motion capture is one of the most accurate methods for measurement of human kinematics [1]. In addition to the fact that the use of this technology is expensive, it limits mobility to specific areas and, in most cases, bulky markers and special suits must be carried by the user. Outside of a controlled environment, a common solution is the use of inertial measurements units (IMUs), which in some cases are small and wireless, and are capable of obtaining sample measurements at high speeds [2]. These sensors may be suitable for short periods of time where the accumulated error is not significant. Nevertheless, a high demand of hardware resources is used for data processing as filtering, integration and trigonometry operations are involved to estimate joint angular kinematics [3,4]. Users should also consider movement complexity, sensor placement, the studied joint, biomechanical models used and calibration procedure.

The era of flexible systems is on the rise, and a new generation of motion sensors is emerging. The wearable flexible sensors (WFSs) are created with flexible materials which are inexpensive to manufacture, have better mechanical and thermal properties than non-flexible sensors and are lightweight and comfortable for motion capture [5]. Still, there are important features to consider, such as stretching, compression, bending and twisting [6]. With the use of wearable systems, there is a promising path to contribute to a meaningful diagnosis of shoulder conditions, as well as a concise follow-up for rehabilitation evolution [7]. Upper extremities of the human body have complex kinematics and contain a large number of degrees of freedom (DOF) [8]; the glenohumeral (shoulder) joint, for instance, is a complex joint with more than three DOF [9]. WFSs could properly estimate the kinematics of the shoulder due to its physical characteristics by eliminating the use of rigid parts and even communication cables in some cases [10–13]. It has been proved that it is possible to estimate the angles of the arm with respect to the trunk by placing sensors on the body [14–17]. Additionally, the use of compression jackets, combined with soft sensor arrays, makes it possible to accurately estimate the position of the limb [18,19], as well as to place the sensors onto the skin without the use of adhesives or other preparations such as invasive intrusions in the user's body. However, a disadvantage of compression garments is that sweat can cause damage when it comes into contact with electronic devices.

Work-related studies using IMU systems for shoulder orientation estimation reported a RMSE of 15° for flexion/extension movements, a RMSE less than 20° for abduction/adduction movement and from 1 to 60° for rotation movement [20]. The combination of IMU with electromyography sensors (EMGs) shows a RMSE of 10.24° in complex tasks performed with the shoulder [21]. Another study using an IMU system as reference and a smart-textile with printed strain sensors showed a mean error of 9.6° in planar motions measurements of shoulder joint [22]. In the case of lower limbs using WFSs, the maximum RMS error was nearly 15° for the knee sensors [23]. The authors of [24] developed a dynamic measurement system for the movement of the legs, which can detect the squat position with an accuracy of 3° and walking with an accuracy of 5°. WFSs made of elastomers were used for sensing hand gestures, obtaining an error of 5° [25], which is acceptable to the majority of requirements of motion capture.

In robotics, the end-effector position is calculated using kinematics equations by knowing the angles of each joint and the length of each link; this means that, to estimate the position of the wrist, the angles of the arm and forearm and its lengths must be known. In this work, the goal is to sense four DOF in the arm [26,27], three DOF in the shoulder and one in the elbow. In addition, a kinematic algorithm is proposed to find the position of the elbow and wrist. These, using mainly the signals from the WFSs and for one single DOF, constitute the IMU system. This document describes the method to recreate a WFS to obtain orientation and position for the upper limbs, so forth applied to the human right arm. A calibration algorithm to estimate the length of the arm and forearm of each subject and an algorithm for the estimation of the position of the elbow and the wrist from the shoulder are proposed. In Section 3, the placement of the sensors and the required calibration for each user are described. Fusion data methods and the filters applied to the resulting signals are discussed. The device presented here eliminates the rigid elements that might interfere in daily tasks and movements, allowing the user freedom and mobility. Furthermore, compared with previous work by the authors, described in Section 2, the number of sensors was reduced, and the computation cost was improved.

2. Previous Work by the Authors

It was proved that it is possible to obtain 95% of the variance of the main components for shoulder gestures with an array of seven single-axis resistive sensors [19]. Other results showed that it is possible to estimate the gestures of the shoulder with a performance 95.4% using an array of four WFSs and EMG signals [28]. In this work, a rigorous extension was performed using the two-axis sADS whose operation is explained and detailed in [29,30]. Features of the sADS include linear and bidirectional response, measurement of angular displacement in two orthogonal planes with a sensitivity of 0.016° and a repeatability of 0.18°. The capacitive sensors are made using layered medical grade silicone elastomers doped with conductive and nonconductive fillers.

Initially, four sADS were placed in the intermediate positions of the seven single-axis resistive sensors configuration recommended by [19]. Replicating the proposed 20-layer hidden neural network method, with a configuration for the acquired data from the four sADS of [70%, 15%, 15%] for training, cross-validation and test stages, respectively, an overfitting was identified. In order to lessen the chance of overfitting, a principal component analysis (PCA) was performed; the sensor placed over the middle deltoid muscle was found to contain the most activity on pure abduction and adduction movements, while the sensors at the rear, placed over the posterior deltoid, were representative for horizontal adduction and flexion and extension movements. A 92% representation of the ROM was obtained using only two sADS; the study and location of each sensor is detailed in the following subsection.

sADS Array Location

Three different arrangements were made in different locations at the shoulder as shown in Figure 1. The arrangement resulting from the analyses was the placement of two rotated sADS 90° between two planes that represent 92% of the variance of the data (See Table 1).

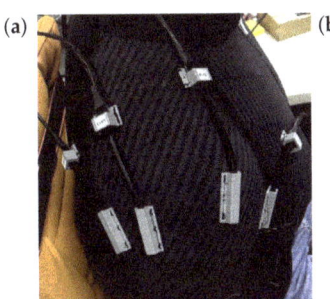
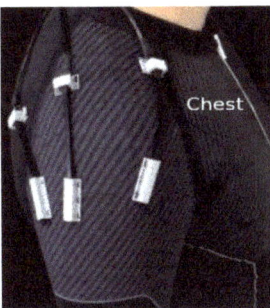
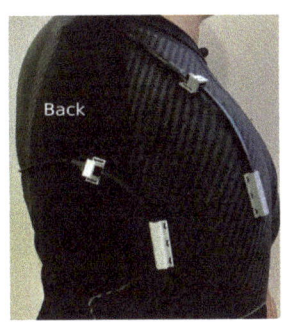

Figure 1. Different locations for the variance estimation. (**a**) Four soft angular displacement sensors (sADS) were placed in the recommended intermediate poses. (**b**) The frontal sADS was eliminated due to its low representation in the variance; it also generated obstructions and poor measurements in the horizontal gestures. The three previous poses were preserved. (**c**) Placement of two sADS, one in the centre of the two sADS of the top three sensor array, and the other in the rear, generating an angle of 90° between the two planes with respect to the first.

Table 1. Result of the estimated variance for different sADS arrays.

Type of Sensor	Amount of Sensors	Variance
Single-axis resistive	7	95%
Two-axis capacitive	4	93%
Two-axis capacitive	3	92%
Two-axis capacitive	2	92%

3. System Overview

This study was performed on a single healthy limb without reduced mobility, the right arm. However, it can be replicated for both arms. The areas considered in the estimation started from the centre of the head of the humerus to the centre of the junction of the radius and the ulna at the wrist. The supination and pronation gestures were not considered.

3.1. Working Range

The arm at rest was considered as the natural pose, making a full extension of the elbow as shown in Figure 2a.

The zero-position of the system occurred when a pure shoulder abduction gesture reaching 90° (without performing any flexion or extension of the shoulder) and a full extension of the elbow were performed, starting from the natural pose.

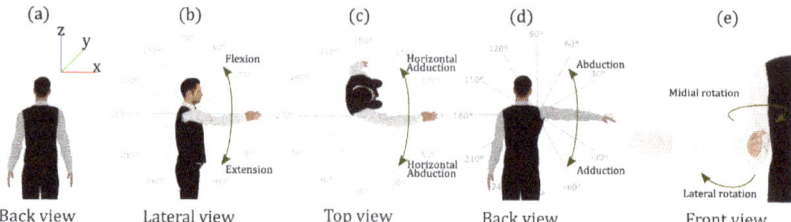

Figure 2. Gestures that define the work space of the right arm. (**a**) Rest position. (**b**) Flexion/extension gesture corresponding to the YZ plane. (**c**) Horizontal abduction/adduction corresponding to the plane XY. (**d**) Abduction/adduction gesture corresponding to the XZ plane. (**e**) Depiction of the rotation of the shoulder, named δ_1.

3.2. Sensors Placement

Placing sensors on a compression jacket presents various difficulties, the most important being wrinkles and folds in the fabric and skin tightening in specific areas. To eliminate such problems, two small rigid parts were designed to pose and guide the two-axis sADS of BendLabs [30]. One of them holds the sensor in a fixed location and the other allows it to slide inside it, not only eliminating the problem of skin stretching but also creating a straight line formed by the limb, which allows the accurate measurement of the angle (see Appendix A.1). The pieces are sewn on the shirt and do not impede the free mobility of the user in any way.

As a result of the PCA for the location of the sADS on the shoulder, the best arrangement was selected with respect to the number of sensors and the representation of movements performed. It is worth mentioning that the locations of each sensor were initially placed in the way recommended by the previous study. The adjustments made to the final positions were identified when making several data captures for subsequent analysis. The location description is detailed on Appendix A.2.

The IMUs were placed on opposite sides of the arm (Figure 3). IMU_1 was located just where the shoulder ends and IMU_2 was located just before the beginning of the elbow. The orientation of the IMUs should be towards the same direction of the arm.

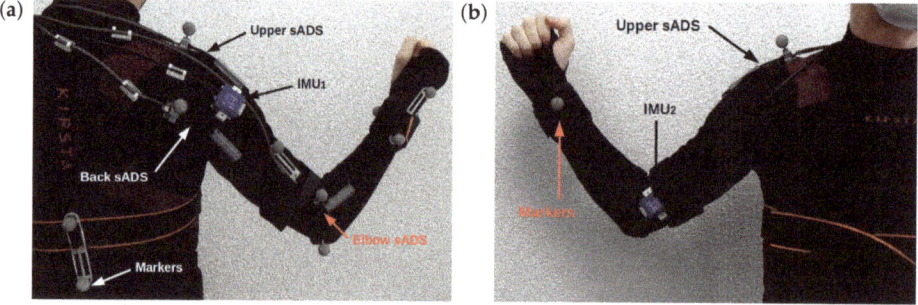

Figure 3. Location of sensors on the compression jacket. (**a**) Back view. The reflective markers are shown in bright grey, the IMU_1 and the two sADS on the shoulder (upper and back) and the sADS on the elbow. (**b**) Front view, which shows two reflective markers and the IMU_2.

3.3. Shoulder Rotation

As the study presented in this document was implemented in an Exosuit developed in our group [31], these solutions were discarded for the first two DOF (abduction/adduction and flexion/extension). The third DOF of the shoulder (Figure 2e medial/lateral rotation) is revealed at the forearm and can be measured at the elbow. Given that the shoulder sADS array does not detect the rotation gesture, the use of IMU is proposed exclusively for this gesture.

Two IMUs were placed on the arm (same link) as shown in Figure 3. The rotation was calculated as the difference of the rotation angles on the x-axis of the IMU. This angle was generated by the shoulder rotation, thus completing the variables necessary to estimate the elbow and wrist position δ_1.

$$\delta_1 = \Delta \left(IMU1_{yaw}, IMU2_{yaw} \right) \tag{1}$$

3.4. Ground Truth

To verify the estimation proposed in this article, the OptiTrack system was used for ground truth data. A total of 10 reflective pointers and four cameras from the OptiTrack system [32] were placed, providing submillimetre precision. The markers placement generated straight lines between each section to be analysed. Two markers were placed on the back to know the inclination of the user—two on the shoulder (just above the fixed parts of the shoulder sADS), two on the arm, two on the forearm, one on the elbow and two on the wrist [33], as shown in Figure 3.

3.5. Data Acquisition

The three sADS were connected to a custom acquisition board based on the LAUNCHXL-F28379D development board and communicated with the micro-controller via I2C protocol at a frequency of 200 Hz. The IMUs and the custom acquisition board were connected to a NVIDIA Jetson Nano via LpBUS and SPI at 400 Hz and 500 Hz, respectively (Figure 4). The LPMS-URS2 9-axis IMU manufactured by LP-RESEARCH, with a Kalman processing stage on board and gyroscope, accelerometer and magnetometer, was selected. This sensor delivers filtered data as output at frequencies up to 400 Hz with a resolution of 0.01. Software was developed on the Jetson Nano board to trigger sensors and store all sensor data along with a timestamp.

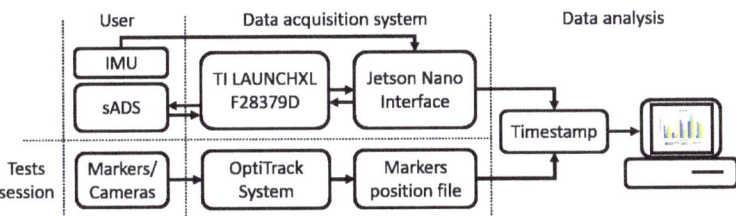

Figure 4. Flow diagram of the data acquisition system. On the left side, the movements of the user, the generated angles and the poses of the markers are shown; in the centre, the acquisition of data and communication between boards as well as the storage of positions of the reflective pointers; on the right side, the data analysis based on the timestamp of each file.

To perform data collection for session testing, the compression jacket with sADS and IMUS was placed on the subject. Then, OptiTrack markers were located as shown in Figure 3 in order to obtain the real position of the subject's arm. Both systems started the data capture operation almost at the same time, first in the OptiTrack software and then in the Jetson Nano. The Jetson Nano stored the following in a file (with the start time in milliseconds): the six angles received from the sADS, the Euler angles, the quaternions and a timestamp of each of the two IMUs and the gesture performed in that timestamp, in addition to a timestamp generated by the Jetson Nano itself. The OptiTrack software stored the points in coordinates x, y and z in the space of each reflective pointer, whose name is the start time in milliseconds, in a file. To synchronise the data of the files of each session (Appendix A.3), the start time and the sampling frequency in each file were considered.

3.6. sADS Behaviour

The angular displacement of the sADS was obtained by a differential capacitance measurement. The sensor repeatability, according to the manufacturer, is 0.18°. However, when taking measures from the sensor at 200 Hz, a noise of a maximum amplitude near 3° was observed. A set of sensor samples obtained while bending the sensor was stored and a frequency domain analysis was realised over those samples. Following frequency spectrum analysis, a low-pass first order infinite impulse response (IIR) digital filter with a cut-off frequency of 10 Hz was applied to the raw data provided by the sensor to reduce noise. Finally, a ±0.15° dead zone for sampling data was added to the filter (see Figure 5).

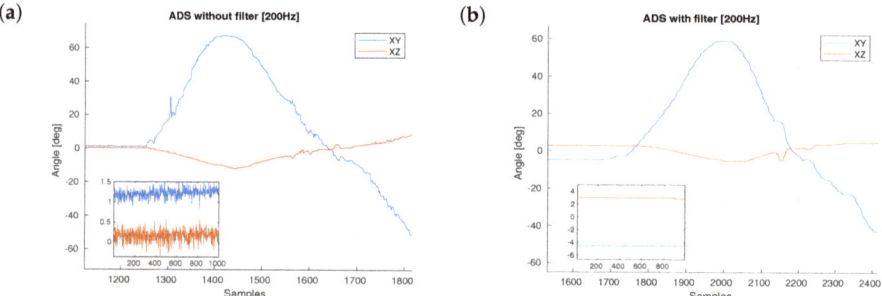

Figure 5. Example of similar gestures in two different takes. (**a**) First take shows the behaviour of the sensor without the filter. (**b**) Second take of a similar gesture shows the behaviour with the filter.

4. Estimation Methods

4.1. Angle Fusion Algorithm

The fusion of the sensor signals is done by using the four angles given by two sADS sensors. Sensor positions and definition of planes are described in Section 3.1. To find the angle in the XY plane, the xy upper sADS and xz back sADS angles are used: for the XZ plane, the xz upper sADS and xy back sADS angles are needed (see Table 2). Data fusion algorithm is detailed on Appendix B.1.

Table 2. Merged data is obtained in two different fusions using the shoulder ADS sensors.

Fusion	Upper sADS	Back sADS
Plane XY (α_1)	xy-axis $\rightarrow \theta_1$	xz-axis $\rightarrow \theta_2$
Plane XZ (ϕ_1)	xz-axis $\rightarrow \theta_1$	xy-axis $\rightarrow \theta_2$

4.2. Method to Estimate Arm and Forearm Length

An important error for the calculation of the position in space of the wrist and elbow with respect to the shoulder—the use of a measuring tape to determine the length of each link (length of the arm and forearm)—was detected. In order to reduce this error, an L-shaped structure was proposed. This calibration method consists of a plane marked by four points at known distances to estimate arm and forearm lengths by trigonometric methods.

This structure was created with the purpose of marking a fixed distance from the shoulder to a point in space, and it was arranged in four points: two fixed and two movable; over each one of the four points, there was a vertical pin with a magnet on top of it, which paired with a bracelet for the user that locates the magnet in the centre of the wrist. By performing a series of defined movements (Appendix B.2), the ADS sensors were calibrated and the arm length was calculated with trigonometric equations.

4.3. Elbow and Wrist Position Estimation

To estimate the position of the shoulder and the wrist, it is necessary to know the angles α_1 (Plane XY), ϕ_1 (Plane XZ), the rotation of the shoulder δ_1 (Equation (1)) and the elbow flexion angle α_2, as well as the distances of each segment: shoulder to elbow (Equation (A16) arm_{length}) and elbow to wrist (Equation (A17) $forearm_{length}$). The kinematic model considered in this work consists of 4 rotating joints. The first three joints take into account the glenohumeral joint. It is commonly accepted that said articulation contains two translational DOF. However, since the surfaces of the head of the humerus are more than 99% spherical [34], it is modelled as a spherical joint. The fourth joint represents the elbow, where pronation and supination are neglected. Finally, to estimate the position of the arm and elbow, the Denavit–Hartenberg notation is used (Appendix B.4).

5. Experiment

The experiment depended on two scenarios. The first one consisted of a table, a chair and the structure described in Section 4.2 in order to perform the length estimation (system calibration). The second one was needed to acquire the positions with the ground truth system (GTS) and to perform the analysis of acquired data (ground truth pose). A graphical user interface developed on the Jetson Nano board allowed calibrations to be performed by saving the values for each user and the gesture performed and guiding the speed and kind of movement of the participants while performing the gestures. Once the estimates of arm and forearm length were saved, these data were used for position estimation. In this document, all the acquired data that were stored to be analysed by the MATLAB R2020a software tool.

The study involved nine subjects: two females and seven males for both scenarios. The subjects were aged 27 ± 4.4 years (mean ± standard deviation (SD)), with a body weight of 81.7 ± 15.6 kg and a height of 1.83 ± 0.16 m. All participants had no evidence or known history of skeletal and neurological diseases, and they exhibited normal joint ROM and muscle strength. All experimental procedures were carried out in accordance with the Declaration of Helsinki on research involving human subjects and approved by the ethical committee of the Polytechnic University of Madrid.

5.1. System Calibration

The arm calibration algorithm (Section 4.2) was tested with nine subjects, measuring the arm length (from shoulder flexion point to elbow flexion point) and the forearm length (from the point of flexion of the elbow to the centre of the point of flexion of the wrist) with a tape measure and placing the reflectors of the OptiTrack ground truth system (GTS) at each point (see Table 3).

Table 3. Comparison between the estimation made by the proposed algorithm with the ground truth system (GTS) and the tape measure of the arm and forearm lengths of the subjects (mm).

Subject	Arm			Forearm		
	Tape	Estimated	GTS	Tape	Estimated	GTS
1	300.0	311.52	310.98	250.0	246.20	246.83
2	330.0	331.40	332.08	270.0	260.44	261.32
3	345.0	340.78	339.12	300.0	291.83	290.55
4	310.0	312.86	311.98	260.0	272.08	273.56
5	334.0	332.27	332.98	260.0	258.40	256.56
6	295.0	305.89	304.63	250.0	**249.32**	**249.12**
7	330.0	**328.63**	**326.35**	270.0	277.42	278.77
8	315.0	309.43	308.66	255.0	260.18	260.80
9	340.0	337.82	339.63	295.0	**302.81**	**299.68**

The angles were captured by the interface, which displayed them on screen along with the time of capture and the estimation of arm and forearm length, obtained using the Equations (A14) and (A15) described in Appendix B.2 with a distance $\overline{AB} = 39.5$ cm. The calibration frame is shown in Figure 6. Then, the distances estimated were compared with the GTS.

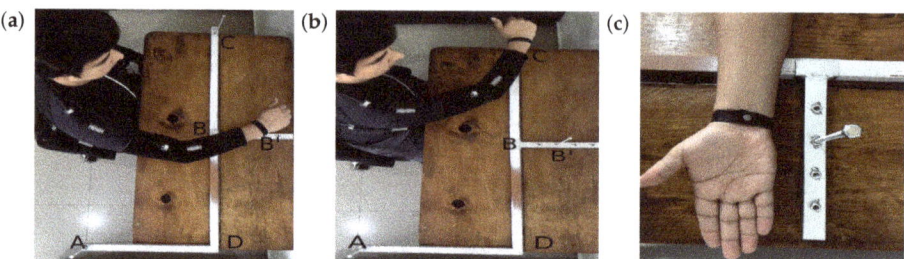

Figure 6. Calibration frame top view. (a) Shows arm pose at the point B of the frame to estimate the length of the arm and forearm with a known distance $\overline{AB}$. (b) Gesture performed for redundant calculation towards point C. (c) It shows the bracelet tight and a magnet to guarantee the same pose of the wrist with the pin on the frame.

The performance of the frame developed is shown on Table 4 and presents an RMSE of [0.540, 2.280 mm] (best, worse case) for the arm and RMSE of [0.200, 3.130 mm] for the forearm.

Table 4. Performance of the proposed frame (RMSE). Comparison between measurements.

	Tape vs. Estimated	Tape vs. GT	Estimated vs. GT
Arm	5.96 mm	5.87 mm	1.31 mm
Forearm	7.18 mm	7.48 mm	1.50 mm

5.2. Ground Truth Pose

The tests were carried out in four different sessions and the data acquired in the tests were analysed later. The first session consisted of a sequence of five abductions/adductions, five flexions/extensions and five horizontal abductions. This session was performed with visual feedback through a graphical interface projected on a monitor, where the time of each gesture (e.g., flexion) was four seconds with one second of rest—that is, each complete movement (e.g., flexion + extension) had a duration of ten seconds. In the second session, free movements were performed for 30 s through the lower shoulder area—that is, only obtaining negative values according to the range of work shown in Figure 2. The third session consisted of making free movements in the upper area. In the fourth session, free movements were performed throughout the entire working range. The subject performed each whole session five times.

The shoulder, elbow and wrist markers were used to make a comparison of the position of the GTS with the estimation made by the proposed algorithm. The back, arm, forearm and shoulder markers were used to find the angles generated by the poses. The shoulder marker was placed on a 12 mm raised pin on the z-axis; therefore, this elevation was subtracted to make the comparison, this being the reference point (P) of the system (X_0, Y_0, Z_0). The pose of the other markers was defined by subtracting the reference point from the position of each marker given by the GTS—that is, $x_n = x_{n_{GT}} - x_0$.

5.3. Orientation Method

The performance of the orientation estimation was evaluated offline using the RMSE for two aspects: the angles acquired by the sADS and the position estimation of the elbow and wrist compared to the GTS, obtained with the L-shaped structure (Figure 7). The estimation of the elbow and shoulder position depended on the angles measured by the sADS in the experiments. The position of the GTS markers was used to find the error of the angles. The angle between the markers of the OptiTrack system was obtained by calculating the angle generated between markers on the arm (placed on the shoulder acromion bone) and the ones on the back. The data from the experiments were classified into cyclical movements, free movements, movements under the shoulder, movements over the shoulder and each gesture performed. The angles acquired by the different sensors and the angles generated by the location of the markers were compared.

It can be seen in Table 5 that free movements and movements carried out over the shoulder had a greater error than cyclical movements and those carried out below the shoulder. In addition, it was observed that the sensor placed on the back measured the gestures of flexion/extension and abduction/adduction more easily, while the sensor placed on the top was a better solution for horizontal adduction movements and shoulder movements.

Table 5. Orientation error in root-mean-square error (RMSE) obtained by the ground truth system (GTS) when performing the movements and gestures. Elbow orientation error was compared even in gestures that did not involve elbow movement.

Sensor	Cyclic Mov.	Free Mov.	Below the Shoulder	Over the Shoulder	Flexion/ Extension	Abd./ Add.	Horizontal Adduction	Rotation
Upper sADS	6.84°	7.33°	1.52°	4.18°	10.53°	4.22°	3.71°	n/a
Back sADS	4.50°	5.67°	2.01°	8.39°	2.97°	1.93°	9.66°	n/a
IMU	1.93°	2.86°	2.96°	1.66°	2.30°	1.89°	2.23°	1.51°
Elbow sADS	0.43°	0.93°	1.73°	1.53°	0.54°	0.38°	0.78°	n/a
Mean	3.42°	4.19°	2.05°	3.94°	4.08°	2.10°	4.09°	n/a

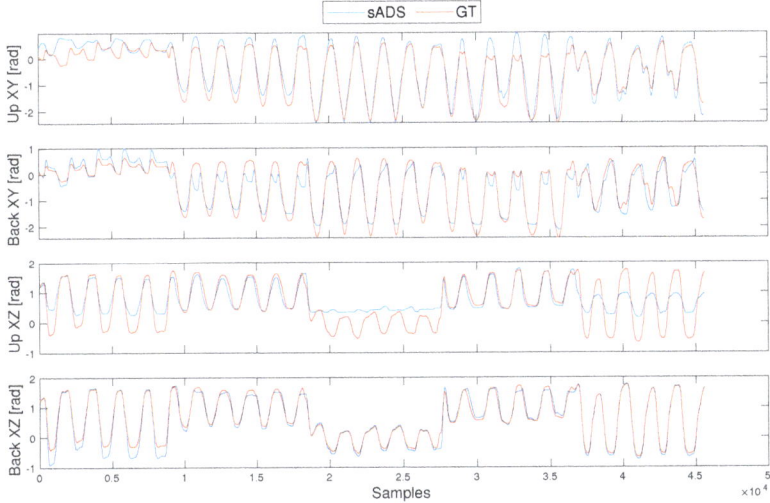

Figure 7. Performance of the sADS angles compared with the GTS in a series test.

Using the algorithm proposed in the Section 4.3 and the angles captured from the elbow and wrist experiments, it was possible to compare the positions with the GTS. The largest error obtained in the entire experiment was 124.3 mm, which corresponded to the position of the wrist in a free movement exercise on the shoulder, and the smallest error was 36 mm, which corresponded to the elbow in a cyclical movement below the shoulder. Table 6 shows the RMSE of all captured movements classified in the elbow and wrist in free and cyclical movements, above and below the shoulder.

The mean error of the position estimate was 43.4 mm for the elbow and 57.2 mm for the wrist in all three axes. If the length of the arm of an average adult is $\approx$ 300 mm, the error would be equivalent to 9.53% of the length from shoulder to the elbow, or 14.47% from the shoulder to the wrist and, in the worst case up to 27%. This means that, when extending the arm entirely, it can be said that the error is as large as half of the palm of an adult's hand in space.

Table 6. Error for the estimated position by the shoulder sADS given in RMSE (mm).

	Elbow Position				Wrist Position			
	Cyclic Mov.	Free Mov.	Below the Shoulder	Over the Shoulder	Cyclic Mov.	Free Mov.	Below Shoulder	Over the Shoulder
Upper sADS	39.7	61.5	31.7	46.5	59.3	79.2	58.0	49.7
Back sADS	35.4	43.8	30.3	58.6	36.3	48.8	44.3	82.2

To improve performance in cyclical movements, a classifier was developed; the classifier identifies the gestures performed and also identifies the movements that correspond to the lower and upper area with respect to the shoulder. The classifier was generated by making a comparison with 24 different methods (see Table A2 in Appendix C.1). Once the best method was obtained and trained, a function was created in MATLAB 2020a using the upper sADS and back sADS angles to classify the motion.

After the classification algorithm found which gesture the movement belonged to, the method described in Appendix C.2 was used, applying a different "weight" for each case, through Equation (A11). The weights (Table 7) were found through an empirical method using the data of the participants of the first test.

Table 7. Weights used in Equation (A11) to reduce the estimation error.

	Below Shoulder	Over the Shoulder	Flexion/ Extension	Abduction/ Adduction	Horizontal Adduction
Upper sADS XY → aFactor	0.4	2.5	2.3	1.6	2.3
Back sADS XZ → bFactor	2.2	1.7	1.9	2.5	1.0
Upper sADS XZ → aFactor	2.0	2.5	0.4	2.5	1.2
Back sADS XZ → bFactor	2.2	2.3	2.7	1.8	2.7

By evaluating the fusion algorithm with the gesture classifier, an overall improvement in angle measurement was observed. This algorithm used the sensor signal that performed best (upper or back sensor) for each type of gesture, resulting in the smallest measurement error of the shoulder angles. The RMSE for cyclical movements was 2.93°. In the case of free movements, the algorithm was allowed to interpret each signal from the sADS sensors and classify the movements, obtaining a significant improvement in angles with an RMSE of 3.71°. Because the mean angle error decreased, the position estimate improved (Table 8). It should be mentioned that the largest error obtained for the position estimation using the weighted fusion algorithm was 60.7 mm, 43% less than the largest error without the weighting. The smallest was 12 mm, only 19 mm better than the smallest without the weighting.

Table 8. Fusion RMSE for position estimation (mm).

	Cyclic Mov.	Free Mov.	Below the Shoulder	Over the Shoulder
Elbow	12.3	31.6	14.1	39.5
Wrist	14.9	40.9	20.3	40.4

The overall RMSE was 26.7 mm. In case the movements were performed below the shoulder or cyclically (as is the case in rehabilitation processes), the error decreased. The horizontal adduction gesture generated a greater error in the estimation, since it was carried out in the limit of the movements that were classified in the upper and lower part of the shoulder. Furthermore, this gesture also shared zones of movement with all the other gestures.

6. Discussion

During the calibration process, it was difficult to correctly place the frame without the appropriate measurement system for the angles generated by the shoulder. It was identified that initial position calibration can be improved using structures fixed to the ground or to the user's hip. With an abduction of more than 90°, a scapular movement was generated, causing a displacement of the superior sADS and, consequently, errors in the measurement. In experiments of over 30 min with the users using the shirt, no evident change in the behaviour of the sADS signals was observed due to prolonged periods of time; the IMUs were re-calibrated in each data collection. In this work, IMUs were used only for the shoulder rotation gesture. For defined tasks, the sensing of shoulder rotation could have been eliminated, removing the use of IMUs and facilitating donning-doffing and estimation calculations. This work will be applied on an exosuit and integrated into an online system; it may use a different classification method than used on this study due to the time response, and a robustness investigation is needed.

The maximum calculated error of the calibration of the OptiTrack cameras was 0.343 mm and can be considered in the comparison of the method of estimating the length of the arm and forearm, being able to improve or worsen within that range. If the noise from the sADS is not reduced, a projected noise is produced at the wrist. Similarly, not using the arm and forearm distances estimated by the L-shaped structure method increases the error. These behaviours increase the error up to 3.5° and are projected in the final position (wrist), increasing up to $\approx$ 50 mm.

Our results are similar to [35], where, on a cyclic movement, there is an RMSE of [1.42°, 3.89°] (best, worst) and, on free or random movements [1.88°, 4.41°]. We also searched for the optimal sensor arrangement, finding four essential sensors for the estimation of the orientation. On the contrary, we found that two sensors can represent 92% of the ROM without adding scapular movement. Similar studies used piezoresistive strain sensors directly adhered to the skin to estimate shoulder ROM; the comparison between reference data from OptiTrack and the strain sensors showed a RMSE less than 10° in shoulder flexion/extension and abduction/adduction estimation [36]. In the case of [37], which used a smart compression garment, the best result for angle measurement of the elbow with 9.98° of error was obtained. An interesting study using 20 self-made soft strain sensors [38] showed an overall error position of the full-body motion tracking of [29.5 mm, 38.7 mm] (best, worst case) and results for the shoulder joint with just two sensors of [30.9 mm, 47.1 mm] for the elbow [13.5 mm and 34.7 mm] and for the wrist [27.3 and 43.5] using OptiTrack as ground truth.

7. Conclusions

Wearable flexible sensors are becoming common as a technology used for motion capture. The shoulder is a complex joint and plays an important role in daily living activities. Therefore, designing portable and accurate arm motion capture system can be challenging. This document reports a device capable of obtaining a mean RMSE of 3.54° in the angle measurement of the shoulder. Using the angles and the length of the arm and forearm and compared with a GTS, a RMSE of 29.1 mm was found for the estimation of the position of the wrist. This performance may be useful in applications of physiotherapy, kinesiology or gaming. However, due to the lack of accuracy at a millimetre level, the use of this device for robotic or biomechanical systems could limit its approaches. Still, a great possibility can be exploited in different applications that require monitoring of the human body in open spaces.

Author Contributions: Conceptualization, A.-F.C.-G.; Data curation, F.J.S.-S.; Formal analysis, A.-F.C.-G.; Investigation, A.-F.C.-G.; Project administration, M.F.; Supervision, M.F., M.Á.S.-U. and F.B.H.; Writing—original draft, A.-F.C.-G.; Writing—review & editing, A.-F.C.-G. All authors have read and agreed to the published version of the manuscript.

Funding: This work has been partially supported by the project "LUXBIT: Lightweight Upper limbs eXosuit for BImanual Task Enhancement" under RTI2018-094346-B-I00 grant, funded by the Spanish "Ministerio de Ciencia, Innovación y Universidades".

Conflicts of Interest: The authors declare no conflict of interest.

Appendix A. System Overview Detailed Description

Appendix A.1. 3D Printed Parts for sADS

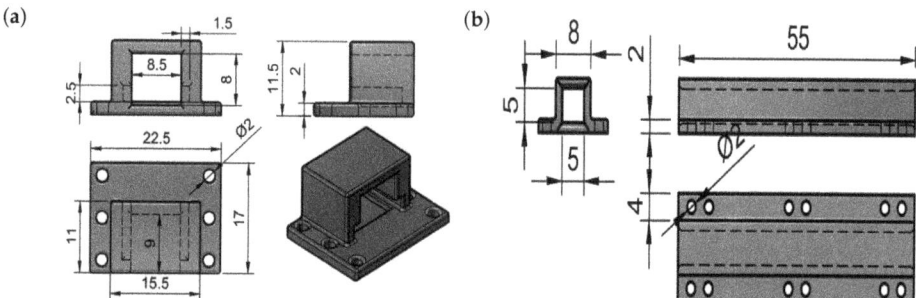

Figure A1. Design of the parts for the sADS sensors. (**a**) Ensures the correct posing on the fixed part. (**b**) Allows correct sliding on the movable part, not only eliminating the problem of skin stretching but also creating a straight line formed by the limb.

Appendix A.2. sADS Placement

We created two identical shirts using the following method to place two sensors (see Figure 3) for the shoulder and one for the elbow:

1. With the shoulder abducted at 90°, a sADS is placed over the printed parts and perched on top of the shoulder. Then, the arm is centred in the XY plane. The user is placed at rest. The fixed part is placed 25.0 mm from the corner of the generated angle and the long sliding part is placed on the vertical part of the arm. The distance between the pieces must be between 50 and 60 mm.
2. The back sADS is placed 40° achieving 90° from the abduction, right in the centre of the arm and drawing a straight line from the sADS on the upper shoulder.
3. The elbow sADS is placed on the outside of the arm, with the centre of the sensor coinciding with the elbow hinge. The distance between the pieces should be between 50 and 60 mm.

Appendix A.3. Synchronisation Algorithm

To synchronise the files, the frequencies of each device, the start time and the duration time of each shot are used. The file that starts first is trimmed until it has the same start time. The file that ends at the end is trimmed until it has the same end time. Finally, a linear interpolation is performed to ensure the same number of samples in each file:

1. The start time of each file is acquired. The file that started first is identified as file A, the other as file B: $tInitA$ and $tInitB$ and the amount of samples of each file is obtained:

$$lenA = length(A)$$
$$lenB = length(B)$$
(A1)

2. The final time and the real frequency of each file are obtained: $tEndA = tInitA + lastTimestampA$ and $tEndB = tInitB + lastTimestampB$; and the frequency is given by:

$$fqA = \frac{lenA}{tEndA - tInitA}$$
$$fqB = \frac{lenB}{tEndB - tInitB}$$
(A2)

3. Cut out the initial n samples from file A:

$$n = ceil((tInitB - tInitA) * fqA) \qquad (A3)$$

4. Check which file ends first. The difference between the end times is calculated as $diff = abs(tEndA - tEndB)$. Cut out the final m samples from the file:

$$if(tEndA > tEndB) \rightarrow m = ceil(diff * fqA)$$
$$else \rightarrow m = ceil(diff * fqB) \qquad (A4)$$

5. Calculate a $factor = (length(fileA)/length(fileB))$ and generate a new vector containing the new length from the shortest:

$$newVec = linspace(1, length(fileA), length(fileA) * factor) \qquad (A5)$$

The interpolation for each column of the original file is performed:

$$fileAInterpol = interp1(fileA, newVec,'linear') \qquad (A6)$$

MATLAB Software is used in this algorithm to perform line-space and data interpolation.

Appendix B. Estimation Method Detailed Description

Appendix B.1. Fusion Sensor Algorithm

Applying the Central Limit Theorem [39], it is assumed that θ_1 and θ_2 denote the two sADS measurements on the same plane with noise variances σ_1^2 and σ_2^2, respectively.

$$\theta_3 = \sigma_3^2(\sigma_1^{-2} * \theta_1 + \sigma_2^{-2} * \theta_2) \qquad (A7)$$

where the variance of the combined estimate is:

$$\sigma_3^2 = ((\sigma_1)^{-2} + (\sigma_2)^{-2})^{-1} \qquad (A8)$$

where variance is defined as:

$$\sigma = \frac{1}{N-1}\sum_{i=1}^{N}|A_i - \mu|^2 \qquad (A9)$$

and μ is the mean of A,

$$\mu = \frac{1}{N}\sum_{i=1}^{N}A_i \qquad (A10)$$

The estimated value of variance for the sensors in both planes is: $\sigma_{XY} = (203.013 + 218.315)/2$ and $\sigma_{XZ} = (205.523 + 239.986)/2$. Therefore: $\sigma_3^2 = (20860.176 + 26079.470)/2$. For the fusion of the sensors with the compensation of the classification by gesture, it is evaluated by adding two factors as follows:

$$\theta_3 = \sigma_3^2\left(\frac{\sigma_1^{-2}}{aFactor} * \theta_1 + \frac{\sigma_2^{-2}}{bFactor} * \theta_2\right) \qquad (A11)$$

Appendix B.2. L-Shaped Structure Details

In the design of the structure, it is recommended that the distance of the segment $\overline{AB}$ be approximately 60 cm, since it is the average length of an adult's arm, as well as the magnitude of the segment $\overline{DC}$ to be 1.33 times the segment $\overline{AD}$. The length of the vertical pins is irrelevant, since its projection is considered in the calculations. It is worth mentioning that this method can be applied on both arms, replicating the structure in mirror mode for the opposite side. Points B and B' must move together on the x-axis, and point B' moves also on the y-axis. Points A and C are fixed to the structure, as shown in Figure A2.

The structure (Figure 6) is located on a table, with the point A on the right side of the user (to align with the z-axis) and point B in front of them. The steps to make the estimation are the following:

1. An abduction of the shoulder is performed at 90°, leaving the elbow at 0°, and achieving an angle in the XY and XZ planes of 0° ± 3°. While the user maintains this pose, the entire structure is moved so that the magnet on the pin in the fixed point A touches the magnet in the centre of the wrist.
2. The user extends the arm to the front performing a shoulder flexion at 90° and keeping the elbow at 0°. The movable point B is adjusted on the x-axis of the structure by making it coincide with the forearm. The movable point B' is then adjusted along the y-axis until it coincides with the new point of the magnet on the wrist, preserving the previous point (A). This way, a right angle is generated between the point A and B as shown in Figure A2.
3. The wrist is then moved from point B' to point B generating a flexion in the elbow. The angles generated with this gesture are acquired (see gesture Figure) with the help of the sADS.
4. Finally, the centre of the wrist is placed on the point C, preserving the pose of the structure, and the angles generated with this gesture are acquired (see gesture (Figure A2b) with the help of the sADS.

Conditions:

- The angles generated in steps 1 and 2 towards the point A and B must be 0° ± 3° and 90° ± 3° in the XY plane, respectively. At the elbow, they must be 0° ± 3° in XY in both steps.
- Step 3 is generated with the shoulder angle greater than 40° and the elbow angle greater than 10°, both in the XY plane.
- Step 4 is generated with the shoulder angle greater than 90° and the elbow angle greater than 10°, both in the XY plane.

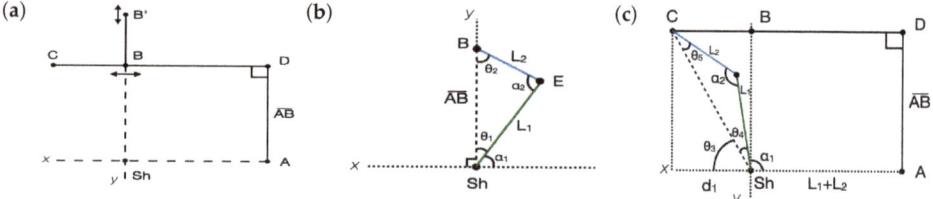

Figure A2. A top view representation of the structure and the generated angles by the arm: (a) The solid black line represents the structure and its properties, and the dotted line represents the pose that the user must adopt in the main gestures. (b) Shows arm pose at the point B to estimate the length of the arm (green colour) and forearm (blue colour) with the known distance $\overline{AB}$. (c) Gesture performed for redundant calculation towards point C.

To obtain the length estimates of the segments of an upper limb, the angle of the shoulder in the XY plane is considered to be α_1 and in the XZ plane is ϕ_1. The angle of the elbow is defined as α_2.

L_1 and L_2 are the projection on the XY plane of the segment of the humerus and the segment generated by the radius and ulna bones. The value of the segment $\overline{AB}$ is a distance known from the structure. Therefore, for the gesture generated in step 3 it can be said that:

$$\theta_1 = \frac{\pi}{2} - \alpha_1 \qquad (A12)$$

and by Euclid's fifth postulate,

$$\theta_2 = \pi - (\theta_1 + \alpha_2) \qquad (A13)$$

By the law of sines, and considering the angle of the plane XZ:

$$arm_{length} = \frac{\overline{AB} * \sin(\theta_2)}{\sin(\alpha_2)} * \cos(\phi_1) \tag{A14}$$

$$forearm_{length} = \frac{\overline{AB} * \sin(\theta_1)}{\sin(\alpha_2)} * \cos(\phi_1) \tag{A15}$$

In step four, point C is used only as a redundant point in the calculation using the first two estimated distances L1 and L2. By the law of sines, and considering the angle of the plane XZ, the redundant estimation is found as:

$$arm_{length} = \frac{\overline{SC} * \sin \theta_5}{\sin \alpha_2} * \cos(\phi_1) \tag{A16}$$

$$forearm_{length} = \frac{\overline{SC} * \sin \theta_4}{\sin \alpha_2} * \cos(\phi_1) \tag{A17}$$

The explanation to get to this point is presented in Appendix B.3. This arm and forearm length estimation process needs to be done only once per user.

Appendix B.3. Redundant Calculation of Arm and Forearm Length

Redundant calculations are possible once the first estimate is obtained. Considering the Figure A2, using the first two estimated distances L1 and L2, it is possible to estimate d_1 distance, where d_1 is the projection of the total length of the frame minus the length of the extended arm

$$d_1 = \overline{CD} - (L_1 + L_2) \tag{A18}$$

and that the distance $\overline{SC}$ generates a right angle being the hypotenuse for AB $\overline{AB}$ y d_1

$$\overline{SC} = \sqrt{\overline{AB}^2 + d_1^2} \tag{A19}$$

Then, the angle θ_3 can be easily calculated as:

$$\theta_3 = \tan^{-1}\left(\frac{\overline{AB}}{d_1}\right) \tag{A20}$$

since the angle generated by the arm α_1 is known, and, having calculated θ_3, it can be said that:

$$\theta_4 = \pi - (\theta_3 + \alpha_1) \tag{A21}$$

and from Euclid's fifth postulate,

$$\theta_5 = \pi - (\theta_4 + \alpha_2) \tag{A22}$$

By the law of sines and considering the angle of the plane XZ, the redundant estimation is found as:

$$arm_{length} = \frac{\overline{SC} * \sin \theta_5}{\sin \alpha_2} * \cos(\phi_1) \tag{A23}$$

$$forearm_{length} = \frac{\overline{SC} * \sin \theta_4}{\sin \alpha_2} * \cos(\phi_1) \tag{A24}$$

Appendix B.4. Denavit–Hartenberg Parameters

The Denavit–Hartenberg parameters and A_i definitions of the kinematic chain are represented in Table A1. A_1, A_2, A_3, A_4 and A_5 are given by the Equation (A25) where the four quantities, a_i, d_i, α_i and θ_i associated with link i and joint i corresponding to the $axis_i$ on the Table A1. The arm length is ($arm_{length} \to a_l$) and forearm length ($forearm_{length} \to f_l$).

$$A_i = \begin{pmatrix} \cos(\theta_i) & -\sin(\theta_i)\cos(\alpha_i) & \sin(\theta_i)\sin(\alpha_i) & a_i\cos(\theta_i) \\ \sin(\theta_i) & \cos(\theta_i)\cos(\alpha_i) & -\cos(\theta_i)\sin(\alpha_i) & a_i\sin(\theta_i) \\ 0 & \sin(\alpha_i) & \cos(\alpha_i) & d_i \\ 0 & 0 & 0 & 1 \end{pmatrix} \quad (A25)$$

Table A1. Denavit–Hartenberg parameters of the kinematic model.

Axis, i	a_i	d_i	α_i	θ_i
1	0	0	$\pi/2$	α_1
2	0	0	$\pi/2$	ϕ_1
3	0	a_l	$-\pi/2$	δ_1
4	0	0	$-\pi/2$	α_2
5	0	f_l	0	0

The T-matrices are thus given by:

$$T_3^0 = A_1 A_2 A_3 \quad (A26)$$

and

$$T_5^0 = A_1 A_2 A_3 A_4 A_5 \quad (A27)$$

The first three rows of the last column of T_3^0 are the x, y and z components of the origin in the elbow; that is,

$$elbow_x = a_l c(\alpha_1) s(\phi_1) \quad (A28)$$

$$elbow_y = a_l s(\alpha_1) s(\phi_1) \quad (A29)$$

$$elbow_z = -a_l c(\phi_1) \quad (A30)$$

and the location for the wrist is defined by T_5^0:

$$wrist_x = a_l c(\alpha_1) s(\phi_1) - f_l \left(s(\alpha_2) s(\alpha_1) s(\delta_1) + c(\alpha_1) c(\phi_1) c(\delta_1) + c(\alpha_1) c(\alpha_2) s(\phi_1) \right) \quad (A31)$$

$$wrist_y = f_l \left(s(\alpha_2) c(\alpha_1) s(\delta_1) - c(\phi_1) c(\delta_1) s(\alpha_1) - c(\alpha_2) s(\alpha_1) s(\phi_1) + a_l s(\alpha_1) s(\phi_1) \right) \quad (A32)$$

$$wrist_z = f_l \left(c(\phi_1) c(\alpha_2) - c(\delta_1) s(\phi_1) s(\alpha_2) \right) - a_l c(\phi_1) \quad (A33)$$

Appendix C. Experiment Detailed Description

Appendix C.1. Classifier

As training data, the signals obtained from the sADS sensors were used, as well as the type of movement, which was the response to the classifier, captured in the interface during the sequential sessions. Movement types were stored as numeric variables. The Classification learner tool was used to train the different models using supervised machine learning with the Statistics and Machine learning Toolbox 11.7. The cross-validation was selected on five folds and the PCA enabled with a 95% of the explained variance. All 24 methods were trained with 70% of the dataset, 15% for validation and 15% for testing.

Table A2. Gesture classification training results. The model with the shortest training time and smaller misclassification cost were chosen among the models with the highest accuracy (%).

Model Type	Accuracy	Model Type	Accuracy	Model Type	Accuracy
Fine Tree	92.3	Quadratic SVM	83.9	Cosine KNN	95.7
Medium Tree	77.5	Cubic SVM	74.1	Cubic KNN	99.7
Coarse Tree	59.6	Fine Gaussian SVM	95.1	Weighted KNN	99.9
Linear Discriminant	65.6	Medium Gaussian SVM	86.0	Boosted Trees	84.3
Quadratic Discriminant	76.9	Coarse Gaussian SVM	74.8	Bagged Trees	99.7
Gaussian Naive Bayes	61.4	**Fine KNN**	99.9	Subspace Discriminant	65.9
Kernel Naive Bayes	67.8	Medium KNN	99.7	Subspace KNN	98.3
Linear SVM	68.5	Coarse KNN	94.6	RUSBoosted Trees	77.5

There are different models that could be used. For this study, the nearest neighbour classifier (k-NN) was selected, which typically has good predictive accuracy in low dimensions. This classifier has an average prediction speed ($\approx$ 1 s) and an average memory usage ($\approx$ 4 MB). Another model, such as the Fine Tree, could have been selected if the required response time should be less ($\approx$ 0.01 s). The k-NN response is shown in the Figure A3 which shows a 99.9% score in the classification. The values 1 to 5 are the representation of the gestures, the true positive rate (TPR) is mostly 100% accurate. The false negative rate (FNR) is 0.1% on the over the shoulder movement.

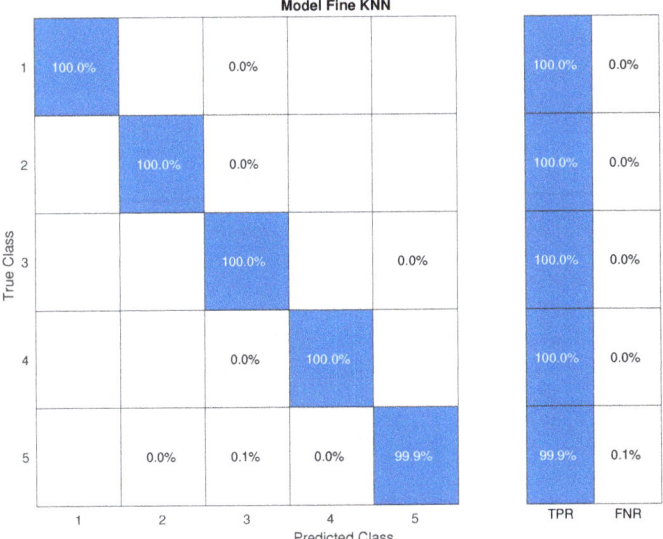

Figure A3. Confusion matrix from the fine nearest neighbour classifier.

Appendix C.2. Weighting Algorithm

Algorithm A1: Movement Classification

Result: Sensor fusion with classification compensation
[ADS_Data] = getsADSdata(fileName);
yfit = trainedModel.predictFcn(ADS_Data);
switch *yfit* **do**
    case *flexion* do
        | fusionCompensationFlexion();
    end
    case *Abduction* do
        | fusionCompensationAbduction();
    end
    ⋮
    otherwise do
        | break;
    end
end

References

1. Van der Kruk, E.; Reijne, M.M. Accuracy of human motion capture systems for sport applications; state-of-the-art review. *Eur. J. Sport Sci.* **2018**, *18*, 806–819. [CrossRef] [PubMed]
2. Rigoni, M.; Gill, S.; Babazadeh, S.; Elsewaisy, O.; Gillies, H.; Nguyen, N.; Pathirana, P.N.; Page, R. Assessment of shoulder range of motion using a wireless inertial motion capture device—A validation study. *Sensors* **2019**, *19*, 1781. [CrossRef] [PubMed]
3. Fong, D.T.P.; Chan, Y.Y. The use of wearable inertial motion sensors in human lower limb biomechanics studies: A systematic review. *Sensors* **2010**, *10*, 11556–11565. [CrossRef] [PubMed]
4. Patel, S.; Park, H.; Bonato, P.; Chan, L.; Rodgers, M. A review of wearable sensors and systems with application in rehabilitation. *J. Neuroeng. Rehabil.* **2012**, *9*, 1–17. [CrossRef]
5. Nag, A.; Mukhopadhyay, S.C.; Kosel, J. Wearable flexible sensors: A review. *IEEE Sens. J.* **2017**, *17*, 3949–3960. [CrossRef]
6. Liu, H.; Li, Q.; Zhang, S.; Yin, R.; Liu, X.; He, Y.; Dai, K.; Shan, C.; Guo, J.; Liu, C.; et al. Electrically conductive polymer composites for smart flexible strain sensors: A critical review. *J. Mater. Chem. C* **2018**, *6*, 12121–12141. [CrossRef]
7. Carnevale, A.; Longo, U.G.; Schena, E.; Massaroni, C.; Presti, D.L.; Berton, A.; Candela, V.; Denaro, V. Wearable systems for shoulder kinematics assessment: A systematic review. *BMC Musculoskelet. Disord.* **2019**, *20*, 546. [CrossRef]
8. Sugimoto, S.I.; Takei, A.; Ogino, M. Finite element analysis with tens of billions of degrees of freedom in a high-frequency electromagnetic field. *Mech. Eng. Lett.* **2017**, *3*, 16-00667. [CrossRef]
9. Winter, J.; Allen, T.J.; Proske, U. Muscle spindle signals combine with the sense of effort to indicate limb position. *J. Physiol.* **2005**, *568*, 1035–1046. [CrossRef]
10. Xu, K.; Lu, Y.; Takei, K. Multifunctional Skin-Inspired Flexible Sensor Systems for Wearable Electronics. *Adv. Mater. Technol.* **2019**, *4*, 1800628. [CrossRef]
11. Lou, Z.; Wang, L.; Jiang, K.; Shen, G. Programmable three-dimensional advanced materials based on nanostructures as building blocks for flexible sensors. *Nano Today* **2019**. *26*, 176–198. [CrossRef]
12. Chen, W.; Yan, X. Progress in achieving high-performance piezoresistive and capacitive flexible pressure sensors: A review. *J. Mater. Sci. Technol.* **2020**, *43*, 175–188. [CrossRef]
13. Yang, Y.; Gao, W. Wearable and flexible electronics for continuous molecular monitoring. *Chem. Soc. Rev.* **2019**, *48*, 1465–1491. [CrossRef] [PubMed]

14. Nguyen, K.D.; Chen, I.M.; Luo, Z.; Yeo, S.H.; Duh, H.B.L. A wearable sensing system for tracking and monitoring of functional arm movement. *IEEE/ASME Trans. Mechatron.* **2010**, *16*, 213–220. [CrossRef]
15. Varghese, R.J.; Lo, B.P.L.; Yang, G.Z. Design and prototyping of a bio-inspired kinematic sensing suit for the shoulder joint: Precursor to a multi-dof shoulder exosuit. *IEEE Robot. Autom. Lett.* **2020**, *5*, 540–547. [CrossRef]
16. Proske, U.; Gandevia, S.C. The kinaesthetic senses. *J. Physiol.* **2009**, *587*, 4139–4146. [CrossRef] [PubMed]
17. Varghese, R.J.; Guo, X.; Freer, D.; Liu, J.; Yang, G.Z. A simulation-based feasibility study of a proprioception-inspired sensing framework for a multi-dof shoulder exosuit. In Proceedings of the 2019 IEEE 16th International Conference on Wearable and Implantable Body Sensor Networks (BSN), Chicago, IL, USA, 19–22 May 2019; pp. 1–4.
18. Xiong, Y.; Tao, X. Compression garments for medical therapy and sports. *Polymers* **2018**, *10*, 663. [CrossRef]
19. Samper-Escudero, J.L.; Contreras-González, A.F.; Ferre, M.; Sánchez-Urán, M.A.; Pont-Esteban, D. Efficient Multiaxial Shoulder-Motion Tracking Based on Flexible Resistive Sensors Applied to Exosuits. *Soft Robot.* **2020**, *7*, 370–385. [CrossRef]
20. Poitras, I.; Dupuis, F.; Bielmann, M.; Campeau-Lecours, A.; Mercier, C.; Bouyer, L.J.; Roy, J.S. Validity and reliability of wearable sensors for joint angle estimation: A systematic review. *Sensors* **2019**, *19*, 1555. [CrossRef]
21. Poitras, I.; Bielmann, M.; Campeau-Lecours, A.; Mercier, C.; Bouyer, L.J.; Roy, J.S. Validity of wearable sensors at the shoulder joint: Combining wireless electromyography sensors and inertial measurement units to perform physical workplace assessments. *Sensors* **2019**, *19*, 1885. [CrossRef]
22. Esfahani, M.I.M.; Nussbaum, M.A. A "smart" undershirt for tracking upper body motions: Task classification and angle estimation. *IEEE Sens. J.* **2018**, *18*, 7650–7658. [CrossRef]
23. Mengüç, Y.; Park, Y.L.; Pei, H.; Vogt, D.; Aubin, P.M.; Winchell, E.; Fluke, L.; Stirling, L.; Wood, R.J.; Walsh, C.J. Wearable soft sensing suit for human gait measurement. *Int. J. Robot. Res.* **2014**, *33*, 1748–1764. [CrossRef]
24. Feng, Y.; Li, Y.; McCoul, D.; Qin, S.; Jin, T.; Huang, B.; Zhao, J. Dynamic Measurement of Legs Motion in Sagittal Plane Based on Soft Wearable Sensors. *J. Sens.* **2020**, *2020*, 1–10. [CrossRef]
25. Huang, B.; Li, M.; Mei, T.; McCoul, D.; Qin, S.; Zhao, Z.; Zhao, J. Wearable stretch sensors for motion measurement of the wrist joint based on dielectric elastomers. *Sensors* **2017**, *17*, 2708. [CrossRef]
26. Rosen, J.; Perry, J.C.; Manning, N.; Burns, S.; Hannaford, B. The human arm kinematics and dynamics during daily activities-toward a 7 DOF upper limb powered exoskeleton. In Proceedings of the ICAR'05 12th International Conference on Advanced Robotics, Seattle, WA, USA, 18–20 July 2005; pp. 532–539.
27. Zanchettin, A.M.; Rocco, P.; Bascetta, L.; Symeonidis, I.; Peldschus, S. Kinematic motion analysis of the human arm during a manipulation task. In Proceedings of the ISR 2010 (41st International Symposium on Robotics) and ROBOTIK 2010 (6th German Conference on Robotics), Munich, Germany, 7–9 June 2010; pp. 1–6.
28. Contreras-González, A.F.; Samper-Escudero, J.L.; Pont-Esteban, D.; Sáez-Sáez, F.J.; Sánchez-Urán, M.Á.; Ferre, M. Soft-Wearable Device for the Estimation of Shoulder Orientation and Gesture. In *International Conference on Human Haptic Sensing and Touch Enabled Computer Applications*; Springer: Berlin/Heidelberg, Germany, 2020; pp. 371–379.
29. Reese, S.P. Angular Displacement Sensor of Compliant Material. U.S. Patent 8,941,392, 27 January 2015.
30. Labs, B. Bend Labs. Internet Draft, 2020. Available online: http://xxx.lanl.gov/abs/https://www.bendlabs.com/products/2-axis-soft-flex-sensor/ (accessed on 22 June 2020).
31. Pont, D.; Contreras, A.F.; Samper, J.L.; Sáez, F.J.; Ferre, M.; Sánchez, M.Á.; Ruiz, R.; García, Á. ExoFlex: An Upper-Limb Cable-Driven Exosuit. In *Iberian Robotics Conference*; Springer: Berlin/Heidelberg, Germany, 2019; pp. 417–428.
32. OptiTrack. OptiTrack for Movement Sciences. Internet Draft, 2020. Available online: https://optitrack.com/ (accessed on 25 June 2020).
33. Schmidt, R.; Disselhorst-Klug, C.; Silny, J.; Rau, G. A marker-based measurement procedure for unconstrained wrist and elbow motions. *J. Biomech.* **1999**, *32*, 615–621. [CrossRef]
34. Soslowsky, L.; Flatow, E.; Bigliani, L.; Mow, V. Articular geometry of the glenohumeral joint. *Clin. Orthop. Relat. Res.* **1992**, *285*, 181–190.

35. Jin, Y.; Glover, C.M.; Cho, H.; Araromi, O.A.; Graule, M.A.; Li, N.; Wood, R.J.; Walsh, C.J. Soft Sensing Shirt for Shoulder Kinematics Estimation. In Proceedings of the 2020 IEEE International Conference on Robotics and Automation (ICRA), Paris, France, 31 May–31 August 2020; pp. 4863–4869.
36. Lee, H.; Cho, J.; Kim, J. Printable skin adhesive stretch sensor for measuring multi-axis human joint angles. In Proceedings of the 2016 IEEE International Conference on Robotics and Automation (ICRA), Stockholm, Sweden, 16–21 May 2016; pp. 4975–4980.
37. Greenspan, B.; Lobo, M.A. Design and Initial Testing of an Affordable and Accessible Smart Compression Garment to Measure Physical Activity Using Conductive Paint Stretch Sensors. *Multimodal Technol. Interact.* **2020**, *4*, 45. [CrossRef]
38. Kim, D.; Kwon, J.; Han, S.; Park, Y.L.; Jo, S. Deep full-body motion network for a soft wearable motion sensing suit. *IEEE/ASME Trans. Mechatron.* **2018**, *24*, 56–66. [CrossRef]
39. Maybeck, P.S. *Stochastic Models, Estimation, and Control*; Academic Press: Cambridge, MA, USA, 1982.

Publisher's Note: MDPI stays neutral with regard to jurisdictional claims in published maps and institutional affiliations.

© 2020 by the authors. Licensee MDPI, Basel, Switzerland. This article is an open access article distributed under the terms and conditions of the Creative Commons Attribution (CC BY) license (http://creativecommons.org/licenses/by/4.0/).

Article

British Sign Language Recognition via Late Fusion of Computer Vision and Leap Motion with Transfer Learning to American Sign Language

Jordan J. Bird [1,*], Anikó Ekárt [2] and Diego R. Faria [1]

[1] ARVIS Lab—Aston Robotics Vision and Intelligent Systems, Aston University, Birmingham B4 7ET, UK; d.faria@aston.ac.uk
[2] School of Engineering and Applied Science, Aston University, Birmingham B4 7ET, UK; a.ekart@aston.ac.uk
* Correspondence: birdj1@aston.ac.uk

Received: 6 August 2020; Accepted: 4 September 2020; Published: 9 September 2020

Abstract: In this work, we show that a late fusion approach to multimodality in sign language recognition improves the overall ability of the model in comparison to the singular approaches of image classification (88.14%) and Leap Motion data classification (72.73%). With a large synchronous dataset of 18 BSL gestures collected from multiple subjects, two deep neural networks are benchmarked and compared to derive a best topology for each. The Vision model is implemented by a Convolutional Neural Network and optimised Artificial Neural Network, and the Leap Motion model is implemented by an evolutionary search of Artificial Neural Network topology. Next, the two best networks are fused for synchronised processing, which results in a better overall result (94.44%) as complementary features are learnt in addition to the original task. The hypothesis is further supported by application of the three models to a set of completely unseen data where a multimodality approach achieves the best results relative to the single sensor method. When transfer learning with the weights trained via British Sign Language, all three models outperform standard random weight distribution when classifying American Sign Language (ASL), and the best model overall for ASL classification was the transfer learning multimodality approach, which scored 82.55% accuracy.

Keywords: sign language recognition; multimodality; late fusion

---

1. Introduction

Sign language is the ability to converse mainly by use of the hands, as well as in some cases the body, face and head. Recognition and understanding of Sign Language is thus an entirely visuo-temporal process performed by human beings. In the United Kingdom alone, there are 145,000 deaf adults and children who use British Sign Language (BSL) [1]. Of those people, 15,000 report BSL as their main language of communication [2], which implies a difficulty of communication with those who cannot interpret the language. Unfortunately, when another person cannot interpret sign language (of who are the vast majority), a serious language barrier is present due to disability.

In addition to the individuals who act as interpreters for those who can only converse in Sign Language, or who only feel comfortable doing so, this work aims to improve autonomous classification techniques towards dictation of Sign Language in real-time. The philosophy behind this work is based on a simple argument: If a building were to have a ramp in addition to stairs for easier access of the disabled, then why should a computer system not be present in order to aid with those hard of hearing or deaf? In this work, we initially benchmark two popular methods of sign language recognition with an RGB camera and a Leap Motion 3D hand tracking camera after gathering a large dataset of gestures. Following these initial experiments, we then present a multimodality approach which fuses the two forms of data in order to achieve better results for two main reasons: first, mistakes and anomalous data received by either sensor has the chance to be mitigated by the other, and second, a deep neural network can learn to extract useful complimentary data from each sensor as well as the standard approach of extracting information towards the class itself. The driving force behind improving the ability of these two sensors is mainly cost, in that the solution presented is of extremely minimal cost and, with further improvement beyond the 18 gestures explored in this study, could easily be implemented within public places such as restaurants, schools, libraries, etc. in order to improve the lives of disabled individuals and enable communication with those they otherwise could not communicate with.

In this work, the approaches of single modality learning and classification are compared to multimodality late fusion. The main scientific contributions presented by this work are as follows.

1. Collection of a large BSL dataset from five subjects and a medium-sized ASL dataset from two subjects (The dataset is publicly available at https://www.kaggle.com/birdy654/sign-language-recognition-leap-motion).
2. Tuning of classification models for the RGB camera (processing layer prior to output), Leap Motion Classification (evolutionary topology search) and multimodality late fusion of the two via concatenation to a neural layer. Findings show that multimodality is the strongest approach for BSL classification compared to the two single-modality inputs as well as state of the art statistical learning techniques.
3. Transfer learning from BSL to improve ASL classification. Findings show that weight transfer to the multimodality model is the strongest approach for ASL classification.

The remainder of this work is as follows. Section 2 explores the current state-of-the-art for Sign Language Classification. Section 3 details the method followed for these experiments, which includes data collection, data preprocessing and the machine learning pipeline followed. The results for all of the experiments are presented in Section 4, including indirect comparison to other state-of-the-art works in the field, before conclusions are drawn and future work is suggested in Section 5.

2. Related Work

Sign Language Recognition (SLR) is a collaboration of multiple fields of research which can involve pattern matching, computer vision, natural language processing and linguistics [3–5]. The core of SLR is often times focused around a feature engineering and learning model-based approach to recognising hand-shapes [6]. Classically, SLR was usually performed by temporal models trained on sequences of video. Many works from the late 1990s through to the mid-2000s found best results when applying varying forms of Hidden Markov Models (HMMs) to videos [7–10]; HMMs are predictive models of transition (prior distribution) and emission probabilities (conditional distribution) of hidden states. To give a specific example, researchers found in [7] that hand-tracking via a camera and classification of hand gestures while wearing solidly coloured gloves (similar to chroma key) was superior to hand-tracking without a glove. In this work, a vector of eight features was extracted from the hands including 2-dimensional X,Y positions, the angle of the axis of with the least inertia and the eccentricity of a bounding ellipse around the hand. That is, four features for each hand. These vectors then provided features as input to the HMM. More recently though, given affordable sensors that provide more useful information than a video clip, studies have focused upon introducing this information towards stronger and more robust real-time classification of non-verbal languages. Sign language recognition with depth-sensing cameras such as Kinect and Leap Motion is an exciting area within the field due to the possibility of accessing accurate 3D information from the hand through stereoscopy similar to human depth perception via images from two eyeballs. Kinect allows researchers to access RGBD channels via a single colour camera and a single infrared depth-sensing camera. A Microsoft Kinect camera was used to gather data in [11], and features were extracted using a Support Vector Machine from depth and motion profiles. Researchers in [12] found that generating synchronised colour-coded joint distance topographic descriptor and joint angle topographical descriptor and used as input to a two-steam CNN produced effective results; the CNNs in this study were concatenated by late fusion similar to the multimodality method in this study and results were ~92% for a 20-class dataset. In terms of RGB classification specifically, many state-of-the-art works have argued in favour of the VGG16 architecture [13] for hand gesture recognition towards sign language classification [14]. These works include British [15], American [16], Brazilian [17] and Bengali [18] Sign Languages, among others. Given the computational complexity of multimodality when visual methods are concerned in part, multimodality is a growing approach to hand gesture recognition. Researchers have shown that the approach of fusing the LMC and flexible sensors attached to the hand via Kalman filtering [19] is promising. Likewise in this regard, recent work has also shown that RGBD (Realsense) along with a physical sensor-endowed glove can also improve hand-tracking algorithms [20]. Given the nature of SLR, physically-worn devices are an unrealistic expectation for users to accept when real-world situations are considered, e.g., should someone wish to sign in a hotel lobby for staff who do not know sign language. For this reason, we follow the approach of two non-physical sensors that are placed in front of the subject as a "terminal". That is, facing towards a camera and Leap Motion sensor are similar to natural social interaction and do not require the adoption of a physical device on the body.

Transfer Learning is a relatively new idea applied to the field of Sign Language recognition. In [21], researchers found it promising that knowledge could be transferred between a large text corpora and BSL via both LSTM and MLP methods, given that sign language data is often scarcely available. In this work, rather than transferring between syntax-annotated text corpora, we aim to follow the multisensor experiments with transfer learning between two different sign languages, i.e., transferring between the same task but in two entirely different languages (British Sign Language and American Sign Language).

The Leap Motion Controller, a sketch of which can be observed in Figure 1, is a device that combines stereoscopy and depth-sensing in order to accurately locate the individual bones and joints of the human hand. An example of the view of the two cameras translated to a 3D representation of the hand can be seen in Figure 2. The device measures $3.5 \times 1.2 \times 0.5$ inches and is thus a more portable option compared to the Microsoft Kinect. Features recorded from the 26 letters of the alphabet in American Sign Language were observed to be classified at 79.83% accuracy by a Support Vector Machine algorithm [22]. Similarly to the aforementioned work, researchers found that a different dataset also consisting of 26 ASL letters were classifiable at 93.81% accuracy with a Deep Neural Network [23]. Another example achieved 96.15% with a deep learning approach on a limited set of 520 samples (20 per letter) [24]. Data fusion via Coupled Hidden Markov Models was performed in [25] between Leap Motion and Kinect, which achieved 90.8% accuracy on a set of 25 Indian Sign Language gestures.

Additionally, studies often fail to apply trained models to unseen data, and therefore towards real-time classification (the ultimate goal of SL recognition). With this in mind, Wang et al. proposed that sign language recognition systems are often affected by noise, which may negatively impact real-time recognition abilities [26]. In this work, we benchmark two single-modality approaches as well as a multimodality late fusion approach of the two both during training, and on unseen data towards benchmarking a more realistic real-time ability. Additionally, we also show that it is possible to perform transfer learning between two ethnologues with the proposed approaches for British and American Sign Languages.

In much of the state-of-the-art work in Sign Language recognition, a single modality approach is followed, with multimodality experiments being some of the latest studies in the field.

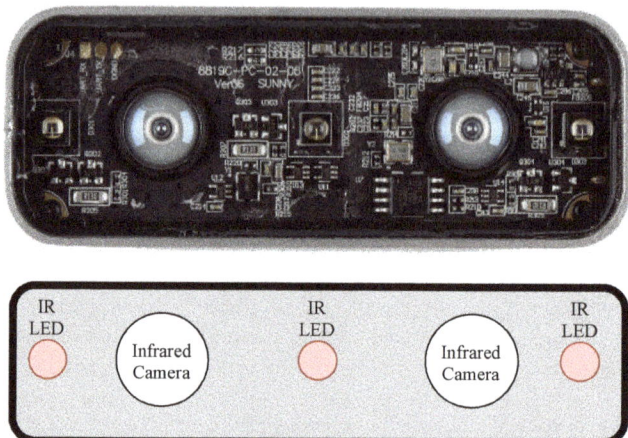

Figure 1. Photograph and labelled sketch of the stereoscopic infrared camera array within a Leap Motion Controller, illuminated by three infrared light-emitting diodes (IR LEDs).

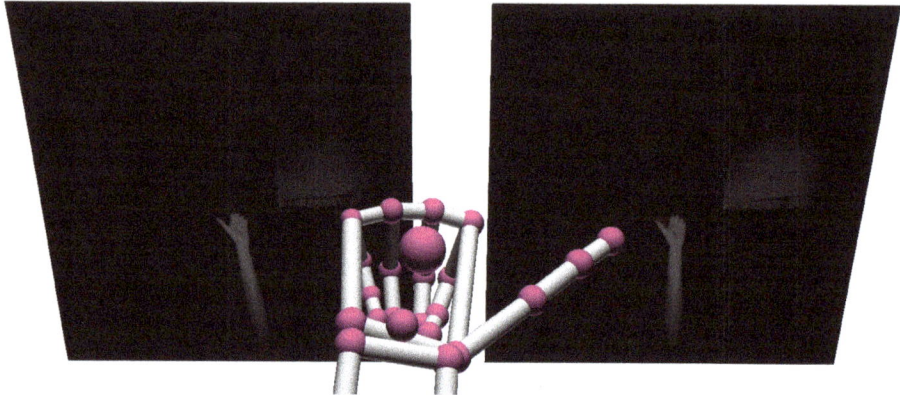

Figure 2. Screenshot of the view from Leap's two infrared cameras and the detected hand reproduced in 3D. Note that this study uses a front-facing view rather than up-facing as shown in the screenshot.

The inspiration for the network topology and method of fusion in this work comes from the work in [27] (albeit applied to scene recognition in this instance), similarly, this work fuses two differing synchronous data types via late-fusion by benchmarking network topologies at each step. In the aforementioned work however, weights of the networks were frozen for late fusion layer training (derived from benchmarking the two separate models). In this experiment, all weights are able to train from the start of the late fusion network from scratch, and thus the networks can extract complimentary features from each form of data for classification in addition to the usual method of extracting features for direct classification and prediction.

Table 1 shows a comparison of state-of-the-art approaches to Sign Language recognition. The training accuracy found in this work is given as comparison as other works report such metric, but it is worth noting that this work showed that classification of unseen data is often lower than the training process. For example, the multimodality approach score of 94.44% was reduced to 76.5% when being applied to completely unseen data.

Table 1. Other state-of-the-art works in autonomous Sign Language Recognition, indirectly compared due to operation on different datasets and with different sensors. Note: It was observed in this study that classification of unseen data is often lower than results found during training, but many works do not benchmark this activity.

Study	Sensor	Input	Approach	Classes	Score (%)
Huang et al. [28]	Kinect	Skeleton	DNN	26	97.8
Filho et al. [29]	Kinect	Depth	KNN	200	96.31
Morales et al. [30]	Kinect	Depth	HMM	20	96.2
Hisham et al. [31]	LMC	Point Cloud	DTW	28	95
Kumar et al. [32]	LMC	Point Cloud	HMM, BLSTM	50	94.55
Quesada et al. [33]	RealSense	Skeleton	SVM	26	92.31
Kumar et al. [12]	MoCap	Skeleton	2-CNN	20	92.14
Yang [34]	Kinect	Depth	HCRF	24	90.4
Cao Dong et al. [35]	Kinect	Depth	RF	24	90
Elons et al. [36]	LMC	Point Cloud	MLP	50	88
Kumar et al. [37]	Kinect	Skeleton	HMM	30	83.77
Chansri et al. [38]	Kinect	RGB, Depth	HOG, ANN	42	80.05
Chuan et al. [22]	LMC	Point Cloud	SVM	26	79.83
Quesada et al. [33]	LMC	Skeleton	SVM	26	74.59
Chuan et al. [22]	LMC	Point Cloud	KNN	26	72.78
This study	LMC, RGB	Hand feats, RGB	CNN-MLP-LF	18	94.44

3. Proposed Approach: Multimodality Late Fusion of Deep Networks

Within this section, the proposed approach for the late fusion experiments is described. The experiments that this section mainly refers to can be observed in Figure 3, which outlines the image classification, Leap Motion classification and multimodality late fusion networks. The camera is used to record an image, and features are extracted via the VGG16 CNN and MLP. The Leap motion is used to record a numerical vector representing the 3D hand features previously described, which serves as input to an evolutionarily optimised deep MLP. Given that data is recorded synchronously, that is, the image from the camera and the numerical vector from the Leap Motion are captured at the same moment in time, the data objects are used as the two inputs to the multimodality network as they both describe the same frame captured.

3.1. Dataset Collection and Preprocessing

Five subjects contributed to a dataset of British Sign Language, where each of the gestures was recorded for thirty seconds each, 15 s per dominant hand. Rather than specific execution times, subjects are requested to repeat the gesture at a comfortable speed for the duration of the recording; a recording of 15 s in length prevents fatigue from occurring and thus affecting the quality of the data. An example of recorded image data can be observed in Figure 4. Eighteen differing gestures were recorded at a frequency of 0.2 s each using a laptop, an image was captured using the laptop's webcam and Leap Motion data are recorded from the device situated above the camera facing the subject. This allowed for "face-to-face" communication, as the subject was asked to communicate as if across from another human being. The "task-giver" was situated behind the laptop and stopped data recording if the subject made an error while performing the gesture. Each 0.2 s recording provides a data object that is inserted into the dataset as a numerical vector to be classified.

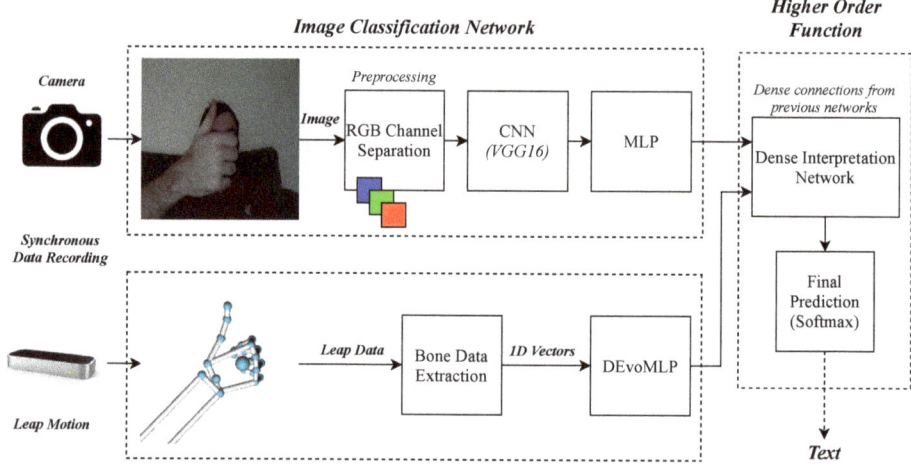

Figure 3. An overall diagram of the three benchmarking experiments. Above shows the process of image classification and below shows Leap Motion data classification for the same problem of sign language recognition. The higher order function network shows the late fusion of the two to form a multimodality solution.

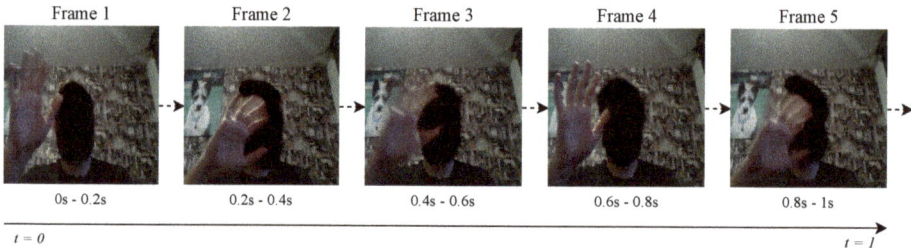

Figure 4. An example of one second of RGB image data collected at a frequency of 0.2 s per frame (5 Hz). Alongside each image that is taken is a numerical vector collected from the Leap Motion Controller.

From the Leap Motion sensor, data were recorded for each of the thumb, index, middle, ring and pinky fingers within the frame (labelled "left" or "right"). The names of the fingers and bones can be observed in the labelled diagram in Figure 5. For each hand, the start and end positions; 3D angles between start and end positions; and velocities of the arm, palm and finger bones (metacarpal, proximal, intermediate and distal bones) were recorded in order to numerically represent the gesture being performed. The pitch, yaw and roll of the hands were also recorded. If one of the two hands were not detected, then its values were recorded as "0" (e.g., a left handed action will also feature a vector of zeroes for the right hand). If the sensor did not detect either hand, data collection was automatically paused until the hands were detected in order to prevent empty frames. Thus, every 0.2 s, a numerical vector is output to describe the action of either one or two hands. The θ angle is computed using two 3D vectors by taking the inverse cosine of the dot product of the two vectors divided by the magnitudes of each vector, as shown below.

$$\theta = arccos\left(\frac{ab}{|a||b|}\right), \tag{1}$$

where $|a|$ and $|b|$ are

$$|a| = \sqrt{a_x^2 + a_y^2 + a_z^2}$$
$$|b| = \sqrt{b_x^2 + b_y^2 + b_z^2},$$
(2)

with regards to the x, y and z co-ordinates of each point in space. The start and end points of each bone in the hand from the LMC are treated as the two points.

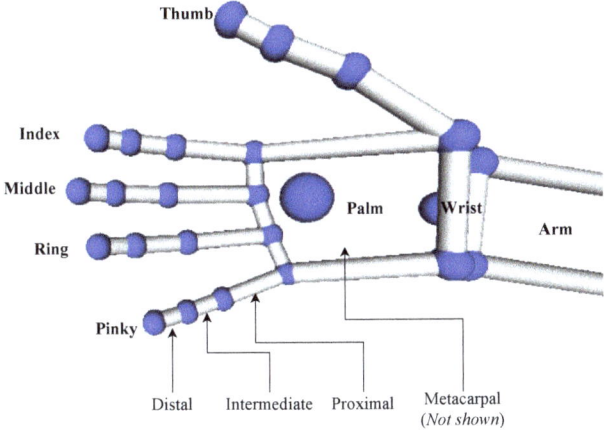

Figure 5. Labelled diagram of the bone data detected by the Leap Motion sensor. Metacarpal bones are not rendered by the LMC Visualiser.

The following is a summary of each feature collected from the hierarchy of arm to finger joint.

- For each arm:
    - Start position of the arm (X, Y and Z)
    - End position of the arm (X, Y and Z)
    - 3D angle between start and end positions of the arm
    - Velocity of the arm (X, Y and Z)
- For each elbow:
    - Position of the elbow (X, Y and Z)
- For each wrist:
    - Position of the wrist (X, Y and Z)
- For each palm:
    - Pitch
    - Yaw
    - Roll
    - 3D angle of the palm
    - Position of the palm (X, Y and Z)
    - Velocity of the palm (X, Y and Z)
    - Normal of the palm (X, Y and Z)

- For each finger:
  - Direction of the finger (X, Y and Z)
  - Position of the finger (X, Y and Z)
  - Velocity of the finger (X, Y and Z)
- For each finger joint:
  - Start position of the joint (X, Y and Z)
  - End position of the joint (X, Y and Z)
  - 3D angle of the joint
  - Direction of the finger (X, Y and Z)
  - Position of the joint (X, Y and Z)
  - Velocity of the joint (X, Y and Z)

Each feature was pre-processed via a minmax scaler between 0 (*min*) and 1 (*max*): $Feat = Feat_{std}(max - min) + min$, where $Feat_{std} = (\frac{Feat - Feat_{min}}{Feat_{max} - Feat_{min}})$. Thus, each feature value is reduced to a value between 0 and 1. This was performed as it was observed that non-processed feature values caused issues for the model and often resulted in classification accuracy scores of only approximately 4%, showing a failure to generalise. The 18 British Sign Language (Visual examples of the BSL gestures can be viewed at https://www.british-sign.co.uk/british-sign-language/dictionary/) gestures recorded were selected due to them being common useful words or phrases in language. A mixture of one and two-handed gestures were chosen. Each gesture was recorded twice where subjects switched dominant hands.

The useful gestures for general conversation were

1. Hello/Goodbye
2. You/Yourself
3. Me/Myself
4. Name
5. Sorry
6. Good
7. Bad
8. Excuse Me
9. Thanks/Thank you
10. Time

The gestures for useful entities were

1. Airport
2. Bus
3. Car
4. Aeroplane
5. Taxi
6. Restaurant
7. Drink
8. Food

Following this, a smaller set of the same 18 gestures, but in American Sign Language (Visual examples of the ASL gestures can be viewed at https://www.handspeak.com/), are collected from two subjects for thirty seconds each (15 per hand) towards the transfer learning experiment. "Airport" and "Aeroplane/Airplane" in ASL are similar, and so "Airport" and "Jet Plane" are recorded instead.

Figures 6 and 7 show a comparison of how one signs "hello" in British and American sign languages; though the gestures differ, the hand is waved and as such it is likely that useful knowledge can be transferred between the two languages.

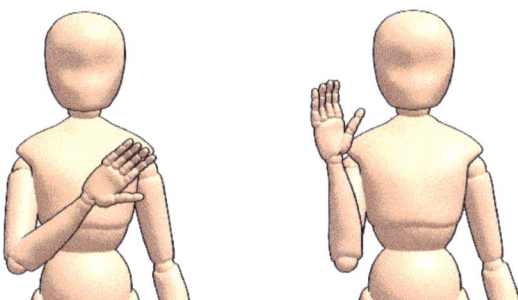

Figure 6. The sign for "Hello" in British Sign Language.

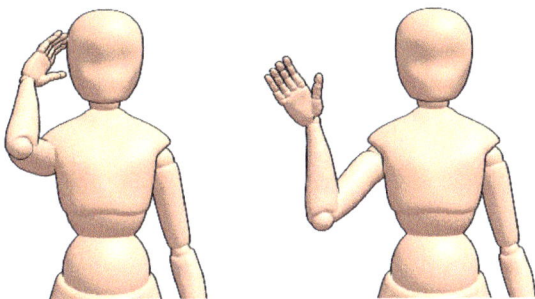

Figure 7. The sign for "Hello" in American Sign Language.

3.2. Deep Learning Approaches

For the image classification network, VGG16 [39] convolutional layers are used as a starting point for feature extraction from image data, as can be seen in Figure 8, where the three 4096 neuron hidden layers are removed. The convolutional layers are followed by $2, 4, 8, \ldots, 4096$ ReLu neuron layers in each of the ten benchmarking experiments to ascertain a best-performing interpretation layer. For the Leap Motion data classification problem, an evolutionary search is performed [40] to also ascertain a best-performing neural network topology; the search is set to a population of 20 for 15 generations, as during manual exploration, stabilisation of a final best result tends to occur at approximately generation 11. The evolutionary search is run three times in order to mitigate the risk of a local maxima being carried forward to the latter experiments.

With the best CNN and Leap Motion ANN networks derived, a third set of experiments is then run. The best topologies (with softmax layers removed) are fused into a single layer of ReLu neurons in the range $2, 4, 8, \ldots, 4096$.

All experiments are benchmarked with randomised 10-fold cross-validation, and training time is uncapped to a number of epochs and rather executed until no improvement of accuracy occurs after 25 epochs. Thus, the results presented are the maximum results attainable by the network within this boundary of early stopping.

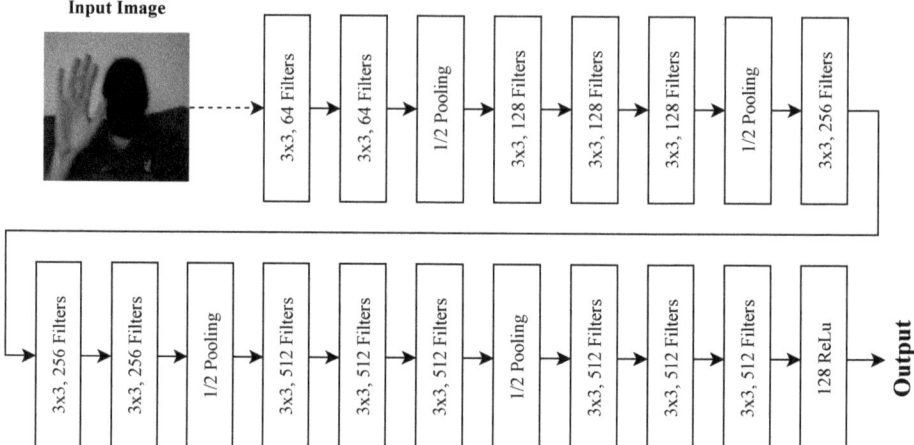

Figure 8. Feature extraction from the RGB branch of the network, the input image is passed through a fine-tuned VGG16 CNN [39] and then a layer of 128 ReLu neurons provide output. The network is trained via softmax output, but this softmax layer is later removed and the 128 outputs are used in late fusion with the Leap Motion network.

Following the experiments on BSL, initial preliminary experiments for Transfer Learning between languages are performed. Figure 9 shows the outline for the transfer experiments, in which the learnt weights from the three BSL models are transferred to their ASL counterparts as initial starting weight distributions and ultimately compared to the usual method of beginning with a random distribution. This experiment is performed in order to benchmark whether there is useful knowledge to be transferred between each of the model pairs.

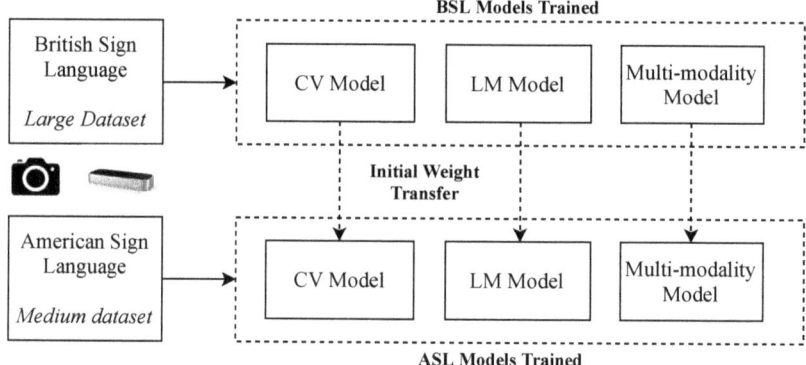

Figure 9. Transfer Learning Experiments which train on BSL and produce initial starting weight distributions for the ASL models.

3.3. Experimental Software and Hardware

The deep learning experiments in this study were performed on an Nvidia GTX 980Ti which has 2816 CUDA cores (1190 MHz) and 6 GB of GDDR5 memory. Given the memory constraints, images are resized to 128 × 128 although they were initially captured in larger resolutions. All deep learning experiments were written in Python for the Keras [41] library and TensorFlow [42] backend.

The statistical models trained in this study were performed with a Coffee Lake Intel Core i7 at a clock speed of 3.7 GHz. All statistical learning experiments were written in Python for the SciKit-Learn library [43].

4. Experimental Results

4.1. Fine Tuning of VGG16 Weights and Interpretation Topology

Figure 10 shows the results for tuning of the VGG network for image classification. Each result is given as the classification ability when a layer of neurons are introduced beyond the CNN operations and prior to output. The best result was a layer of 128 neurons prior to output, which resulted in a classification accuracy of 88.14%. Most of the results were relatively strong except for 2–8 neurons and, interestingly, layers of 256 and 2048 neurons. Thus, the CNN followed by 128 neurons forms the first branch of the multimodality system for image processing alongside the best Leap Motion network (in the next section). The SoftMax output layer is removed for purposes of concatenation, and the 128 neuron layer feeds into the interpretation layer prior to output.

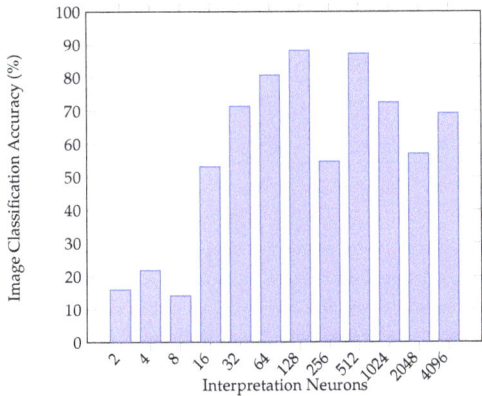

Figure 10. Mean image 10-fold classification accuracy corresponding to interpretation neuron numbers.

4.2. Evolutionary Search of Leap Motion Dnn Topology

The evolutionary search algorithm is applied three times for a population of 20 through 15 generations, which can be observed in Figure 11. The maximum number of neurons was 1024, and the maximum number of layers was 5. After an initial random initialisation of solutions, the algorithm performs roulette selection for each solution and generates an offspring (where number of layers and number of neurons per layer are bred). At the start of each new generation, the worst performing solutions outside of the population size 20 range are deleted and the process runs again. The final best result is reported at the end of the simulation. Table 2 shows the best results for three runs of the Leap Motion classification networks. Of the three, the best model was a deep neural network of 171, 292, 387 neurons which resulted in a classification accuracy of 72.73%. Interestingly, the most complex model found was actually the worst performing of the best three results selected. This forms the second branch of the multimodality network for Leap Motion classification in order to compliment the image processing network. Similarly to the image processing and network, the SoftMax output layer is removed and the final layer of 387 neurons for Leap Motion data classification is connected to the dense interpretation network layer along with the 128 hidden neurons of the image network. In terms of mean and standard deviations of the runs on a generational basis, Run 1 was 65.48% (5.37), Run 2 was 66.98% (4.87) and Run 3 was 68.02% (5.05). With regards to the mean and standard deviation of the three final results, they were 70.5% (1.14).

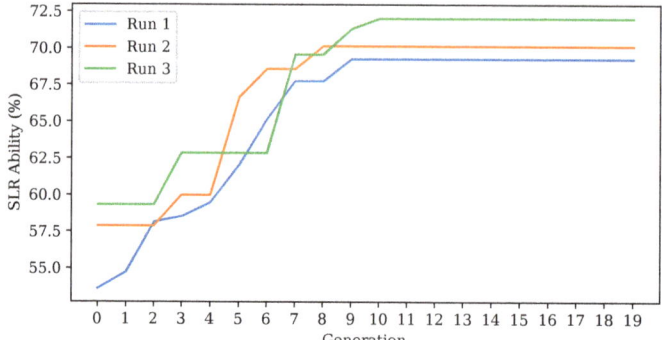

Figure 11. Three executions of optimisation of neural network topologies via an evolutionary algorithm.

Table 2. Final results of the three evolutionary searches sorted by 10-fold validation accuracy along with the total number of connections within the network.

Hidden Neurons	Connections	Accuracy
171, 292, and 387	243,090	72.73%
57, 329, and 313	151,760	70.17%
309, 423, and 277	385,116	69.29%

4.3. Fine-Tuning the Final Model

Figure 12 shows the results of fine-tuning the best number of interpretation neurons within the late fusion layer; the best set of hyperparameters found to fuse the two prior networks was a layer of 16 neurons, which achieved an overall mean classification ability of 94.44%. This best-performing layer of 16 neurons receives input from the Image and Leap Motion classification networks and is connected to a final SoftMax output. Given the nature of backpropagation, the learning process enables the two input networks to perform as they were prior (that is, to extract features and classify data) but a new task is also then possible; to extract features and useful information from either data format which may compliment the other, for example, for correction of common errors, or for contributing to confidence behind a decision.

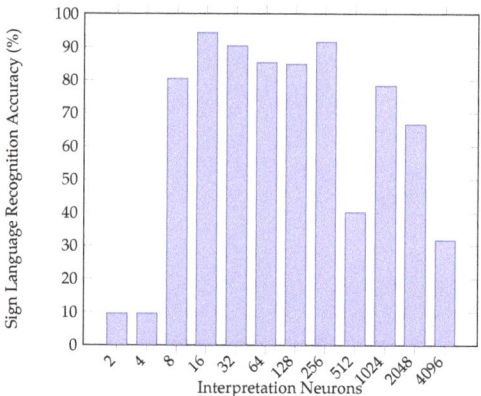

Figure 12. Multimodality 10-fold classification accuracy corresponding to interpretation neuron numbers towards benchmarking the late-fusion network.

4.4. Comparison and Analysis of Models

Table 3 shows a comparison of the final three tuned model performances for recognition of British Sign Language through the classification of photographic images (RGB) and bone data (Leap Motion) compared to the multimodality approach that fuses the two networks together. The maximum classification accuracy of the CV model achieved 88.14%, the Leap Motion model achieved 72.73% but the fusion of the two allowed for a large increase towards 94.44% accuracy. A further comparison to other statistical approaches can be observed in Table 4, within which the different algorithms applied to the same dataset are shown and directly compared; although the DNN approach is relatively weak compared to all statistical models except for Gaussian Naive Bayes, it contributes to the multimodality approach by extracting features complimentary to the CNN prior to late fusion as well as the task of classification—this, in turn, leads to the multimodality approach attaining the best overall result. The best statistical model, the Random Forest, was outperformed by the CNN by 1.07% and the multimodality approach by 7.37%. Performance aside, it must be noted that the statistical approaches are far less computationally complex than deep learning approaches; should the host machine for the task not have access to a GPU with CUDA abilities, a single-modality statistical approach is likely the most realistic candidate. Should the host machine, on the other hand, have access to a physical or cloud-based GPU or TPU, then it would be possible to enable the most superior model, which was the deep learning multimodality approach.

Table 3. Sign Language Recognition scores of the three models trained on the dataset.

Model	Sign Language Recognition Ability
RGB	88.14%
Leap Motion	72.73%
Multi-modality	94.44%

Table 4. Comparison of other statistical models and the approaches presented in this work.; Deep Neural Network (DNN), Convolutional Neural Network (CNN), Random Forest (RF), Sequential Minimal Optimisation Support Vector Machine (SMO SVM), Quadratic Discriminant Analysis (QDA), Linear Discriminant Analysis (LDA), Logistic Regression (LR), and Naïve Bayes (NB).

Model	Input Sensor(s)	Sign Language Recognition Ability
MM(DNN, CNN)	LMC, Camera	94.44%
CNN	Camera	88.14%
RF	LMC	87.07%
SMO SVM	LMC	86.78%
QDA	LMC	85.46%
LDA	LMC	81.31%
LR	LMC	80.97%
Bayesian Net	LMC	73.48%
DNN	LMC	72.73%
Gaussian NB	LMC	34.91%

Table 5 shows the ten highest scoring features gathered from the Leap Motion Controller by measure of their information gain or relative entropy. Right handed features are seemingly the most useful, which is possibly due to the most common dominant hand being the right. Though all features shown have relatively high values, it can be noted that the roll of the right hand is the most useful when it comes to classification of the dataset.

Table 6 shows the final comparison of all three models when tasked with predicting the class labels of unseen data objects (100 per class (18 classes)). The error matrix for the best model, which was the multimodality approach at 76.5% accuracy can be observed in Figure 13. Interestingly, most classes were classified with high confidence with the exception of three main outliers: "thanks" was misclassified as "bus" in almost all cases, "restaurant" was misclassified as a multitude of other classes and "food" was often mistaken for "drink", although this did not occur vice versa. Outside of the anomalous classes which must be improved in the future with more training examples, the multimodality model was able to confidently classify the majority of all other phrases. Though it would require further experiments to pinpoint, it is likely that the poor performance of the leap motion suggests that such data is difficult to generalise outside of the learning process. Though, on the other hand, useful knowledge is still retained given the high accuracy of the multimodality model which considers it as input alongside a synchronised image.

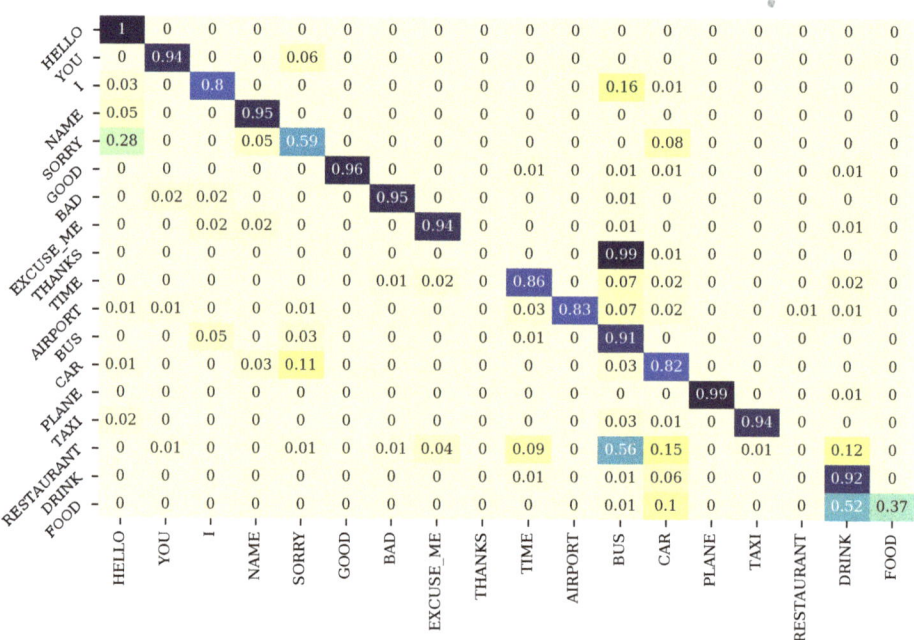

Figure 13. Confusion matrix for the best model (multimodality, 76.5%) on the set of unseen data (not present during training).

Table 5. The top ten features by relative entropy gathered from the Leap Motion Controller.

Leap Motion Feature	Information Gain (Relative Entropy)
right_hand_roll	0.8809
right_index_metacarpal_end_x	0.8034
right_thumb_metacarpal_end_x	0.8034
right_pinky_metacarpal_end_x	0.8034
left_palm_position_x	0.8033
right_index_proximal_start_x	0.8028
left_index_proximal_start_x	0.8024
right_middle_proximal_start_x	0.8024
left_middle_proximal_start_x	0.8023
right_ring_proximal_start_x	0.8021

Table 6. Results of the three trained models applied to unseen data.

Approach	Correct/Incorrect	Classification Accuracy
RGB	1250/1800	69.44%
Leap Motion	752/1800	41.78%
Multi-modality	1377/1800	76.5%

4.5. Leave-One-Subject-Out Validation

Table 7 shows the training metrics for each model with a leave-one-subject-out approach. That is, training on all subjects but one, and then validation upon the left out subject. All models performed relatively well, with the interesting exception of the RGB camera when classifying subject 2, which scored only 68.24%. On average, the best approach remained the multimodality model, which scored 92.12% accuracy (+6.69% over RGB, +3.55% over Leap Motion). This finding is similar to the outcomes of the other experiments, where the multimodality model always outperformed the singular sensor approaches.

Table 7. Results for the models when trained via leave-one-subject-out validation. Each subject column shows the classification accuracy of that subject when the model is trained on the other four.

Model	Subject Left Out Accuracy (%)					Mean	Std.
	1	2	3	4	5		
RGB	81.12	68.24	93.82	89.82	94.15	85.43	9.79
Leap Motion	89.21	88.85	86.97	89.27	88.54	88.57	0.84
Multi-modality	85.52	96.7	87.51	93.82	97.1	92.12	4.76

4.6. Transfer Learning from BSL to ASL

Table 8 shows the results for transfer learning from BSL to ASL. Interestingly, with the medium-sized ASL dataset and no transfer learning, the multimodality approach is worse than both the Computer Vision and Leap Motion models singularly. This, and considering that the best model overall for ASL classification was the multimodality model with weight transfer from the BSL model, suggests that data scarcity poses an issue for multimodality models for this problem.

Table 8. Results of pre-training and classification abilities of ASL models, with and without weight transfer from the BSL models.

Model	Non-Transfer from BSL		Transfer from BSL	
	Epoch 0	Final Ability	Epoch 0	Final Ability
RGB	2.98	80.68	13.28	81.82
Leap Motion	5.12	67.82	7.77	70.95
Multi-modality	5.12	65.4	21.31	82.55

The results show that transfer learning improves the abilities of the Leap Motion and multimodality classification approaches to sign language recognition. With this in mind, availability of trained weights may be useful to improve the classification of other datasets regardless of whether or not they are in the same sign language. Overall, the best model for ASL classification was the multimodality model when weights are transferred from the BSL model. This approach scored 82.55% classification ability on the ASL dataset. The results suggest that useful knowledge can be transferred between sign languages for image classification, Leap Motion classification and late-fusion of the two towards multimodality classification.

Though future work is needed for further explore the transfer learning hypotheses, the results in these initial experiments suggest the possibility of success when transferring knowledge between models and ultimately improving their recognition performances.

5. Conclusions and Future Work

This work has presented multiple experiments for the singular sensor and multimodality approaches to British and American Sign Language. The results from the experiments suggest that a multimodality approach outperforms the two singular sensors during both training and classification of unseen data. This work also presented a preliminary Transfer Learning experiment from the large BSL dataset to a medium-sized ASL dataset, in which the best model for classification of ASL was found to be the multimodality model when weights are transferred from the BSL model. All of the network topologies in this work that were trained, compared and ultimately fused together towards multimodality were benchmarked and studied for the first time. Accurate classification of Sign Language, especially unseen data, enables the ability to perform the task autonomously and thus provide a digital method to interpretation of non-spoken language within a situation where interpretation is required but unavailable. In order to realise this possibility, future work is needed. The hypotheses in these experiments were argued through a set of 18 common gestures in both British and American Sign Languages. In future, additional classes are required to allow for interpretation of conversations rather than the symbolic communication enabled by this study. In addition, as multimodality classification proved effective, further tuning of hyperparameters could enable better results, and other methods of data fusion could be explored in addition to the late fusion approach used in this work. Transfer learning could be explored with other forms of non-spoken language, for example, Indo-Pakistani SL, which has an ethnologue of 1.5 million people and Brazilian SL with an ethnologue of 200,000 people. The aim of this work was to explore the viability and ability of multimodality in Sign Language Recognition by comparing Leap Motion and RGB classification with their late-fusion counterpart. In addition, the 0.2s data collection frame poses a limitation to this study, and as such, further work could be performed to derive a best window length for data collection.

A cause for concern that was noted in this work was the reduction of ability when unseen data is considered, which is often the case in machine learning exercises. Such experiments and metrics (ability on unseen dataset and per-class abilities) are rarely performed and noted in the state-of-the-art works within sign language recognition. As the main goal of autonomous sign language recognition is to provide a users with a system which can aid those who otherwise may not have access to a method of translation and communication, it is important to consider how such a system would perform when using trained models to classify data that was not present in the training set. That is, real-time classification of data during usage of the system and subsequently the trained classification models. In this work, high training results were found for both modalities and multimodality, deriving abilities that are competitive when indirectly compared to the state of the art works in the field. When the best performing 94.44% classification ability model (multimodality) was applied to unseen data, it achieved 76.5% accuracy mainly due to confusion within the "thanks" and "restaurant" classes. Likewise, the RGB model reduced from 88.14% to 69.44% and the Leap Motion model reduced from 72.73% to 41.78% when comparing training accuracy and unseen data classification ability. Future work is needed to enable the models a better ability to generalise towards real-time classification abilities that closely resemble their abilities observed during training.

Ethics

The requirements of the ethics procedure of Aston University are based on UK laws and were incorporated into the definition of the guidelines. All participants were informed in detail on the project characteristics and written informed consent was obtained. Special attention was given to the trial in order to ensure the compliance with ethical requirements, confidentiality and protection of personal data. No trials were performed without previous approval by the ethical committee and data protection based on the Ethics committee of the Aston University. All experiments were done in accordance with the highest ethical standards from the UK.

We ensured that the information given to the participants was easy to understand, and all written information was in accordance to the "Easy to Read" guidelines. All participants agreed with the "Informed Consent Form".

Author Contributions: Conceptualisation, J.J.B. and D.R.F.; Investigation, J.J.B.; Methodology, J.J.B. and D.R.F.; Software, J.J.B.; Writing—original draft, J.J.B.; Writing—review and editing, J.J.B. and D.R.F. Supervision; A.E. and D.R.F.; J.J.B.'s PhD Supervisors: D.R.F. and A.E. All authors have read and agreed to the published version of the manuscript.

Funding: This research received no external funding.

Conflicts of Interest: The authors declare no conflict of interest.

References

1. Ipsos MORI. *GP Patient Survey—National Summary Report*; NHS England: London, UK, 2016.
2. ONS. *2011 Census: Key statistics for England and Wales, March 2011*; ONS: Pittsburgh, PA, USA, 2012.
3. Al-Ahdal, M.E.; Nooritawati, M.T. Review in sign language recognition systems. In Proceedings of the 2012 IEEE Symposium on Computers & Informatics (ISCI), Penang, Malaysia, 18–20 March 2012; pp. 52–57.
4. Cheok, M.J.; Omar, Z.; Jaward, M.H. A review of hand gesture and sign language recognition techniques. *Int. J. Mach. Learn. Cybern.* **2019**, *10*, 131–153. [CrossRef]
5. Wadhawan, A.; Kumar, P. Sign Language Recognition Systems: A Decade Systematic Literature Review. *Arch. Comput. Methods Eng.* **2019**, 1–29. [CrossRef]
6. Kapuscinski, T.; Organisciak, P. Handshape Recognition Using Skeletal Data. *Sensors* **2018**, *18*, 2577. [CrossRef] [PubMed]
7. Starner, T.; Pentland, A. Real-time american sign language recognition from video using hidden markov models. In *Motion-Based Recognition*; Springer: Berlin/Heidelberg, Germany, 1997; pp. 227–243.
8. Assan, M.; Grobel, K. Video-based sign language recognition using hidden markov models. In *International Gesture Workshop*; Springer: Berlin/Heidelberg, Germany, 1997; pp. 97–109.
9. Vogler, C.; Metaxas, D. Parallel hidden markov models for american sign language recognition. In Proceedings of the Seventh IEEE International Conference on Computer Vision, Kerkyra, Greece, 20–27 September 1999; Volume 1, pp. 116–122.
10. Haberdar, H.; Albayrak, S. Real time isolated turkish sign language recognition from video using hidden markov models with global features. In *International Symposium on Computer and Information Sciences*; Springer: Berlin/Heidelberg, Germany, 2005; pp. 677–687.
11. Agarwal, A.; Thakur, M.K. Sign language recognition using Microsoft Kinect. In Proceedings of the IEEE 2013 Sixth International Conference on Contemporary Computing (IC3), Noida, India, 8–10 August 2013; pp. 181–185.
12. Kumar, E.K.; Kishore, P.; Kumar, M.T.K.; Kumar, D.A. 3D sign language recognition with joint distance and angular coded color topographical descriptor on a 2-stream CNN. *Neurocomputing* **2020**, *372*, 40–54. [CrossRef]
13. Simonyan, K.; Zisserman, A. Very deep convolutional networks for large-scale image recognition. *arXiv* **2014**, arXiv:1409.1556.
14. Kulhandjian, H.; Sharma, P.; Kulhandjian, M.; D'Amours, C. Sign language gesture recognition using doppler radar and deep learning. In Proceedings of the 2019 IEEE Globecom Workshops (GC Wkshps), Waikoloa, HI, USA, 9–13 December 2019; pp. 1–6.
15. Liang, X.; Woll, B.; Epaminondas, K.; Angelopoulou, A.; Al-Batat, R. Machine Learning for Enhancing Dementia Screening in Ageing Deaf Signers of British Sign Language. In Proceedings of the LREC2020 9th Workshop on the Representation and Processing of Sign Languages: Sign Language Resources in the Service of the Language Community, Technological Challenges and Application Perspectives, Marseille, France, 11–16 May 2020; pp. 135–138.

16. Masood, S.; Thuwal, H.C.; Srivastava, A. American sign language character recognition using convolution neural network. In *Smart Computing and Informatics*; Springer: Berlin/Heidelberg, Germany, 2018; pp. 403–412.
17. Lima, D.F.; Neto, A.S.S.; Santos, E.N.; Araujo, T.M.U.; Rêgo, T.G.D. Using convolutional neural networks for fingerspelling sign recognition in brazilian sign language. In Proceedings of the 25th Brazillian Symposium on Multimedia and the Web, Rio de Janeiro, Brazil, 29 October–1 November 2019; pp. 109–115.
18. Hossen, M.; Govindaiah, A.; Sultana, S.; Bhuiyan, A. Bengali sign language recognition using deep convolutional neural network. In Proceedings of the 2018 Joint 7th International Conference on Informatics, Electronics & Vision (ICIEV) and 2018 IEEE 2nd International Conference on Imaging, Vision & Pattern Recognition (icIVPR), Kitakyushu, Japan, 25–29 June 2018; pp. 369–373.
19. Ponraj, G.; Ren, H. Sensor fusion of leap motion controller and flex sensors using Kalman filter for human finger tracking. *IEEE Sens. J.* **2018**, *18*, 2042–2049. [CrossRef]
20. Jiang, L.; Xia, H.; Guo, C. A Model-Based System for Real-Time Articulated Hand Tracking Using a Simple Data Glove and a Depth Camera. *Sensors* **2019**, *19*, 4680. [CrossRef] [PubMed]
21. Mocialov, B.; Turner, G.; Hastie, H. Transfer learning for british sign language modelling. *arXiv* **2020**, arXiv:2006.02144.
22. Chuan, C.H.; Regina, E.; Guardino, C. American sign language recognition using leap motion sensor. In Proceedings of the 2014 IEEE 13th International Conference on Machine Learning and Applications, Detroit, MI, USA, 3–6 December 2014; pp. 541–544.
23. Chong, T.W.; Lee, B.G. American sign language recognition using leap motion controller with machine learning approach. *Sensors* **2018**, *18*, 3554. [CrossRef] [PubMed]
24. Naglot, D.; Kulkarni, M. Real time sign language recognition using the leap motion controller. In Proceedings of the 2016 IEEE International Conference on Inventive Computation Technologies (ICICT), Coimbatore, India, 26–27 August 2016; Volume 3, pp. 1–5.
25. Kumar, P.; Gauba, H.; Roy, P.P.; Dogra, D.P. Coupled HMM-based multi-sensor data fusion for sign language recognition. *Pattern Recognit. Lett.* **2017**, *86*, 1–8. [CrossRef]
26. Wang, X.; Jiang, F.; Yao, H. DTW/ISODATA algorithm and Multilayer architecture in Sign Language Recognition with large vocabulary. In Proceedings of the 2008 IEEE International Conference on Intelligent Information Hiding and Multimedia Signal Processing, Harbin, China, 15–17 August 2008; pp. 1399–1402.
27. Bird, J.J.; Faria, D.R.; Premebida, C.; Ekárt, A.; Vogiatzis, G. Look and Listen: A Multi-modality Late Fusion Approach to Scene Classification for Autonomous Machines. *arXiv* **2020**, arXiv:2007.10175.
28. Huang, J.; Zhou, W.; Li, H.; Li, W. Sign language recognition using real-sense. In Proceedings of the 2015 IEEE China Summit and International Conference on Signal and Information Processing (ChinaSIP), Chengdu, China, 12–15 July 2015; pp. 166–170.
29. Costa Filho, C.F.F.; Souza, R.S.D.; Santos, J.R.D.; Santos, B.L.D.; Costa, M.G.F. A fully automatic method for recognizing hand configurations of Brazilian sign language. *Res. Biomed. Eng.* **2017**, *33*, 78–89. [CrossRef]
30. Caballero Morales, S.O.; Trujillo Romero, F. 3D modeling of the mexican sign language for a speech-to-sign language system. *Comput. Sist.* **2013**, *17*, 593–608.
31. Hisham, B.; Hamouda, A. Arabic Static and Dynamic Gestures Recognition Using Leap Motion. *J. Comput. Sci.* **2017**, *13*, 337–354. [CrossRef]
32. Kumar, P.; Gauba, H.; Roy, P.P.; Dogra, D.P. A multimodal framework for sensor based sign language recognition. *Neurocomputing* **2017**, *259*, 21–38. [CrossRef]
33. Quesada, L.; López, G.; Guerrero, L. Automatic recognition of the American sign language fingerspelling alphabet to assist people living with speech or hearing impairments. *J. Ambient. Intell. Humaniz. Comput.* **2017**, *8*, 625–635. [CrossRef]
34. Yang, H.D. Sign language recognition with the kinect sensor based on conditional random fields. *Sensors* **2015**, *15*, 135–147. [CrossRef] [PubMed]
35. Dong, C.; Leu, M.C.; Yin, Z. American sign language alphabet recognition using microsoft kinect. In Proceedings of the IEEE Conference on Computer Vision and Pattern Recognition Workshops, Boston, MA, USA, 7–12 June 2015; pp. 44–52.
36. Elons, A.; Ahmed, M.; Shedid, H.; Tolba, M. Arabic sign language recognition using leap motion sensor. In Proceedings of the 2014 IEEE 9th International Conference on Computer Engineering & Systems (ICCES), Cairo, Egypt, 22–23 December 2014; pp. 368–373.

37. Kumar, P.; Saini, R.; Roy, P.P.; Dogra, D.P. A position and rotation invariant framework for sign language recognition (SLR) using Kinect. *Multimed. Tools Appl.* **2018**, *77*, 8823–8846. [CrossRef]
38. Chansri, C.; Srinonchat, J. Hand gesture recognition for Thai sign language in complex background using fusion of depth and color video. *Procedia Comput. Sci.* **2016**, *86*, 257–260. [CrossRef]
39. Simonyan, K.; Zisserman, A. Very Deep Convolutional Networks for Large-Scale Image Recognition. In Proceedings of the International Conference on Learning Representations, San Diego, CA, USA, 7–9 May 2015.
40. Bird, J.J.; Ekart, A.; Buckingham, C.D.; Faria, D.R. Evolutionary optimisation of fully connected artificial neural network topology. In *Intelligent Computing-Proceedings of the Computing Conference*; Springer: Berlin/Heidelberg, Germany, 2019; pp. 751–762.
41. Keras. Available online: https://keras.io/getting_started/faq/ (accessed on 8 September 2020).
42. Abadi, M.; Agarwal, A.; Barham, P.; Brevdo, E.; Chen, Z.; Citro, C.; Corrado, G.S.; Davis, A.; Dean, J.; Devin, M.; et al. TensorFlow: Large-Scale Machine Learning on Heterogeneous Systems. 2015. Available online: https://www.tensorflow.org (accessed on 8 September 2020.)
43. Pedregosa, F.; Varoquaux, G.; Gramfort, A.; Michel, V.; Thirion, B.; Grisel, O.; Blondel, M.; Prettenhofer, P.; Weiss, R.; Dubourg, V.; et al. Scikit-learn: Machine Learning in Python. *J. Mach. Learn. Res.* **2011**, *12*, 2825–2830.

© 2020 by the authors. Licensee MDPI, Basel, Switzerland. This article is an open access article distributed under the terms and conditions of the Creative Commons Attribution (CC BY) license (http://creativecommons.org/licenses/by/4.0/).

Article

TUHAD: Taekwondo Unit Technique Human Action Dataset with Key Frame-Based CNN Action Recognition

Jinkue Lee and Hoeryong Jung *

Department of Mechanical Engineering, Konkuk University, 120 Neungdong-ro, Jayang-dong, Gwangjin-gu, Seoul 05029, Korea; ejk0502@naver.com

* Correspondence: junghl80@konkuk.ac.kr; Tel.: +82-02-450-3903

Received: 7 August 2020; Accepted: 26 August 2020; Published: 28 August 2020

Abstract: In taekwondo, poomsae (i.e., form) competitions have no quantitative scoring standards, unlike gyeorugi (i.e., full-contact sparring) in the Olympics. Consequently, there are diverse fairness issues regarding poomsae evaluation, and the demand for quantitative evaluation tools is increasing. Action recognition is a promising approach, but the extreme and rapid actions of taekwondo complicate its application. This study established the Taekwondo Unit technique Human Action Dataset (TUHAD), which consists of multimodal image sequences of poomsae actions. TUHAD contains 1936 action samples of eight unit techniques performed by 10 experts and captured by two camera views. A key frame-based convolutional neural network architecture was developed for taekwondo action recognition, and its accuracy was validated for various input configurations. A correlation analysis of the input configuration and accuracy demonstrated that the proposed model achieved a recognition accuracy of up to 95.833% (lowest accuracy of 74.49%). This study contributes to the research and development of taekwondo action recognition.

Keywords: gesture recognition; action recognition; convolutional neural network; taekwondo; poomsae; human action dataset

1. Introduction

Vision-based action recognition is an important research topic in the domain of human action recognition. Many action recognition studies have adopted vision sensors because of the rich information they provide, despite their limited field of view and sensitivity to lighting changes [1]. Recent advances in artificial intelligence technology and vision sensors have promoted vision-based action recognition for various applications, such as education [2], entertainment [3,4], and sports [5–12]. Various studies have proposed novel algorithms [13–23] or established datasets [1,24–27] for vision-based action recognition.

Sports is one sector with significant adoption of vision-based action recognition. Several action recognition algorithms have been proposed for sports, including soccer [5], golf [6,7], tennis [8–10], table tennis [11], and baseball [12]. Vision-based action recognition systems have been applied to provide quantitative scoring standards or systems to assist referees. However, relatively few studies have investigated the application of vision-based action recognition to martial arts. The actions of martial arts are significantly more rapid than normal movements, which complicates the acquisition of continuous actions with sufficient clarity and without the loss of inter-frames. In addition, martial arts poses require rapid posture changes and an extreme range of action, which complicates the application of existing human action databases and software libraries developed for normal actions [28]. Many studies have used skeleton data obtained with RGB-D sensors for action recognition [16,19–23,29,30]. Such skeleton data provide information on the locations of joints over time, which can be utilized for action recognition [29]. In the literature, skeleton data have been combined with machine learning algorithms such as the convolutional neural network (CNN) [16,19,21–23] or recurrent neural network [29,30] for human action recognition. However, using such data for martial arts with a wide range of movements, and extreme and rapid actions is difficult because the RGB-D sensors have low skeleton extraction accuracy for those actions [31,32]. Several studies on action recognition for martial arts have sought to address these challenges. Zang et al. [32] and Soomro et al. [33,34] proposed action recognition methods that can be applied to martial arts as well as general sports and routine movements, and Heinz et al. [35] attached sensors to users for kung fu action recognition. Salazar et al. [36] proposed using Kinect to automate the evaluation process of martial arts forms, and Stasinopoulos and Maragos [37] proposed an algorithm based on the historiographic method and hidden Markov model for martial arts action recognition from videos. However, while studies focused on typical human action recognition could leverage various action datasets and recognition algorithms, previous studies on martial arts action recognition had no public datasets and recognition algorithms specific to martial arts that were available to them.

Taekwondo is an official Olympic sport consisting of two major categories: gyeorugi and poomsae. Gyeorugi is a type of full-contact sparring between opponents that uses a quantitative and accurate electronic scoring system to facilitate objective judgment. In contrast, poomsae is a form competition where a single competitor arranges basic attack and defense techniques in a certain order. Unlike *gyeorugi*, which has quantitative and accurate scoring, poomsae is scored by judges. Except for certain penalties such as timeouts and borderline violations, the judging is subjective and qualitative. In addition, situational constraints mean that judges must often evaluate multiple competitors simultaneously. Therefore, issues have arisen over scoring fairness and consistency for poomsae, not only in competitive events but also in promotion examinations.

Several studies have focused on vision-based action recognition for taekwondo. De Goma et al. [28] proposed a taekwondo kick detection algorithm with skeleton data preprocessing. Choi et al. [38] proposed a system for remotely scoring poomsae by comparing actions acquired from multiple vision sensors with corresponding reference actions. Seo et al. [39] suggested a Poisson distribution-based recognition algorithm that uses one-dimensional spatial information extracted from image sequences as its input. Kong et al. [40] extracted taekwondo actions from a broadcast competition video and classified them with high accuracy by applying a support vector machine and defining a taekwondo action as a set of poses. However, these studies had limitations such as low accuracy despite a complex recognition system [38], restricted applicability arising from limited movements [28], and vulnerability to the movement of subjects because of the exclusive use of histogram images [39]. Despite a high recognition accuracy rate, Kong et al.'s method [40] requires two training and recognition models each for a single frame and action classification process, and the pose order needs to be defined for all action classes. This results in unique actions that greatly influence the behavior definition. Thus, if an action is performed in a different pose order (e.g., a transitional action), the recognition accuracy can decrease [40]. Furthermore, the task of labeling 16 poses requires a significant amount of time and resources.

To address these problems, a simpler system, dataset optimized for taekwondo, and method to minimize manual intervention in the action recognition process are required. In this study, the Taekwondo Unit technique Human Action Dataset (TUHAD see Supplementary Materials) was compiled for taekwondo action recognition, and a key frame-based action recognition algorithm was proposed. The proposed algorithm was validated through an accuracy analysis for various input configurations. The main contributions of this study are as follows:

1. TUHAD was constructed for application to taekwondo action recognition, and it includes the representative unit techniques of taekwondo. All actions were performed by taekwondo experts and were collected in a controlled environment for high reliability.
2. A key frame-based CNN architecture was developed for taekwondo action recognition. The accuracy of the proposed model was analyzed according to various input configurations regarding the image modality, key frame position, camera view, and target action to determine the optimal settings for data gathering and action recognition based on taekwondo-specific characteristics.

2. Materials and Methods

Figure 1 shows the proposed method for taekwondo action recognition, which includes data collection, action recognition, and accuracy analysis. For data collection, image sequences of the taekwondo unit techniques were acquired to establish TUHAD. All unit techniques in TUHAD are from the first three chapters of Poomsae Taegeuk (i.e., set of forms), and they were performed by professional taekwondo experts. A mono RGB-D camera was used to acquire the multimodal image sequences. The key frame-based CNN action recognition architecture was trained with TUHAD. The accuracy of the recognition model was then tested with various input configurations to determine the optimal configuration for taekwondo action recognition.

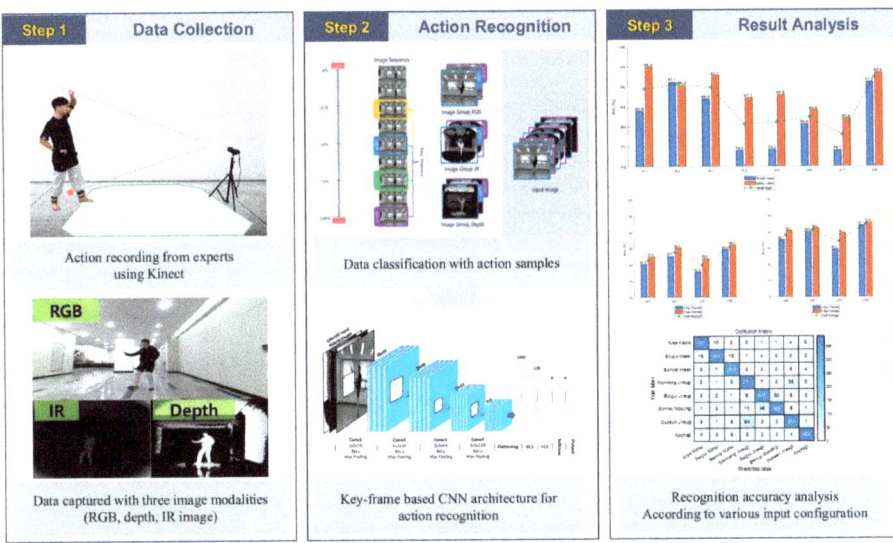

Figure 1. Overall process of the proposed action recognition method.

2.1. TUHAD: Taekwondo Unit Technique Human Action Dataset

TUHAD consists of approximately 100,000 image sequences of eight basic unit techniques of taekwondo performed by 10 experts. All actions were recorded from the front and side views. The experimental protocol was approved by the Konkuk University Institutional Review Board (7001355-202004-HR-375).

2.1.1. Subjects

Ten professional taekwondo poomsae demonstrators (or equivalent) of various heights and body types participated in the experiment to collect action data for TUHAD. No clothing restrictions were imposed on the subjects. The subjects were designated as T1–T10.

2.1.2. Data Modalities

Microsoft Kinect v2 was used to collect image sequences and capture RGB, depth, and infrared images concurrently. The depth and infrared images that were input to the dataset had a raw resolution of 512 × 424 pixels. The RGB images were down-sampled from 1980 × 1080 pixels to 786 × 424 pixels to reduce memory requirements and match the horizontal resolution of the depth and infrared images. All images were captured from two different camera views: front and side. The front-view images were filmed so that the subject approached the camera from the starting point, and the side-view images captured the movements of the subject from the starting point to the right of the camera. In total, 99,982 image frames were captured for each image modality and input to TUHAD.

2.1.3. Capture Setup

Figure 2 shows the setup for capturing actions from the front and side views with a single RGB-D sensor. During data collection, each subject performed eight unit techniques in a predefined order while the sensor recorded the action from a fixed location. The capture space was a 5 × 5 m square set up so that the subjects would remain within sensing range considering the range of movement of the unit techniques. The camera was located 0.5 m from the center of the reference wall. To capture the front- and side-view images, the subjects performed the same actions twice in different directions. For the front-view image capture, a subject performed an action while moving towards the sensor from the starting point located 4 m away from the center of the reference wall. For the side-view image capture, the subject moved to the other starting point, which was 1 m to the left of the front-view starting point, and repeated the same action while moving parallel to the reference wall. All movements were recorded indoors and under artificial lighting. To reduce the influence of background elements on the training process, 30% of the subjects were recorded in another environment under different background and lighting conditions, as shown in Figure 3.

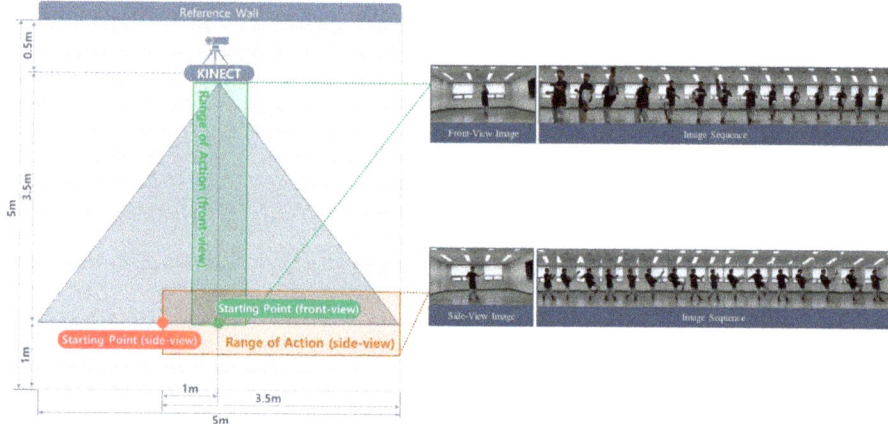

Figure 2. Capture space and setup for front and side view images.

Figure 3. Two image capture environments: (**a**) 70% of the dataset images recorded here; (**b**) the remaining 30% recorded here.

2.1.4. Action Classes and Action Samples

Figure 4 shows the hierarchical structure of TUHAD. The dataset is classified first by subject (T1–T10) and then by camera view (F, S) in the subsequent child node. Each view subset comprised eight action classes (A1–A8) corresponding to the eight unit techniques of the first three chapters of Poomsae Taegeuk. Figure 5 shows front and side views of a representative pose for each action. These unit techniques are the basics of taekwondo and comprise three makki (block), three jireugi (punch), one chigi (strike), and one chagi (kick). For each subject, one action class set comprised 12 action samples (S1–S12), each representing a set of consecutive images for one-unit technique. Each action sample consisted of three different image modalities: RGB, depth, and infrared. For data collection, four action samples were captured in a single take as the subject performed the same action continuously four times while moving forward from the starting point. This procedure was repeated three times, with the subject returning to the starting point each time, to acquire 12 action samples for one action class. There were no restrictions on the stride or standing posture to allow for variability within the actions. Therefore, different subjects executed the same unit technique with variations in the standing posture, position on the screen, and transitional actions. Figure 6a shows the differences between the standing postures of subjects T2 and T4 performing action class A3, and Figure 6b shows the difference between subjects T5 and T3 performing A8. Some of the unit techniques were mistakenly performed four times, and the additional samples were added to the dataset in the same manner as the other data samples without any modification. However, action samples (e.g., A3 by subject T5) that were performed incorrectly were excluded from the dataset. There should normally be 96 samples for each camera view (eight action classes × 12 action samples), but these mistakes are the reason for the irregularities in the number of samples among subjects as given in Table 1.

Table 1. The number of acquired action samples by subject and camera view.

View	T1	T2	T3	T4	T5	T6	T7	T8	T9	T10	Total
Front	96	100	96	100	88	100	96	104	100	96	976
Side	96	96	96	104	84	96	96	96	96	100	960

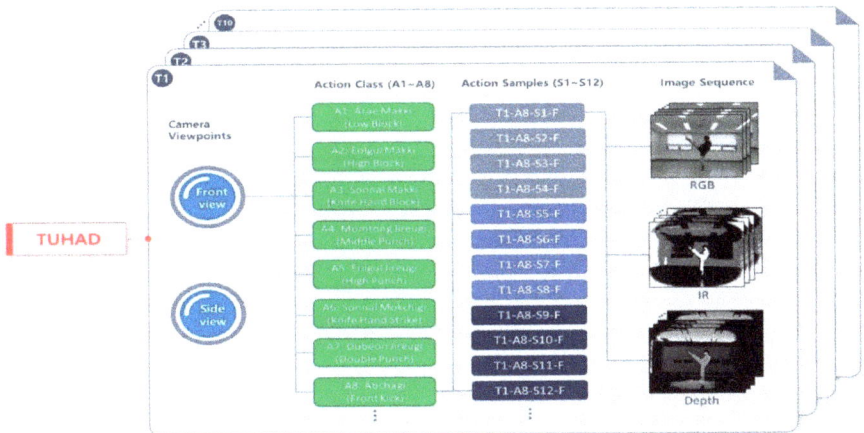

Figure 4. Hierarchy of action classes and action samples in Taekwondo Unit technique Human Action Dataset (TUHAD). Each hierarchy level is repeated at a higher layer.

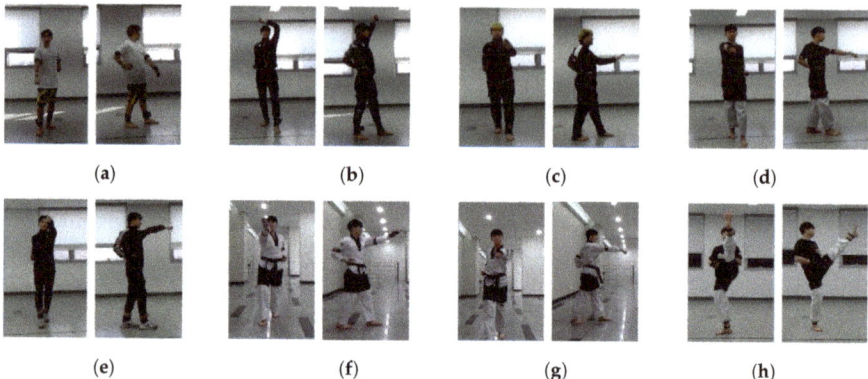

Figure 5. Eight taekwondo actions in TUHAD: (**a**) arae makki (low block, A1), (**b**) eolgul makki (high block, A2), (**c**) sonnal makki (knife hand block, A3), (**d**) momtong jireugi (middle punch, A4), (**e**) eolgul jireugi (high punch, A5), (**f**) sonnal mokchigi (knife hand strike, A6), (**g**) dubeon jireugi (double punch, A7), and (**h**) abchagi (front kick, A8). All actions were recorded with two camera views.

Figure 6. Differences between the subjects when performing unit techniques: (**a**) standing postures for apseogi (left, walking stance) and dwisgubi (right, back stance); (**b**) transitional actions of abchagi (front kick, A8).

2.1.5. Data Organization

An action class captured in a single take was manually divided into four action samples, where the beginning and ending frames were marked for each unit technique as shown in Figure 7. Three annotators indexed and crosschecked the data several times to ensure data reliability. First, each annotator individually searched the frames corresponding to the beginning and end of an action while watching the image sequence frame by frame and recorded the frame number in a separate document. Second, the initial indexing results produced by each annotator were compared, and the correct indexing result was selected by majority. If there was no majority indexing result, then all annotators searched the beginning and end frames of an action together again, and a final agreement was derived through discussion. Third, the final indexing results were carefully verified one more time by the annotators to ensure the integrity of the database. Finally, the action samples separated from the long take were placed in hierarchical data folders, as shown in Figure 4.

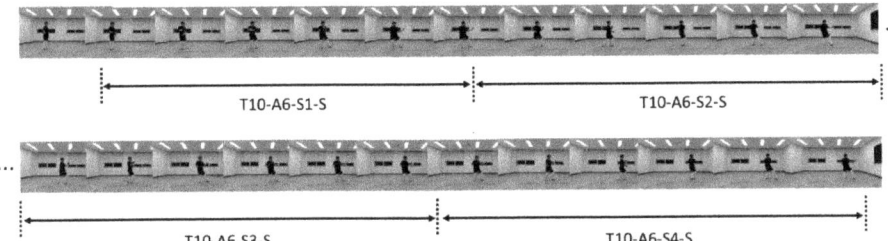

Figure 7. Data organization process: take image sequence including four action samples. The start and end frames of each action sample are marked to distinguish individual action samples.

2.2. Key Frame-Based Action Recognition with CNN

In studies on vision-based action recognition, image frames extracted from the action sequence (i.e., static pose images) have been used to recognize complex human actions [17,40,41]. Kong et al. [40] defined 16 preset poses and assumed that all taekwondo actions could be represented as a combination of these poses. Although their method achieved a mean classification accuracy of up to 91.3%, the recognition rate was relatively low for transitional actions (i.e., movements connecting different actions or poses). This was because their method strongly depended on manual adjustments to set each pose combination. In this study, a key frame-based action recognition algorithm is proposed that is based on a CNN architecture, which is known to be effective for image pattern recognition. The key frames are the set of images representing the distinct features of a target action and are used as the input for the CNN classifier. Regardless of differences in the action speed and technique of subjects, poses corresponding to the moment as a proportion of the entire action sequence can be assumed similar because unit techniques need to be performed in certain ways in taekwondo. Under this assumption, key frames can be selected automatically according to a predefined proportional position with the entire action sequence. The CNN classifier was customized for key frame-based taekwondo action recognition, and the optimal key frame positions were determined through recognition accuracy analysis.

2.2.1. CNN Input Data

One set of multichannel images was used as the input for the key frame-based CNN classifier. The size of each input image was set to 120 × 120 pixels, and the images used for training and testing were resized to match. All RGB images needed their edges cropped before resolution adjustment because they had different resolution ratios compared to the depth and IR images. As shown in Figure 8, the input images comprised a stack of image groups of a specific data modality, and each image group comprised two to four key frames extracted from the action samples of the unit techniques. Various input data configurations were obtained for the three independent variables: image modality, key frame position, and camera view. The dependence of accuracy on the input data configuration was analyzed as follows.

Image modalities: Action samples of the unit techniques were acquired with three different image modalities: RGB, depth, and infrared. Previous studies have employed methods that superimpose different image modalities into one multichannel image to improve the classification and action recognition performances [41,42]. In this study, various modalities of key frame images were simply stacked into one multichannel image, which was used as the input for the CNN classifier. Seven input image configurations were created from different combinations of the three modalities. The seven input configurations were used to analyze their correlation with the recognition accuracy, and the optimal configuration was selected for subsequent analyses.

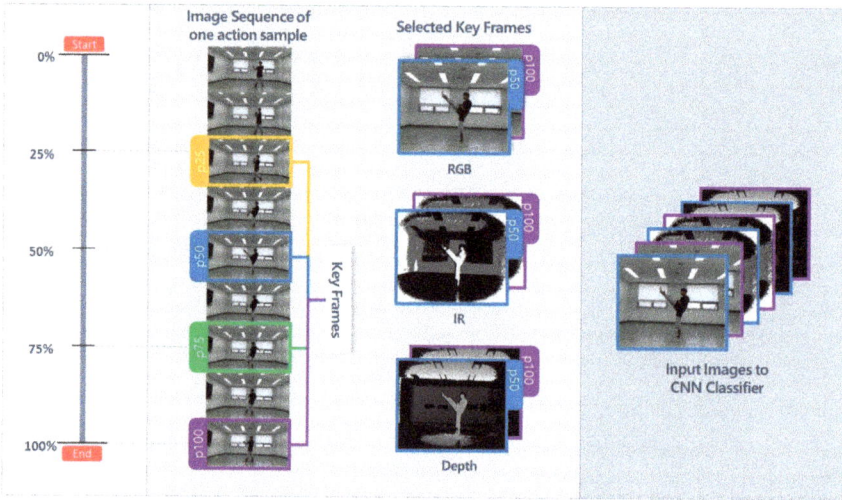

Figure 8. Process of constructing the key frame-based multimodal input images for the convolutional neural network (CNN) classifier.

Key frames: A minimum of two images was required for accurate recognition because all unit techniques consist of changes in poses over time. Several key frames were defined and used to extract multiple images from one action sequence. The images located at a constant ratio were extracted based on the start and end of an image sequence. The first image of each action image sequence was designated as the 0% position, and the last image was taken as the 100% position. The frame images located at 25%, 50%, 75%, and 100% of the image sequence were then defined as key frames and were labeled as p25, p50, p75, and p100, respectively. There was no designation of p0 because the first image of the action sequence was intentionally excluded in consideration of the characteristics of taekwondo: even for the same technique, the initial pose and movement depend on the previous technique. For example, arae makki (low block, A1), which begins in the preparation stance and is performed following other techniques, does not always have the same initial stance. Therefore, the initial image frame of actions did not have generality, and only the other key frame positions were used. Two to four key frames were used as the input data for the different training models. This yielded six input configurations with two key frames, four input configurations with three key frames, and one input configuration with four key frames. The correlation between the number of key frames and recognition accuracy was analyzed, and the optimal key frame containing the most important features of an action was identified.

Camera views and action classes: The actions of unit techniques were captured in two different viewpoints: front and side viewpoints. All unit techniques were sampled independently in each view. These separate action samples were used to analyze the variation in the recognition accuracy as a function of the camera view. In addition, the accuracy for each action class was analyzed to detect taekwondo characteristics that could be utilized in action recognition.

2.2.2. CNN Architecture

The CNN architecture for action classification was constructed by considering existing CNN-based action recognition architectures [11,16,41,43]. In total, four convolutional layers were used with 16 5 × 5 filters, 32 3 × 3 filters, 64 3 × 3 filters, and 128 3 × 3 filters. All hidden layers used the rectified linear unit (ReLU) as the activation function. Max pooling was performed after each convolutional layer over 2 × 2 spatial windows with a stride of 2. After the data were passed through two fully connected layers, a softmax layer was applied to obtain the classification score. Figure 9 shows the proposed CNN architecture for taekwondo action recognition, and Table 2 presents the number of training parameters and the output shapes of each layer.

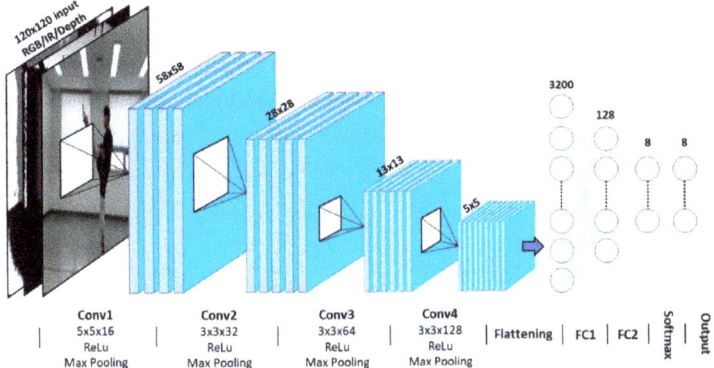

Figure 9. Proposed architecture of the key frame-based CNN.

Table 2. Details of the structure of the key frame-based CNN.

Layer Index	Conv1	Conv2	Conv3	Conv4	FC1	FC2	Total
Output shape	58 × 58 × 16	28 × 28 × 32	13 × 13 × 64	5 × 5 × 128	3200 × 1	128 × 1	-
# of parameters [1]	3216	4640	18,496	73,856	409,728	1032	514,168

[1] Number of parameters from the training model using the RGB+D modality and p50 + p100 key frames.

2.2.3. Training Steps

Parametric training was conducted with 90% of the samples, and the remaining 10% were used to test the trained model. The training and test samples were selected randomly from the entire dataset that contains action samples of all subjects. During the training process, fivefold cross-validation was used to obtain the generalization accuracy of the predictive models. All data were flipped left and right during the training process because taekwondo is divided into right-handed and left-handed actions, even for the same technique. However, these actions have perfect bilateral symmetry, and there are no other differences. Therefore, the images were flipped to double the number of training samples. The ADAM optimizer was applied to train the parameters [44]. The maximum number of epochs was set to 200. The cross-entropy loss was used as the objective function. Table 3 summarizes the characteristics of the training and test data.

For a multichannel input image set of n samples:

- Flipped samples: $2n$;
- Number of test samples: $2n \times 0.1$;
- Number of validation samples: $2n \times 0.9 \times 0.2$;
- Number of training samples: $2n \times 0.9 \times 0.8$.

Table 3. Types and number of training and test samples.

Camera View	Action Samples	Flipped Samples	Validation Samples	Training Samples	Test Samples
Front	976	1952	352	1404	196
Side	960	1920	343	1382	192

3. Results

The experimental results and recognition accuracy of the proposed method for the various input configurations are presented here. The recognition accuracy was analyzed with regard to the image modality, key frames, camera view, and action class.

3.1. Image Modalities

The recognition accuracy was evaluated for seven input configurations comprising various combinations of the three image modalities, as given in Table 4. All four key frames (i.e., p25, p50, p75, and p100) were used for the multimodal input data to prevent them from influencing the accuracy. Table 4 and Figure 10 present the accuracy of the proposed method according to the input image modalities. The accuracy was measured by using test samples that were not used during the training process. To evaluate the recognition accuracy, 196 and 192 test samples were used for the front and side views, respectively. Combining the RGB and depth image modalities provided the highest accuracy for both the front and side views at 87.7% and 94.2%, respectively. The lowest accuracy was obtained by using only the infrared image modality for both the front and side views at 77.0% and 80.2%, respectively.

Table 4. Recognition accuracy with different image modality combinations.

Modality	Accuracy (%)	
	Front View	Side View
RGB	85.7	89.5
Infrared	77.0	80.2
Depth	83.1	93.7
Infrared + Depth	77.0	84.3
RGB + IR	82.1	88.5
RGB + D	87.7	94.2
RGB + IR + D	77.5	83.3

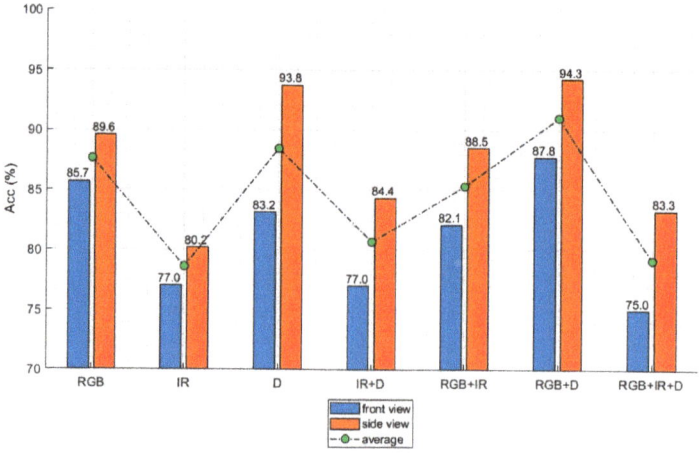

Figure 10. Recognition accuracy according to the image modality.

3.2. Key Frames

The effect of each key frame on the recognition accuracy was analyzed. In total, 11 input configurations were created from various combinations of the four key frames (i.e., p25, p50, p75, and p100). Table 5 and Figure 11 present the key frame combinations and obtained recognition accuracy for the front and side views. The recognition accuracy was evaluated with 196 and 192 test samples for the front and side views, respectively. The highest recognition accuracy with two key frames was obtained by combining p50 and p100 at 88.2% and 95.8% for the front and side views, respectively. With three key frames, the highest accuracy was obtained for the combination of p25, p50, and p100 at 89.7% and 95.3% for the front and side views, respectively. The combinations with the highest accuracy were p25, p50, and p100 for the front view and p50 and p100 for the side view.

Table 5. Recognition accuracy according to key frames.

Number of Key Frames	Key Frames Used				Accuracy	
					Front View	Side View
2	p25	p50			81.1	90.6
	p25		p75		74.4	81.2
	p25			p100	85.2	91.1
		p50	p75		78.5	83.8
		p50		p100	88.2	95.8
			p75	p100	80.6	89.2
3	p25	p50	p75		77.5	86.9
	p25	p50		p100	89.7	95.3
	p25		p75	p100	80.1	90.6
		p50	p75	p100	88.2	92.7
4	p25	p50	p75	p100	87.7	94.2

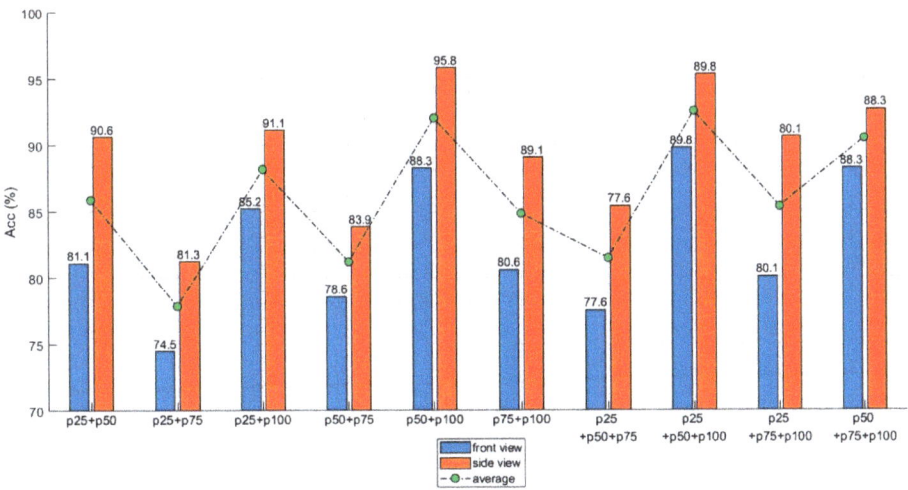

Figure 11. Recognition accuracy according to the selected key frames.

Table 6 and Figure 12 present the average recognition accuracy for a specific key frame. In Table 6, the accuracy of each key frame indicates the average accuracy of all combinations that includes this key frame. If p25 is taken as an example, the accuracy for two key frames was calculated by averaging the accuracies of (p25 + p50), (p25 + p75), and (p25 + p100). The accuracy for three key frames was calculated by averaging the accuracies of (p25 + p50 + p75), (p25 + p50 + p100), and (p25 + p75 + p100). The accuracies of the other key frames were calculated in the same manner. The highest average accuracy was obtained with p100, and the lowest average accuracy was obtained with p75.

Table 6. Average recognition accuracy by key frames.

Key Frame	Two Key Frames		Three Key Frames		Total Average Accuracy
	Front View	Side View	Front View	Side View	
p25	80.2	87.6	82.4	83.4	85.2
p50	82.6	90.1	85.2	85.9	87.2
p75	77.8	84.7	81.9	81.5	83.5
p100	84.6	92.0	86.0	87.5	88.9

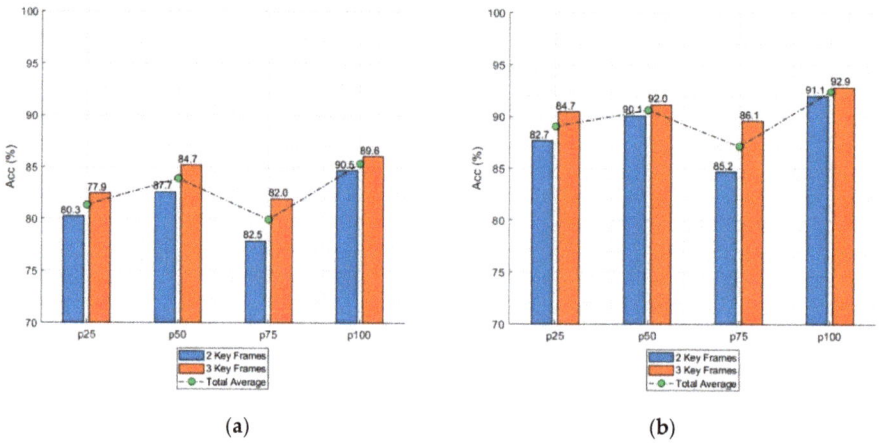

Figure 12. Average accuracy by key frames for each camera view: (a) front and (b) side.

3.3. Camera Views and Action Classes

Table 7 presents the recognition accuracy for each action class and camera view. As indicated in Tables 4 and 5, the accuracy was about 2–10% higher with the side view than the front view for almost all analyses. The same trend can be observed in Table 7. The average accuracy was 88.8% with the side view and 81.8% with the front view. This tendency was confirmed for each unit technique except for A2. With regard to action classes, the three jireugi actions (A4, A5, and A7) and one chigi action (A6) had lower accuracies than the others, as shown in Figure 13. Figure 14 shows the confusion matrices for the action classification. The most frequently confused actions were momtong jireugi (middle punch, A4) versus dubeon jireugi (double punch, A7) and sonnal mokchigi (neck-high knife hand strike, A6) versus eolgul jireugi (high punch, A5).

Table 7. Recognition accuracy according to the camera view and action class.

Action Class	Accuracy (# of Test Samples)	
	Front View	Side View
A1	83.9 (398)	94.6 (408)
A2	91.1 (414)	90.2 (396)
A3	86.9 (374)	92.7 (356)
A4	74.0 (396)	87.1 (426)
A5	74.3 (447)	87.8 (395)
A6	80.6 (443)	83.9 (436)
A7	74.1 (432)	81.9 (437)
A8	91.1 (428)	93.4 (410)
Average	81.9 (3332)	88.8 (3264)

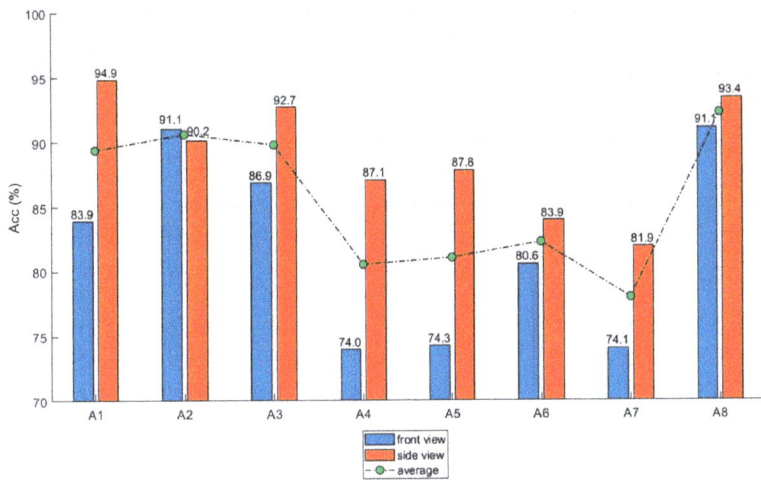

Figure 13. Recognition accuracy according to the action class: front view (blue) and side view (red).

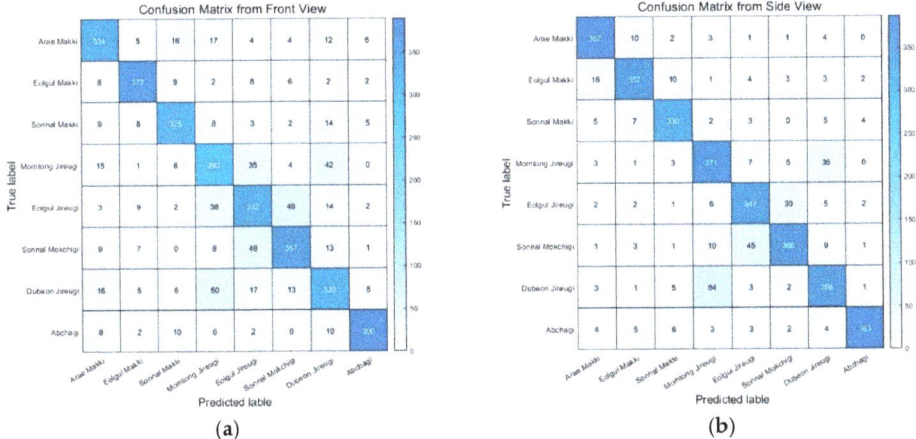

Figure 14. Confusion matrices of the cumulative test results: (**a**) front view and (**b**) side view.

3.4. Backgrounds

Table 8 shows the effect of the background to the recognition accuracy. TUHAD was captured in two different backgrounds as shown in Figure 3. In total, 70% of images were captured in a background shown in Figure 3a and remaining 30% of images were captured in the other background shown in Figure 3b. To compare the recognition accuracy regarding the backgrounds, the accuracies were evaluated for five sets of training and test samples having different background configurations as shown in Table 8. The recognition accuracy of the model trained with the samples captured in the background A and tested with the images captured in the background B was 44.2% and 47.4% for the front and the side viewpoint, respectively. On the contrary, when training was conducted with images captured in the background B and tested with the images captured in the background A, the accuracy was 30.0% and 30.7% for front and side viewpoints, respectively. These cases, in which training and testing were conducted with images of different backgrounds, showed significantly lower accuracy than the model trained with the images of both backgrounds. However, there were no significant differences in recognition accuracy for the cases in which the training was conducted with the images of both backgrounds. These results imply that the problem of such overfitting may arise if the training data is captured in a specific environment.

Table 8. Recognition accuracy according to the backgrounds.

Training Samples	Test Samples	Accuracy (%)	
		Front View	Side View
Background A	Background B	44.2	47.4
Background B	Background A	30.0	30.7
Background A + B	Background A	85.3	93.7
Background A + B	Background B	88.3	94.1
Background A + B	Random	88.3	95.8

3.5. Comparison with Previous Datasets and Recognition Algorithms

In this paper, we proposed the dataset and the recognition algorithm specialized for taekwondo action recognition. This section compares the proposed dataset (TUHAD) and the recognition algorithm with the existing datasets and recognition algorithms, respectively. Table 9 shows the comparison of the proposed dataset with the previous one containing sports and martial arts actions. The datasets were compared regarding the field, recording environment, modality, number of action classes, samples, and subjects. The comparison with previous datasets demonstrates that the proposed dataset contains sufficient action samples, subjects, and classes with various image modalities for a relatively narrow field of taekwondo compared to the previous datasets.

Table 9. The comparison between datasets containing sports and martial arts.

Datasets	Field	Recording Environment	Modality	# of Classes (Martial Arts)	# of Subjects	# of Samples
MAHD [27]	Routine human actions, including some sports	Studio captured	RGB-D, Skeleton, IMU	27 (0)	8	861
UCF Sports Action Dataset	Overall sports	Broadcasting video	RGB	10 (0)	150	150
TTStroke-21 [11]	Sports (table tennis)	Video with similar camera position	RGB	20 (0)	129	129
MADS [32]	Martial arts, dancing, sports	Studio captured	RGB-D, Skeleton	36 (12)	5	216
TUHAD	Martial arts (taekwondo)	Studio captured	RGB-D, IR	8 (8)	10	1936

The performance of the proposed key frame-based taekwondo action recognition algorithm was quantitatively compared with the previous algorithms [39,40] applied for taekwondo action recognition regarding the recognition accuracy and computation time required for the action recognition. Since the previous algorithms were specialized for their own datasets, it was difficult to apply the algorithms to TUHAD. Thus, the previous algorithms have been slightly modified to fit into our dataset while maintaining their methodology. RGB image of key-frame p100, which shows highest recognition accuracy among the key frames, was given as the input to the previous algorithms receiving single input image. The recognition accuracy of the proposed method was evaluated as the average recognition accuracy of the key frame p100 shown in Table 6 for fair comparison. The computation time was measured in the machine equipped with NVDIA GeForce RTX 2060 GPU, Intel i7-9700 CPU, and 64 GB Ram. Table 10 shows the results of performance comparison. For the recognition accuracy, the proposed method was 24.7% and 8.5% higher than that of the previous method [40]. For the computation time, the proposed method also showed the superior result which was two times faster than the previous method [40].

Table 10. The comparison with taekwondo action recognition algorithm.

Method	Accuracy (%)		Computation Time (ms)
	Front View	Side View	
Seo at al. [39] + Yolo V3/SVM	50.0	51.1	42.8
Kong et al. without SPOT [40]	52.1	56.8	16.4
Kong et al. with SPOT [40]	60.7	81.3	48.4
Proposed method	85.4	89.8	7.57

4. Discussion

Implications and insights obtained from the analysis of how the various input configurations affected the recognition accuracy are presented here. They are pertinent to understanding the important features of taekwondo action recognition and can be utilized for improved accuracy and reliability in further research.

4.1. Image Modalities

The analysis of the input image modalities indicated that combining RGB and depth images provided the highest recognition accuracy. In contrast, image modality combinations that included infrared images achieved relatively low accuracy compared to the other combinations. For example, adding infrared images to the RGB and depth images lowered the recognition accuracies by 14.5% and 11.6% for the front and side views, respectively. This result is interesting because the accuracy declined even though more information was given to the action classifier. The results confirmed that simply stacking image modalities is a feasible approach to improving the recognition accuracy, rather than using various image preprocessing techniques or creating new types of images [11,40,41].

4.2. Key Frames

The proposed action recognition algorithm uses 2–4 key frames extracted from a sequence of images of the target action. Using only the key frames rather than the entire image sequence allows the proposed algorithm to achieve acceptable recognition accuracy while maintaining computational efficiency. The correlation between the recognition accuracy and different combinations of key frames (p25, p50, p75, and p100) were analyzed. As shown in Figure 11, the highest accuracy for the side view was achieved by combining p50 and p100, followed by combining p25, p50, and p100. For the front view, the highest accuracy was achieved by combining p25, p50, and p100, followed by combining p50 and p100. This implies no relationship between the number of key frames and recognition accuracy. If a critical key frame presents a distinct feature of an action, sufficient recognition accuracy can be achieved even without using the information from all frames. This conclusion is further supported by the fact that the accuracy was higher with p50 and p100 than with all of the key frames for both the front and side views. However, the position of the key frame greatly affected the recognition accuracy, as demonstrated in Table 6 and Figure 13. Regardless of the camera view, p100 provided the highest recognition accuracy followed by p50, p25, and p75. This implies that the last pose of a taekwondo action contains its most distinct features.

4.3. Camera Views and Action Classes

The recognition accuracy was 2–10% higher with the side view than with the front view for all action classes except for A2, as shown in Figure 13. This was expected because of the nature of taekwondo actions, in which many movements are made while looking forward. When a limb is extended toward the front (e.g., jireugi (punch)), extracting shape information for the arms and legs from the front view is difficult. Therefore, action features can be observed more easily from the side than from the front. Four action classes (three jireugi (middle punch, A4; high punch, A5; double punch, A7) and one chigi (neck-high knife hand strike, A6)) had lower recognition accuracies than the other classes for both the front and side views. For the four action classes, a common feature was the arms were swung while straight. In particular, the recognition accuracy was below 80% for the three jireugi actions from the front view, which can be attributed to their high visual similarity. As discussed previously, determining the angles of the arms from the front view was difficult. In addition, the fist may overlap the torso, which makes it difficult to recognize. In contrast, these techniques can be distinguished more clearly from the side view because the front of the arm does not overlap with the torso. This conclusion is supported by the fact that the recognition accuracy for the jireugi actions was relatively high from the side view.

The low recognition accuracy for the front view due to visual similarity is also shown in Figure 14. The most frequently confused movements were momtong jireugi (middle punch, A4) versus dubeon jireugi (double punch, A7) and sonnal mokchigi (neck-high knife hand strike, A6) versus eolgul jireugi (high punch, A5). A4 and A7 only differ in the number of punches performed, and the punching action and target point are the same; thus, these two actions result in the same pose at p100. A5 and A6 are aimed at the face and neck, respectively, so they have similar heights for the hand position at p100. Obviously, these actions can be sufficiently distinguished by considering the entire trajectory, but discerning them by analyzing only key frames is a challenge. In particular, the similarity in poses at p100, which is the most critical key frame, had a large influence on the reduced recognition accuracy.

In contrast, high recognition accuracy was achieved for the rest of the action classes, which had little visual similarity. Abchagi (front kick, A8) is the only kick motion, and it achieved the highest and second-highest recognition accuracies for the side and the front views, respectively. This is because it involves unique lower-body movements that can be clearly distinguished from the other actions. A1, A2, and A3 also have distinct visual characteristics. Arae makki (low block, A1) and sonnal makki (knife hand block, A3) have huge differences in the movement of the arm and the final pose at p100. Eolgul makki (high block, A2) is a unique motion in which the arms are placed above the subject's head horizontal to the ground, as shown in Figure 8. Due to these characteristics, A1, A2, A3, and A8 all had high recognition accuracies above 90% with the side view, and they had higher recognition accuracies than other actions with the front view. Eolgul makki (high block, A2) was unique because it achieved a high recognition accuracy with the front view, while most of the other action classes obtained a high recognition accuracy with the side view. This may be because the arms blocked the face when they were above the head or horizontal, which made the features of this action class more apparent from the front view.

Several studies have used multi-view images that were captured simultaneously using multiple cameras for improving the recognition accuracy [32,38]. Although TUHAD provides images captured in two camera viewpoints, the recognition accuracy of the multi-view images cannot be evaluated because the action samples of the front and side views were captured separately. This is one limitation of TUHAD.

4.4. Backgrounds

The results of cross-background test show lower recognition accuracy compared to the test result of the model trained with both backgrounds as represented in Figure 8. This results clearly demonstrates that background feature was reflected in the training process and affected the resulting recognition accuracy. In the case of a model that trained with both backgrounds, there was no significant difference in recognition accuracy between two background samples, even though the number of samples with that background A is more than twice of the background B. This implies that features other than actions can be intervened in the training process even when a high-performance feature extractor such as CNN is used in the action recognition process. However, at the same time, it is possible to prevent the model becoming overfitted to secondary features like background by adding a few different types of samples to the dataset.

4.5. Comparison with Previous Recognition Algorithms

Table 10 shows the comparison result between recognition algorithms. The proposed method trained with TUHAD achieved the higher accuracy and less computation time compared to the previous taekwondo action recognition algorithms. However, as mentioned above, the previous recognition algorithm is specialized in their own dataset, some degree of accuracy decline was inevitable. The recognition algorithm proposed by Seo at al. [39] has a simple structure that calculates the image histogram and classifies it. However, due to the limitations of the method using simple histogram, it seems that the accuracy decreases in the dataset with diversity of brightness and subjects. Kong et al. [40] recognized the actions of taekwondo in the broadcast image with high accuracy. However, it also showed a limitation that it cannot be used in an action class that is not defined preliminarily. For this reason, only one input image was used in the performance evaluation without motion sequence information. For this reason, the accuracy of this method was evaluated relatively low compared to the value presented in their paper. However, the recognition accuracy improvement through the de-noising technique with modified SPOT was remarkable. Despite the additional computational time, it seems that it can be adopted to the proposed algorithm to improve recognition accuracy.

5. Conclusions

In this study, TUHAD was established to provide data for accurate vision-based action recognition of taekwondo. TUHAD contains 1936 samples representing eight fundamental unit techniques performed by 10 taekwondo experts who were recorded from two camera views. A key frame-based CNN classifier was developed, and the recognition accuracy was analyzed according to the image modality, key frame, and camera view. The results demonstrated that the CNN classifier achieved a recognition accuracy of up to 95.833%. TUHAD and the proposed classifier can contribute to advancing research regarding taekwondo action recognition, and the results on the optimal image capture setup can have broader applicability. For example, this information may also be applicable to other situations entailing the recognition of rapid actions outside the range of normal human movements. However, a critical prerequisite for applying the proposed method to action recognition is that the beginning and ending frames of the action (i.e., action detection) should be given prior to action classification. This will be explored in following research papers. TUHAD will be expanded to include more unit techniques as well as combinations of various unit techniques to recognize more complex and diverse taekwondo actions. In addition, more advanced action recognition and detection algorithms, such as trajectory-based and multi-view conditions, will be investigated.

Supplementary Materials: The following is available online at http://gofile.me/6AOtN/UePI6h55H, Data S1: Taekwondo Unit technique Human Action Dataset (TUHAD).

Author Contributions: Conceptualization, H.J. and J.L.; methodology, H.J. and J.L.; software, J.L.; validation, J.L.; formal analysis, J.L.; investigation, J.L.; resources, H.J.; data curation, J.L.; writing—original draft preparation, J.L.; writing—review and editing, H.J.; visualization, J.L.; supervision, H.J.; project administration, H.J.; funding acquisition, H.J. All authors have read and agreed to the published version of the manuscript.

Funding: This paper was supported by Konkuk University in 2017.

Conflicts of Interest: The authors declare no conflict of interest.

References

1. Wei, H.; Chopada, P.; Kehtarnavaz, N. C-MHAD: Continuous Multimodal Human Action Dataset of Simultaneous Video and Inertial Sensing. *Sensors* **2020**, *20*, 2905. [CrossRef] [PubMed]
2. Ren, H.; Xu, G. Human action recognition in smart classroom. In Proceedings of the Fifth IEEE International Conference on Automatic Face Gesture Recognition, Washington, DC, USA, 21–21 May 2002; pp. 417–422.
3. Rautaray, S.S.; Agrawal, A. Interaction with virtual game through hand gesture recognition. In Proceedings of the 2011 International Conference on Multimedia, Signal Processing and Communication Technologies, Aligarh, India, 17–19 December 2011.
4. Kong, Y.; Zhang, X.; Wei, Q.; Hu, W.; Jia, Y. Group action recognition in soccer videos. In Proceedings of the 2008 19th International Conference on Pattern Recognition, Tampa, FL, USA, 8–11 December 2008; pp. 1–4.

5. Zhang, L.; Hsieh, J.-C.; Ting, T.-T.; Huang, Y.-C.; Ho, Y.-C.; Ku, L.-K. A Kinect based Golf Swing Score and Grade System using GMM and SVM. In Proceedings of the 2012 5th International Congress on Image and Signal Processing, Chongqing, China, 16–18 October 2012; pp. 711–715.
6. Zhang, L.; Hsieh, J.C.; Wang, J. A Kinect-based golf swing classification system using HMM and Neuro-Fuzzy. In Proceedings of the 2012 International Conference on Computer Science and Information Processing (CSIP), Xian, China, 24–26 August 2012; pp. 1163–1166.
7. Zhu, G.; Xu, C.; Huang, Q.; Gao, W.; Xing, L. Player action recognition in broadcast tennis video with applications to semantic analysis of sports game. In Proceedings of the 14th Annual ACM International Conference on Multimedia—MULTIMEDIA'06, Santa Barbara, CA, USA, 12–16 October 2006; p. 431.
8. FarajiDavar, N.; de Campos, T.; Kittler, J.; Yan, F. Transductive transfer learning for action recognition in tennis games. In Proceedings of the 2011 IEEE International Conference on Computer Vision Workshops (ICCV Workshops), Barcelona, Spain, 6–13 November 2011; pp. 1548–1553.
9. Zhu, G.; Xu, C.; Huang, Q.; Gao, W. Action Recognition in Broadcast Tennis Video. In Proceedings of the 18th International Conference on Pattern Recognition (ICPR'06), Hong Kong, China, 20–24 August 2006; pp. 251–254.
10. Martin, P.-E.; Benois-Pineau, J.; Peteri, R.; Morlier, J. Sport Action Recognition with Siamese Spatio-Temporal CNNs: Application to Table Tennis. In Proceedings of the 2018 International Conference on Content-Based Multimedia Indexing (CBMI), La Rochelle, France, 4–6 September 2018; pp. 1–6.
11. Piergiovanni, A.J.; Ryoo, M.S. Fine-grained Activity Recognition in Baseball Videos. *arXiv* **2018**, arXiv:1804.03247.
12. Pham, H.H.; Salmane, H.; Khoudour, L.; Crouzil, A.; Velastin, S.A.; Zegers, P. A Unified Deep Framework for Joint 3D Pose Estimation and Action Recognition from a Single RGB Camera. *Sensors* **2020**, *20*, 1825. [CrossRef] [PubMed]
13. Dong, J.; Gao, Y.; Lee, H.J.; Zhou, H.; Yao, Y.; Fang, Z.; Huang, B. Action Recognition Based on the Fusion of Graph Convolutional Networks with High Order Features. *Appl. Sci.* **2020**, *10*, 1482. [CrossRef]
14. Wang, H.; Song, Z.; Li, W.; Wang, P. A Hybrid Network for Large-Scale Action Recognition from RGB and Depth Modalities. *Sensors* **2020**, *20*, 3305. [CrossRef] [PubMed]
15. Du, Y.; Fu, Y.; Wang, L. Skeleton based action recognition with convolutional neural network. In Proceedings of the 2015 3rd IAPR Asian Conference on Pattern Recognition (ACPR), Kuala Lumpur, Malaysia, 3–6 November 2015; pp. 579–583.
16. Ravanbakhsh, M.; Mousavi, H.; Rastegari, M.; Murino, V.; Davis, L.S. Action Recognition with Image Based CNN Features. *arXiv* **2015**, arXiv:1512.03980.
17. Feichtenhofer, C.; Pinz, A.; Zisserman, A. Convolutional Two-Stream Network Fusion for Video Action Recognition. *arXiv* **2016**, arXiv:1604.06573.
18. Li, B.; Dai, Y.; Cheng, X.; Chen, H.; Lin, Y.; He, M. Skeleton based action recognition using translation-scale invariant image mapping and multi-scale deep CNN. In Proceedings of the 2017 IEEE International Conference on Multimedia & Expo Workshops (ICMEW), Hong Kong, China, 10–14 July 2017; pp. 601–604.
19. Ercolano, G.; Riccio, D.; Rossi, S. Two deep approaches for ADL recognition: A multi-scale LSTM and a CNN-LSTM with a 3D matrix skeleton representation. In Proceedings of the 2017 26th IEEE International Symposium on Robot and Human Interactive Communication (RO-MAN), Lisbon, Portugal, 28 August–1 September 2017; pp. 877–882.
20. Ke, Q.; Bennamoun, M.; An, S.; Sohel, F.; Boussaid, F. A New Representation of Skeleton Sequences for 3D Action Recognition. In Proceedings of the 2017 IEEE Conference on Computer Vision and Pattern Recognition (CVPR), Honolulu, HI, USA, 21–26 July 2017; pp. 4570–4579.
21. Li, B.; He, M.; Dai, Y.; Cheng, X.; Chen, Y. 3D skeleton based action recognition by video-domain translation-scale invariant mapping and multi-scale dilated CNN. *Multimed. Tools Appl.* **2018**, *77*, 22901–22921. [CrossRef]
22. Ding, Z.; Wang, P.; Ogunbona, P.O.; Li, W. Investigation of different skeleton features for CNN-based 3D action recognition. In Proceedings of the 2017 IEEE International Conference on Multimedia & Expo Workshops (ICMEW), Hong Kong, China, 10–14 July 2017; pp. 617–622.
23. Liu, C.; Hu, Y.; Li, Y.; Song, S.; Liu, J. PKU-MMD: A Large Scale Benchmark for Continuous Multi-Modal Human Action Understanding. *arXiv* **2017**, arXiv:1703.07475.

24. Shahroudy, A.; Liu, J.; Ng, T.-T.; Wang, G. NTU RGB+D: A Large Scale Dataset for 3D Human Activity Analysis. *arXiv* **2016**, arXiv:1604.02808.
25. Liu, J.; Shahroudy, A.; Perez, M.; Wang, G.; Duan, L.-Y.; Kot, A.C. NTU RGB+D 120: A Large-Scale Benchmark for 3D Human Activity Understanding. *IEEE Trans. Pattern Anal. Mach. Intell.* **2019**, *1*. [CrossRef] [PubMed]
26. Chen, C.; Jafari, R.; Kehtarnavaz, N. UTD-MHAD: A multimodal dataset for human action recognition utilizing a depth camera and a wearable inertial sensor. In Proceedings of the 2015 IEEE International Conference on Image Processing (ICIP), Quebec City, QC, Canada, 27–30 September 2015; pp. 168–172.
27. Goma, J.C.; Bustos, M.S.; Sebastian, J.A.; Macrohon, J.J.E. Detection of Taekwondo Kicks Using RGB-D Sensors. In Proceedings of the 2019 3rd International Conference on Software and e-Business, Tokyo, Japan, 9–11 December 2019; pp. 129–133.
28. Liu, J.; Shahroudy, A.; Wang, G.; Duan, L.-Y.; Kot, A.C. Skeleton-Based Online Action Prediction Using Scale Selection Network. *IEEE Trans. Pattern Anal. Mach. Intell.* **2020**, *42*, 1453–1467. [CrossRef] [PubMed]
29. Liu, J.; Shahroudy, A.; Xu, D.; Kot, A.C.; Wang, G. Skeleton-Based Action Recognition Using Spatio-Temporal LSTM Network with Trust Gates. *IEEE Trans. Pattern Anal. Mach. Intell.* **2018**, *40*, 3007–3021. [CrossRef] [PubMed]
30. Livingston, M.A.; Sebastian, J.; Ai, Z.; Decker, J.W. Performance measurements for the Microsoft Kinect skeleton. In Proceedings of the 2012 IEEE Virtual Reality (VR), Costa Mesa, CA, USA, 4–8 March 2012; pp. 119–120.
31. Zhang, W.; Liu, Z.; Zhou, L.; Leung, H.; Chan, A.B. Martial Arts, Dancing and Sports dataset: A challenging stereo and multi-view dataset for 3D human pose estimation. *Image Vis. Comput.* **2017**, *61*, 22–39. [CrossRef]
32. Soomro, K.; Zamir, A.R. Action Recognition in Realistic Sports Videos. In *Computer Vision in Sports*; Advances in Computer Vision and Pattern, Recognition; Moeslund, T.B., Thomas, G., Hilton, A., Eds.; Springer International Publishing: Cham, Switzerland, 2014; pp. 181–208, ISBN 978-3-319-09395-6.
33. Soomro, K.; Zamir, A.R.; Shah, M. UCF101: A Dataset of 101 Human Actions Classes from Videos in the Wild. *arXiv* **2012**, arXiv:1212.0402.
34. Heinz, E.A.; Kunze, K.S.; Gruber, M.; Bannach, D.; Lukowicz, P. Using Wearable Sensors for Real-Time Recognition Tasks in Games of Martial Arts—An Initial Experiment. In Proceedings of the 2006 IEEE Symposium on Computational Intelligence and Games, Reno, NV, USA, 22–24 May 2006; pp. 98–102.
35. Salazar, K.A.; Sibaja Garcia, J.E.; Mateus, A.S.; Percybrooks, W.S. Autonomous recognition of martial arts forms using RGB-D cameras. In Proceedings of the 2017 Congreso Internacional de Innovacion y Tendencias en Ingenieria (CONIITI), Bogota, Colombia, 4–6 October 2017; pp. 1–5.
36. Stasinopoulos, S.; Maragos, P. Human action recognition using Histographic methods and hidden Markov models for visual martial arts applications. In Proceedings of the 2012 19th IEEE International Conference on Image Processing, Orlando, FL, USA, 30 September–3 October 2012; pp. 745–748.
37. Choi, C.-H.; Joo, H.-J. Motion recognition technology based remote Taekwondo Poomsae evaluation system. *Multimed. Tools Appl.* **2016**, *75*, 13135–13148. [CrossRef]
38. Seo, J.M.; Jang, I.K.; Choi, J.H.; Lee, S.M. A Study of the Taekwondo Poomsae Recognition System Used by Motion Recognition Techniques. In Proceedings of the 2009 International Conference on Multimedia Information Technology and Applications, Osaka, Japan, 20–22 August 2009.
39. Kong, Y.; Wei, Z.; Huang, S. Automatic analysis of complex athlete techniques in broadcast taekwondo video. *Multimed. Tools Appl.* **2018**, *77*, 13643–13660. [CrossRef]
40. Simonyan, K.; Zisserman, A. Two-Stream Convolutional Networks for Action Recognition in Videos. *arXiv* **2014**, arXiv:1406.2199.
41. Zhang, B.; Wang, L.; Wang, Z.; Qiao, Y.; Wang, H. Real-Time Action Recognition with Enhanced Motion Vector CNNs. In Proceedings of the 2016 IEEE Conference on Computer Vision and Pattern Recognition (CVPR), Las Vegas, NV, USA, 27–30 June 2016; pp. 2718–2726.
42. Dehzangi, O.; Taherisadr, M.; ChangalVala, R. IMU-Based Gait Recognition Using Convolutional Neural Networks and Multi-Sensor Fusion. *Sensors* **2017**, *17*, 2735. [CrossRef]
43. Kingma, D.P.; Ba, J. Adam: A Method for Stochastic Optimization. *arXiv* **2017**, arXiv:1412.6980.
44. UCF Sports Action Data Set. Available online: https://www.crcv.ucf.edu/data/UCF_Sports_Action.php (accessed on 7 August 2020).

© 2020 by the authors. Licensee MDPI, Basel, Switzerland. This article is an open access article distributed under the terms and conditions of the Creative Commons Attribution (CC BY) license (http://creativecommons.org/licenses/by/4.0/).

Article

An Acoustic Sensing Gesture Recognition System Design Based on a Hidden Markov Model

Bruna Salles Moreira *, Angelo Perkusich and Saulo O. D. Luiz

Embedded Systems and Pervasive Computing Laboratory, Electrical Engineering Department, Federal University of Campina Grande, Campina Grande, Paraíba 58429-900, Brazil; perkusic@embedded.ufcg.edu.br (A.P.); saulo@dee.ufcg.edu.br (S.O.D.L.)
* Correspondence: bruna.moreira@ee.ufcg.edu.br

Received: 7 July 2020; Accepted: 24 August 2020; Published: 26 August 2020

Abstract: Many human activities are tactile. Recognizing how a person touches an object or a surface surrounding them is an active area of research and it has generated keen interest within the interactive surface community. In this paper, we compare two machine learning techniques, namely Artificial Neural Network (ANN) and Hidden Markov Models (HMM), as they are some of the most common techniques with low computational cost used to classify an acoustic-based input. We employ a small and low-cost hardware design composed of a microphone, a stethoscope, a conditioning circuit, and a microcontroller. Together with an appropriate surface, we integrated these components into a passive gesture recognition input system for experimental evaluation. To perform the evaluation, we acquire the signals using a small microphone and send it through the microcontroller to MATLAB's toolboxes to implement and evaluate the ANN and HMM models. We also present the hardware and software implementation and discuss the advantages and limitations of these techniques in gesture recognition while using a simple alphabet of three geometrical figures: circle, square, and triangle. The results validate the robustness of the HMM technique that achieved a success rate of 90%, with a shorter training time than the ANN.

Keywords: gesture recognition; acoustic-based input; artificial neural network; Hidden Markov models

1. Introduction

Day-to-day activities are a combination of tactile and auditory sensations. We play, listen, and interact with a variety of objects every day. Some of these objects are recording our activities, such as the touch screens of smartphones or tablets. Thus, adding sensory perception to objects and surfaces that surround us daily is an active area of research, and it has generated keen interest within the interactive surface community [1–4].

By connecting a microphone to a surface, a signal is acquired by an acoustic sensor, and it is then possible to analyze the acquired signal to identify information for the development of tangible acoustic interfaces [5]. These interfaces work based on the principle that, when an object is touched and manipulated, the vibrations it produces can be acquired and analyzed to infer how interaction with the object occurs [6].

Acoustic sensing has been explored as a powerful tool to retrieve information from a user's interaction with a surface or object. Some of this information can be used by developers to enhance interfaces with new features, or, most importantly, to improve interaction on current interfaces [6], which can provide more expression to user-defined gestures and expand the interaction input language.

In contrast to camera-based gesture recognition systems, all sensor elements of the acoustic detection technique can be integrated into the surface, and this method does not suffer from lighting and occlusion problems [7].

Researchers have explored several acoustic-based input techniques. These techniques are classified either as passive or active approaches. Passive approaches detect a user's input, acquiring and analyzing sounds generated by the user's actions, without the need for an active component, only depending on the properties of the object used (its structure, material, or exclusive properties). Besides, for active approaches, an actuator must be used to interact with a surface, such as a loudspeaker.

Acoustic detection has been the subject of intense research in recent decades. Various algorithms for processing acoustic information have been explored. These include Artificial Neural Networks [8,9], Convolution Neural Networks (CNN) [10], Support Vector Machine (SVM) [11,12], Decision Trees [13], and Hidden Markov Models [14]. These efforts led to the development of systems used in various acoustic tasks, including gesture and textures recognition, the spatial location of the surface touch, and object classification.

In the context of this work, our focus is to answer the following Research Questions (RQ):

- RQ1: What are the tools, applications, and trends involving these machine learning classifiers?
- RQ2: What are the signal characteristics when using a machine learning technique to recognize acoustic patterns?
- RQ3: What is the most suitable machine learning technique for acoustic gesture recognition applications?

We distinguish from previous work by implementing acoustic-based input in gesture recognition applications comparing two different techniques: Artificial Neural Network (ANN) and Hidden Markov Models (HMM). First, we present a low-cost hardware design that is composed of a microphone, a stethoscope, a conditioning circuit, and a microcontroller. Subsequently, we integrated these components with a surface to implement a passive gesture recognition system. Second, we evaluated the dataset acquired for developing and training the ANN and HMM models. For ANNs, we investigate algorithms to process the signal to achieve higher accuracy rates due to the low success rate obtained using unprocessed signals. Finally, we evaluated the HNN model. The results validate the robustness of the HMM technique that achieved a success rate of 90%, with a shorter training time than the ANN. We also discuss how to generate code from the trained HMM, cross-compile it automatically, and embed it into low-cost hardware. Thus, after training, the system would be independent of MATLAB software, which has a higher cost.

The rest of the paper is organized, as follows. In Section 2, we introduce a review of the related works, while in Section 3 we present the materials and methods. In Section 4, we present the experiments and, in Section 5, the discussion of the results against the defined research questions. Finally, in Section 6 we present the conclusions and future work.

2. Acoustic Sensing Related Works

In this section, we present a review of scientific papers that use the acoustic detection technique, focusing on the three research questions defined in the introduction.

Nine keywords were defined in order to search for papers aiming to answer the research question enumerated in the introduction, and are as follows:

Acoustic Sensing, Scratch Input, Acoustic Tracking, Tactile Input, Gesture Classification, Sound based classification, Sound Sensing, Acoustic-based input, and Fingertip Gesture.

Besides, we defined two general selection criteria: (i) the papers were peer-reviewed and (ii) English was the language used to write the paper.

Scratch Input [13] is an acoustic input technique that is based on the sound originated when a nail is dragged over the surface of textured material. Harrison and Hudson [13] used a microphone attached to a modified stethoscope, particularly suitable for amplifying sound and detecting high-frequency noise. A microphone converts the sound into an electrical signal, which is then amplified and acquired by a computer using an audio input connector. This hardware can be effortlessly attached to existing surfaces, turning them into large, non-powered, ad hoc entry surfaces.

The acoustic pattern recognizer proposed by Harrison and Hudson [13] employs a decision tree based on peak count and amplitude variation. A more sophisticated recognition mechanism can incorporate other dimensions, e.g., frequency and duration, and it may support a broader set of gestures and higher precision. Subsequently, other works started to use more advanced techniques, such as Hambone [14] with HMM, Stane [8] with ANN, and TapSense [12] with SVM.

Hambone [14] is a light and discreet system that offers quick access and the ability to multitask for the interaction of mobile devices. Hambone [14] uses two small piezoelectric sensors placed on the wrist or ankle of the user. When a user moves either the hands or feet, the sounds generated voyage to the device via bone conduction. Subsequently, it transmits the signals digitally to a mobile device or computer for processing using HMMs. Afterwards, the signals are mapped to a set of commands that control applications.

Two limitations were found in the current implementation of Hambone [14]. Whenever a user makes a gesture, there is a two-second lag from the initiation of the gesture to have the final command issued and, when training the system to recognize more than four gestures, the HMM training sessions become time-consuming.

Stane [8] is a small device with an embedded microphone and several textures projected onto its surface. The device classifies the sounds produced when rubbing different areas. Stane [8] uses a two-stage classification process, with instantaneous low-level classification and higher-level classifiers that aggregate the evidence of the first stage over time. For instant classification, the input audio is classified by Multi-Layer Perceptron (MLP). However, Stane [8] needs a textured device case and it cannot be used on any surface, differently of what we are proposing in this paper: a passive acoustic-based input classification easily incorporated into a surface.

TapSense [12] uses a microphone connected to an interactive surface to differentiate between touches of different objects and parts of the finger, and it uses the SVM classifier. Nevertheless, the following amounts of data points were collected per participant to train this classifier: 200 data points for the mobile input set, 160 data points for the table finger set, and 280 data points for the table toolset. It has been identified that the user boredom and fatigue became problematic in more extended study durations.

Most recently, we can find papers using machine learning techniques with high computational costs, such as a combination of motion and audio features to train the neural network, such as Pentelligence [9], or even using Convolutional Neural Network, such as Mingshi et al. [10]. Indeed, it is required massive amounts of data, millions of samples.

For example, Pentelligence [9] is based on a pen for handwritten digit recognition. It can be used on regular paper, and no separate dedicated tracking device is required. The authors of Pentelligence [9] found that combining the strengths of audio and motion features produces better results when motion data are classified first. Neural networks trained on the sound emissions of the pen tip are used for evaluation purposes. However, the authors of Pentelligence [9] have used a contact sensor, a microphone, an accelerometer, and a gyroscope in order to achieve a reasonable recognition rate. All of these sensors and the high computational cost became problematic in low-cost applications.

Chen et al. [10] explore the possibility of extending the input and interactions beyond the screen of the mobile device by using ad hoc adjacent surfaces. The proposed system Ipanel uses the acoustic signals from the fingers' sliding on the table for tracking. Different features are extracted by exploiting the spatio-temporal and frequency domain properties of the produced acoustic signals. The features are transformed into images, and then Chen et al. [10] employed CNN to recognize the finger movement on the table. Ipanel can support not only commonly used gestures (such as click, flip, scroll, and zoom) recognition and handwriting (10 numbers and 26 letters) recognition at high accuracy.

Further, Ipanel's performance is robust against different levels of ambient noise and different surface materials. Although, the recognition accuracy significantly decreases when the fingers are

20 cm away from the mobile, mainly because the signals become too weak to be used for recognition, and the five-layer CNN adopted has a high computational cost.

3. Materials and Methods

We conducted an experiment focusing on the dataset input for the classifiers in the gesture classification problem to improve the analysis. Our goal is to have simple hardware and low computational cost for the machine learning algorithm that can achieve high success rate with at most ten drawings per gesture and short training time (maximum two minutes per gesture), wherefore the user is not fatigued in the training stage. Such a goal is similar to the one that motivated the authors of TapSense [12].

Based on a previous study, several papers focus on gesture recognition using a subset of machine learning techniques, but some of the most common techniques with low computational cost are ANN and HMM. Therefore, the next section presents our platform, analyzes these two machine learning techniques, and compares them.

Platform

Figure 1 illustrates the operation of the proposed system. When a nail (A) scratches a surface, it produces a series of mechanical vibrations, which propagate through the surface and they are acquired by the microphone (C), which is connected to the stethoscope cannula (B). The use of stethoscopes to acquire sounds naturally provides a high level of suppression of environmental noise. The microphone converts the sound into an electrical signal. By covering the microphone with the stethoscope, the first may pick up a less noisy signal from the environment. This allows for impacts to be promptly segmented from any background noise with a simple amplitude threshold [15]. The microphone signal is then filtered and amplified by a conditioning circuit (D), and acquired by an analog to digital converter of a microcontroller. Then the microcontroller sends the digital signal via serial communication (UART) to the computer (E), which finally will be capable of recognizing the gesture performed (F) on the surface by one of the machine learning applications developed in MATLAB.

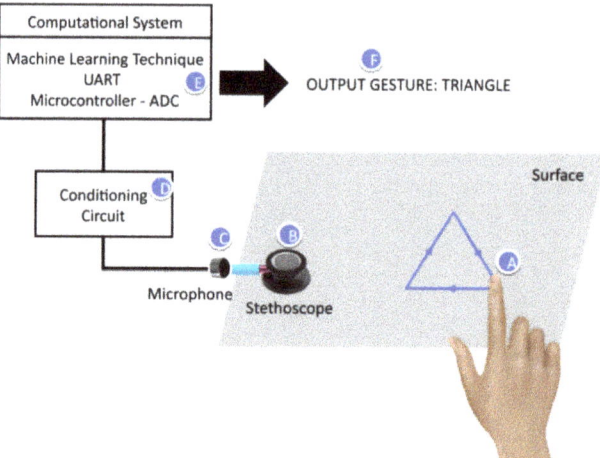

Figure 1. Functioning of the proposed system.

The stethoscope has a dual lumen design. The mini electret microphone dimensions are 0.16 × 0.06 inches, and it has to be small enough to fit inside the stethoscope cannula. The conditioning circuit is a low-cost microphone amplifier by Adafruit MAX4466. This circuit has a trimmer pot to adjust the gain from 25× to 125×. The output is rail-to-rail and the supply voltage operation is 2.4 V to 5.5 V.

The microcontroller used in this project is the Arduino Nano V3.0, which has, as primary characteristics, its small size and low cost, allowing greater flexibility for the use of this board in projects whose size is essential. The ADC of this microcontroller is a 10-bit, and the UART transmission rate used in this project is 115,200 bits/s.

Because sound travels through solid and liquid materials much more efficiently than through the air, the surface's importance is reaffirmed. Thus, while the friction of the nail on a surface only produces an audible and smooth noise, the signal is propagated considerably better through the solid material. This superior sound propagation means that a signal is propagated over a longer distance, but it is also better-preserved [13]. As the speed of sound propagation in aluminum is among the highest among the common materials, around 6300 m/s, an aluminum surface was chosen to carry out the experiments. The stethoscope provides a high level of suppression of environmental noise to the microphone. Still, all of the experiments were performed against the maximum level of ambient noise of 45 dB.

This work aims to compare the robustness of the HMM and the ANN techniques to recognize gestures on surfaces while using a low-cost acoustic sensing gesture recognition system concerning time and physical memory usage. Accordingly, we established the following requirements: ten drawings per gesture at the most, and short training time, a maximum of two minutes per gesture. We defined, for the initial alphabet, three geometrical figures: circle, square, and triangle. Such a small initial alphabet thus prevents time-consuming training. Hence, at the beginning of the application, the user is notified to start drawing one of those figures.

In contrast, for training the recognition of four parts of the finger (tip, pad, nail, and knuckle), Tapsense [12] requires collecting per participant 200 data points for the mobile input set, 160 data points for the table finger set, and 280 data points for the table toolset. When training Hambone [14] to recognize more than 3–4 gestures, the HMM training sessions become extremely tedious. The authors of Tapsense and Hambone found that user boredom and fatigue became problematic in a longer study duration. Furthermore, an excessive number of gestures in the dictionary may lead to high computational costs.

4. Experiments

This section describes experiments in order to evaluate the performance of the proposed methods and analyzes them using the machine learning techniques ANN and HMM.

4.1. Artificial Neural Networks Experiment

Finding an optimal setup for neural networks is challenging because many parameters have to be considered. Determining the optimal number of hidden layers and neurons for all classifiers is a crucial aspect. If the network's complexity is too low to model the dataset's characteristics, the error rates are higher. If the complexity is too high, extended training and recall times are the consequence [16].

Hence, to train the ANN, we collected ten drawings of each gesture (circle, square, and triangle). Subsequently, all of the data were concatenated to be used as input for MATLAB's Neural Net Pattern Recognition Toolbox. The configuration offered by this toolbox is a two-layer feed-forward network with sigmoid hidden and softmax output neurons. The network is trained with scaled conjugate gradient backpropagation. By setting the number of neurons in the hidden layer to 10 neurons, we had the best performance, because we have minimized the cross-entropy while constraining overfitting. If more than ten neutrons were placed in the hidden layer, the model started to overfit the data and decrease the estimation accuracy.

4.1.1. Dataset for ANN

Achieving a high generalization in one neural network is challenging due to the differences that were observed in our dataset's scratching styles. The complexity of the optimal topology is possibly too high to be sufficiently trained, given our limited set of training samples. For that reason, we had to process the signal that was presented to train the neural network.

4.1.2. Raw Time Signal

The first dataset we have used to train the ANN was the raw time signal, as shown in Figure 2. We can see the difference between the square (Figure 2b) and the triangle (Figure 2c) due to the difference in the number of peaks related to the stops at the edges of the drawing. However for the ANN, all of these peaks representing the gesture in the surface (Figure 2) make the ANN classification more complex, because each gesture will have a completely different number and position of peaks and grooves.

Another complicating factor for the neural network is that each person can start the gesture at a different time, making it difficult for the ANN to identify this first peak and classify the signal correctly because each gesture possibly starts at a different time instant. Accordingly, with this dataset, we only had 33% of success.

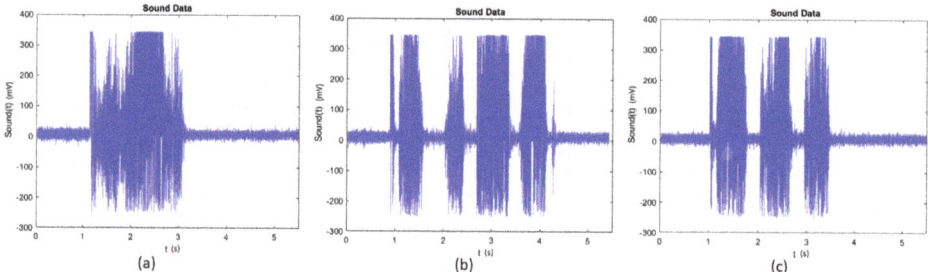

Figure 2. (a) Time signal for Circle. (b) Time signal for Square. (c) Time signal for Triangle.

4.1.3. FFT Signal

The second dataset attempt to train the ANN was using the Fast Fourier Transform (FFT) signal, as shown in Figure 3, but it was even harder for the ANN to make the recognition and we had a success rate of 15%.

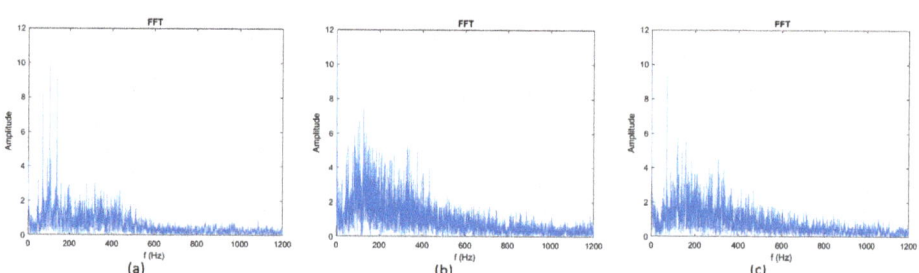

Figure 3. (a) Fast Fourier Transform (FFT) signal for Circle. (b) FFT signal for Square. (c) FFT signal for Triangle.

4.1.4. Envelope Time Signal

We have decided to process the raw time signal, as the FFT signal's performance was worse than that of the raw time signal in the ANN training set. We have used the envelope MATLAB function that returns the upper and lower root-mean-square envelopes of the time signal. The envelope is determined using a sliding window of 200 samples, defined by the author. A sliding window greater than 200 samples results in a signal not generalized enough for the ANN. A sliding window smaller than 200 samples results in a signal which does not preserve the raw signal's original shape. As shown in Figure 4, the output of the envelope function is greater than or equal to zero, because it returns the root-mean-square envelope of the time signal. The 200 samples sliding window smooths the peaks and preserves the signal shape. Accordingly, it will be more general for the ANN to recognize the gesture, but we still have the problem of when the gesture started to be drawn. For this dataset, we had a success rate of 65%.

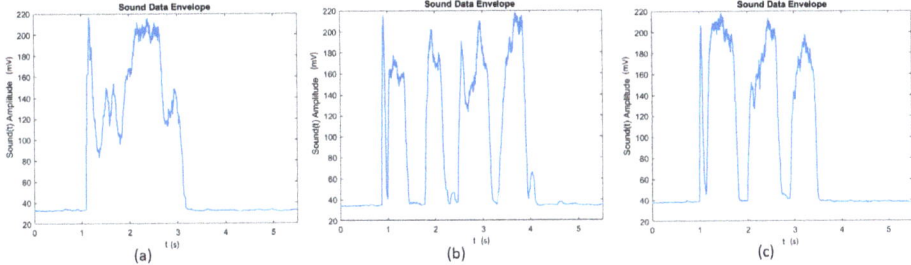

Figure 4. (a) Envelope time signal for the Circle. (b) Envelope time signal for the Square. (c) Envelope time signal for the Triangle.

4.1.5. Time Scaled Envelope Signal

Finally, we have time scaled the envelope signal employing the algorithm developed in this work and presented in Figure 5. In this data set, we first identify the initial touch, when considering that there is a peak every time the finger touches the surface, and we shift this data set to time 0 (zero). We identify the last touch, and we time scale the data set to the time interval [0, 1], with 100 samples in between. Thus, the instant that the user begins to draw is no longer relevant. The second improvement was making the algorithm robust to the drawing speed, because users have different rhythms. We used time scaling to maintain the time scale of the data across different datasets.

Furthermore, all of the data sets were the same length of 100 samples. With the find peaks MATLAB function, and the options MinPeakHeight and MinPeakDistance, we could find peaks that had a minimum amplitude and ignored peaks that were very close to each other. Therefore, we have smoothed the peaks and preserved the initial shape of the signal. All of these improvements made it much easier for the ANN recognition task with the enhanced signals shown in Figure 6. Hence, for this dataset, we had the highest accuracy of 90% of success.

Table 1 presents the rate of success of each dataset evaluated to train the neural network. As explained before, the best result was with the time-scaled envelope signal, making it easier for the ANN recognition task.

Table 1. Success rate results for the different datasets that trained the ANN.

Signal	Success Rate
Raw time signal	33.00%
FFT signal	15.00%
Envelope signal	65.00%
Time scaled envelope signal	90.00%

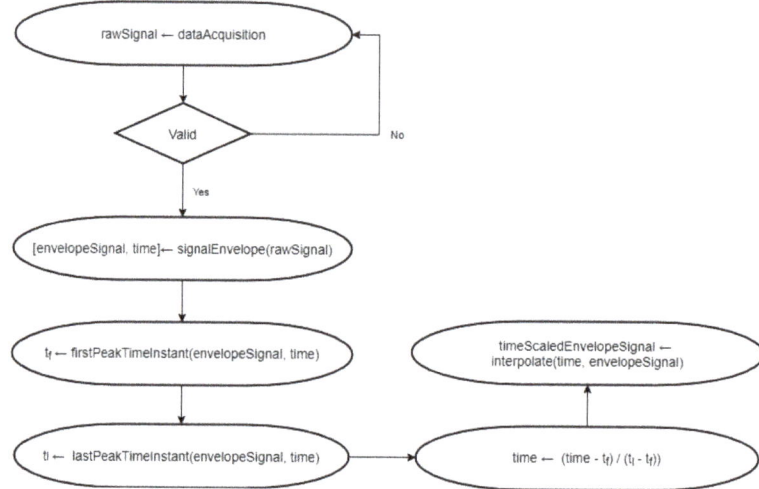

Figure 5. Proposed algorithm for processing the signal.

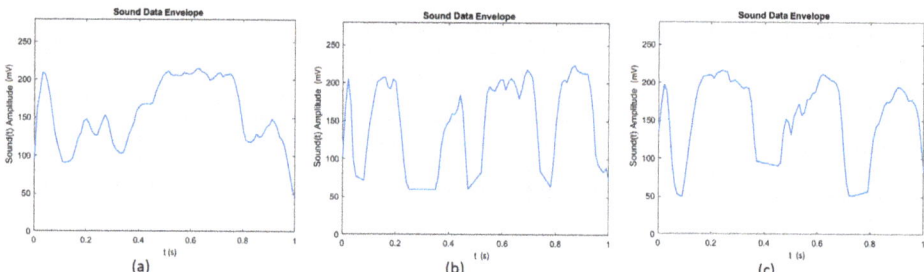

Figure 6. (a) Time scaled envelope signal for Circle. (b) Time scaled envelope signal for Square. (c) Time scaled envelope signal for Triangle.

From Figure 7, one can observe the development of the signal processing for the circle, from the raw signal in time until the time-scaled envelope signal that was evaluated by the algorithm proposed by the authors, as explained in Figure 5. We can see the improvements, as in Figure 7a, we have many more samples (more than 15,000) in the drawing, more peaks, and grooves, and the signal is not general enough for the ANN to have a high (above 85%) recognition rate. In Figure 7b, we have a cleaner signal, with fewer samples and peaks, although we still cannot be general to realize when the drawing has started or the speed of the drawing. Finally, in Figure 7c, we observe the time-scaled envelope signal with only 100 samples. The proposed algorithm smooths the peaks and preserves the initial shape of the signal.

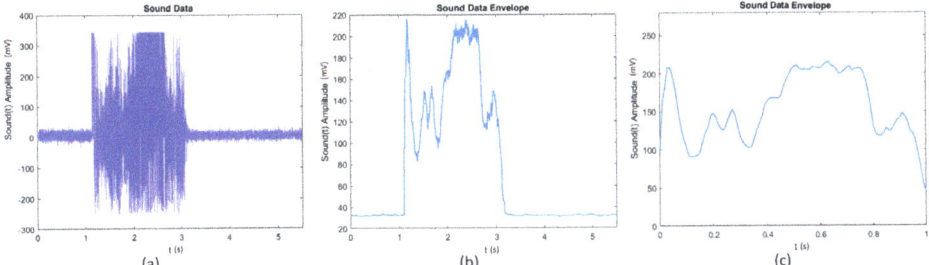

Figure 7. (a) Time signal for Circle. (b) Time envelope signal for Circle. (c) Time scaled envelope signal for Circle.

4.2. Hidden Markov Models Experiment

A stochastic approach for modeling an acoustic-based input is the Hidden Markov Model technique. A first-order Markov model is a finite set of states, where transitions between states are modeled by a transition probability matrix A, while assuming that the probability of being in state S_i at time t only depends on the state occupied at time $t-1$. If the state probability vector π is known for $t = 0$, the probability vector for the next observation moments can be recursively computed by [17]:

$$\pi_t = A \times \pi_{t-1} \tag{1}$$

$$\pi_t = A_0^t \tag{2}$$

The state sequence of a Hidden Markov Model cannot be observed directly (hidden), and only the observation sequence is known. A Probability Density Function describes the probability of P_i for the observation vector, given that the process is in a given state [17].

Over the past years, hidden Markov modeling has been one of the most popular and effective modeling techniques for acoustic time series. The HMMs are suitable for the classification from one or two-dimensional signals and it can be used when the information is incomplete or uncertain [18]. The reasons why this method has become so popular are the inherent (mathematically accurate) statistical structure; the facility and availability of training algorithms to estimate model parameters from finite sets of speech data training; the flexibility of the resulting recognition system in which you can easily change the size, type, or model architecture to suit words and sounds [19].

Taking into account that the acoustic speech signal has characteristics that are similar to the acoustic signal produced when a nail is dragged over a surface, previous works on speech recognition using HMMs were used as a basis and inspiration for this experiment. It is worth mentioning that the acoustic signal structure is similar, but the complexity of the signal dragged by a nail as compared to the speech signal is lower, since it is neither necessary to search for a range of phonemes nor to have a large database to train the model.

The choice of a topological configuration and the number of states in the model generally reflect the prior knowledge of the specific sound source to be modeled and is not related to mathematical treatability or implementation considerations [19]. The ideal number of states is best determined by executing experiments, because the relationship between the number of states and the HMM performance is very imprecise.

Luigi Rosa [20] proposed a fast and reliable algorithm for speech recognition based on Hidden Markov Models. The proposed approach uses frequency-related features robust to most types of noise.

The topological structure of the HMM implemented is left-right. These settings were pre-chosen by the toolbox of Luigi Rosa and his team [20] because they present good results in recognizing gestures on surfaces. We choose the left-right topology, because the gesture starts and ends in well-identified moments, and a sequential HMM well represents the sequential behavior of the movement.

We developed an application in MATLAB to support gesture data collection and hidden Markov model training. For each gesture, the application prompts the user to start drawing, and then records the microphone signal for a three-second interval and saves it as a .wav extension by the audio write MATLAB function. Once recording completes, the system asks the user whether it should retain the particular drawing. After the application collects five drawings for a particular gesture, it repeats the same data collection process with the next gesture. After collecting data for all three gestures (circle, square, and triangle), the application generates a hidden Markov gesture model via the Luigi Rosa toolbox [20].

Figure 8 presents Luigi Rosa interface toolbox in MATLAB. We used the tab *Add a new sound from files* to train the model (it only accepts .wav file extensions).

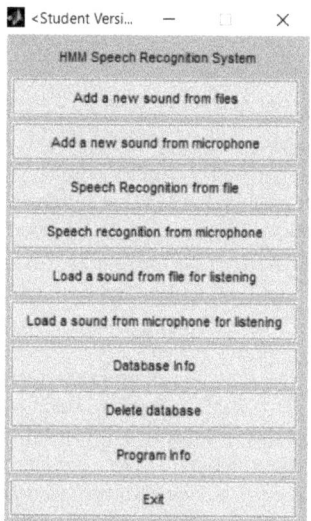

Figure 8. Luigi Rosa [20] interface toolbox in MATLAB.

The first dataset attempt to train the HMM was the raw time signal, such as for the ANN. We added five drawings for each gesture. Subsequently, using the tab *Speech recognition from file* in Luigi Rosa toolbox [20], we loaded a new sample to be recognized, and we obtained a recognition rate of 90%.

5. Discussion

We address the research questions and the limitations of our proposed platform in this section when considering the literature review and the experimental results presented in this work.

5.1. Addressing RQ1

The *RQ1* is widely addressed in the Acoustic sensing Related Works Section. Nevertheless, based on the related works presented, this section considers the tools that this work uses in more detail.

This paper has no intention of developing the toolboxes to train and build the neural network or the Markov model. Our focus is on the hardware and the embedded software development to acquire and process the signal and improve and test the datasets to feed the models. We used MATLAB's Neural Net Pattern Recognition Toolbox to train the network using scaled conjugate gradient backpropagation. In this toolbox, we can choose the network parameters, such as the number of neurons in the pattern recognition network's hidden layer, select samples for validation and testing, and it is possible to evaluate the ANN performance while using cross-entropy and confusion matrices.

If the network's performance is not good enough, we can train it again, adjust the network size, or even import a larger data set to improve the network performance.

For the HMM, we have researched and found some toolboxes for speech recognition, such as the Georgia Tech Gesture Toolkit (GT2k) [21] and the gpdsHMM [18]. However, we had some issues in making them work, and we could not find support. Subsequently, we have tried the MATLAB toolbox implemented by the team of Luigi Rosa [20]. Accordingly, after collecting data for all of the gestures, the application generates a hidden Markov gesture model via Speech Recognition using Hidden Markov Models by Luigi Rosa [20]. We exchanged information with the Luigi Rosa team, and it was straightforward to make it work. Nevertheless, differently from the ANN toolbox, we have used, in this one, we can only supply the data to train the model, and we cannot choose any other parameter of the model. Therefore, the ANN toolbox is more configurable, gives the user more freedom to choose the parameters, and provides graphs that make it possible to evaluate the network's performance.

5.2. Addressing RQ2

A central question when developing systems using machine learning is how much data are needed for training before accuracy levels off. In our work, we have chosen the target precision rate of at least 90%, taking into account the precision rates from most of the related works: 89.5% from Scratch input [13], 90–95% from Hambone [14], 95% from Tapsense[12], 78.4% from Pentelligence [9], 75% from Stane [8], and 91.3% from Ipanel [10]. We have tried the raw time signal and then the FFT signal for the ANN. The latter had the worst performance. We have then processed the raw time signal by taking the envelope and made some improvements such as interpolation to make the peaks and grooves smoother. After all these attempts, we have reached a success rate of 90%, using for each gesture a ten drawings dataset, each composed of 100 samples, 1000 samples per gesture. Finally, for the HMM, we have achieved a success rate higher than 90% by training the model with the raw time signal and five drawings of each gesture, each drawing composed of 15,000 samples, which is, 75,000 samples per gesture.

Consequently, the choice of the dataset and the number of drawings for each machine learning technique is essential. For some drawings, the HMM has mistaken the square for the triangle and vice versa, but for the circle, we had a 100% successful recognition. It is essential to point out that HMM with a smaller number of drawings per gesture, shorter time to train, and smaller computational cost, then the ANN achieved the best precision rate.

5.3. Addressing RQ3

A previous work that inspired us was the Ipanel [10], because we have the same problems of tracking the acoustic signals that are generated by sliding fingers on a surface, and Ipanel's reached a robust performance against different levels of ambient noise and varying surface material. However, Ipanel [10] transformed the features into images and then employed the CNN to recognize the finger movement on the table. We have also tried to develop a CNN in this work, with MATLAB Deep Learning Toolbox. However, to train a network from scratch, the architect is required to define the number of layers and filters, along with other tunable parameters. Training an accurate model from scratch also requires massive amounts of data, on the order of millions of samples ([Online] The MathWorks, Inc, "Convolutional Neural Network" Available: Footnotes are not allowed in this journal, we moved it to here, please confirm. https://www.mathworks.com/solutions/deep-learning/convolutional-neural-network.html, accessed 28 December 2019).

Deep neural networks with a higher amount of training data and different topologies can achieve high recognition rates, as well as the impact of different surfaces or background noises [9]. Nevertheless, as we were looking for a simple and low computational cost solution, the CNN approach (or any deep neural network) turned out to be much more laborious, because of the need for this huge dataset and the longer time to train the network.

Similarly, works, like TapSense [12], also inspired us. For the classification, they use the SVM technique provided in the Weka machine learning toolkit. However, as we can see in their works, training this classifier requires the collection of over 160 data points per gesture. Moreover, SVM also has some weakness when applied to tasks with low computational effort requirement, due to the large memory requirement and computation time of this training algorithm [22]. Consequently, the need for thousands of samples to train the model and the high computational effort would not fit our requirement of at most ten drawings per gesture and short training time (maximum of 2 min per gesture). These SVM limitations led us to try other techniques, such as HMM and ANN.

When considering the success rates for both machine learning techniques presented in Section 4, we achieved the highest success rate through the Markov model technique, which indicates that the proposed solution with HMM is simpler to implement and train than the ANN technique, and it is sufficient to solve the problem stated in the research questions. Therefore, HMM with a smaller dataset, shorter time to train, and computational cost lower than ANN achieved the best result.

5.4. Discussion in How to Embed the HMM Trained into the Low-Cost Hardware

In this section, we discuss how to generate code from the trained HMM automatically, cross-compile it, and then embed it into low-cost hardware. Thus, after training, the system would be independent of MATLAB software, which has a higher cost.

The first step is the installation of the hardware support package in Simulink. Second, develop the model, as shown in Figure 9. In this model, the Analog input acquires the raw signal. If the signal value is greater than 60, which means that someone is drawing on the surface, the *Compare To Constant* block applies a True value into the import *In1* of the *Enable Subsystem* block, which has a memory block saving the raw signal during three seconds. The raw signal is then fed into the hidden Markov model previously generated through the MATLAB HMMModel function. Finally, the gesture recognition result (circle, triangle, or square) is printed on the serial output by the *Serial Transmit* block.

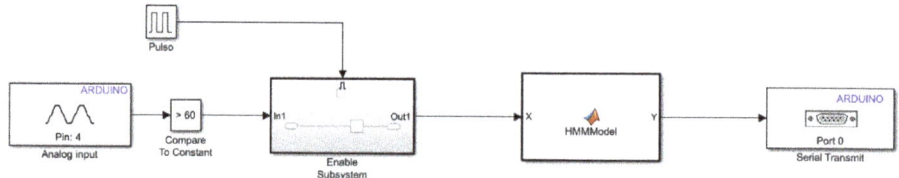

Figure 9. Model developed in Simulink to embedded on the hardware.

It is necessary to load, on the Arduino Nano, 25 MATLAB files, which exceed 140 KB, with a specific input and output relationships, generated by Luigi Rosa's toolbox [20]. Hence, it is crucial to consider the memory specifications of the microcontroller that the developed HMM is to be embedded.

5.5. Limitations

We had some limitations on our platform, as we set our goal to use simple hardware and low computational cost for the machine learning algorithm. First, the maximum level of ambient noise had to be 45 dB. We chose the aluminum surface to carry out the experiments because of its high speed of sound propagation, and the use of stethoscopes to acquire sounds was crucial, because it provides a high level of suppression of environmental noise. Second, we used a simple initial alphabet of geometrical figures: circle, square, and triangle.

We found that small variations in sensor placement caused significant variations in signal characteristics. Thus, repeatable sensor placement is critical for practical inter-session training and recognition.

6. Conclusions

In this paper, we presented the design of a low-cost acoustic sensing gesture recognition system based on surface scratch input. In the context of the design, we validated the robustness of the HMM technique to recognizing gestures on surfaces and with low computational costs concerning time and physical memory use. We obtained at least a 90% success rate with five drawings per gesture, and a short training time, a maximum of two minutes per gesture.

Besides the design of the system, we focused on processing the dataset that trains the models to achieve better performance. To do so, we implemented two machine learning techniques, namely ANN and HMM, to support answering the research questions. The solution proposed with the HMM classifier is simpler to implement and train than the ANN technique and it is sufficient to solve the problem. For the training stage, with five drawings per gesture and the raw time signal, the HMM achieved a success rate of 90%. Therefore, the HMM with a smaller number of drawings, shorter signal processing time, and training time obtained the best result. The results also demonstrated the importance of data representation for the efficient processing of sensory information for the ANNs.

In future work, we are investigating the use of multiple microphones for the physical sensing setup providing an extension of using location and improve the classification precision. Additionally, a hardware implementation, e.g., FPGA (Field Programmable Gate Array), can be considered.

Author Contributions: Conceptualization, B.S.M.; Formal analysis, A.P. and S.O.D.L.; Investigation, B.S.M., A.P. and S.O.D.L.; Methodology, A.P. and S.O.D.L.; Project administration, A.P. and S.O.D.L.; Software, B.S.M.; Supervision, A.P. and S.O.D.L.; Writing—original draft, B.S.M.; Writing—review & editing, A.P., S.O.D.L. and B.S.M. All authors have read and agreed to the published version of the manuscript.

Funding: This research was funded by CNPq (Brazilian National Research Council) grant.

Acknowledgments: The authors would like to thank the CNPq for the financial support and everyone from the LIEC (Electronic Instrumentation and Control Laboratory UFCG) and Embedded (Embedded Systems and Pervasive Computing Laboratory) who supported the development of this work. We also thank COPELE (Graduate Course in Electrical Engineering), Federal University of Campina Grande, Brazil.

Conflicts of Interest: The authors declare no conflict of interest.

References

1. Lopes, P.; Jota, R.; Jorge, J.A. Augmenting touch interaction through acoustic sensing. In Proceedings of the ACM International Conference on Interactive Tabletops and Surfaces 2011, Kobe, Japan, 13–16 November 2011; ACM: New York, NY, USA, 2011; pp. 53–56.
2. Yin, H.; Zhou, A.; Liu, L.; Wang, N.; Ma, H. Ubiquitous Writer: Robust Text Input for Small Mobile Devices via Acoustic Sensing. *IEEE Int. Things J.* **2019**, *6*, 5285–5296. [CrossRef]
3. Luo, G.; Yang, P.; Chen, M.; Li, P. HCI on the Table: Robust Gesture Recognition Using Acoustic Sensing in Your Hand. *IEEE Access* **2020**, *8*, 31481–31498. [CrossRef]
4. Alonso-Martín, F.; Gamboa-Montero, J.J.; Castillo, J.C.; Castro-González, Á.; Salichs, M.Á. Detecting and Classifying Human Touches in a Social Robot Through Acoustic Sensing and Machine Learning. *Sensors* **2017**, *17*, 1138. [CrossRef] [PubMed]
5. Chou, T.-R.; Lo, J.-C. Research on tangible acoustic interface and its applications. In Proceedings of the 2nd International Conference on Computer Science and Electronics Engineering, Hangzhou, China, 22–23 March 2013; Atlantis Press: Amsterdam, The Netherlands, 2013.
6. Soldado, P.M.G. Toolkit for Gesture Classification through Acoustic Sensing. Master's Thesis, Técnico Lisboa, Lisboa, Portugal, 2015.
7. Rekimoto, J. Smartskin: An infrastructure for freehand manipulation on interactive surfaces. In Proceedings of the SIGCHI Conference on Human Factors in Computing Systems, Minneapolis, MN, USA, 20–25 April 2002; ACM: New York, NY, USA, 2002; pp. 113–120.
8. Murray-Smith, R.; Williamson, J.; Hughes, S.; Quaade, T. Stane: Synthesized surfaces for tactile input. In Proceedings of the SIGCHI Conference on Human Factors in Computing Systems, Florence, Italy, 5–10 April 2008; ACM: New York, NY, USA, 2008; pp. 1299–1302.

9. Schrapel, M.; Stadler, M.-L.; Rohs, M. Pentelligence: Combining pen tip motion and writing sounds for handwritten digit recognition. In Proceedings of the 2018 CHI Conference on Human Factors in Computing Systems, Montreal, QC, Canada, 21–26 April 2018; ACM: New York, NY, USA, 2018; pp. 1–11.
10. Chen, M.; Yang, P.; Xiong, J.; Zhang, M.; Lee, Y.; Xiang, C.; Tian, C. Your table can be an input panel: Acoustic-based device-free interaction recognition. *Proc. ACM Interact. Mob. Wearable Ubiquitous Technol.* **2019**, *3*, 1–21. [CrossRef]
11. Harrison, C.; Tan, D.; Morris, D.; Starner, T. Skinput: Appropriating the body as an input surface. In Proceedings of the SIGCHI Conference on Human Factors in Computing Systems, Atlanta, GA, USA, 10–15 April 2010; ACM: New York, NY, USA, 2010; pp. 453–462.
12. Harrison, C.; Schwarz, J.; Hudson, S.E. Tapsense: Enhancing finger interaction on touch surfaces. In Proceedings of the 24th Annual ACM Symposium on User Interface Software and Technology, Santa Barbara, CA, USA, 16–19 October 2011; ACM: New York, NY, USA, 2011; pp. 627–636.
13. Harrison, C.; Hudson, S.E. Scratch input: Creating large, inexpensive, unpowered and mobile finger input surfaces. In Proceedings of the 21st Annual ACM Symposium on User Interface Software and Technology, Monterey, CA, USA, 19–22 October 2008; ACM: New York, NY, USA, 2008; pp. 205–208.
14. Deyle, T.; Palinko, S.; Poole, E.S.; Starner, T. Hambone: A bio-acoustic gesture interface. In Proceedings of the 2007 11th IEEE International Symposium on Wearable Computers, Boston, MA, USA, 11–13 October 2007; pp. 3–10.
15. Braun, A.; Krepp, S.; Kuijper, A. Acoustic tracking of hand activities on surfaces. In Proceedings of the 2nd International Workshop on Sensor-Based Activity Recognition and Interaction, Rostock, Germany, 24–25 June 2015; ACM: New York, NY, USA, 2015; pp. 1–5.
16. Vujicic, T.; Matijevic, T.; Ljucovic, J.; Balota, A.; Sevarac, Z. Comparative analysis of methods for determining number of hidden neurons in artificial neural network. In Proceedings of the 27th Central European Conference on Information and Intelligent Systems (CECIIS 2016), Varazdin, Croatia, 21–23 September 2016; Faculty of Organization and Informatics Varazdin: Varaždin, Croatia, 2016; pp. 219–223.
17. Price, J.; Eydgahi, A. Design of MATLAB-based automatic speaker recognition systems. In Proceedings of the 9th International Conference on Engineering Education-T4J-1, San Juan, Puerto Rico, 23–28 July 2006.
18. David, S.; Ferrer, M.; Travieso, C.; Alonso, J.B. gpdsHMM: A hidden Markov model toolbox in the MATLAB environment. In Proceedings of the Complex Systems, Intelligence and Modern Technological Applications Conference, Cherbourg, France, 19–22 September 2004; pp. 476–479.
19. Juang, B.H.; Rabiner, L.R. Hidden markov models for speech recognition. *Technometrics* **1991**, *33*, 251–272. [CrossRef]
20. Rosa, L. Speech Recognition Using Hidden Markov Models. Available online: http://www.advancedsourcecode.com/hmmspeech.asp (accessed on 3 December 2019).
21. Westeyn, T.; Brashear, H.; Atrash, A.; Starner, T. Georgia tech gesture toolkit: Supporting experiments in gesture recognition. In Proceedings of the International Conference on Multimodal Interfaces, Vancouver, BC, Canada, 5–7 November 2003; ACM: New York, NY, USA, 2003; pp. 85–92.
22. Lopes, C.; Perdigão, F. Event detection by HMM, SVM and ANN: A comparative study. In Proceedings of the International Conference on Computational Processing of the Portuguese Language, Canela, Brazil, 24–26 September 2018; Springer: Aveiro, Portugal, 2008; pp. 1–10.

© 2020 by the authors. Licensee MDPI, Basel, Switzerland. This article is an open access article distributed under the terms and conditions of the Creative Commons Attribution (CC BY) license (http://creativecommons.org/licenses/by/4.0/).

Article

Development of Real-Time Hand Gesture Recognition for Tabletop Holographic Display Interaction Using Azure Kinect

Chanhwi Lee [1], Jaehan Kim [2], Seoungbae Cho [2], Jinwoong Kim [2], Jisang Yoo [1] and Soonchul Kwon [3,*]

[1] Department of Electronic Engineering, Kwangwoon University, Seoul 01897, Korea; chanheui0102@gmail.com (C.L.); jsyoo@kw.ac.kr (J.Y.)
[2] Electronics and Telecommunications Research Institute (ETRI), Daejeon 34129, Korea; kimjhan@etri.re.kr (J.K.); csb60237@etri.re.kr (S.C.); jwkim@etri.re.kr (J.K.)
[3] Graduate School of Smart Convergence, Kwangwoon University, Seoul 01897, Korea
* Correspondence: ksc0226@kw.ac.kr; Tel.: +82-2-940-8637

Received: 8 July 2020; Accepted:12 August 2020; Published: 14 August 2020

Abstract: The use of human gesturing to interact with devices such as computers or smartphones has presented several problems. This form of interaction relies on gesture interaction technology such as Leap Motion from Leap Motion, Inc, which enables humans to use hand gestures to interact with a computer. The technology has excellent hand detection performance, and even allows simple games to be played using gestures. Another example is the contactless use of a smartphone to take a photograph by simply folding and opening the palm. Research on interaction with other devices via hand gestures is in progress. Similarly, studies on the creation of a hologram display from objects that actually exist are also underway. We propose a hand gesture recognition system that can control the Tabletop holographic display based on an actual object. The depth image obtained using the latest Time-of-Flight based depth camera Azure Kinect is used to obtain information about the hand and hand joints by using the deep-learning model CrossInfoNet. Using this information, we developed a real time system that defines and recognizes gestures indicating left, right, up, and down basic rotation, and zoom in, zoom out, and continuous rotation to the left and right.

Keywords: azure kinect; deep-learning; gesture interaction; hand detection; hologram display

1. Introduction

Gesture interaction technology that measures and analyzes the movement of the user's body to control information devices or to link with content has been the topic of many studies [1–7]. Among them, the hand is the most easily used and is a medium capable of various formations owing to its high degree of freedom. Therefore, most gesture interactions include gestures that involve the use of the hands. Human interaction with a computer by way of gesturing relies on gesture interaction technology, representative examples of which are Azure Kinect and Leap Motion from Leap Motion, Inc. This technology enables gesture interaction to be used to easily control a variety of devices.

Recently, gesture recognition using a sensor such as Azure Kinect has been applied to a wide range of fields from smart home applications, medical applications, to automotive applications [8–13]. Through the gesture interaction of the smart home, household appliances are available without touching them directly. In medical applications, gesture interaction helps remote remedial exercise of burn patients to rehabilitate. In the automotive field, it is difficult for a driver to use a touch screen while driving. Gesture interaction allows drivers to control touch screen operations with gestures.

Tabletop holographic display is a device that allows the viewer to observe 3D hologram contents created from various angles with multiple cameras and view them anywhere from 360 degrees [14–16].

The system allows multiple viewers to view digital hologram images in the horizontal 360-degree direction by using digital micromirror device (DMD) capable of high-speed operation as a spatial light modulator (SLM). In addition, by applying a lenticular lens, holographic images can be viewed in a range of 15 degrees or more in the vertical direction. The device can display 22,000 binary hologram image data per second, with 1024 and 768 pixels in the horizontal and vertical directions, respectively.

A color hologram display device consisting of a total reflection prism illuminates the DMD and a prism capable of separating and recombining the three primary colors of light by applying three DMDs, a laser source emitting red, green and blue laser light, and the use of a fiber-based laser combination of the wavelengths 660, 532, and 473 nm. Because the holographic image is created by the interference of light, the hologram resulting from the tabletop holographic display must be observed in a dark environment from which all light is excluded. Therefore, in a dark environment without light, the display needs to be controlled by a computer to control the image displayed on the tabletop holographic display.

Since light is not present in the experimental environment, only depth information is used to develop gesture interaction using hand gestures. Thus, high accuracy hand detection using color information is not applicable. In this experiment, we use only the depth image with the high quality depth camera Azure Kinect. In addition, depth images are disturbed by structures such as optical components and eye-tracking cameras attached to tabletop holographic displays. To interact with the tabletop hologram display, we designed a new pipeline as shown in Figure 1. This pipeline is described in full in the next sections, beginning with the physical setup, to our proposed method for gesture interaction.

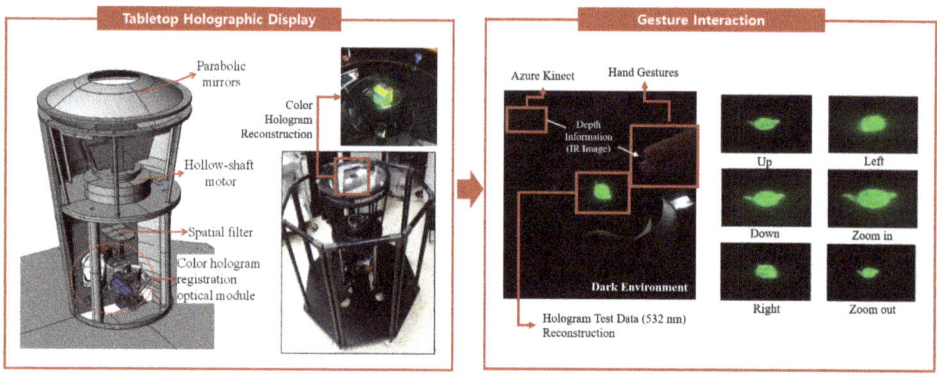

Figure 1. Overview of the gesture recognition for the tabletop holographic display.

2. Background Theory

2.1. Azure Kinect

3D depth recognition technology consists of stereo-type, structured light, and Time-of-Flight (ToF). Stereo-type uses a viewpoint mismatch between two 2D cameras, similar to the principle that a person measures distance using both eyes. The structured light method recognizes the depth by calculating the amount of change in a pattern by scanning a specific light pattern on an object. The ToF method recognizes depth by calculating the travel time of light reflected from an object. The ToF method can acquire a better depth quality than other methods in an indoor environment. Azure Kinect is a Microsoft's ToF-based depth camera released in 2019. Figure 2a shows the configuration of Azure Kinect. Azure Kinect provides high quality depth information. Figure 2b shows the Azure Kinect view field. Depth Narrow-Field of view (NFOV) is a mode that provides depth information of a narrow area, and Depth Wide-Field of view (WFOV) is a mode that provides depth information of a wide area.

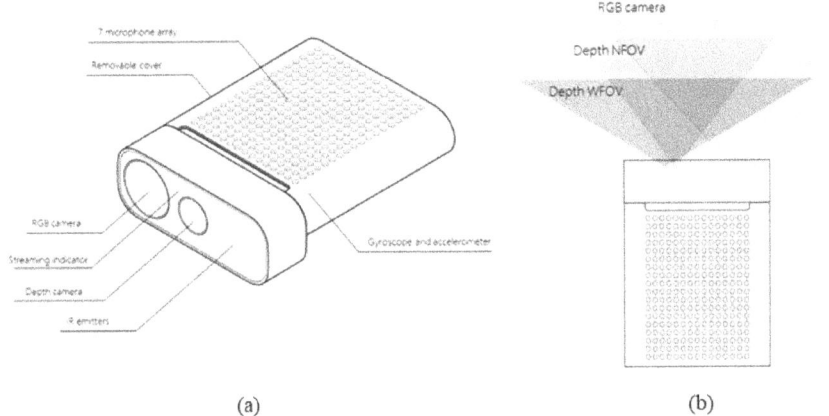

Figure 2. Azure Kinect. (**a**) Azure Kinect configuration; (**b**) Azure Kinect view field. (source: www.docs.microsoft.com)

2.2. Gesture Interaction

Gesture interaction takes place when a user makes a gesture to command a device such as a computer. In other words, it entails noncontact interaction between the user and the computer. Among the human limbs, the hand is the most easily used and is a medium capable of conveying various expressions; thus, gesture interaction mostly occurs by using hand gesture interaction, which requires the use of the hands. Hand gesture interaction necessitates accurate hand detection and hand joint information [17,18].

CrossInfoNet [19] is a deep learning model that detects hands using depth information. Figure 3 shows the structure of CrossInfoNet. Unlike other existing models that detect the entire hand image to find joint information [20–25], CrossInfoNet detects the entire hand once, and then redetects the palm and fingers, respectively. First, the entire hand is detected to obtain approximate finger and palm joint information. The acquired palm and finger joint information is re-extracted from each of the two different branches. The joint information that is found again is transferred to the other branch. In other words, the information about the palm of the hand is delivered to the branch where the finger is found, and the information about the finger is transferred to the branch on which the palm is found. The branch containing the palm information also contains rough palm joint information received via a skip connection together with details of fine finger information shared with the palm joint information. When these types of information are subtracted, the coarse palm information and the fine palm information disappear, and only the fine finger information remains. In this way, finger joint information is obtained. In addition, in the branch in which the finger is found precisely, subtracting is performed using the approximate finger joint information received via the skip connection, the finger joint information found finely, and the sophisticated palm information shared. The result is elaborate palm information. Finger and palm information obtained by using this process is continuously shared with each finding as learning progresses, resulting in more accurate finger and palm joint information. The joint information of the last finger and palm joint is acquired to obtain the joint information of the entire hand. When hand detection and hand joint information are obtained, it is defined using the hand joint information obtained by the user.

It is important that each gesture should be defined such that it is intuitive and easy for the user to learn [26]. As a good example, operating a smartphone is similar to the operations performed when handling a book or paper in real life, such as switching the screen by swiping to the next page or pushing and lowering it, thus users are easily able to use the phone without the need to learn. Gesture interaction allows users to control the device they intend using without having to touch the mouse, keyboard, remote control, or screen. In addition, people with disabilities can control the device with simple hand gestures, thereby improving usability and convenience. In addition, gesture interaction is useful in situations in which it is difficult to operate other devices, such as a doctor working in an operating room while wearing work gloves.

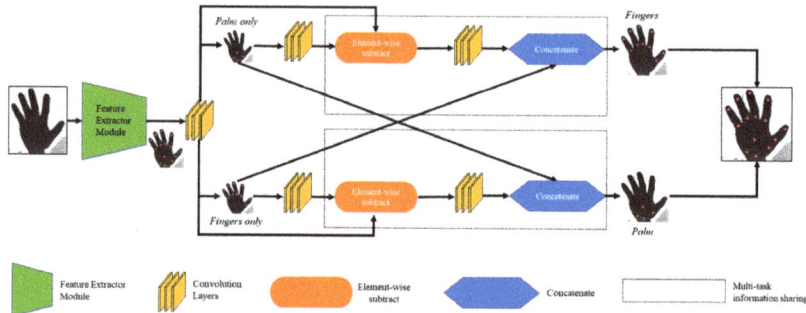

Figure 3. CrossInfoNet structure.

3. Proposed Method

3.1. System Configuration

When the gesture determined in the video is input to the server using UDP/IP socket communication, the server transmits the corresponding hologram to the sending end. The hologram reads the received signal and shows the hologram display corresponding to the signal. The 3D hologram data created via computer-generated holography (CGH) are stored in the hologram data storage section. The information of the user's hand gesture obtained from the Azure Kinect video is transferred to the Interaction Controller section using UDP/IP socket communication. In the Interaction Controller section, the hologram sending unit requests new hologram contents that have undergone appropriate actions for the corresponding gesture. The hologram transmitter that receives the request displays the hologram image with the gesture on the 360-degree Viewable Tabletop Holographic Display. The user can observe the new hologram display by viewing the gesture action taken in real time. Figure 4 shows the overall structure of the 3D holographic display system capable of interacting with hand gestures.

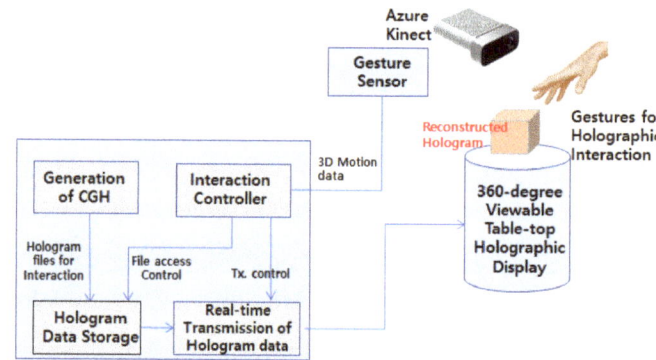

Figure 4. Block diagram of real-time interactive holographic display by hand gestures.

3.2. Proposed Gesture Interaction

Color information is used for most high performance hand detection models [27]. However, color information cannot be used in the tabletop holographic display environment. Therefore, using only depth information, the characteristics of the tabletop holographic display installed in many other structures are taken into account. Then, the necessary depth information is retrieved using background subtraction and Region of Interest (ROI) to detect the hand. The ROI is the area limited to processing only the region of interest in the image. Furthermore, gestures are defined using the joint information of the detected hand. Then, when a gesture corresponding to the subject's motion is detected, the gesture prediction is output in real time. The system was designed to operate with a delay of one second between gestures. Figure 5 shows the framework of the hand gesture recognition system based on depth frames.

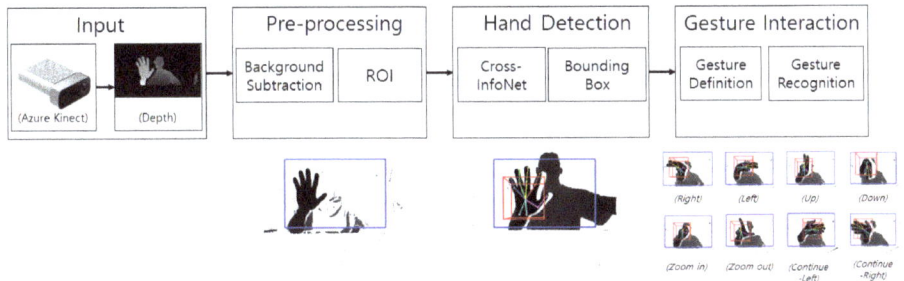

Figure 5. Framework of the hand gesture recognition system based on depth frames.

3.2.1. Background Subtraction

We use the depth difference between the first frame and the next frame when the image is turned on, and we used a threshold to obtain the depth information of the image when it exceeds the threshold. Figure 6 shows the background subtraction method. When the camera is turned on, only the background or structures other than the user are present on the screen in the first frame that is received. Thereafter, the user exists in the incoming frames, and the depth difference is continuously calculated from the first frame. The background and surrounding structures are erased using only the depth information of the image with a depth difference value exceeding a predetermined threshold, it becomes the image in which only the depth information of the user and the user's hand exists.

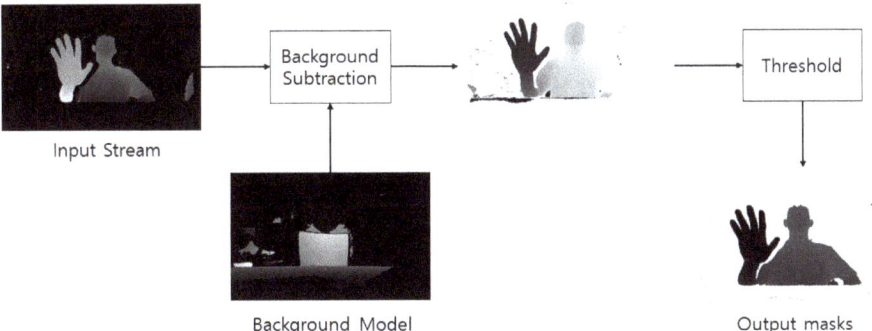

Figure 6. Background subtraction.

In a tabletop holographic display using Azure Kinect, the bottom part of the tabletop is closer than the hand. In addition, several cameras for gaze tracking are attached to the tabletop holographic display, which also causes depth information and interferes with accurate hand detection. Therefore, the depth information of the remaining parts except the moving person has to be erased. Thus, the depth information of the background and the structure is erased using background subtraction [28].

3.2.2. Set ROI

The background and structure were erased with background subtraction. However, a certain amount of noise remains, thus the ROI is set such that the hand can be detected only within the ROI. In the holographic display environment, the position of the camera and the position at which the gesture is made is always constant, thus the ROI is set statically. The mouse pointer is dragged to where the person actually stands in the image to find the coordinates. The ROI is drawn based on these coordinates.

3.2.3. Hand Detection and Bounding Box

Background subtraction erases the depth of the surrounding structures and uses only the depth information of the user to find the user's hand in the ROI using CrossInfoNet. We trained CrossInfoNet with the NYU hand dataset. As a result, information on 14 joints of the hands, including the center of the palm, can be obtained. The information of each of the 14 joints includes x, y, and z information. After the hand is detected, a bounding box is drawn based on the center of the hand. Bounding box is necessary to visualize the threshold of outputting the up, down, left, right, continuous rotation left and right gestures. The bounding box was drawn as large as the threshold in each of the up, down, left, and right directions, centering on the hand. In addition, the front and back were drawn with the size of 15cm around the hand. Thus, this bounding box was drawn in consideration of the threshold used when recognizing the gesture, and when the finger passes over this bounding box, the corresponding gesture is output.

3.2.4. Gesture Definition and Gesture Recognition

Eight possible gestures can be made: basic rotation up, down, left, right, and zoom in, zoom out, and continuous rotation to the left and right. Figure 7 shows 8 hand gestures. First, the basic rotation is divided into the motion of swiping the index finger and middle finger all the way up, down, left, and right. Intuitively, when swiping in the up, down, left, and right directions, the same gestures as swiping directions are output. Second, the thumb and index finger are used to zoom in and out. The distance between the thumb and forefinger is collected, and the two fingers are spread apart to output the gesture of zooming in. Spreading the thumb and index finger and pinching the two fingers together outputs a zoom out action. Lastly, continuous rotation to the left and right is recognized as a gesture of spreading all fingers and swiping to the left and right.

Each gesture was defined using the relative positional relationship of 14 joints obtained from the result of hand detection, the inner product for each finger, and the distance between fingers. The inner product uses the vector inner product between each finger and the center of the finger and hand. We normalized the value of the inner product from -1 to 1. When a finger is bent, the value of the inner product becomes a negative value close to -1 by the nature of the inner product of the vector, and when the finger is not included, the value of the inner product of the vector approaches 1. This method is used to distinguish gestures based on whether they are bent or stretched for each of the five fingers.

Up, down, left, and right gestures are output when the relative positions of the middle, upper, lower, left, and right joints of the middle finger relative to the center of the hand exceed the threshold, and the inner product of the ring finger and the palm of each finger is negative. The zoom-in and zoom-out gestures use a heap-like arrangement, which continuously stores the distance between the thumb and index finger. When the distance value between the two fingers stacked in the array shows a tendency to increase to exceed the threshold, a zoom in gesture is displayed, and if this distance decreases to exceed the threshold, a zoom out gesture is output. In continuous rotation to the left and right gestures, for all five fingers, the inner product value of the vector with the palm exceeds the threshold, and unlike basic left and right rotation, the ring finger and the little finger are also positioned relative to the palm center. When each threshold is exceeded, a gesture is output. Because the rotation gesture overlaps with the basic left and right gestures and the continuous left and right gestures, it is classified by using the inner product of the vector between the finger and the palm, respectively.

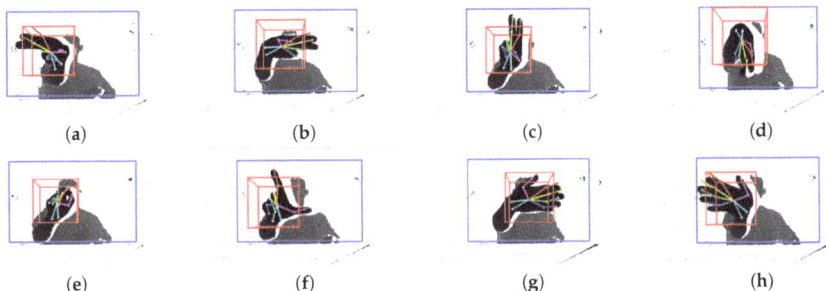

Figure 7. 8 hand gestures. (**a**) Left; (**b**) Right; (**c**) Up; (**d**) Down; (**e**) Zoom-out; (**f**) Zoom-in; (**g**) Continuous rotation right; (**h**) Continuous rotation left.

4. Experiment Method

In the experiment, a hologram using only a green laser was used. We conducted experiments at various distances. First, We experimented with 10 people on a total of 8 features we defined. Figure 8a shows the environment of the tabletop holographic display. All the subjects were aware of the gesture operation method and the delay of 1 second and conducted 10 experiments per gesture. All subjects were tested in the same test environment. As shown in Figure 8b, the distance between the camera and the subject's hand was kept constant at 35–50 cm. The subject performed the experiment in line with the Azure Kinect installed on the tabletop holographic display. Each subject made eight gestures that were tested 80 times. That is, 100 experiments were performed for each gesture. Second, the distance between the camera and the subject's hand was kept constant at 50–60 cm. Finally, the distance between the camera and the subject's hand was changed to 60–70 cm.

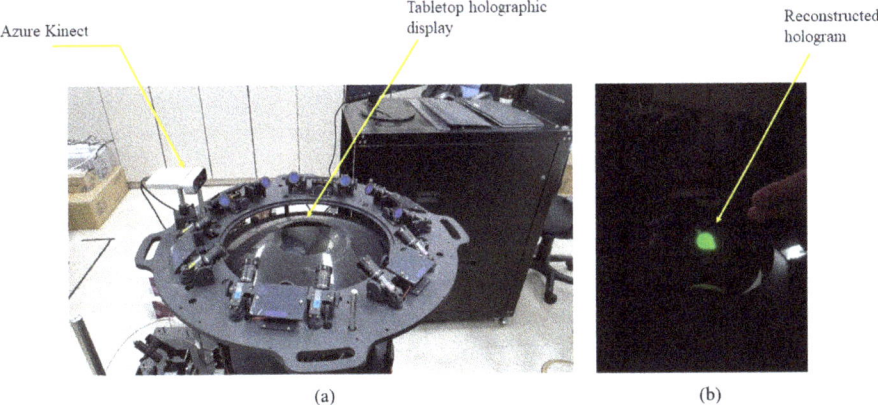

Figure 8. Experiment environment. (**a**) Tabletop holographic environment; (**b**) Gesture interaction environment.

5. Results and Discussions

5.1. Results

Figure 9 shows the result of background subtraction. Figure 9a shows an image that not only includes the depth information of the user but also the structures and backgrounds. As shown in Figure 9b, the depth information of the structure and the background is removed through the background subtraction, and only the depth information of the user is shown.

Figure 9. The experimental result before (**a**) and after (**b**) of applying the background subtraction.

Figure 10a shows the result of setting the area to find the user's hand as an ROI. Figure 10b shows a 3D bounding box that shows the result of detecting the hand joint information and the threshold within the ROI.

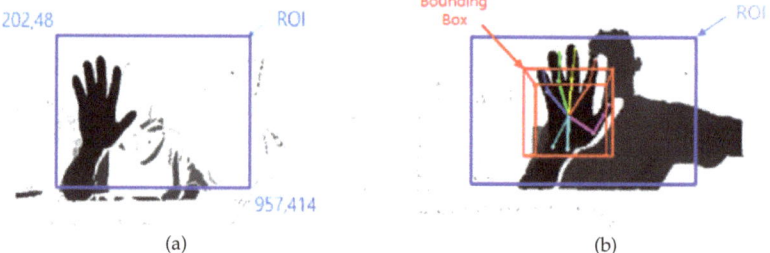

Figure 10. Result of Region of Interest (ROI) and Bounding box. (**a**) Applied ROI; (**b**) Hand detection with 14 joint points and Bounding box.

Figure 11 shows the result for the basic rotation gesture. In the default state, if the up gesture is made, the hologram image rotates upward, and when the down gesture is made, the hologram image rotates downward. Gesturing to the right and left has the effect of rotating the hologram image to the right and left, respectively.

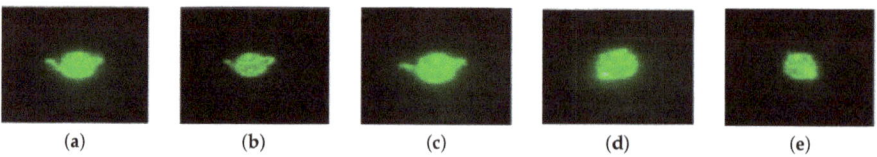

Figure 11. Result of basic rotation gestures. (**a**) Default state; (**b**) Up; (**c**) Down; (**d**) Right; (**e**) Left.

Figure 12 shows the results of the zoom in and zoom out gestures. In the default state, the hologram image becomes larger when the zoom in gesture is detected, and the hologram image becomes smaller when the zoom out gesture is performed.

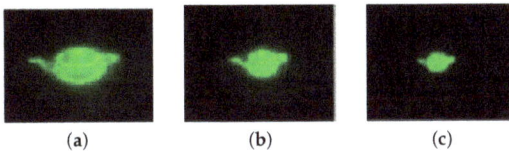

(a) (b) (c)

Figure 12. Result of zoom in and out gestures. (**a**) Zoom in; (**b**) Default state; (**c**) Zoom out.

Table 1 lists the True Positive (TP), False Positive (FP), False Negative (FN), Precision, Recall, and F1 scores [29,30] of each gesture tested 100 times. TP means a condition when a gesture is properly output as a result of performing the gesture. FP means a condition when a gesture is performed, but another gesture is output as a result. FN means a condition when a gesture is performed, but no gesture is output as a result. Table 1 shows the results at a distance of 35–50 cm. For the up gesture, two FN results were obtained, and for the enlarge and reduce gestures, one FP result was obtained. For gesturing to the right with continuous rotation, seven FN results were obtained. The Precision, Recall, and F1 scores were calculated using these results. All the gestures had a precision value of 100, except for the zoom in and zoom out gestures, which yielded a precision value of 99 each. A Recall value of 100 was obtained for all gestures except the right gesture above and continuous rotation right. The Recall values of the up and right hand gestures were 98 and 93, respectively. The F1 score that was calculated using the Precision and Recall values was 98.98 for the up gesture, 99.49 for the zoom in and zoom out gesture, and 96.37 for gesturing to the right with continuous rotation. The F1 score of the remaining gestures was 100.

Table 1. Experiment results of precision error, recall error, and F1 score about each gesture of 10 subject at 35–50 cm.

Gesture	Left	Right	Up	Down	Zoom-In	Zoom-Out	Continue Left	Continue Right
Total Attempts	100	100	100	100	100	100	100	100
True Positive	100	100	98	100	99	99	100	93
False Positive	0	0	0	0	1	1	0	0
False Negative	0	0	2	0	0	0	0	7
Precision	100	100	100	100	99	99	100	100
Recall	100	100	98	100	100	100	100	93
F1 score	100	100	98.98	100	99.49	99.49	100	96.37

Table 2 shows the results at a distance of 50–60 cm. For the zoom in and zoom out gestures, Table 2 also obtained 1 false positive result each. False Negative results were obtained for 6 times for the left gesture, 9 times for the right gesture, 2 times for the down gesture, 7 times for the continuous rotation left gesture, and 12 times for the continuous rotation right gesture. All the gestures had a precision value of 100, except for the zoom in and zoom out gestures, which yielded a precision value of 99 each. A Recall value of 100 was obtained for the up gesture, zoom in gesture, zoom out gesture, and continuous rotation left gesture. The Recall value of the left gesture was 94, the right gesture was 91, the down gesture was 98, the continuous rotation left gesture was 93, and the continuous rotation right gesture was 88. The F1 score was 96.90 for the left gesture, 95.28 for the right gesture, 100 for the up gesture, 98.98 for the down gesture, 99.49 for the zoom in and zoom out gesture, 96.37 for the continuous rotation left gesture, and 93.61 for the continuous rotation right gesture.

Table 2. Experiment results of precision error, recall error, and F1 score about each gesture of 10 subjects at 50–60 cm.

Gesture	Left	Right	Up	Down	Zoom-in	Zoom-out	Continue Left	Continue Right
Total Attempts	100	100	100	100	100	100	100	100
True Positive	94	91	100	98	99	99	93	88
False Positive	0	0	0	0	1	1	0	0
False Negative	6	9	0	2	0	0	7	12
Precision	100	100	100	100	99	99	100	100
Recall	94	91	100	98	100	100	93	88
F1 score	96.90	95.28	100	98.98	99.49	99.49	96.37	93.61

Table 3 shows the results at a distance of 60–70 cm. For the zoom in and zoom out gestures, Table 3 also obtained 1 false positive result each. False Negative results were obtained for 10 times for the left gesture, 10 times for the right gesture, 9 times for the up gesture, 6 times for the down gesture, 17 times for the continuous rotation left gesture, and 21 times for the continuous rotation right gesture. All the gestures had a precision value of 100, except for the zoom in and zoom out gestures, which yielded a precision value of 99 each. A Recall value of 100 was obtained for the zoom in gesture and zoom out gesture. The Recall value of the left gesture was 90, the right gesture was 90, the up gesture was 91, the down gesture was 94, the continuous rotation left gesture was 83, and the continuous rotation right gesture was 79. The F1 score was 94.73 for the left gesture, 94.73 for the right gesture, 95.28 for the up gesture, 96.90 for the down gesture, 99.49 for the zoom in and zoom out gesture, 90.71 for the continuous rotation left gesture, and 88.26 for the continuous rotation right gesture.

Table 3. Experiment results of precision error, recall error, and F1 score about each gesture of 10 subjects at 60–70 cm.

Gesture	Left	Right	Up	Down	Zoom-In	Zoom-Out	Continue Left	Continue Right
Total Attempts	100	100	100	100	100	100	100	100
True Positive	90	90	91	94	99	99	83	79
False Positive	0	0	0	0	1	1	0	0
False Negative	10	10	9	6	0	0	17	21
Precision	100	100	100	100	99	99	100	100
Recall	90	90	91	94	100	100	83	79
F1 score	94.73	94.73	95.28	96.90	99.49	99.49	90.71	88.26

Table 4 combines the results of all gestures of 10 subjects at 35–50 cm, 50–60 cm, and 60–70 cm. The combined results of all the gestures at 35–50 cm were: Precision was 0.99747, Recall was 0.98872, and the F1 score was 0.99307. The combined results of all the gestures at 50–60 cm were: Precision was 0.99747, Recall was 0.95500, and the F1 score was 0.97577. The combined results of all the gestures at 60–70 cm were: Precision was 0.99747, Recall was 0.90875, and the F1 score was 0.95104.

Table 4. Experiment results of total precision error, total recall error, and total F1 score.

Distance	35–50 cm	50–60 cm	60–70 cm
Precision	0.99747	0.99747	0.99747
Recall	0.98872	0.95500	0.90875
F1 score	0.99307	0.97577	0.95104

5.2. Discussions

Tables 1–3 show one false positive result for each of the zoom in and zoom out gestures. The reason for the false positive is the occurrence of a delay of 1 second each time a gesture is output, because the duration of the gesture is shorter than the delay. In Table 1, nine gestures remained undetected, including two up gestures and seven gestures to the continuous rotation right. The false positive result among the up gestures and also among the continuous rotation to the right occurred because the threshold is not exceeded. The hand of an inexperienced subject was smaller than that of the other subjects. In particular, the hand movement in the case of the continuous rotation to the right gesture was more unnatural than the other gestures; thus, the subject with small hands was not able to easily exceed the specified threshold.

Tables 2 and 3 were tested at a greater distance than Table 1. The amount of the undetected increases as the distance increases. As shown in Table 4, The best results were obtained at 35–50 cm. Especially, the undetected result of a person with a small hand increased significantly. In most ordinary hand-sized people, the amount of the undetected did not increase significantly until the distance between the camera and the user was 70 cm. The experiment was conducted at 70 cm or more, but the hand was not accurately detected and almost no gesture was output. In addition, in the case of a subject whose wrist movement range was not normal, it was difficult to perform the right gesture and the continuous rotation right gesture. Because of the difficulty of performing the right gesture and the continuous rotation right gesture, false negative results often occurred.

If the user and the camera are not in a straight line or are turned more than 30 degrees, the system cannot properly detect the hand. Furthermore, when the camera is rotated more than 30 degrees, the shape of the hand visible on the camera no longer looks like a hand. In addition, only 10 subjects participated in the experiment, thus personal characteristics can influence the outcome. This can be solved by increasing the number of subjects to obtain more objective results.

The field of gesture interaction using Azure Kinect is expanding, such as gesture interaction for drivers in the automotive field and gesture interaction in home appliances by using Azure Kinect. Unlike the approach of these studies, this study developed gesture interaction using only depth information in situations where no light is available. This is a gesture interaction that is more robust to environmental changes than other approaches. If the above problems are solved, gesture interaction using only depth information can be applied to the smart home and automobile fields.

6. Conclusions

In this study, we designed a gesture interaction system that uses Azure Kinect to enable the hologram displayed on the tabletop holographic display to be controlled in real time without any equipment. Because the tabletop holographic display requires complete darkness, only depth information is available. Thus, we used Azure Kinect to implement a gesture interaction system that provides high-performance depth information and defined intuitive and easy gestures to render the system user friendly. As a result, precision and recall values of 0.99747 and 0.98872 were obtained, respectively, and finally, an excellent F1 score of 0.99307 was achieved. However, people with small hands could encounter the problem of undetectableness. The false positive rate caused by this problem could be reduced by allowing the threshold to change flexibly by considering the size of the user's hand. In the future, we plan to improve the system to allow users with small hands to use it without any prior exploration. In addition, through experiments, we found that people's right wrist bending behavior was more difficult than others. Therefore, it was assumed that it was necessary to lower the threshold of the gesture to twist the wrist to the right compared to other gestures. This system enables the user to control the hologram of the tabletop holographic display without using other equipment. As the demand for holograms increases and the amount of research in this field increases, the implementation of a larger number of gestures in the future would enable the user to control the hologram more freely with their own hands without requiring additional equipment.

Author Contributions: Conceptualization, J.K. (Jaehan Kim), S.C., and S.K.; Data curation, C.L. and S.K.; Formal analysis, C.L.; Methodology, C.L.; Project administration, J.K. (Jinwoong Kim) and S.K.; Software, C.L; Supervision, J.Y. and S.K.; Validation, J.K. (Jaehan Kim), S.C., and J.K. (Jinwoong Kim); Visualization, C.L. All authors have read and agreed to the published version of the manuscript.

Funding: This research received no external funding.

Acknowledgments: This work was supported by the "Giga KOREA Project" granted from the Ministry of Science and ICT, KOREA. (GK20D0100: Development of Telecommunications Terminal with Digital Holographic Tabletop Display).

Conflicts of Interest: The authors declare no conflict of interest.

References

1. Ren, Z.; Yuan, J.; Meng, J.; Zhang, Z. Robust part-based hand gesture recognition using kinect sensor. *IEEE Trans. Multimed.* **2013**, *15*, 1110–1120. [CrossRef]
2. Biswas, K.K.; Basu S.K. Gesture recognition using microsoft kinect. In Proceeding of the 5th International Conference on Automation, Robotics and Applications, James Cook Hotel, Wellington, New Zealand, 6–8 December 2011; pp. 100–103.
3. Li, Y. Hand gesture recognition using Kinect. In Proceeding of the 2012 IEEE International Conference on Computer Science and Automation Engineering, Zhangjiajie, China, 25–27 May 2012; pp. 196–199.
4. Marin, G.; Dominio, F.; Zanuttigh, P. Hand gesture recognition with leap motion and kinect devices. In Proceeding of the 2014 IEEE International Conference on Image Processing, La Defense, Paris, France, 27–30 October 2014; pp. 1565–1569.
5. Patsadu, O.; Nukoolkit, C.; Watanapa, B. Human gesture recognition using Kinect camera. In Proceeding of the 2012 Ninth International Conference on Computer Science and Software Engineering, Bangkok, Thailand, 30 May–1 June 2012; pp. 28–32.
6. Guzsvinecz, T.; Szucs, V.; Sik-Lanyi, C. Suitability of the Kinect sensor and Leap Motion controller—A literature review. *Sensors* **2019**, *19*, 1072. [CrossRef] [PubMed]
7. He, G.F.; Kang, S.K.; Song, W.C.; Jung, S.T. Real-time gesture recognition using 3D depth camera. In Proceeding of the 2011 IEEE 2nd International Conference on Software Engineering and Service Science, Beijing, China, 15 July 2011; pp. 187–190.
8. Ito, A.; Nakada, K. UI Design based on Traditional Japanese Gesture. In Proceeding of the 2019 10th IEEE International Conference on Cognitive Infocommunications, Naples, Italy, 23–25 October 2019; pp. 85–90.
9. Ferri, J.; Llinares Llopis, R.; Moreno, J.; Ibañez Civera, J.; Garcia-Breijo, E. A wearable textile 3D gesture recognition sensor based on screen-printing technology. *Sensors* **2019**, *19*, 5068. [CrossRef] [PubMed]
10. Zsolczay, R.; Brown, R.; Maire, F.; Turkay, S. Vague gesture control: Implications for burns patients. In Proceeding of the 31st Australian Conference on Human-Computer-Interaction, Fremantle, Australia, 3–5 December 2019; pp. 524–528.
11. Jiang, L.; Xia, M.; Liu, X.; Bai, F. Givs: Fine-Grained Gesture Control for Mobile Devices in Driving Environments. *IEEE Access* **2020**, *8*, 49229–49243. [CrossRef]
12. Streeter, L.; Gauch, J. Detecting Gestures Through a Gesture-Based Interface to Teach Introductory Programming Concepts. In Proceeding of the International Conference on Human-Computer Interaction, Vienna, Austria, 29–30 July 2020; pp. 137–153.
13. Bakken, J.P.; Varidireddy, N.; Uskov, V.L. Smart Universities: Gesture Recognition Systems for College Students with Disabilities. In Proceeding of the 7th International KES Conference on Smart Education and e-Learning, Split, Croatia, 17–19 June 2020; pp. 393–411.
14. Kim, J.; Lim, Y.; Hong, K.; Kim, H.; Kim, H.E.; Nam, J.; Park, J.; Hahn, J.; Kim, Y.J. Electronic tabletop holographic display: Design, implementation, and evaluation. *Appl. Sci.* **2019**, *9*, 705. [CrossRef]
15. Lim, Y.; Hong, K.; Kim, H.E.; Chang, E.Y.; Lee, S.; Kim, T.; Nam, J.; Choo, H.G.; Kim, J.; Hahn, J. 360-degree tabletop electronic holographic display. *Opt. Express* **2016**, *24*, 24999–25009. [CrossRef] [PubMed]
16. Chang, E.Y.; Choi, J.; Lee, S.; Kwon, S.; Yoo, J.; Park, M.; Kim, J. 360-degree color hologram generation for real 3D objects. *Appl. Opt.* **2018**, *57*, A91–A100. [CrossRef] [PubMed]
17. Nguyen, X.S.; Brun, L.; Lézoray, O.; Bougleux, S.A neural network based on SPD manifold learning for skeleton-based hand gesture recognition. In Proceedings of the IEEE Conference on Computer Vision and Pattern Recognition, Long Beach, CA, USA, 16–20 June 2019; pp. 12036–12045.
18. Wan, C.; Probst, T.; Gool, L.V.; Yao, A. Self-supervised 3d hand pose estimation through training by fitting. In Proceedings of the IEEE Conference on Computer Vision and Pattern Recognition, Long Beach, CA, USA, 16–20 June 2019; pp. 10853–10862.

19. Du, K.; Lin, X.; Sun, Y.; Ma, X. Crossinfonet: Multi-task information sharing based hand pose estimation. In Proceedings of the 2019 IEEE Conference on Computer Vision and Pattern Recognition, Long Beach, CA, USA, 16–20 June 2019; pp. 9896–9905.
20. Wang, C.; Liu, Z.; Chan, S.C. Superpixel-based hand gesture recognition with kinect depth camera. *IEEE Trans. Multimed.* **2014**, *17*, 29–39. [CrossRef]
21. Supancic, J.S.; Rogez, G.; Yang, Y.; Shotton, J.; Ramanan, D. Depth-based hand pose estimation: Data, methods, and challenges. In Proceedings of the IEEE International Conference on Computer Vision, Santiago, Chile, 7–13 December 2015; pp. 1868–1876.
22. Joo, S.I.; Weon, S.H.; Choi, H.I. Real-time depth-based hand detection and tracking. *Sci. World J.* **2014**, *2014*, 1–17. [CrossRef] [PubMed]
23. Liu, X.; Fujimura, K. Hand gesture recognition using depth data. In Proceedings of the Sixth IEEE International Conference on Automatic Face and Gesture Recognition, Seoul, Korea, 19 May 2004; pp. 529–534.
24. Poularakis, S.; Katsavounidis, I. Finger detection and hand posture recognition based on depth information. In Proceedings of the 2014 IEEE International Conference on Acoustics, Speech and Signal Processing, Florence, Italy, 4–9 May 2014; pp. 4329–4333.
25. Ren, Z.; Meng, J.; Yuan, J. Depth camera based hand gesture recognition and its applications in human-computer-interaction. In Proceedings of the 2011 8th International Conference on Information, Communications Signal Processing, Singapore, 13–16 December 2011; pp. 1–5.
26. Yu, M.; Kim, N.; Jung, Y.; Lee, S. A Frame Detection Method for Real-Time Hand Gesture Recognition Systems Using CW-Radar. *Sensors* **2020**, *20*, 2321. [CrossRef] [PubMed]
27. Abavisani, M.; Joze, H.R.V.; Patel, V.M. Improving the performance of unimodal dynamic hand-gesture recognition with multimodal training. In Proceedings of the IEEE Conference on Computer Vision and Pattern Recognition, Long Beach, CA, USA, 16–20 June 2019; pp. 1165–1174.
28. Lee, S.H.; Lee, G.C.; Yoo, J.; Kwon, S. Wisenetmd: Motion detection using dynamic background region analysis. *Symmetry* **2019**, *11*, 621. [CrossRef]
29. Yin, Y.; Randall, D. Gesture spotting and recognition using salience detection and concatenated hidden markov models. In Proceedings of the 15th ACM on International conference on multimodal interaction, Coogee Bay Hotel, Sydney, Australia, 9–12 December 2013; pp. 489–494.
30. Kim, J.H.; Hong, G.S.; Kim, B.G.; Dogra, D.P. deepGesture: Deep learning-based gesture recognition scheme using motion sensors. *Displays* **2018**, *55*, 38–45. [CrossRef]

© 2020 by the authors. Licensee MDPI, Basel, Switzerland. This article is an open access article distributed under the terms and conditions of the Creative Commons Attribution (CC BY) license (http://creativecommons.org/licenses/by/4.0/).

Article

A Portable Fuzzy Driver Drowsiness Estimation System

Alimed Celecia [1], Karla Figueiredo [2,*], Marley Vellasco [1,*] and René González [3]

1   Electrical Engineering Department, PUC-Rio, Rio de Janeiro 22451900, Brazil; acelecia@aluno.puc-rio.br
2   Department of Informatics and Computer Science, Institute of Mathematics and Statistics, State University of Rio de Janeiro (UERJ), Rio de Janeiro 20550-900, Brazil
3   Research & Development Department, Solinftec, Araçatuba 16013337, Brazil; rene.hernandez@solinftec.com
*   Correspondence: karla@ele.puc-rio.br (K.F.); marley@ele.puc-rio.br (M.V.)

Received: 31 May 2020; Accepted: 6 July 2020; Published: 23 July 2020

Abstract: The adequate automatic detection of driver fatigue is a very valuable approach for the prevention of traffic accidents. Devices that can determine drowsiness conditions accurately must inherently be portable, adaptable to different vehicles and drivers, and robust to conditions such as illumination changes or visual occlusion. With the advent of a new generation of computationally powerful embedded systems such as the Raspberry Pi, a new category of real-time and low-cost portable drowsiness detection systems could become standard tools. Usually, the proposed solutions using this platform are limited to the definition of thresholds for some defined drowsiness indicator or the application of computationally expensive classification models that limits their use in real-time. In this research, we propose the development of a new portable, low-cost, accurate, and robust drowsiness recognition device. The proposed device combines complementary drowsiness measures derived from a temporal window of eyes (PERCLOS, ECD) and mouth (AOT) states through a fuzzy inference system deployed in a Raspberry Pi with the capability of real-time response. The system provides three degrees of drowsiness (Low-Normal State, Medium-Drowsy State, and High-Severe Drowsiness State), and was assessed in terms of its computational performance and efficiency, resulting in a significant accuracy of 95.5% in state recognition that demonstrates the feasibility of the approach.

Keywords: drowsiness detection; drowsiness measures; fuzzy inference system; Raspberry Pi; embedded hardware; eyes closing detection

---

1. Introduction

Driver fatigue and drowsiness constitute one of the leading causes of traffic accidents, being involved in 9.5% of crashes in the US [1] and 6% of fatal accidents in Brazil [2]. To alleviate these figures, authorities, research groups, and automobile manufacturers have concentrated their efforts on developing awareness campaigns, promoting the implementation and use of rest stops, and developing automatic devices that assist drivers by detecting fatigue or drowsiness [3]. Particularly, automatic devices have shown promising capabilities [4,5], offering alternative solutions to alert drivers depending on the data obtained from multiple types of sensors.

There are three categories of drowsiness detection systems, based on the measures of these sensors [4]: Vehicle-Based, physiological, and behavioral. Vehicle-based measures rely on monitoring car parts or sensors (e.g., the steering wheel, pedals, or external cameras) to infer drivers' level of fatigue or drowsiness based on driving habit modifications (e.g., a variation in steering wheel micro-corrections) or abnormal behavior (crossing lanes or leaving the road). Physiological measures include electroencephalography (EEG), electrooculography (EoG), electrocardiography (ECG), and electromyography (EMG) signals, and systems detect their deviation from the characteristics of the subject's standard signals, and then analyze if the new state is related to drowsiness. Behavioral measures are mostly related to monitoring the driver's face, focusing on facial features like eyes, brows, mouth, head inclination, or facial expression to determine the drowsiness level.

All three referred categories have some limitations that must be considered when developing a drowsiness detection device [4–6]. Vehicle-based measurements are associated with vehicle types, and are profoundly affected by many factors, such as: the driver's habits, abilities, and experience; road characteristics (quality, marking status, lighting, geometry); and climate conditions. On the other hand, physiological measures are intrusive systems that demand that the user be connected to electrodes, which in turn are connected to some electronic processing device (even with the advances in wireless devices, the electrode would have to be on the subject). This setup involves noise and artefacts that can deteriorate the signal quality and therefore decrease the drowsiness detection accuracy. Additionally, EEG signals present a high variability among different subjects, as well as among measures from the same subject over time [7], demanding a very robust signal processing model to maintain the accuracy in continuous time. Limitations of the behavioral measures are strictly related to the sensors employed (i.e., camera(s)), which are affected by ambient lightning and vision obstruction (specifically when the subject uses glasses).

Among these different methods, behavioral measures are associated with lower cost, and are non-invasive, adaptable to any vehicle, and independent of road conditions. Therefore, a versatile and fully portable device which can function in real-time with an affordable price should be based on those measures. Drowsiness detection systems that employ these strategies have shown outstanding performance in experiments in both controlled laboratory and real conditions [8–10], given the limitations that behavioral measures can present (related to the sensors).

Usually, systems based on behavioral measures comprise a recording device for driver image acquisition, face recognition and identification of patterns indicating drowsiness, and an output signal of alarm. To ensure accurate performance, the most critical component is the hardware that processes the images and generates the alarm. Due to the high computing power demanded by computer vision algorithms, most of the portable drowsiness detection systems reported in the literature [5,8–12] are computer-based, employing a laptop for data processing. As a result, the cost of these systems is elevated, and their application is limited to specific scenarios, not being adaptable to different vehicle conditions.

Alternative processing hardware employed in these applications are smartphones [13–18] and semi-custom hardware devices [19–21]. In smartphone applications, the camera of the phone records the image of the subject, and drowsiness indicators are computed to generate the alarm signal. Given the high computing power and storage space of smartphone devices, these applications are capable of running, in real time (from 10 to 14 frames per second), complex algorithms like ensemble of classifiers [14] or deep neural networks [16,18] for face and drowsiness indicators recognition. On the other hand, due to hardware limitations, semi-custom hardware devices like field-programmable gate arrays (FPGAs) [19] and digital signal processors (DSPs) [20,21] are limited to methods which are less computationally expensive. In the case of one more complex drowsiness detection methodology [21], the response of the system was able to process at a reduced speed of only three frames per second (fps).

Given recent advances in the processing capacity of embedded hardware and single-board computers like the Raspberry Pi [22], Nvidia Jetson Nano [23], Asus Tinker Board [24], or Rock64 [25], such powerful hardware can represent a new step in the establishment of a low-cost drowsiness detection standard tool for driver safety maintenance. In particular, Raspberry Pi single-board computers are low-cost devices with impressive computing power, and have recently been applied in drowsiness detection systems [26–30]. In [26–28], the drowsy state was recognized, establishing a threshold for individual drowsiness indicators like percentage of eyelid closure (PERCLOS) [31] or detecting eye closure for a predefined time, which can limit the performance of the model in case of variations in the blinking frequency [8] or eye closure misclassifications. On the other hand, the application of convolutional neural networks in these devices is explored in [29,30], and due to the high computing capacity demanded by these algorithms, it was acknowledged that the response in real-time was limited, reporting a frame rate of 2.15 fps in [30]. This limitation led to an enhanced server-based processing model in a mobile phone device, which achieved 4.47 fps. From these results, authors in [26,27] tackled the limitations related to the variation of ambient lightning and vision obstruction, based on the addition of an infrared (IR) illuminator and camera system.

Therefore, to design a low-cost portable device applicable to any vehicle, it is necessary to overcome the limitations of the sensors employed in image acquisition. Additionally, it is necessary to develop a processing model with a balanced demand of computing capacity, robustness to facial features state misclassifications, and adaptable to characteristics from different subjects. In this sense, the combination of varying drowsiness indicators (including various facial features) such as PERCLOS, eye closing duration (ECD) [8], percentage of mouth yawn [9], and average mouth opening time (AOT) [10] can improve the robustness of the system. The use of multiple indicators overcomes the limitations of partially losing one of the facial features in the image, and of erroneous values from individual measures.

One of the suitable algorithms for the combination of these different modalities is a fuzzy inference system (FIS). Fuzzy inference systems are computationally inexpensive interpretable models which can consider various drowsiness indicators without establishing strict thresholds. These advantages were exploited in [32,33] for computer-based devices which evaluated only indicators extracted from the eyes region (PERCLOS, eyelid distance changes, eye closure rate, or ECD) to recognize if the driver was drowsy without addressing the problem of changes in the ambient illumination.

The main objective of this work was therefore to develop a new portable, low-cost, accurate, and robust drowsiness recognition device which incorporates complementary measures from eyes (PERCLOS, ECD) and mouth (AOT). The proposed equipment is based on a fuzzy inference system and deployed in a Raspberry Pi complemented with a NoIR camera and illumination system, which limits the influence of variations in ambient illumination and vision obstruction in drivers wearing glasses. The resultant device should be adaptable to any vehicle, indicating the drowsiness level of the user in three states: Normal State, Drowsy State, and Severe Drowsiness State.

The remainder of this paper is organized as follows: Section 2 describes the materials and methods employed to develop the hardware, software and processing algorithms; Section 3 describes the results obtained from testing the proposed device and associated algorithms under different conditions; finally, Section 4 provides the conclusions of the work.

2. Materials and Methods

The proposed Portable Fuzzy Drowsiness Estimation System (PFDESys) is defined as observed in Figure 1.

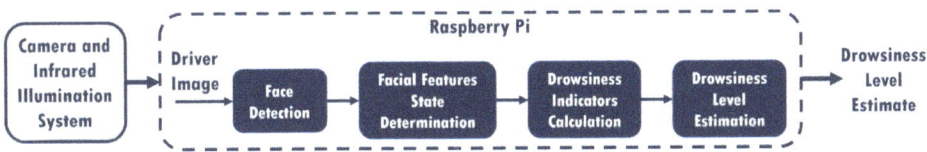

Figure 1. Portable Fuzzy Drowsiness Estimation System (PFDESys).

The PFDESys is composed of five functional blocks: (i) a camera and infrared illumination system for the acquisition of the driver image; (ii) a face detection module to define the possible area in which the driver's face is situated in the image; (iii) a module to determine the position of the facial features (eyes and mouth) and their states (closed or open); (iv) drowsiness indicators calculation module (PERCLOS, ECD, and AOT); and the driver drowsiness level estimation. The Raspberry Pi is the base hardware to run all algorithms defined for each functional block. The following subsections detail the methods applied in each processing block, finishing with a subsection that describes the hardware of the device.

2.1. Face Detection

Face detection is the first step when processing each driver's image. In this work, we investigate two approaches: a cascade classifier that employs Haar-like filter features as proposed in [34], and a linear support vector machine (SVM) with histogram of oriented gradients (HOG) features, as proposed in [35]. Those approaches were chosen due to their reduced computational cost compared to deep learning approaches and proved accuracy.

The model proposed in [34] detects faces in an image with high velocity and accuracy, which is why it has been extensively utilized in the image processing community, extending its use to object detection applications. The algorithm defines a set of features derived from Haar filters that are applied to the image on a defined scale. The algorithm provides a high-dimensional set of features that is combined with an Adaboost model [36] to select a reduced number of those features and train a cascade of successive linear classifiers that best separate faces from no-faces in the images.

The second approach for face detection evaluated in this work is based on a feature set known as HOG features [35]. This feature extraction algorithm firstly divides the image into a grid of small cells, and then computes, for each image cell, the histogram of the orientation of the gradients weighted by their magnitude. Each cell histogram is stacked in a vector of features of high dimensionality after normalizing the values over a measure of the spatial energy on more extensive regions of the image. Face detection windows overlap with grids of HOG descriptors, providing a feature vector that can be employed with any classifiers. In this case, a linear SVM classifier was used.

2.2. Facial Features State Determination

After obtaining the possible region of the frame in which the face is situated, the algorithm reported in [37] is employed to determine the positions of facial landmarks. Facial landmarks describe main facial elements such as nose, eyes, eyebrows, and mouth, among others, through a series of marks as illustrated in Figure 2. The algorithm consists of a cascade of regression trees in which each regressor updates the estimated landmark positions employing the previous value and the intensity of a sparse set of pixels selected from the original estimate. The ensemble of regression trees is trained by gradient boosting with a squared error function, which in addition to improving the accuracy of the model assists in the selection of the sparse set of pixels in combination with the prior probability of the distances between pairs of pixels. The model presents a response on the order of milliseconds, being well suited for the application at hand. The training process used the 300-W dataset [38], which consists of 300 images obtained indoors and 300 in outdoor conditions with spontaneous expressions, all manually annotated. This dataset includes face images collected during several outdoor activities such as sports, parties, or protests, presenting large variations in both illumination conditions (including poor illumination) and facial expressions. Therefore, it is particularly useful for our application, given that it is required to robustly detect facial landmarks in different illumination conditions when driving.

After obtaining the facial landmarks, the proposed model focuses on the recognition of opening and closing of eyes and mouth. With this objective, markers for the right eye (38,39,41,42), left eye (44,45,47,48), and mouth (62–64,66–68) are tracked for computing the distance between eyelids and lips. Eyes are considered closed when the space between eyelids is less than 20% of the open eye area (as defined in [39]), and the mouth is considered opened when its aspect ratio ($mar = Height/Width$) is greater than 0.7, as defined in [10].

Given the different characteristics of subjects' facial features (eyes and mouth) and opening area, the developed system includes a setup step of at least one minute in which the subject is monitored to determine a personalized threshold value of open eyes and mouth areas. When switching on the device, the driver is prompted to maintain their position in front of the camera while continuing with the driving activities (leaving their mouth open at least twice for a small period). Then, for each frame obtained during the selected time window (in our case the duration was defined as 1 min), the device measures the *mar* metric and the space between eyelids (at a 30 fps rate, 1800 values for each eye and *mar* are obtained). The average of 5% most significant distances (which indicates opened eyes and mouth) is employed to calculate the thresholds that determine eyes or mouth openings. Therefore, the system can adapt to different drivers without any variation in its accuracy for recognizing eyes closing or mouth opening.

Figure 2. Facial landmarks included in the 300-W dataset.

2.3. Driver Drowsiness Indicators

The selected driver drowsiness indicators are based on the principle that a combination of complementary measures can produce a more robust system, overcoming the limitations of each one separately. The selected indicators are: PERCLOS [8], ECD [8], and AOT [10]. Each of those measures is computed based on the states obtained for eyes (PERCLOS, ECD) and mouth (AOT).

PERCLOS is a prevalent indicator of drowsiness in behavioral-measures-based systems. It is defined as the proportion of frames in which the driver has their eyes closed in a determined temporal window [8]:

$$PERCLOS[i] = \frac{\sum_{j=i-n+1}^{i} frame[j]}{n} \quad (1)$$

where $PERCLOS[i]$ indicates the value of PERCLOS for the selected window at instant i, n is the number of frames obtained in the temporal window, and $frame[j]$ is a binary value that indicates if the eye was closed in $frame\ j$.

ECD is defined as the mean duration of intervals in which eyes are closed in a determined temporal window:

$$ECD[i] = \frac{\sum_{j=1}^{p} Duration[j]}{p} \quad (2)$$

where $ECD[i]$ represents the values of ECD at time i, p is the number of intervals in a defined temporal window, and $Duration[j]$ is the duration of the lapse between closing and reopening the eyes.

AOT is defined as the mean duration of intervals in which the subject kept their mouth open during a specific time window. It can be expressed as:

$$AOT[i] = \frac{1}{N_y} \sum_{j=1}^{N_y} t_j \quad (3)$$

where $AOT[i]$ defines the AOT magnitude at instant i, N_y is the number of yawns during the time window, and t_j is the duration of yawn j. Yawning is considered as the action of keeping the mouth open for more than three seconds [10]. In our application, the yawning duration value begins after those three seconds.

These indicators are complementary, in the sense that if one of them gives a false positive, the others act as validators of the drowsiness condition. Moreover, the combination of PERCLOS and ECD strengthens the robustness of the system to variations in blinking frequency and eye state misclassifications [8].

2.4. Fuzzy Inference System Applied to Drowsiness Level Estimation

The combination of the three drowsiness indicators is performed by a Mamdani Fuzzy Inference System [40]. Therefore, the proposed Drowsiness Level Estimation module provides a nonlinear and interpretable mapping from the input indicators (PERCLOS, ECD and AOT) to the drowsiness level output (Low-Normal State, Medium-Drowsy State, and High-Severe Drowsiness State). The three indicators are calculated based on a temporal window size of one minute, computed each second.

One essential aspect of the proposed system's design is the specification of the limits that determine if a person is drowsy or not. In the literature, there is no consensus about these values for each of the metrics, defining the drowsiness threshold based on experimental results without any clinical validation. Table 1 presents, as an example, the different drowsiness thresholds for the PERCLOS indicator. This disagreement among experts makes the use of a fuzzy inference system even more critical, as FIS is known for being able to deal with these uncertainties. The values of the fuzzy sets corresponding to each variable were set considering the selected window size, experimental results, and reference values in the literature.

Table 1. Drowsiness thresholds reported in the literature for percentage of eyelid closure (PERCLOS).

Drowsiness Threshold	Window Size	FPS	Reference
0.02	1, 2 min	25	[32]
0.3, 0.25		4–5	[41]
0.2		25	[42]
0.2	8, 10 s	25	[8]
0.4	24–25 s	25	[12]
0.15, 0.18	30 s	7	[9]

The developed FIS is defined by the membership functions shown in Figures 3–6 and a set of rules illustrated in Figure 7. The three output drowsiness levels (Low-Normal State, Medium-Drowsy State, and High-Severe Drowsiness State) are represented by singleton fuzzy sets (Figure 6). The rules were defined following the principle that the selected indicators (PERCLOS, ECD, and AOT) complement each other, allowing the system to reduce the effect of individual false positives and eye state misclassifications. Therefore, a Medium drowsiness level is produced by two eye states indicators increasing their level to medium, one of them increasing its level to high, or a combination of AOT at a high level and any of the other indicators at medium. Particularly, AOT influences an increment in the output drowsiness level when its level is high due to undesired effects on the metric produced by driver activities such as conversation or singing.

The fuzzy operator employed for AND connective and the Mamdani implication was the minimum; the maximum was chosen as the aggregation operator. The minimum of maximum was selected as the defuzzification method to provide the final classification output, given that the output membership functions are singletons.

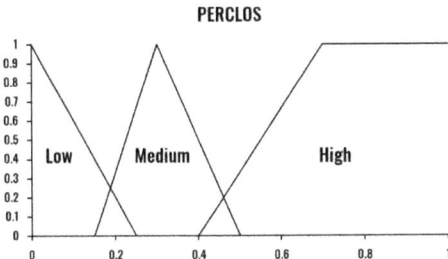

Figure 3. Fuzzy membership functions for PERCLOS.

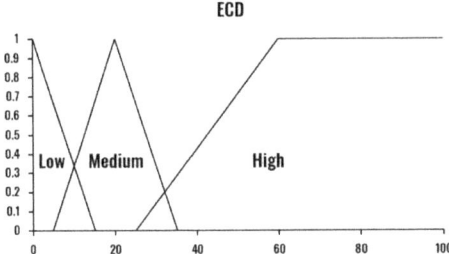

Figure 4. Fuzzy membership functions for eye closing duration (ECD).

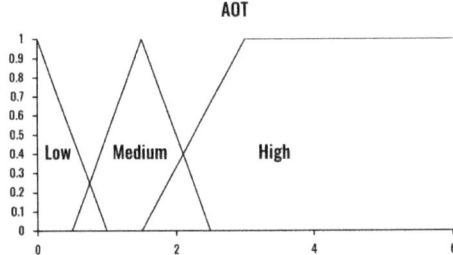

Figure 5. Fuzzy membership functions for average mouth opening time (AOT).

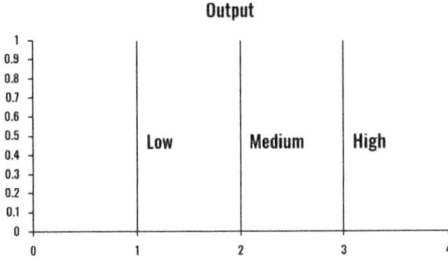

Figure 6. Fuzzy membership functions for drowsiness level output.

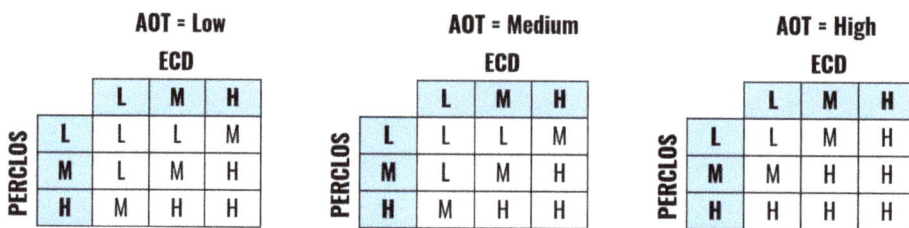

Figure 7. Fuzzy rules (L = Low, M = Medium, H = High).

2.5. Hardware

The main hardware component is the Raspberry Pi 3 Model B [43], which possesses a Quad Core 1.2 GHz Broadcom BCM2837 64 bit processor combined with a memory of 1 GB. The device operates as a minicomputer that executes the operating system Raspbian [44] (an operating system based on Debian and optimized for that hardware) that allows the developed software to be integrated in Python language and processes each frame with the other components. The device relies on a 5 V power source with 3 A, and an SD card with 16 GB of storage capacity to run the operating system.

Infrared (IR)-sensitive cameras, combined with proper external IR illumination, can generate excellent images for environments with little or no lightning and eliminate reflections caused by drivers' glasses [45]. Therefore, this type of camera was selected to produce a system robust to ambient lightning variations and vision obstruction. The camera utilized in our device is the NoIR v2 of 8 MP, built for the Raspberry Pi hardware, combined with an external IR illumination of 48 LEDs that require a power source of 12 V and 1 A. The camera and IR illumination system are designed to be located on the dashboard above the steering wheel, with a direct vision of the driver.

3. Results and Discussion

The proposed model was evaluated through two different analyses. The first investigation was directed to the examination of the processing capacity of the portable hardware to analyze real-time images and the effects of continuous work on the device's response. The second analysis focused on the determination of the performance obtained by the proposed model in recognizing different drowsiness states. In both cases, the portable device's results were compared with those of a processing model deployed in a laptop, offering a benchmark comparison of the response of the model in a more powerful hardware setup. In this way, it was possible to compare how the drowsiness recognition accuracy of the model was affected by variations in the hardware computing capacity.

The laptop was equipped with an integrated webcam model Camera L 80WK HD 720P, an Intel Core I7-7700HQ processor, and 16 GB of RAM. The metrics were computed each second, employing samples with a one-minute window size. In each hardware setup, the model was developed in Python 3.6, running in the Anaconda environment on the Microsoft Windows 10 Operating System for the laptop and in the Raspbian Operating System for the Raspberry Pi.

3.1. Computational Performance of the Model in Real-Time

The objective of this analysis was to verify the computational performance offered by the proposed model in combination with the portable hardware. Additionally, we wanted to compare this response with the one produced by a standard hardware setup (a laptop). We also wished to assess the effects of continuous working time on the processing capacity of the device. The evaluation was conducted using ten sample videos of approximately 50 min of users during work activities in front of the camera. Figures 8 and 9 illustrate the mean frames per second of the two face recognition models and the two hardware setups.

The difference between hardware setups is evident when comparing Figures 8 and 9. On the one hand, the laptop configuration was able to maintain the average number of processed frames per second over 32 for both facial recognition models. On the other hand, the Raspberry Pi was limited to values between 7–9.5 and 7–7.3 for the Haar-features-based and HOG models, respectively. This remarkable difference is a result of the massive computing power demanded by those facial recognition models (the most time-consuming stage of the processing model). Another effect observed is a small tendency (in all cases) to decrease the fps with time. Although a more profound analysis should be implemented to derive more accurate conclusions related to this issue, it can be stated that the continuous processing imposes a limit on the processing capacity, with probable overheating in both laptop and Raspberry Pi devices.

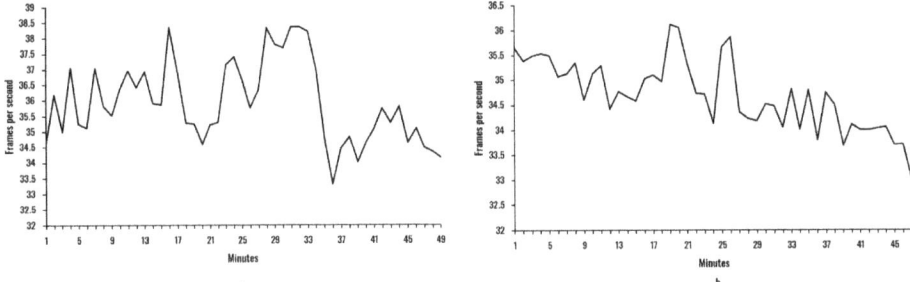

Figure 8. Mean of the fps per minute for the laptop hardware: (**a**) Haar model; (**b**) HOG model.

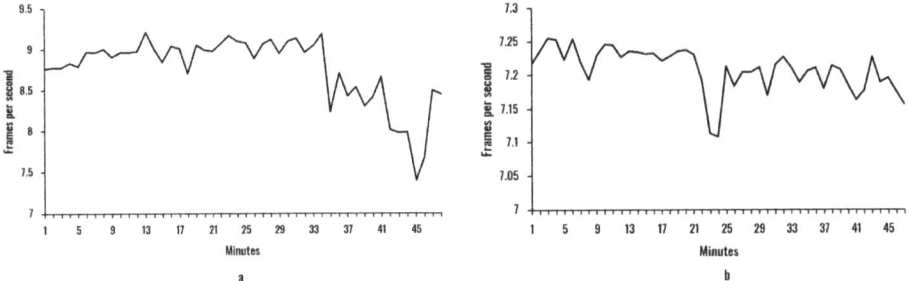

Figure 9. Mean of the fps per minute for the Raspberry Pi hardware: (**a**) Haar model; (**b**) HOG model.

When comparing the Haar and HOG models, it can be seen that for both hardware setups, the HOG model presented a reduction in the fps values, with fewer variations than the fps of the Haar model (see Table 2). Specifically, the Haar model offered an average of 35.93 and 8.75 fps for laptop and Raspberry Pi setups, respectively, with standard deviations of 1.31 and 0.59. Remarkably, the Raspberry Pi setup, even with a much slower response, presented less variability in the fps rate, reducing a standard deviation of 0.72. The HOG model resulted in smaller values, with 34.70 fps for the laptop and 7.21 fps for the Raspberry Pi. The standard deviation, on the other hand, was lower when compared to the Haar models, with 0.70 and 0.07 for both hardware setups. Particularly, during the experiments, it was perceived that for the Haar model, face rotation of more than 30° resulted in instability in the face recognition, while the HOG model was more robust in this aspect.

Table 2. Real-time response of face detection models in different hardware.

Model	Haar		HOG	
Hardware Setup	Mean fps	Standard Deviation	Mean fps	Standard Deviation
Laptop	35.93	1.31	34.70	0.70
Raspberry Pi	8.75	0.59	7.21	0.07

To improve the fps rate in the Raspberry Pi (our proposed portable model), we explored a computing performance improvement strategy based on the experimental evidence that the facial recognition is the stage in which the algorithms take a longer time. Therefore, the size of the image employed in the facial recognition stage was reduced, maintaining the aspect ratio. After obtaining the coordinates of the region of the smaller image in which the face is situated, these values were resized to represent the equivalent region in the original image resolution (area of the original image that contains the face). This strategy produced the improvements in computing performance described in Table 3. As expected, rescaling the image had an inversely proportional influence on the fps rate of the system, with steady increments when reducing the reduction factor until doubling the performance (15.94 fps for the Haar model and 14.77 for the HOG model) for a reduction factor of 0.5. The standard deviation generally presented a small increment for both models, indicating that smaller images produced more pronounced variations of the fps.

Table 3. Performance obtained with fps enhancement strategies.

Model	Haar		HOG	
Reduction Factor	Mean fps	Standard Deviation	Mean fps	Standard Deviation
Original	8.75	0.59	7.21	0.07
0.7	10.58	0.52	9.6	0.11
0.6	12.14	0.7	11.17	0.16
0.5	15.94	0.66	14.77	0.29

These results confirm our conclusions related to the face recognition models. In all cases, the mean fps of the Haar model was superior to the mean fps of the HOG model by around 1 fps, but with a more significant standard deviation. By reducing the image to half its original size, the performance doubled.

3.2. Accuracy of the Drowsiness Recognition System

To evaluate the accuracy of the proposed model, four acquisition experiments were designed based on video streams of approximately 50 min from two subjects (two videos by subject) of 24 and 28 years old, each without preexisting medical conditions. The recorded videos were scripted and contained simulations of different combinations of eyes and mouth states that defined different drowsiness conditions. The acquisition setup emulated the position of the subject and the inclination of the camera when installed in a car. Given those specific conditions, the simulations can be compared to the real drowsiness level provided by the fuzzy inference system, producing an assessment of the accuracy of the proposed device. The video resolution was set to 640 × 480. Table 4 summarizes the total number of different drowsiness states included in the experiments, divided into segments with a size of approximately 1 min.

Table 4. Testing drowsiness data.

Drowsiness Level	Segments of Approximately 1 min Duration
Normal State	100
Drowsy State	60
Severe Drowsiness State	40

The accuracy of the model was evaluated by comparing the subject's state in each moment (segments of the experiment in which the subject simulated drowsiness symptoms) with the FIS output. The results of this assessment for the laptop- and Raspberry-Pi-based models are presented in Figure 10.

When analyzing the results of the proposed model in the portable hardware configuration, it can be stated that the proposed system presented a high accuracy (95.5%). Remarkably, the recognition errors were produced by misclassifications of Normal State segments as Drowsy State segments (five for the Raspberry Pi and three for the laptop) and Drowsy State segments as Severe Drowsiness State segments (four for the Raspberry Pi and one for the laptop). Although these errors indicate some limitations of the proposed system in some specific segments, they are not as relevant as a misclassification of drowsiness states into the normal state (not present in our model), which would fail the purpose of the device (to alarm the subject when tired). Additionally, the high accuracy obtained for the two subjects in the four experiments confirms the relevance of the adaptation stage included in the system setup. Through this process, different threshold values were defined for each test when determining eyes closure and mouth opening, adjusting the device to different conditions.

		Laptop True Level					Raspberry Pi True Level		
		Normal State	Drowsy State	Severe Drowsiness State			Normal State	Drowsy State	Severe Drowsiness State
Predicted Level	Normal State	97	0	0	Predicted Level	Normal State	95	0	0
	Drowsy State	3	59	0		Drowsy State	5	56	0
	Severe Drowsiness State	0	1	40		Severe Drowsiness State	0	4	40
	Precision per class	97.0%	98.3%	100.0%		Precision per class	95.0%	93.3%	100.0%
	Total Accuracy		98.0%			Total Accuracy		95.5%	

Figure 10. Confusion matrices describing the performance of the model.

There was a 2.5% difference between the results of the laptop and the Raspberry Pi in terms of total accuracy. Notably, the laptop-based model recognized both Normal and Drowsy States with higher accuracy. Both approaches were able to accurately identify the segments representing Severe Drowsiness. Those results indicate that the differences in frames processed per second (see Section 3.1) did not produce a significant difference in the performance of the model.

An example of the output of the portable model for a given user is illustrated in Figure 11. Items (a), (b), and (c) are the magnitudes of PERCLOS, ECD, and AOT per second, respectively. The graph represented in (d) is the subject's estimated Drowsiness Level. The time segment begins with the driver in an alert state, transitioning to a simulated drowsy state after the 40th second.

Note that in our proposed system we are monitoring only facial features, which might prevent the accurate recognition of the drowsiness state in some specific situations that can generate total facial occlusion or head-turning. Additionally, cases where the driver presents a behavior deviating from their usual one when driving (e.g., an extremely high number of blinks in a short time or frequently opening their mouth) can generate imprecisions in the recognition. Nevertheless, as described in Sections 2.3 and 2.4, the selected facial features are complementary, and the FIS is designed to avoid false-positive drowsiness detection from only one of the measures. To generate a more robust system based on behavioral measures, one can add the detection of head inclination and turning.

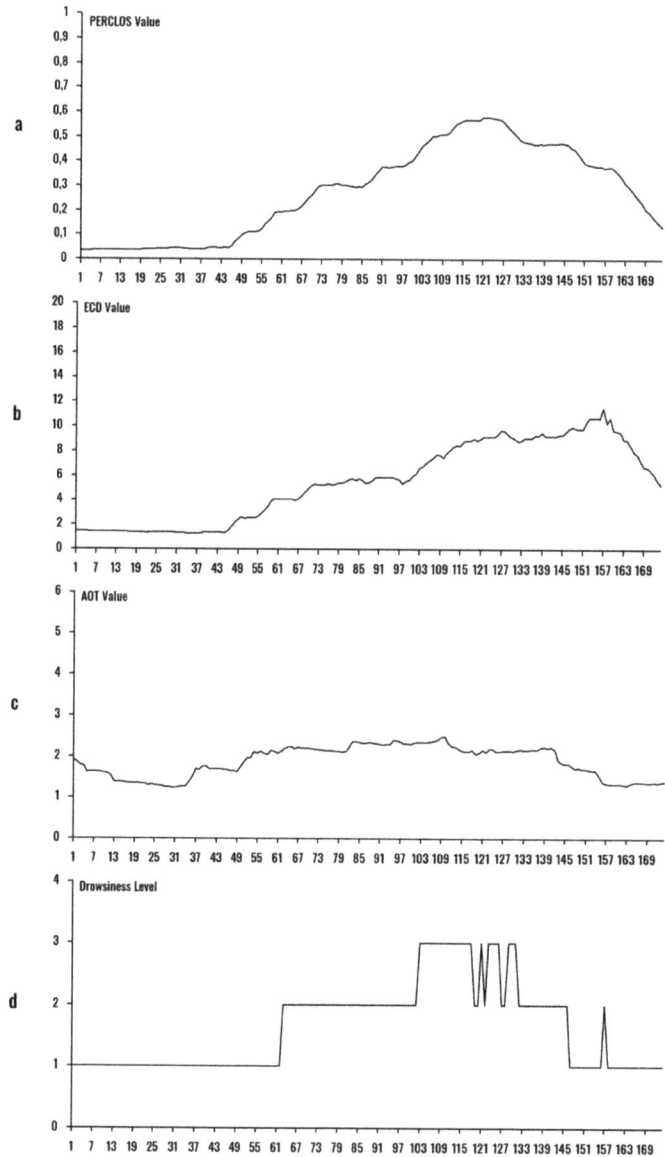

Figure 11. Example of output of the model for 175 s processing: (**a**) PERCLOS; (**b**) ECD; (**c**) AOT; (**d**) Drowsiness level.

Extended Performance Validation

To extend the analysis of the system's performance and to validate its adaptability to different users, new tests were performed over a more significant set of subjects, with a broader range of ages and genders, following the same protocol (50 min duration). Eight new subjects were included, with six males and four females in total: two in the range of 20 to 30 years; one in the range of 30 to 40 years; one in the range from 40 to 50 years; two in the range from 50 to 60; and two in the range of 70 to 80 years. The tests were applied using laptops, but emulating the limitations of the Raspberry Pi setup by eliminating frames from the stream and designing the system to process images only in the corresponding time instants (frames per second reduced to 14). The resulting quantities of ~1-min segments from these experiments were: 500 of Normal State, 300 of Drowsy State, and 200 of Severe Drowsiness State. The obtained accuracy of the system in this extended dataset is shown in Figure 12.

		Laptop True Level					Raspberry Pi (Emulated) True Level		
		Normal State	Drowsy State	Severe Drowsiness State			Normal State	Drowsy State	Severe Drowsiness State
Predicted Level	Normal State	481	0	0	Predicted Level	Normal State	465	0	0
	Drowsy State	19	290	0		Drowsy State	35	274	1
	Severe Drowsiness State	0	10	200		Severe Drowsiness State	0	26	199
	Precision per class	96.2%	96.7%	100.0%		Precision per class	93.0%	91.3%	99.5%
	Total Accuracy		97.1%			Total Accuracy		93.5%	

Figure 12. Confusion matrices describing the performance of the model for a more significant number of subjects.

When applied on a larger number of subjects, the performance of the model dropped slightly for the laptop setup (from 98.0% total accuracy to 97.1%) and more significantly for the emulated Raspberry Pi setup (from 95.5% total accuracy to 93.5%). In general, the tendency of the model was maintained when misclassifying examples, mistakenly assigning Drowsy State labels to Normal State ones (19 samples for the laptop and 35 for the emulated Raspberry Pi), and Severe Drowsiness State labels to Drowsy State examples (10 and 26 cases for the laptop and emulated Raspberry Pi, respectively). For both setups, an outstanding performance for Severe Drowsiness State recognition was observed, with only one example misclassified as Drowsy State for the emulated Raspberry Pi. These preliminary results validate the model's capacity to accurately recognize the drowsiness level of subjects of different ages in laboratory conditions. Extensive tests should be conducted to validate the model in real driving situations, including even more subjects.

4. Conclusions

This paper introduced the development of a low-cost portable device that assesses the drowsiness level of a driver. The device is based on an IR illuminator and a camera that streams the image acquired to a Raspberry Pi 3 Model B, resulting in a device which is robust to variations in the ambient lighting condition and vision obstruction. The processing model combines measures obtained from the eyes and mouth (PERCLOS, ECD, and AOT) and provides the drowsiness level as the output of a fuzzy inference system (Low-Normal State, Medium-Drowsy State, and High-Severe Drowsiness State). Two different facial features recognition methods were evaluated: one that employed a cascade classifier and Haar-like filter features and another that applied a linear support vector machine SVM with HOG features.

The proposed device was tested in four experiments comprising two subjects in different simulated drowsiness conditions with approximately 50 min duration. The average accuracy of the system in recognizing different drowsiness states was 95.5%. The processing model was also implemented in a laptop to compare the effects of reducing the computational power (using the Raspberry Pi) for the portable hardware. The difference in the recognition accuracy was only 2.5%, even with a difference in the mean number of frames processed by the hardware of approximately 17 frames. Additional tests were implemented with more subjects, covering a broader age range, resulting in a significant accuracy of 97.1% and 93.5% for the laptop and emulated Raspberry Pi based models, respectively.

The main advantages of the proposed device are: adaptability to different drivers' facial features, low cost, robustness to changes in ambient illumination and vision occlusion, and freedom in the design (allowing the device owner to modify the fuzzy membership functions domains and temporal window for the calculation of PERCLOS, ECD, and AOT). This last feature allows the adjustment of the device to specific conditions desired for the application, such as a faster response of the output (by decreasing the temporal window size) or new drowsiness indications (modifying the limits of the fuzzy membership functions).

As future work, the model should be evaluated on real driving conditions and a more significant number of subjects in order to validate the conclusions obtained in this work on a practical application. Additionally, we intend to investigate the enhancement of the fps obtained from the portable model (the fps obtained by the Raspberry Pi was far from the fps rate achieved with the laptop-based setup). This improvement can be explored by different approaches. In the first case, more powerful portable hardware devices can be evaluated, like the Raspberry Pi 4, Nvidia Jetson Nano, Asus Tinker Board, or Rock64 embedded systems. Secondly, the possibility of coupling the Raspberry Pi with a neural stick such as the Intel Neural Compute Stick 2 could be explored, which, for a medium increment in the price, would make it possible to explore deep-learning-based image processing in real time. We also intend to set up the proposed model in real vehicles to assess the effects of actual driving conditions on its operation. Given the lack of information in the literature about specific thresholds for the drowsiness measures (PERCLOS, ECD, AOT), and the divergences between the research that reported such information, it would be interesting to conduct a broader investigation that helps to unify the decision criteria. Additionally, the monitoring of head inclination and turning in the system could be included, which could enhance the system's robustness by adding a measure not limited to facial features without modifying the proposed hardware.

Author Contributions: Conceptualization, A.C., K.F., M.V., and R.G.; methodology, A.C., K.F., and M.V.; software, A.C.; validation, A.C. and K.F.; formal analysis, A.C., K.F., and M.V.; investigation, A.C.; resources, K.F., M.V., and R.G.; writing-original draft preparation, A.C.; writing-review and editing, K.F. and M.V.; supervision, K.F. and M.V.; project administration, R.G.; funding acquisition, M.V. All authors have read and agreed to the published version of the manuscript.

Funding: This research was funded by two Brazilian Agencies—CNPq, grants number 304497/2017-7 and 161404/2017-0, and FAPERJ, grant number E-26/203.004/2018—and by Solinftec Company, contract number 201800502.

Conflicts of Interest: The authors declare no conflicts of interest. The funders had no role in the design of the study; in the collection, analysis, or interpretation of data; in the writing of the manuscript; or in the decision to publish the results.

References

1. Owens, J.M.; Dingus, T.A.; Guo, F.; Fang, Y.; Perez, M.; McClafferty, J.; Tefft, B. *Prevalence of Drowsy-Driving Crashes: Estimates from a Large-Scale Naturalistic Driving Study;* AAA Foundation for Traffic Safety: Washington, DC, USA, 2018.
2. Veruska Narciso, F.I.; Túlio de Mello, M.I.; Túlio de Mello, M. Segurança e saúde dos motoristas profissionais que trafegam nas rodovias do Brasil. *Rev. Saude Publica* **2017**, *51*, 26. [CrossRef]
3. Higgins, J.S.; Michael, J.; Austin, R.; Åkerstedt, T.; Van Dongen, H.P.; Watson, N.; Czeisler, C.; Pack, A.I.; Rosekind, M.R. Asleep at the wheel-the road to addressing drowsy driving. *Sleep* **2017**, *40*, zsx001. [CrossRef] [PubMed]
4. Sahayadhas, A.; Sundaraj, K.; Murugappan, M. Detecting driver drowsiness based on sensors: A review. *Sensors* **2012**, *12*, 16937–16953. [CrossRef] [PubMed]
5. Kaplan, S.; Guvensan, M.A.; Yavuz, A.G.; Karalurt, Y. Driver behavior analysis for safe driving: A survey. *IEEE Trans. Intell. Transp. Syst.* **2015**, *16*, 3017–3032. [CrossRef]
6. Wang, Q.; Yang, J.; Ren, M.; Zheng, Y. Driver fatigue detection: A survey. *Proc. World Congr. Intell. Control Autom.* **2006**, *2*, 8587–8591. [CrossRef]

7. Ramos, A.C.; Vellasco, M. Quantum-inspired evolutionary algorithm for feature selection in motor imagery EEG classification. In Proceedings of the 2018 IEEE Congress on Evolutionary Computation, CEC 2018, Rio de Janeiro, Brazil, 8–13 July 2018; Institute of Electrical and Electronics Engineers Inc.: Piscataway, NJ, USA, 2018.
8. Jo, J.; Lee, S.J.; Park, K.R.; Kim, I.J.; Kim, J. Detecting driver drowsiness using feature-level fusion and user-specific classification. *Expert Syst. Appl.* **2014**, *41*, 1139–1152. [CrossRef]
9. Zheng, R.; Tian, C.; Li, H.; Li, M.; Wei, W. Fatigue detection based on fast facial feature analysis. In Proceedings of the Lecture Notes in Computer Science (Including Subseries Lecture Notes in Artificial Intelligence and Lecture Notes in Bioinformatics); Springer: New York, NY, USA, 2015; Volume 9315, pp. 477–487.
10. Zhu, W.; Yang, H.; Jin, Y.; Liu, B. A method for recognizing fatigue driving based on dempster-shafer theory and fuzzy neural network. *Math. Probl. Eng.* **2017**, 10. [CrossRef]
11. Lin, L.; Huang, C.; Ni, X.; Wang, J.; Zhang, H.; Li, X.; Qian, Z. Driver fatigue detection based on eye state. *Technol. Heal. Care* **2015**, *23*, S453–S463. [CrossRef] [PubMed]
12. Zhang, C.; Wei, L.; Zheng, P. Research on driving fatigue detection based on PERCLOS. In Proceedings of the 4th International Conference on Vehicle, Mechanical and Electrical Engineering, ICVMEE 2017, Taiyuan, China, 24–25 July 2017; DEStech Publications: Lancaster, PA, USA, 2017; pp. 207–211. [CrossRef]
13. Abulkhair, M.; Alsahli, A.H.; Taleb, K.M.; Bahran, A.M.; Alzahrani, F.M.; Alzahrani, H.A.; Ibrahim, L.F. Mobile platform detect and alerts system for driver fatigue. *Procedia Comput. Sci.* **2015**, *62*, 555–564. [CrossRef]
14. Kong, W.; Zhou, L.; Wang, Y.; Zhang, J.; Liu, J.; Gao, S. A system of driving fatigue detection based on machine vision and its application on smart device. *J. Sens.* **2015**, 11. [CrossRef]
15. Manoharan, R.; Chandrakala, S. Android OpenCV based effective driver fatigue and distraction monitoring system. In Proceedings of the International Conference on Computing and Communications Technologies, ICCCT 2015, Chennai, India, 26–27 February 2015; Institute of Electrical and Electronics Engineers Inc.: Piscataway, NJ, USA, 2015; pp. 262–266.
16. Jabbar, R.; Al-Khalifa, K.; Kharbeche, M.; Alhajyaseen, W.; Jafari, M.; Jiang, S. Real-time driver drowsiness detection for android application using deep neural networks techniques. In Proceedings of the 9th International Conference on Ambient Systems, Networks and Technologies, Porto, Portugal, 8–11 May 2018; pp. 400–407.
17. Galarza, E.E.; Egas, F.D.; Silva, F.M.; Velasco, P.M.; Galarza, E.D. Real time driver drowsiness detection based on driver's face image behavior using a system of human computer interaction implemented in a smartphone. In Proceedings of the International Conference on Information Technology & Systems, La Libertad, Ecuador, 10–12 January 2018; pp. 563–572.
18. Wijnands, J.S.; Thompson, J.; Nice, K.A.; Aschwanden, G.D.P.A.; Stevenson, M. Real-time monitoring of driver drowsiness on mobile platforms using 3D neural networks. *Neural Comput. Appl.* **2019**, 1–13. [CrossRef]
19. Fei, W.; Huabiao, Q. A FPGA based driver drowsiness detecting system. In Proceedings of the 2005 IEEE International Conference on Vehicular Electronics and Safety, ICVES 2005, Shaan'xi, China, 14–16 October 2005; pp. 358–363. [CrossRef]
20. Li, Z.; Zhang, F.; Sun, G.; Zhao, D.; Zheng, K. Driver fatigue detection system based on DSP platform. In Proceedings of the 22nd International Conference on Multimedia Modeling, Miami, FL, USA, 4–6 January 2016; pp. 47–53.
21. Selvakumar, K.; Jerome, J.; Rajamani, K.; Shankar, N. Real-time vision based driver drowsiness detection using partial least squares analysis. *J. Signal Process. Syst.* **2016**, *85*, 263–274. [CrossRef]
22. Teach, Learn, and Make with Raspberry Pi–Raspberry Pi. Available online: https://www.raspberrypi.org/ (accessed on 10 December 2019).
23. The Power of Modern AI to Millions of Devices | NVIDIA Jetson Nano. Available online: https://www.nvidia.com/en-us/autonomous-machines/embedded-systems/jetson-nano/ (accessed on 10 December 2019).
24. Tinker Board | Single Board Computer | ASUS Global. Available online: https://www.asus.com/Single-Board-Computer/Tinker-Board/ (accessed on 10 December 2019).
25. ROCK64 | PINE64. Available online: https://www.pine64.org/devices/single-board-computers/rock64/ (accessed on 10 December 2019).
26. Mavely, A.G.; Judith, J.E.; Sahal, P.A.; Kuruvilla, S.A. Eye gaze tracking based driver monitoring system. In Proceedings of the IEEE International Conference on Circuits and Systems, Thiruvananthapuram, India, 20–21 December 2017; pp. 364–367.

27. Mena, D.M.L.; Rosero, A.F.C. Portable artificial vision system to determine fatigue in a person using a raspberry PI3 card. In Proceedings of the 2017 International Conference on Information Systems and Computer Science, Quito, Ecuador, 23–25 November 2017; pp. 87–91.
28. Hossain, M.Y.; George, F.P. IOT based real-time drowsy driving detection system for the prevention of road accidents. In Proceedings of the 2018 International Conference on Intelligent Informatics and Biomedical Sciences, Bangkok, Thailand, 21–24 October 2018; pp. 190–195.
29. Ghazal, M.; Abu Haeyeh, Y.; Abed, A.; Ghazal, S. Embedded fatigue detection using convolutional neural networks with mobile integration. In Proceedings of the IEEE 6th International Conference on Future Internet of Things and Cloud Workshops, Barcelona, Spain, 6–8 August 2018; pp. 129–133.
30. Kim, W.; Jung, W.-S.; Choi, H.K. Lightweight driver monitoring system based on multi-task mobilenets. *Sensors* **2019**, *19*, 3200. [CrossRef] [PubMed]
31. Wierwille, W.W.; Wreggit, S.S.; Kirn, C.L.; Ellsworth, L.A.; Fairbanks, R.J. *Research on Vehicle-Based Driver Status/Performance Monitoring; Development, Validation, and Refinement of Algorithms for Detection of Driver Drowsiness*; U.S. Department of Transportation: Virginia, VA, USA, 1994.
32. Sigari, M.H.; Fathy, M.; Soryani, M. A driver face monitoring system for fatigue and distraction detection. *Int. J. Veh. Technol.* **2013**, 11. [CrossRef]
33. Rigane, O.; Abbes, K.; Abdelmoula, C.; Masmoudi, M. A fuzzy based method for driver drowsiness detection. In Proceedings of the IEEE/ACS 14th International Conference on Computer Systems and Applications, AICCSA, Hammamet, Tunisia, 30 October–3 November 2017; pp. 143–147.
34. Viola, P.; Jones, M. Rapid object detection using a boosted cascade of simple features. In Proceedings of the IEEE Computer Society Conference on Computer Vision and Pattern Recognition, Kauai, HI, USA, 8–14 December 2001.
35. Dalal, N.; Triggs, B. Histograms of oriented gradients for human detection. In Proceedings of the 2005 IEEE Computer Society Conference on Computer Vision and Pattern Recognition, CVPR 2005, San Diego, CA, USA, 20–26 June 2005; Volume 1, pp. 886–893.
36. Schapire, R.E. Explaining adaboost. In *Empirical Inference: Festschrift in Honor of Vladimir, N. Vapnik*; Schoelkopf, B., Luo, Z., Vovk, V., Eds.; Springer: Berlin/Heidelberg, Germany, 2013; pp. 37–52.
37. Kazemi, V.; Sullivan, J. One millisecond face alignment with an ensemble of regression trees. In Proceedings of the IEEE Computer Society Conference on Computer Vision and Pattern Recognition, San Francisco, CA, USA, 18–20 June 1996; IEEE Computer Society: Washington, DC, USA, 2014; pp. 1867–1874.
38. Sagonas, C.; Tzimiropoulos, G.; Zafeiriou, S.; Pantic, M. 300 faces in-the-wild challenge: The first facial landmark Localization Challenge. In Proceedings of the 2013 IEEE International Conference on Computer Vision, Sydney, Australia, 2–8 December 2013; pp. 397–403.
39. Lin, L.; Huang, C.; Ni, X.; Wang, J.; Zhang, H.; Li, X.; Qian, Z. Driver fatigue detection based on eye state. In Proceedings of the 3rd International Conference on Biomedical Engineering and Technology, Beijing, China, 25–28 September 2014; pp. 453–463.
40. Mamdani, E.H.; Assilian, S. An experiment in linguistic synthesis with a fuzzy logic controller. *Int. J. Man. Mach. Stud.* **1975**, *7*, 1–13. [CrossRef]
41. Flores, M.J.; Armingol, M.J.M.; de la Escalera, A. Sistema avanzado de asistencia a la conducción para la detección de la somnolencia. *Rev. Iberoam. Autom. Inform. Ind. RIAI* **2011**, *8*, 216–228. [CrossRef]
42. Jo, J. Vision-based method for detecting driver drowsiness and distraction in driver monitoring system. *Opt. Eng.* **2011**, *50*, 127202. [CrossRef]
43. Buy a Raspberry Pi 3 Model B–Raspberry Pi. Available online: https://www.raspberrypi.org/products/raspberry-pi-3-model-b/ (accessed on 31 December 2019).
44. Front Page-Raspbian. Available online: https://www.raspbian.org/ (accessed on 31 December 2019).
45. Shoja Ghiass, R.; Arandjelović, O.; Bendada, A.; Maldague, X. Infrared face recognition: A comprehensive review of methodologies and databases. *Pattern Recognit.* **2014**, *47*, 2807–2824. [CrossRef]

© 2020 by the authors. Licensee MDPI, Basel, Switzerland. This article is an open access article distributed under the terms and conditions of the Creative Commons Attribution (CC BY) license (http://creativecommons.org/licenses/by/4.0/).

Article

Sign Language Recognition Using Wearable Electronics: Implementing k-Nearest Neighbors with Dynamic Time Warping and Convolutional Neural Network Algorithms

Giovanni Saggio [1], Pietro Cavallo [2], Mariachiara Ricci [1], Vito Errico [1,*], Jonathan Zea [3] and Marco E. Benalcázar [3]

1. Department of Electronic Engineering, University of Rome "Tor Vergata", Via Politecnico 1, 00133 Rome, Italy; saggio@uniroma2.it (G.S.); maryclair_91@hotmail.it (M.R.)
2. Data Analysis Group, MathWorks, Matrix House, Cambridge Business Park, Cambridge CB4 0HH, UK; p.cavallo85@gmail.com
3. Department of Informatics and Computer Science, Escuela Politécnica Nacional, Quito 170517, Ecuador; marco.benalcazar@epn.edu.ec (M.E.B.); z_tjalezea@yahoo.com (J.Z.)
* Correspondence: vito.errico@uniroma2.it

Received: 27 April 2020; Accepted: 8 July 2020; Published: 11 July 2020

Abstract: We propose a sign language recognition system based on wearable electronics and two different classification algorithms. The wearable electronics were made of a sensory glove and inertial measurement units to gather fingers, wrist, and arm/forearm movements. The classifiers were k-Nearest Neighbors with Dynamic Time Warping (that is a non-parametric method) and Convolutional Neural Networks (that is a parametric method). Ten sign-words were considered from the Italian Sign Language: cose, grazie, maestra, together with words with international meaning such as google, internet, jogging, pizza, television, twitter, and ciao. The signs were repeated one-hundred times each by seven people, five male and two females, aged 29–54 y ± 10.34 (SD). The adopted classifiers performed with an accuracy of 96.6% ± 3.4 (SD) for the k-Nearest Neighbors plus the Dynamic Time Warping and of 98.0% ± 2.0 (SD) for the Convolutional Neural Networks. Our system was made of wearable electronics among the most complete ones, and the classifiers top performed in comparison with other relevant works reported in the literature.

Keywords: wearable electronics; gesture recognition; sign language; sensory glove; IMU; classifiers

1. Introduction

Generally speaking, standardized signs or gestures improve communication [1], as it occurs in army and aircraft security scenarios [2], or improve interaction, as it occurs in human–machine systems [3–5] and in tele-control [6], or improve efficiency, as it occurs in surgery [7], just to mention a few. Specifically, signs that are structured with syntax, semantics, grammar, pragmatics morphology, and phonology become "sign languages" [8], which allow us the expression of thoughts and feelings, in the same way as a "natural language" can do.

Sign languages spread worldwide. This occurs especially because of a large amount of hearing disabilities, suffered by more than 466 million people, as pointed out by the World Health Organization (WHO, 2018) [9]. Sign languages are used by muted, deaf, aurally challenged, and hear impaired people, along as with their relatives and educators. Unfortunately, most of the people are not used to, or do not know, sign languages so their communication with hearing and speaking impaired people is quite difficult. Fortunately, more and more technologies focus on solving this challenging issue, measuring signs and assigning to each gesture the appropriate meaning.

Signs consist of sequences of movements of the upper limbs [10]. Therefore, we have to focus on the measures of these movements, and rests, of each finger, of the wrist and of the arm and forearm too [11]. Such measures can be performed by means of two main approaches, namely image-based and sensor-based methods [8,12]. In particular, the image-based approach demands less-expensive technology, but appropriate light and unobstructed-view conditions, and usually demand of high computational resources. On the other hand, the sensor-based approach requires the signers to wear devices, which can be of some discomfort, but the user is not limited by the scene conditions, since there is no need to stay in front of a camera.

For this work, we decided the use of the sensor-based approach. In particular, we used wearable electronics composed of a homemade sensory glove, used for measuring the movements of the fingers, and inertial measurement units (IMUs), used for measuring the movements of the wrist, forearm, and arm. The potential discomfort of the signers wearing these sensors is minimized, because we built the sensory glove according to the needs and requests of the users, and applied the IMUs with simple Velcro self-gripping straps.

Our research focused on the Italian sign language (Lingua Italiana dei Segni, LIS), that is the Italian one, but our methodology applies to whatever sign language. Our dataset consisted of seven thousand instances of ten gestures measured on seven signers, who performed one hundred instances of each gesture.

For the sign recognition, we considered two classifiers: one based on the k-Nearest Neighbors (k-NN) plus the Dynamic Time Warping (DTW) algorithms (i.e., a non-parametric method), and the other based on Convolutional Neural Networks (CNNs) (i.e., a parametric method). In particular, the k-NN method is applied for the recognition of gestures that may vary in speed, but having similar patterns in the shape of the temporal sequences, whereas the CNN has been more and more proving state of the art accuracies for different kind of signals (in particular for 1D, images, and video).

From the side of measurements, our efforts were particularly devoted to implement a full set of wearable devices, measuring both hand/forearms/arms and fingers of the dominant hand, to realize a dataset with an important number of gesture repetitions (100), and to enroll non-native gesture-speakers, so as to rely on low-repeatability gestures in order to stress the classification algorithms. From the side of classification, we adopted two different approaches, competing or even better performing related works on sign language recognition.

2. Related Works

In the scientific literature, the works that adopt a sensor-based approach use a sensory glove with embedded flex sensors, or inertial measurement units (IMUs), or both [13]. Flex sensors are used for measuring flexion and extension of the fingers' joints [14,15]; IMUs are used for measuring the accelerations and rotations of the palm/wrist and/or the arm/forearm. The number of involved signers, the number of measured signs, and the number of sign repetitions can vary from work to work. Moreover, a number of different classification algorithms have been reported in the literature, underlying the challenging issues to be solved towards the optimal solution for sign language recognition. Within this frame, in the remainder of this section, we present some relevant works for comparison purposes.

Mohandes et al. [16] used the PowerGlove, which provides hand's space position, wrist roll, and four bending finger movements [17]. The glove was used to repeat 10 signs for 20 times. The adopted support vector machine (SVM) algorithm reached an accuracy greater than 90% ± 10(SD).

Mohandes and Deriche [18] measured finger movements using two CyberGloves, with 22 embedded sensors each, and hand movements using the so-called 6-Degrees of Freedom (DOF) "Flock of Birds" device. One signer performed 20 repetitions of 100 two-handed signs. The data dimensionality was reduced by means of Linear Discriminant Analysis (LDA), and the classification was based on the minimum distance (MD) algorithm, reaching an accuracy of 96.2% ± 0.78 (SD).

Two DG5-VHand data gloves, both equipped with five flex sensors and a three-axes accelerometer, were adopted by Tubaiz et al. [19]. Those two gloves measured gestures performed by one signer, who repeated ten times 40 sentences, later divided into 80 words by means of manual labeling separation. With the use of a Modified k-Nearest Neighbors classifier (Mk-NN), researchers obtained the best result as 82% ± 4.88 (SD).

Abualola et al. [20] used a glove equipped with six IMUs to measure fingers and palm movements of nine participants, while signing 24 static letters, one sample per letter per user. Linear Discriminant Analysis (LDA) was applied to reduce the data complexity later analyzed by the Euclidean distance-based classification algorithm, resulting with an accuracy of 85%.

Hernandez et al. [21] adopted a technology based on the "AcceleGlove" and a two-link arm skeleton. Their database consisted of data coming from 17 signers who repeated 30 times one-hand gestures. The classification was based on Conditional Template Matching (CTM) and the resulting recognition rate was equal to 98%.

Lu et al. [22] used the "YoBu" sensory glove, made of eighteen low-cost inertial and magnetic measurement units. This sensor was used to acquire both arm and hand motions, simultaneously. The glove acquired data of 10 types of static gestures. The classification was based on Extreme Learning Machine kernel (ELM-kernel) and on Support Vector Machine (SVM) algorithms, with classification accuracies of 89.59% and 83.65%, respectively.

A work done by Saengsri et al. [23] measured signs by means of a sensory glove and a motion tracker. The first was the "5DT Data Glove 14 Ultra", with 14 sensors for measuring both flexures and abductions of the fingers. The latter provided 3D spatial coordinates of the hand. The dataset consisted of 16 signs, 4 samples for each sign made by a professional signer. The adopted Elman Back Propagation Neural Network (ENN) algorithm resulted with an accuracy of 94.44%.

Silva et al. [24] used a sensory glove, which was equipped with a flex sensor, a gyroscope and an accelerometer attached on the distal phalanx of each finger. The signs were alphabet characters, measured 100 times each. An Artificial Neural Network (ANN) reached 95.8% of recognition accuracy.

Although the aforementioned papers demonstrate important efforts to solve the problem of sign language recognition, the optimal solution remains a challenging problem. This is because there is a lack in defining the best measurement technology and the best classifier, all having advantages and drawbacks too.

We present two different classification algorithms, both competing or even better performing similar literature works. The algorithm based on convolutional neural networks is well suited for training sets from few to thousands, while the algorithm based on the k-nearest neighbors, combined with dynamic time warping, is a good option for scenarios with training sets made of examples in the order of dozens or hundreds.

This work explores possibilities gathered from a double technology measurement approach (a sensory glove plus IMUs), from a huge number of repetitions (100) of each gesture, and from a two-model classification approach (k-NN with DTW and CNN algorithms). In addition, given that native signers sign in highly repeatable manner, we adopted language signs performed by trainees (with lower repetition ability) in order to evidence the robustness of the system, if any.

3. Materials and Methods

Our wearable electronics (simply called wearables hereafter) is composed of a sensory glove and IMUs. In particular, the sensory glove allows measuring the movements of the fingers' joints of the dominant hand (specifically the right one) for every signer (Figure 1a,b), and the IMUs allow measuring the spatial arrangements of the upper limbs (Figure 1c,d).

In general, for the most part of sign languages (and in particular for the here adopted Italian one), the meaning concerns the movements of the fingers of dominant hand, the non-dominant one acting symmetrically or to intensify the meaning only. Therefore, here we adopted a single glove for the dominant hand. Figure 2 shows the overall system.

Data, wireless send via Zigbee protocol to a receiving unit, are stored on a personal computer (Intel i5, 8GB RAM) and reproduced on a screen via avatar (Figure 2).

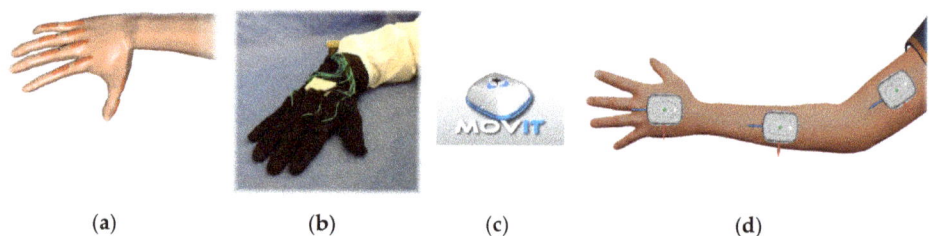

(a) (b) (c) (d)

Figure 1. (**a**) Arrangement of the ten flex sensors on top of the carpal–metacarpal and metacarpal–phalangeal joints of the fingers. (**b**) The sensory glove equipped with the ten flex sensors, singularly hosted in one pocket each. (**c**) The inertial measurement units termed Movit. (**d**) Arrangement of the inertial measurement units (IMUs) on the dorsal aspect of the hand, on the forearm and arm, for both of the upper limbs.

3.1. Sensory Glove

We adopted an indigenously developed sensory glove, termed Hiteg Glove, in order to take into account the requests of comfort and usability evidenced by the signers. Our sensory glove consists of a 70% Lycra and 30% cotton fabric with 10 slim pockets, each hosting one flex sensor [25,26]. An on-purpose hardware translates the analog data from the flex sensors into 12-bit digital values at a 40 Hz sampling frequency. The pockets were sewn onto the regions of the carpal–metacarpal and the metacarpal–phalangeal joints to measure the flexion/extension movements of all fingers.

3.2. IMUs

We used six inertial measurement units (IMUs), three for the left and three for the right upper limb, so as to measure the space arrangement and the movements of the wrists, arms, and forearms. The IMU, previously validated [27–29], is termed "Movit G1" (by Captiks Srl Rome, Italy) (Figure 1c), and hosts three-axial accelerometer, gyroscope and a compass (plus a barometer and a thermometer too, but not used for our purposes). The sampling rate for measurement can be set within 4–200 Hz, the acceleration within ±2 g to ±16 g (gravities), the angular velocity within ±250 dps to ±2000 dps (degree per seconds). Each IMU can store the measured data and/or provide the data to a unique receiver via a proprietary wireless protocol, or through a USB cable.

3.3. Calibration and Data Acquisition

The "Captiks Motion Studio" software store data and reproduce gestures by means of an avatar on a computer screen. The starting procedure consists of a calibration step both for the sensory glove and for the IMUs. In particular for the glove, on the hypothesis of a linear response of the bend sensors, it is requested to the wearer to place the hand completely open (flat) and completely closed (wrist), so that the software will interpolate all the intermediate angles of the joints of the fingers.

For the IMUs, a patented calibration procedure consists of placing the IMUs on a support turned on three orthogonal planes in sequence, and then wearer by the subject posed in a "T" condition (the arms parallel to the floor) to assign a starting plane to each sensor.

The software synchronizes all acquired data by adding timestamps. Thus, the LIS recognition can benefit from simultaneous, multiple sensors, multiple technologies, synchronized data collection, and real-time kinematic reconstruction. The open-source universal messaging ZeroMQ socket (http://zeromq.org/) is configured for transferring the streaming of the acquired data from Motion Studio to MATLAB® and here saved in MATLAB tables. The proposed off-line study permits to identify the most appropriate method for real-time LIS word recognition, further improvable for the

LIS consecutive sentence recognition. For this work, we selected 40 Hz sampling rate from the glove's flex sensors and 200 Hz sampling rate for the IMUs. Delays in the signal chain resulted in an effective average of 37.5 Hz data rate from IMUs. Moreover, we selected ±2 g and ±2000 dps for the acceleration and angular degree scales, respectively.

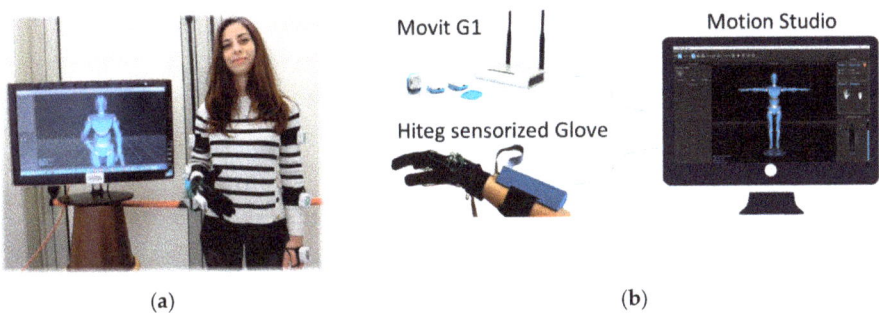

(a)   (b)

Figure 2. (a) A signer with the sensory glove and the six IMUs on the hand/forearm/arm. (b) Block diagram of the system: an avatar reproduces gestures on a computer screen, to visually control that the correct data flow from the sensors; the software manages the data stream and the synchronization of the two system.

3.4. Signers and Signs

Seven signers were recruited for the experiments, five males and two females aged 29–54 y ± 10.34 (SD). All signers were right-handed and with similar hand dimensions, so that a unique-size right-hand sensory glove was used.

The signers were asked to replicate, as accurately as possible, 10 common sign gestures, as showed by a professional language signer. The 10 signs were selected among the most used in LIS (the Italian Sign Language), such as ciao, cose (things), grazie (thanks), maestra (teacher), google, internet, jogging, pizza, TV, and twitter. Most of these 10 signs refers to words internationally known.

Each signer, in turn, wore the sensory glove and the six IMUs by means of Velcro straps, and performed signs when sitting on a chair in front of a table, with his/her right hand resting on the table. The time duration of each sign depended on the natural performance of the user, without any constraint. For each user and each sign, a continuous stream of data, generated by the electronic wearables, was stored on a personal computer. For a mere qualitative correct data flow control, an avatar replicated the signer's movements (Figure 2).

4. Classifiers

We applied two different classification models on the same dataset: the first is a non-parametric method based on the k-Nearest Neighbors (k-NN) classifier and the Dynamic Time Warping (DTW) algorithm, and the second is based on Convolutional Neural Networks (CNNs) [30].

4.1. k-NN with DTW

Data representation: The data acquired when a user performs a gesture, or class, is represented as a tuple $H = (\underline{F}, \overline{\underline{A}}, \overline{\underline{W}}, L)$. The matrix $\underline{F}$ contains the data acquired by the flex sensors from the sensory glove, the hyper-matrices $\overline{\underline{A}}$ and $\overline{\underline{W}}$ contain the data from the accelerometers and the gyroscopes, respectively. The categorical variable $L = 1, 2, \ldots, c$, with $c \in \mathbb{Z}^+$, denotes the corresponding label of the signals $\underline{F}, \overline{\underline{A}}, \overline{\underline{W}}$.

The matrix $\underline{F} = (\mathbf{F}^{(1)}, \ldots, \mathbf{F}^{(i)}, \ldots, \mathbf{F}^{(10)})$ is formed by 10 column vectors of the form $\mathbf{F}^{(i)} = (f_1^{(i)}, \ldots, f_n^{(i)}, \ldots, f_N^{(i)})^T \in \mathbb{R}^{N \times 1}$, with $i = 1, 2, \ldots, 10$ and $N \in \mathbb{Z}^+$. The value of $f_n^{(i)}$ represents the electric resistance, in ohms, measured at the nth instant in the ith flex sensor of the Hiteg Glove, at a sampling frequency of 40 Hz. The hypermatrix $\overline{\mathbf{A}} = (\overline{\mathbf{A}}^{(1)}, \ldots, \overline{\mathbf{A}}^{(j)}, \ldots, \overline{\mathbf{A}}^{(6)}) \in \mathbb{R}^{M \times 6 \times 3}$ is formed by the hypermatrices $\overline{\mathbf{A}}^{(j)} = ({}^x\mathbf{A}^{(j)}, {}^y\mathbf{A}^{(j)}, {}^z\mathbf{A}^{(j)}) \in \mathbb{R}^{M \times 1 \times 3}$, with $j = 1, 2, \ldots, 6$ and $M \in \mathbb{Z}^+$. The vector ${}^s\mathbf{A}^{(j)} = ({}^s a_1^{(j)}, \ldots, {}^s a_m^{(j)}, \ldots, {}^s a_M^{(j)})^T \in \mathbb{R}^{M \times 1}$ is the measurement returned by the jth inertial sensor of the Movit G1 in the sth coordinate axis, with $s \in \{x,y,z\}$. The value of ${}^s a_m^{(j)}$ represents the acceleration, in fractions of gravity, measured at a sampling frequency of 37.5 Hz at the mth instant of time.

Similarly, the hypermatrix $\overline{\mathbf{W}} = (\overline{\mathbf{W}}^{(1)}, \ldots, \overline{\mathbf{W}}^{(j)}, \ldots, \overline{\mathbf{W}}^{(6)}) \in \mathbb{R}^{M \times 6 \times 3}$ corresponds to the angular velocity, in degrees per second, measured at a sampling frequency of 37.5 Hz, and it is formed by the hypermatrices $\overline{\mathbf{W}}^{(j)} = ({}^x\mathbf{W}^{(j)}, {}^y\mathbf{W}^{(j)}, {}^z\mathbf{W}^{(j)}) \in \mathbb{R}^{M \times 1 \times 3}$. The column vector ${}^s\mathbf{W}^{(j)} = ({}^s w_1^{(j)}, \ldots, {}^s w_m^{(j)}, \ldots, {}^s w_M^{(j)})^T \in \mathbb{R}^{M \times 1}$ contains the data of the jth inertial sensor in the sth coordinate axis, with $s \in \{x,y,z\}$.

The length N of the column vectors $\mathbf{F}^{(i)}$ of the flex sensors and the length M of the vectors ${}^s\mathbf{A}^{(j)}$ of the accelerometer and the vectors ${}^s\mathbf{W}^{(j)}$ of the angular velocity are not equal. This is because of the difference in the sampling rate of each sensor: 40 Hz for the flex sensors and 37.5 Hz for the IMU sensors.

Datasets: The signs are grouped to form a dataset $\mathcal{H} = \{\mathcal{H}_1, \ldots, \mathcal{H}_1, \ldots, \mathcal{H}_U\}$, with $U \in \mathbb{Z}^+$, where the example $\mathcal{H}_u = (\underline{\mathbf{F}}_u, \overline{\mathbf{A}}_u, \overline{\mathbf{W}}_u, L_u)$ is the uth instance of a gesture labeled with L_u, where $u = 1, 2, \ldots, U$. Data were randomly split into a test set (with 20% of the original dataset) and a training set (with the remaining 80% of the original dataset).

Training and testing sets: A subset $\mathcal{H}_1^v$ from the set $\mathcal{H}$ was used for training and the remaining subset $\mathcal{H} - \mathcal{H}_1^v$ was used for testing, where $0 < v < U$, with $v \in \mathbb{Z}^+$. Since the k-NN with DTW algorithm does not need any training (but only the adjustment of the number of neighbors used for the classification), here the term training refers to differentiate data used to find the k-nearest neighbors to the signal being classified, which comes from the testing set used to estimate the accuracy of the classification model. Therefore, we should be clear that.

Pre-processing: In this stage, we first normalized the amplitude and then filtered the noise of the time series contained in the column vectors of the examples $(\underline{\mathbf{F}}, \overline{\mathbf{A}}, \overline{\mathbf{W}})$ from the set $\mathcal{H}_1^v$.

For the normalization, we used the function $\mathcal{L} : \mathbb{R}^{N \times 1} \to \mathbb{R}^{N \times 1}$ defined through the following equation:

$$\mathcal{L}(\mathbf{V}) = \frac{\mathbf{V} - \overline{\mathbf{V}}_{\min}}{\overline{\mathbf{V}}_{\max} - \overline{\mathbf{V}}_{\min}}, \qquad (1)$$

In this equation, $\mathbf{V} \in \{\underline{\mathbf{F}}, \overline{\mathbf{A}}, \overline{\mathbf{W}}\}$ denotes the vector to normalize and $\mathcal{L}(\mathbf{V})$ denotes the normalized vector. The values of $\overline{\mathbf{V}}_{\max}$ and $\overline{\mathbf{V}}_{\min}$ are computed among the values of the element from the set $\{\underline{\mathbf{F}}, \overline{\mathbf{A}}, \overline{\mathbf{W}}\}$ that $\mathbf{V}$ takes. For example, if we want to normalize the values of the vector $\mathbf{F}^{(i)} \in \underline{\mathbf{F}}$, being $\mathbf{V} = \mathbf{F}^{(i)}$, the $\overline{\mathbf{V}}_{\max}$ and $\overline{\mathbf{V}}_{\min}$ are the maximum and minimum values, respectively, computed among all the values of the column vectors that form the set $\{\underline{\mathbf{F}}_1, \ldots, \underline{\mathbf{F}}_v\}$. A similar process is applied for the case where $\mathbf{V} = {}^s\mathbf{A}^{(j)}$ and $\mathbf{V} = {}^s\mathbf{W}^{(j)}$. This normalization function $\mathcal{L}$ is applied over all the time series of each example from the training set $\mathcal{H}_1^v$, so that each component of the new vectors is in the range $[0,1]$. Applying this normalization over all the instances (i.e., tuples) of the training set, we obtain the new set $\mathcal{L}(\mathcal{H}_1^v) = \{(\mathcal{L}(\underline{\mathbf{F}}_u), \mathcal{L}(\overline{\mathbf{A}}_u), \mathcal{L}(\overline{\mathbf{W}}_u), L_u)\}_{u=1}^v$.

For filtering, we apply a low pass filter ψ to the normalized time series $\mathcal{L}(\overline{\mathbf{A}}_u)$ and $\mathcal{L}(\overline{\mathbf{W}}_u)$ of the inertial sensors only. The function ψ is a digital Butterworth filter [31] of 4th order, where the cutoff frequency is $f_c = 0.05 \pi f_s$, where f_s is the value of the sampling frequency in Hz. From this step, we obtain the set:

$$\psi(\mathcal{L}(\mathcal{H}_1^v)) = \{(\mathcal{L}(\underline{\mathbf{F}}_u), \psi(\mathcal{L}(\overline{\mathbf{A}}_u)), \psi(\mathcal{L}(\overline{\mathbf{W}}_u)), L_u)\}_{u=1}^v \qquad (2)$$

Classification: The classification assigns a label to a gesture $\mathbf{X} \in \mathcal{H}_{v+1}^U$ of the testing set based on the k-Nearest Neighbors (k-NN) classifier and the Dynamic Time Warping (DTW) algorithm [32].

We computed a distance value $d \in \mathbb{R}^+$ that represents the similarity between the unlabeled preprocessed gesture $\psi(\mathcal{L}(\mathbf{X}))$, with $\mathbf{X} = (\mathbf{F}, \overline{\mathbf{A}}, \overline{\mathbf{W}})$, and the 3 first elements of each tuple from the preprocessed training set $\psi(\mathcal{L}(\mathcal{H}_1^v))$. We used the DTW algorithm [33] to optimally align the corresponding channels of $\psi(\mathcal{L}(\mathbf{X}))$ and each tuple from the set $\psi(\mathcal{L}(\mathcal{H}_1^v))$. For computing the distance d between $\psi(\mathcal{L}(\mathbf{X}))$ and the three first elements of each tuple from the set $\psi(\mathcal{L}(\mathcal{H}_1^v))$, we first computed the DTW distance $d(\mathbf{F}^{(i)})$ between the corresponding channels of the flex sensors (Equation (3)), the distance $d(^{(s)}\mathbf{A}^{(j)})$ between the corresponding channels of the accelerometers (Equation (4)), and the distance $d(^{(s)}\mathbf{W}^{(j)})$ between the corresponding channels of the angular velocity (Equation (5)).

$$d(\mathbf{F}^{(i)}) = DTW\left(\mathcal{L}(\mathbf{F}^{(i)}), \mathcal{L}(F_u^{(i)})\right), \mathbf{F}^{(i)} \in \mathbf{X}, \tag{3}$$

$$d(^{(s)}\mathbf{A}^{(j)}) = DTW\left(\psi\left(\mathcal{L}(^{(s)}\mathbf{A}^{(j)})\right), \psi\left(\mathcal{L}(^{(s)}\mathbf{A}_u^{(j)})\right)\right), {}^{(s)}\mathbf{A}^{(j)} \in \mathbf{X}, \tag{4}$$

$$d(^{(s)}\mathbf{W}^{(j)}) = DTW\left(\psi\left(\mathcal{L}(^{(s)}\mathbf{W}^{(j)})\right), \psi\left(\mathcal{L}(^{(s)}\mathbf{W}_u^{(j)})\right)\right), {}^{(s)}\mathbf{W}^{(j)} \in \mathbf{X}, \tag{5}$$

with $u = 1, 2, \ldots, U$, where $U \in \mathbb{Z}^+$ is the size of the training set.

For computing the total distance d_u between $\psi(\mathcal{L}(\mathbf{X}))$ and the uth tuple from the preprocessed training set $\psi(\mathcal{L}(\mathcal{H}_{u=1}^v))$, we summed all the DTW distances obtained using the Equations (3)–(5):

$$d_u = \sum_{i=1}^{10} d(\mathbf{F}^{(i)}) + \sum_{j=1}^{6}\left(\sum_{s \in \{x,y,z\}} d(^{(s)}\mathbf{A}^{(j)}) + d(^{(s)}\mathbf{W}^{(j)})\right). \tag{6}$$

The label Y, with $Y \in \{1, 2, \ldots, c\}$, that the classifier returns for the unknown gesture $\mathbf{X}$ corresponds to the most voted label among the k-nearest neighbors in terms of the DTW distance, [34,35] found in the preprocessed training set $\psi(\mathcal{L}(\mathcal{H}_1^v))$.

For the kNN and DTW classification algorithm, we evaluated several implementations of DTW. The options that we tested range from evaluating the whole matrix of distances between the two signals to find the best path of alignment and more efficient implementations based on dynamic programming and window constraints of the space of search for the best path of alignment of the signals. The criteria that we used for evaluating different implementations of DTW was the gain in the classification accuracy versus the increase in the time of processing of the classification algorithm. For all the implementations that we tested, there was not a significant difference in terms of the classification accuracy, but there was an important difference in the time of processing. Based on this analysis, we chose the option based on dynamic programming with a window constraint in the space of search space of length 50 [36].

4.2. CNN

Datasets: In the same way as for the k-NN with the DTW algorithm, for the CNN classifier data were randomly split into a test set (20% of the original dataset) and a training set (the remaining 80%). The training set was further split into two subsets to create a validation set. As common practice in literature, we used a holdout validation scheme considering 20% of the training samples for model selection and hyper-parameters tuning and the remaining 80% for training the model.

Pre-processing: All signals were re-sampled to a fix number of 120 samples by means of a cubic spline interpolation using not-a-knot end conditions. Signals were further normalized, dividing each dimension by its maximum across the training set, using the normalization function $\mathcal{L} : \mathbb{R}^{N \times 1} \to \mathbb{R}^{N \times 1}$:

$$\mathcal{L}(\mathbf{V}) = \frac{\mathbf{V}}{\overline{\mathbf{V}}_{max}}. \tag{7}$$

Network architecture: We tried several network architectures and hyper-parameter values for Convolutional Neural Networks (CNN) [30] including different numbers and complexity of the convolutional layers, various learning rates and mini-batch sizes. We also tried Long Short Term Memory (LSTM) networks [37]. Among all the architectures and the hyper-parameters values that we tried, the best validation accuracy was achieved by a CNN network with only one convolutional layer with 20 filters of size 16, ReLU activation and batch normalization [38], no pooling layers, and 16 × 16 sized kernel. A fully connected layer was then used to obtain the vector $\mathbf{Z} = (Z_1, \ldots, Z_c) \in \mathbb{R}^{c \times 1}$, where c is the number of classes, being $c = 10$ in our case (Figure 3).

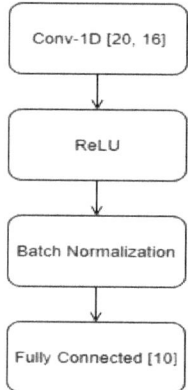

Figure 3. Convolutional Neural Network (CNN) architecture used in this work.

Training phase: We chose to optimize the cross-entropy loss function of the Matlab softmax function applied to the resulting vector $\mathbf{Z}$ together with L2 weights regularizes, where the jth component of the softmax is defined as follows:

$$p_j = \frac{e^{Z_j}}{\sum_{k=1}^{c} e^{Z_k}}, \tag{8}$$

with $j = 1, \ldots, c$. The cross-entropy between the resulting vector of probabilities $\mathbf{p} = (p_1, \ldots, p_c)$ predicted by the network and the expected one-hot encoding $\mathbf{Y} = (Y_1, \ldots, Y_c)$ of the actual label Y of the gesture $\mathbf{X}$ is defined as follows:

$$H(\mathbf{Y}, \mathbf{p}) = -\sum_{i=1}^{c} Y_i \times \log(p_i). \tag{9}$$

The CNN was trained using stochastic gradient descent with momentum, with a learning rate of 10^{-4} and a mini-batch size of 200. The training went on for 9600 iterations and was stopped when the validation loss did not increase for five consecutive times. This took a total time of 244 s using a Tesla K40 GPU and MATLAB® with its Neural Network Toolbox.

5. Results and Discussion

For this work, we used a dataset composed of 10 different gestures, repeated 100 times each by 7 users, obtaining a dataset of $U = 7000$ tuples. This dataset $\mathcal{H}_1^U$ was divided into two subsets: one subset $\mathcal{H}_1^{5600}$ contains 80% of the examples for designing and training the classification models, and the other subset $\mathcal{H}_{5601}^{7000}$, 20% of $\mathcal{H}_1^U$, was used for testing the models. Before performing this partition, the elements of the original dataset were randomly shuffled.

5.1. Results with the k-NN and DTW Algorithm

For defining the model composed of the k-NN classifier with DTW algorithm, we tested this model varying two parameters: the size N of the training set and the number k of neighbors. Each training set $\mathcal{H}_1^N$ was formed by selecting the first N elements from $\mathcal{H}_1^{5600}$, where $N = 70, 140, 210, 280, 350$, i.e., with an incremental step of 70 tuples, so that to balance the tuples added from each user. Moreover, the training set had the same number of tuples for each sign to recognize in order to be balanced. The number k of neighbors varies from 1 to N/7, where (N/7) $\in \mathbb{Z}^+$ is the number of tuples per gesture in the training set $\mathcal{H}_1^N$. It is worth noting that, for the classification using the k-NN with the DTW algorithm, we only used a small fraction of the training set in order to reduce the time of classification without reducing significantly the accuracy of the model. The accuracies reported in Figure 4a were computed by applying each model tested to all the tuples in the test set $\mathcal{H}_{5601}^{7000}$. Figure 4b shows the variation of the time of classification versus the size N of the training set. Each point of Figure 4b was obtained as the average of the times of classifying each tuple from the test set.

As Figure 4 shows, the accuracy of the classification model improves with the increase of the size N of the training set; however, the time required for training a model with a larger number of examples increases at a growth rate of approximately O(N). Table 1 shows the confusion matrix related to the results obtained when the classification model was trained using N = 140 examples (2 repetitions per user for each gesture) and just one neighbor, k = 1, for the k-NN algorithm. It is worth mentioning that these settings correspond to a balance between a good accuracy and a low processing time. In the confusion matrix, the predicted gestures are in the rows, whereas the actual gestures are in the columns. The percentage shown in each cell, except for the cells of the last column and the last row, is obtained by diving the value that accompanies the percentage by the sum of the values of all the cells of the matrix, except for the last row and the last column. Therefore, the accuracy of each method (the last value of the main diagonal) is obtained by adding up the percentages along the main diagonal, except for the last value. The precisions (percentages are shown in the last column) are computed by dividing the value of the main diagonal, in each row, by the sum of the values of that row. The sensitivities (percentages shown in the last row) are computed by dividing the value of the main diagonal, in each column, by the sum of the values of that column.

Table 1 shows two main results related to the confusion: on the lower row the sensitivity rates (i.e., percentage of gestures correctly classified over the total of gestures performed for a given class), and on the right column the precision rates (i.e., percentage of gestures correctly classified over the total of gestures predicted for a given class). Three gestures reach 100% of sensitivity rate: jogging, pizza, and twitter. On the other hand, the worst sensitivity is for the gesture cose with 87.5%, while its precision is 100%. This means that every time that cose was predicted, it was correct, but many cose signs were not identified as such. Interestingly, the sign google has an opposite behavior, because its precision is just 89.4% (the worst among all precisions), but its sensitivity is 96.4%. Finally, the overall recognition accuracy of the k-NN with DTW model is 96.6%.

5.2. Results with the CNN Algorithm

Table 2 shows the classification accuracy obtained by the CNN classifier. The experiments were repeated 10 times using different random seeds for hyperparameters initialization and the mean accuracy is reported with results equal to 98% on the test set, 98.04% on the validation set, and 99.8% on the training set. Deeper architectures with more than one convolutional layer and pooling layers led to comparable if not worse results. This was somehow expected, since the small number of classes. Among all the architectures that gave us comparable results, we picked the smallest since we envision this application to run in real time and a smaller network would lead to faster performances. It is worth mentioning that the time performance of the training phase on GPU is also very fast.

Table 1. Confusion matrix for the k-NN and DTW classification model.

	Google	Internet	Jogging	Pizza	Television	Twitter	Ciao	Cose	Grazie	Maestra	PRECISION
Google	135; 9.6%	0; 0%	0; 0%	0; 0%	1; 0.1%	0; 0%	0; 0%	13; 0.9%	2; 0.1%	0; 0%	89.4%
Internet	0; 0%	132; 9.4%	0; 0%	0; 0%	0; 0%	0; 0%	0; 0%	4; 0.3%	0; 0%	0; 0%	97.1%
Jogging	2; 0.1%	0; 0.0%	140; 10%	0; 0%	8; 0%	0; 0%	0; 0%	0; 0%	0; 0%	0; 0%	93.3%
Pizza	0; 0%	0; 0%	0; 0%	140; 10%	0; 0%	0; 0%	0; 0%	0; 0%	0; 0%	0; 0%	100%
Television	3; 0.2%	0; 0.0%	0; 0%	0; 0.0%	131; 9.4%	0; 0%	0; 0%	0; 0%	0; 0%	1; 0.1%	97.0%
Twitter	0; 0%	0; 0%	0; 0%	0; 0%	0; 0%	140; 10%	0; 0%	0; 0%	0; 0%	0; 0.0%	100%
Ciao	0; 0%	0; 0%	0; 0%	0; 0%	0; 0%	0; 0%	139; 9.9%	0; 0%	0; 0%	0; 0%	100%
Cose	0; 0%	0; 0%	0; 0%	0; 0%	0; 0%	0; 0%	0; 0%	120; 8.6%	0; 0%	0; 0%	100%
Grazie	0; 0%	8; 0.6%	0; 0%	0; 0%	0; 0%	0; 0%	1; 0.1%	3; 0.2%	138; 9.9%	1; 0.1%	91.4%
Maestra	0; 0%	0; 0%	0; 0%	0; 0%	0; 0%	0; 0%	0; 0%	0; 0%	0; 0%	138; 9.9%	100%;
SENSITIVITY	96.4%	94.3%	100%	100%	93.6%	100%	99.3%	85.7%	98.6%	98.6%	96.6%

Table 2. Confusion matrix for the CNN classification model.

	Google	Internet	Jogging	Pizza	Television	Twitter	Ciao	Cose	Grazie	Maestra	PRECISION
Google	139; 9.9%	0; 0%	1; 0.1%	0; 0%	0; 0%	0; 0%	0; 0%	0; 0%	1; 0.1%	0; 0%	98.6%
Internet	0; 0%	139; 9.9%	0; 0%	0; 0%	0; 0%	0; 0%	1; 0.1%	0; 0%	0; 0%	1; 0.1%	98.6%
Jogging	0; 0%	0; 0%	135; 9.6%	1; 0.1%	0; 0%	1; 0.1%	2; 0.1%	2; 0.1%	1; 0.1%	0; 0%	95.1%
Pizza	0; 0%	0; 0%	0; 0%	138; 9.9%	0; 0%	0; 0%	0; 0%	0; 0%	0; 0%	0; 0%	100%
Television	0; 0%	0; 0%	0; 0%	0; 0%	140; 10.0%	0; 0%	0; 0%	0; 0%	0; 0%	0; 0%	100%
Twitter	0; 0%	0; 0%	0; 0%	1; 0.1%	0; 0%	139; 9.9%	0; 0%	0; 0%	0; 0%	0; 0%	99.3%
Ciao	0; 0%	0; 0%	2; 0.1%	0; 0%	0; 0%	0; 0%	133; 9.5%	0; 0%	0; 0%	0; 0%	98.5%
Cose	1; 0.1%	0; 0%	0; 0%	0; 0%	0; 0%	0; 0%	0; 0%	137; 9.8%	1; 0.1%	2; 0.1%	97.2%
Grazie	0; 0%	0; 0%	0; 0%	0; 0%	0; 0%	0; 0%	0; 0%	1; 0.1%	135; 9.6%	0; 0%	99.3%
Maestra	0; 0%	1; 0.1%	2; 0.1%	0; 0%	0; 0%	0; 0%	4; 0.3%	0; 0%	2; 0.1%	137; 9.8%	93.8%
SENSITIVITY	99.3%	99.3%	96.4%	98.6%	100%	99.3%;	95.0%	97.9%	96.4%	97.9%	98.0%

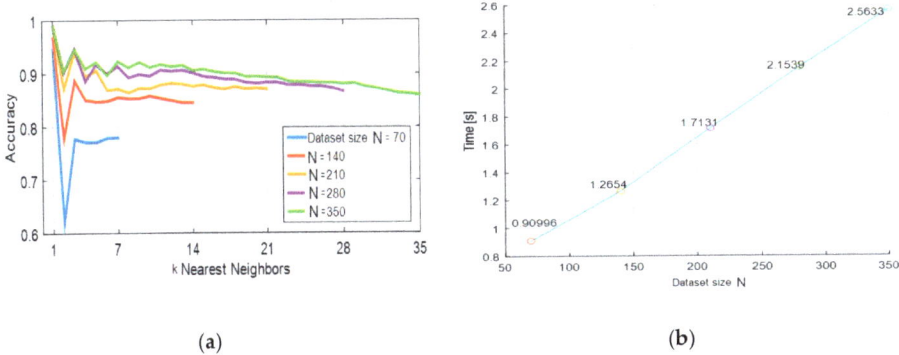

(a) (b)

Figure 4. Related to the *k*-Nearest Neighbors (*k*-NN) and Dynamic Time Warping (DTW) classification algorithm: (**a**) Accuracy for different dataset sizes N and number of neighbors k; (**b**) Average time of classification versus the size N of the training set.

5.3. Comparison of Results with Related Works

The relevant works about sign language recognition were already discussed in Section 2. Now, after reporting our results, we present in Table 3 a comparison of our work with the technologies and the classification accuracies of the works reviewed in this paper. According to this comparison, our method performed better than the other methods. As far as we know, we consider this as a very promising result.

Table 3. Confusion matrix for the CNN classification model.

Reference	Sensor(s)	Signers, Signs, Repetitions	Classifier	Accuracy $m \pm s$ [%]
Mohandes et al., 1996 [16]	PowerGlove	n/a, 10, 20	SVM	90 ± 10
Mohandes and Deriche, 2013 [18]	CyberGloves	1, 100, 20	LDA + MD	96.2 ± 0.78
Tubaiz et al., 2015 [19]	DG5 - VHand	1, 40, 10	MKNN	82 ± 4.88
Abualola et al., 2016 [20]	AcceleGlove + skeleton	17, 1, 30	CTM	98 ± n/a
Lu et al., 2016 [22]	YoBuGlove	n/a, 10, n/a	ELM-kernel SVM	89.59 ± n/a 83.65 ± n/a
Saengsri et al., 2012 [23]	5DTGlove + tracker	1, 16, 4	ENN	94.44 ± n/a
Silva et al., 2017 [24]	Glove + IMU	1, 26, 100	ANN	95.8 ± n/a
Our work	HitegGlove + Movit G1 IMU	7, 10, 100	kNN + DTW CNN	96.6 ± 3.4 98 ± 2.0

6. Conclusions

The non-parametric model that combines the *k*-NN classifier with the DTW algorithm has good classification accuracy (96.6%) and its time complexity has a linear growth with the number of examples used to find the *k*-nearest neighbors for classification. The classification accuracy of this model improves with the increase of the number of training examples, but at the cost of increasing also the time of classification. Therefore, practical applications of sign language classification, especially in real time, using the *k*-NN and DTW model demand a tradeoff between accuracy and time of processing. Even though the time of classification is a big drawback for this model when we have a large dataset, its high accuracy has to be considered, especially for scenarios where the number of examples for the classification is limited. As it is usual, the computing time of this and other models depends highly on the hardware used to run the model. The *k*-NN and DTW model was tested on a desktop computer with an Intel® Core™ i7-3770S processor (Intel Corporation, Santa Clara, CA, USA) and 4 GB of RAM.

The relatively high classification accuracy and linear time complexity of the k-NN and DTW model suggest that it can be a good option for applications where the processing and storage capabilities are limited and the number of available data is in the order of the dozens.

The CNN parametric classifier performed with a very high accuracy value, quite close to 100%. We also tried to run inference of this model using a CPU, and we got up to 500 gestures per second on computer with an Intel® Core™ i7-7700 processor ((Intel Corporation, Santa Clara, CA, USA) and 16 GB of RAM. This speed of processing means that inference in real time is possible using the CNN classifier.

The difference between the accuracies of both models tested in this work might occur because the CNN model captures better the distribution underlying the data of the ten gestures that we used here. However, with the increase of the number of training examples, the k-NN and DTW model might lead to similar or even better results than the CNN model at the cost of a higher time of processing. However, increasing the number of training examples will increase the time of training of the CNN, but its time of prediction will be fixed since the complexity of the CNN does not change with the increase of the size of the training set. This last feature of the CNN and the results obtained in this work evidence that this model is an interesting option for sign language classification in scenarios with many training examples.

We reported comparisons of our results with those from other relevant works published in the scientific literature. Although a perfect fit among all the works is almost impossible, since there are differences in terms of the types of wearables and signs, and number of signers and signs, the higher accuracies obtained in this work suggest how our approach can be valuable for sign recognition purposes. There are some major differences with respect to other studies. In particular, the number of used sensors, that constitute a complete set for full fingers, hands/arms/forearms joints analysis; the 100 gesture repetitions for each LIS sign from each signer, that constitute a comprehensive set of valuable data, permit us a fair and reliable comparison between two different data analysis approach. Moreover, the data from the sensory glove and the IMUs are collected and synchronized, providing real-time data-fusion from both sensory glove and IMUs.

As a meaningful further consideration, our database was constructed with signs performed by trainees rather than expert native signers, which adds a sort of "robustness" to the tested classification algorithms. Indeed, a non-native speaker typically repeats a specific gesture with minor precision with respect to a native speaker. Thus, the analysis applies to more dispersed values, thus enabling an expected better performance in case of native-speaker better-accuracy gestures (to be demonstrated in a future work).

Further research includes improvements on the k-NN and DTW model using an efficient reduction of the data dimensionality. In this way, better and faster results might be obtained, which in turn may also allow us to recognize more gestures for real-time applications. Finally, both models need to be tested at classifying more classes for different sign languages and for the recognition of consecutive sentences.

Author Contributions: Conceptualization, G.S. and M.E.B.; methodology, G.S., P.C., J.Z., and M.E.B.; software, P.C., M.R., and J.Z.; validation, G.S., P.C., and M.E.B.; formal analysis, P.C. and J.Z.; investigation, G.S., M.R., V.E., J.Z., and M.E.B.; resources, G.S. and M.E.B.; data curation, G.S., P.C., M.R., V.E., J.Z., and M.E.B.; writing—original draft preparation, G.S., P.C., and M.E.B.; writing—review and editing, G.S. and M.E.B.; visualization, G.S. and M.E.B.; supervision, G.S. and M.E.B.; project administration, G.S. and M.E.B.; funding acquisition, G.S. and M.E.B. All authors have read and agreed to the published version of the manuscript.

Funding: Authors gratefully acknowledge the financial support provided by Escuela Politécnica Nacional for the development of the research project PIJ-16-13 "Clasificación de señales electromiográficas del brazo humano usando técnicas de reconocimiento de patrones y machine learning".

Conflicts of Interest: The authors declare no conflict of interest. The funders had no role in the design of the study; in the collection, analyses, or interpretation of data; in the writing of the manuscript, or in the decision to publish the results.

References

1. Saggio, G.; Cavrini, F.; Di Paolo, F. Inedited SVM application to automatically tracking and recognizing arm-and-hand visual signals to aircraft. In Proceedings of the 7th International Joint Conference on Computational Intelligence 3, Lisbon, Portugal, 12–14 November 2015; pp. 157–162.
2. Saggio, G.; Cavrini, F.; Pinto, C.A. Recognition of arm-and-hand visual signals by means of SVM to increase aircraft security. *Stud. Comput. Intell.* **2017**, *669*, 444–461.
3. León, M.; Romero, P.; Quevedo, W.; Arteaga, O.; Terán, C.; Benalcázar, M.E.; Andaluz, V.H. Virtual rehabilitation system for fine motor skills using a functional hand orthosis. In Proceedings of the International Conference on Augmented Reality, Virtual Reality and Computer Graphics, Otranto, Italy, 24–27 June 2018; pp. 78–94.
4. Ramírez, F.; Segura-Morales, M.; Benalcázar, M.E. Design of a software architecture and practical applications to exploit the capabilities of a human arm gesture recognition system. In Proceedings of the 3rd IEEE Ecuador Technical Chapters Meeting (ETCM), Cuenca, Ecuador, 15–19 October 2018; pp. 1–6.
5. Tsironi, E.; Barros, P.; Weber, C.; Wermter, S. An analysis of convolutional long short-term memory recurrent neural networks for gesture recognition. *Neurocomputing* **2017**, *268*, 76–86. [CrossRef]
6. Saggio, G.; Bizzarri, M. Feasibility of teleoperations with multi-fingered robotic hand for safe extravehicular manipulations. *Aerosp. Sci. Tech.* **2014**, *39*, 666–674. [CrossRef]
7. Saggio, G.; Lazzaro, A.; Sbernini, L.; Carrano, F.M.; Passi, D.; Corona, A.; Panetta, V.; Gaspari, A.L.; Di Lorenzo, N. Objective surgical skill assessment: An initial experience by means of a sensory glove paving the way to open surgery simulation? *J. Surg. Educ.* **2015**, *72*, 910–917. [CrossRef] [PubMed]
8. Mohandes, M.; Deriche, M.; Liu, J. Image-Based and sensor-based approaches to Arabic sign language recognition. *IEEE Trans. Hum. Mach. Syst.* **2014**, *44*, 551–557. [CrossRef]
9. Who.int. Available online: http://www.who.int/mediacentre/factsheets/fs300/en/ (accessed on 2 May 2018).
10. Valli, C.; Lucas, C. *Linguistics of American Sign Language: An Introduction*, 4th ed.; University Press: Washington, DC, USA, 2000.
11. Yi, B.; Wang, X.; Harris, F.C.; Dascalu, S.M. sEditor: A prototype for a sign language interfacing system. *IEEE Trans. Hum. Mach. Syst.* **2014**, *44*, 499–510. [CrossRef]
12. Saggio, G.; Sbernini, L. New scenarios in human trunk posture measurements for clinical applications. In Proceedings of the IEEE International Symposium on Medical Measurements and Applications (MeMeA 2011), Bari, Italy, 30–31 May 2011.
13. Estrada, L.; Benalcázar, M.E.; Sotomayor, N. Gesture recognition and machine learning applied to sign language translation. In Proceedings of the 7th Latin American Congress on Biomedical Engineering CLAIB 2016, Bucaramanga, Colombia, 26–28 October 2016; pp. 233–236.
14. Orengo, G.; Lagati, A.; Saggio, G. Modeling wearable bend sensor behavior for human motion capture. *IEEE Sens. J.* **2014**, *14*, 2307–2316. [CrossRef]
15. Saggio, G.; Bocchetti, S.; Pinto, C.A.; Orengo, G.; Giannini, F. A novel application method for wearable bend sensors. In Proceedings of the 2nd IEEE International Symposium on Applied Sciences in Biomedical and Communication Technologies, Bratislava, Slovakia, 24–27 November 2009; pp. 1–39.
16. Mohandes, M.; A-Buraiky, S.; Halawani, T.; Al-Baiyat, S. Automation of the Arabic sign language recognition. In Proceedings of the IEEE International Conference on Information and Communication Technologies: From Theory to Applications, Damascus, Syria, 19–23 April 2004; pp. 479–480.
17. Kadous, M.W. Machine recognition of auslan signs using powergloves: Towards large-lexicon recognition of sign language. In Proceedings of the Workshop on the Integration of Gesture in Language and Speech, Wilmington, DE, USA, 7–8 October 1996.
18. Mohandes, M.; Deriche, M. Arabic sign language recognition by decisions fusion using Dempster-Shafer theory of evidence. In Proceedings of the IEEE Computing, Communications and IT Applications Conference, Hong Kong, China, 2–3 April 2013; pp. 90–94.
19. Tubaiz, N.; Shanableh, T.; Assaleh, K. Glove-Based continuous arabic sign language recognition in user-dependent mode. *IEEE Trans. Hum. Mach. Syst.* **2015**, *45*, 526–533. [CrossRef]
20. Abualola, H.; Al Ghothani, H.; Eddin, A.N.; Almoosa, N.; Poon, K. Flexible gesture recognition using wearable inertial sensors. In Proceedings of the 59th IEEE International Midwest Symposium on Circuits and Systems, Abu Dhabi, UAE, 16–19 October 2016; pp. 1–4.

21. Hernandez-Rebollar, J.L.; Kyriakopoulos, N.; Lindeman, R.W. A new instrumented approach for translating American sign language into sound and text. In Proceedings of the 6th IEEE International Conference on Automatic Face and Gesture Recognition, Seoul, Korea, 17–19 May 2004; pp. 547–552.
22. Lu, D.; Yu, Y.; Liu, H. Gesture recognition using data glove: An extreme learning machine method. In Proceedings of the IEEE International Conference on Robotics and Biomimetics, Qingdao, China, 3–7 December 2016; pp. 1349–1354.
23. Saengsri, S.; Niennattrakul, V.; Ratanamahatana, C.A. TFRS: Thai finger-spelling sign language recognition system. In Proceedings of the 2nd IEEE International Conference on Digital Information and Communication Technology and its Applications, Bangkok, Thailand, 16–18 May 2012; pp. 457–462.
24. Silva, B.C.R.; Furriel, G.P.; Pacheco, W.C.; Bulhoes, J.S. Methodology and comparison of devices for recognition of sign language characters. In Proceedings of the 18th IEEE International Scientific Conference on Electric Power Engineering, Kouty nad Desnou, Czech Republic, 17–19 May 2017; pp. 1–6.
25. Saggio, G.; Cavallo, P.; Fabrizio, A.; Ibe, S.O. Gesture recognition through HITEG data glove to provide a new way of communication. In Proceedings of the 4th International Symposium on Applied Sciences in Biomedical and Communication Technologies (ISABEL'11), Barcelona, Spain, 26 October 2011.
26. Saggio, G.; Orengo, G. Flex sensor characterization against shape and curvature changes. *Sens. Actuators A Phys.* **2018**, *273*, 221–223. [CrossRef]
27. Costantini, G.; Casali, D.; Paolizzo, F.; Alessandrini, M.; Micarelli, A.; Viziano, A.; Saggio, G. Towards the enhancement of body standing balance recovery by means of a wireless audio-biofeedback system. *Med. Eng. Phys.* **2018**, *54*, 74–81. [CrossRef] [PubMed]
28. Ricci, M.; Terribili, M.; Giannini, F.; Errico, V.; Pallotti, A.; Galasso, C.; Tomasello, L.; Sias, S.; Saggio, G. Wearable-Based electronics to objectively support diagnosis of motor impairments in school-aged children. *J. Biomech.* **2019**, *83*, 243–252. [CrossRef] [PubMed]
29. Ricci, M.; Di Lazzaro, G.; Pisani, A.; Mercuri, N.B.; Giannini, F.; Saggio, G. Assessment of Motor Impairments in Early Untreated Parkinson's Disease Patients: The Wearable Electronics Impact. *IEEE J. Biomed. Health Inform.* **2020**, *24*, 120–130. [CrossRef] [PubMed]
30. LeCun, Y.; Bengio, Y.; Hinton, G. Deep learning. *Nature* **2015**, *521*, 436–444. [CrossRef] [PubMed]
31. Oppenheim, A.V.; Schafer, R.W. *Digital Filter Design Techniques of Digital Signal Processing*, 1st ed.; Prentice Hall: Upper Saddle River, NJ, USA, 1978.
32. Benalcázar, M.E.; Jaramillo, A.; Zea, J.; Páez, A.; Andaluz, V.H. Hand gesture recognition using machine learning and the Myo armband. In Proceedings of the 25th European Signal Processing Conference (EUSIPCO), Kos, Greece, 28 August–2 September 2017; pp. 1040–1044.
33. Müller, M. *Information Retrieval for Music and Motion*; Springer: Berlin, Germany, 2007.
34. Devroye, L.; Györfi, L.; Lugosi, G. *A Probabilistic Theory of Pattern Recognition. Applications of Mathematics. Stochastic Modelling and Applied Probability*; Springer: Berlin, Germany, 1991; Volume 31, pp. 61–81.
35. Benalcázar, M.E.; Motoche, C.; Zea, J.; Jaramillo, A.; Anchundia, C.; Zambrano, P.; Segura, M.; Benalcázar, F.; Pérez, M. Real-Time hand gesture recognition using the myo armband and muscle activity detection. In Proceedings of the 2nd IEEE Ecuador Technical Chapters Meeting (ETCM), Salinas, Ecuador, 18–20 October 2017; pp. 1–6.
36. Wang, Q. Dynamic Time Warping. MATLAB Central File Exchange. Available online: https://www.mathworks.com/matlabcentral/fileexchange/43156-dynamic-time-warping-dtw (accessed on 22 June 2020).
37. Hochreiter, S.; Schmidhuber, J. Long short-term memory. *Neural Comput.* **1997**, *9*, 1735–1780. [CrossRef] [PubMed]
38. Ioffe, S.; Szegedy, C. Batch normalization: Accelerating deep network training by reducing internal covariate shift. In Proceedings of the 32nd International Conference on Machine Learning, Lille, France, 6–11 July 2015.

© 2020 by the authors. Licensee MDPI, Basel, Switzerland. This article is an open access article distributed under the terms and conditions of the Creative Commons Attribution (CC BY) license (http://creativecommons.org/licenses/by/4.0/).

Article

Analysis of Control Characteristics between Dominant and Non-Dominant Hands by Transient Responses of Circular Tracking Movements in 3D Virtual Reality Space

Wookhyun Park [1], Woong Choi [2,*], Hanjin Jo [1], Geonhui Lee [1] and Jaehyo Kim [1,*]

1. Department of Mechanical and Control Engineering, Handong Global University, Pohang 37554, Korea; 21834002@handong.edu (W.P.); 21834006@handong.edu (H.J.); 21834004@handong.edu (G.L.)
2. Department of Information and Computer Engineering, National Institute of Technology, Gunma College, Maebashi 371-8530, Japan
* Correspondence: wchoi@ice.gunma-ct.ac.jp (W.C.); jhkim@handong.edu (J.K.)

Received: 28 May 2020; Accepted: 18 June 2020; Published: 19 June 2020

Abstract: Human movement is a controlled result of the sensory-motor system, and the motor control mechanism has been studied through diverse movements. The present study examined control characteristics of dominant and non-dominant hands by analyzing the transient responses of circular tracking movements in 3D virtual reality space. A visual target rotated in a circular trajectory at four different speeds, and 29 participants tracked the target with their hands. The position of each subject's hand was measured, and the following three parameters were investigated: normalized initial peak velocity ($IPV2$), initial peak time ($IPT2$), and time delay ($TD2$). The $IPV2$ of both hands decreased as target speed increased. The results of $IPT2$ revealed that the dominant hand reached its peak velocity 0.0423 s earlier than the non-dominant hand, regardless of target speed. The $TD2$ of the hands diminished by 0.0218 s on average as target speed increased, but the dominant hand statistically revealed a 0.0417-s shorter $TD2$ than the non-dominant hand. Velocity-control performances from the $IPV2$ and $IPT2$ suggested that an identical internal model controls movement in both hands, whereas the dominant hand is likely more experienced than the non-dominant hand in reacting to neural commands, resulting in better reactivity in the movement task.

Keywords: circular tracking movement; motor control; virtual reality; dominant hand; transient response

---

1. Introduction

Researchers in various academic areas have studied human movement to better understand human motor control mechanisms [1–25]. In particular, the human body produces a single movement through the combined coordination of multiple joints and muscles [18,26], while the human brain controls physiological movements by receiving sensory feedback and transmitting neural commands. As such, many individual movements involve a variety of motor control behaviors [19–48].

Various target-tracking movements have been studied using a multi-joint upper-limb to analyze human visuo-motor systems [26–48]. Several studies have used a visual target moving in a straight line [44–47] or a sinusoidal waveform [26–29] to examine motor characteristics on a 1-DOF arm movement, and many have used target-tracking on a circular trajectory to investigate the velocity-dependent behaviors of upper-limb movement [33–39]. The control characteristics of the visuo-motor system have also been examined to ascertain their contribution to intermittency [28–32] and proactiveness in response to a predictable target [26,39–41].

Handedness and hand usage are another important aspect of upper-limb movement [47–53]. Several efforts have been made in the physiological field to elucidate which factors determine the preferred or dominant hand (*DH*) [52,53]. Functional comparisons between the *DH* and non-*DH* (*NDH*), as well as between right- and left-handed individuals, have investigated the control characteristics of upper-extremity movement [47–51]. These studies revealed that control performance differed between the hands when the given movement task required a high level of accuracy or dexterity [47,48], although handedness does not directly cause the performance differences between the hands [49,50].

Recently, we implemented a system that measures the Cartesian movement of an end-effector within a three-dimensional virtual reality environment, enabling quantitative evaluation of human hand movement during various movements, such as reaching and tracking [37,38]. In one study, we examined a visual target rotated along a specific circular trajectory, as well as subjects' tracking performances under monocular and binocular vision [37]. In another, we analyzed how the human visuo-motor system controls temporo-spatial parameters during circular tracking movements [38].

Circular target-tracking tasks have been distinguished from other movement tasks because the continuous motion allows researchers to analyze the velocity properties of upper-limb end-point movement [25,32,33]. Previous studies have compared subjects' control of stable behaviors at different target speeds during circular tracking tasks [37,38].

To comprehend the control mechanisms of the human upper-extremity, researchers must examine the initial behaviors in a tracking movement. In control engineering, the time-domain response of a controlled system is classified into a transient response and a steady-state response [54]. For instance, assuming a step signal is given to a system, the rise time and overshoot are frequently evaluated in the performance analysis of the system's transient response. Steady-state error is often determined to examine the stability of a control system's steady-state response. Considering the human visuo-motor system as a controlled system, the transient responses of the target-tracking movement under various target speeds are thought to indicate the velocity-dependent motor control mechanism.

Therefore, in the present study, velocity-dependent motor control characteristics were examined using the transient responses of the circular tracking movements of the *DH* and *NDH* in a 3D space. Temporal behaviors in response to a moving target were analyzed using three parameters: the normalized magnitude of the hand's initial peak velocity on the 2D plane (*IPV2*), the corresponding initial-peak time (*IPT2*), and the calculated time delay of the hand (*TD2*). Participants used their *DH* and *NDH* to track a visual target rotating in a circular trajectory at four different speeds.

2. Materials and Methods

2.1. Subjects and Experimental Setup

The present study involved 29 subjects: 19 males and 10 females (Table 1). Their mean age was 24.67 ± 3.1 years, and 26 of them were right-handed while the others were left-handed. All subjects had normal or corrected-to-normal vision and decent physical condition without any medical history regarding their upper limbs. The subjects had no experience of similar studies or any relevant measurement devices utilized in this experiment, and all of them provided written consent prior to participation in the research. All experiments were performed in compliance with relevant guidelines and regulations. The protocol was approved by the ethics committee of the National Institute of Technology, Gunma College.

Table 1. Characteristics of 29 Subjects.

Subject No.	Age (Years)	Sex	Dominant Hand
1	25	M	R
2	24	M	R
3	24	F	L
4	24	M	R
5	25	M	R
6	22	F	R
7	22	F	R
8	22	F	R
9	22	F	R
10	24	M	L
11	26	M	R
12	22	M	R
13	22	F	R
14	23	F	R
15	23	F	R
16	22	F	R
17	35	M	R
18	24	F	R
19	26	M	R
20	25	M	R
21	23	M	R
22	26	M	R
23	26	M	R
24	24	M	R
25	23	M	R
26	23	M	L
27	25	M	R
28	33	M	R
29	30	M	R

The experiment aimed to investigate visuo-motor control characteristics at different target speeds at the beginning of visual guided tracking tasks using a virtual-reality (VR) system. Such VR systems must (1) provide an immersive 3D audio-visual environment, (2) visualize preprogramed 3D objects and operate them in real-time, and (3) record and display the movement of the user's hand in the environment [37]. HTC Vive was used to give visually guided tracking tasks to the subjects and to display the position of their hands in real time. The head-mounted display (HMD) offered 2160 × 1200-pixel graphic resolution at a refresh rate of 90 Hz. The compatible controller weighed 200 g and was virtually illustrated as 20 cm long with a white stick in the VR space.

An experimental chair designed for the research was placed in the center of the camera-viewed space. The subjects sat on this chair, and two belts fixed on each side were used to fasten their upper bodies to prevent undesired shoulder movements.

2.2. Experimental Procedures

The subjects were fully informed about the research and safely prepared for the experiment. To start with, they were instructed to read the written notice thoroughly and given verbal instructions by the experimenter. They were then asked to fill in a consent form and assigned to the experimental chair. After they were seated, they were carefully fastened onto the chair and received a VR face-protection cover. They were then equipped with the HMD and grasped a hand-held controller (Figure 1A). To become acquainted with and to practice interaction within the provided VR environment, individual subjects were assigned 20 min of a familiarization session with basic VR programs embedded in the HTC Vive system.

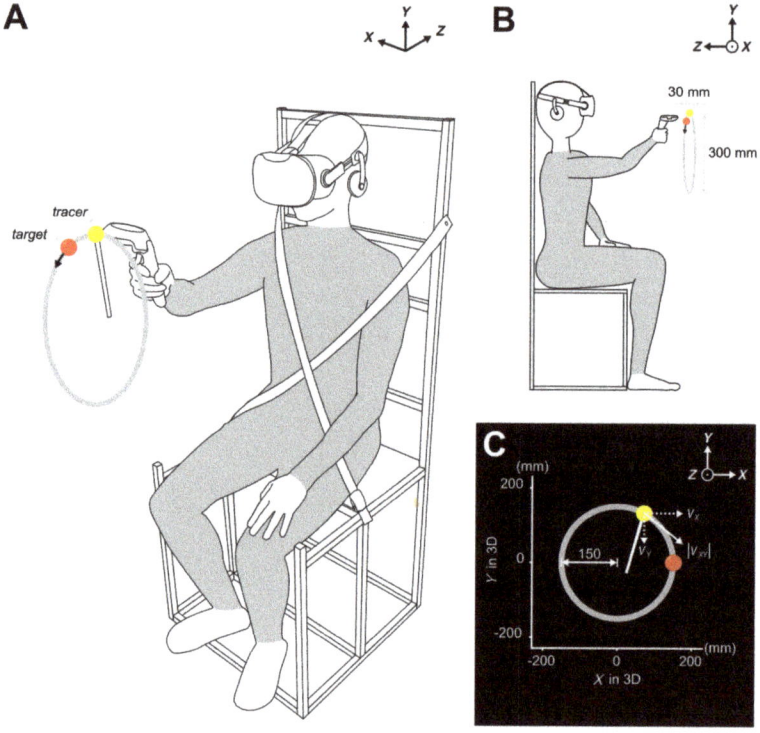

* Only the target and the tracer are displayed in the VR environment.

Figure 1. Experimental procedure for the circular tracking experiment. (**A**) Subject sitting on an experimental chair and holding a hand-held controller to conduct the target tracking movement with the virtual reality (VR) head-mounted display on. To restrict upper-body interference, belts are crossed on the subject's chest. The target (red ball) is only visible in the 3D VR environment, while the tracer (yellow ball) indicates the current 3D location of the controller. The orbit of the target is invisible to the subject. (**B**) The sizes and trajectory of the balls. The target must move along a virtual trajectory with a diameter of 300 mm. They are instructed to follow the target with the tracer. (**C**) The target moves within the frontal plane and the velocity of the tracer is examined.

Once the subjects sufficiently performed the session, a brief checkup was given to verify if the subjects find any inconvenience prior to the experiment, and the experimental program was initiated. The HMD showed a target with a red, ball-shaped sphere and a tracer with a yellow, ball-shaped sphere that had a white stick attached to it. Both had a radius of 15 mm but differed in size depending on their depths (Figure 1B). The background was black (Figure 1C).

The controller was custom calibrated to the arms of each individual subject. Specifically, the subject initially placed the controller immediately beneath their jaw and pulled the trigger. The experimenter then told the subject to reach their arm straight forward and release the trigger after full reaching. The tracer was continuously displayed on the HMD, and the target appeared after the trigger was released. The target was set at a position of 200 mm in the positive direction on the Z-axis and 150 mm in the positive direction on the Y-axis from the position of the tracer. This process was executed when the subject changed their hand to grab the controller.

The subjects were asked to place the tracer in the center of the target to verify whether the calibration was appropriate. They were then given verbal corrections to ensure they were aware of the initial position of the target. No physical adjustment was applied to the subjects.

The subjects were then directed to maintain the position of the tracer. They were also informed that four "beep" sounds would be played to indicate a 3-s countdown and that the subjects should start to track the target as closely as possible using the tracer after the 4th beep sound, regardless of the target speed. When they accurately placed the tracer and maintained their posture, the experimenter notified the start of a task and ran the program. The speaker on the HMD produced the beep sounds, and the subject started tracking immediately after hearing the last sound.

2.3. Movement Tasks

The experiment consisted of two main tasks. The first was to track the target with the tracer using the *DH*. The target, displayed at the initially calibrated position (0, 150, 0 mm), moved in a circular trajectory in the clockwise direction on the frontal (*X-Y*) plane. The radius of the orbit was 150 mm, and the target revolved six times at a constant speed. The target speeds were set at 0.250 π, 0.500 π, 1.000 π, and 1.500 π rad/s along the trajectory. Only one trial was carried out at each speed, and the subjects were told that the target would move faster in the next trial. A break of 30 s was given after each trial.

The second task was to perform the same type of tracking movement using the *NDH*. At the beginning of the experiment, each subject was randomly assigned which hand would start the tracking movement: *DH* or *NDH*. The controller was re-calibrated for each hand.

2.4. Data Analysis

Real-time positions of the tracer in the Cartesian coordinates (*X,Y,Z*) were used for data analysis. The sampling frequency was 90 Hz and the transient response of the circular tracking motion was examined using the data measured after the target started moving. As a transient response of a controlled system illustrates behavior to instantaneous changes in its reference input and a process of reaching a steady-state response, so the initial performance of the tracer indicated a transient response of how the subject instantly started the target-tracking movement.

Three parameters were chosen to analyze the performance of the transient response. The first was the *IPV2*, the initial peak velocity of the tracer on the frontal plane. The measured *X* and *Y* values were numerically differentiated and computed with respect to the speed of the tracer. Considering the target speed as a referenced input, the *IPV2* could be interpreted as an overshoot of the transient response in a controlled system. The *IPV2* was normalized to the corresponding target speed to allow comparisons with other *IPV2* values at different target speeds. The *IPV2* was calculated as a percentage.

$$v_{x,trc}[t] = \begin{cases} \frac{x_{trc}[t] - x_{trc}[t-1]}{T_s} & \text{for } t > 1 \\ 0 & \text{for } t = 1 \end{cases} \quad (1)$$

$$v_{y,trc}[t] = \begin{cases} \frac{y_{trc}[t] - y_{trc}[t-1]}{T_s} & \text{for } t > 1 \\ 0 & \text{for } t = 1 \end{cases} \quad (2)$$

$$v_{xy,trc}[t] = \sqrt{v_{x,trc}[t]^2 + v_{y,trc}[t]^2} \quad (3)$$

$$v_{xy,trc}^{peak} = \max(v_{xy,trc}[t])\big|_{t=1}^{n_{hr}} \quad (4)$$

$$v_{xy,trg} = r_{traj} \times \omega_{trg} \quad (5)$$

$$IPV2 = \frac{v_{xy,trc}^{peak}}{v_{xy,trg}} \times 100 \quad (6)$$

Constant n_{hr} denotes the length of data measured at a sample rate of 90 Hz while the target rotated through half of the first orbit. The n_{hr} values at each speed were 360 (0.250 π rad/s), 180 (0.500 π rad/s), 90 (1.000 π rad/s), and 60 (1.500 π rad/s). The abbreviations *trg* and *trc* represent the target and tracer, respectively. The velocity of the target on the frontal plane, $v_{xy,trg}$, was decided by the target's angular speed ω_{trg} which was one of 0.250 π, 0.500 π, 1.000 π, and 1.500 π rad/s. The radius of the target's trajectory r_{traj} was fixed to 150 mm and the $v_{xy,trg}$ was considered as a constant because the target rotated the circular trajectory at a constant velocity during a single trial.

The second parameter was *IPT2*, the initial peak time, which is the time at which *IPV2* occurred.

$$IPT2 = t\left[v_{xy,trc}^{peak}\right]\Big|_{t=1}^{n} \tag{7}$$

The last parameter was *TD2*, the time delay or reaction time of the tracer on the frontal plane. In order to examine the transient response, it is essential to know the starting moment of the response. Other studies could easily distinguish the moment of when the subject actually started to move since they employed measurement devices with 1- or 2-DOF [26–48]. Such devices were fixed on a certain spot or plane, and the measured data did not fluctuate for a stationary movement, allowing easy detection of positional changes of the tracer. The VR environment of this experiment, however, did not physically restrict any movement of our subjects. In fact, they placed their hands in the air without any structural support. Though the subjects were told to stay still, physiological factors such as cardiac impulses or a hand tremor may cause positional fluctuation of the hands. These unintentional movements hinder the detection of the starting moment of the response. By identifying features of the involuntary movements, the transient response of the target tracking movement can be discriminated from the unintentional fluctuation.

In statistics, one standard deviation of a normal distribution denotes how much difference each data point has from its mean value, expressing the broadness of the data. In a normal distribution, 68.2% of the data lies within one standard deviation of the mean, and three standard deviations cover 99.6% of the sample.

Applying this theory to our experiment, one standard deviation of the tracer during a 3-s countdown (*STDtrc*) represented a statistic feature of the involuntary movements prior to the tracking movement. That is, *STDtrc* could be referred to as a magnitude of the hand's tremor or how widely the tracer was fluctuated irrespective of the subject's intention. If the displacement of the tracer from its initial position was greater than three standard deviations, this could be interpreted as the subject moves the tracer with clear intention. The *TD2* value expressed the moment at which the tracer's displacement from its initial position became more than three times that of the *STDtrc*.

$$disp_{trc}[t] = \sqrt{(x_{trc}[t] - 0)^2 + (y_{trc}[t] - 150)^2} \text{ for } -270 \leq t \leq -1 \tag{8}$$

$$disp_{trc}^{mean} = \frac{\sum_{t=-270}^{-1} disp_{trc}[t]}{n} \tag{9}$$

$$STD_{trc} = \sqrt{\frac{\sum_{t=-270}^{-1}\left(disp_{trc}[t] - disp_{trc}^{mean}\right)^2}{n-1}} \tag{10}$$

$$d_{xy,trc}[t] \text{ [mm]} = \sqrt{\left(x_{trc}(t) - x_{trc}^{init}\right)^2 + \left(y_{trc}(t) - y_{trc}^{init}\right)^2} \text{ for } t > 0 \tag{11}$$

$$TD2 = \min\left(t[d_{xy,trc}(t) \geq 3 \times STD_{trc}]\right)\Big|_{t=1}^{n_{hr}} \tag{12}$$

$disp_{trc}$ represented a displacement of the tracer from the target's position (0, 150, 0 mm) on the frontal plane. Since the sampling frequency was 90 Hz, 270 position data were measured during the 3-s countdown (the time indices ranged from −270 to −1 to distinguish from the data measured after the countdown). Equation (8) indicated that displacements were calculated for the three seconds before the start. $disp_{trc}^{mean}$ in Equation (9) is a mean value of the collected $disp_{trc}$, which is used for computing the value of $STDtrc$ in Equation (10). After the 4th beep, the subject may initiate to move the tracer, but the initial position of the tracer may differ from that of the target, although the subjects were told to place the tracer in the center of the target prior to the experiment. The tracer is on the frontal plane $(x_{trc}^{init}, y_{trc}^{init})$ at the start of each trial. Displacements after the start were calculated as $d_{xy,trc}$ as shown in Equation (11), and the moment that the displacement becomes greater than triple of $STDtrc$ was considered as $TD2$.

All these parameters were calculated from data measured for two types of hand factors: DH and NDH, as well as four types of speed factors: $S1$, $0.250\ \pi$ rad/s; $S2$, $0.500\ \pi$ rad/s; $S3$, $1.000\ \pi$ rad/s; $S4$: $1.500\ \pi$ rad/s. Through examinations of each parameter, hand and speed-dependent motor characteristics are to be studied. To be specific, the control mechanism of how humans respond to an instantaneous velocity input is to be investigated. Through $IPV2$, a magnitude-related property in velocity-control process and accuracy of velocity prediction can be examined while $IPT2$ and $TD2$ directly propose temporal behaviors of velocity-control performance such as reactivity or sensitivity to a given velocity input.

Performances of the 29 subjects were analyzed using MATLAB 2019a, MathWorks (Natick, Massachusetts, United States). A Butterworth IIR digital filter (3rd-ordered low-pass with a cutoff frequency of 7.5 Hz) was applied to all the data prior to analysis. SPSS statistics V26 (IBM) was used to carry out two-way repeated-measures analysis of variance (ANOVA) tests to numerically analyze differences in performances of the circular tracking movements with the hand and speed factors. Mauchly's sphericity test ($p > 0.05$) was also executed to validate the results of ANOVA. For the results whose sphericity was not assumed ($p < 0.05$), the values corrected with Greenhouse–Geisser in tests of within-subjects effects were employed. The post hoc test was performed by Bonferroni pairwise comparison ($p < 0.05$) to verify the significance of each condition for hand and speed factors.

3. Results

The designed experiment was to investigate initial motor characteristics in the target tracking movements. To examine speed-dependent characteristics of the transient responses and the differences between the DH and NDH, 29 subjects participated in the experiment using their DH and NDH at the four speeds. The obtained tracer's position data was transformed into three parameters: $IPV2$, $IPT2$, and $TD2$.

Figure 2 shows typical examples of the calculated velocities of target-tracking movements at $S2$, while the target rotated through the first half-orbit of the circular trajectory. The measured trajectories of the DH and NDH are illustrated on the frontal plane (Figure 2A,B). The velocity components of the hands are depicted on the X-axis (Figure 2C1,D1) and Y-axis (Figure 2C2,D2). The normalized speeds are displayed in Figure 2C3,D3 in terms of the target speed $S2$; the computed $IPV2$, $IPT2$, and $TD2$ are marked.

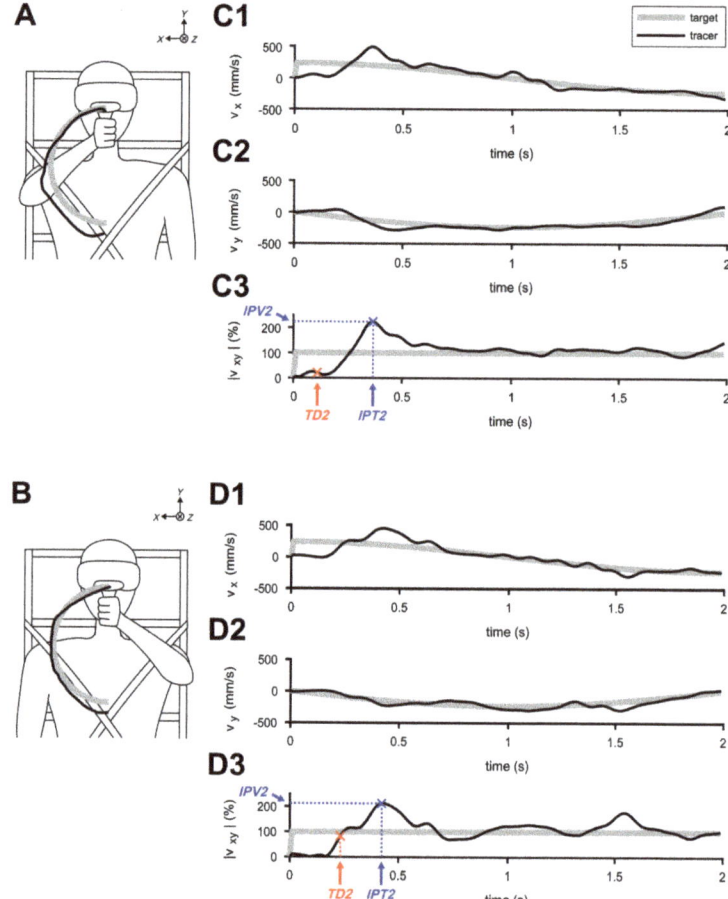

Figure 2. Typical examples of velocities during the first half-orbit of circular tracking movements at 0.500 π rad/s (S2). (**A**) Trajectories of the target and tracer performed by the dominant hand (*DH*) on the frontal plane. (**B**) Trajectories of the target and tracer performed by the non-dominant hand (*NDH*) on the frontal plane. (**C1**) Velocity of the *DH* calculated on the *X*-axis and (**C2**) on the *Y*-axis. (**C3**) Computed speeds on the frontal plane, normalized to *S2*. (**D1**) Velocity of the *NDH* calculated on the *X*-axis and (**D2**) on the *Y*-axis. (**D3**) Computed speeds on the frontal plane, normalized to *S2*.

3.1. Differences in the Transient Response of Tracking Movement Based on IPV2

ANOVA of the *IPV2* demonstrated that only the speed factor caused a significant difference in the *IPV2* of the transient responses of the circular tracking movement (item A in Table S1). The hand factor and the interaction between the hand and speed factors did not significantly affect the *IPV2*.

Figure 3 illustrates the *IPV2* results of the *DH* and *NDH* in terms of the transient responses of the tracking movement on the 2D frontal plane. The statistical values of *IPV2* are listed as the variable *IPV2* in Table 2. There was no significant difference in *IPV2* between the *DH* and *NDH* (Figure 3A,B; item B in Table S1). The *IPV2* of the *DH* indicated that the maximum speed differences between the target and the tracer were approximately 37.70% and 26.22% larger at *S1* and *S2*, respectively, than at *S4* (Figure 3C; item C in Table S1). The *IPV2* of the *NDH* indicated that the maximum speed differences between the target and the tracer were approximately 55.05% and 35.30% larger, respectively, at *S1* and *S2* than at *S3* as well as 62.79% and 43.04% larger at *S1* and *S2* than at *S4* (Figure 3D; item D in

Table S1). The combined *IPV2* suggested that the maximum speed differences between the target and the tracer were approximately 39.25% and 23.63% larger at *S1* and *S2* than at *S3* as well as 50.25% and 34.63% larger at *S1* and *S2* than at *S4* (Figure 3E; item E in Table S1).

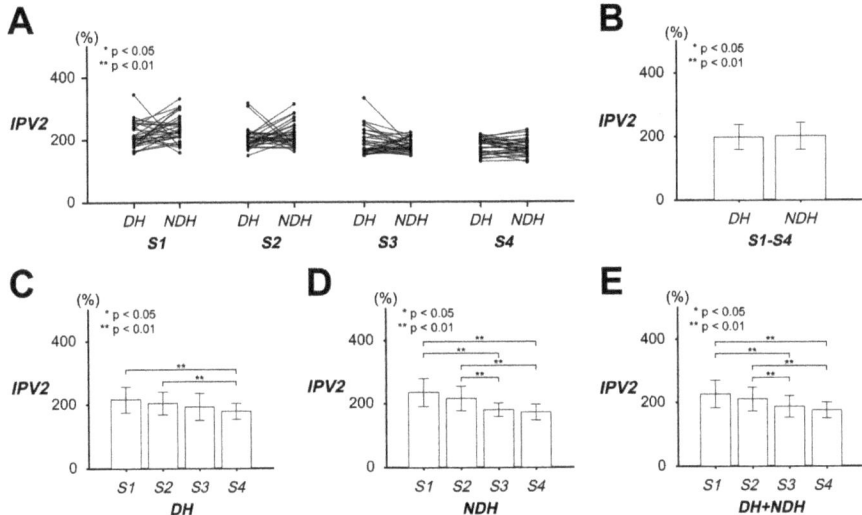

Figure 3. Evaluation of transient responses of the circular tracking movement based on initial peak velocity (*IPV2*) on the frontal plane. (**A**) The values of *IPV2* of 29 subjects for four speed factor levels. (**B**) The pairwise comparison between the dominant hand (*DH*) and *NDH* was shown for *IPV2* of all the speed factors. (**C**) Pairwise comparisons of *IPV2* were represented for the speed factor within *DH* and (**D**) within *NDH*. (**E**) The results of pairwise comparison of *IPV2* in both *DH* and *NDH*.

Table 2. Statistical results of each parameter.

Variable	Hand Factor	Speed Factor				Total
		S1	S2	S3	S4	
IPV2 (%)	DH	216.01 (±40.992)	204.53 (±36.119)	192.56 (±42.834)	178.31 (±24.868)	197.85 (±39.011)
	NDH	235.65 (±44.350)	215.90 (±38.679)	180.60 (±20.895)	172.86 (±25.152)	201.25 (±42.034)
	DH + NDH	225.83 (±43.471)	210.21 (±37.532)	186.58 (±33.944)	175.58 (±24.942)	
IPT2 (s)	DH	0.4299 (±0.1142)	0.4789 (±0.1126)	0.4954 (±0.1126)	0.4540 (±0.1105)	0.4646 (±0.1138)
	NDH	0.4966 (±0.1513)	0.4966 (±0.1306)	0.5084 (±0.1087)	0.5261 (±0.1837)	0.5069 (±0.1448)
	DH + NDH	0.4632 (±0.1371)	0.4877 (±0.1212)	0.5019 (±0.1099)	0.4900 (+0.1546)	
TD2 (s)	DH	0.2092 (±0.0571)	0.1686 (±0.0645)	0.1720 (±0.0626)	0.1525 (±0.0768)	0.1756 (±0.0681)
	NDH	0.2586 (±0.0579)	0.2395 (±0.0571)	0.1870 (±0.0637)	0.1843 (±0.0626)	0.2173 (±0.0679)
	DH + NDH	0.2339 (±0.0622)	0.2040 (±0.0701)	0.1795 (±0.0631)	0.1684 (±0.0713)	

* These values are recorded in terms of 'mean (± standard deviation)'.

These results signified that *IPV2* was likely to decrease as the target speed became faster on the 2D frontal plane regardless of the hand. In other words, the subjects' hands showed clear tendencies to reduce the initial speed difference by approximately 16.75% at a faster speed.

3.2. Differences in Transient Response of Tracking Movement Based on IPT2

ANOVA of the *IPT2* revealed that only the hand factor caused significant differences in the *IPT2* of the transient responses of the circular tracking movement (item A in Table S2). The speed factor and the interaction between the hand and speed factors did not significantly affect the *IPT2*.

Figure 4 illustrates the *IPT2* results of the *DH* and *NDH* in terms of the transient responses of the tracking movement on the 2D frontal plane. The statistical values of *IPT2* are listed as variable *IPT2* in Table 2. Although no significant differences were found in the paired *IPT2* (Figure 4A; item B in Table S2), the *IPT2* of the hands revealed that the *DH* reached the initial peak speed approximately 0.0423 s before the *NDH* did, regardless of the target speed (Figure 4B). The *IPT2* values of the *DH* and *NDH* indicated that there were no significant differences in the speed factor (Figure 4C–E; items C–E in Table S2).

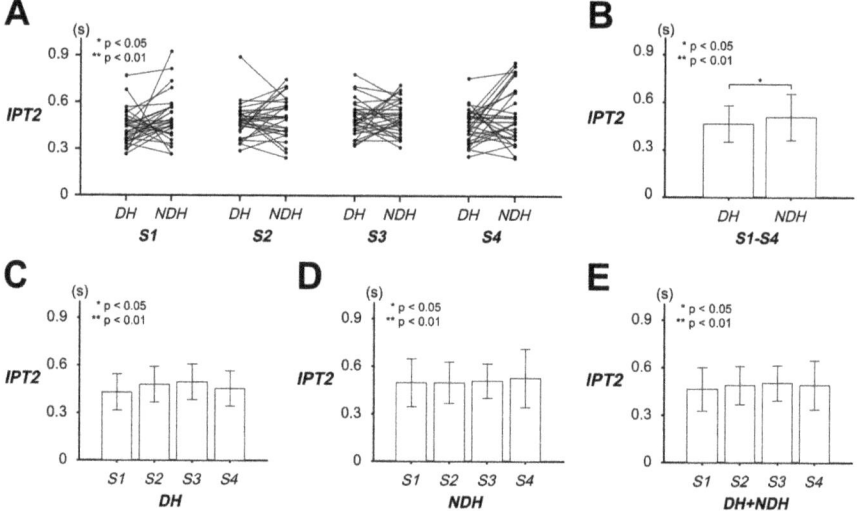

Figure 4. Evaluation of the transient responses of the circular tracking movement based on the initial peak time (*IPT2*) on the frontal plane. (**A**) The values of *IPT2* of the 29 subjects at four speed factor levels. (**B**) The pairwise comparison between dominant hand (*DH*) and non-dominant hand (*NDH*) is shown for the *IPT2* of all the speed factors. (**C**) Pairwise comparisons of the *IPT2* are represented in terms of the speed factor within *DH* and (**D**) *NDH*. (**E**) Pairwise comparison of *IPT2* for both *DH* and *NDH*.

The stated results implied that the *IPT2* had a significant relationship with the hand factor on the 2D frontal plane. Specifically, the subjects' *DH* attained its initial peak velocity 0.0423 s before the *NDH* did at the beginning of the tracking movement while both the hands disclosed no clear tendency on the target speed.

3.3. Differences in Transient Response of Tracking Movement Based on TD2

ANOVA of the *TD2* indicated that all the factors and their interaction caused significant differences in the *TD2* of the transient responses of the circular tracking movement (item A in Table S3).

Figure 5 illustrates the *TD2* results of the *DH* and *NDH* during the transient responses of the tracking movement on the 2D frontal plane. The statistical values of *TD2* are listed as variable *TD2* in Table 2. Paired analysis of *TD2* implied that the subjects initiated tracking approximately 0.0494 s earlier at *S1* when using the *DH* than when using the *NDH*; at *S2*, they initiated tracking 0.0709 s earlier (Figure 5A; item B in Table S3). The *TD2* of the hands revealed that the *DH* started moving the tracer approximately 0.0417 s earlier than the *NDH*, irrespective of the target speed (Figure 5B).

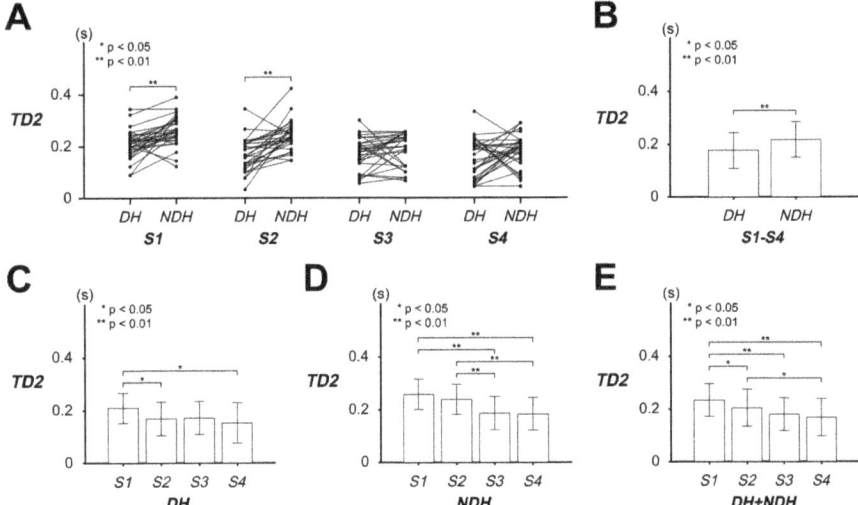

Figure 5. Evaluation of transient responses of the circular tracking movement based on the time delay (TD2) on the frontal plane. (**A**) The values of TD2 of 29 subjects at four speed factor levels. (**B**) The pairwise comparison between dominant hand (DH) and non-dominant hand (NDH) is shown for the TD2 of all speed factors. (**C**) Pairwise comparisons of TD2 are represented for each speed factor with the DH and (**D**) NDH. (**E**) Pairwise comparison of TD2 with both the DH and NDH.

The *TD2* of the *DH* indicated that the subjects initiated tracking approximately 0.0406 s earlier at *S2* than at *S1*, and 0.0567 s earlier at *S4* than at *S1* (Figure 5C; item C in Table S3), whereas the *TD2* of the *NDH* indicated that the subjects reacted to the target approximately 0.0716 and 0.0743 s earlier at *S3* and *S4* than at *S1*, and that they reacted 0.0525 and 0.0552 s earlier at *S3* and *S4* than at *S2* (Figure 5D; item D in Table S3). The combined *TD2* suggested that the subjects started moving the tracer approximately 0.0299, 0.0544, and 0.0655 s earlier at *S2*, *S3*, and *S4*, respectively, than at *S1*, as well as 0.0356 s earlier at *S2* than at *S4* (Figure 5E; item E in Table S3).

These results signified that *TD2* showed significant differences between slow (*S1*, *S2*) and fast (*S3*, *S4*) speeds. In other words, the subjects reacted to the target approximately 0.0218 s more quickly at fast target speeds in the circular tracking movement. Moreover, the *TD2* of the *DH* and *NDH* showed different statistical features; specifically, the subjects had a transient response that was approximately 0.0417 s earlier with the *DH* than with the *NDH*.

4. Discussion

This study quantitatively analyzed the transient responses of the circular tracking movement of the *DH* and *NDH* to investigate initial motor control characteristics at different target speeds. Three parameters were examined: *IPV2*, the normalized magnitude of initial peak velocity, *IPT2*, initial peak velocity time, and *TD2*, the reaction time the subject took to react to the target. All parameters were investigated at *S1*–*S4* with the *DH* and *NDH*.

The following discussion mainly focuses on: (1) speed-dependent features of *IPV2*, (2) temporal analysis of *IPT2* and *TD2*, and (3) clinical applications and future work.

4.1. Speed-Dependent Features of IPV2

The subjects performed the target-tracking movement by immediately moving the tracer faster than the target after they perceived target movement. As overshoot is a key component of transient response analysis in control theories [54], the speed of the tracer exceeded that of the target and, after the target was caught up, the subjects continued the tracking task by adjusting the speed of the tracer (Figure 2). Particularly at *S4*, the subjects controlled the speed of the tracer rather than reducing the position error between the target and the tracer. This implied that they deemed the target too fast to track and that they simply decided to maintain a certain level of the tracer's speed.

Analyzing the immediate movements of the tracer when the target started moving, we showed that the *IPV2* decreased as the target speed increased, indicating that the initial prediction about the target speed was more accurate at faster speeds. The subjects could barely apprehend the next target speed because the given instruction was not quantitative, so the initial target-tracking movement was executed based solely on the subject's predicted speed. The *DH* and *NDH* commonly had lower *IPV2* values at faster speeds and showed nearly identical behavior in overall speed, indicating that both hands have the same internal model for initiating tracking movement.

4.2. Temporal Analysis of IPT2 and TD2

The *IPT2* represents the time corresponding to *IPV2* and therefore indicates the moment when the subject first corrected the speed of the tracer toward the moving target. In other words, *IPT2* expresses the actual initiation of speed control. The *IPT2* showed no significant difference among the different speeds, but had a 0.0423-s difference between the *DH* and *NDH*. It follows that both hands may have nearly the same reactivity to the target speed. This also suggests that an identical internal model controls motor performances of the hands. Such an idea coincides with motor equivalence, the theoretical concept that the central nervous system (CNS) rather stores abstract forms of information on actions than records neural commands to specific muscles for performing actions [55]. The possibility for the hands to receive not distinct commands from the CNS but similar forms of information intimates that the *IPT2* could be a personal motor characteristic rather than an externally affected trait.

TD2, the time when the subject perceived the target's positional change and initiated tracer movement, showed significant differences between the hands and among the various speeds. In the *DH* and *NDH*, the *TD2* reduced as the target became faster, showing clear differences in average values. Specifically, mutual differences were found between the slow (*S1*, *S2*) and fast (*S3*, *S4*) speeds, indicating that when the subjects performed more trials, they predicted the starting moment of trials more accurately. In addition, the *DH* had less *TD2* than the *NDH* at all the speeds, showing that the subjects were more proficient at controlling the *DH* than the *NDH*. Otherwise stated, the *DH*, comparatively the more experienced hand, reacted to the target faster than the *NDH*. Assuming that the same internal model controlled the movements of the *DH* and *NDH*, the tracers might have started moving at a nearly identical moment in each case. Since the *TD2* showed a significant difference between the hands, we concluded that the *DH* showed better performance at controlling objects in reacting to motor commands and catching the moving target.

4.3. Clinical Application and Future Work

Assessing of motor functions and analysis of possible recovery processes will be feasible by applying the protocol of this study to patients with restrictions on upper limb movements. The experimental system can measure performance of a circular target tracking movement and can evaluate motor characteristics of an upper limb quantitatively. The examined results can be integrated with conventional indicators which inspect motor capability of individual joint movements and diagnose current recovery processes from deficits of a neurological disorder, such as Fugl-Meyer assessment (FMA) and manual function test (MFT). After appropriate correlation analysis, the present protocol will be employed in estimating the patients' physical conditions, for example, spasticity of their impaired limbs, and in speculating potential recovery phases.

The results of this research can benefit the clinical population with neural impairment by providing valuable information which can be employed in navigating suitable treatment. Such patients have difficulties in performing continuous multi-joint movements for a long time because of sensorimotor malfunction caused by the impairment. Motor characteristics of the patients can be examined by simply conducting a half orbit of the circular tracking movement. The obtained information can be effectively useful for therapists in planning proper rehabilitation goals or in designing customized treatment programs for the patients. The outcome of this research is expected to provide clinical improvement to those whose motor functions are deteriorated by a stroke, spatial neglect, or lesion in the cerebellum.

In future, we will investigate target-tracking performance at random target speeds without notifying the subjects about the target speed. Without any clues about the target speed, it will likely be difficult for subjects to make any predictions. The motor control characteristics of individuals will be studied by analyzing reactivity to a moving target.

$TD2$ represented time delay or reaction time of the target tracking movement in this research. In neuroscience and biological engineering, reaction time is defined as the time taken when a neural command from the brain is transmitted to its musculoskeletal system for a joint movement, and the time is estimated as approximately 200 msec [45,46]. A time delay in control theories is normally referred to as a time necessary to reach 50% of the final value in a step response of a controlled system [54]. Both definitions were difficult to apply in this research since the measured data did not clearly indicate the starting moment of the reaction and final values of the subjects' angular velocities in their tracking movement. We will evaluate these definitions by executing the same tasks within a dynamically-limited environment in future work.

A mathematical model to explain the tradeoff characteristic between speed and accuracy could be developed in the future. Our previous studies verified that the subjects could stably perform the tracking tasks after the first orbit of the trajectory [37,38]. In terms of control strategies, the subjects employed relatively more intermittent feedback control at the slow target speeds whereas feedforward control was dominant at the fast target speeds. This tradeoff relationship has been interpreted between speed and accuracy by establishing computational models [56,57]. Applying those mathematical models in our results is anticipated to better explain the speed-dependent characteristics of the human motor control mechanism.

Furthermore, an identical experiment with different weights of the hand-held controller will be conducted to investigate the effects of weight on the circular tracking movement. Applying a constant weight to the gravitational direction will probably influence the transient response of the tracking movement. Such an experiment should elucidate any differences in the impedance characteristics of DH and NDH, and analyze the motor characteristics of the hands from various perspectives.

5. Conclusions

The initial motor control characteristics of DH and NDH in the circular tracking movement were examined in a 3D VR space. The transient responses of the hands in the tracking movement were analyzed for $S1$–$S4$ on the frontal plane. The $IPV2$ decreased as the target speed increased, irrespective of the hand, suggesting that the subjects improved velocity-prediction accuracy by approximately 16.75% at faster speeds. The $IPT2$ did not vary with the speed factor but showed a 0.0423-s difference between the DH and NDH, indicating that the DH reached its maximum speed earlier than the NDH. The $TD2$ revealed significant differences in both the hand and speed factors, implying that the subjects reacted to the target 0.0218 s earlier as the target speed increased, and that the DH reacted to the target 0.0417 s earlier than the NDH. The performances of the $IPV2$ and $IPT2$ suggested that the same internal model controls tracking movements of both the hands whereas the results of $TD2$ proposed that the DH generally had better reactivity in its transient response. The target tracking movements can be utilized in clinic environments to evaluate motor functions of patients and to set up treatment plans for rehabilitation. Effects of different experimental factors such as random speeds or weights will be analyzed as well as applying different methods of calculating reaction time and mathematical models of the tradeoff characteristics to the target tracking movements. This study examined the motor control characteristics of the *DH* and *NDH* in their transient responses of the circular tracking movements in the 3D VR space.

Supplementary Materials: The following are available online at http://www.mdpi.com/1424-8220/20/12/3477/s1, Table S1: a summary of statistical analysis of *IPV2* for the circular tracking movement, Table S2: a summary of statistical analysis of *IPT2* for the circular tracking movement, Table S3: a summary of statistical analysis of *TD2* for the circular tracking movement.

Author Contributions: Conceptualization, W.P., J.K., and W.C.; methodology, W.P. and W.C.; resources, J.K.; software, W.C.; data curation, W.P. and W.C.; investigation, W.P. and W.C.; validation, W.P., W.C., formal analysis, W.P., W.C., H.J., and G.L.; writing—original draft, W.P., H.J., and G.L.; writing—review and editing, W.P., W.C., and J.K.; All authors have read and agreed to the published version of the manuscript.

Funding: This research was funded by the Korea National Research Foundation (KNRF) grant funded by the Korean government (MOE) (No. 2020R1I1A3A04038203).

Conflicts of Interest: The authors declare no conflicts of interest.

References

1. Wolpert, D.M.; Ghahramani, Z.; Jordan, M.I. An internal model for sensorimotor integration. *Science* **1995**, *269*, 1880. [CrossRef] [PubMed]
2. Wolpert, D.M.; Miall, R.C.; Kawato, M. Internal models in the cerebellum. *Trends Cogn. Sci.* **1998**, *2*, 338–347. [CrossRef]
3. Flash, T.; Hogan, N. The coordination of arm movements: An experimentally confirmed mathematical model. *J. Neurosci.* **1985**, *5*, 1688–1703. [CrossRef] [PubMed]
4. Uno, Y.; Kawato, M.; Suzuki, R. Formation and control of optimal trajectory in human multijoint arm movement. *Biol. Cybern.* **1989**, *61*, 89–101. [CrossRef] [PubMed]
5. Takahashi, C.D.; Scheidt, R.A.; Reinkensmeyer, D.J. Impedance control and internal model formation when reaching in a randomly varying dynamical environment. *J. Neurophysiol.* **2001**, *86*, 1047–1051. [CrossRef] [PubMed]
6. Kakei, S.; Hoffman, D.S.; Strick, P.L. Muscle and movement representations in the primary motor cortex. *Science* **1999**, *285*, 2136–2139. [CrossRef]
7. Bastian, A.J. Learning to predict the future: The cerebellum adapts feedforward movement control. *Curr. Opin. Neurol.* **2006**, *16*, 645–649. [CrossRef]
8. Todorov, E. Optimality principles in sensorimotor control. *Nat. Neurosci.* **2004**, *7*, 907–915. [CrossRef]
9. Kakei, S.; Hoffman, D.S.; Strick, P.L. Sensorimotor transformations in cortical motor areas. *Neurosci. Res.* **2003**, *46*, 1–10. [CrossRef]
10. Kambara, H.; Shin, D.; Koike, Y. A computational model for optimal muscle activity considering muscle viscoelasticity in wrist movements. *J. Neurophysiol.* **2013**, *109*, 2145–2160. [CrossRef]
11. Yokota, H.; Naito, M.; Mizuno, N.; Ohshima, S. Framework for visual-feedback training based on a modified self-organizing map to imitate complex motion. *Proc. Inst. Mech. Eng. Part P* **2020**, *234*, 49–58. [CrossRef]
12. Giannousi, M.; Kioumourtzoglou, E. The effects of verbal and visual feedback on performance and learning freestyle swimming in novice swimmers. *Kinesiology* **2017**, *49*, 65–73. [CrossRef]
13. Ewerton, M.; Rother, D.; Weimar, J.; Kollegger, G.; Wiemeyer, J.; Peters, J.; Maeda, G. Assisting movement training and execution with visual and haptic feedback. *Front. Neurorobot.* **2018**, *12*, 1–18. [CrossRef]
14. Steinberg, F.; Pixa, N.H.; Doppelmayr, M. Mirror visual feedback training improves intermanual transfer in a sport-specific task: A comparison between different skill levels. *Neural Plast.* **2016**, 1–11. [CrossRef]
15. Knudsen, E.W.; Holledig, M.; Knudsen, E.W.; Holledig, M.; Bach-Nielsen, S.S.; Peterson, R.K.; Zanescu, B.-C.; Nielsen, M.J.; Helweg, K.; Overholt, D.; et al. Audio-visual feedback for self-monitoring posture in ballet training. In Proceedings of the NIME 2017, Copenhagen, Denmark, 15–18 May 2017; 2017; pp. 71–76.
16. Zajac, F.E. Muscle coordination of movement: A perspective. *J. Biomech.* **1993**, *26*, 109–124. [CrossRef]

17. Scott, S.H.; Cluff, T.; Lowrey, C.R.; Takei, T. Feedback control during voluntary motor actions. *Curr. Opin. Neurobiol.* **2015**, *33*, 85–94. [CrossRef] [PubMed]
18. Wakeling, J.M.; Blake, O.M.; Chan, H.K. Muscle coordination is key to the power output and mechanical efficiency of limb movements. *J. Exp. Biol.* **2010**, *213*, 487–492. [CrossRef]
19. Sabes, P.N. The planning and control of reaching movements. *Curr. Opin. Neurol.* **2000**, *10*, 740–746. [CrossRef]
20. Krakauer, J.W.; Ghilardi, M.-F.; Ghez, C. Independent learning of internal models for kinematic and dynamic control of reaching. *Nat. Neurosci.* **1999**, *2*, 1026–1031. [CrossRef]
21. Georgopoulos, A.P.; Grillner, S. Visuomotor coordination in reaching and locomotion. *Science* **1989**, *245*, 1209–1210. [CrossRef] [PubMed]
22. Jeannerod, M.; Arbib, M.A.; Rizzolatti, G.; Sakata, H. Grasping objects: The cortical mechanisms of visuomotor transformation. *Trends Neurosci.* **1995**, *18*, 314–320. [CrossRef]
23. Lacquaniti, F.; Caminiti, R. Visuo-motor transformations for arm reaching. *Eur. J. Neurosci.* **1998**, *10*, 195–203. [CrossRef]
24. Zelaznik, H.N.; Hawkins, B.; Kisselburgh, L. Rapid visual feedback processing in single aiming movements. *J. Mot. Behav.* **1983**, *15*, 217–236. [CrossRef] [PubMed]
25. Engel, K.C.; Soechting, J.F. Manual tracking in two dimensions. *J. Neurophysiol.* **2000**, *83*, 3483–3496. [CrossRef] [PubMed]
26. Ishida, F.; Sawada, Y.E. Human hand moves proactively to the external stimulus: An evolutional strategy for minimizing transient error. *Phys. Rev. Lett.* **2004**, *93*, 1–4. [CrossRef] [PubMed]
27. Miall, R.; Weir, D.; Stein, J. Planning of movement parameters in a visuo-motor tracking task. *Behav. Brain Res.* **1988**, *27*, 1–8. [CrossRef]
28. Russell, D.M.; Sternad, D. Sinusoidal visuomotor tracking: Intermittent servo-control or coupled oscillations? *J. Mot. Behav.* **2001**, *33*, 329–349. [CrossRef]
29. Miall, R.; Weir, D.; Stein, J. Manual tracking of visual targets by trained monkeys. *Behav. Brain Res.* **1986**, *20*, 185–201. [CrossRef]
30. Gollee, H.; Mamma, A.; Loram, I.D.; Gawthrop, P.J. Frequency-domain identification of the human controller. *Biol. Cybern.* **2012**, *106*, 359–372. [CrossRef]
31. Miall, R.; Weir, D.; Stein, J. Intermittency in human manual tracking tasks. *J. Mot. Behav.* **1993**, *27*, 53–63. [CrossRef] [PubMed]
32. Inoue, Y.; Sakaguchi, Y. Periodic change in phase relationship between target and hand motion during visuo-manual tracking task: Behavioral evidence for intermittent control. *Hum. Mov. Sci.* **2014**, *33*, 211–226. [CrossRef] [PubMed]
33. Roitman, A.V.; Massaquoi, S.G.; Takahashi, K.; Ebner, T.J. Kinematic analysis of manual tracking in monkeys: Characterization of movement intermittencies during a circular tracking task. *J. Neurophysiol.* **2004**, *91*, 901–911. [CrossRef] [PubMed]
34. Roitman, A.V.; Pasalar, S.; Johnson, M.T.V.; Ebner, T.J. Position, direction of movement, and speed tuning of cerebellar purkinje cells during circular manual tracking in monkey. *J. Neurosci.* **2005**, *25*, 9244–9257. [CrossRef] [PubMed]
35. Roitman, A.V.; Pasalar, S.; Ebner, T.J. Single trial coupling of purkinje cell activity to speed and error signals during circular manual tracking. *Exp. Brain Res.* **2008**, *192*, 241–251. [CrossRef]
36. Kim, J.; Lee, J.; Kakei, S.; Kim, J. Motor control characteristics for circular tracking movements of human wrist. *Adv. Robot.* **2017**, *31*, 29–39. [CrossRef]
37. Choi, W.; Lee, J.; Yanagihara, N.; Li, L.; Kim, J. Development of a quantitative evaluation system for visuo-motor control in three-dimensional virtual reality space. *Sci. Rep.* **2018**, *8*, 134–139. [CrossRef]
38. Choi, W.; Lee, J.; Li, L. Analysis of three-dimensional circular tracking movements based on temporo-spatial parameters in polar coordintates. *Appl. Sci.* **2020**, *10*, 621. [CrossRef]
39. Yoshikatsu, H.; Yurie, T.; Kazuya, S.; Ken, S.; Yasuji, S. Intermittently-visual tracking experiments reveal the roles of error-correction and predictive mechanisms in the human visual-motor control system. *Proc. Soc. Instrum. Control Eng.* **2010**, *46*, 391–400.
40. Fine, J.M.; Ward, K.L.; Amazeen, E.L. Manual coordination with intermittent targets: Velocity information for prospective control. *Acta Psychol.* **2014**, *149*, 24–31. [CrossRef]

41. Hayashi, Y.; Sawada, Y. Transition from an antiphase error-correction mode to a synchronization mode in interaction hand tracking. *Phys. Rev. E* **2013**, *88*, 1–7. [CrossRef] [PubMed]
42. Keele, S.W.; Posner, M.I. Processing of visual feedback in rapid movements. *J. Exp. Psychol.* **1968**, *77*, 155–158. [CrossRef] [PubMed]
43. Lee, J.; Kagamihara, Y.; Tomatsu, S.; Kakei, S. The functional role of the cerebellum in visually guided tracking movement. *Cerebellum* **2012**, *11*, 426–433. [CrossRef] [PubMed]
44. Nagaoka, M.; Tanaka, R. Contribution of kinesthesia on human visuomotor elbow tracking movements. *Neurosci. Lett.* **1981**, *26*, 245–249. [CrossRef]
45. Beppu, H.; Nagaoka, M.; Tanaka, R. Analysis of cerebellar motor disorders by visually-guided elbow tracking movement. *Brain* **1984**, *107*, 787–809. [CrossRef]
46. Beppu, H.; Nagaoka, M.; Tanaka, R. Analysis of cerebellar motor disorders by visually-guided elbow tracking movement. 2. contribution of the visual cues on slow ramp pursuit. *Brain* **1987**, *110*, 1–18. [CrossRef]
47. Mathew, J.; Sarlegna, F.R.; Bernier, P.-M.; Danion, F.R. Handedness matters for motor control but not for prediction. *eNeuro* **2019**, *93*, 1–4. [CrossRef]
48. Hoffmann, E.R. Movement time of right- and left-handers using their preferred and non-preferred hands. *Int. J. Ind. Ergon.* **1997**, *19*, 49–57. [CrossRef]
49. Simon, J.R.; De Crow, T.W.; Lincoln, R.S.; Smith, K.U. Effects of handedness on tracking accuracy. *Mot. Skills Res. Exchange* **1952**, *4*, 53–57. [CrossRef]
50. Flowers, K. Handedness and controlled movement. *Br. J. Psychol.* **1975**, *66*, 39–52. [CrossRef]
51. Todor, J.I.; Kyprie, P.M.; Price, H.L. Lateral asymmetries in arm, wrist and finger movements. *Cortex* **1982**, *18*, 515–523. [CrossRef]
52. Wiberg, A.; Ng, M.; Omran, Y.A.; Alfaro-Almagro, F.; McCarthy, P.; Marchini, J.; Bennett, D.L.; Smith, S.; Douaud, G.; Furniss, D. Handedness, language areas and neuropsychiatric diseases: Insights from brain imaging and genetics. *Brain* **2019**, *142*, 2938–2947. [CrossRef] [PubMed]
53. Parma, V.; Brasselet, R.; Zoia, S.; Bulgheroni, M.; Castiello, U. The origin of human handedness and its role in pre-birth motor control. *Sci. Rep.* **2017**, *7*, 1–9. [CrossRef] [PubMed]
54. Golnarafhi, F.; Kuo, B.C. *Automatic Control Systems*, 9th ed.; Wiley: Hoboken, NJ, USA, 2009; pp. 283–293.
55. Wing, A.M. Motor control: Mechanisms of motor equivalence in handwriting. *Curr. Biol.* **2000**, *10*, 245–248. [CrossRef]
56. Plamondon, R.; Alimi, A.M. Speed/accuracy trade-offs in target-directed movements. *Behav. Brain Sci.* **1997**, *20*, 279–303. [CrossRef] [PubMed]
57. Parziale, A.; Senatore, R.; Marcelli, A. Exploring speed–accuracy tradeoff in reaching movements: A neurocomputational model. *Neural Comput. Appl.* **2020**, 1–27. [CrossRef]

© 2020 by the authors. Licensee MDPI, Basel, Switzerland. This article is an open access article distributed under the terms and conditions of the Creative Commons Attribution (CC BY) license (http://creativecommons.org/licenses/by/4.0/).

Article

Turning Characteristics of the More-Affected Side in Parkinson's Disease Patients with Freezing of Gait

Hwayoung Park [1], Changhong Youm [1,2,*], Myeounggon Lee [1], Byungjoo Noh [2] and Sang-Myung Cheon [3]

1. Biomechanics Laboratory, College of Health Sciences, Dong-A University, Busan 49315, Korea; app00113@dau.ac.kr (H.P.); ssam011@dau.ac.kr (M.L.)
2. Department of Healthcare and Science, College of Health Sciences, Dong-A University, Busan 49315, Korea; bnoh@dau.ac.kr
3. Department of Neurology, School of Medicine, Dong-A University, Dongdaesin-dong 3-ga, Seo-gu, Busan 49315, Korea; smcheon@dau.ac.kr
* Correspondence: chyoum@dau.ac.kr; Tel.: +82-51-200-7830; Fax: +82-51-200-7505

Received: 8 May 2020; Accepted: 29 May 2020; Published: 30 May 2020

Abstract: This study investigated the turning characteristics of the more-affected limbs in Parkinson's disease (PD) patients in comparison with that of a control group, and in PD patients with freezing of gait (FOG; freezers) in comparison with those without FOG (non-freezers) for 360° and 540° turning tasks at the maximum speed. A total of 12 freezers, 12 non-freezers, and 12 controls participated in this study. The PD patients showed significantly longer total durations, shorter inner and outer step lengths, and greater anterior–posterior (AP) root mean square (RMS) center of mass (COM) distances compared to those for the controls. The freezers showed significantly greater AP and medial-lateral (ML) RMS COM distances compared to those of non-freezers. The turning task toward the inner step of the more-affected side (IMA) in PD patients showed significantly greater step width, total steps, and AP and ML RMS COM distances than that toward the outer step of the more-affected side (OMA). The corresponding results for freezers revealed significantly higher total steps and shorter inner step length during the 540° turn toward the IMA than that toward the OMA. Therefore, PD patients and freezers exhibited greater turning difficulty in performing challenging turning tasks such as turning with an increased angle and speed and toward the more-affected side.

Keywords: Parkinson's disease; freezing of gait; gait; turning; fall; kinematics

---

1. Introduction

Parkinson's disease (PD) is one of the most common neurodegenerative disorders [1]. A total of 60%–80% of patients with PD eventually develop the freezing of gait (FOG) [1], which is defined as the "episodic absence or marked reduction in forward progression of the feet despite the intention to walk" [2]. The FOG is most commonly experienced during turning tasks, gait initiation, walking through narrow passages, timed up and go (TUG) tasks, dual tasks, and while approaching a destination or avoiding an obstacle [3]. In particular, PD patients with FOG (freezers) encounter greater challenges and need to pay greater attention when performing turning tasks [4]. They face increased risk of falls caused by the instability of their body because it requires the center of mass (COM) to momentarily shift outside the lateral boundaries of the base of support [5].

Previous studies have reported the turning characteristics of 0°, 90°, 120°, and 180° turns [6]; 180° and 360° turns while walking [7]; and 180° turns while walking and 360° turns in place with a narrower range [1] in PD patients and freezers. These studies have revealed that freezers encounter greater difficulty in performing turning tasks than non-freezers, as evidenced by the higher number of steps, slower turning speed, shorter step length, and wider step width with an increasing turning angle. In addition, freezers impose greater demand on lower limb coordination and experience an increased risk of falling and frequent freezing episodes in daily life [6,7].

More than 50% of PD patients exhibit motor impairments, in which unilateral predominance may persist throughout the progression of the disease [8,9]. However, most patients present bilateral impairments at a later stage of the disease [10]. One reason for the unilateral predominance of disease symptoms appears to be the differences in the striatal uptake between the caudate and putamen nuclei [11]. Additionally, the dominant cerebral hemisphere extensively distributed throughout the circuitry of basal ganglia [12]. The asymmetrical gait characteristics of PD patients affect both the upper and lower limbs, and they appear to affect balance control during turning tasks [13]. However, although PD patients show unilateral predominance of disease symptoms, turning tasks assigned in studies so far have been used to evaluate the preferred turning direction toward one side or both sides, without considering the turning task in the direction of the more-affected side.

Spildooren et al. [14] reported that freezers showed higher cadence while turning toward the more-affected side compared to non-freezers. Their findings suggested that freezers experienced greater turning difficulty when turning toward the more-affected side. However, it is still unclear whether there is a difference in the turning characteristics while turning toward the more-affected side in PD patients and freezers. Although PD patients and freezers are affected by the turning speed [15,16], there has been limited research on the characteristics of turning tasks performed at the maximum speed.

Several studies have shown that greater attention and postural stability are required when increasing the turning angle [1,16]. An experimental choice was made to select a 540° turning angle as the challenging condition that would threaten posture stability. This study investigated the characteristics of the turning direction toward the more-affected side in PD patients in comparison with controls, and in freezers in comparison with non-freezers for 360° and 540° turning tasks at the maximum speed. We hypothesized that, for the turning direction of the more-affected side, the turning characteristics with regard to the turning direction may significantly differ between PD patients and controls, and freezers and non-freezers.

2. Materials and Methods

2.1. Participants

A total of 60 PD patients were recruited. However, 36 of them could not be considered because of reasons such as the withdrawal of informed consent, refusal to participate in the experiment, or inability to participate in the experiment. Eventually, 24 PD patients, which included 12 freezers and 12 non-freezers, were considered, and 12 age-matched older adults also participated as controls. The consort diagram containing the details of the study participants is shown in Figure 1 and Table 1. Idiopathic PD patients were diagnosed by a neurologist using the UK Parkinson's Disease Society Brain Bank criteria [17]. The inclusion criteria were: (a) Age 50–75 years; (b) capable of walking and moving independently and with a modified Hoehn and Yahr (H&Y) stage of 2–3 [18,19]; (c) mini-mental state examination (MMSE) score of >24 [20]; (d) stable response to antiparkinsonian medications; and (e) classified as freezers with a score of >3 according to the new freezing of gait questionnaire (NFOGQ) [21].

None of the participants (PD patients and controls) reported any history of musculoskeletal injuries or other cardiovascular and neurological diseases in the past six months. The PD patients that required movement assistive devices and those with dyskinesia (uncontrollable muscle movements induced by drug therapy) were excluded. All participants provided written informed consent before participating in this study. The experimental protocols were approved by the institutional review board (IRB) of Dong-A University Medical Center (IRB number: DAUHIRB-17-033 (See Supplementary file S1. IRB number)).

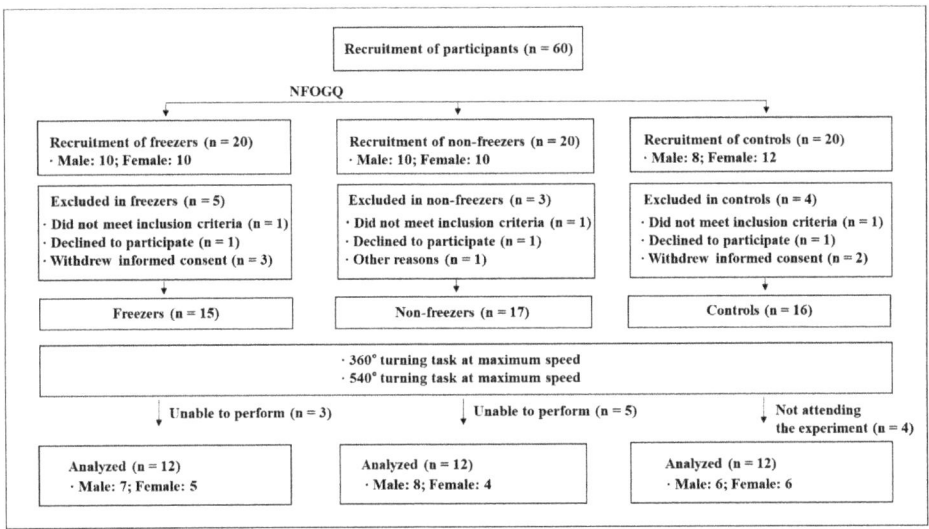

Figure 1. Consort flow diagram. NFOGQ: New freezing of gait questionnaire.

Table 1. Physical characteristics of all participants.

	PD Patients		Controls (n = 12)	p-Value
	Freezers (n = 12)	Non-Freezers (n = 12)		
Sex (male/female)	7/5	8/4	6/6	-
Age (years)	66.67 ± 4.38	68.83 ± 6.00	68.25 ± 3.47	0.517
Height (cm)	158.83 ± 9.08	157.73 ± 7.22	160.30 ± 9.29	0.765
Body weight (kg)	57.88 ± 8.97	61.07 ± 8.43	61.53 ± 9.54	0.563
BMI (kg/m^2)	22.86 ± 2.24	24.55 ± 3.13	23.84 ± 2.20	0.281
MMSE (scores)	27.33 ± 2.06	26.67 ± 2.57	26.00 ± 1.76	0.330
Disease duration (years)	9.83 ± 4.26	5.96 ± 1.83	-	**0.008**
Treatment duration (years)	8.95 ± 4.35	3.52 ± 2.26	-	**0.001**
UPDRS Total (scores)	60.47 ± 9.59	38.13 ± 5.90	-	**<0.001**
UPDRS III (scores)	33.38 ± 6.16	27.96 ± 4.38	-	**0.023**
Hoehn and Yahr scale	2.55 ± 0.27	2.38 ± 0.31	-	0.176
NFOGQ (scores)	19.18 ± 5.62	-	-	-
L-Dopa equivalent dose (mg/day)	1142.50 ± 418.20	682.92 ± 239.17	-	**0.003**
More affected side (left/right)	11/1	8/4	All right-handed	-

All data represent the mean ± standard deviation; PD: Parkinson's disease; BMI: Body mass index; MMSE: Mini-mental state examination; UPDRS: Unified Parkinson's disease rating scale; L-dopa: Levodopa. Boldface denotes a significant difference between freezers and non-freezers. Significant difference: $p < 0.05$.

2.2. Test Procedures

The PD patients were in the "On" state, which was induced by dopaminergic medication that was administered approximately 2–3 h before the tests. They were sufficiently under the effect of the medication [22]. The experiments were performed in two sessions. In the first session, the participants completed the informed consent form and were assessed according to the Unified Parkinson disease rating scale (UPDRS) [23], modified H&Y stage, NFOGQ, and MMSE (Table 1). In the second session, the participants warmed up for approximately 5 min before performing the turning tasks and practiced such tasks. After 5 min of rest, the test started, and the participants were instructed to successfully complete the 360° and 540° turning tasks at the maximum speed three times.

The orientation of body segments in a global coordinate system was captured using nine cameras (Vicon MX-T10, Oxford Metrics, Oxford, UK). The data sampling frequency was 100 Hz [24]. Three-dimensional motion data were captured using the Vicon Nexus software (version 1.83; Oxford Metrics, UK). The appropriate metrics were measured bilaterally to estimate the joint kinematic data. The plug-in gait marker set was attached with 39 14-mm spherical reflective markers, which is a modified version of the Helen Hayes marker set [25].

The 360° and 540° turning tasks were conducted with maximum speed, which was defined as the fastest speed at which the patients choose to perform the tasks, in both the directions of the inner step of the more-affected side (IMA) and the outer step of the more-affected side (OMA). The turning directions for the more-affected sides (IMA and OMA) were classified by a neurologist. The 360° and 540° turning tasks with maximum speed used in this study were modified from the TUG test (Figure 2).

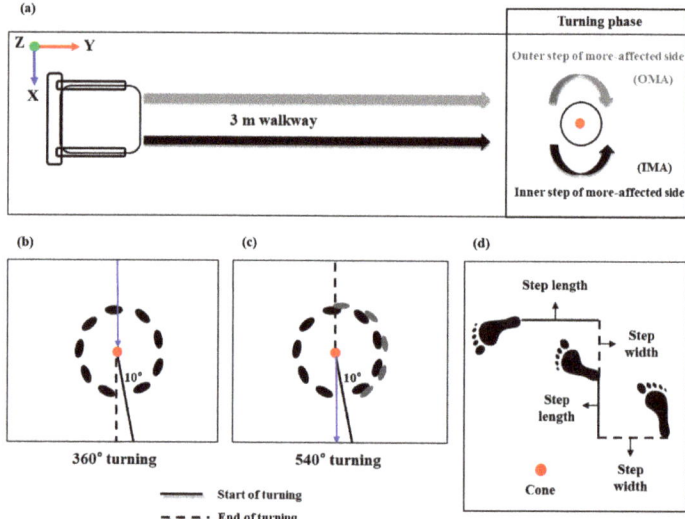

Figure 2. Schematic of the data collection and analysis phase. (**a**) The 360° turning task involved sitting on the chair, getting up from the chair, turning around the cone at the 3-m point, and reaching the final target point as quickly as possible. The 540° turning task involved sitting on the chair, getting up from the chair, turning around the cone at the 3-m point, and reaching the chair as quickly as possible. (**b**,**c**) In the analysis phase of the 360° and 540° turning tasks, the start event was defined as the event when the angle between the pelvic vector and the left and right vectors passed 10°. After the turning movement was completed, the event when the two vectors completed 360° and 540° was defined as the end of the rotation. (**d**) Step width was defined as the length between the initial foot heel contact of one leg and the initial foot heel contact of the other leg. The inner and outer step lengths were defined as the lengths of the initial foot heel contact of the left/right leg and the initial foot heel contact of the other leg, respectively.

2.3. Data Analysis

The 360° and 540° turning data was a fourth-order Butterworth low-pass filtered with a cutoff frequency of 10 Hz [24]. The measurements were performed three times and the averaged value was used for the analysis.

The variables for the analysis were the total steps, total duration, step width, inner and outer step lengths, area of the 95% confidence interval (CI), and the anterior–posterior (AP) and medial–lateral (ML) root mean square (RMS) distances of the center of mass (COM) during the 360° and 540° turning tasks performed at maximum speed. A weighted sum of the COM of all segments was calculated, where the segments were defined by markers. The COM was the COM of all modeled segments. In addition, the area of the 95% CI (Equation (1)) and the AP and ML RMS distances of the COM on the horizontal plane (Equation (2)) were computed as [26]:

$$\text{Area} = \pi ab, \quad (1)$$

where a and b denote the major and minor axis, respectively.

$$a = \left[3\left(SD_{AP}^2 + SD_{ML}^2 + D\right)\right]^{\frac{1}{2}}; \, b = \left[3\left(SD_{AP}^2 + SD_{ML}^2 - D\right)\right]^{\frac{1}{2}}, \quad (2)$$

where SD_{AP} and SD_{ML} denote the standard deviations of the AP and ML RMS distances of the COM, respectively.

$$D = \left[\left(SD_{AP}^2 + SD_{ML}^2\right) - 4\left(SD_{AP}^2 SD_{ML}^2 - SD_{APML}^2\right)\right]^{\frac{1}{2}}, \quad (3)$$

where D denotes the distance from the center to the focus for the AP and ML RMS distances of the COM.

$$SD_{APML} = \frac{1}{N}\left(\sum_{n=1}^{N} X_{AP(n)} X_{ML(n)}\right), \quad (4)$$

where X_{AP} and X_{ML} denote the position of the AP and ML of the COM, respectively.

$$RMS_{AP} = \left[\frac{1}{N}\sum_{n=1}^{N}\left(X_{AP(n)} - \overline{X}_{AP}\right)^2\right]^{\frac{1}{2}}; \, RMS_{ML} = \left[\frac{1}{N}\sum_{n=1}^{N}\left(X_{ML(n)} - \overline{X}_{ML}\right)^2\right]^{\frac{1}{2}}, \quad (5)$$

where $\overline{X}_{AP}$ and $\overline{X}_{ML}$ denote the mean of AP and ML of the COM, respectively.

2.4. Statistical Analysis

The Shapiro–Wilk test revealed that data followed a normal distribution. A two-way analysis of variance (ANOVA) with repeated measures was performed to analyze the differences between the groups (PD patients compared with controls and freezers compared with non-freezers) and between the turning directions (IMA and OMA) during the 360° and 540° turning tasks at maximum speed. Post-hoc tests were performed using the independent sample t-test between the groups and the paired samples t-test was used to analyze the turning directions. To compare the differences of physical characteristics between all participants, one-way ANOVAs were performed.

In addition, the responsiveness between the groups and the turning directions were expressed as the effect size (ES). Univariate and multivariate logistic regression analyses and stepwise binary logistic regression analysis were performed to identify the classifier variables for PD patients and freezers, and for the turning directions. Classifier variables were expressed as odds ratios (OR) with a 95% CI (min to max). All statistical analyses were performed using SPSS 22.0 (SPSS Inc., Chicago, IL, USA), and the statistical significance was set at 0.05.

3. Results

3.1. Differences between PD Patients and Controls

In the results of the 360° turning task at the maximum speed, the total steps (IMA, $p = 0.035$), total duration (IMA, $p = 0.006$; OMA, $p = 0.047$), inner (IMA, $p = 0.003$; OMA, $p < 0.001$) and outer (IMA, $p = 0.001$; OMA, $p < 0.001$) step lengths, and ML RMS distance of the COM (IMA, $p = 0.042$; OMA, $p = 0.016$) of the turning tasks in the directions of the IMA and OMA showed significant differences between PD patients and controls (Table 2). In the results of the 540° turning task at the maximum speed, the inner (OMA, $p = 0.018$) and outer (IMA, $p = 0.001$) step lengths and AP RMS distance of the COM (IMA, $p = 0.042$; OMA, $p = 0.016$) of the turning tasks in the directions of the IMA and OMA showed significant differences between the PD patients and controls (Table 3).

Table 2. Comparison of turning characteristics of PD patients and controls for the 360° turning task at maximum speed.

		PD	Controls	p^a-Value	ES
Total steps	IMA	9.17 ± 2.59	7.39 ± 1.52	**0.035**	0.09
	OMA	9.96 ± 2.53	9.11 ± 2.14	0.328	0.24
	p^b-value	0.060	0.037		0.04
Total duration (s)	IMA	4.34 ± 1.18	3.25 ± 0.66	**0.006**	0.18
	OMA	4.67 ± 2.03	3.42 ± 0.70	**0.047**	0.03
	p^b-value	0.338	0.566		0.00
Step width (m)	IMA	0.13 ± 0.08	0.17 ± 0.08	0.133	0.18
	OMA	0.09 ± 0.04	0.15 ± 0.07	**0.006**	0.11
	p^b-value	**0.042**	0.353		0.00
Inner step length (m)	IMA	0.40 ± 0.07	0.47 ± 0.05	**0.003**	0.32
	OMA	0.41 ± 0.06	0.49 ± 0.05	**<0.001**	0.05
	p^b-value	0.605	0.156		0.01
Outer step length (m)	IMA	0.40 ± 0.07	0.49 ± 0.06	**0.001**	0.32
	OMA	0.40 ± 0.07	0.49 ± 0.04	**<0.001**	0.01
	p^b-value	0.588	0.914		0.00
Area of horizontal plane of the COM (m²)	IMA	2.43 ± 0.59	2.67 ± 0.35	0.140	0.14
	OMA	2.23 ± 0.69	2.56 ± 0.31	0.050	0.03
	p^b-value	0.347	0.149		0.00
Anterior-posterior RMS distance of the COM (m)	IMA	0.29 ± 0.13	0.24 ± 0.06	0.258	0.01
	OMA	0.20 ± 0.08	0.22 ± 0.04	0.403	0.14
	p^b-value	**0.009**	0.218		0.07
Medial-lateral RMS distance of the COM (m)	IMA	0.29 ± 0.13	0.22 ± 0.05	**0.042**	0.01
	OMA	0.16 ± 0.06	0.20 ± 0.03	**0.016**	0.19
	p^b-value	**0.002**	0.182		0.12

All data represent the mean ± standard deviation (95% confidence interval). p^a-value (groups): Independent t-tests; p^b-value (turning direction): Paired samples t-tests; ES: Effect size; IMA: Inner step of the more affected side; OMA: Outer step of the more affected side; COM: Center of mass; RMS: Root mean square. Boldface indicates a significant difference ($p < 0.05$).

3.2. Classifier Variables for PD Patients and Controls

Stepwise binary logistic regression analysis for the PD patients and controls revealed that the total duration (OR: 0.271; 95% CI: 0.077–0.957; $R_N^2 = 0.532$; $p = 0.043$) and outer step length (OR: 4.826; 95% CI: 1.248–18.659; $R_N^2 = 0.532$; $p = 0.023$) of the turning task performed in the direction of the IMA and inner step length (OR: 7.218; 95% CI: 1.831–28.463; $R_N^2 = 0.607$; $p = 0.005$) of the turning task performed in the direction of the OMA were significantly different during the 360° turning task at the maximum speed. In addition, the outer step length (OR: 5.642; 95% CI: 1.578–20.167; $R_N^2 = 0.390$; $p = 0.008$) of the turning task performed in the direction of the IMA and inner step length (OR: 2.984; 95% CI: 1.092–8.152; $R_N^2 = 0.223$; $p = 0.033$) of the turning task performed in the direction of the OMA were significantly different during the 540° turning task at the maximum speed.

Table 3. Comparison of turning characteristics of PD patients and controls for the 540° turning task at maximum speed.

		PD	Controls	p^a-Value	ES
Total steps	IMA	12.33 ± 2.64	10.61 ± 2.12	0.058	0.03
	OMA	10.75 ± 2.55	10.89 ± 3.11	0.886	0.05
	p^b-value	**0.008**	0.760		0.09
Total duration (s)	IMA	6.51 ± 1.77	6.30 ± 3.01	0.789	0.02
	OMA	6.30 ± 3.14	5.43 ± 1.55	0.372	0.02
	p^b-value	0.759	0.381		0.01
Step width (m)	IMA	0.14 ± 0.08	0.16 ± 0.06	0.377	0.02
	OMA	0.12 ± 0.04	0.12 ± 0.07	0.945	0.08
	p^b-value	0.390	0.158		0.01
Inner step length (m)	IMA	0.44 ± 0.09	0.50 ± 0.11	0.141	0.20
	OMA	0.41 ± 0.10	0.49 ± 0.07	**0.018**	0.01
	p^b-value	0.351	0.915		0.01
Outer step length (m)	IMA	0.39 ± 0.08	0.48 ± 0.05	**0.001**	0.19
	OMA	0.42 ± 0.09	0.47 ± 0.05	0.100	0.02
	p^b-value	0.057	0.180		0.10
Area of horizontal plane of the COM (m^2)	IMA	2.40 ± 0.59	2.48 ± 0.42	0.645	0.06
	OMA	2.05 ± 0.57	2.33 ± 0.27	0.058	0.10
	p^b-value	0.068	0.114		0.02
Anterior-posterior RMS distance of the COM (m)	IMA	0.28 ± 0.13	0.23 ± 0.09	0.315	0.01
	OMA	0.18 ± 0.06	0.19 ± 0.03	0.577	0.20
	p^b-value	**0.005**	0.109		0.04
Medial-lateral RMS distance of the COM (m)	IMA	0.26 ± 0.13	0.19 ± 0.03	0.059	0.03
	OMA	0.15 ± 0.06	0.19 ± 0.03	0.058	0.14
	p^b-value	**0.003**	0.660		0.13

All data represent the mean ± standard deviation (95% confidence interval). p^a-value (groups): Independent t-tests; p^b-value (turning direction): Paired samples t-tests. Boldface indicates a significant difference ($p < 0.05$).

3.3. Differences between Freezers and Non-Freezers

The AP (360° turn, $p < 0.001$; 540° turn, $p < 0.001$) and ML (360° turn, $p < 0.001$; 540° turn, $p < 0.001$) RMS distances of the COM in the turning task performed in the direction of the IMA (Figure 3) and the ML RMS distance of the COM (360° turn, $p = 0.003$; 540° turn, $p = 0.013$) in the turning task performed in the direction of the OMA were significantly different for freezers and non-freezers during the 360° and 540° turning tasks at the maximum speed (Tables 4 and 5).

3.4. Classifier Variables for Freezers and Non-Freezers

Stepwise binary logistic regression analysis for freezers and non-freezers showed that the ML RMS distance of the COM in the turning tasks performed in the directions of the IMA (OR: 10.188; 95% CI: 1.699–61.100; $R_N^2 = 0.596$; $p = 0.011$) and OMA (OR: 0.193; 95% CI: 0.053–0.708; $R_N^2 = 0.437$; $p = 0.013$) were significantly different during the 360° turning task at the maximum speed. In addition, the inner step length (OR: 0.047; 95% CI: 0.004–0.560; $R_N^2 = 0.665$; $p = 0.016$) of the turning task performed in the direction of the IMA and the ML RMS distance of the COM (OR: 0.276; 95% CI: 0.086–0.883; $R_N^2 = 0.324$; $p = 0.030$) in the turning task performed in the direction of the OMA were significantly different during the 540° turning task at the maximum speed.

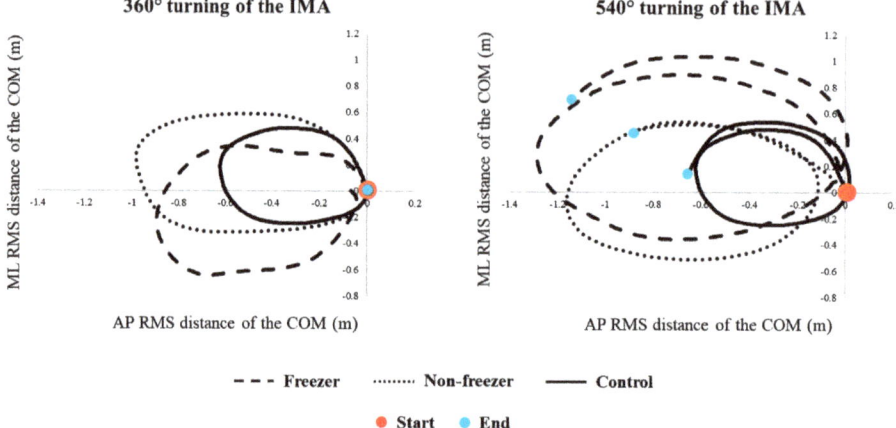

Figure 3. Single participant trial of freezers, non-freezers, and controls during the 360° and 540° turning tasks. This figure presented the horizontal trajectory of the center of mass presented by large (a freezer) and small (a non-freezer) solid dots, and full line (a control), respectively.

Table 4. Comparison of turning characteristics of freezers and non-freezers for the 360° turning task at maximum speed.

		Freezers	Non-Freezers	p^a-Value	ES
Total steps	IMA	9.78 ± 2.52	8.56 ± 2.61	0.256	0.02
	OMA	9.94 ± 2.76	9.97 ± 2.40	0.979	0.16
	p^b-value	0.750	**0.034**		0.11
Total duration (s)	IMA	4.31 ± 1.09	4.37 ± 1.32	0.899	0.02
	OMA	5.07 ± 2.34	4.27 ± 1.67	0.346	0.04
	p^b-value	0.211	0.787		0.07
Step width (m)	IMA	0.14 ± 0.10	0.12 ± 0.05	0.503	0.00
	OMA	0.09 ± 0.04	0.10 ± 0.03	0.424	0.18
	p^b-value	0.058	0.407		0.05
Inner step length (m)	IMA	0.39 ± 0.08	0.41 ± 0.06	0.554	0.05
	OMA	0.39 ± 0.07	0.42 ± 0.05	0.212	0.01
	p^b-value	0.935	0.226		0.02
Outer step length (m)	IMA	0.39 ± 0.06	0.41 ± 0.09	0.572	0.01
	OMA	0.40 ± 0.06	0.41 ± 0.08	0.837	0.01
	p^b-value	0.327	0.957		0.02
Area of horizontal plane of the COM (m²)	IMA	2.39 ± 0.44	2.47 ± 0.72	0.722	0.02
	OMA	2.38 ± 0.43	2.07 ± 0.86	0.276	0.04
	p^b-value	0.969	0.349		0.04
Anterior-posterior RMS distance of the COM (m)	IMA	0.20 ± 0.05	0.17 ± 0.03	**<0.001**	0.28
	OMA	0.20 ± 0.05	0.20 ± 0.11	0.887	0.38
	p^b-value	0.674	**0.002**		0.41
Medial-lateral RMS distance of the COM (m)	IMA	0.19 ± 0.05	0.17 ± 0.03	**<0.001**	0.27
	OMA	0.19 ± 0.04	0.12 ± 0.06	**0.003**	0.54
	p^b-value	0.818	**<0.001**		0.53

All data represent the mean ± standard deviation (95% confidence interval). p^a-value (groups): Independent t-tests; p^b-value (turning direction): Paired samples t-tests. Boldface indicates a significant difference ($p < 0.05$).

Table 5. Comparison of turning characteristics of freezers and non-freezers for the 540° turning task at maximum speed.

		Freezers	Non-Freezers	p^a-Value	ES
Total steps	IMA	12.72 ± 2.25	11.94 ± 3.03	0.482	0.00
	OMA	10.61 ± 2.55	10.89 ± 2.66	0.797	0.28
	p^b-value	**0.026**	0.168		0.04
Total duration (s)	IMA	5.89 ± 1.00	6.29 ± 1.02	0.340	0.05
	OMA	6.23 ± 3.52	6.37 ± 2.86	0.912	0.00
	p^b-value	0.739	0.917		0.05
Step width (m)	IMA	0.15 ± 0.11	0.13 ± 0.05	0.456	0.00
	OMA	0.11 ± 0.04	0.14 ± 0.03	**0.043**	0.04
	p^b-value	0.210	0.526		0.09
Inner step length (m)	IMA	0.51 ± 0.06	0.38 ± 0.07	**<0.001**	0.06
	OMA	0.38 ± 0.10	0.45 ± 0.07	0.055	0.07
	p^b-value	**0.007**	**0.008**		0.48
Outer step length (m)	IMA	0.38 ± 0.07	0.40 ± 0.09	0.628	0.06
	OMA	0.39 ± 0.07	0.45 ± 0.10	0.106	0.16
	p^b-value	0.555	0.072		0.10
Area of horizontal plane of the COM (m²)	IMA	2.22 ± 0.48	2.59 ± 0.65	0.127	0.00
	OMA	2.21 ± 0.56	1.90 ± 0.56	0.182	0.16
	p^b-value	0.949	0.051		0.15
Anterior-posterior RMS distance of the COM (m)	IMA	0.19 ± 0.05	0.16 ± 0.02	**<0.001**	0.36
	OMA	0.19 ± 0.06	0.17 ± 0.07	0.646	0.42
	p^b-value	0.925	0.550		0.41
Medial-lateral RMS distance of the COM (m)	IMA	0.18 ± 0.05	0.15 ± 0.03	**<0.001**	0.27
	OMA	0.18 ± 0.06	0.12 ± 0.05	**0.013**	0.49
	p^b-value	0.810	**0.001**		0.50

All data represent the mean ± standard deviation (95% confidence interval). p^a-value (groups): Independent t-tests; p^b-value (turning direction): Paired samples t-tests. Boldface indicates a significant difference ($p < 0.05$).

3.5. Differences between Turning Characteristics in the Directions of the IMA and OMA

In the results of the PD patients, the step width ($p = 0.042$) and AP ($p = 0.009$) and ML ($p = 0.002$) RMS distances of the COM in the turning tasks performed in the direction of the IMA were significantly higher than those in the direction of the OMA during the 360° turning task at the maximum speed (Table 2). In addition, the total steps ($p = 0.008$) and AP ($p = 0.005$) and ML ($p = 0.003$) RMS distances of the COM in the turning tasks performed in the direction of the IMA were significantly higher than those in the direction of the OMA during the 540° turning task at the maximum speed (Table 3). In the results of the freezers, the total steps ($p = 0.026$) and inner step length ($p = 0.007$) of the turning tasks performed in the direction of the IMA were significantly higher than those in the direction of the OMA during the 540° turning task at the maximum speed (Table 5).

3.6. Classifier Variables for Turning Tasks in the Directions of the IMA and OMA

Stepwise binary logistic regression analysis for the PD patients revealed that the ML RMS distance of the COM was significantly different in the turning task performed in the direction of the IMA during the 360° (OR: 0.000; 95% CI: 0.000–0.005; $R_N^2 = 0.301$; $p = 0.002$) and 540° (OR: 0.000; 95% CI: 0.000–0.021; $R_N^2 = 0.231$; $p = 0.004$) turning tasks at the maximum speed. In addition, the results for freezers revealed that the ML RMS distance of the COM was significantly different in the turning direction of the IMA during the 360° (OR: 0.000; 95% CI: 0.000–0.010; $R_N^2 = 0.405$; $p = 0.005$) and 540° (OR: 0.000; 95% CI: 0.000–0.014; $R_N^2 = 0.426$; $p = 0.004$) turning tasks at the maximum speed. Significant differences were found for the total steps (OR: 0.755; 95% CI: 0.574–0.993; $R_N^2 = 0.426$; $p = 0.045$) in the 540° turning task performed in the direction of the IMA at the maximum speed.

4. Discussion

4.1. Differences between PD Patients and Controls, and Freezers and Non-Freezers

We found that PD patients showed a significantly longer total duration, shorter inner and outer step lengths, and greater ML RMS distance of the COM during the 360° turning task at the maximum speed compared to those of the controls. The total duration and outer step length of the 360° and 540° turning tasks performed in the direction of the IMA and the inner step length of the 360° and 540° turning tasks performed in the direction of the OMA at the maximum speed were revealed as the classifier variables for the PD patients. In addition, the freezers showed significantly greater AP and ML RMS distances of the COM in the 360° and 540° turning tasks performed in the direction of the IMA, and greater ML RMS distance of the COM in the 360° and 540° turning tasks performed in the direction of the OMA at the maximum speed in comparison with those of the non-freezers. The ML RMS distance of the COM in the 360° and 540° turning tasks performed in the directions of the IMA and OMA at the maximum speed were revealed as the classifier variables for the freezers. These results demonstrated our hypothesis that turning tasks under challenging conditions might be more difficult for PD patients than for controls, and for freezers than for non-freezers.

Turning tasks threaten the stability of PD patients more than any other freezing trigger, and they require the precise control of each limb [26]. Therefore, PD patients may experience greater challenge and distraction in performing turning tasks. Previous studies have reported that PD patients showed significantly greater total steps, wider step width, shorter step length, and slower turning speed to maintain their center of gravity between the two feet [27]. Increased turning angle and speed were observed during 90° and 180° turning tasks at the preferred speed [28], 180° turning tasks at comfortable and faster speeds [29], and 30° to 180° turning tasks at the self-selected preferred, slower, and faster speeds [15]. Thus, these turning characteristics may be a compensatory strategy for postural instability in PD patients [30].

The motor cortex closely cooperates with the basal ganglia, and the cerebellum is involved in some functions such as attention, executive and visuospatial functions, and control motor tasks [31]. The motor symptoms in PD patients are the results of incrementally impaired motor functions and impaired basal ganglia cells in the substantia nigra, which initiate and control body movements and balance [32]. Further, the degeneration of the substantia nigra is reflected as a loss of dopaminergic innervation, which may influence the control of automatized behavior. Therefore, PD patients may experience difficulty in automatic movements without attention [33]. The abnormalities in the basal ganglia or spinal cord circuit behavior have been suggested to be important factors influencing PD patients because of the greater decline in voluntary contractions [34]. The turning tasks thus require more attention and involve greater interlimb coordination, increased coupling between posture and gait [35], and modifications of locomotor patterns requiring frontal lobe cognitive and executive functions that control postural transitions [36]. Thus, these results suggest that challenging turning tasks may indicate postural instabilities, which imply that PD patients are more likely to be vulnerable to functional impairments [37] because turning is inherently asymmetrical and cannot stem from central pattern generators unlike walking in a straight line [38].

The results of our study show that PD patients might experience greater difficulty in 360° and 540° turning tasks in the directions of the IMA and OMA at the maximum speed in comparison with the controls, as evidenced by longer total turn durations, shorter inner and outer step lengths, and greater ML RMS distances of the COM (Figure 3). These differences were associated with relatively small effect sizes (d = 0.01–0.32). In addition, this study demonstrated classifier variables for the PD patients. We found that the total duration and the inner and outer step length may be considered when comparing PD patients and controls in addition to classifier variables to identify turning difficulty during the 360° and 540° turning tasks performed in the direction of the IMA and OMA at the maximum speed. Our results are useful for determining the decline in dynamic stability and the posture control of PD patients, and they can potentially be used in clinical environments to measure the effectiveness of interventions meant to prevent risk of falls.

In previous studies, the freezers showed higher total steps, longer total durations, slower turning speeds, wider step widths, and shorter step lengths than the non-freezers, as well as increased turning angles and speeds while performing tasks such as 0°, 90°, 120°, 180°, and 360° turning tasks at the preferred and faster speeds [1,6,16]. Turning difficulty has been related to disorders of the frontocortical areas, which may be more severe in freezers than in non-freezers because freezers present a lower supplementary motor area activity than non-freezers [39]. The dysfunction of the supplementary motor area may require the functional reorganization of the spinal circuitry, given the abnormal projections from this area through the reticulospinal tract [40]. As the reticulospinal tract connects to the spinal interneurons that mediate one of the most powerful spinal inhibitory mechanisms, presynaptic inhibition [41], it is possible that presynaptic inhibition during challenging turning tasks may be deficient in freezers compared to those in controls and non-freezers. Therefore, increasing the turning angle and turning speed might pose additional difficulties in threatening situations, where dynamic stability while performing turning tasks with a small turning angle at the normal speed is potentially related to difficulties in coupling the inter-limb coordination and postural control [1,6]. In addition, such turning tasks in freezers may lead to an increased risk of fall because these conditions are not commonly experienced in daily life and therefore require greater attention and postural stability [15,29,42].

Further, our results show that freezers might experience greater difficulty in turning at 360° and 540° angles in the directions of the IMA and OMA at the maximum speed compared to non-freezers, as evidenced by the greater AP and ML RMS distances of the COM (Figure 3). These differences were associated with a relatively moderate effect size ($d = 0.27$–0.54). In addition, we found that the ML RMS distance of the COM may be considered when comparing freezers and non-freezers in addition to classifier variables to identify disease severity during the 360° and 540° turning tasks performed in the direction of the IMA and OMA at the maximum speed. Therefore, we suggest that preventive training to reduce risk of falling may require practicing around a larger radius to complete a turn [28,43].

4.2. Differences between Turning Characteristics in the Directions of the IMA and OMA

We found that PD patients showed significantly greater step widths, higher total steps, and greater AP and ML RMS distances of the COM in the 360° and 540° turning tasks performed at the maximum speed in the direction of the IMA than those in the direction of the OMA. In addition, the ML RMS distance of the COM while turning by 360° and 540° at the maximum speed in the direction of the IMA was revealed as the classifier variable for the PD patients and controls. The 540° turning task performed by the freezers at the maximum speed revealed significantly higher total steps and shorter inner step length in the direction of the IMA than those in the direction of the OMA. Moreover, the ML RMS distance of the COM during the 360° turning task in the direction of the IMA and the total steps and ML RMS distance of the COM during the 540° turning task in the direction of the IMA at the maximum speed were revealed as the classifier variables for freezers and non-freezers. The study results proved our hypothesis that turning in the direction of the more-affected side might present more difficulties in PD patients and freezers.

Only one study on turning tasks toward the more-affected and less-affected sides in PD patients and freezers [14] reported that such patients showed higher turning steps and a greater duration of turn while turning 180° and 360° toward the more-affected side. Thus, PD patients and freezers might experience greater difficulty in turning toward the more-affected side [14], which increases the risk of falls [9].

Previous studies reported that the less-affected side assumes the function of the more-affected side during a turning task, as a compensatory strategy between the lower limbs in PD patients and freezers [9,44]. This asymmetry in performing the turning tasks is responsible for the motor manifestation characteristics of PD patients [45]. The cause of this asymmetry is not known [46]. However, it might reflect a different vulnerability of the substantia nigra pars compacta neurons to the factors involved in the generation of the disorder. Therefore, these results suggest that freezers with higher asymmetry may experience greater difficulty than non-freezers and controls with symmetrical motor involvement [45]. The motor manifestations are predominantly observed while performing challenging turning tasks [46].

Lee et al. [47] suggested that the more-affected side of the PD patients tends to be affected predominantly throughout disease progression. Therefore, this dominant tendency may promote greater motor deficits on the more-affected side. These results suggest that turning difficulty may be related to asymmetry between the more-affected and less-affected sides of the lower limbs [47]. Moreover, shorter step lengths may be related to weakened muscle strength, which could influence the alterations in the lower limb kinematics [48]. In addition, freezers may have greater difficulty in adapting postural control during turning and switching their motor pattern to meet the asymmetrical demands while turning in the direction of the more-affected side [5]. These results suggest that the efforts made by PD patients and freezers to increase the postural stability during the turning tasks may help compensate the reduced lower limb strength of the more-affected side [48].

The findings presented in this study have some important implications. First, PD patients and freezers might experience greater difficulty in turning toward the direction of the more-affected side, which may be useful in the clinical assessment of the disease severity and FOG. Thus, fall prevention training may require focus on improving the turning performances, particularly turning toward the more-affected side, by practicing wider turns, turning more slowly, or practicing to sustain a wider base of support. Second, the ML RMS distance of the COM was shown as a marker that can distinguish between the severity of the motor symptoms in PD patients and controls, or freezers and non-freezers.

However, our study presents some limitations. First, the sample size was small for the generalization of the results obtained. Although a different sample size was used in this study, the lack of influences may have been obtained in the results. Second, the comparison of antiparkinsonian medication effects was not performed while evaluating the turning tasks of this study. Third, this study was based on difficult turning tasks that do not appear in daily life activities. Finally, this study, which used 39 markers, was considered to observe turning movements such as upper and lower limb coordination and posture control and dynamic stability of PD patients. However, we did not consider these results of upper limbs movement in our study because we focused on only lower limb movements.

5. Conclusions

Our study investigated the characteristics of turning performance in the direction of the more-affected side in PD patients in comparison with controls, and in freezers in comparison with non-freezers during 360° and 540° turning tasks at the maximum speed. We found that the PD patients and freezers exhibited higher turning difficulty during challenging turning tasks such as those requiring increasing turning angles and speeds. Further, PD patients and freezers may be in greater danger of falling while turning in the direction of the more-affected side. Therefore, turning tasks involving 360° and 540° turning tasks in the direction of the IMA and OMA at the maximum speed may be useful for evaluating the turning characteristics to distinguish between PD patients and freezers. Further studies are needed to evaluate turning characteristics according to motor symptoms in PD patients at more various conditions during turning tasks.

Ethics approval and consent to participate: All procedures performed in studies involving human participants were performed in accordance with the ethical standards of the institutional and/or national research committee and with the 1964 Helsinki declaration and its later amendments or comparable ethical standards. All subjects gave their informed consent for inclusion before they participated in the study. The study was approved by the Institutional Review Board of Dong-A University Hospital (IRB number: DAUHIRB-17-033; see "Ethical approval letter IRB").

Supplementary Materials: The following are available online at http://www.mdpi.com/1424-8220/20/11/3098/s1, Supplementary File S1: IRB number, Supplementary File S2: Research data (raw data), Supplementary Table S1: List of levodopa-equivalent doses.

Author Contributions: Conceptualization, H.P., C.Y., M.L., B.N., and S.-M.C.; methodology, H.P., C.Y., M.L., B.N., and S.-M.C.; formal analysis, H.P., C.Y., M.L., B.N., and S.-M.C.; investigation, H.P., C.Y., M.L., and B.N.; resources, H.P., M.L., B.N., and S.-M.C.; data acquisition, H.P., C.Y., M.L., B.N., and S.-M.C.; writing—original draft preparation, H.P., C.Y., and S.-M.C.; writing—review and editing, H.P., C.Y., M.L., B.N., and S.-M.C. All authors have read and agreed to the published version of the manuscript.

Funding: This research was funded by Dong-A University research fund. This research did not receive any specific grant from funding agencies in the public, commercial, or not-for-profit sectors.

Acknowledgments: The authors would like to thank the Biomechanics Laboratory staff at Dong-A University for their assistance with data collection.

Conflicts of Interest: The authors declare no conflict of interest.

Availability of data and materials: The datasets generated and/or analyzed during the current study are not publicly available due to intellectual property reasons, but these are available upon a reasonable request.

References

1. Bertoli, M.; Della, C.U.; Cereatti, A.; Mancini, M. Objective measures to investigate turning impairments and freezing of gait in people with Parkinson's disease. *Gait Posture* **2019**, *74*, 187–193. [CrossRef] [PubMed]
2. Giladi, N.; McMahon, D.; Przedborski, S.; Flaster, E.; Guillory, S.; Kostic, V.; Fahn, S. Motor blocks in Parkinson's disease. *Neurol.* **1992**, *42*, 333–339. [CrossRef] [PubMed]
3. Mirelman, A.; Bonato, P.; Camicioli, R.; Ellis, T.D.; Giladi, N.; Hamilton, J.L.; Hass, C.J.; Hausdorff, J.M.; Pelosin, E.; Almeida, Q.J. Gait impairments in Parkinson's disease. *Lancet Neurol.* **2019**, *18*, 697–708. [CrossRef]
4. Mitchell, T.; Conradsson, D.; Paquette, C. Gait and trunk kinematics during prolonged turning in Parkinson's disease with freezing of gait. *Parkinsonism Relat. Disord.* **2019**, *64*, 188–193. [CrossRef]
5. Bengevoord, A.; Vervoort, G.; Spildooren, J.; Heremans, E.; Vandenberghe, W.; Bloem, B.R.; Nieuwboer, A. Center of mass trajectories during turning in patients with Parkinson's disease with and without freezing of gait. *Gait Posture* **2016**, *43*, 54–59. [CrossRef]
6. Bhatt, H.; Pieruccini-Faria, F.; Almeida, Q.J. Dynamics of turning sharpness influences freezing of gait in Parkinson's disease. *Parkinsonism Relat. Disord.* **2013**, *19*, 181–185. [CrossRef]
7. Stuart, S.; Mancini, M. Prefrontal cortical activation with open and closed-loop tactile cueing when walking and turning in Parkinson disease: A pilot study. *J. Neurol. Phys. Ther.* **2020**, *44*, 121–131. [CrossRef]
8. Uitti, R.J.; Baba, Y.; Whaley, N.R.; Wszolek, Z.K.; Putzke, J.D. Parkinson disease: Handedness predicts asymmetry. *Neurol.* **2005**, *64*, 1925–1930. [CrossRef]
9. Beretta, V.S.; Gobbi, L.T.B.; Lirani-Silva, E.; Simieli, L.; Orcioli-Silva, D.; Barbieri, F.A. Challenging postural tasks increase asymmetry in patients with Parkinson's disease. *PLoS ONE* **2015**, *10*, e0137722. [CrossRef]
10. Bekkers, E.M.J.; Van Rossom, S.; Heremans, E.; Dockx, K.; Devan, S.; Verschueren, S.M.P.; Nieuwboer, A. Adaptations to postural perturbations in patients with freezing of gait. *Front. Neurol.* **2018**, *9*, 540. [CrossRef]
11. Knable, M.B.; Jones, D.W.; Coppola, R.; Hyde, T.M.; Lee, K.S.; Gorey, J.; Weinberger, D.R. Lateralized differences in iodine-123-IBZM uptake in the basal ganglia in asymmetric Parkinson's disease. *J. Nucl. Med.* **1995**, *36*, 1216–1225. [PubMed]
12. Potgieser, A.R.E.; de Jong, B.M. Different distal-proximal movement balances in right- and left-hand writing may hint at differential premotor cortex involvement. *Hum. Mov. Sci.* **2011**, *30*, 1072–1078. [CrossRef] [PubMed]
13. Rocchi, L.; Chiari, L.; Horak, F.B. Effects of deep brain stimulation and levodopa on postural sway in Parkinson's disease. *J. Neurol. Neurosurg. Psychiatry* **2002**, *73*, 267–274. [CrossRef] [PubMed]
14. Spildooren, J.; Vercruysse, S.; Meyns, P.; Vandenbossche, J.; Heremans, E.; Desloovere, K.; Vandenberghe, W.; Nieuwboer, A. Turning and unilateral cueing in Parkinson's disease patients with and without freezing of gait. *Neurosci.* **2012**, *207*, 298–306. [CrossRef] [PubMed]
15. Mellone, S.; Mancini, M.; King, L.A.; Horak, F.B.; Chiari, L. The quality of turning in Parkinson's disease: A compensatory strategy to prevent postural instability? *J. Neuroeng. Rehab.* **2016**, *13*, 39. [CrossRef] [PubMed]
16. Snijders, A.H.; Haaxma, C.A.; Hagen, Y.J.; Munneke, M.; Bloem, B.R. Freezer or non-freezer: Clinical assessment of freezing of gait. *Parkinsonism Relat. Disord.* **2012**, *18*, 149–154. [CrossRef] [PubMed]

17. Hughes, A.J.; Daniel, S.E.; Lees, A.J. Improved accuracy of clinical diagnosis of Lewy body Parkinson's disease. *Neurol.* **2001**, *57*, 1497–1499. [CrossRef]
18. Hoehn, M.M.; Yahr, M.D. Parkinsonism: Onset, progression, and mortality. *Neurol.* **1967**, *17*, 427–442. [CrossRef]
19. Goetz, C.G.; Poewe, W.; Rascol, O.; Sampaio, C.; Stebbins, G.T.; Counsell, C.; Giladi, N.; Holloway, R.G.; Moore, C.G.; Wenning, G.K.; et al. Movement Disorder Society Task Force report on the Hoehn and Yahr staging scale: Status and recommendations. *Mov. Disord.* **2004**, *19*, 1020–1028. [CrossRef]
20. Folstein, M.F.; Folstein, S.E.; McHugh, P.R. "Mini-mental state": A practical method for grading the cognitive state of patients for the clinician. *J. Psychiatr. Res.* **1975**, *12*, 189–198. [CrossRef]
21. Nieuwboer, A.; Rochester, L.; Herman, T.; Vandenberghe, W.; Emil, G.E.; Thomaes, T.; Giladi, N. Reliability of the new freezing of gait questionnaire: Agreement between patients with Parkinson's disease and their carers. *Gait Posture* **2009**, *30*, 459–463. [CrossRef] [PubMed]
22. Willemssen, R.; Müller, T.; Schwarz, M.; Hohnsbein, J.; Falkenstein, M. Error processing in patients with Parkinson's disease: The influence of medication state. *J. Neural Transm.* **2008**, *115*, 461–468. [CrossRef] [PubMed]
23. Fahn, S.; Elton, R. Unified Parkinson's disease rating scale. In *Recent developments in Parkinson's disease*; Fahn, S., Marsden, C.D., Calne, D.B., Goldstein, M., Eds.; Macmillan Health Care Information: Florham Park, NJ, USA, 1987; Volume 2, pp. 153–163.
24. Jones, G.D.; James, D.C.; Thacker, M.; Jones, E.J.; Green, D.A. Sit-to-walk and sit-to-stand-and-walk task dynamics are maintained during rising at an elevated seat-height independent of lead-limb in healthy individuals. *Gait Posture* **2016**, *48*, 226–229. [CrossRef] [PubMed]
25. Davis, R.O.; Katz, D.F. Standardization and comparability of CASA instruments. *J. Androl.* **1992**, *13*, 81–86. [PubMed]
26. Youm, C.H.; Park, Y.H.; Seo, K.W. Assessment of single-leg stance balance using COP 95% confidence ellipse area. *Korean J. Sports Med.* **2008**, *18*, 19–27.
27. Cohen, J. A power primer. *Psychological Bull.* **1992**, *112*, 155. [CrossRef]
28. Courtine, G.; Schieppati, M. Human walking along a curved path. I. Body trajectory, segment orientation and the effect of vision. *Eur. J. Neurosci.* **2003**, *18*, 177–190. [CrossRef]
29. Taylor, M.J.D.; Dabnichki, P.; Strike, S.C. A three-dimensional biomechanical comparison between turning strategies during the stance phase of walking. *Hum. Mov. Sci.* **2005**, *24*, 558–573. [CrossRef]
30. Adamson, M.B.; Gilmore, G.; Stratton, T.W.; Baktash, N.; Jog, M.S. Medication status and dual-tasking on turning strategies in Parkinson disease. *J. Neurol. Sci.* **2019**, *396*, 206–212. [CrossRef]
31. Peterson, D.S.; Mancini, M.; Fino, P.C.; Horak, F.; Smulders, K. Speeding up gait in Parkinson's disease. *J. Parkinson's Dis.* **2020**, *10*, 245–253. [CrossRef]
32. Stack, E.L.; Ashburn, A.M.; Jupp, K.E. Strategies used by people with Parkinson's disease who report difficulty turning. *Parkinsonism Relat. Disord.* **2006**, *12*, 87–92. [CrossRef] [PubMed]
33. Holtzer, R.; Epstein, N.; Mahoney, J.R.; Izzetoglu, M.; Blumen, H.M. Neuroimaging of mobility in aging: A targeted review. *J. Gerontol. A Biol. Sci. Med. Sci.* **2014**, *69*, 1375–1388. [CrossRef] [PubMed]
34. Hausdorff, J.M. Gait dynamics in Parkinson's disease: Common and distinct behavior among stride length, gait variability, and fractal-like scaling. *Chaos* **2009**, *19*, 026113. [CrossRef] [PubMed]
35. Nonnekes, J.; Růžička, E.; Nieuwboer, A.; Hallett, M.; Fasano, A.; Bloem, B.R. Compensation strategies for gait impairments in Parkinson disease: A review. *JAMA Neurol.* **2019**, *76*, 718–725. [CrossRef] [PubMed]
36. Klass, M.; Baudry, S.; Duchateau, J. Age-related decline in rate of torque development is accompanied by lower maximal motor unit discharge frequency during fast contractions. *J. Appl. Physiol.* **2008**, *104*, 739–746. [CrossRef] [PubMed]
37. Patla, A.E.; Adkin, A.; Ballard, T. Online steering: Coordination and control of body center of mass, head and body reorientation. *Exp. Brain Res.* **1999**, *129*, 629–634. [CrossRef]
38. Herman, T.; Giladi, N.; Hausdorff, J.M. Properties of the 'timed up and go' test: More than meets the eye. *Gerontology* **2011**, *57*, 203–210. [CrossRef]
39. Mancini, M.; Fling, B.W.; Gendreau, A.; Lapidus, J.; Horak, F.B.; Chung, K.; Nutt, J.G. Effect of augmenting cholinergic function on gait and balance. *BMC Neurol.* **2015**, *15*, 264. [CrossRef]
40. McNeely, M.E.; Earhart, G.M. The effects of medication on turning in people with Parkinson disease with and without freezing of gait. *J. Parkinson's Dis.* **2011**, *1*, 259–270. [CrossRef]

41. Butler, J.S.; Fearon, C.; Killane, I.; Waechter, S.M.; Reilly, R.B.; Lynch, T. Motor preparation rather than decision-making differentiates Parkinson's disease patients with and without freezing of gait. *Clin. Neurophysiol.* **2017**, *128*, 463–471. [CrossRef]
42. Takakusaki, K. Functional neuroanatomy for posture and gait control. *J. Mov. Disord.* **2017**, *10*, 1–17. [CrossRef] [PubMed]
43. Sirois, J.; Frigon, A.; Gossard, J.P. Independent control of presynaptic inhibition by reticulospinal and sensory inputs at rest and during rhythmic activities in the cat. *J. Neurosci.* **2013**, *33*, 8055–8067. [CrossRef] [PubMed]
44. Plotnik, M.; Bartsch, R.P.; Zeev, A.; Giladi, N.; Hausdorff, J.M. Effects of walking speed on asymmetry and bilateral coordination of gait. *Gait Posture* **2013**, *38*, 864–869. [CrossRef] [PubMed]
45. Conradsson, D.; Paquette, C.; Franzén, E. Turning stability in individuals with Parkinson disease. *J. Neurol. Phys. Ther.* **2018**, *42*, 241–247. [CrossRef]
46. Boonstra, T.A.; van Kordelaar, J.; Engelhart, D.; van Vugt, J.P.P.; van der Kooij, H. Asymmetries in reactive and anticipatory balance control are of similar magnitude in Parkinson's disease patients. *Gait Posture* **2016**, *43*, 108–113. [CrossRef]
47. Lee, C.S.; Schulzer, M.; Mak, E.; Hammerstad, J.P.; Calne, S.; Calne, D.B. Patterns of asymmetry do not change over the course of idiopathic parkinsonism: Implications for pathogenesis. *Neurology* **1995**, *45*, 435–439. [CrossRef]
48. Aboutorabi, A.; Arazpour, M.; Bahramizadeh, M.; Hutchins, S.W.; Fadayevatan, R. The effect of aging on gait parameters in able-bodied older subjects: A literature review. *Aging Clin. Exp. Res.* **2016**, *28*, 393–405. [CrossRef]

© 2020 by the authors. Licensee MDPI, Basel, Switzerland. This article is an open access article distributed under the terms and conditions of the Creative Commons Attribution (CC BY) license (http://creativecommons.org/licenses/by/4.0/).

Article

Simultaneous Hand Gesture Classification and Finger Angle Estimation via a Novel Dual-Output Deep Learning Model

Qinghua Gao [†], Shuo Jiang [†] and Peter B. Shull *

The State Key Laboratory of Mechanical System and Vibration, School of Mechanical Engineering, Shanghai Jiao Tong University, Shanghai 200240, China; gaoqinghua@sjtu.edu.cn (Q.G.); jiangshuo@sjtu.edu.cn (S.J.)
* Correspondence: pshull@sjtu.edu.cn
† These authors contributed equally to this work.

Received: 21 April 2020; Accepted: 22 May 2020; Published: 24 May 2020

Abstract: Hand gesture classification and finger angle estimation are both critical for intuitive human–computer interaction. However, most approaches study them in isolation. We thus propose a dual-output deep learning model to enable simultaneous hand gesture classification and finger angle estimation. Data augmentation and deep learning were used to detect spatial-temporal features via a wristband with ten modified barometric sensors. Ten subjects performed experimental testing by flexing/extending each finger at the metacarpophalangeal joint while the proposed model was used to classify each hand gesture and estimate continuous finger angles simultaneously. A data glove was worn to record ground-truth finger angles. Overall hand gesture classification accuracy was 97.5% and finger angle estimation R^2 was 0.922, both of which were significantly higher than shallow existing learning approaches used in isolation. The proposed method could be used in applications related to the human–computer interaction and in control environments with both discrete and continuous variables.

Keywords: modified barometric sensor; gesture recognition; convolutional neural network; dual-output model

1. Introduction

With the rapid development of computer technology and the widespread use of sensors, there is an emerging demand for more intuitive human–computer interaction (HCI) [1]. HCI approaches have been investigated for various applications, including touch interaction, voice control, and emotion perception. Gesture recognition is a promising HCI area, including a wide range of potential applications: sign language recognition [2], navigation and manipulation in virtual environments [3], automotive manufacturing [4], and control for home service robots [5]. The hands are a logical choice for gesture recognition because of their dexterity, and intricate movements involving multiple degrees of freedom [6–8].

Hand gestures can be classified as static or dynamic. Static hand gesture recognition considers the shape characteristics of the hand at a point in time, and dynamic hand gestures focus on a series of hand movements over a time interval. Dynamic hand gestures can involve both hand gesture classification and finger angle estimation. Hand gesture classification can decode human intentions as discrete commands for interacting with and controlling physical hardware. Finger angle estimation can be utilized to achieve the continuous operation of physical devices. For example, varying finger angles could be mapped to operate dynamic realistic tasks, such as game joysticks in virtual reality.

Various machine learning-based algorithms have been proposed for hand gesture classification. Jiang et al. [9] recognized four surface gestures and eight air gestures based on a fusion of surface electromyography and inertial measurement unit signals, utilizing linear discriminant analysis (LDA). Zhang et al. [10] presented Tomo, which employed electrical impedance tomography to evaluate two gesture sets with a support vector machine (SVM). Jiang et al. [11] classified singer-finger gestures and American Sign Language 0–9 number gestures with LDA, k Nearest Neighbor (KNN), and random forests (RF). Deep learning has also been studied in hand gesture classification. Wang et al. [12] proposed a combination of convolutional and recurrent neural networks (RNN) with Google's Soli sensor to recognize 11 dynamic gestures. Kim et al. [13] used Doppler radar to recognize hand gestures with a convolutional neural network (CNN).

Machine learning approaches have also been proposed for finger angle estimation. Kawaguchi et al. [14] detected finger movement from wrist deformation and used multiple regression models to estimate finger joint angles. Zhou et al. [15] estimated finger motion through forearm muscle deformation measured by A-mode ultrasound-sensing approaches with a linear ridge model and a least-squares SVM model. Deep learning has also been investigated in the continuous angle estimation of fingers. Smith et al. [16] asynchronously decoded metacarpophalangeal (MCP) joint angles of five fingers using a backpropagation neural network classifier with a Levenberg–Marquardt training algorithm. Hioki et al. [17] estimated proximal interphalangeal finger joint angles by streaming feedback into a recurrent artificial neural network with time delay factors.

Some have also proposed simultaneous hand gesture classification and finger angle estimation. Pan et al. [18] proposed a switching regime, including one LDA classifier to identify wrist movements and two state space models to continuously decode the finger angle from electromyogram (EMG) signals. Antfolk et al. [19] classified finger movements and produced finger joint angle outputs using local approximation and lazy learning, consequently controlling the prosthetic hand.

Some studies simultaneously output the results of classification and regression for other areas. Abraham et al. [20] presented a joint regression and classification framework to predict the future values of a zero-inflated time series. A linear regression model was used to predict the value of the time series, and the regression results were input to the SVM classifier to determine whether the predicted value should be adjusted to zero. Wang et al. [21] proposed a hybrid CNN model integrating a classification network and a regression network for object pose estimation from a single image, but their algorithms were based on static image data and thus not suitable for low-dimensional and dynamic time-series signals in our application.

However, current approaches suffer from several limitations. First, previous machine learning models produced limited accuracy because features were typically extracted independently from time-series signals in an ad-hoc manner [22], and the correlations among different signals were often overlooked. Although deep learning avoids the tedious process of manually extracting features, it relies on proper data structures. If the dimension of data is too small, the model may overfit and lead to low accuracy and poor performance. Second, shallow learning approaches cannot output classification values and regression values simultaneously. Although some articles investigated the output of hand gesture categories and finger angle estimation at the same time, they still relied on two superimposed algorithm models: one for classification and the other for regression. But this pattern has inherent drawbacks: (1) since the model parameters are derived from the data features, the attributes of multiple models are statistically relevant, and two separate models may create system redundancies. (2) When data changes, the classification and regression models require retraining, and the parameters of the two models cannot be adjusted simultaneously. (3) In the practical prediction applications, compared to the parallel structure that simultaneously derives the category and the regression values, the ordinal structure of first predicting the category and then estimating the angle values increases the complexity and inconvenience of the system.

Therefore, an improved compact model that can fully explore the spatial-temporal features should be built to enable two simultaneous outputs. To the best of our knowledge, there are currently no approaches for simultaneous outputs of hand gesture classification and finger angle estimation based on deep learning.

The purpose of this paper is to address the previous two limitations by introducing a novel framework to simultaneously detect hand gestures during finger movement with high accuracy, including identifying which finger is flexing and determining the joint angle of each finger. To improve the accuracy of the model, we present a new spatial-temporal method to explore the hidden relationships between different sensors and useful information contained in historical data. For simultaneous hand gesture classification and finger angle estimation, we propose a dual-output model structure. We hypothesized that the framework would enable classification of the hand gestures and estimation of finger angles simultaneously via a single deep learning model with dual outputs, and this framework would have better performance than single-output, shallow learning models.

2. Materials and Methods

2.1. Wristband Prototype and Experiment Protocol

2.1.1. Wristband prototype

While current wearable approaches are limited because of low sensitivity or poor linearity, our prototype takes advantage of the fact that hand motion changes the shape of the wrist due to the expansions and contractions of the muscles, which brings position and thickness transformations of tendons and muscles, producing deformations on the surface contour of the wrist. We thus used a wristband with ten embedded modified barometric sensors with high sensitivity and excellent linearity to measure the activity of the tendons and muscles that cause finger movement [23]. The deformations apply pressure to the surface of modified barometric sensors. When a subject with the wristband performs various gestures, a corresponding contact pressure distribution can be obtained from the wristband (Figure 1).

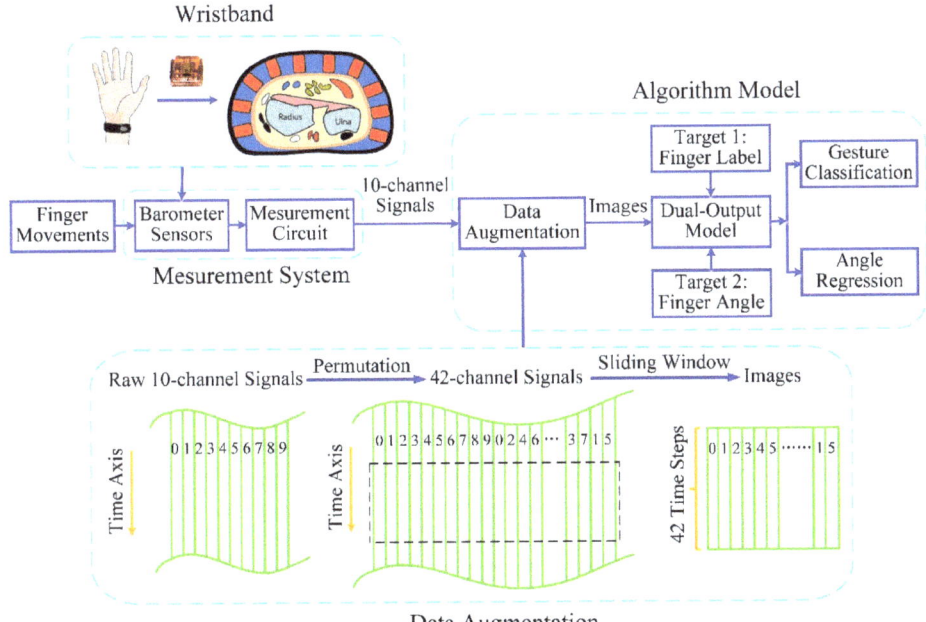

Figure 1. System framework of the novel dual-output convolutional neural network (CNN) model for simultaneous hand gesture recognition and finger angle estimation.

2.1.2. Gesture Set

When handling actual tasks by hand, multiple fingers often work in concert. The Taiwanese Sign Language includes 50 fundamental gestures [24], and many of them are the linkage of multiple fingers. Most studies about interlocking multiple fingers used static positions. However, we studied the dynamic process of finger movement. The dynamic recognition process of multiple fingers is complicated because the flexion angles of different fingers are different, and it involves a lot of research on hand anatomy. Multi-finger movements include thumb opposition, multi-finger flexion/extension, multi-finger adduction/abduction, etc. These multi-finger movements can be decomposed into multiple single-finger movements. Analyzing single-finger movements is the basis of multi-finger movements. At present, most studies on finger movement are based on single finger movement [15,25]. Therefore, we chose 5 single fingers as the gesture set to identify the moving fingers and estimate the finger joint angle.

2.1.3. Experiment Protocol

Ten subjects (8 male, 2 female, age: 22–26 year, height: 166–184 cm, weight: 57–76 kg, wrist circumference: 15.3–16.9 cm) participated in the experiment. All subjects gave their informed consent in accordance with the Declaration of Helsinki before they participated in the study. During each trial, subjects flexed/extended one finger at the MCP joint repeatedly at their self-selected frequency. The minimum and maximum angles of thumb were required to be 0° and 55°, and of other 4 fingers were required to be 0° and 90°. Some subjects could not bend their fingers to 90° [26]. Therefore, the actual maximum and minimum angles were decided by the subjects themselves. Fingers were flexed in the order of thumb, index finger, middle finger, ring finger, and pinky finger, and the data were encoded into 5 categories and recorded. We used a data glove (5DT Data Glove 14 Ultra, South Africa, Gauteng, Pretoria), which is widely used and regarded as the gold standard for measurement in the estimation of finger joint angles, to record the real finger angle relative to the ground at the same time [14]. Each finger was flexed/extended for 25 s, there were 5 fingers per trial (Figure 2), and the sampling frequency was 40 Hz, so $25 \times 5 \times 40 = 1000$ samples were collected per trial. Each subject performed 10 trials [27], so $10 \times 10 = 100$ trials were performed. Thus, there was a total of $1000 \times 100 = 100,000$ samples.

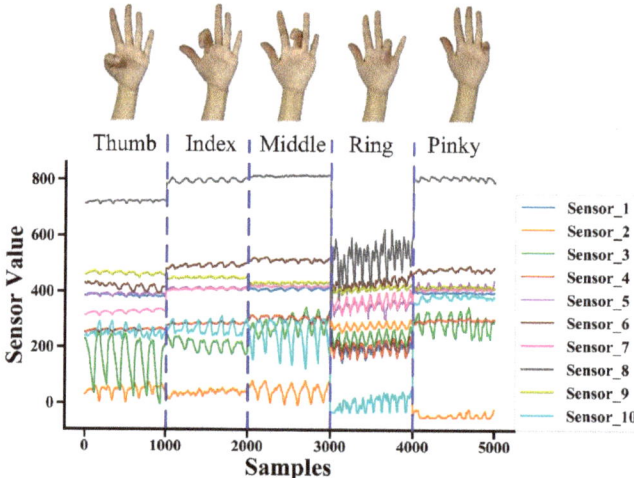

Figure 2. Raw signals from 10 modified barometric sensors for a typical trial (subject 1, trial 1) showing distinct patterns between each gesture.

For each trial, we had 10 columns of modified barometric sensing data, corresponding finger categories and finger angle data. The data dimension was (1000, 12). Given these data, we aimed to learn a mapping f from the pressure sensing data $x \in X$ to dual outputs $[y_1, y_2] \in Y$, where y_1 represents the label of the finger, totaling 5 classes, and y_2 represents the corresponding MCP angle measured by the data glove.

2.2. Data Augmentation

Sequential data were usually represented as a multivariate time series, and so the 10 columns of modified barometric sensing data were encoded as 10 features. However, there are restrictions on this data form. According to our sensing scheme and physiological structure of users, spatial locations between different sensors are related, but multivariate time-series form cannot distinguish a relationship between sensors that are far away. Suppose there are N-channel signals arranged in columns. For the column k signal, it is only adjacent to the column $k-1$ signal and column $k+1$ signal. When referring to the spatial information of the column k signal, only the correlation between column k signal and the column $k-1$ signal, and the correlation between the column k signal and column $k+1$ signal are considered, while the spatial positional relationships with signals of other columns are ignored. Therefore, we propose a data augmentation method to explore the hidden spatial–temporal relationships between different sensors.

We propose to convert time-series signals collected from sensors to new movement images that contain hidden relationships between any pair of signals (Figure 1). Features would be extracted from the newly generated movement image, providing additional potential spatial information between the signals.

The algorithm steps are as follows:

1. N-channel signals are arranged into a 2D array $L \times N$, where L is the time length of signal sequences, which is the original signal array.
2. The 2D array from Step 1 is permutated into $L \times M$, where M is the dimension of a newly generated array so that each signal sequence is adjacent to every other sequence [28]. For example, 3-channel signals [1, 2, 3], wherein the column 3 signal and column 1 signal are not adjacent, can be rearranged into 2D array signals [1, 2, 3, 1]. Then, each column of signals can be adjacent to other columns of signals, which takes into account the spatial information between each column of signals, and $M = 4$ in this example.
3. The new signal array from Step 2 is converted into a movement image by windowing, and the image size is $Ls \times M$, where Ls is the length of the window.
4. The window slides along the time axis to generate different movement images that are utilized as new inputs of the model.

Our signal data have 10 signal sequences [1, 2, 3, 4, 5, 6, 7, 8, 9, 10]. After Step 1 and Step 2, a movement image is generated with the size of $42 \times Ls$, where Ls is the time length of signal sequences. For each trial, $Ls = 1000$. The 42-dimensional vectors are [1, 2, 3, 4, 5, 6, 7, 8, 9, 10, 1, 3, 5, 7, 9, 1, 4, 6, 8, 10, 2, 4, 7, 10, 3, 6, 9, 2, 5, 8, 1, 5, 9, 3, 7, 1, 6, 10, 4, 8, 2, 6], and each column from 1 to 10 is adjacent to the other nine columns. A time window is utilized to crop the signals based on Step 3. The window length is 42, and the size of our movement image is finalized as 42×42. The window slides 1-time step along the time axis to generate a new movement image, and after Step 4, $Ls - 42$ images are ultimately obtained. These images are new samples of the model, and the dimension of the samples is $(Ls - 42, 42, 42)$.

For each newly generated movement image, there are 42 finger labels and angles corresponding to window length. We select the finger category with the highest frequency as the label for this movement image, and the finger angle of the last time step as angle regression value for this image. For speeding up the convergence, the sensor features and finger angle data are standardized with a mean of 0 and a standard deviation of 1.

2.3. Model Architecture

We proposed a deep learning model with dual outputs to enable the classification of finger gestures and the estimation of finger angles simultaneously (Figure 3). We built a dual-output model based on CNN. We used 10 sensor units to measure the pressure changes of 10 tendons related to the finger movement. The pressure can be converted into a force myography (FMG). CNN can be used to identify specific FMG patterns. CNN is a deep learning model that extracts local features of data through convolution operations and weight sharing and is widespread in computer vision and pattern recognition.

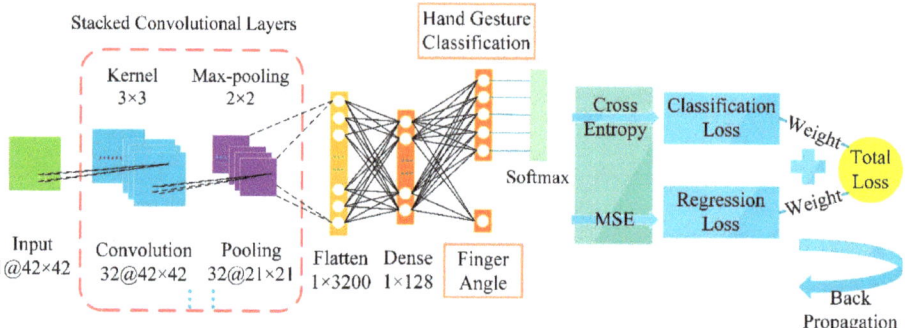

Figure 3. Dual-output CNN model structure diagram.

2.3.1. Convolutional Layer

The convolutional layer includes multiple convolutional filters that extract the signal features by the convolution process. The sparse connection and weight sharing of the convolution kernels allow the convolutional layer to learn features with a small amount of calculations.

An activation function is used after the convolutional filter to solve non-linear problems. Deep learning currently employs a Rectified Linear Unit (ReLU) function as activation function, $f(x) = max(0, x)$. This function defines the non-linear output after the linear transformation of the neuron.

The pooling layer is used for reducing data dimensions and preventing network overfitting after the convolutional layer. Several convolutional layers and pooling layers are often stacked to extract gradually more abstract features.

2.3.2. Dual Outputs

A flatten layer is utilized to transform a multi-dimensional array to a one-dimensional vector, which then flows into a dense layer to reduce the dimension of neurons. Finally, the model takes two parallel dense layers as outputs: one with K neurons to export the category attribute, and the other with 1 neuron to export the regression attribute, where K is the number of hand gesture categories (Figure 3).

The dense layer used for classification requires a K-way softmax activation function to obtain the probability distribution over different categories:

$$y_i = \frac{e^{z_i}}{\sum_{j=1}^{K} e^{z_j}}, \quad i = 1, 2, 3, \ldots, K \tag{1}$$

where z is the output vector of the dense layer, y_i is the probability that the sample belongs to the category i. The category with the highest probability is the predicted label of the sample.

2.3.3. Loss Weighting and Training Algorithm

Angle estimation is a scalar regression task, while hand gesture recognition is a multi-category task. The training model needs to assign different loss functions to the two outputs. The mean-squared error can be used as the loss of regression output:

$$loss_r = MSE = \frac{1}{n}\sum_{i=0}^{n-1}(y_i - \hat{y}_i)^2 \quad (2a)$$

where $loss_r$ is the regression loss, y_i is the true value of sample i, $\hat{y}_i$ is the predicted value of sample i, and n is the number of samples.

Categorical cross entropy can be used as the loss of classification output:

$$loss_c = J = -\frac{1}{n}\sum_{i=0}^{n-1}\sum_{j=0}^{K-1} y_{i,j} \log(p_{i,j}) \quad (2b)$$

where $loss_c$ is the classification loss, $y_{i,j} \in (0, 1)$ indicates whether the sample i is predicted to be the label j, $p_{i,j}$ is the probability that the sample i is predicted to be the label j, and K is the number of hand gesture categories.

Two losses need to be combined into a total loss. The scale of the two losses is different, which leads to the total loss being dominated by one of the tasks, and the loss of other task cannot affect the learning process of the network. A practical way to solve the problem is loss weighting, and thus, we weighted the losses to get a global loss. The goal of model optimization is to minimize total loss during training.

$$loss_{total} = w_c loss_c + w_r loss_r \quad (2c)$$

where $loss_{total}$ is a total loss, w_c is the weight of classification loss, and w_r is the weight of regression loss. The ratio of w_r to w_c is the weight ratio, which is a hyperparameter.

The coefficients of convolution filters and dense layers are obtained by training a dataset. The dual-output model is multi-task learning based on parameter sharing. Multiple tasks share the representation at shallow layers, which can reduce network overfitting and improve the generalization effect.

Our dual-output CNN model was established according to the principle described above and was trained in Keras 2.2. The first convolutional layer filtered the 42 × 42 input movement image with 32 kernels of size 3 × 3, followed by a max-pooling layer of size 2 × 2. The second convolutional layer filtered the output of the first pooling layer with 32 kernels of size 3 × 3, followed by a 2 × 2 max-pooling layer. The flatten layer vectorized the output into a 128-dimension feature vector. The dense layer consisted of 32 units. The network ended with a 5-way dense layer as classification output and a 1-way dense layer as the regression output. We adopted: (1) a ReLU activation function in each hidden layer, (2) a Softmax function in the 5-way dense layer, (3) a 4:1 weight ratio between the finger angle regression loss and the finger gesture classification loss, and (4) an RMSprop function as the optimizer with a batch size of 32 and 10 epochs in model training.

2.4. Model Performance Evaluation

Leave-one-trial-out cross validation was utilized to assess the performance of the model. For each subject, the network was trained based on his training subset and evaluated based on his test subset. Each subject had 10 sets of experimental data, and we conducted 10 verifications for each subject. Each verification used 9 sets of data as the training set, the remaining set of data as the test set. Therefore, for the training set, the time length $Ls = 9 \times 1000 = 9000$, and the dimension of features was (9000 − 42, 42, 42). For the test set, the time length $Ls = 1000$, and the dimension of the features was (1000 − 42, 42, 42). The test set selected for each verification was different from each other.

For each subject, the proportion of correctly recognized finger gestures in all test samples was used as the accuracy index of finger classification:

$$Accuracy = \frac{n_{correct}}{n_{total}} \quad (3)$$

where $n_{correct}$ is the number of samples classified correctly, and n_{total} is the number of all test samples. The R^2 was used to access the accuracy of finger angle estimation:

$$R^2 = 1 - \frac{\sum_i (y_i - \hat{y}_i)^2}{\sum_i (y_i - \overline{y}_i)^2} \quad (4)$$

where y_i is the true value, $\hat{y}_i$ is the predicted value, and $\overline{y}_i$ is the mean value of test samples. The larger the R^2 score, the better the model fitting effect. The average accuracy over all subjects was calculated as the ultimate gesture classification accuracy and the average R^2 score over all subjects was calculated as the ultimate R^2 score.

2.5. Benchmarking against Other Machine Learning Models

For validating the performance of our proposed dual-output model, we established the following benchmarks: CNN without data augmentation, RNN, single-output classification models, and single-output regression models. SVM and RF can be utilized for both classification and regression, so they were chosen as the benchmarks of the single-output models.

A paired t-test was used to assess whether there were significant differences between any benchmark and the proposed method. Since there were only 10 subjects, and the size of the samples was small, the data might not conform to the normal distribution. The nonparametric test does not require a population distribution, so a nonparametric paired t-test was ultimately selected. SPSS was used to perform the nonparametric paired t-test on the results of 10 subjects. When $p < 0.05$, we considered it a significant difference between the two groups of samples.

2.5.1. CNN without Data Augmentation

A dual-output CNN without data augmentation model was established to observe the impact of our proposed data augmentation method on the dual-output deep learning model. The original signal was composed of 10 columns of features, and we took a time window with a length of 10. The size of the movement image was finalized as 10×10, and the dimension of the samples was $(Ls - 10, 10, 10)$. Other selections, namely (1) the processing of finger labels and angles to keep up with each image, (2) the structures and parameters of the dual-output model, (3) the parameters of model training, were the same as the CNN with data augmentation model.

2.5.2. RNN

RNN is a deep learning model with memory and is widely used to process time-series signals. Base on the gating mechanism, long short-term memory (LSTM) retains long-term sequence information and alleviates the gradient disappearance problem [29]. The gated recurrent unit (GRU) is a simplified variant of the LSTM [30]. The GRU network does not maintain additional state vectors and has less computation and faster training than the LSTM.

We built a dual-output model based on GRU to compare with the CNN dual-output model. The network structure and parameters were as follows: (1) the 10 columns of original signals were taken as the input, so the dimension of the input was 10, (2) the length of time step was 10, (3) the finger category with the highest frequency in 10-length time step was taken as the true label, and the last angle value in 10-length time step was taken as true angle value, (4) 1 GRU layer was used, (5) the dimension of the output was 32, (6) the dropout of input unit was 0.2, and the dropout of the recurrent unit was 0.2.

The GRU layer was followed by the dual-output structure, which was the same as the principle described in the dual-output CNN model. Other selections of the weight ratio, the optimizer, the batch size, and the epoch, were the same as the CNN model parameters.

2.5.3. SVM

SVM is a widely adopted approach in the realm of hand gesture recognition. It uses hinge loss to calculate empirical risk and uses regularization to optimize structural risk. SVM can be used for classification with support vector classification (SVC) and regression with support vector regression (SVR). SVC is a classifier with sparsity and robustness. It can be nonlinearly classified by the kernel method. Its goal is to maximize the margin between support vectors and the hyperplane. Different from SVC, the goal of SVR is to minimize the total deviation of all sample points from the hyperplane.

We used the RBF kernel function and tuned the penalty coefficient (C) and the kernel parameter gamma (γ) to obtain higher accuracy and R^2 score. An SVC model with the parameters $C = 5$ and $\gamma = 0.1$ was established to classify finger gestures, and an SVR model with parameters $C = 10$ and $\gamma = 0.1$ was established to estimate the finger angle.

2.5.4. RF

RF is a bagging-based ensemble learning method composed of multiple weak learners. RF can be used for classification with RF classifier and regression with RF regressor. RF classifier randomly generates k decision trees from the training set to form a random forest by the bootstrap resampling technique. The classification result is determined by decision tree voting scores. Different from classification, the RF regression result is the average of the outputs of decision trees.

We tuned the parameters of the number of decision trees and the maximum number of features selected when dividing leaf nodes. For the RF classifier, the number of decision trees was 100, and the maximum number of features was $\sqrt{n_{features}}$, where $n_{features}$ is the number of total features. For the RF regressor, the number of decision trees was 60, and the maximum number of features was $log_2 n_{features}$.

2.6. The Impact of Sensor Numbers on the Dual-Output Model

We compared the results of different sensor numbers between 1 and 10. Tree-based feature selection was used to calculate the importance of features. The RF classifier and RF regressor were, respectively, applied as tree models to obtain the feature importance α_c on classification attributes and α_r on regression attributes. The mean value α_i of α_c and α_r for each subject was taken as the total importance of this subject, where $i = 1, 2, \ldots, 10$. We calculated the average of total importance for all subjects as the ultimate results of feature importance, which was sorted in reverse order as [8, 1, 3, 7, 5, 6, 2, 4, 9, 10]. We selected 1 to 10 features with the highest feature importance and used the proposed data augmentation method and dual-output model to obtain the results of different sensor numbers.

3. Results

The mean classification accuracy of hand gesture was 97.5% across the subjects. A confusion matrix was drawn from subject 10 (Figure 4), and there was no obvious confusion in the classification. The thumb had the highest classification accuracy at 100.0%, while the middle finger had the lowest classification accuracy at 97.5%. The predicted label typically confused the middle finger and ring finger. The mean R^2 score of the finger angle estimation over all subjects was 0.922. The fitting effect was better in the rising and falling phases of the curve, but there were deviations in the peaks and valleys (Figure 5).

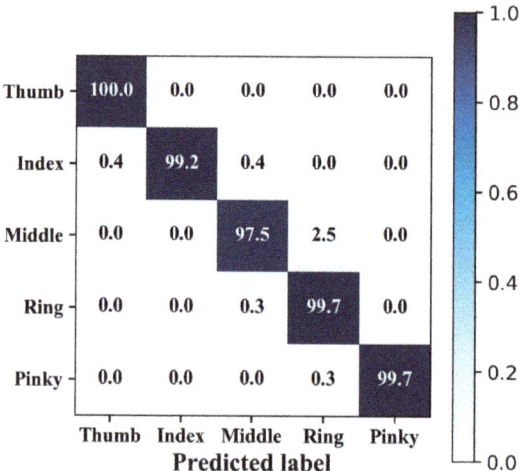

Figure 4. Confusion matrix of hand gesture classification from a typical subject (subject 10). The overall classification accuracy for this trial was 99.2%.

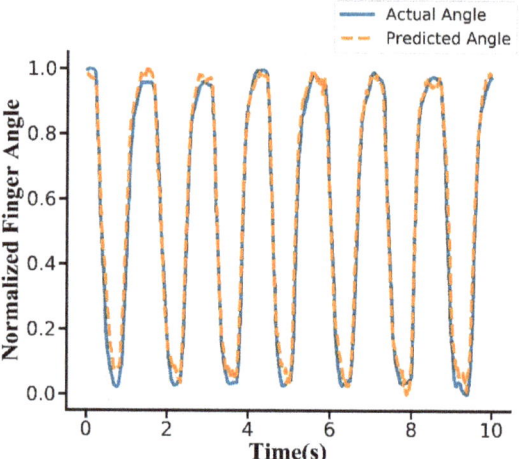

Figure 5. Typical trial showing actual and predicted normalized finger angles (subject 10, thumb). The R^2 score for this trial was 0.965. Finger angles were normalized from 0 and 1.

The results (Figure 6) of four benchmarks were as follows: (1) CNN without data augmentation had a classification accuracy of 96.3% and angle R^2 score of 0.916. (2) RNN had a classification accuracy of 95.6% and an angle R^2 score of 0.881. (3) SVM had a classification accuracy of 96.5% and an angle R^2 score of 0.887. (4) RF had a classification accuracy of 95.8% and an angle R^2 score of 0.905.

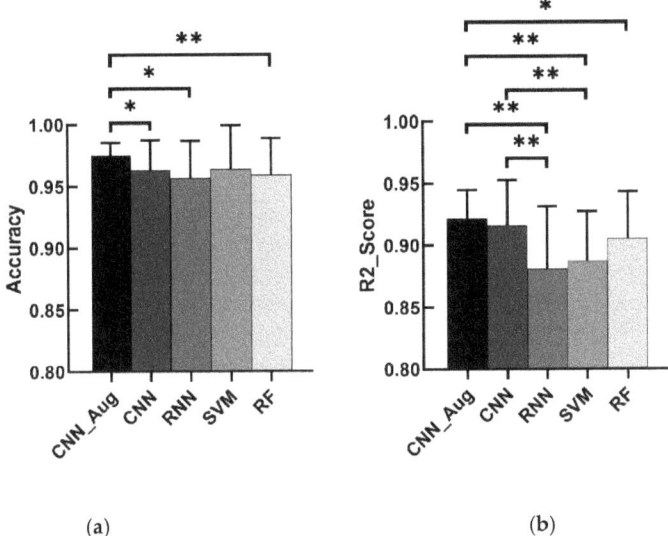

(a)   (b)

Figure 6. Overall results for different models: CNN_Aug (presented model) = convolutional neural network with data augmentation, CNN = convolutional neural network without data augmentation, RNN = recurrent neural network, SVM = support vector machine, and RF = random forest. (**a**) The results of hand gesture classification accuracy for different models. (**b**) The results of finger angle estimation fitting for different models. ** denotes $p < 0.001$ and * denotes $p < 0.05$.

The results (Figure 7) of different sensor numbers between 1 and 9 were as follows: (1) one sensor had a classification accuracy of 76.4% and an angle R^2 score of 0.528; (2) two sensors had a classification accuracy of 87.8% and an angle R^2 score of 0.729; (3) three sensors had a classification accuracy of 91.5% and an angle R^2 score of 0.820; (4) four sensors had a classification accuracy of 93.2% and an angle R^2 score of 0.855; (5) five sensors had a classification accuracy of 95.7% and an angle R^2 score of 0.889; (6) six sensors had a classification accuracy of 96.9% and an angle R^2 score of 0.909; (7) seven sensors had a classification accuracy of 97.3% and an angle R^2 score of 0.916; (8) eight sensors had a classification accuracy of 97.3% and an angle R^2 score of 0.918; (9) nine sensors had a classification accuracy of 97.4% and an angle R^2 score of 0.920.

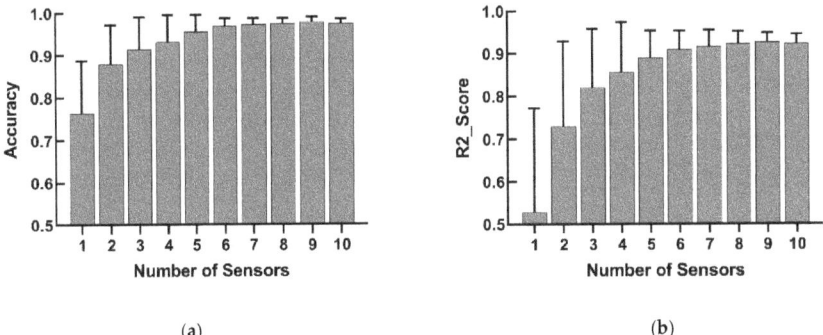

(a)   (b)

Figure 7. Overall results for different sensor numbers between 1 and 10. (**a**) The results of hand gesture classification accuracy for different sensor numbers. (**b**) The results of finger angle estimation fitting for different sensor numbers.

4. Discussion

4.1. Comparison with Previous Results

This paper presents a novel framework to output hand gesture classification and finger angle estimation simultaneously via a deep learning model with dual outputs. Compared with previous methods, this scheme enables outputs of both classification and regression attributes simultaneously with higher accuracy. For hand gesture recognition with shallow learning, Al-Timemy et al. [31] achieved 98% accuracy for the classification of 15 classes of different finger movements with time-domain autoregression, orthogonal fuzzy neighborhood discriminant analysis, and LDA. For hand gesture recognition with deep learning, Geng et al. [32] used EMG images and a deep convolutional network for an 8-gesture within-subject recognition. The recognition accuracy reached 89.3% on a frame of the image and 99.0% using the majority voting algorithm over 40 frames. For finger angle estimation with shallow learning, Huang et al. [25] employed an ultrasound image to predict the MCP joint angles of all fingers in nonperiod movements and got an average correlation of 0.89 ± 0.07. For finger angle estimation with deep learning, Ngeo et al. [33] utilized a fast feedforward artificial neural network and a nonparametric Gaussian process (GP) regressor to capture finger angles during finger flexion and extension. This method yielded an R^2 of 0.78. For hand gesture classification and finger angle estimation simultaneously with two superimposed models, Yang et al. [34] reported a class-specific proportional control system and utilized LDA for gesture recognition and GP regression for muscle contraction force estimation via wearable ultrasound sensing. The accuracy of this model was 93.7%, and the R^2 was 0.927. Previous research [27] used the SVM, LDA, and KNN models for the recognition of three sets of static hand gesture, and an RF model for dynamic single finger angle estimation. Thus, the classification and regression attributes of gesture data were not considered jointly. In addition, previous research achieved a classification accuracy of 94.4% on a set of static single finger flexion gestures. However, we obtained a classification accuracy of 97.5% on a set of dynamic single finger flexion gestures. Both studies examined finger angle estimation based on a dynamic single finger flexion experiment, but we got a higher R^2 of 0.922 compared with 0.79 in previous research. Therefore, our model implemented more functions and exhibited higher accuracy.

4.2. Analysis of Confusion Matrix and Fitting Curve

The least frequent misclassification occurred in the thumb, while the most frequent misclassification occurred in the middle finger (Figure 4). This happens because the flexion and extension movements of the thumb are on the sagittal axis, while the flexion and extension movement of the other four fingers are on the coronal axis. Therefore, the flexion and extension of the thumb are rarely affected, and the classification is not easily confused with the other four fingers. When the middle finger was flexing and stretching, it was easily confused with the index finger and ring finger because the same ligament drives the index finger and ring finger at the same time.

Angle estimation did not fit as well at the peaks and troughs in some cases (Figure 5). The reason might be that the activities of the tendons and muscles that caused finger movement were very complicated when the fingers varied from a flexed state to a stretched state or vice versa, and the model could not statistically excavate the principles.

4.3. Effects of Hyperparameters

The effects of hyperparameters on the performance of the model were investigated.

4.3.1. Window Length

The window length indicated the length of each movement image. The longer the window length, the more past information each image contained, which could improve the performance of the model. However, when the window length was too long, each image contained too much past information, which caused the model to be overburdened and make it overfit. Therefore, the appropriate window length should be selected. In the model training, we found that the model performance was best when the window length was between 40 and 50. Considering that the channel dimensions after data augmentation were 42, the window length was ultimately selected to be 42.

4.3.2. Network Structure of the Model

We also assessed the impact of the network structure on the performance of the model and found that, with the increases in the model depth, the performance did not improve significantly. Therefore, a shallow network structure was suitable because a very large and deeper network structure would learn noise and other interference errors and could result in performance degradation or increased computational cost and network burden.

4.3.3. Batch Size and Epoch

The batch size and the epoch followed a similar trend that, as they increased, the performance of the model decreased. So, a smaller batch size and epoch should be selected. The reason for the shallow network structure and small batch size and epoch might be that our data was less complicated, so a lightweight network was sufficient to extract features.

4.3.4. Weight Ratio

The weight ratio was a hyperparameter introduced to make the scales of classification loss and regression loss close. In the model training, we adjusted the weight ratio from 20:1 to 1:20 and found fluctuations in performance. A possible reason for this is related to the decay rate of the loss function. In the model training, the decay rates of the two loss functions were inconsistent. Therefore, a fixed weight ratio might not be effective enough. In the weight ratios we tested, when the weight ratio was 4:1, the effect was best, so we used 4:1 as the final weight ratio.

4.4. Feature Extraction in Sequential Signals and Image Signals for CNN

4.4.1. Feature Extraction in Sequential Signals for CNN

CNN can be well applied to sequential signals, such as inertial measurement units (IMU) signals and audio signals. Time can be viewed as a spatial dimension. The 1D convolution layer can extract and recognize local patterns in a sequence. Because the same transformation is performed on every patch, a pattern learned at a specific position can be recognized at a different position later, making 1D CNN translation-invariant for temporal translations.

4.4.2. Feature Extraction in Converted Image Signals for CNN

When the time series data are converted into images, the convolutional kernel of 2D CNN slides on the image. The temporal information is extracted when the convolutional kernel slides from top to bottom on the image. The spatial information between different sensors is extracted when the convolutional kernel slides from left to right on the image.

When the convolutional kernel slides from top to bottom on the image, it is very similar to 1D CNN. When the convolutional kernel slides from left to right on the image, and the data of one sensor changes to the data of an adjacent sensor, a drastic change will occur, thus generating a high-frequency signal. Through the convolution operation between the convolution kernel and the high-frequency signal, the frequency information will be selected, so CNN can extract the position information between the sensors.

4.5. Comparison with Other Machine Learning Models

From the comparison of the dual-output models based on CNN with data augmentation and other models (Figure 6), we found that the model built by CNN with data augmentation performed best. This model had the highest accuracy, highest R^2 score, and the smallest deviations.

4.5.1. Comparison between Dual-Output Models with and without Data Augmentation

From the comparison between the dual-output CNN models with and without data augmentation (Figure 6), for hand gesture classification, the CNN without data augmentation model had a classification accuracy of 96.3%, and the CNN with data augmentation model had a classification accuracy of 97.5%. A nonparametric paired t-test indicated significant differences between the CNN with data augmentation and the CNN without data augmentation. The data augmentation method not only made classification accuracy higher but it also made deviation smaller. For finger angle estimation, the CNN without data augmentation model had a R^2 score of 0.916, and CNN with data augmentation model had a R^2 score of 0.922. Although a nonparametric paired t-test indicated no significant difference between dual-output models with and without data augmentation, there was a smaller deviation in the CNN with data augmentation model.

The results show that the data augmentation method achieved better results. This is because the data augmentation method took into account the hidden relationships between different sensors and useful information contained in history data.

4.5.2. Comparison between Dual-Output Models Based on CNN with Data Augmentation and RNN

From the comparison between dual-output models based on CNN with data augmentation and RNN (Figure 6), the RNN model had a classification accuracy of 95.6% for hand gesture classification and had an R^2 score of 0.881 for finger angle estimation. A nonparametric paired t-test indicated significant differences between the CNN with data augmentation model and RNN model both in hand gesture classification and finger angle estimation. CNN with the data augmentation model had a smaller deviation. Similarly, CNN without the data augmentation model was also better than the RNN model. Therefore, the models built by CNN performed better than RNN.

RNN is mainly utilized to describe the continuous output in time and to connect spatial states together. It is more suitable for predicting future data from past data, such as the prediction of the next moment of the video, the prediction of the context of the document, and the prediction of future temperature. CNN, however, is more suitable for describing the state of a certain space and feature extraction. Our research tends to perform feature extraction on data to identify patterns in gesture data, rather than predicting what gesture will be made or what angle the finger will bend at the next moment.

RNN only considers the temporal information of the data and does not consider the spatial information. We have 10 sensors around the wrist, and there are positional relationships between the 10 sensors. CNN can extract the position information between the sensors.

CNN is more appropriate for hand gesture classification and finger angle estimation by the above discussion. The results further show that although a dual-output model could be implemented based on deep learning, our proposed method had better results.

4.5.3. Comparison between Dual-Output Models and Single-Output Models

From the comparison between the dual-output models based on deep learning and the single-output models based on other machine learning (Figure 6), we found that the performance of the dual-output models based on deep learning was not necessarily higher than the single-output model based on shallow learning, and sometimes even worse. For example, in terms of finger angle estimation, the result of CNN without data augmentation was higher than SVM and RF, but the result of RNN was much lower than RF. In terms of hand gesture classification, although the result of CNN was higher than RF, the result of RNN was much lower than SVM. However, in general, our proposed method was superior to shallow learning models in both hand gesture recognition and finger angle estimation.

The results of the above comparisons can verify our hypothesis. The newly proposed data augmentation method can discover hidden spatial position relationships in time-series signals and improve the accuracy of the results. Deep learning models can learn different attributes of the signal at the same time rather than in succession. When the model adjusts its internal features, other features associated with them can automatically adapt and adjust. This is more powerful than stacked shallow learning models.

4.6. Comparison of Results with Different Sensor Numbers

The classification accuracy and angle fitting degree improved with the increase in sensors (Figure 7). When using the optimal six or more sensors, the classification accuracy reached more than 96% and the R^2 value reached more than 0.9. When using the optimal three to five sensors, the classification accuracy reached more than 90% and the R^2 value reached more than 0.8. When using the optimal one or two sensors, the results dropped sharply, and the model performance was poor. Therefore, the performance of the model could be improved by increasing the number of sensors. However, when the optimal number of sensors exceeded six, the performance of the model improved more slowly, and the device became more complicated.

4.7. Calculation Time and Real-Time Application

In practical application, the time duration for each gesture was about 2 to 3s. Therefore, after the dual-output model was trained offline, we selected samples of 2 s in a test set (subject 10, trial 1) to calculate the prediction time. We got the prediction time 0.0444 s on the proposed dual-output model (Table 1). For gesture recognition, when the time delay was less than 0.08 s, the model could be employed in a real-time system [35]. Therefore, we think the dual-output model could be used in real-time. For the other two dual-output model benchmarks, their time delays were also less than 0.08 s (Table 1), so they could also be used in real-time systems.

Table 1. Calculation time of three dual-output models.

Model	Time (s)
CNN with data augmentation	0.0444
CNN without data augmentation	0.0489
RNN	0.0424

4.8. Improvement of Dual-Output Model

A loss weighting method was used to define the total loss in our dual-output model, but this method introduced a hyperparameter, and the fixed weight ratio might not perform well due to the different decay rates of loss functions. Therefore, an adaptive weight variable could be introduced to replace the weight ratio.

Our model used an optimizer after defining the total loss. In practice, it might appear that no matter how the weight ratio was adjusted, only part of the losses was dominant, while the losses of other tasks did not work. In addition to dynamically adjusting the weight parameters, different learning rates could be assigned to the optimizers for different losses.

4.9. Benefits of the Dual-Output Model Compared with Stacked Single-Output Models

Compared with stacked two single-output models to obtain classification attribute and regression attribute, respectively, a dual-output model can receive two characteristics simultaneously by only one model. Benefits of the dual-output model compared with stacked single-output models are as follows:

1. Avoiding the analysis for the internal relationships of multi-model structure

When stacking multiple single-output models, the output and input of different models and the connections between the models need to be considered. In addition, when numerous models are cascaded, the output of the previous model may affect the decision of the latter model, and the output of the latter model may also affect the results of the previous model, so the internal process and the final output can be very complicated. The multi-output model has only one model and does not need to consider the intermediate output, which saves a lot of intermediate analysis.

2. Tuning parameter and training model more conveniently

Some shallow learning models have multiple hyperparameters. The total hyperparameters will become more with stacked models. When stacked models are retrained, all hyperparameters need to retune, and the process can be very complicated. In a dual-output model, only one model requires tuning and training. Thus, the process is more convenient.

3. Performing tasks in a more effective way.

When used in practical tasks, the parallel output model is more effective in control than the sequential output model. For example, in prosthesis control, if a sequential model composed of multiple single-output models is used first to classify which finger to manipulate, and then predict the angle of the finger joint, the task decision-making process will be time consuming [36]. With the parallel output model simultaneously, the classification and regression tasks are solved at the same time, and the task decision-making process becomes more efficient.

4.10. Limitations and Future Work

Our model only achieved better results than the four model benchmarks and thus provided one promising solution in similar hand gesture recognition scenarios. However, future studies should be performed to see whether the proposed model can still perform best in other applications and data set. We only studied single finger movements and did not consider multiple coupled finger movements due to complex hand anatomy, which is common in practical tasks. Therefore, this is a potential limitation in our research. Future work would involve the coupling of multiple fingers. In addition, we only used modified barometric sensors to measure the muscle force of the wrist, so the information obtained was limited. EMG has been widely applied to hand gesture recognition. The fusion of multiple sensors could obtain more information and higher recognition accuracy. Future work would involve applying multiple sensors to a dual-output model. When re-wearing the wearable device, the positions of sensors may shift, resulting in a different distribution of the collected data. Future studies would involve the reproducibility of the device location.

4.11. Potential Applications

Although this paper only considered establishing a dual-output model, the research could potentially be extended to multiple outputs. For gesture recognition, in addition to hand gesture classification and finger angle estimation, the wrist angle could also be output simultaneously. In practical application, this method could be used in a controlled environment with both discrete and continuous variables: hand gesture classification for controlling discrete variables, and finger angle estimation for controlling continuous variables. For example, gesture recognition is used to control the direction and displacement of mobile robots. In this application, the direction is a discrete variable, and the displacement is a continuous variable. This method could pave the way for human–machine interaction [37], home automation [38], rehabilitation systems [39], robot control [40], consumer electronics [41], and other related applications.

5. Conclusions

In this paper, we presented a novel framework to enable both hand gesture classification and finger angle estimation simultaneously via a deep learning model with dual outputs. A dual-output deep learning model and a data augmentation method were proposed and evaluated by finger flexion/extension trials. The results show that the dual-output deep learning model can output hand gesture and finger angle at the same time and that data augmentation methods can improve the accuracy of results. This approach could be widely utilized in medical rehabilitation, virtual and augmented reality, sign language recognition, and other HCI-related applications.

Author Contributions: Conceptualization, S.J. and P.B.S.; Funding acquisition, P.B.S.; Investigation, Q.G. and S.J.; Methodology, Q.G., S.J. and P.B.S.; Experimental data acquisition, S.J.; Project administration, P.B.S.; Software, Q.G.; Supervision, P.B.S.; Validation, Q.G. and S.J.; Visualization, Q.G.; Writing—original draft, Q.G.; Writing—review & editing, S.J. and P.B.S. All authors have read and agreed to the published version of the manuscript.

Funding: This work was funded by the National Natural Science Foundation of China, grant number 51950410602. The work of S.J. is also supported by the Chinese Scholarship Council (CSC).

Conflicts of Interest: The authors declare no conflict of interest.

References

1. Mitra, S.; Acharya, T. Gesture Recognition: A Survey. *IEEE Trans. Syst. Man Cybern. Part C Appl. Rev.* **2007**, *37*, 311–324. [CrossRef]
2. Galka, J.; Masior, M.; Zaborski, M.; Barczewska, K. Inertial Motion Sensing Glove for Sign Language Gesture Acquisition and Recognition. *IEEE Sens. J.* **2016**, *16*, 6310–6316. [CrossRef]
3. Xu, D. A neural network approach for hand gesture recognition in virtual reality driving training system of SPG. In Proceedings of the 18th International Conference on Pattern Recognition (ICPR'06), Hong Kong, China, 20–24 August 2006.
4. Lee, S.; Hara, S.; Yamada, Y. A safety measure for control mode switching of skill-assist for effective automotive manufacturing. *IEEE Trans. Autom. Sci. Eng.* **2009**, *7*, 817–825. [CrossRef]
5. Chen, F.; Lv, H.; Pang, Z.; Zhang, J.; Hou, Y.; Gu, Y.; Yang, H.; Yang, G. WristCam: A Wearable Sensor for Hand Trajectory Gesture Recognition and Intelligent Human-Robot Interaction. *IEEE Sens. J.* **2019**, *19*, 8441–8451. [CrossRef]
6. Ren, Z.; Meng, J.; Yuan, J.; Zhang, Z. Robust hand gesture recognition with Kinect sensor. In Proceedings of the 19th ACM international conference on Multimedia, Scottsdale, AZ, USA, 28 November–1 December 2011.
7. Pu, Q.; Gupta, S.; Gollakota, S.; Patel, S. Whole-home gesture recognition using wireless signals. In Proceedings of the 19th Annual International Conference on Mobile Computing & Networking, Miami, FL, USA, 30 September–4 October 2013.
8. Liu, J.; Zhong, L.; Wickramasuriya, J.; Vasudevan, V. uWave: Accelerometer-based personalized gesture recognition and its applications. *Pervasive Mob. Comput.* **2009**, *5*, 657–675. [CrossRef]
9. Jiang, S.; Lv, B.; Guo, W.; Zhang, C.; Wang, H.; Sheng, X.; Shull, P.B. Feasibility of Wrist-Worn, Real-Time Hand, and Surface Gesture Recognition via sEMG and IMU Sensing. *IEEE Trans. Ind. Inf.* **2018**, *14*, 3376–3385. [CrossRef]
10. Zhang, Y.; Harrison, C. Tomo: Wearable, low-cost electrical impedance tomography for hand gesture recognition. In Proceedings of the 28th Annual ACM Symposium on User Interface Software & Technology, Charlotte, NC, USA, 1–4 November 2015.
11. Jiang, S.; Li, L.; Xu, H.; Xu, J.; Gu, G.; Shull, P.B. Stretchable e-Skin Patch for Gesture Recognition on the Back of the Hand. *IEEE Trans. Ind. Electron.* **2020**, *67*, 647–657. [CrossRef]
12. Wang, S.; Song, J.; Lien, J.; Poupyrev, I.; Hilliges, O. Interacting with soli: Exploring fine-grained dynamic gesture recognition in the radio-frequency spectrum. In Proceedings of the 29th Annual Symposium on User Interface Software and Technology, Tokyo, Japan, 16–19 October 2016.
13. Kim, Y.; Toomajian, B. Hand Gesture Recognition Using Micro-Doppler Signatures with Convolutional Neural Network. *IEEE Access* **2016**, *4*, 7125–7130. [CrossRef]
14. Kawaguchi, J.; Yoshimoto, S.; Kuroda, Y.; Oshiro, O. Estimation of Finger Joint Angles Based on Electromechanical Sensing of Wrist Shape. *IEEE Trans. Neural Syst. Rehabil. Eng.* **2017**, *25*, 1409–1418. [CrossRef]
15. Zhou, Y.; Zeng, J.; Li, K.; Fang, Y.; Liu, H. Voluntary and FES-induced Finger Movement Estimation Using Muscle Deformation Features. *IEEE Trans. Ind. Electron.* **2020**, *67*, 4002–4012. [CrossRef]
16. Smith, R.J.; Tenore, F.; Huberdeau, D.; Etienne-Cummings, R.; Thakor, N.V. Continuous decoding of finger position from surface EMG signals for the control of powered prostheses. In Proceedings of the 2008 30th Annual International Conference of the IEEE Engineering in Medicine and Biology Society, Vancouver, BC, Canada, 20–25 August 2008.

17. Hioki, M.; Kawasaki, H. Estimation of finger joint angles from sEMG using a neural network including time delay factor and recurrent structure. *ISRN Rehabil.* **2012**, *2012*, 604314. [CrossRef]
18. Pan, L.; Zhang, D.; Liu, J.; Sheng, X.; Zhu, X. Continuous estimation of finger joint angles under different static wrist motions from surface EMG signals. *Biomed. Signal Process. Control* **2014**, *14*, 265–271. [CrossRef]
19. Antfolk, C.; Cipriani, C.; Controzzi, M.; Carrozza, M.C.; Lundborg, G.; Rosén, B.; Sebelius, F. Using EMG for real-time prediction of joint angles to control a prosthetic hand equipped with a sensory feedback system. *J. Med. Biol. Eng.* **2010**, *30*, 399–406. [CrossRef]
20. Abraham, Z.; Tan, P.N. An integrated framework for simultaneous classification and regression of time-series data. In Proceedings of the 2010 SIAM International Conference on Data Mining, Columbus, OH, USA, 29 April–1 May 2010.
21. Wang, Z.; Li, W.; Kao, Y.; Zou, D.; Wang, Q.; Ahn, M.; Hong, S. HCR-Net: A Hybrid of Classification and Regression Network for Object Pose Estimation. In Proceedings of the 2018 IJCAI, Stockholm, Sweden, 13–19 July 2018.
22. Anguita, D.; Ghio, A.; Oneto, L.; Parra, X. A public domain dataset for human activity recognition using smartphones. In Proceedings of the ESANN, Bruges, Belgium, 24–26 April 2013.
23. Jiang, S.; Gao, Q.; Liu, H.; Shull, P.B. A novel, co-located EMG-FMG-sensing wearable armband for hand gesture recognition. *Sens. Actuators A.* **2020**, *301*, 111738. [CrossRef]
24. Liang, R.H.; Ouhyoung, M. A sign language recognition system using hidden markov model and context sensitive search. In Proceedings of the ACM Symposium on Virtual Reality Software and Technology, Hong Kong, China, 1–4 July 1996.
25. Huang, Y.; Yang, X.; Li, Y.; Zhou, D.; He, K.; Liu, H. Ultrasound-based sensing models for finger motion classification. *IEEE J. Biomed. Health Inf.* **2017**, *22*, 1395–1405. [CrossRef]
26. Dwivedi, S.K.; Ngeo, J.G.; Shibata, T. Extraction of Nonlinear Synergies for Proportional and Simultaneous Estimation of Finger Kinematics. *IEEE Trans. Biomed Eng.* **2020**. [CrossRef]
27. Shull, P.B.; Jiang, S.; Zhu, Y.; Zhu, X. Hand Gesture Recognition and Finger Angle Estimation via Wrist-Worn Modified Barometric Pressure Sensing. *IEEE Trans. Neural Syst. Rehabil. Eng.* **2019**, *27*, 724–732. [CrossRef]
28. Murthy, G.; Jadon, R. Hand gesture recognition using neural networks. In Proceedings of the 2010 IEEE 2nd International Advance Computing Conference (IACC), Patiala, India, 19–20 February 2010.
29. Gers, F.A.; Schmidhuber, J.; Cummins, F. Learning to forget: Continual prediction with LSTM. In Proceedings of the 9th International Conference on Artificial Neural Networks: ICANN '99, Edinburgh, UK, 7–10 September 1999.
30. Zhao, R.; Wang, D.; Yan, R.; Mao, K.; Shen, F.; Wang, J. Machine health monitoring using local feature-based gated recurrent unit networks. *IEEE Trans. Ind. Electron.* **2017**, *65*, 1539–1548. [CrossRef]
31. Al-Timemy, A.H.; Bugmann, G.; Escudero, J.; Outram, N. Classification of finger movements for the dexterous hand prosthesis control with surface electromyography. *IEEE J. Biomed. Health Inf.* **2013**, *17*, 608–618. [CrossRef]
32. Geng, W.; Du, Y.; Jin, W.; Wei, W.; Hu, Y.; Li, J. Gesture recognition by instantaneous surface EMG images. *Sci. Rep.* **2016**, *6*, 36571. [CrossRef]
33. Ngeo, J.G.; Tamei, T.; Shibata, T. Continuous and simultaneous estimation of finger kinematics using inputs from an EMG-to-muscle activation model. *J. Neuroeng. Rehabil.* **2014**, *11*, 122. [CrossRef]
34. Yang, X.; Yan, J.; Chen, Z.; Ding, H.; Liu, H. A Proportional Pattern Recognition Control Scheme for Wearable A-mode Ultrasound Sensing. *IEEE Trans. Ind. Electron.* **2020**, *67*, 800–808. [CrossRef]
35. Ma, X.; Zhao, Y.; Zhang, L.; Gao, Q.; Pan, M.; Wang, J. Practical Device-Free Gesture Recognition Using WiFi Signals Based on Metalearning. *IEEE Trans. Ind. Inf.* **2020**, *16*, 228–237. [CrossRef]
36. Farina, D.; Jiang, N.; Rehbaum, H.; Holobar, A.; Graimann, B.; Dietl, H.; Aszmann, O.C. The extraction of neural information from the surface EMG for the control of upper-limb prostheses: Emerging avenues and challenges. *IEEE Trans. Neural Syst. Rehabil. Eng.* **2014**, *22*, 797–809. [CrossRef]
37. Gupta, H.P.; Chudgar, H.S.; Mukherjee, S.; Dutta, T.; Sharma, K. A Continuous Hand Gestures Recognition Technique for Human-Machine Interaction using Accelerometer and Gyroscope sensors. *IEEE Sens. J.* **2016**, *16*, 6425–6432. [CrossRef]
38. Cenedese, A.; Susto, G.A.; Belgioioso, G.; Cirillo, G.I.; Fraccaroli, F. Home automation oriented gesture classification from inertial measurements. *IEEE Trans. Autom. Sci. Eng.* **2015**, *12*, 1200–1210. [CrossRef]
39. Megalingam, R.K.; Rangan, V.; Krishnan, S.; Edichery Alinkeezhil, A.B. IR sensor based Gesture Control Wheelchair for Stroke and SCI Patients. *IEEE Sens. J.* **2016**, *16*, 6755–6765. [CrossRef]

40. Kruse, D.; Wen, J.T.; Radke, R.J. A sensor-based dual-arm tele-robotic system. *IEEE Trans. Autom. Sci. Eng.* **2014**, *12*, 4–18. [CrossRef]
41. Premaratne, P.; Nguyen, Q. Consumer electronics control system based on hand gesture moment invariants. *IET Comput. Vis.* **2007**, *1*, 35–41. [CrossRef]

© 2020 by the authors. Licensee MDPI, Basel, Switzerland. This article is an open access article distributed under the terms and conditions of the Creative Commons Attribution (CC BY) license (http://creativecommons.org/licenses/by/4.0/).

Article

A Frame Detection Method for Real-Time Hand Gesture Recognition Systems Using CW-Radar

Myoungseok Yu [1], Narae Kim [1], Yunho Jung [2] and Seongjoo Lee [1,*]

[1] Dept. Information and Communication Engineering, Sejong University, Gunja-dong, Gwangjin-gu, Seoul 05006, Korea; myoungseok@itsoc.sejong.ac.kr (M.Y.); narae@itsoc.sejong.ac.kr (N.K.)
[2] School of Electronics and Information Engineering, Korea Aerospace University, Goyang, Gyeonggi-do 10540, Korea; yjung@kau.ac.kr
* Correspondence: seongjoo@sejong.ac.kr

Received: 17 February 2020; Accepted: 16 April 2020; Published: 18 April 2020

Abstract: In this paper, a method to detect frames was described that can be used as hand gesture data when configuring a real-time hand gesture recognition system using continuous wave (CW) radar. Detecting valid frames raises accuracy which recognizes gestures. Therefore, it is essential to detect valid frames in the real-time hand gesture recognition system using CW radar. The conventional research on hand gesture recognition systems has not been conducted on detecting valid frames. We took the R-wave on electrocardiogram (ECG) detection as the conventional method. The detection probability of the conventional method was 85.04%. It has a low accuracy to use the hand gesture recognition system. The proposal consists of 2-stages to improve accuracy. We measured the performance of the detection method of hand gestures provided by the detection probability and the recognition probability. By comparing the performance of each detection method, we proposed an optimal detection method. The proposal detects valid frames with an accuracy of 96.88%, 11.84% higher than the accuracy of the conventional method. Also, the recognition probability of the proposal method was 94.21%, which was 3.71% lower than the ideal method.

Keywords: hand gesture; micro-Doppler signatures; CW radar; convolutional neural network; real-time process; detection

1. Introduction

HUMAN-computer interaction (HCI) recognizes the purpose of humans and operates a device. Hand gesture recognition is a type of HCI that gets the hand gestures of humans sorted and steers the device for each gesture. According to the advance of hand gesture recognition, the hand gesture recognition system can be applied to various devices, such as drones and robots. There is a representative advantage in hand gesture recognition, so a user can control a device remotely. In particular, it is a great merit when steering a drone, because the flying is separated between a user and a drone. In addition, hand gesture recognition has an advantage, because the movement of the hand is intuitive. The intuitive hand movement does not require a special explanation for the user.

The research of hand gesture recognition is being studied and developed [1–3]. Hand gesture recognition systems based mainly on camera sensors and accelerometer sensors are widely used. Camera sensors shoot the hand gesture and go through the process of recognizing the photographed data. Since the photographed data contains shape information, it can be effectively utilized for hand gestures with various image processing techniques [4,5]. However, there are disadvantages that arise from using the photographed data such as recognition environment and privacy violations. For example, vision sensors such as cameras may have difficulty in recognition in severe environments such as foggy or dark place. Also, camera sensors may cause privacy violations if they are hacked or personal privacy can be filmed. Recently, noncooperative space targets detection is being studied with vision sensors [6,7]. The target can be detected by finding the pose (position and attitude) of the noncooperative space target. However, the shape of the target must be circular or near-circular and the algorithm cannot be applied to real-time recognition systems due to the large amount of computation. Accelerometer sensors will be also utilized with wearable devices like gloves or bracelet for hand gesture recognition [8,9]. Accelerometer sensors have the advantage of being able to recognize minute movements, such as the gestures of a finger, but have an inconvenience of always wearing a sensor. Radar sensors are less sensitive to recognition environments and privacy violations and are being actively studied for hand gesture recognition [10–15]. In addition, the sensors do not need to be worn unlike accelerometer sensors. Therefore, this paper also adopts radar sensors for hand gesture recognition.

When using a radar sensor, frequency modulated continuous wave (FMCW) and continuous wave (CW) radar are used [10–12]. The reason for using the FMCW radar and the CW radar is to measure the micro-Doppler signatures of hand gestures [13–15]. The measured micro-Doppler signal can generate spectrogram via short term Fourier transform (STFT). The spectrogram expresses the frequency component of a hand gesture with time in the image. Therefore, the spectrogram can be used to use powerful machine learning for image recognition, such as the convolutional neural network (CNN). Previous research has only focused on hand gesture recognition and not on detecting a valid frame [16–18]. A valid frame is a frame that contains whole information of hand gestures, while an invalid frame contains partial information of hand gestures or does not have any information. Hand gestures can be correctly recognized only after detecting a valid frame. It is very important to detect a valid frame in order to process the real-time hand gesture system. We undertook this study about a valid frame detection to construct the real-time hand gesture system.

Signal detection has been studied in many fields, such as communications, voice activity detection (VAD) and constant false alarm rate (CFAR). However, it is impossible to use the above detection methods for a real-time hand gesture recognition system using CW radar. Communication detection methods are not suitable for the system using CW radar, because they require signals, such as pilots or preambles. Also, the CW radar detection method is not appropriate for using a VAD method because of the difference of the voice and the CW radar signal. The VAD method requires a sustained time but the CW radar signal appears in the form of an impulse signal in a shorter time than the voice signal.

Real-time hand gesture recognition using FMCW radar employs an exponentially weighted moving average (EWMA), which is one of the CFAR algorithms used to detect valid frames [19]. EWMA defines detection as the change in average energy increases. Also, EWMA is not suitable for detecting sensitive energy changes. FMCW radar calculates signals by beat frequency, so it does not reflect energy fluctuations significantly. Thus, the hand gesture recognition system using FMCW radar can get a high accuracy when EWMA is applied as a detection method. On the other hand, CW radar calculates hand gestures with energy change, so it is sensitive to energy fluctuations. Therefore, a hand gesture recognition system that uses CW radar cannot use EWMA. Since the detection method described above cannot be used, the detection method of an electrocardiogram (ECG) was selected as a conventional method. A CW radar signal is similar to an R-wave on an ECG. Both signals appear in the form of an impulse signal in a short time. R-wave detection in ECG uses a shifting window difference threshold (SWDT) [20]. Hence, SWDT was selected as a conventional method. In this paper, methods were provided to detect frames that can be used in real-time hand gesture recognition using CW radar. Also, the performances of the proposed and conventional method were compared. Section 2 explains roughly the hand gesture recognition system using CW radar. The conventional method is entered into the details, and the proposed methods are presented in Section 2. Section 4 accounts for the experiment environment and displays the experimental result. Section 5 summarizes the results and concludes this paper.

2. System Overview

Hand gesture recognition is a method of measuring hand gesture features from a sensor and analyzing and recognizing the measured data. Therefore, in the hand gesture recognition system, the sensor can be used in various ways. Among the various sensors, this paper describes a hand gesture recognition system using CW radar. Figure 1 shows a diagram of hand gesture recognition using CW radar. The hand gesture recognition system using CW radar is divided into three major parts: the analog signal processing part, the digital signal processing part and the software part.

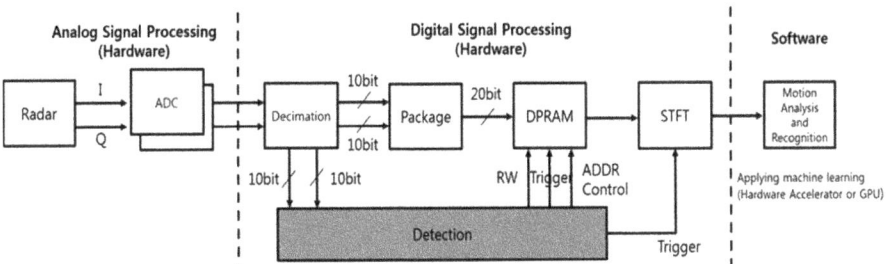

Figure 1. Diagram of Hand Gesture Recognition System Using CW radar Sensor.

The analog signal processing part measures the micro-Doppler signatures of the hand gesture from the CW radar and converts the analog signals to the digital signal. First, the analog signal processing part measures the hand gesture's micro-Doppler signal through the CW radar. The micro-Doppler signal is measured on two channels as I/Q data. Then, the I/Q data are converted to a digital signal using an analog-to-digital converter (ADC) for digital signal processing.

The digital signal processing part processes digital signals converted through the ADC. First, the digital signal which is transmitted by the analog signal processing part is preprocessed. Pre-Processing includes processing that proceeds to easily signal process the raw data coming in from the ADC. The pre-processing module consists of Decimation, Re-formation. The reason for proceeding with decimation is that using a sampling rate that is too high can increase the complexity and have processing times that are too high relative to the accuracy of the spectrogram. The decimated signal proceeds through the re-formation process. Re-formation is the process of converting the signal coming from the ADC to make it easier to perform bit operations. Pre-processed signals are connected on both sides by package and detection. The package is a module that combines I/Q data into one. The reason why I/Q data from the package is put together is to make it easy to save and access data measured at the same time of dual-ported random-access memory (DPRAM). The data generated from the package is transferred and stored to the space of DPRAM appointed by each ADDRESS. When a valid frame is detected, the detection module analyzes the received decimation signal to determine if a valid frame has been detected. Then the detection module informs the DPRAM and the STFT modules that the available frame has been detected via the trigger signal. The detection module also notifies the DPRAM of the ADDRESS where there is a valid frame of data stored in the DPRAM via the ADDRESS control signal. Finally, the detection module indicates whether to write that it is to read data from the DPRAM using the R/W signal. The DPRAM module saves and outputs decimation data based on the signal from the detection. The STFT module makes from a valid frame to the spectrogram. When the trigger signal comes in, the STFT module receives a valid frame from the DPRAM; this frame is output to spectrogram by STFT. The software part analyzes and recognizes motion using the spectrogram transmitted by the digital signal processing part. The software part performs machine learning using a hardware accelerator or a graphics processing unit (GPU) on the spectrogram. It makes possible to recognize any motion according to the spectrogram using a machine learning model generated through machine learning.

In this paper, a CNN model was employed as the software part. The CNN model was trained by the spectrogram of hand gestures. Then, hand gestures were inferred using the CNN model. The inference was taken within 0.1 s using a computer. It is enough time for the real-time process.

3. Detection Methods

In this section, the conventional method [20] and the proposed method are presented. The conventional method calculates a trigger value from the raw data. Then, a trigger value is compared with the threshold. The proposed method consists of a 2-stage detection method. The first stage of the proposed method roughly detects the valid data. After that, the second stage proceeds with detection where it has the largest energy near the detection position of the first stage. Figure 2 shows a spectrogram created on the valid frame data detected in raw data.

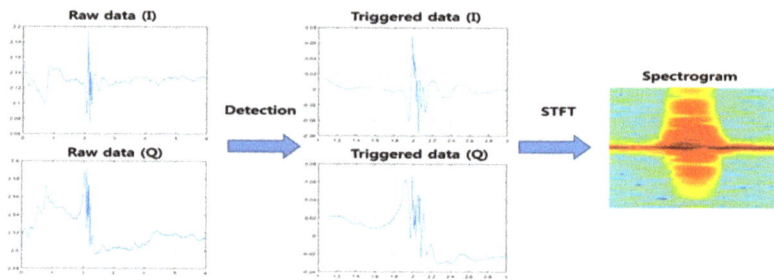

Figure 2. Example of detection.

The conventional method divides the raw data into frames and calculates the trigger value. First, to calculate the trigger value, which is shown in Equation (1), D is calculated, which means the difference between adjacent samples in the frame. In Equation (1), F means the value of the sample present in the frame and abs means the absolute value in Equation (1). The absolute value of the complex number is the square root of the sum of the values where the real value and the imaginary value are, respectively, squared. However, the absolute magnitude of a complex number can be obtained without using the square root as in Equation (2). Therefore, abs use Equation (2) in the conventional method to reduce the computational complexity.

$$D[k] = abs(F[k] - F[k+1]) \tag{1}$$

$$abs(R) = I^2 + Q^2 \tag{2}$$

D is calculated for all values in a frame. Therefore, the value in the range corresponding to $k = (1, 2, \ldots sizeof(F))$ is calculated. Also, all the calculated D values are summed. Equation (3) shows a value obtained by adding up all the D values of the frame. The value of Equation (3) is defined as the trigger value.

$$T = \sum_{k=1}^{n} D[k] \tag{3}$$

After calculating the trigger value, the trigger value compares the magnitude with a threshold. If the trigger value is smaller than the threshold, the next frame recalculates the trigger value. Conversely, when the trigger value is greater than the threshold, it is defined that a valid frame is detected. Since the conventional method has a threshold set to a constant and the trigger value exists as an absolute numerical value, there is a disadvantage that the detection probability may change depending on the magnitude of the hand movement.

The proposed methods consist of two stages to compensate for and overcome the disadvantages of the conventional method, thereby increasing the detection probability. Stage 1 searches for an approximate valid frame location. The frames existing around the frame position detected in Stage 1 are defined as the window. Stage 2 proceeds in a way that finds the maximum trigger value in the window.

The proposed method 1 uses the conventional method in Stage 1. In the proposed method 1a window is defined as a frame located behind in time in the frame detected in Stage 1. The reason for defining the window by the above method is that it is not necessary to recalculate the trigger value, which is calculated previously. Stage 2 calculates the trigger value of the frame present in the window, and then a frame that has the largest trigger value in the window is defined as a valid frame. As shown in Figure 3, the conventional method consists of single stage and determines the valid frame by using the frame with a trigger value exceeding the threshold. However, the proposed method 1 uses the trigger values of all frames within the window in Stage 2 and finds out the valid frame, which results in getting high accuracy than the conventional method. The proposed method 2 detects in Stage 1 using the rate of change of the trigger value. The change ratio of the trigger value is defined as the trigger ratio; the trigger ratio is calculated as shown in Equation (4). The trigger ratio is calculated using the trigger value calculated in a present frame and the trigger value of a frame existing after delay. $T[n]$ means the present trigger value and $T[n+delay]$ means the delayed trigger value in Equation (4). The trigger ratio does not grasp the magnitude of the trigger value, but it grasps the change ratio of the trigger value. Therefore, the method using the trigger ratio has an advantage, because the detection probability doesn't change according to the magnitude of the hand movement. In this paper, the delay was 50 milliseconds, a half of the size of window 1.

$$R = \frac{T[n+delay]}{T[n]} \tag{4}$$

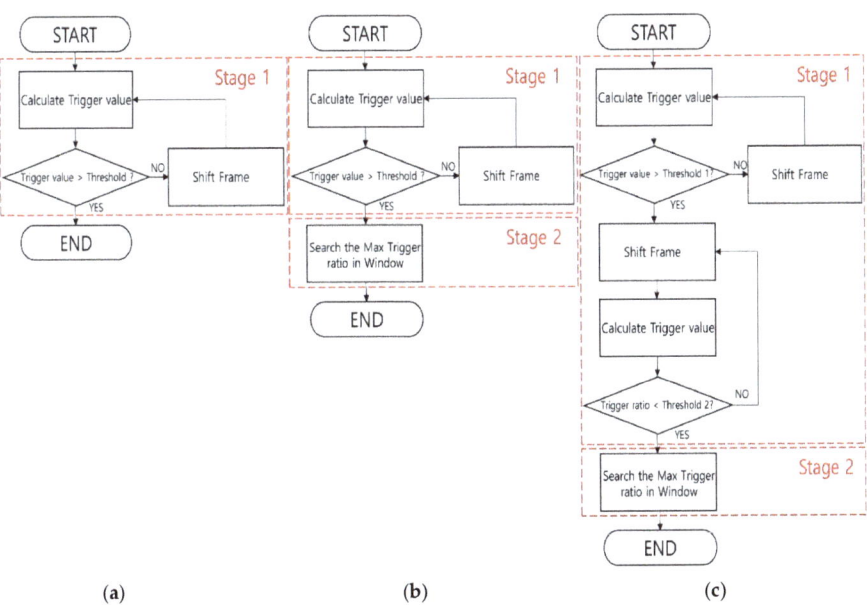

Figure 3. Flowchart of proposed methods. (a) conventional method; (b) proposed method 1; (c) proposed method 2.

The trigger ratio calculated via (4) is displayed in Figure 4. The trigger ratio can find the starting point of the hand gesture and the endpoint of the hand gesture. Looking at Figure 4, the trigger ratio keeps a value of around 1 but increases to more than 1 significantly later. The reason the trigger ratio is kept around 1 is that a delayed trigger value and the present trigger value are almost equal. Before the hand gesture is started, the delayed trigger is kept similar to the present trigger value. The reason for an increase in the trigger ratio is that the delayed trigger value is bigger than the present trigger value. When the hand gesture is started, the delayed trigger increases. The high peak of the trigger ratio means the hand gesture is begun. The red circle at the upper left side in Figure 4 signifies a start point. After this, the trigger ratio reduces to around 1, and it maintains its value. While the hand gesture is sustained, the present trigger value increases as much as the delayed trigger value. Then, the trigger ratio decreases to less than 1, because the delayed trigger value is smaller than the present trigger value. When the hand gesture ends, the delayed trigger decreases. The red circle at the lower right side in Figure 4 signifies the low peak of the trigger ratio, which means that the hand gesture has ended. The threshold of the proposed method 2 has a threshold of the start point and a threshold of the endpoint. The threshold of the point where the hand gesture starts is defined as threshold 1, which has a value of more than 1. Also, the threshold of the point where the hand gesture ends is defined as threshold 2 which has a value of less than 1. The proposed method 2 detects the start point and the endpoint using both thresholds in first stage. When the trigger ratio exceeds threshold 1, that point is defined as the start point. After that, when the trigger ratio is lower than threshold 2, that point is defined as the endpoint. The middle point of the start points, and the endpoint is defined as the temporary valid frame. The window of proposed method 2 is defined as a frame before and a frame after the temporary valid frame. The reason for defining the window by the above method is that it is not possible to know whether the frame that has the maximum trigger value exists before or after the temporary valid frame. Stage 2 of proposed method 2 detects a frame that has a maximum trigger value in the window like proposed method 1. The frame having the largest trigger value in the second stage is defined as a valid frame. The method using the trigger ratio cannot detect the frame with the largest trigger value accurately but considers the relative change of data, so finding the approximate position of the frame with the largest trigger value is powerful. In this paper, we experimented with assuming real-time processing. Real-time processing requires a short processing time. Therefore, real-time processing is impossible if the window size is too long. For the above reasons, the window size was fixed within 0.1 s and 0.2 s in the second stage of the proposed methods. A window with a size of 0.1 s is defined as window 1; a window with a size of 0.2 s is defined as window 2.

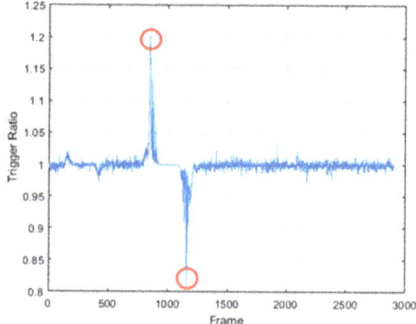

Figure 4. Example of the trigger ratio.

4. Experiment

This section describes experiments to confirm the performance of the proposed methods and analyzes the results. First, the experimenter's hand gestures were measured as a micro-Doppler signal via the CW radar. Next, the measured data were created in a spectrogram and the CNN model was trained using the spectrogram. The detection range was defined using the CNN model and the raw data. The detection probability was the result of calculating the probability that the valid frame of each method was included within the detection range. Finally, spectrograms made from the valid frame of each method calculate the recognition probability through the inference process of the CNN model. In the experiment, a K-MC1 radar, ST200 hardware and RFbeam signal explorer software were used. The operating frequency of the K-MC1 was 24 GHz (K-Band), and it uses 180 MHz sweep FM (frequency modulation) input. The ST200 has a 16-bit data acquisition at the speed of 250 ksps (sample per second) sampling rate. We employed 6 hand gestures.

Figure 5 shows the hand gestures. The six hand gestures consist of right-to-left, left-to-right, up-to-down, down-to-up, finger stretch and finger pinch. The distance to the hand was set to about 30 cm in the radar module. Also, we measured the micro-Doppler signal of the hand gesture in front of the radar module. The gestures of right-to-left and left-to-right consisted of 45 degrees of movement from the radar line of sight. The gestures of Up to down and Down to up had 45 degrees of movement from the horizontal position of the radar. The maximum angle of outstretched fingers was 90 degrees for finger gestures. Four people took part in the experiments. Before measuring the raw data, each hand gesture was ready to the initial pose as shown in the left part of Figure 5. Each hand gesture was performed with undetermined time delay after the start of data gathering system. One person did repeatedly an action 100 times for each gesture, which resulted in the collection of 400 data for each gesture. The raw data were measured for 6 s, in which the hand gesture frames were included for 1.8 s with unknown time position. The starting point (valid frame) of hand gesture should be correctly determined by the detection algorithm before the start of recognition process.

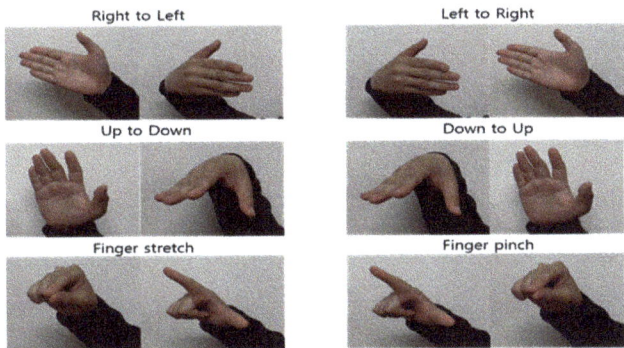

Figure 5. Types of hand gestures.

Figure 6 depicts the spectrogram of each of the hand gestures. The conditions of STFT in this paper were as follows. The size of the FFT configured in STFT was 512 samples, the number of non-overlapping samples was 5 samples; color mapping uses jet color mapping [18]. The spectrogram of Figure 6 used the ideal method. The ideal method detects a frame that has a maximum trigger value within 6 s of the measured raw data. In the ideal method, all data samples of Micro-doppler signal were stored and evaluated from the start of experiment to the end of it before finding the valid frame. The ideal method can compare the overall Micro-doppler signal data and show the best detection performance, but cannot be performed in real-time, because it has to be waiting for the end of entire data gathering process. Also, the detection range was defined based on a frame detected using the ideal method.

As shown at Figure 7, the convolutional neural network (CNN) model was constructed using a spectrogram created using the ideal method. We utilized the data for training with 90% of the obtained micro-Doppler signals. And the rest of the measured data were used for both the inference and the accuracy estimation. The CNN consisted of three convolutional layers, each of which contained the combination of convolution filters, an activation function and a pooling. Through experiment optimization, 16 convolution filters and an average-pooling scheme were used. An activation function was a sigmoid function.

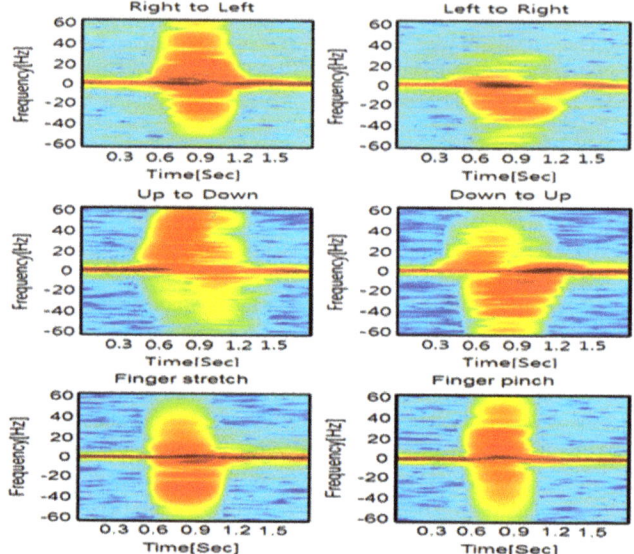

Figure 6. Spectrograms of each hand gesture.

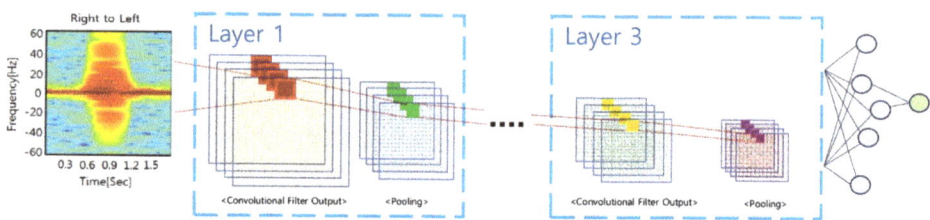

Figure 7. Structure in convolutional neural network (CNN) with three layers.

Figure 8 displays the performance drop according to the detection offset. To define the detection range, we used the performance drop according to the detection offset. The frame detected by the ideal method was set to 0 in the x-axis in Figure 8. Detection offset means the error frame. Error frames were made with an error in 0.01 s units based on the ideal method. Then, error frames were inferred using the CNN model and calculated the recognition probability. Recognition probability was defined as the accuracy when the inference of pre-trained deep learning model was correct from the data detected from a spectrogram. Commercial recognition systems require more than 95% accuracy, so we established a detection range where the performance drop was up to 5%.

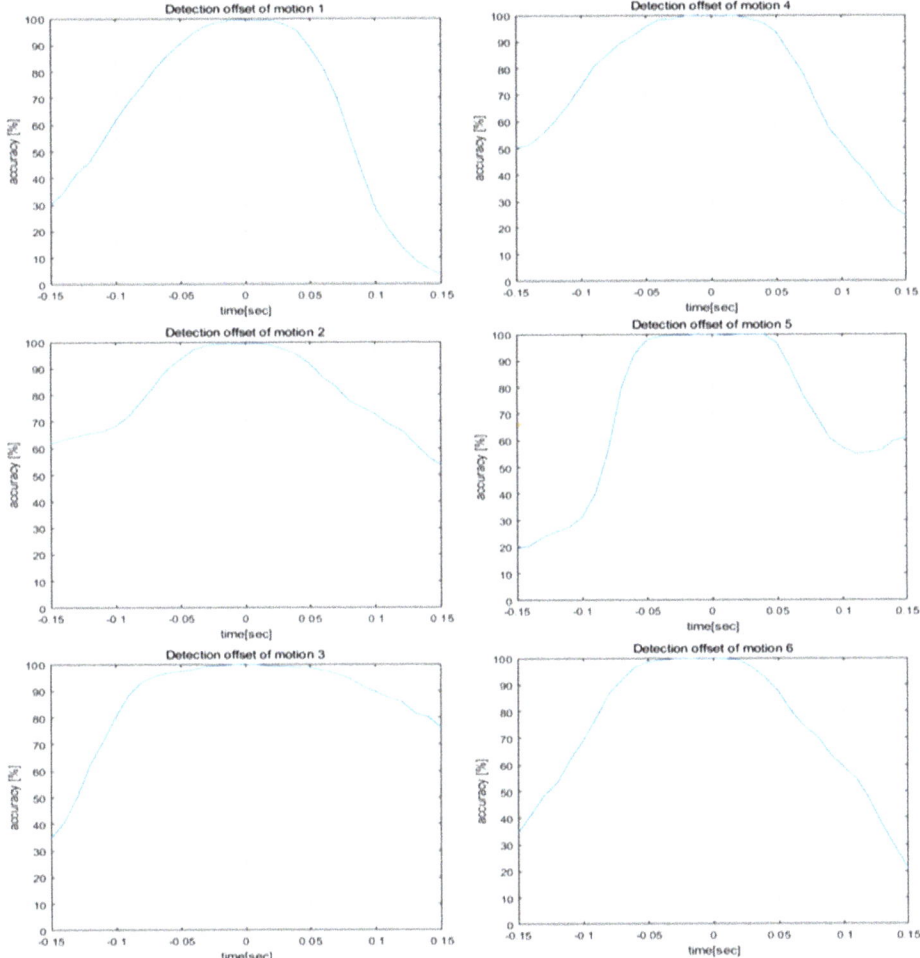

Figure 8. The performance drops caused by detection offset in motion 1 to 6.

Table 1 indicates a detection range based on the performance drop according to the detection offset. The detection range was calculated for each detection offset where the performance drops were 1%, 3% and 5%. Detection probability uses the detection range described in Table 1 to calculate the probability that the spectrogram configured using each method enters the detection range. Figures 9–13 depict the detection probability of each method. Each graph was created according to the detection range for each offset. A window does not exist in the conventional method, but the proposed method consists of a 2-stage and a window exists. The size of window 1 was 0.1 s; the size of window 2 was 0.2 s. The window of the proposed method 1 consists of a frame after the frame detected in the first stage and proposed method 2 consists of a frame before and a frame after the frame detected in the first stage. Looking at Figure 9's conventional method detection probability, it can be seen that the detection probability changes significantly based on each threshold. The gestures 1–4 were large movements that use the whole hand, so it was possible to see a high detection probability when the threshold was high, but a low detection probability when the threshold was low. However, since the gestures 5–6 were small movements using only two fingers, it can be seen that the detection probability was low when the threshold was large, and detection probability was high when the threshold was small. Large gestures cause the trigger value to fluctuate more than small gestures. Therefore, there was a probability that early detection occurs when the threshold was small for large gestures. Early detection means an error detecting a frame exists before a valid frame. Conversely, small gestures were indicated by small changes in the trigger value. Thus, small gestures have a probability that a miss will occur if the threshold was large. A miss means passing without detecting a valid frame. As each performance drop increases, the detection range expands more. Therefore, when the performance drop was high, it can be seen that the detection probability becomes the same as or higher than when the performance drop was low. The conventional method has the advantage of being the simplest over the other methods However, the conventional method has the disadvantage of a low detection probability. Looking at Figures 9–11 and Tables 2–4, the proposed method 1 shows a higher detection probability than the conventional method, because the first stage was added in the conventional method. Also, when the window size was 0.2, the detection probability was higher than when the window size was 0.1. The reason why the detection probability was high when the window size was large was it has found the maximum value of the trigger value in a wider range. However, if the window size was large, it may need more time with the real-time process, so the difference in the size of the window size has advantages and disadvantages. The detection and recognition probabilities of the proposed method 1 increase up to 86–92% and up to 86–67%, respectively. The proposed method 1 shows a higher performance than the conventional method. However, since Stage 1 of the proposed method 1 uses the conventional method, the detection probability and the recognition probability change greatly according to the magnitude of the threshold. As described in the previous conventional method, a large gesture indicates a higher detection probability if the threshold was large; a small gesture indicates a higher detection probability if the threshold was small in the proposed method 1. Therefore, the proposed method 1 has problems such as the conventional method. After all, the proposed method 1 shows a higher performance than the conventional method, but it shows a performance that was not sufficient to configure the recognition system.

Table 1. Detection range of each hand gesture.

Hand Gesture	Detection Range [sec]		
Perf. Drop	1% Drop	3% Drop	5% Drop
1	−0.02–0.03	−0.04–0.04	−0.04–0.05
2	−0.02–0.02	−0.04–0.04	−0.05–0.05
3	−0.03–0.03	−0.06–0.07	−0.08–0.08
4	−0.03–0.03	−0.05–0.04	−0.06–0.05
5	−0.04–0.05	−0.06–0.05	−0.06–0.06
6	−0.05–0.03	−0.06–0.03	−0.07–0.04

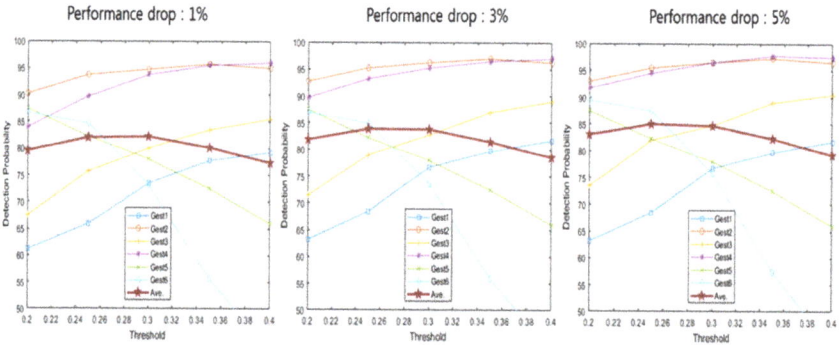

Figure 9. Detection probability of conventional method [20].

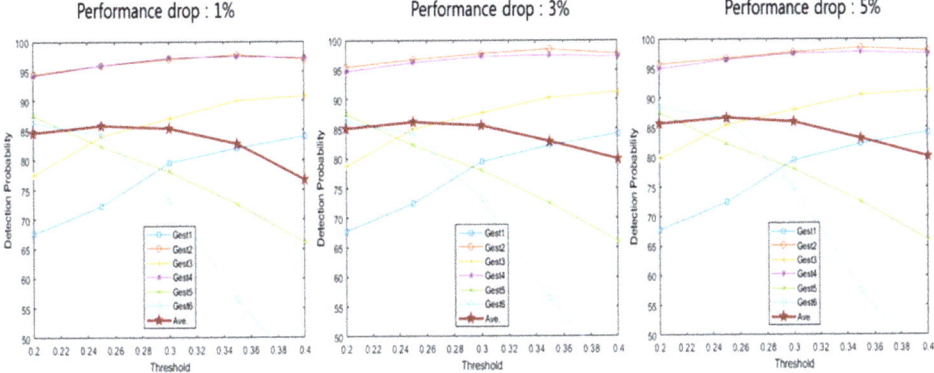

Figure 10. Detection probability of proposed method 1 (window 1).

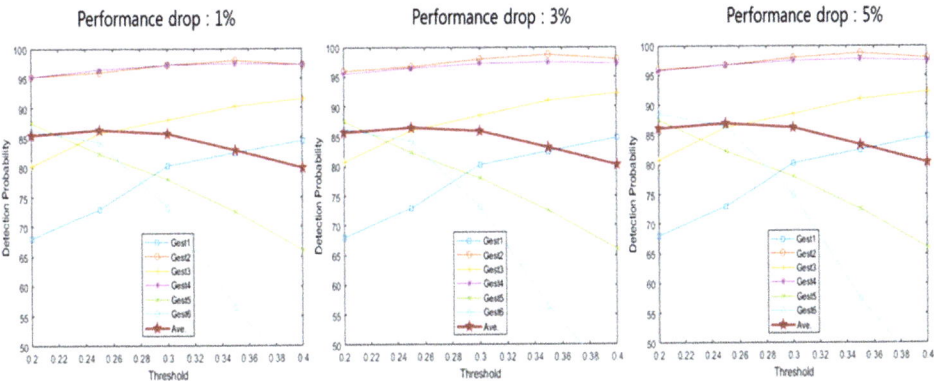

Figure 11. Detection probability of proposed method 1 (window 2).

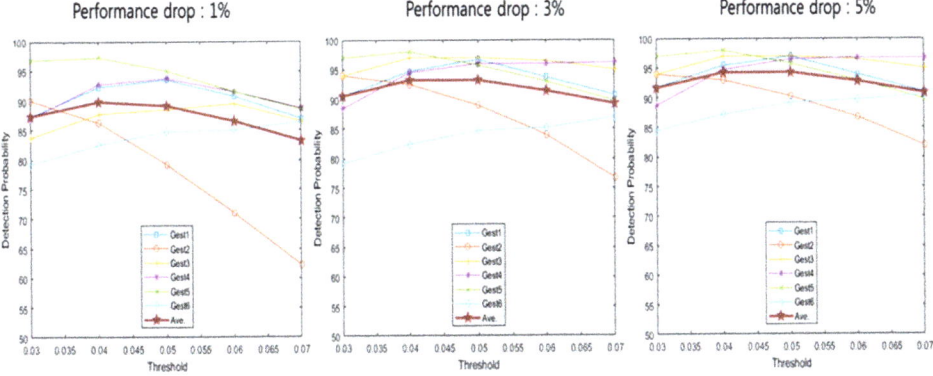

Figure 12. Detection probability of proposed method 2 (window 1).

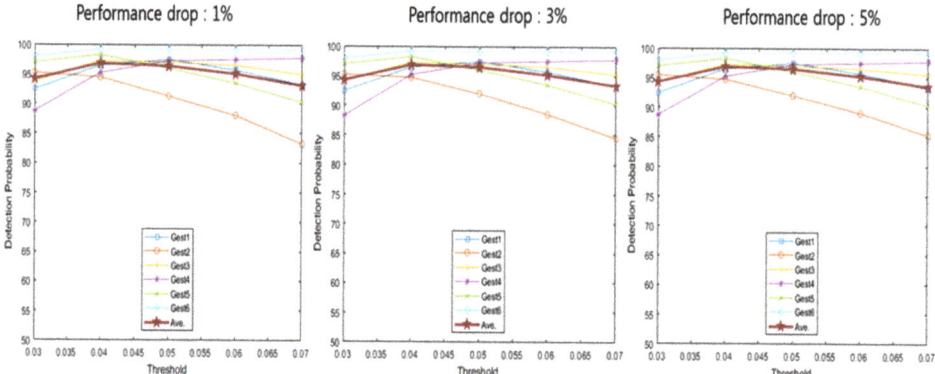

Figure 13. Detection probability of proposed method 2 (window 2).

Table 2. Averaged detection probabilities of conventional methods [20].

Offset	Threshold				
	0.4	0.35	0.3	0.25	0.2
1%	77.33%	80.13%	82.21%	82.04%	79.54%
2%	78.58%	81.46%	83.79%	83.88%	81.88%
3%	79.29%	82.29%	84.71%	85.04%	83.08%

Table 3. Averaged detection probabilities of proposal 1 (window 1).

Offset	Threshold				
	0.4	0.35	0.3	0.25	0.2
1%	79.67%	82.71%	85.33%	85.79%	84.58%
2%	79.92%	82.92%	85.58%	86.17%	85.08%
3%	80.13%	83.17%	85.96%	86.67%	85.71%

Table 4. Averaged detection probabilities of proposal 1 (window 2).

Offset	Threshold				
	0.4	0.35	0.3	0.25	0.2
1%	79.92%	82.88%	85.67%	86.29%	85.42%
2%	80.21%	83.13%	85.88%	86.46%	85.67%
3%	80.38%	83.33%	86.21%	86.92%	86.08%

The proposed method 2 has no significant difference in the detection probability of a specific hand gesture based on the threshold. This was because the proposed method 2 does not use the trigger value but uses the trigger ratio. The trigger ratio signifies the relative change of the trigger value, so there was no difference between a large hand gesture and a small hand gesture. The proposed method 2 shows a higher detection probability than the conventional method and the proposed method 1, and was not limited to a specific hand gesture. Also, it shows a detection probability of about 90% for all hand gestures. In summary, from the results of Figures 9–13, Tables 2–6 depict the averaged detection probabilities of all hand gestures for the methods evaluated with varying threshold values. As shown in Tables 2–6, we found that the optimum threshold values having the maximum detection probabilities were changed depending on not only the offset values but the detection methods. For example, as shown in Table 7, in the conventional method [20], the optimum threshold value was 0.3 when the offset value was 1%. At 3% offset, the optimal value of threshold was changed to 0.25. Hence, the optimal detection can find the positions having the maximum recognition probability.

Table 5. Averaged detection probabilities of proposal 2 (window 1).

Offset	Threshold				
	±0.07	±0.06	±0.05	±0.04	±0.03
1%	83.25%	86.54%	89.13%	89.79%	87.33%
2%	89.25%	91.42%	93.21%	93.21%	90.54%
3%	90.83%	92.79%	94.29%	94.25%	91.67%

Table 6. Averaged detection probabilities of proposal 2 (window 2).

Offset	Threshold				
	±0.07	±0.06	±0.05	±0.04	±0.03
1%	93.13%	95.08%	96.38%	96.83%	94.21%
2%	93.38%	95.17%	96.50%	96.83%	94.29%
3%	93.54%	95.25%	96.50%	96.83%	94.33%

Table 7. Optimum thresholds of methods.

Offset	Conventional	Proposal 1		Proposal 2	
	-	Window1	Window2	Window1	Window2
1%	0.3	0.25	0.25	1 ± 0.04	1 ± 0.04
2%	0.25	0.25	0.25	1 ± 0.04	1 ± 0.04
3%	0.25	0.25	0.25	1 ± 0.05	1 ± 0.04

Table 7 indicates the optimum threshold with the highest detection probability. The detection probability and the recognition probability of each method were compared using the optimum threshold.

Table 8 displays the detection probability of each method; Table 9 displays the recognition probability of each method. To measure the performance of the proposed method, Table 8 shows how much the detection probability was improved over conventional methods; Table 9 presents the recognition performance of proposed methods. The percentage in parentheses shows the performance drop compared with the method adopting the ideal (perfect) detection. The existing detection methods provided robustness in terms of false alarm. However, they had a weakness to miss the correct frames. Unlike the existing algorithms, the proposed method could have a strength with respect to the miss issue without increasing false alarm probabilities. In order to verify the false alarm issue, we measured the micro-Doppler signal for 6 seconds including hand gesture and inactivity. During the idle time, we evaluated whether or not the proposed method declared false alarms. In addition, the two-stage processing in the proposed scheme could have more reliable performance in terms of position accuracy of valid frames compared with the existing algorithms. The two proposed methods have a higher performance than the convention method. In particular, the proposed method 2 improves the detection probability by about 10% compared to the conventional method and decreases the recognition probability by 5% compared to the ideal method.

In order to verify the suitability for real-time processing, experiments were also conducted on the detection of raw data with multiple hand gestures and Table 10 shows the computational time of each methods. Since the proposed method 2 consists of two stages, it was about 0.06 s slower than the conventional method. However, the proposed method 2 can improve both a detection probability (96.88%) and a recognition probability (94.21%) significantly compared to the conventional one even satisfying real-time processing requirements. The computational time was measured on an Intel Core i7-8700 CPU and 16 G RAM. The experiments measured micro-Doppler signals of three hand gestures for 10 s. The measurements about continuous three hand gestures were performed for 100 times, and the proposed method 2 was evaluated in the experiments. Figure 14 shows an example of valid frame detection results for three hand gestures from the micro-Doppler signals containing three hand gestures. Figure 14a depicts the raw data of the micro-Doppler signals with continuous three hand gestures; we can see three detected gestures from Figure 14b–d. Figure 15 shows the spectrograms of three gestures, which were obtained from the detected frames. As shown in Figure 15, we can find that the spectrograms of all gestures were clearly generated. The detection probability was 93.33%.

Table 8. Detection probability of methods.

Offset	Proposal 1	
	Window 1	Window2
1%	85.79% (3.58%↑)	86.29% (4.08%↑)
2%	86.17% (2.29%↑)	86.46% (2.58%↑)
3%	86.67% (1.63%↑)	86.92% (1.88%↑)
Offset	Proposal 2	
	Window 1	Window2
1%	89.79% (7.58%↑)	96.83% (14.62%↑)
2%	93.21% (9.33%↑)	96.88% (13.00%↑)
3%	94.29% (9.25%↑)	96.88% (11.84%↑)

Table 9. Recognition probability of methods.

Gesture	Proposal 1	
	Window 1	Window2
1	72.50% (26.00%↓)	72.50% (26.00%↓)
2	87.50% (8.00%↓)	87.50% (8.00%↓)
3	85.00% (13.00%↓)	84.75% (13.25%↓)
4	94.50% (3.00%↓)	94.75% (2.75%↓)
5	88.25% (11.00%↓)	90.00% (9.25%↓)
6	90.50% (8.25%↓)	90.50% (8.25%↓)
Ave.	86.38% (11.54%↓)	86.67% (11.25%↓)
Gesture	Proposal 2	
	Window 1	Window2
1	96.25% (2.25%↓)	96.00% (2.50%↓)
2	85.75% (9.75%↓)	87.00% (8.50%↓)
3	93.75% (4.25%↓)	94.50% (3.50%↓)
4	94.50% (3.00%↓)	93.25% (4.25%↓)
5	96.25% (3.00%↓)	97.75% (1.50%↓)
6	96.00% (2.75%↓)	96.75% (2.00%↓)
Ave.	93.75% (4.17%↓)	94.21% (3.71%↓)

Table 10. Computational time of methods.

Conventional	Proposal 1		Proposal 2	
	Window1	Window2	Window1	Window2
0.108715	0.109328	0.109716	0.163992	0.164874

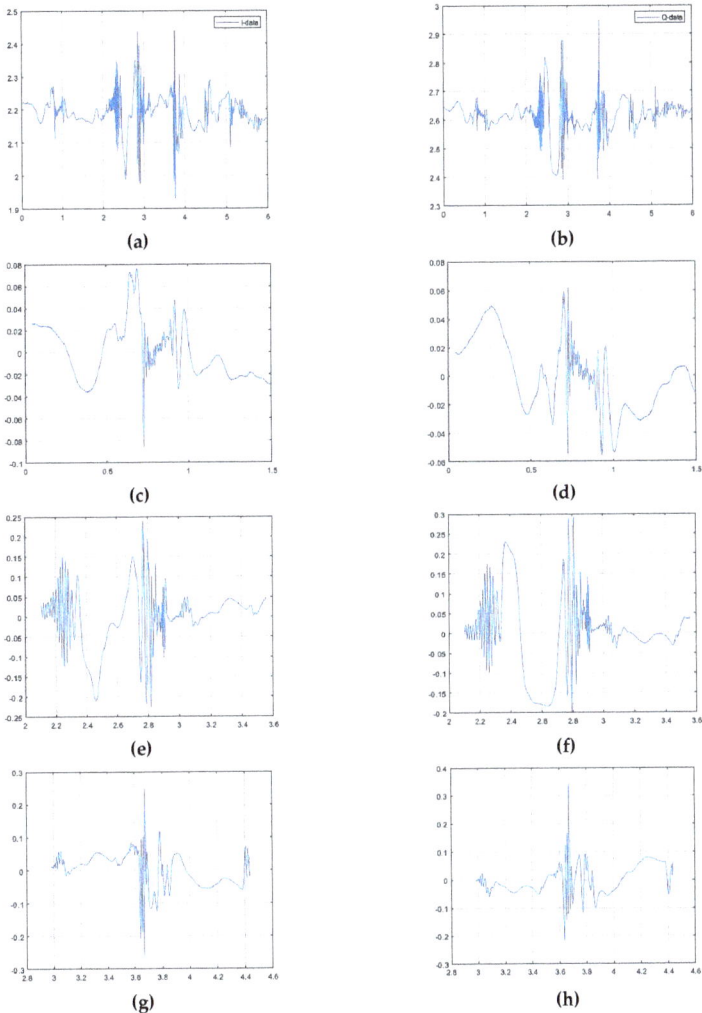

Figure 14. Detection probability of multiple hand gestures: (**a**) I-data of raw data; (**b**) Q-data of raw data; (**c**) I-data of the first hand gesture; (**d**) Q-data of the first hand gesture; (**e**) I-data of the second hand gesture; (**f**) Q-data of the second hand gesture; (**g**) I-data of the third hand gesture; (**h**) I-data of the third hand gesture.

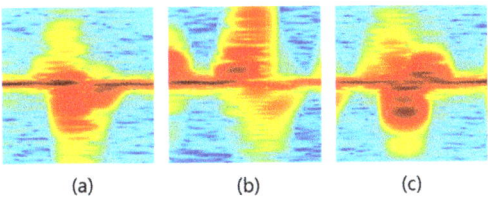

Figure 15. Spectrograms of multiple hand gestures: (**a**) spectrogram of the first hand gesture (right-to-left); (**b**) spectrogram of the second hand gesture (up-to-down); (**c**) spectrogram of the third hand gesture (finger stretch).

5. Conclusions

In this paper, we proposed a method to detect frames that can be used to construct a real-time hand gesture recognition system using CW radar. To measure the performance of the proposed method, experiments were performed to measure hand gesture with CW radar. Hand gesture performed four hundred measurements in six divisions. The measured hand gesture was created in spectrogram; the CNN model was constructed using that spectrogram. The recognition probability and the detection probability were defined using the constructed CNN model. The conventional method has a detection probability of up to 85.04% and a recognition probability of up to 85.29%. Also, the proposed method 1 has a detection probability of up to 86.92% and a recognition probability of up to 86.67%. Therefore, the conventional method and the proposed method 1 show a performance that was not sufficient to construct a real-time hand recognition system using CW radar. The proposed method 2 has a detection probability of up to 96.88% and a recognition probability of up to 94.21%. In conclusion, based on these performance measurements, we believe that the proposed method 2 could be used to construct a real-time hand gesture recognition system using CW radar. Future research will create a detection method that exhibits higher detection probability to construct a real-time hand gesture recognition system using CW radar. In the direction of other research, we plan to take a wide detection range and construct a CNN model that can improve the recognition probability even using a simple detection method.

Author Contributions: Conceptualization, S.L.; Formal analysis, N.K.; Investigation, M.Y.; Methodology, N.K. and Y.J.; Project administration, S.L.; Software, M.Y.; Supervision, S.L.; Writing—original draft, M.Y.; Writing—review & editing, N.K., Y.J. and S.L. All authors have read and agreed to the published version of the manuscript.

Funding: This research was supported by the National Research Foundation of Korea (NRF) grant funded by the Korea government (MOE) [Grant Number NRF-2017R1D1A1B03033422] and the MSIT (Ministry of Science and ICT), Korea, under the ITRC (Information Technology Research Center) support program (IITP-2020-2018-0-01423) supervised by the IITP (Institute for Information & communications Technology Promotion); the EDA tools were supported by the IC Design Education Center (IDEC), Korea.

Conflicts of Interest: The authors declare no conflict of interest.

References

1. Sonkusare, J.S.; Chopade, N.B.; Sor, R.; Tade, S.L. A review on hand gesture recognition system. In Proceedings of the 2015 International Conference on Computing Communication Control and Automation, Pune, India, 26–27 Febuary 2015.
2. Cheng, H.; Yang, L.; Liu, Z. Survey on 3D Hand Gesture Recognition. *IEEE Trans. Circuits Syst. Video Technol.* **2015**, *26*, 1659–1673. [CrossRef]
3. Sun, J.; Ji, T.; Zhang, S.; Yang, J.; Ji, G. Survey on 3D hand gesture recognition. In Proceedings of the IEEE International Conference 12th International Symposium on Antennas, Propagation and EM Theory, Hangzhou, China, 7 Febuary 2019.
4. Zhang, Y.; Cao, C.; Cheng, J.; Lu, H. EgoGesture: A new dataset and benchmark for egocentric hand gesture recognition. *IEEE Trans. Multimed.* **2018**, *20*, 1038–1050. [CrossRef]
5. Wang, C.; Liu, Z.; Chan, S. Superpixel-based hand gesture recognition with kinect depth camera. *IEEE Trans. Multimed.* **2014**, *17*, 29–39. [CrossRef]
6. Peng, J.; Xu, W.; Yan, L.; Pan, E.; Liang, B.; Wu, A. A pose measurement method of a space non-cooperative target based on maximum outer contour recognition. *IEEE Trans. Aerosp. Electron. Syst.* **2019**, *56*, 512–516. [CrossRef]
7. Peng, J.; Xu, W.; Yuan, H. An efficient pose measurement method of a space non-cooperative target based on stereo vision. *IEEE Access* **2017**, *5*, 22344–22362. [CrossRef]
8. Lian, K.; Chiu, C.; Hong, Y.; Sung, W. Wearable armband for real time hand gesture recognition. In Proceedings of the IEEE Internatonal Conference IEEE Internatonal Conference on Systems, Man, and Cybernetics, Banff, AB, Canada, 5–8 October 2017.

9. Siddiqui, N.; Chan, R.H.M. A wearable hand gesture recognition device based on acoustic measurements at wrist. In Proceedings of the IEEE International Conference 39th Annual International Conference of the IEEE Engineering in Medicine and Biology Society, Seogwipo, Korea, 11–15 July 2017.
10. Sakamoto, T.; Gao, X.; Yavari, E.; Rahman, A.; Boric-Lubecke, O.; Lubecke, V.M. Radar-based hand gesture recognition using I-Q echo plot and convolutional neural network. In Proceedings of the IEEE International Conference IEEE Conference on Antenna Measurements and Applications, Tsukuba, Japan, 4–6 December 2017.
11. Dekker, B.; Jacobs, S.; Kossen, A.S.; Kruithof, M.C.; Huizing, A.G.; Geurts, M. Gesture recognition with a low power FMCW radar and a deep convolutional neural network. In Proceedings of the IEEE International Conference European Radar Conference, Nuremberg, Germany, 11–13 October 2017.
12. Kim, S.; Han, H.; Kim, J.; Lee, S.; Kim, T. A hand gesture recognition sensor using reflected impulses. *IEEE Sens.* **2017**, *17*, 2975–2976. [CrossRef]
13. Zhang, S.; Li, G.; Ritchie, M.; Fioranelli, F.; Griffiths, H. Dynamic hand gesture classification based on radar micro-doppler signatures. In Proceedings of the IEEE International Conference CIE International Conference on Radar, Guangzhou, China, 10–13 October 2016.
14. Ryu, S.; Suh, J.; Baek, S.; Hong, S.; Kim, J. Feature-based hand gesture recognition using an fmcw radar and its temporal feature analysis. *IEEE Sens.* **2018**, *18*, 7593–7602. [CrossRef]
15. Zhang, Z.; Tian, Z.; Zhou, M. Latern: Dynamic continuous hand gesture recognition using FMCW radar sensor. *IEEE Sens.* **2018**, *18*, 3278–3289. [CrossRef]
16. Skaria, S.; Al-Hourani, A.; Lech, M.; Evans, R.J. Hand-gesture recognition using two-antenna doppler radar with deep convolutional neural networks. *IEEE Sens. J.* **2019**, *19*, 3041–3048. [CrossRef]
17. Kim, Y.; Toomajian, B. Application of Doppler Radar for the recognition of hand gestures using optimized deep convolutional neural networks. In Proceedings of the IEEE International Conference 11th European Conference on Antennas and Propagation, Paris, France, 19–24 March 2017.
18. Kim, Y.; Toomajian, B. Hand gesture recognition using micro-doppler signatureswith convolutional neural network. *IEEE Access* **2016**, *4*, 7125–7130. [CrossRef]
19. Choi, J.; Ryu, S.; Kim, J. Short-range radar based real-time hand gesture recognition using LSTM encoder. *IEEE Access* **2019**, *7*, 33610–33618. [CrossRef]
20. She, L.; Wang, G.; Zhang, S.; Zhao, J. An adaptive threshold algorithm combining shifting window difference and forward-backward difference in real-time r-wave detection. In Proceedings of the IEEE International Conference 2009 Internatonal Congress on Image and Signal Processing, Tianjin, China, 17–19 October 2009.

© 2020 by the authors. Licensee MDPI, Basel, Switzerland. This article is an open access article distributed under the terms and conditions of the Creative Commons Attribution (CC BY) license (http://creativecommons.org/licenses/by/4.0/).

Review

Motion Detection Using Tactile Sensors Based on Pressure-Sensitive Transistor Arrays

Jiuk Jang [1,2,3,†], **Yoon Sun Jun** [1,2,3,†], **Hunkyu Seo** [1,2,3,†], **Moohyun Kim** [1,2,3,†] **and Jang-Ung Park** [1,2,3,*]

1. Nano Science Technology Institute, Department of Materials Science and Engineering, Yonsei University, Seoul 03722, Korea; jiukjang@wearablelab.net (J.J.); yoonsun17@wearablelab.net (Y.S.J.); hunkyu1359@wearablelab.net (H.S.); moohyunkim@wearablelab.net (M.K.)
2. Center for Nanomedicine, Institute for Basic Science (IBS), Seoul 03722, Korea
3. Graduate Program of Nano Biomedical Engineering (NanoBME), Advanced Science Institute, Yonsei University, Seoul 03722, Korea
* Correspondence: jang-ung@yonsei.ac.kr; Tel.: +82-(0)2-2123-2851
† These authors contributed equally to this work.

Received: 1 June 2020; Accepted: 23 June 2020; Published: 28 June 2020

Abstract: In recent years, to develop more spontaneous and instant interfaces between a system and users, technology has evolved toward designing efficient and simple gesture recognition (GR) techniques. As a tool for acquiring human motion, a tactile sensor system, which converts the human touch signal into a single datum and executes a command by translating a bundle of data into a text language or triggering a preset sequence as a haptic motion, has been developed. The tactile sensor aims to collect comprehensive data on various motions, from the touch of a fingertip to large body movements. The sensor devices have different characteristics that are important for target applications. Furthermore, devices can be fabricated using various principles, and include piezoelectric, capacitive, piezoresistive, and field-effect transistor types, depending on the parameters to be achieved. Here, we introduce tactile sensors consisting of field-effect transistors (FETs). GR requires a process involving the acquisition of a large amount of data in an array rather than a single sensor, suggesting the importance of fabricating a tactile sensor as an array. In this case, an FET-type pressure sensor can exploit the advantages of active-matrix sensor arrays that allow high-array uniformity, high spatial contrast, and facile integration with electrical circuitry. We envision that tactile sensors based on FETs will be beneficial for GR as well as future applications, and these sensors will provide substantial opportunities for next-generation motion sensing systems.

Keywords: transistor; tactile sensor; pressure sensor; gesture recognition

1. Introduction

Since computer systems were first developed, they have been able to perform simple computing operations, as well as analysis and evaluation of the collected data. Gesture recognition (GR) is referred to as computer recognition and the digitization of human movement, such as the touch of a finger or the motion of a hand [1]. In recent years, to develop more spontaneous and instant interfaces between this system and users, technology has evolved that can design efficient and simple GR techniques. This advanced form of GR technology is essential for quick command systems and feedback between computers and people in real situations, such as computer games and machine control. As the computational speed and amount of data that can be processed increase, these interfaces can be applied to advanced functions, including big data-based behavior models and robotics, followed by expansion of GR applications to the public.

In terms of the data collection method, GR can be largely divided into contact and non-contact interfaces. In the case of non-contact interfaces, most are based on tracking visual signals [2,3]. Signal processing is conducted by recognizing a specific part of the user and consequently analyzing the pose of the object. However, this method requires extensive use of the camera roll (e.g., the photodetector), and it depends significantly on environmental changes, such as brightness and humidity. In addition, it provides poor signal accuracy and currently has many limitations for handling numerous signals in series. Therefore, this form of GR is used mainly with arranged gestures at a predetermined location. In contrast, the command system, with its contact interface, consists of direct contact between the user and machines. The invention of the keyboard and mouse as input devices suggests that the principal and standard means of human interaction with a machine is the detection of tactile stimulations. Generally, the system converts the signal created by human touch into a single datum, and executes the command by translating a bundle of data into a text language or by triggering a preset sequence as a haptic motion. Compared to vision-based signal processing, the touch-based contact interface has a similar processing flow, but has less complexity, a small signal, and substantially better intuition.

After the development of principal input devices, predominantly keyboards, user interface technology has been developed and refined further with the emergence of a smartphone implemented with a touch sensor that enables the provision of information for the machine (i.e., the circuitry system) by a touch of a finger [4,5]. Among future technologies, GR has attracted attention as a key technology for facile communications with machines. Due to these industrial and research trends, research has been accelerated on motion sensing systems, which consist of tactile detection in various fields, such as robotics [6,7], artificial intelligence (AI) [8,9], human-machine interface (HMI), [10–12], and Internet of Things (IoT) [13]. Users can perform complex tasks through the provision of motion, including simple touch, and such systems can also exhibit very high efficiency, particularly in terms of augmented reality (AR) and virtual reality (VR). The characteristics required for effective motion sensing are (1) the sensitivity of the motion sensing device, (2) the size of the threshold for tactile stimulus, and (3) the speed with which the device can respond to the stimulus. These characteristics are considered important for fundamental GR performance. For example, the device developed for a GR application must be able to detect several tens of kilopascals (kPas) because the tactile pressure of a gentle human touch is in the range of 10 to 100 kPa. In addition, the realization of 3D touch technology, which can convert the magnitude of tactile pressures to other factors, such as the thickness of a line, should consider the sensitivity factor that affects how many steps the pen pressure can be divided into. Numerous studies have been reported on the assumption that the target application is based on a pen or finger touch, and have focused mainly on measuring more sensitive and wider ranges. In addition, the time delay from the moment of tactile touch until the device responds and the reliability of multiple contacts are significant factors in assessing the validity of the sensor.

Recently, tactile sensors for GR have been developed to provide convenience to users and acquire additional information by integrating various functions in addition to the detection of touch. As an example, a device exists that can detect a normal force and a shear force simultaneously, thereby providing detailed information about human touch. In addition, integrated tactile sensors for visual and auditory feedback to users are attracting attention in the field of human–machine interfaces [14]. Proximity sensors that can detect approaching objects can also be representative tactile sensors for sensing motion. Their principle follows that of a contact interface-based tactile sensor, but can also be used as a non-contact interface. In addition, advanced fabrication techniques have been studied in order to produce a highly-integrated, multi-functional sensor device [15–18]. As the development of flexible and stretchable electronics-based technologies has accelerated, tactile sensors are being developed that can operate even in harsh environments where reliable mechanical deformations, such as bending and stretching, are required [19–23]. These characteristics will provide a substantial technical basis for next-stage augmented reality and virtual reality (Figure 1).

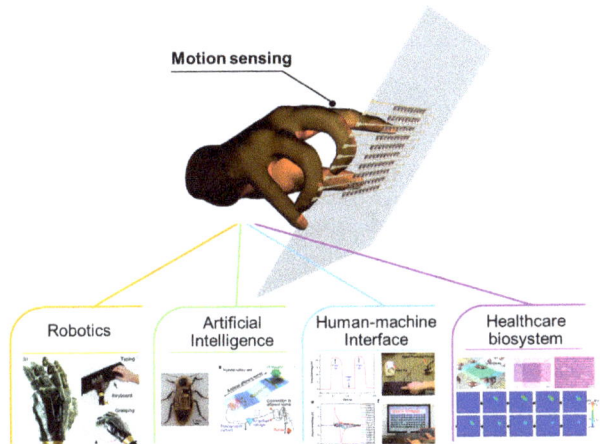

Figure 1. Tactile sensors for motion sensing. Reproduced with permission [24]. Copyright 2014, Springer Nature. Reproduced with permission [9]. Copyright 2018, American Association for the Advancement of Science. Reproduced with permission [10]. Copyright 2015, American Chemical Society. Reproduced with permission [25]. Copyright 2020, American Chemical Society.

2. Tactile Sensor Arrays

Tactile sensors can collect comprehensive data on various motions of the human body, from the touch of a fingertip to the movements of the entire body. The sensor devices have different characteristics that are important for target applications, and can be fabricated using various principles. The forms include piezoelectric [26,27], capacitive [28–30], piezoresistive [31,32] and field-effect transistor types, depending on the parameters to be achieved [33–36]. Here, we present basic information about the tactile sensor array device, which is used extensively as a tool for recognizing gestures, so that readers can gain a better understanding of the fundamental mechanisms involved.

2.1. Parameters of Tactile Sensors and Their Arrays

A tactile sensor is a device that acquires the applied force quantitatively as an electrical signal or some other indicator. Parameters for evaluating tactile sensors include their sensitivity, range of detectable pressure, minimum sensing pressure, response and recovery times, and reliability [33]. Sensitivity is the most intuitive parameter that can display the accuracy and characteristics of the tactile pressure sensor. The sensitivity of the pressure sensor is defined as follows:

$$S = \Delta X / \Delta P \tag{1}$$

where S is sensitivity, X is an arbitrary conversion signal (e.g., current, voltage, or capacitance), and P is pressure. High sensitivity suggests that a high-magnitude conversion signal can be obtained with only a small change in the input signal, which is an advantage when fine pressures must be measured. From the perspective of the recognition of motion and gestures, human motion can include a comprehensive range of movements, ranging from a feathery touch of the fingertip to large movements, such as footsteps or jumping. Therefore, it is better for the detectable tactile pressure range for data acquisition to cover a wide range, i.e., from subtle pressure to high pressure for the target application, because this will provide advantages in the use of a pressure sensor for sensing motion.

Response time is considered to be an important factor for real-time and repetitive detection, and refers to the time that is required to reach more than 90% of the output signal after the application of tactile pressure. Generally, pressure sensors can be approximated by first-order differential equations for time as follows:

$$X = X_{max}\left(1 - e^{-\frac{t}{c}}\right) \quad (2)$$

where X is an arbitrary conversion signal, X_{max} is 100% of the conversion signal for a specific stimulus, t is time, and c is a time constant for the sensor device.

For the recognition of motion, a tactile sensor device should be integrated as a large-scale or high-resolution two-dimensional (2D) array. The array-type pressure sensor scans a plurality of pixels over time, and this array device, which has a large number of pixels, may have limitations due to the time delay associated with the successive scan times for each of the pixels. Therefore, fast response time and the fast recovery time of individual pixels are essential to acquire array data simultaneously. In the case of an array device, the uniformity of the previously-mentioned parameters (e.g., sensitivity and range of detectable pressures) should be considered when the device is used in industrial applications.

As advanced, human-friendly electronics evolve, including wearable electronics, robotics, and artificial intelligence, motion sensing devices are being integrated radially into wearable devices with flexible or skin-attachable forms, and this can require a high level of reliability against mechanical deformation and cyclic folding and stretching.

2.2. Various Types of Tactile Sensors

Tactile sensors for converting tactile stimuli into electrical signals (e.g., current, voltage, capacitance) are being developed based on various principles, such as piezoresistive, piezoelectric, capacitive, optical, and transistors, in accordance with the purpose of the target application. Figure 2 shows the fundamental schematics of the types of tactile sensors with their transduction principles.

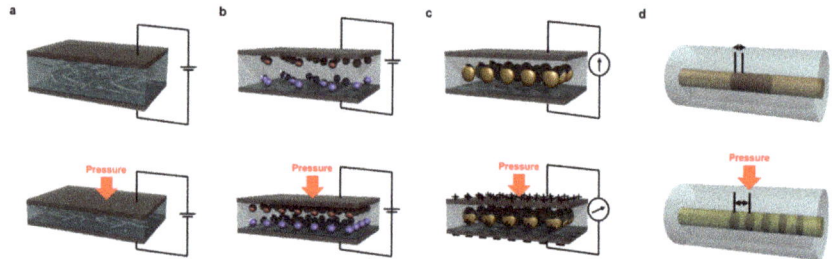

Figure 2. Schematic illustrations of transduction mechanisms of tactile sensors: (**a**) piezoresistivity; (**b**) capacitance; (**c**) piezoelectricity; (**d**) optics.

The transduction principle of a piezoresistive tactile sensor is to convert the change in the resistance of the device due to the application of external pressure into an electrical signal, with the current flowing mainly along the sensors. This mechanism is similar to that of a resistive tactile sensor, which utilizes change in contact resistance between two conductors upon physical force. These devices are fabricated from simple interlocked microstructures where physical deformation leads to change in contact resistance. Devices utilizing the piezoresistive principle have been studied in various forms and materials due to their excellent linearity, simple structure, method of operation, and the convenience of processing the output signal due to the facile mechanism [37–40]. Piezoresistive tactile sensors are suitable for measuring large pressure stimuli. These devices are mainly made using the complicated serpentine pattern of thin-film metal or the changes in the conducting path by three-dimensional percolation networks of one-dimensional or two-dimensional metal filler, such as metal nanoparticles and nanowires, within the elastomer matrix, inducing the resistance changes that are followed by current changes. Generally, compared to other types of devices, piezoresistive tactile sensors have fast response time and wide ranges in which they can detect pressure.

Piezoelectric-type tactile sensors use materials that induce changes in the internal electric dipole moment due to the pressure as their active materials [41]. This type of sensor has relatively high sensitivity and fast response time, and such sensors easily can be utilized for measuring dynamic pressure, such as vibration and friction [42–44]. A tactile sensor using a triboelectric material also generates triboelectric potential due to the friction and electrification with electrostatic induction, which broadly can be included in the piezoelectric method [45,46]. A triboelectric material-based device can detect various types of forces, including normal and shear forces, because of the friction-based potential changes within the material. However, these active materials are generally affected by external environments, such as temperature, because, in most cases, their piezoelectric properties are accompanied by pyroelectric properties [47], so these limitations must be solved when the device is used as a wearable device.

Optical operation mechanisms, such as light wavelength, phase, polarization, color, and intensity, are other mechanisms for flexible pressure sensors [48–50]. A tactile sensor using an optical mechanism prevents stray capacitances and thermal noise, and has lower crosstalk and a high spatial solution. Despite of these properties, medium power consumption is a representative problem of optical mechanisms, so this problem should be addressed for the future technology of tactile sensors [51].

Capacitive devices detect the tensile stimuli by sensing the change in capacitance that naturally is formed in an insulating layer between two conductive plates [52,53]. When the thickness of a material changes due to the pressure that is applied between two parallel plate electrodes, the distance between the two plates is changed by physical contact, and this results in a change in capacitance due to changes in the distance between the electrodes. This device has a simple structure and is particularly easy to make into an array structure, so many studies have used this structure when developing an array-type tactile sensor [54–58]. Even though there are various tactile sensors with several principles, they have several limitations in their applications in GR technology since the data acquisition system is unable to fully analyze the motion-detection data and capacitance data are hard to handle in constructing a measurement system compared to the current or voltage system. Furthermore, sensor arrays using these three types of transduction mechanism are controlled electrically by addressing the passive matrix, which cannot prevent the low contrast ratio and the crosstalk effect. Therefore, there is a need to identify solutions to these issues and provide direction for the future development of the technology.

2.3. Field Effect Transistor (FET)-Based Tactile Sensor Arrays

Gesture recognition and motion sensing require a specific process, such as acquiring a large amount of data in an array rather than using a single sensor, and this suggests the importance of fabricating a tactile sensor as an array [59–61]. At this time, in order to manufacture a device in the form of an active matrix, an FET array must be added to each sensor pixel. The FET is a transistor that controls the magnitude of current using an electric field applied inside the device. Therefore, by placing the FET in each pixel and connecting electrodes with terminals of the FET to measure the current flowing, independent information can be obtained from each pixel. Since the integration of an FET as a component of a tactile sensor array was reported by the Someya et al. (2014) [62], the role of FETs in tactile sensor arrays has begun to grow.

An FET-type pressure sensor can exploit the advantages of active-matrix sensor arrays that allow high-array uniformity, high spatial contrast, and facile integration with electrical circuitry [63]. Figure 3 shows typical tactile sensor arrays utilizing an FET. First, the FET can be added on the source or drain electrode, so that the current modulation has a direct effect on the drain current. Second, FET materials can be reconstructed using the piezoelectric or triboelectric materials as channel materials within the FET. Third, the gate dielectric layer of the FET can be modified as an elastomer, such as polydimethylsiloxane (PDMS, Dow Corning) or Ecoflex 0030. By integrating FETs with the pressure-sensor array, large-scale fabrication is made much easier and the consumption of power is reduced due to the extremely low off-current compared to the previously-mentioned pressure sensors. Further, the intrinsic implementation of FETs enables the device to operate as an active-matrix array;

therefore, the specific characteristics of an active matrix, such as low crosstalk and high contrast ratio, are accompanied by the integration. As a result, FET-type pressure sensors make it easy to realize future sensor systems in terms of the GR.

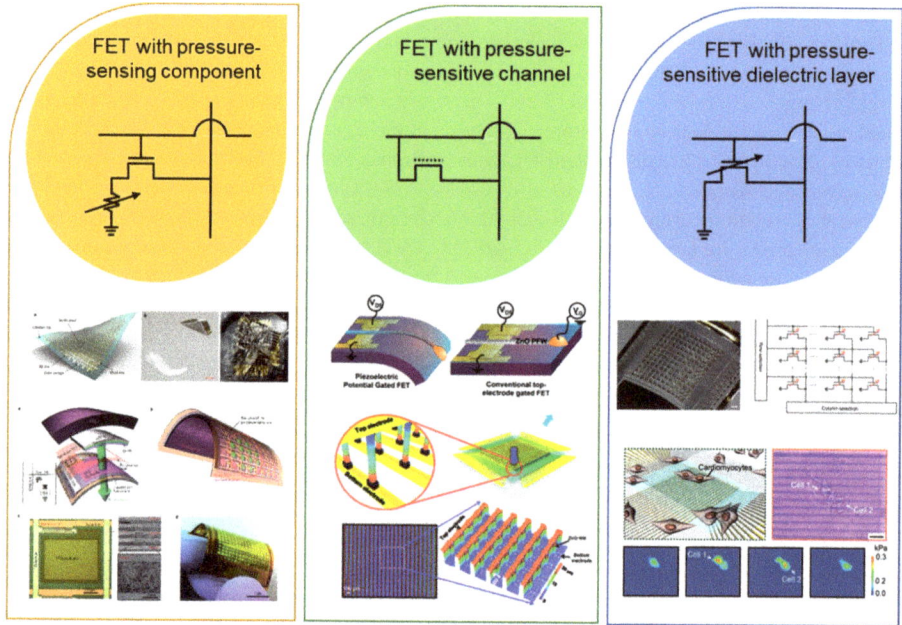

Figure 3. Representative tactile sensor arrays with active-matrix driving with circuits. Reproduced with permission [63]. Copyright 2013, Springer Nature. Reproduced with permission [64]. Copyright 2019, Springer Nature. Reproduced with permission [65]. Copyright 2010, Elsevier. Reproduced with permission [66]. Copyright 2013, American Association for the Advancement of Science. Reproduced with permission [67]. Copyright 2017, Springer Nature. Reproduced with permission [15]. Copyright 2020, American Chemical Society.

3. Pressure-Sensitive Transistor Arrays

Pressure-sensitive transistor arrays were first theorized using a transistor as an electronic on–off switch for tactile sensing applications. The presence of an isolated, pressure-sensitive component that stimulates and controls the drain current of the transistor array can be classified as an extrinsic, pressure-sensitive device. Someya et al. (2004) demonstrated the nature of this application using a pressure-sensitive component as an intermediate resistance variable between the source and drain electrodes [62]. The change in the value of the drain current of the transistor arrays with respect to the resistance variations in the pressure-sensitive component when strain was applied has provided a 2D visualization of pressure-sensing detection. The integration of pressure-sensitive rubber (PSR) and organic field effect transistors have been reported to be first modifications of such tactile sensing applications. In recent work, there have been attempts to evaluate the idea of a transistor array-integrated sensor device. The concept of an intrinsic, pressure-sensitive device implements direct dynamic change in the electrical output of field effect transistors upon onset of physical strain, thereby increasing the on–off ratio and sensitivity of such sensor devices. By removing the need for the integration of pressure-sensitive components, intrinsic pressure-sensitive devices are less complex and provide superior mechanoelectrical output readings. This novel pressure-sensitive FET device has shown enhanced detection capabilities, detecting even up to cellular motion [15]. These sensor devices have achieved high signal-to-noise ratios in active-matrix pressure detection while maintaining their excellent mechanical properties. Table 1 presents the representative studies on the active-matrix transistor arrays for tactile pressure sensing.

3.1. FET-Based Tactile Sensor Arrays with Pressure-Sensing Components

There are two strategies involved in the application of extrinsic pressure-sensitive transistor devices in active-matrix motion sensing. First, the structural design and layout implementation of pressure-sensing components are specified in a way that yield mechanoelectrical readings that correspond to an applied force. These components are connected to data scan lines that transfer their mechanoelectrical outputs into transistor arrays. These transistor arrays enable the determination of the pressure-sensing specifications and sensitivities of these pressure-sensing devices. Another experimental strategy uses novel materials that are susceptible and receptive to physical stimuli. These novel materials intrinsically enable electrical signals when paired with a transistor array, which enhances the capability to sense pressure. However, these transistor devices are not affected dynamically by mechanical stimuli; instead, the electrical signal from the drain current is enhanced when these pressure-sensing components are deformed. Other work on pressure-sensing devices has used piezoelectric [68–70], capacitive [71,72], triboelectric [73,74], piezoelectric [75,76], and optical methods [77,78] as the mechanoelectrical mechanism to detect physical stimuli. However, the use of such materials in pressure-sensing devices has shown overall mechanical limitations. These materials also have shown difficulty in producing large-scale active-matrix application for tactile pressure sensing compared to transistor-based sensor devices. Transistor-based pressure sensors have been proven to have lower power consumption enabled by high on–off ratio, low signal cross-talk, and dynamic mechanoelectrical physical detection, as well as enhanced sensitivities of the sensor devices. When implemented onto thin polymer films, these devices showed a promising degree of flexibility and transparency.

Table 1. Comparison of active-matrix transistor array device for tactile pressure sensing.

	Device Composition	Pressure-Sensing Range	Response Time	Spatial Resolution	Sensitivity	Reference
Structure-Modified	PSR	Minimal pressure down to 1 kPa		12 × 12		[63]
Structure-Modified	2D graphene sheet	5 kPa~40 kPa		4 × 4	0.12 kPa^{-1}	[59]
Structure-Modified	PZT		0.1 ms	8 × 8	0.005 Pa^{-1}	[79]
Structure-Modified	AgNWs	0–10 kPa	10 ms		1090 kPa^{-1}	[80]
Material-Modified	PSR	2–15 kPa		32 × 32		[62]
Material-Modified	PSR		0.1 s	19 × 18	~11.5 µS kPa^{-1}	[81]
Material-Modified	Carbon-nanotube, PSR	1–7.2 kPa	<30 ms	20 × 20	~800% kPa^{-1}	[82]
Material-Modified	OLED, PSR	5–98 kPa	1 ms	16 × 16	~42.7 Cd m^{-2} kPa^{-1}	[64]
Material-Modified	Ferroelectric nanoparticle	2–22 MPa				[83]

3.1.1. Transistor with Structure-Modified, Pressure-Resistive Component

Due to their intrinsic high on–off ratios and superior mechanoelectrical properties, transistors are used in tactile pressure sensors as electrical signal enhancers to pressure-sensing components. With the increasing interest in flexible sensor electronics, an array of transistors is placed on thin polymer films to fabricate ideal flexible sensor devices. Structure-modified extrinsic pressure sensors are designed in a way that the array of transistors is isolated from the pressure-sensing components. The array of transistors works solely as an electrical signal enhancer for the mechanoelectrical outputs of pressure-sensitive components. The change in the value of the drain current with the onset of external pressure via these components is the basic principle that governs the detection of the active-matrix pressure of these pressure sensors.

One work that demonstrated the use of a structure-modified, pressure-resistive component was the implementation of a transistor matrix array with a resistive tactile sensor (Figure 4a). Kaltenbrunner et al. (2013) demonstrated a 12 × 12 active-matrix tactile sensor array by integrating the transistor array with the physically receptive components [63]. This tactile pressure sensor has shown promising mechanical properties due to its ultra-thin dimension and deformation durability. The authors reported a high on–off ratio ($\sim 10^7$), indicating low power consumption, which is similar to most transistor-based sensor devices. This device can detect pressures are low as 1 kPa when using the pressure-sensitive, rubber-layer lamination. However, this device has limitations in detecting objects with non-conducting surfaces. Hence, pressure-sensitive rubber is laminated onto the tactile sensing array to detect non-conducting objects. Another work by Sun et al. (2014) used a 2D graphene sheet over a serpentine source channel as a structural modification to an array of tactile transistors [59]. The use of graphene enabled high transparency (80%) while maintaining excellent mechanical properties, such as a sensitivity of 0.12 kPa^{-1} and durability exceeding 2500 cycles. The 4 × 4 matrix showed a minimal pressure detection down to 5 kPa and a maximum of 40 kPa as the contact region between the source channel and the graphene sheet increased gradually after 5 kPa. However, the use of the ion-gel gate dielectric in this device limited its high range pressure detection. Similar to most transistor-based tactile sensors, this device had low power consumption, which was enabled by its high on–off ratio. Dagdeviren et al. (2014) developed a similar structure-modified transistor array sensor using piezoelectric material (Figure 4b) [79]. The device uses an 8 × 8 array of lead zirconate titanate (PZT) as the physically receptive component to a transistor amplifier for drain current output. This array is connected to the gate electrode of an adjacent FET, which enables the capability to sense pressure. The piezoelectric responses from the PZT with the onset of pressure control the value of the gate voltage of the connected transistor, ultimately giving a range of drain current values respective to their applied pressures. Although this device had a superior sensitivity of 0.005 Pa^{-1} and a response time of 0.1 ms, it was unable to detect tactile pressure when the PZT array was connected to a single transistor. Hence, the operational model of this device is not feasible for the detection of tactile pressure in a large area. The work by Chen et al. (2017) demonstrated a similar mechanism, but they used silver nanowires to alter the value of the drain current of the connected transistor [80]. The mechanical deformation of PDMS containing silver nanowires (AgNWs) induces a resistance change in the gate channel. This ultimately affects the drain current value in the transistor, thereby enabling the detection of mechanoelectrical pressure. The mechanical property of this pressure device seems relatively inferior to the previously mentioned devices, e.g., it exhibited a sensitivity of 1090 kPa^{-1}, a response time of 10 ms, and a low sensing range of 0–10 kPa. However, when selenophene–diketopyrrolopyrrole donor–acceptor conjugated polymer (PSeDPP) was used as the intermediate layer in the transistor, nonvolatile memory storing capability was enabled, thereby suggesting a new direction towards advanced functional applications.

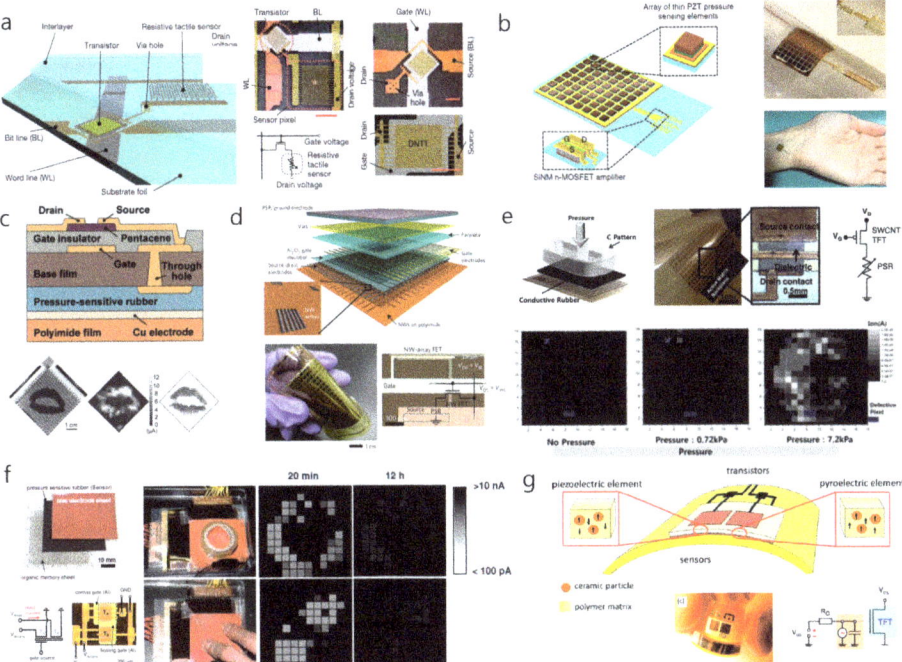

Figure 4. Field-effect transistor (FET)-based tactile sensor arrays with pressure-sensing components. (**a**) Active-matrix tactile pixel sensor comprising a switching transistor and a resistive touch sensor. (**b**) Thin conformal array pressure sensor made of elements of zirconate titanate (PZT) with transistor amplified pressure-sensing capability. (**c**) Tactile pressure sensor with pressure-sensitive component in its active-matrix transistor array. (**d**) Nanowire-based flexible tactile pressure sensor with pressure-sensitive rubber (PSR)-integrated active-matrix transistor array. (**e**) Tactile pressure sensor with carbon nanotube backplane integrated with active-matrix transistor array. (**f**) Nonvolatile tactile pressure sensor with active-matrix two-transistor array with intermediate pressure-sensitive rubber sheet. (**g**) Bifunctional sensor array with flexible ceramic polymer sensor laminated onto transistor backplane. (**a**) Reproduced with permission [80]. Copyright 2013, Springer Nature. (**b**) Reproduced with permission [79]. Copyright 2014, Springer Nature. (**c**) Reproduced with permission [62]. Copyright 2004, National Academy of Sciences. (**d**) Reproduced with permission [81]. Copyright 2010, Springer Nature. (**e**) Reproduced with permission [82]. Copyright 2015, John Wiley and Sons. (**f**) Reproduced with permission [84]. Copyright 2009, The American Association for the Advancement of Science. (**g**) Reproduced with permission [83]. Copyright 2009, Journal of Applied Physics.

3.1.2. Transistor Arrays with a Material-Modified, Pressure-Sensitive Component

Another strategy engineered to create transistor-based, tactile, sensor arrays with pressure-sensing components is to incorporate novel materials that are highly susceptible to physical stimuli into the infrastructure of the transistor. Pressure-sensitive rubber and piezoelectric, ferroelectric, and carbon-based materials commonly are used to enhance or induce the drain current values of transistors in functional sensor devices. The incorporation of these materials induces mechano-electrical readings in arrays of transistors that are related to the physical stimuli applied to the array of transistors. However, devices that are fabricated by orienting the materials of the pressure-sensitive components have increased parasitic capacitance due to the metal interconnections, limited mechanical durability, and limited response speeds.

The first ideal development of an active-matrix array of transistors incorporated with pressure-sensitive components was undertaken (Figure 4c) [62]. A 32 × 32 array of organic field-effect transistors was integrated with pressure-sensitive rubber. The increases in the applied pressure and strain reduced the resistance of the PSR, thereby increasing the value of the drain current of its corresponding transistor. The correlation between physical stimuli and the output drain current enables the transistor array to function as a tactile pressure sensor. Because the sensitivity and response time of a transistor is limited by the PSR, a relatively inferior data collection time was observed in this study when the mechano-electrical mechanism was used. Despite the disappointing performance, high on–off ratios (~10^6) have been reported for this device, as is the case for most transistor-based pressure-sensor devices. Takei et al. (2010) reported a tactile pressure-sensor device that used a pressure-sensitive-rubber integrated field-effect-transistor array (Figure 4d) [81]. This 19 × 18 matrix sensor used parallel Ge/Si NW arrays as the active-matrix backplane to achieve superior mechanical properties despite its slow response time, i.e., ~0.1 s. The conductance change in the PSR, via the shortened tunneling path between the carbon nanoparticles when a physical stimulus is applied, induces high sensitivity to the normal pressure that is applied to the tactile sensor. However, the main limitation of this device seems to be the highly sophisticated steps in its integration process. Defective pixels frequently occur during the production of devices due to the defective sensitivities of the materials used in NW printing and the lithography procedure. Like all transistor-based tactile pressure sensors, this device has low power consumption (<5 V) and superior pressure-sensing capability (2–15 kPa). Yeom et al. (2015) reported a similar device with 20 × 20 active-matrix sensor device that uses a single-wall, carbon-nanotube thin-film transistor backplane with PSR as its conductive pressure-sensitive layer (Figure 4e) [82]. This tactile sensor shows promise for application in large-area tactile pressure sensing, with its pressure range of 1 to 7.2 kPa. With its physically durable, carbon-based layer, the device also demonstrated moderate durability during bending. Its mechano-electrical sensing capability is also notable with a response time of less than 30 ms during 1000 operation cycles. However, similar to the device constructed by Takei et al.'s group, the device exhibits high yield of defective pixels, which is induced by its sophisticated production procedures. The use of organic light-emitting diodes (OLED) in a pressure sensor based on a tactile array of transistors was demonstrated by Wang et al.'s group (2013) [64]. In addition, their device incorporated PSR and OLED layers into the bottom, thin-film transistor backplane as pressure-sensitive components. These 16 × 16 active-matrix devices use light emitted by OLED, with the intensity of the light corresponding to the magnitude of the pressure that is applied. The PSR acts as a pressure contact surface, which enhances the yield of energy transfer from the applied pressure to the intensity of the light emitted by the OLED. The light emitted by the OLED is irradiated onto an indium tin oxide (ITO) electrode that is connected to the data line of the transistor. Using light as an intermediate form of data transfer allowed the device to achieve visual tactile pressure mapping and relatively low response time that was comparable to those of other PSR incorporated devices (i.e., ~1 ms). Likewise, the transistor-based pressure-sensor device enhanced the range for sensing pressure to 5–98 kPa. Although the instantaneous visual representation of tactile pressure sensing without secondary data processing is favorable in a practical platform application, the presence of the multi-layer composition and the fragile ITO layer limit its flexibility and mechanical durability. Sekitani et al.'s group (2009) bonded a conducting PSR film onto a floating-gate transistor array sheet to fabricate a non-volatile, tactile pressure sensor (Figure 4f) [84]. This 26 × 26 active-matrix device provides an independent PSR layer between the electrode sheet and the organic memory sheet to enable the application of erasable memory. The intermediate, pressure-sensitive rubber sheet acts as an element of a pressure-sensitive component to the transistor memory sheet below. The combination of the memory transistor array sheet and the pressure-sensor rubber (PSR) sheet enables the detection of tactile pressure. Since the novelty of this device was to allow the visualization of nonvolatile 2D tactile pressure, its ability to sense active pressure was somewhat limited. The response time and pressure-sensing range of devices that incorporate PSR clearly show their limitations. Graz et al. (2006) created a similar, material-dependent, pressure-sensing array, but they used ferroelectric materials as the pressure-sensitive components [85]. They reported a modulation in the value of the drain current when the polymer matrix film, which contained ferroelectric pressure-sensitive material, was connected to the gate electrode and stimulated physically. The piezoelectric property of the pressure-sensing component contributes to the mechano-electrical mechanism of the device. The transistor sensor that was fabricated showed a promising on–off ratio of $\sim 10^7$ and a significant pressure-sensing range from 2 to 400 kPa. Despite these qualities, this device lacks flexibility, transparency, and reasonable spatial resolution. Similar to the PSR-incorporated device, this work also showed slow response speed during operation, a low signal-to-noise ratio, and low sensitivity. Subsequent work by this group, in which a ferroelectric pressure-sensing component was used, showed slight modification (Figure 4g) [83]. The pressure-sensitive components were based on both piezoelectric and pyroelectric properties, and were connected to a single transistor of the sensor device. This incorporation allowed bifunctional sensing capability, i.e., detecting pressure and temperature independently within the device. The pressure-sensitive component was composed of a ferroelectric polymer that was embedded with piezoelectric nanoparticles, so it displayed both piezoelectric and pyroelectric properties based on its polarity direction-orientation. This sensor consisting of an array of transistors had a superior pressure-sensing range, i.e., 2–22 MPa, which was comparable to the group's previous work. However, the operational stability of all piezoelectric devices is strictly limited by external environmental conditions, and the operation response time is also strictly limited. The measurement of physical stimuli by characterizing the mechano-electrical properties of pressure-sensitive components, such as PSR, has limitations in obtaining fast response speed. By existing as an intermediate sensing layer, PSR has slowed the overall operational speed of these sensor devices. The presence of a pressure-sensitive element seemingly increases the complexity of the devices and ultimately degrades the overall mechano-electrical sensing efficiency of such sensor devices. This, in addition to the naturally slow mechanical property of PSR, slows the operational response speed of pressure detection in extrinsic pressure-sensing FET array devices. Transistor arrays that have intrinsic pressure-sensing capability seem to correct this disability. Dynamic pressure detection by changing the structures of transistor arrays has simplified the overall pressure-sensing process by eliminating the need for a separate component for sensing pressure.

3.2. Pressure-Sensitive Transistor Arrays

An active-matrix structure is required to optimize the pressure sensor in the form of an array [86]. This means that external pressure-sensitive components must be implemented with transistors. Devices of this type accompany the benefits of an active matrix. However, these devices can exhibit some disadvantages, such as a complicated process and low spatial resolution. Therefore, we introduced a transistor array in which the components that make up the transistor are affected by pressure [35]. Unlike the devices introduced above, these devices have gate dielectric materials or channel materials that are sensitive to pressure, and the drain current is modulated by pressure without external pressure-sensitive components. The transistor array without external components has the advantage of an active matrix and can compensate for the shortcomings that have been mentioned. Triboelectric materials and piezoelectric materials were used to make the transistor array pressure sensitive, and the electrical properties of these materials change when pressure is applied [87]. Polarization occurs inside the piezoelectric material by physical deformation. Polarization is caused by the structure of the material, which leads to the piezopotential. The phenomenon in which piezoelectric potential is generated by mechanical force, as described above, is referred to as the piezoelectric effect, and piezoelectric pressure sensors use this piezoelectric effect. The magnitude of the drain current is changed by using the piezopotential directly or by using the generated electric field. Piezoelectric sensors have high sensitivity and fast response time. When the triboelectric material is in contact, electrostatic induction occurs through contact electrification to form a triboelectric charge. A potential difference occurs between two electrodes due to the triboelectric charge. When the triboelectric charge generates a current, the pressure can be measured. The triboelectric sensor has the advantages of low cost, easy process, and simple mechanism. Having the dielectric layer deformable by pressure is another way to make a pressure-sensitive transistor array [67]. In this case, an elastic material generally is generally used as the dielectric layer. When the dielectric layer is deformed under pressure, the distance between the gate and the channel of the transistor changes. The decrease in the distance due to mechanical force causes an increase in the capacitance of the device. The width of the channel increases due to higher capacitance, which results in increased drain current. The pressure applied can be detected by measuring the change in the drain current. This type of pressure-sensitive transistor array has the advantages of fast response time and a wide detection range.

3.2.1. Options for Transistor Channel Materials

In general, transistors with pressure-sensitive channels use materials with piezoelectric or triboelectric properties. Piezoelectric or triboelectric materials are used in the form of strain-gated transistors. Chen et al. (2016) fabricated strain-gated field effect transistors using MoS_2 and ZnO (Figure 5a) [86]. The transistor with ZnO nanowire placed over the channel makes the device pressure sensitive. When piezoelectric ZnO is pressed and polarization occurs inside, an electric field is generated as presented in other work [88]. Therefore, the drain current increases as the width of the channel increases. The pressure measurement was possible up to about 6.25 MPa. Yang et al. (2016) used triboelectric properties to fabricate a pressure sensor (Figure 5b) [89]. The device is called a tribotronic transistor array (TTA). Polytetrafluoroethylene was used as a mobile friction layer to induce charge upon contact with the electrode under pressure. The sensitivity of the device is 1.029/mm, and it can detect distances up to 9 mm based on the distance between the electrode and the polytetrafluoroethylene (PTFE).

Piezotronic transistors, which have been made simpler using piezoelectric properties in the form of conventional transistors, also are being studied [65,90]. Piezotronics basically have a structure in which a semiconductor material is placed between metal electrodes. A semiconductor is piezoelectric and usually made in nanowire form. When a piezoelectric nanowire is inserted between two metal electrodes, it may contract or relax under pressure. At the interface where the metal and semiconductor are in contact, the movement of charge is limited by the barrier. When the deformation occurs, a piezopotential is generated by nonmobile ions in the nanowire. This piezopotential changes the height of the barrier at the interface. As the height of the barrier decreases, the transfer of charges at the interface becomes easier. The basic principle is that the change in the magnitude of the piezopotential due to deformation controls the transfer of charge. Piezotronic transistors differ from conventional FETs in two ways. First, the gate component is not required because the channel material controls the charge transfer in the channel. Second, charge transfer is controlled by the movement of the charge at the interface, not by the width of the channel.

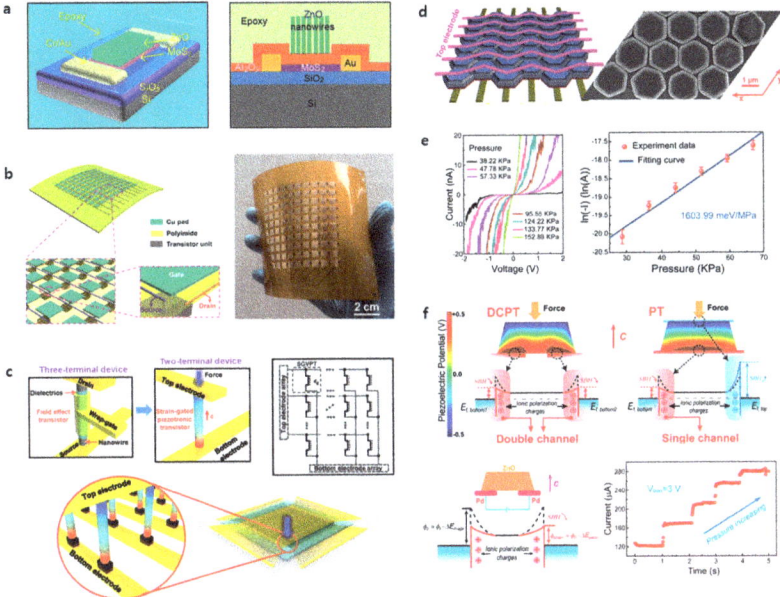

Figure 5. Transistor array using pressure-sensitive channel materials. (**a**) Schematic illustration of a FET based on a MoS$_2$ and ZnO heterostructure (left). Schematic cartoon graphs of the architecture of the device that uses the ZnO nanowire (NW) array and MoS$_2$ flake, separated by a 20-nm atomic layer deposition (ALD)-deposited Al$_2$O$_3$ layer. (**b**) Schematic of a 10 × 10 tribotronic transistor array (TTA) (left). Partial enlarged tilted views of the TTA configuration and pixel structure, respectively (inset). Optical photograph of a fully integrated TTA with each sensing pixel of 5 × 5 mm (right). (**c**) Comparison between three-terminal voltage-gated NW FET and two-terminal strain-gated vertical piezotronic transistor (left). Color gradient in the strained strain-gated vertical piezotronic transistor (SGVPT) represents the strain-induced piezopotential field, in which red and blue indicate positive and negative piezopotential, respectively. ZnO NWs in SGVPT grow along the c axis (red arrow). Equivalent circuit diagram of the 3D SGVPT array (right). Equivalent circuit diagram of the 3D SGVPT array (bottom). The region highlighted by black dashed lines is the unit SGVPT device, in which ε_g represents the mechanical strain gate signal and the vertical dotted line between the two terminals of the SGVPT denotes the modulation effect of ε_g on the conducting characteristics of the device. (**d**) Schematic illustration of a 2D piezotronic transistor (2DPT) array using ZnO nanoplatelet (left). Scanning electron micrograph of 2DPT array with high spatial resolution (≈12,700 dpi) (right). (**e**) The modulation of carrier transport by pressure in a piezotronic transistor based on ZnO twin nanoplatelets, which shows the characteristic of piezotronic effect (left). ln(I)−P curve demonstrates a linear relationship between ln(I) and the applied pressure, showing the extreme sensitivity and indicating the modulation effect of applied pressure on conductance (right). (**f**) Piezopotential distributions and the corresponding energy-band diagrams of double-channel piezotronic transistor (DCPT) and conventional piezotronic transistor (PT) (top). Compared to one rise and another drop in conventional PT, both Schottky barriers in DCPT decrease with increasing pressure. Energy-band diagram of DCPT without (black dashed line) and with (red line) piezotronic effect, in which ΔE_{image} and ΔE_{piezo} represent mirror force and piezopotential-induced Schottky barrier height change, respectively (left). Current increased step-by-step with increasing pressure by a step of 63.5 kPa from 0.75 to 1.00 MPa at a fixed bias (right). (**a**) Reproduced with permission [86]. Copyright 2016, American Chemical Society (**b**) Reproduced with permission [89]. Copyright 2016, American Chemical Society. (**c**) Reproduced with permission [66]. Copyright 2013, American Association for the Advancement of Science. (**d**) Reproduced with permission [91]. Copyright 2017, American Chemical Society. (**e**) Reproduced with permission [88]. Copyright 2017, American Chemical Society. (**f**) Reproduced with permission [92]. Copyright 2018, American Chemical Society.

Wu et al. (2013) published a study on transistor-based pressure-sensor arrays using piezotronics (Figure 5c) [66]. A conventional transistor is a three-terminal device that includes a gate. A dielectric and a gate are required to form a channel between the source and drain. In this study, two terminal devices were fabricated by removing the dielectric and the gate using piezoelectric nanowire. A ZnO piezoelectric nanowire was placed vertically between the top and bottom electrodes of the device to make contact. The response time of the device was 0.15 s, and its sensitivity was 2.1 µS/kPa. The observed sensing range was from a few kPa to 30 kPa. Liu et al. (2017) used a ZnO nanoplatelet for the channel material to compensate for the shortcomings of nanowire (Figure 5d) [91]. When the channel material is inserted into the piezotronic transistor in the form of nanowires, lateral deflection may occur due to external pressure. This is called the buckling effect, which limits the magnitude of the piezopotential generated in the nanowire. In order to prevent the buckling effect, transistors were fabricated by making ZnO into hexagonal nanoplatelets instead of nanowires. The response time of this device is very short, i.e., less than 5 ms, and the sensitivity ranges from 60.97 to 78.23 meV/MPa. It also has a detection range from a few kPa to 3.64 MPa. Wang et al. (2017) showed a device with significantly increased sensitivity (Figure 5e) [88]. ZnO was used as the piezoelectric material, and it was made into a twin nanoplatelet to increase the sensitivity by a factor of 50. This structure lowers the barrier at both interfaces of the top and bottom electrodes. Thus, even small pressure changes can increase charge transfer significantly. The sensitivity ranged from 1448 to 1677 meV/MPa, which is a very high value. The response time was less than 5 ms, and the detection range was from 24.84 to 152.88 kPa. Conventional piezotronic pressure sensors consist of a top electrode, a bottom electrode, and a piezoelectric material between the two electrodes (Figure 5f). Liu et al. (2018) studied piezotronic transistors in which the electrodes were placed on the bottom, unlike the elements mentioned above [92]. The top electrode was removed to change from a three-layer structure to a two-layer structure. This makes the fabrication process simpler and can increase reliability in large-scale production. In addition, it shows a pressure-sensitivity range from 84.2 to 104.4 meV/MPa, which is 1.1 to 1.7 times higher than previous piezoelectric pressure sensors.

3.2.2. Options for the Dielectric Materials of the Transistor Gate

Field effect transistors (FETs) operate based on the principle of flowing electrons or holes in the channel by the electric field generated by the applied gate voltage. Dielectric polarization occurs in the gate dielectric by the electric field due to the gate voltage. It forms an electric field using metal and a semiconductor as a capacitor, and the generated capacitance is expressed as follows:

$$C_i = \frac{\epsilon_0 \epsilon_r}{d}, d = d_0 \times (1 - \varepsilon) = d_0 \times \left(1 - \frac{pressure(P)}{modulus(E)}\right)$$

where capacitance is represented by permittivity (ϵ_0), relative permittivity (ratio of medium permittivity and permittivity, $\varepsilon = \epsilon_0 \epsilon_r$), and thickness of gate dielectric layer, d, when an external force is applied. Thickness, d, can be expressed by multiplying thickness, d_0, which means no force is applied to the dielectric and $\left(1 - \frac{pressure(P)}{modulus(E)}\right)$ [67]. In the FET-based tactile sensor, the thickness of the gate dielectric layer decreases when pressure is applied to the gate dielectric, and, accordingly, the dielectric capacitance increases. When the gate dielectric capacitance has a high sensitivity to pressure, sensing is possible over a wider range of pressures. In addition, it could have smaller output noise and reduce errors due to its delicate acceptance of mechanical stimuli. For these reasons, various channel materials and elastomeric dielectric materials have been studied for the development of the higher pressure-sensitive gate dielectric capacitances. The characteristics of the dielectric and channel materials and the results of the modification of the dielectric layer are summarized in Figure 6 [16,93–96] and Table 2 [55,93,95–104], respectively. Sujie Chen and co-workers proposed a method of one-step processing for a large area microstructure elastomer film that had highly-integrated microfeatures of the air gap (Figure 6a). The porous PDMS was used as a microstructure elastomer film. Due to the air gap inside the PDMS, this sensor has a rapid response time at the ultra-low pressure of 1 Pa, and remains sensitive to high pressures over a wide pressure range up to 250 kPa. It also has superior durability under heavy loads, i.e., loads larger than 1 MPa [94]. D. Kwon et al. (2016) reported a pressure sensor in which they used an ecoflex-porous elastromeric material as the dielectric layer (Figure 6b). Due to the presence of micropores, this device was able to detect pressures over a wide range, i.e., from 0.1 Pa to 130 kPa. In addition, it retained its outstanding electrical properties, such as a high sensitivity of 0.601 kPa^{-1} in a low-pressure region (<5 kPa) and a high resolution of 0.17 µm [95]. Z. Bao's group (2010) used PDMS as an elastomeric component for the first time in dielectric spacing. A low mechanical modulus is required for high mechanical sensitivity, and PDMS has a low modulus of ~2 MPa, which helps to improve the speed of the sensor's response. The use of elastomeric materials, including air gap and the pyramid-shaped PDMS, enhances the deformation of the dielectric so that it has better sensitivity to pressure in the low-pressure region [55]. Viry et al. (2014) demonstrated a three-axial pressure sensor in which an air gap of ~150 µm was formed naturally between copper/tin-coated electrodes. This is possible due to the adhesion properties of fluorosilicone. The air gap acts as a second dielectric layer in the sensor and has high sensitivity at very low pressure (ca. 0–2 kPa) [97]. Our group proposed a simple method of forming a graphene FET pressure sensor with an air dielectric layer. We developed an origami substrate structure in which two plastic panels, one of which was the source/drain panel with the other being the gate panel, were connected to a one-foldable elastic joint, as shown in Figure 6c. By folding two plastic panels, we fabricated the pressure-sensitive graphene FET with an air dielectric layer without any damage. In addition, 50 × 50 integrated array FETs could be used for mapping the 2D pressure distribution over a wide range of pressures [67]. Z. Bao et al. (2013) reported flexible polymer transistors utilizing microstructural PDMS as a dielectric layer (Figure 6d). This pressure-sensitive, organic, thin-film transistor (OTFT) had outstanding sensitivity of 8.4 kPa^{-1}, a rapid response time, high stability, and low power consumption. Due to the excellent mechanical properties of the PDMS dielectric layer, their transistors are suitable for application in electronic skin (e-skin) and health monitoring systems [96]. In addition, our group reported the fabrication of human-interactive displays (Figure 6e). Active-matrix arrays of pressure-sensitive Si transistors with air dielectric layers were fully integrated with the pixels of organic light-emitting diodes (OLEDs). Due to the air dielectric layer, pressure-sensitive transistors have high transconductance and negligible hysteresis, so the transistor can detect pressure with a relatively fast response time [16]. Zhang et al. (2015) demonstrated flexible, suspended-gate, organic, thin-film transistors (SGOTFTs), as shown in Figure 6f. The suspended gate of SGOTFTs was able to detect a wider range of pressures, and had a high sensitivity of 192 kPa^{-1} in a low-range detection pressure of <0.5 kPa. In addition, it had a low power consumption of <100 nW at an operating voltage of 6 V that could effectively detect the human pulse and the pressure of sound. In addition, one of the outstanding properties of SGOTFTs is their fast response time of 10 ms, which makes them suitable for real-time measurement devices [95].

The roughness of the oxide-channel interface of the transistor induced scattering, such as carrier trapping, which degraded the electrical properties of the transistor. To solve this problem, we used an air spacing in the dielectric layer, which allowed the gate dielectric to be formed uniformly, and this helped in avoiding the degradation of the electrical properties of the transistors. In addition, when using the air dielectric, a fast response time was possible due to the negligible hysteresis. Therefore, the elastomeric, dielectric FET-based transistor with an air gap has outstanding properties, such as fast response time, high mobility, and high sensitivity under a wide range of applied pressures, so it could be used effectively in various fields, including robotics, e-skins, and biomachines.

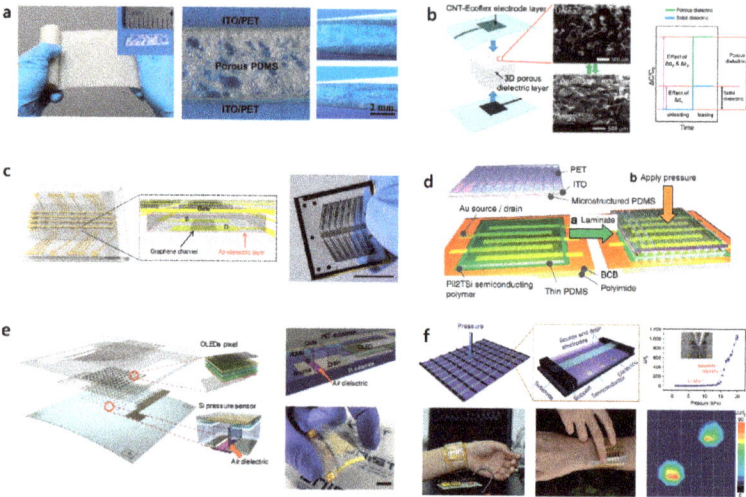

Figure 6. Results of dielectric layer modification. (**a**) The photo image of the fabricated large area microstructured polydimethylsiloxane (PDMS) film (the inset shows the cross-sectional photo image of the microstructured PDMS film) (left); The cross-sectional photo images of the microstructured PDMS film clipped by a tweezer without pressure (upper) and with pressure (bottom) (right). (**b**) Relative changes in the capacitances of pressure sensors using solid and porous elastomeric dielectric layers induced by identical levels of external loading. The synergy of the larger deformation by the reduced stiffness and the increased effective dielectric constant by the closure of the air gap dramatically amplifies the capacitance change. (**c**) Schematic images of pressure-sensitive graphene FETs with air-dielectric layers after the folding. The air-dielectric layer is placed between the graphene channel and the gate electrode as illustrated in the schematic image (inset) (left); Photograph of the fabricated pressure-sensitive graphene FETs; scale bar, 1 cm (right). (**d**) Schematic of the final fabrication step of our pressure-sensitive transistor. (**e**) Schematic of active-matrix pressure-sensitive display, integrating the Si tactile pressure sensors and organic light-emitting diodes (OLEDs). (**f**) Suspended gate organic thin-film transistor pressure sensors. (a) Reproduced with permission [94]. (b) Reproduced with permission [95]. Copyright 2016, ACS Applied Materials & Interfaces. (c) Reproduced with permission [67]. Copyright 2017, Nature Communications. (d) Reproduced with permission [93]. Copyright 2013, Nature Communications. (e) Reproduced with permission [16]. Copyright 2019, Advanced Material Technologies. (f) Reproduced with permission [96]. Copyright 2015, Nature Communications.

Table 2. The tactile sensor characteristics with various gate dielectric and channel materials.

Dielectric Materials	Channel Materials	Pressure-Sensing Range	Response Time	Spatial Resolution	Sensitivity	Reference
Pressure-sensitive rubber (PSR)	50 nm-thick pentacene layer	0 to 30 kPa	~30 ms of cycle time	16 × 16 arrays 10 dpi (254 mm)		[62]
Ecoflex-porous elastomeric		0.1 Pa to ~130 kPa	Fast response time	0.17 μm Position resolution	0.601 kPa^{-1} at 5 kPa	[95]
Microstructured V-shape-groove PDMS (pyramid molding PDMS)	Rubrene single crystal	0 to ~7 kPa		~1 mm	(<2 kPa) 0.55 kPa^{-1} (>2 kPa) to 0.15 kPa^{-1}	[55]
Microstructural PDMS	PiI2T-Si	0 to 60 kPa	< 10 ms	~1.7 mm	(<8 kPa) 8.2 kPa^{-1} (>30 kPa) 0.38 kPa^{-1}	[93]
PDMS with air-gap	Graphene	250 Pa to ~3 MPa	30 ms	1 mm	(<500 kPa) to 2.05 × 10^{-4} kPa^{-1} and (>500 kPa) to 9.43 × 10^{-6} kPa^{-1}	[67]
PDMS + G-PDMS (G-PDMS; synthesis of glycerol and PDMS at 1:10)	MoS$_2$	200 Pa to 5 MPa	25 ms	500 μm	(<500 kPa) 1.8 MPa^{-1} (>500 kPa) 0.018 MPa^{-1}	[15]

3.3. Multimodal, Multifunctional Tactile Sensor Arrays

Development of multimodal, multifunctional FET-based tactile sensors imitating multifunctional properties of human skin that can simultaneously detect various stimuli, or providing the ability of human-readable output through sensing, remain important challenges. Recently, various properties of multimodal, multifunctional tactile sensors have been achieved. Detecting normal and shear forces separately, measuring external forces simultaneously in real-time, or visualizing sensing output with emitting lights are representative examples. In this section, various studies about multimodal, multifunctional tactile sensor arrays will be presented.

Recently, we fabricated tactile sensor arrays consisting of a mechanoluminescent layer and air-dielectric MoS_2 transistors. Cu-doped ZnS (ZnS:Cu) phosphor particles were used as mechanoluminescent (ML) components. When an external force is applied to the ML, light is emitted to the channel, and absorption of light causes a photocurrent to enable high pressure sensitivity in a wide detectable range of pressure as shown in Figure 7a [15]. The Ali Javey group demonstrated multimodal tactile sensors with active-matrix OLEDs for the first time. Outputs of applied pressures to tactile sensors are converted to human-readable information by active-matrix OLEDs. Red, green, and blue pixels comprise the OLEDs and emit light proportional to the intensity of applied pressure (Figure 7b). Pressure-sensitive rubber (PSR) is laminated on the top of the OLEDs, and its conductivity increases by applied forces [64]. In addition, Someya and co-workers made pressure- and thermal-sensitive sensors based on an organic semiconductor. By forming a net-shaped structure of a plastic film with organic transistor-based electronic circuits, conformability is possible [98]. Moreover, the Caofeng Pan group developed a polyimide-based 3D integration structure that allows simultaneous monitoring of seven physical stimuli and demonstrated stretchable multifunctional integrated sensor arrays in which each sensor can be driven independently without crosstalk (Figure 7c) [99]. E. Hwang and co-workers made flexible tactile sensors using polyimide and PDMS. The thin metal strain gauge incorporated in the polymer is used to measure normal and shear force. Each unit tactile sensor in 8×8 tactile sensor arrays evaluates deformations for normal and shear forces. In addition, the sensors have been proposed to measure ground reaction force because of their rigid structures [100]. D. Choi and co-workers used a pyramid-plug structure to detect normal force, shear force, and torsion. By utilizing pyramid-shaped engraved electrodes and ionic gel as neural mechanoreceptors, each mechanical force has its own deformation mechanism, as shown in Figure 7d [101]. Similarly, J. Park et al. developed stress-direction-sensitive, stretchable e-skin inspired from interlocked microstructures found in epidermal-dermal ridges in human skin. Microdome arrays employed for e-skin have a highly sensitive detection capability for various mechanical stimuli, such as normal, shear, stretching, bending, and twisting forces (Figure 7e) [102]. For commercialization of multimodal, multifunctional tactile sensors, the Rogers group proposed the fabrication of epidermal electronics using multimodal, multifunctional tactile sensors for the first time. Unlike basic wafer-based technology, conformal contact is possible using only Van der Waals force on curved skin. By attaching their devices to the back side of a commercial temporary transfer tattoo, they achieved multifunctional invisible epidermal electronic skins as shown in Figure 7f [103].

In short, enhancing the properties of multimodal, multifunctional tactile sensor arrays, such as by monitoring diverse stimuli at the same time, or visualizing the outputs of tactile sensing data, provides potential applications in human-health monitoring and biomachine interface fields, as well as robotics and e-skin.

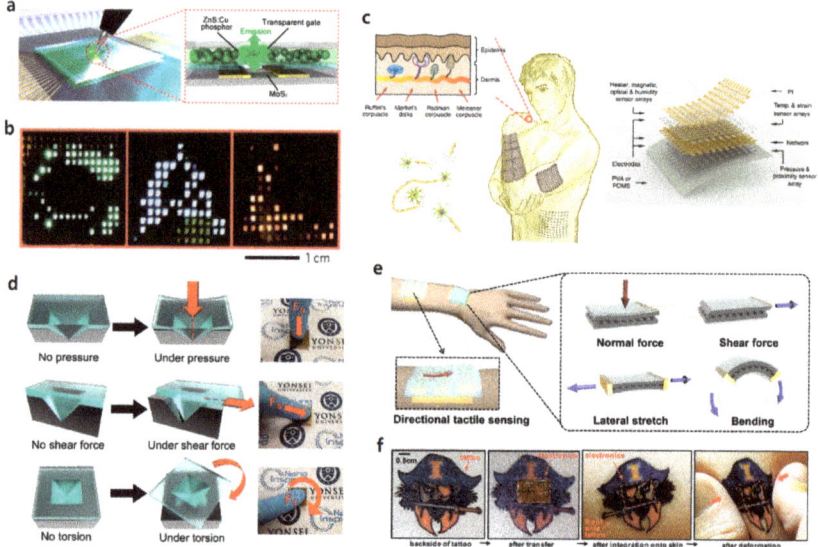

Figure 7. Multimodal, multifunctional tactile sensor arrays based on FETs. (**a**) Schematic layouts of the pressure-sensor array integrated with ZnS:Cu phosphor particles. (**b**) Green, blue, and red color interactive e-skins are used to spatially map and display the pressure applied with C-(left), A-(center) and L-(right) shaped PDMS slabs, respectively. (**c**) Skin-inspired highly stretchable and conformable matrix networks; a schematic illustration of stretchable and conformable matrix networks (SCMNs) conforming to the surface of a human arm and an expanded network (expansion: 200%) conforming to the surface of a human abdomen (right); the tree branch-like connections of neurons (left bottom); the sensory receptors of the glabrous skin (left top). (**d**) Schematic illustrations without stimulus and under three different mechanical stimuli for pressure, shear force, and torsion. There were possible geometric deformations of the pyramid-plug structure with mechanical loadings. (**e**) Schematic of a stress-direction-sensitive electronic skin for the detection and differentiation of various mechanical stimuli including normal, shear, stretching, bending, and twisting forces. (**f**) A commercial temporary transfer tattoo provides an alternative to polyester/polyvinyl alcohol (PVA) for the substrate; in this case, the system includes an adhesive to improve bonding to the skin. Images are of the back side of a tattoo (far left), electronics integrated onto this surface (middle left), and attached to the skin with electronics facing down in undeformed (middle right) and compressed (far right) states. (**a**) Reproduced with permission [15]. Copyright 2020, Nano Letters. (**b**) Reproduced with permission [64]. Copyright 2013, Nature Materials. (**c**) Reproduced with permission [99]. Copyright 2018, Nature Communications. (**d**) Reproduced with permission [101]. Copyright 2019, Advanced Materials Technologies. (**e**) Reproduced with permission [102]. Copyright 2014, ACS Nano. (**f**) Reproduced with permission [103]. Copyright 2011, Science.

4. Future Applications for the Tactile Sensor Arrays Based on FETs

4.1. Robotics

Robotics uses an artificial machine to execute functions previously performed by humans, and can be useful in many academic and industrial fields [104,105]. Currently, robotics is mostly used in manufacturing in the industrial field. However, robotics can be applied in almost any field. Robotics enables access to dangerous and inaccessible locations in various fields such as agriculture, biotechnology, medical, electronics, and engineering. Robotics can replace humans actions, with better performance than humans in many cases. It can also perform tasks that might be limiting for humans. Recently, soft robotics using flexible materials has been studied extensively [106–109]. Soft robotics, which have flexibility, stretchability, and transparency, can have various applications, and can be used, in particular, to create a human-interactive device.

Human skin is one of the largest sensor networks that can detect various stimuli, such as pressure, temperature, strain, humidity, and pain. It also sends signals to the brain through synapses. E-skin is an electronic device that can mimic and reproduce these various characteristics of the human skin in materials, functions, and structures [110–112]. E-skin can be applied to robotics, and is highly useful for medical diagnostics when attached to the skin. It can also be applied to replacement prosthetic devices instead of injured skin and as a monitoring device that monitors physical condition in real time.

Human skin has mechanoreceptors that respond to mechanical stimuli [113,114]. In a mechanoreceptor, when a mechanical stimulus is received from the outside, mechanotransduction occurs that makes the stimulus into a current of ions through the ion channel. The flow of ions generated transmits information of the stimulation to the brain through synapses. A function to be noted in mechanoreceptors is that they can convert external stimuli into electrical signals. In order to transmit the external stimulus and use the detected information, it must be converted into electrical signals. Physical changes, such as the deformation of materials and the shrinkages of thickness or length that occur under pressure, are not readily available information in digital devices. If the tactile sensor array transmits information through a change in electrical information due to a change in pressure, it can be monitored, e.g., the brain receives signals from the body through the delivery of ions, and a signal is received to diagnose the meaning. In addition, such signals can be processed into useful information that can be used more easily.

Mechanical properties are important to use e-skin effectively. The component in which e-skin is used will be attached to actual human skin or robotics that can move like a human body. It must be able to bend or fold like real skin and stretch without damage. Therefore, e-skin requires both flexibility and stretchability. In order to adhere to the skin, the adhesion properties of the device must also be very good [115]. To be used in people, it must be able to withstand the ingress of moisture [116].

Park et al. (2019) fabricated ultrathin, tactile sensors based on MoS_2 (Figure 8a) [117]. In this paper, MoS_2 TFTs were deposited on Al_2O_3 (50 nm)/SU-8 (500 nm)/polymethyl methacrylate (PMMA) (sacrificial layer) and fabricated on a SiO_2/Si substrate. Then, the PMMA was removed and the fabrication of the sensor was completed on a very thin, i.e., 2 mm thick, PDMS with a Young's modulus similar to that of human skin. The tactile sensor was attached directly to the palm, and experiments were conducted to sense pressure for various inputs. Another study used a porous structure as a pressure-sensitive layer. Lou et al. (2017) composed a device by putting a layer of polyaniline hollow nanosphere composite films (PANI-HNSCF) between two electrodes (Figure 8b) [118]. It had a size of 10 × 10 pixels and experiments were conducted in which the device was attached to various parts. It was confirmed that it could be twisted without damage. In addition, it was attached to the back of the hand to measure pressure, and the applied pressure could be mapped. Boutry et al. (2018) fabricated an e-skin that mimics the microstructure of the skin and simultaneously can detect normal and shear forces (Figure 8c) [119]. Carbon nanotubes (CNTs) were fabricated as an array and covered with polyurethane (PU) to form a spherical microstructure of PU that contained CNTs. A sensor manufactured in this way can detect two forces through changes in resistance and capacitance between electrodes. After fabrication, an e-skin capable of pressure sensing was applied to the arm of robot. The pressure sensor was attached to the fingertip of the robot's hand, providing feedback on the pressing action. Figure 8c shows that the robot's hand does not break the raspberry due to feedback. However, there is no feedback in the picture below, which confirmed that the raspberry was broken by pressure. As such, it can be used as a role for feedback on an action. Research has also been conducted on the recognition of braille by applying a pressure sensor at the fingertip (Figure 8d). You et al. (2018) fabricated a tactile sensor array using microparticles [120]. This device, which was assembled by inserting microparticles between two electrodes, has high sensitivity even at very low pressures. Because it can be operated even at low pressure and has high sensitivity, it is suitable for use as a sensor applied to the tip of the finger for research purposes. The device was made of 10 × 10 pixels and was used to recognize a braille sign stating "restroom for handicapped males". The arranged braille was detected accurately by a 10 × 10 pixel sensor. Sundaram et al. (2019) made a scalable tactile glove (STAG) that covered the entire palm with a pressure-sensor array (Figure 8e) [121]. They analyzed the behavior of interacting with 26 objects. The array of 548 sensors was assembled on a knitted glove, and a large-scale tactile dataset with 135,000 frames was recorded. It was confirmed how the pressure acts on each part of the palm depending on the objects. This work proved the worth of tactile sensors, as well as emphasizing the potential for robotics.

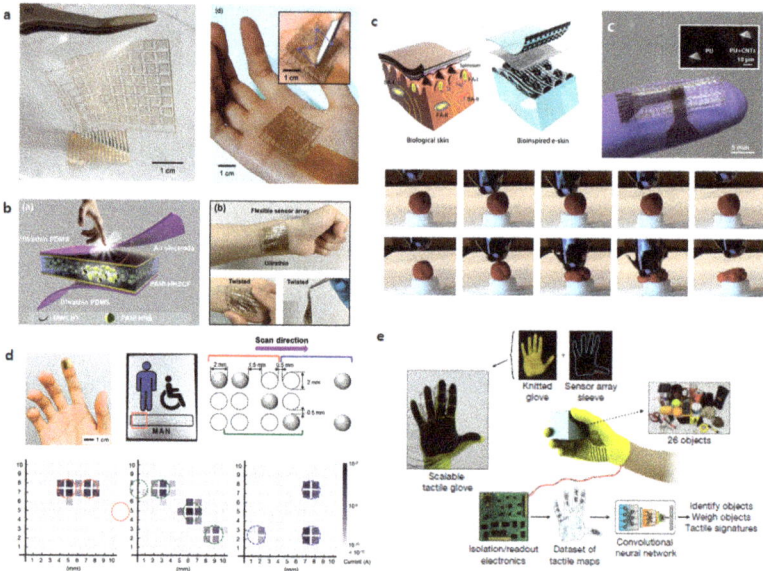

Figure 8. Tactile pressure sensors for e-skin and robotics. (a) Photograph of the large area flexible active-matrix (AM) MoS$_2$ tactile sensor array (left). Photograph of the AM MoS$_2$ tactile sensor on the human palm (right). (b) Primary design concept of flexible e-skin sensor based on polyaniline hollow nanosphere composite films (PANI-HNSCF) (left). Optical image of a wearable ultrathin e-skin sensor array on the wrist and under various mechanical deformations (right). (c) Cross-section of the skin of the fingertip depicting key sensory structures and soft biomimetic e-skin (left). Optical image showing carbon nanotube-polyurethane (CNT-PU) interconnects for signal recording with inductance/capacitance ratio (LCR) meter and SEM picture of the top e-skin layer with molded pyramids (right), showing CNT-PU and PU areas (inset). Tactile feedback prevented flattening of the raspberry. Without tactile feedback, the fruit was crushed (bottom). (d) Digital image of the flexible tactile array sensor attached to the tip of an index finger as an artificial fingertip (left). Digital image of a braille sign stating "restroom for handicapped males" (middle). Illustration denoting the dimensions of the scanned braille (right). Current profiles obtained from the artificial fingertip while scanning the braille (bottom). (e) The scalable tactile glove (STAG) consists of a sensor array with 548 elements covering the entire hand, attached to a custom knit glove. An electrical readout circuit is used to acquire the normal force recorded by each sensor at approximately 7.3 fps. Using this setup allows recording of a dataset of 135,187 tactile maps while interacting with 26 different objects. A deep convolutional neural network trained purely on tactile information can be used to identify or weigh objects and explore the tactile signatures of the human grasp. The glove shown at the center is a rendering. (a) Reproduced with permission [117]. Copyright 2019, American Chemical Society. (b) Reproduced with permission [118]. Copyright 2017, Elsevier. (c) Reproduced with permission [119]. Copyright 2018, American Association for the Advancement of Science. (d) Reproduced with permission [120]. Copyright 2018, John Wiley and Sons. (e) Reproduced with permission [121]. Copyright 2019, Springer Nature.

4.2. Artificial Intelligence (AI)

For the commercialization of tactile sensors, FET-based tactile sensors with outstanding electrical and mechanical properties must be researched and developed, and they must be able to accept and recognize various stimuli of the features of unknown objects through machine learning. Tactile sensors with machine learning can judge how to deal with various unknown objects. This helps the development of future industrial applications that can create self-made solutions to the output after taking measurements, rather than just measuring the stimuli. Spiers et al. (2014) proved that the recognition of an object and the extraction of its features are possible in the sensing process of tactile sensors with machine learning through the training of random forest classifiers. A robot hand with machine learning has high-accuracy data classification and an excellent ability to determine the characteristics of objects [122]. Liu (2016) developed the ability to represent and classify tactile data using the kernel sparse coding method. The use of existing sparse coding has led tactile data to deal with the interference problem when all of the robot's fingers touch an object at the same time. They solved this problem by developing the joint kernel sparse coding model [123]. To analyze the motion of an unknown object, Luo analyzed the features of the object using a new tactile-SIFT (scale-invariant feature transform) descriptor [124]. Mohsen et al. (2017) developed a multi-functional tactile sensor that was capable of sensing multiple stimuli and made it possible to recognize the features of unknown objects through machine learning [125].

To date, various studies of AI tactile sensors capable of the recognition and acquisition of the motion of an object have been published. In addition, after obtaining various data (e.g., shape, color, elasticity, or roughness), research is being conducted actively to develop an application of a human–machine interactive FET-based tactile sensor capable of simultaneously classifying and making decisions about the data through machine learning.

4.3. Human-Machine Interface (HMI)

Multimodal and multifunctional tactile sensors developed to recognize human processes and the results of sensing data measured in real time, not just simply measuring human's motions or external forces, have attracted significant attention recently [126,127]. Optical tactile sensors enable interactive viewing through eyes, which is the most basic method for recognizing data. Thus, the importance of HMI tactile sensors is increasing due to research on devices that can visualize outputs. In this section, we introduce optical tactile sensors as representative examples of HMI tactile sensors.

Optical tactile sensors can reduce stray capacitance (e.g., unwanted capacitance that occurs due to sensor proximity) and thermal noises. In addition, they can reduce the complexity of wiring and crosstalk, thereby enabling high spatial resolution [128]. X. Wang et al. (2015) demonstrated a pressure-sensor matrix capable of recording the pressure, force, and speed of signing applied to each pixel in personalized signing. Pressed mechano-luminescent materials emitted light and were visualized by a pressure-sensor matrix. A piezophotonic mechanism was used to operate this device [78]. E. H. Kim et al. (2019) demonstrated an interactive skin display with an epidermal stimuli electrode. It was based on a two-layer structure with light-emitting inorganic phosphors in a structure with gaps in the two electrodes. The interactive skin display with an epidermal stimuli electrode visualized the motion sensing of the tactile sensor while stimulation was applied by external forces [129]. Our group provided a platform for wireless pressure sensing with a built-in battery and instant visualization. Minimization was achieved by simply using a built-in battery on an FET-based pressure sensor that consisted of a Si channel and an air dielectric. In addition, it made it possible to visualize the real-time output with a smartphone by processing with a wireless device [126].

Devices that have been optimized to operate an interactive display for diverse external stimuli are proposed as potential applications in various fields relative to biomotion, such as health care and biomachines. Current studies can help develop HMI tactile sensors with characteristics of olfactory or auditory capabilities in addition to visualization in the next generation of these devices.

4.4. Healthcare Biosystems

The demand for emerging flexible electronic technologies, such as wearable healthcare devices biomedical prosthesis, robotics, and electronic skin (e-skin), has resulted in profound research interests in developing tactile pressure sensors [130,131]. One of the main reasons for GR is to create a people-friendly environment. For this purpose, motion detection for healthcare systems and biosystems has also become an important research goal, and there are several challenges that must be overcome to produce such a device for biological objects. For example, pressure sensing and monitoring of biological systems, such as cardiac and vascular tissues, joints, cartilage, and spinal cord discs, have clinical importance that requires high-performing sensors in terms of sensitivity and accuracy, wide sensing range, enhanced spatial resolution, and low power consumption. To meet these requirements, many different types of pressure sensors, such as resistive, capacitive, and piezoelectric pressure sensors, have been developed in recent years using various nanomaterials with different structural configurations [132–134]. Despite these advancements, utilization of flexible devices is still limited to specialized applications that require specific sensing ranges, sensitivities, and spatial resolutions, and these devices are inadequate for generalized application in bio-systems.

Kim et al. (2017) reported a wearable smart contact lens with highly transparent and stretchable sensors that continuously and wirelessly monitor glucose and intraocular pressure, which are the risk factors associated with diabetes and glaucoma, respectively [135]. In this work, the authors wirelessly demonstrated real-time, in vivo glucose detection on the eye of a rabbit and in vitro monitoring of the intraocular pressure of a bovine eyeball. This device is the completed form of an integrated system of a pressure sensor and a biochemical sensor, suggesting a substantial platform for future biomedical applications of tactile pressure sensors [136]. Jang et al. (2020) presented the formation of active-matrix, pressure-sensitive, MoS_2 FET arrays with air dielectrics and mechanoluminescence materials for sensing extensive ranges of tactile pressure [15]. In this work, a single FET can operate solely as a pressure sensor, and, therefore, the active-matrix formation using these FETs can be advantageous for high spatial resolutions with miniaturized integrations. In addition, these approaches could enlarge the detectable range of pressure from 70 Pa to 5 MPa by successfully monitoring the pressure distributions of single cell motions and heel footsteps in real time. In particular, the outstanding spatial and temporal resolutions of this active-matrix sensor array enabled single- and/or sub-cellular pressure mapping. This sensor array shows potential for being beneficial for pressure sensing and monitoring multiple events in biology for future applications of prostheses, robotics, and various biomedical electronics, from muscles, joints, and cartilage working under high pressure to cardiac and vascular systems under mild and small pressures. Based on the results of these studies, it is expected that research that confirms the correlation by measuring and analyzing the results of mechanical pressure rather than biological potential with a tactile sensor will be actively conducted.

5. Prospects

As previously discussed, FET-based tactile pressure sensors have advantageous features, such as high pixel resolution, wide range of detectable pressure, fast response time, and reliable performance, and are suitable for numerous applications, including GR technology. In addition, active-matrix arrays, which are inherent properties of FET arrays, can provide a tactile sensor device with low power consumption, low signal crosstalk, and a high contrast ratio. In addition, multi-functional tactile sensors exist that can convert tactile stimuli into visual and auditory signals, suggesting substantial potential for future robotics and motion-detection systems. The tactile sensor devices based on distinct functions and characteristics can be used in various fields, such as robotics, artificial intelligence, human-machine interfaces, and health monitoring systems.

Nonetheless, there are challenges that must be overcome for the recognition of gestures and the detection of motion, and some of these challenges are presented here. First, sophisticated multi-modal and multi-functional sensors are required to detect the various types of stimulus from people's movements. Detection and analysis of a single pattern of tactile stimuli cannot provide sufficient information for a computing system to recognize various gestures. Second, excellent mechanical stability against stretching and bending is required for wearable electronics. Since robotics and HMI technology have attracted the attention of researchers in various fields, tactile sensors can be applied directly to a robot's parts, such as the hand and arm. In this case, it is important to maintain the robot's sensing characteristics during the various types of mechanical deformations. Third, superb biocompatibility of the materials that are used is essential so that the robot can operate in harsh environmental conditions, such as sweat and water. In addition, for e-skin applications, materials that are incompatible with biosystems do not easily interact with the human body because they can cause inflammation and irritation of the skin. Therefore, we plan to concentrate on these challenges that must be solved in order to develop advanced GR technology.

6. Conclusions

In conclusion, excellent research on FET-based tactile pressure sensors has been conducted, followed by accelerated development of pressure sensors, including touch interfaces. Although non-contact interface-based gesture recognition has developed rapidly, environmental restrictions inhibit the application of the systems in practice. In addition, the principles underpinning various tactile sensors have their own advantages and disadvantages, suggesting the sensor type should be appropriately customized and arranged to fulfil target applications. However, the current direction of development is toward interactions frequently performed by humans and machines (e.g., motion detection and gesture recognition), suggesting the implementation of the active matrix, which provides the advantages of low power consumption and signal crosstalk, is essential. We envision that this type of tactile pressure sensor will be beneficial for GR technology, as well as future applications, such as prostheses, robotics, artificial intelligence, and biomedical electronics, and will provide substantial opportunities to develop the next-generation motion sensing systems.

Author Contributions: J.J., Y.S.J., H.S. and M.K. contributed equally to this work. J.J., Y.S.J., H.S. and M.K. wrote the paper. J.-U.P. supervised the work. All authors have read and agreed to the published version of the manuscript.

Funding: This work was supported by the Ministry of Science & ICT (MSIT) and the Ministry of Trade, Industry and Energy (MOTIE) of Korea through the National Research Foundation (2019R1A2B5B03069358, 2016R1A5A1009926, and 2018R1A2A1A05019733), the Bio & Medical Technology Development Program (2018M3A9F1021649), the Nano Material Technology Development Program (2015M3A7B4050308 and 2016M3A7B4910635), and Industry Technology Development Program (10080540). Also, the authors thank financial support by the Institute for Basic Science (IBS-R026-D1) and the Research Program (2018-22-0194) funded by Yonsei University.

Acknowledgments: The authors own many thanks to the anonymous reviewers for their instructive comments.

Conflicts of Interest: The authors declare no conflict of interest.

References

1. Wu, Y.; Huang, T.S. Vision-Based Gesture Recognition: A review. In Proceedings of the Gesture-Based Communication in Human-Computer Interaction, Berlin/Heidelberg, Germany, 17 March 1999; pp. 103–115.
2. Jeon, C.; Kwon, O.J.; Shin, D.; Shin, D. Hand-Mouse Interface Using Virtual Monitor Concept for Natural Interaction. *IEEE Access* **2017**, *5*, 25181–25188. [CrossRef]
3. Dorner, B.; Hagen, E. Towards an American Sign Language Interface. In Proceedings of the Integration of Natural Language and Vision Processing: Computational Models and Systems, Dordrecht, The Netherlands, 31 July 1995; pp. 143–161.
4. An, B.W.; Shin, J.H.; Kim, S.-Y.; Kim, J.; Ji, S.; Park, J.; Lee, Y.; Jang, J.; Park, Y.-G.; Cho, E.; et al. Smart Sensor Systems for Wearable Electronic Devices. *Polymers* **2017**, *9*, 303. [CrossRef] [PubMed]
5. Park, Y.G.; Lee, S.; Park, J.U. Recent Progress in Wireless Sensors for Wearable Electronics. *Sensors* **2019**, *19*, 4353. [CrossRef]
6. Melzer, M.; Kaltenbrunner, M.; Makarov, D.; Karnaushenko, D.; Karnaushenko, D.; Sekitani, T.; Someya, T.; Schmidt, O.G. Imperceptible magnetoelectronics. *Nat. Commun.* **2015**, *6*, 6080. [CrossRef] [PubMed]

7. Wang, X.; Dong, L.; Zhang, H.; Yu, R.; Pan, C.; Wang, Z.L. Recent Progress in Electronic Skin. *Adv. Sci.* **2015**, *2*, 1500169. [CrossRef]
8. Deng, L. A tutorial survey of architectures, algorithms, and applications for deep learning. *APSIPA Trans. Signal Inf. Process.* **2014**, *3*. [CrossRef]
9. Kim, Y.; Chortos, A.; Xu, W.; Liu, Y.; Oh, J.Y.; Son, D.; Kang, J.; Foudeh, A.M.; Zhu, C.; Lee, Y.; et al. A bioinspired flexible organic artificial afferent nerve. *Science* **2018**, *360*, 998–1003. [CrossRef]
10. Chen, J.; Zhu, G.; Yang, J.; Jing, Q.; Bai, P.; Yang, W.; Qi, X.; Su, Y.; Wang, Z.L. Personalized Keystroke Dynamics for Self-Powered Human–Machine Interfacing. *ACS Nano* **2015**, *9*, 105–116. [CrossRef] [PubMed]
11. Luo, J.; Tang, W.; Fan, F.R.; Liu, C.; Pang, Y.; Cao, G.; Wang, Z.L. Transparent and Flexible Self-Charging Power Film and Its Application in a Sliding Unlock System in Touchpad Technology. *ACS Nano* **2016**, *10*, 8078–8086. [CrossRef] [PubMed]
12. Lim, S.; Son, D.; Kim, J.; Lee, Y.B.; Song, J.-K.; Choi, S.; Lee, D.J.; Kim, J.H.; Lee, M.; Hyeon, T.; et al. Transparent and Stretchable Interactive Human Machine Interface Based on Patterned Graphene Heterostructures. *Adv. Funct. Mater.* **2015**, *25*, 375–383. [CrossRef]
13. Zeng, W.; Shu, L.; Li, Q.; Chen, S.; Wang, F.; Tao, X.-M. Fiber-Based Wearable Electronics: A Review of Materials, Fabrication, Devices, and Applications. *Adv. Mater.* **2014**, *26*, 5310–5336. [CrossRef]
14. Jang, J.; Oh, B.; Jo, S.; Park, S.; An, H.S.; Lee, S.; Cheong, W.H.; Yoo, S.; Park, J.-U. Human-Interactive, Active-Matrix Displays for Visualization of Tactile Pressures. *Adv. Mater. Technol.* **2019**, *4*, 1900082. [CrossRef]
15. Park, Y.G.; An, H.S.; Kim, J.Y.; Park, J.U. High-resolution, reconfigurable printing of liquid metals with three-dimensional structures. *Sci. Adv.* **2019**, *5*, eaaw2844. [CrossRef] [PubMed]
16. Park, Y.G.; Min, H.; Kim, H.; Zhexembekova, A.; Lee, C.Y.; Park, J.U. Three-Dimensional, High-Resolution Printing of Carbon Nanotube/Liquid Metal Composites with Mechanical and Electrical Reinforcement. *Nano Lett.* **2019**, *19*, 4866–4872. [CrossRef] [PubMed]
17. Jo, Y.; Kim, J.Y.; Kim, S.Y.; Seo, Y.H.; Jang, K.S.; Lee, S.Y.; Jung, S.; Ryu, B.H.; Kim, H.S.; Park, J.U.; et al. 3D-printable, highly conductive hybrid composites employing chemically-reinforced, complex dimensional fillers and thermoplastic triblock copolymers. *Nanoscale* **2017**, *9*, 5072–5084. [CrossRef] [PubMed]
18. Ji, S.; Jang, J.; Cho, E.; Kim, S.H.; Kang, E.S.; Kim, J.; Kim, H.K.; Kong, H.; Kim, S.K.; Kim, J.Y.; et al. High Dielectric Performances of Flexible and Transparent Cellulose Hybrid Films Controlled by Multidimensional Metal Nanostructures. *Adv. Mater.* **2017**, *29*, 1700538. [CrossRef]
19. Kim, M.; Park, J.; Ji, S.; Shin, S.H.; Kim, S.Y.; Kim, Y.C.; Kim, J.Y.; Park, J.U. Fully-integrated, bezel-less transistor arrays using reversibly foldable interconnects and stretchable origami substrates. *Nanoscale* **2016**, *8*, 9504–9510. [CrossRef]
20. Ji, S.; Hyun, B.G.; Kim, K.; Lee, S.Y.; Kim, S.H.; Kim, J.Y.; Song, M.H.; Park, J.U. Photo-patternable and transparent films using cellulose nanofibers for stretchable origami electronics. *NPG Asia Mater.* **2016**, *8*, e299. [CrossRef]
21. Lee, M.-S.; Kim, J.; Park, J.; Park, J.U. Studies on the mechanical stretchability of transparent conductive film based on graphene-metal nanowire structures. *Nanoscale Res. Lett.* **2015**, *10*, 1–9. [CrossRef]
22. Kim, K.; Park, Y.G.; Hyun, B.G.; Choi, M.; Park, J.U. Recent Advances in Transparent Electronics with Stretchable Forms. *Adv. Mater.* **2019**, *31*, 1804690. [CrossRef]
23. Jang, J.; Hyun, B.G.; Ji, S.; Cho, E.; An, B.W.; Cheong, W.H.; Park, J.U. Rapid production of large-area, transparent and stretchable electrodes using metal nanofibers as wirelessly operated wearable heaters. *NPG Asia Mater.* **2017**, *9*, e432. [CrossRef]
24. Kim, J.; Lee, M.; Shim, H.J.; Ghaffari, R.; Cho, H.R.; Son, D.; Jung, Y.H.; Soh, M.; Choi, C.; Jung, S.; et al. Stretchable silicon nanoribbon electronics for skin prosthesis. *Nat. Commun.* **2014**, *5*, 5747. [CrossRef]
25. Jang, J.; Kim, H.; Ji, S.; Kim, H.J.; Kang, M.S.; Kim, T.S.; Won, J.; Lee, J.-H.; Cheon, J.; Kang, K.; et al. Mechanoluminescent, Air-Dielectric MoS2 Transistors as Active-Matrix Pressure Sensors for Wide Detection Ranges from Footsteps to Cellular Motions. *Nano Lett.* **2020**, *20*, 66–74. [CrossRef] [PubMed]
26. Zhang, Y.; Liu, Y.; Wang, Z.L. Fundamental Theory of Piezotronics. *Adv. Mater.* **2011**, *23*, 3004–3013. [CrossRef] [PubMed]
27. Wang, X.; Zhou, J.; Song, J.; Liu, J.; Xu, N.; Wang, Z.L. Piezoelectric Field Effect Transistor and Nanoforce Sensor Based on a Single ZnO Nanowire. *Nano Lett.* **2006**, *6*, 2768–2772. [CrossRef]
28. M Kalayeh, K.; G Charalambides, P. A Non-Linear Model of an All-Elastomer, in-Plane, Capacitive, Tactile Sensor Under the Application of Normal Forces. *Sensors* **2018**, *18*, 3614. [CrossRef]

29. Guo, S.; Shiraoka, T.; Inada, S.; Mukai, T. A Two-Ply Polymer-Based Flexible Tactile Sensor Sheet Using Electric Capacitance. *Sensors* **2014**, *14*, 2225–2238. [CrossRef]
30. Asano, S.; Muroyama, M.; Nakayama, T.; Hata, Y.; Nonomura, Y.; Tanaka, S. 3-Axis Fully-Integrated Capacitive Tactile Sensor with Flip-Bonded CMOS on LTCC Interposer. *Sensors* **2017**, *17*, 2451. [CrossRef]
31. Yan, C.; Wang, J.; Kang, W.; Cui, M.; Wang, X.; Foo, C.Y.; Chee, K.J.; Lee, P.S. Highly Stretchable Piezoresistive Graphene–Nanocellulose Nanopaper for Strain Sensors. *Adv. Mater.* **2014**, *26*, 2022–2027. [CrossRef]
32. Stassi, S.; Cauda, V.; Canavese, G.; Pirri, C.F. Flexible Tactile Sensing Based on Piezoresistive Composites: A review. *Sensors* **2014**, *14*, 5296–5332. [CrossRef] [PubMed]
33. Zang, Y.; Zhang, F.; Di, C.; Zhu, D. Advances of flexible pressure sensors toward artificial intelligence and health care applications. *Mater. Horiz.* **2015**, *2*, 140–156. [CrossRef]
34. Wang, C.; Dong, L.; Peng, D.; Pan, C. Tactile Sensors for Advanced Intelligent Systems. *Adv. Intell. Syst.* **2019**, *1*, 1900090. [CrossRef]
35. Huo, Z.; Peng, Y.; Zhang, Y.; Gao, G.; Wan, B.; Wu, W.; Yang, Z.; Wang, X.; Pan, C. Recent Advances in Large-Scale Tactile Sensor Arrays Based on a Transistor Matrix. *Adv. Mater. Interfaces* **2018**, *5*, 1801061. [CrossRef]
36. Kim, K.; Song, G.; Park, C.; Yun, K.S. Multifunctional Woven Structure Operating as Triboelectric Energy Harvester, Capacitive Tactile Sensor Array, and Piezoresistive Strain Sensor Array. *Sensors* **2017**, *17*, 2582. [CrossRef] [PubMed]
37. Yao, H.B.; Ge, J.; Wang, C.F.; Wang, X.; Hu, W.; Zheng, Z.J.; Ni, Y.; Yu, S.H. A Flexible and Highly Pressure-Sensitive Graphene–Polyurethane Sponge Based on Fractured Microstructure Design. *Adv. Mater.* **2013**, *25*, 6692–6698. [CrossRef]
38. Park, J.; Kim, M.; Lee, Y.; Lee, H.S.; Ko, H. Fingertip skin–inspired microstructured ferroelectric skins discriminate static/dynamic pressure and temperature stimuli. *Sci. Adv.* **2015**, *1*, e1500661. [CrossRef]
39. Stampfer, C.; Helbling, T.; Obergfell, D.; Schöberle, B.; Tripp, M.K.; Jungen, A.; Roth, S.; Bright, V.M.; Hierold, C. Fabrication of Single-Walled Carbon-Nanotube-Based Pressure Sensors. *Nano Lett.* **2006**, *6*, 233–237. [CrossRef]
40. Gong, S.; Schwalb, W.; Wang, Y.; Chen, Y.; Tang, Y.; Si, J.; Shirinzadeh, B.; Cheng, W. A wearable and highly sensitive pressure sensor with ultrathin gold nanowires. *Nat. Commun.* **2014**, *5*, 3132. [CrossRef]
41. Martins, P.; Lopes, A.C.; Lanceros-Mendez, S. Electroactive phases of poly(vinylidene fluoride): Determination, processing and applications. *Prog. Polym. Sci.* **2014**, *39*, 683–706. [CrossRef]
42. Zhou, J.; Gu, Y.; Fei, P.; Mai, W.; Gao, Y.; Yang, R.; Bao, G.; Wang, Z.L. Flexible Piezotronic Strain Sensor. *Nano Lett.* **2008**, *8*, 3035–3040. [CrossRef]
43. Persano, L.; Dagdeviren, C.; Su, Y.; Zhang, Y.; Girardo, S.; Pisignano, D.; Huang, Y.; Rogers, J.A. High performance piezoelectric devices based on aligned arrays of nanofibers of poly(vinylidenefluoride-co-trifluoroethylene). *Nat. Commun.* **2013**, *4*, 1633. [CrossRef]
44. Fan, F.R.; Tang, W.; Wang, Z.L. Flexible nanogenerators for energy harvesting and self-powered electronics. *Adv. Mater.* **2016**, *28*, 4283–4305. [CrossRef]
45. Pu, X.; Liu, M.; Chen, X.; Sun, J.; Du, C.; Zhang, Y.; Zhai, J.; Hu, W.; Wang, Z.L. Ultrastretchable, transparent triboelectric nanogenerator as electronic skin for biomechanical energy harvesting and tactile sensing. *Sci. Adv.* **2017**, *3*, e1700015. [CrossRef]
46. Yang, Y.; Zhang, H.; Lin, Z.H.; Zhou, Y.S.; Jing, Q.; Su, Y.; Yang, J.; Chen, J.; Hu, C.; Wang, Z.L. Human Skin Based Triboelectric Nanogenerators for Harvesting Biomechanical Energy and as Self-Powered Active Tactile Sensor System. *ACS Nano* **2013**, *7*, 9213–9222. [CrossRef]
47. Busch-Vishniac, I.J. Piezoelectricity and Pyroelectricity. In *Electromechanical Sensors and Actuators*; Mechanical Engineering Series; Busch-Vishniac, I.J., Ed.; Springer: New York, NY, USA, 1999; pp. 140–183. ISBN 978-1-4612-1434-2.
48. Ramuz, M.; Tee, B.C.K.; Tok, J.B.H.; Bao, Z. Transparent, Optical, Pressure-Sensitive Artificial Skin for Large-Area Stretchable Electronics. *Adv. Mater.* **2012**, *24*, 3223–3227. [CrossRef]
49. Yun, S.; Park, S.; Park, B.; Kim, Y.; Park, S.K.; Nam, S.; Kyung, K.U. Polymer-Based Sensors: Polymer-Waveguide-Based Flexible Tactile Sensor Array for Dynamic Response. *Adv. Mater.* **2014**, *26*, 4473. [CrossRef]
50. Arata, J.; Terakawa, S.; Fujimoto, H. Fiber Optic Force Sensor for Medical Applications within a Backbone-shape Structure. *Procedia CIRP* **2013**, *5*, 66–69. [CrossRef]

51. Zou, L.; Ge, C.; Wang, Z.J.; Cretu, E.; Li, X. Novel Tactile Sensor Technology and Smart Tactile Sensing Systems: A review. *Sensors* **2017**, *17*, 2653. [CrossRef] [PubMed]
52. Lee, J.; Kwon, H.; Seo, J.; Shin, S.; Koo, J.H.; Pang, C.; Son, S.; Kim, J.H.; Jang, Y.H.; Kim, D.E.; et al. Conductive Fiber-Based Ultrasensitive Textile Pressure Sensor for Wearable Electronics. *Adv. Mater.* **2015**, *27*, 2433–2439. [CrossRef] [PubMed]
53. Yang, X.; Wang, Y.; Qing, X. A Flexible Capacitive Pressure Sensor Based on Ionic Liquid. *Sensors* **2018**, *18*, 2395. [CrossRef] [PubMed]
54. Yao, S.; Zhu, Y. Wearable multifunctional sensors using printed stretchable conductors made of silver nanowires. *Nanoscale* **2014**, *6*, 2345–2352. [CrossRef] [PubMed]
55. Mannsfeld, S.C.B.; Tee, B.C.K.; Stoltenberg, R.M.; Chen, C.V.H.H.; Barman, S.; Muir, B.V.O.; Sokolov, A.N.; Reese, C.; Bao, Z. Highly sensitive flexible pressure sensors with microstructured rubber dielectric layers. *Nat. Mater.* **2010**, *9*, 859–864. [CrossRef] [PubMed]
56. Hernández-Sebastián, N.; Díaz-Alonso, D.; Renero-Carrillo, F.J.; Villa-Villaseñor, N.; Calleja-Arriaga, W. Design and Simulation of an Integrated Wireless Capacitive Sensors Array for Measuring Ventricular Pressure. *Sensors* **2018**, *18*, 2781. [CrossRef] [PubMed]
57. Wang, J.; Lou, Y.; Wang, B.; Sun, Q.; Zhou, M.; Li, X. Highly Sensitive, Breathable, and Flexible Pressure Sensor Based on Electrospun Membrane with Assistance of AgNW/TPU as Composite Dielectric Layer. *Sensors* **2020**, *20*, 2459. [CrossRef] [PubMed]
58. Li, M.; Liang, J.; Wang, X.; Zhang, M. Ultra-Sensitive Flexible Pressure Sensor Based on Microstructured Electrode. *Sensors* **2020**, *20*, 371. [CrossRef] [PubMed]
59. Sun, Q.; Kim, D.H.; Park, S.S.; Lee, N.Y.; Zhang, Y.; Lee, J.H.; Cho, K.; Cho, J.H. Transparent, Low-Power Pressure Sensor Matrix Based on Coplanar-Gate Graphene Transistors. *Adv. Mater.* **2014**, *26*, 4735–4740. [CrossRef] [PubMed]
60. Tien, N.T.; Jeon, S.; Kim, D.-I.; Trung, T.Q.; Jang, M.; Hwang, B.U.; Byun, K.E.; Bae, J.; Lee, E.; Tok, J.B.H.; et al. A Flexible Bimodal Sensor Array for Simultaneous Sensing of Pressure and Temperature. *Adv. Mater.* **2014**, *26*, 796–804. [CrossRef] [PubMed]
61. Trung, T.Q.; Tien, N.T.; Kim, D.; Jang, M.; Yoon, O.J.; Lee, N.E. A Flexible Reduced Graphene Oxide Field-Effect Transistor for Ultrasensitive Strain Sensing. *Adv. Funct. Mater.* **2014**, *24*, 117–124. [CrossRef]
62. Someya, T.; Sekitani, T.; Iba, S.; Kato, Y.; Kawaguchi, H.; Sakurai, T. A large-area, flexible pressure sensor matrix with organic field-effect transistors for artificial skin applications. *Proc. Natl. Acad. Sci. USA* **2004**, *101*, 9966–9970. [CrossRef] [PubMed]
63. Kaltenbrunner, M.; Sekitani, T.; Reeder, J.; Yokota, T.; Kuribara, K.; Tokuhara, T.; Drack, M.; Schwödiauer, R.; Graz, I.; Bauer-Gogonea, S.; et al. An ultra-lightweight design for imperceptible plastic electronics. *Nature* **2013**, *499*, 458–463. [CrossRef]
64. Wang, C.; Hwang, D.; Yu, Z.; Takei, K.; Park, J.; Chen, T.; Ma, B.; Javey, A. User-interactive electronic skin for instantaneous pressure visualization. *Nat. Mater.* **2013**, *12*, 899–904. [CrossRef]
65. Wang, Z.L. Piezopotential gated nanowire devices: Piezotronics and piezo-phototronics. *Nano Today* **2010**, *5*, 540–552. [CrossRef]
66. Wu, W.; Wen, X.; Wang, Z.L. Taxel-Addressable Matrix of Vertical-Nanowire Piezotronic Transistors for Active/Adaptive Tactile Imaging. *Science* **2013**, 1234855. [CrossRef] [PubMed]
67. Shin, S.H.; Ji, S.; Choi, S.; Pyo, K.H.; Wan An, B.; Park, J.; Kim, J.; Kim, J.Y.; Lee, K.S.; Kwon, S.Y.; et al. Integrated arrays of air-dielectric graphene transistors as transparent active-matrix pressure sensors for wide pressure ranges. *Nat. Commun.* **2017**, *8*, 14950. [CrossRef] [PubMed]
68. Park, J.; Lee, Y.; Hong, J.; Ha, M.; Jung, Y.D.; Lim, H.; Kim, S.Y.; Ko, H. Giant Tunneling Piezoresistance of Composite Elastomers with Interlocked Microdome Arrays for Ultrasensitive and Multimodal Electronic Skins. *ACS Nano* **2014**, *8*, 4689–4697. [CrossRef]
69. Park, M.; Park, Y.J.; Chen, X.; Park, Y.K.; Kim, M.S.; Ahn, J.H. MoS2-Based Tactile Sensor for Electronic Skin Applications. *Adv. Mater.* **2016**, *28*, 2556–2562. [CrossRef] [PubMed]
70. Li, Y.; Luo, S.; Yang, M.-C.; Liang, R.; Zeng, C. Poisson Ratio and Piezoresistive Sensing: A New Route to High-Performance 3D Flexible and Stretchable Sensors of Multimodal Sensing Capability. *Adv. Funct. Mater.* **2016**, *26*, 2900–2908. [CrossRef]
71. Lee, T.; Choi, Y.W.; Lee, G.; Pikhitsa, P.V.; Kang, D.; Kim, S.M.; Choi, M. Transparent ITO mechanical crack-based pressure and strain sensor. *J. Mater. Chem. C* **2016**, *4*, 9947–9953. [CrossRef]

72. Lipomi, D.J.; Vosgueritchian, M.; Tee, B.C.-K.; Hellstrom, S.L.; Lee, J.A.; Fox, C.H.; Bao, Z. Skin-like pressure and strain sensors based on transparent elastic films of carbon nanotubes. *Nat. Nanotechnol.* **2011**, *6*, 788–792. [CrossRef]
73. Ren, Z.; Nie, J.; Shao, J.; Lai, Q.; Wang, L.; Chen, J.; Chen, X.; Wang, Z.L. Fully Elastic and Metal-Free Tactile Sensors for Detecting both Normal and Tangential Forces Based on Triboelectric Nanogenerators. *Adv. Funct. Mater.* **2018**, *28*, 1802989. [CrossRef]
74. Wang, X.; Zhang, H.; Dong, L.; Han, X.; Du, W.; Zhai, J.; Pan, C.; Wang, Z.L. Self-Powered High-Resolution and Pressure-Sensitive Triboelectric Sensor Matrix for Real-Time Tactile Mapping. *Adv. Mater.* **2016**, *28*, 2896–2903. [CrossRef]
75. Wu, W.; Wang, L.; Li, Y.; Zhang, F.; Lin, L.; Niu, S.; Chenet, D.; Zhang, X.; Hao, Y.; Heinz, T.F.; et al. Piezoelectricity of single-atomic-layer MoS 2 for energy conversion and piezotronics. *Nature* **2014**, *514*, 470–474. [CrossRef] [PubMed]
76. Li, F.; Cabral, M.J.; Xu, B.; Cheng, Z.; Dickey, E.C.; LeBeau, J.M.; Wang, J.; Luo, J.; Taylor, S.; Hackenberger, W.; et al. Giant piezoelectricity of Sm-doped Pb(Mg1/3Nb2/3)O3-PbTiO3 single crystals. *Science* **2019**, *364*, 264–268. [CrossRef]
77. Yi, H.; Lee, S.H.; Ko, H.; Lee, D.; Bae, W.G.; Kim, T.; Hwang, D.S.; Jeong, H.E. Ultra-Adaptable and Wearable Photonic Skin Based on a Shape-Memory, Responsive Cellulose Derivative. *Adv. Funct. Mater.* **2019**, *29*, 1902720. [CrossRef]
78. Wang, X.; Zhang, H.; Yu, R.; Dong, L.; Peng, D.; Zhang, A.; Zhang, Y.; Liu, H.; Pan, C.; Wang, Z.L. Dynamic Pressure Mapping of Personalized Handwriting by a Flexible Sensor Matrix Based on the Mechanoluminescence Process. *Adv. Mater.* **2015**, *27*, 2324–2331. [CrossRef] [PubMed]
79. Dagdeviren, C.; Su, Y.; Joe, P.; Yona, R.; Liu, Y.; Kim, Y.-S.; Huang, Y.; Damadoran, A.R.; Xia, J.; Martin, L.W.; et al. Conformable amplified lead zirconate titanate sensors with enhanced piezoelectric response for cutaneous pressure monitoring. *Nat. Commun.* **2014**, *5*, 4496. [CrossRef]
80. Chen, C.T.; Lee, W.Y.; Shen, T.L.; Wu, H.C.; Shih, C.C.; Ye, B.W.; Lin, T.Y.; Chen, W.C.; Chen, Y.F. Highly Reliable and Sensitive Tactile Transistor Memory. *Adv. Electron. Mater.* **2017**, *3*, 1600548. [CrossRef]
81. Takei, K.; Takahashi, T.; Ho, J.C.; Ko, H.; Gillies, A.G.; Leu, P.W.; Fearing, R.S.; Javey, A. Nanowire active-matrix circuitry for low-voltage macroscale artificial skin. *Nat. Mater.* **2010**, *9*, 821–826. [CrossRef]
82. Yeom, C.; Chen, K.; Kiriya, D.; Yu, Z.; Cho, G.; Javey, A. Large-Area Compliant Tactile Sensors Using Printed Carbon Nanotube Active-Matrix Backplanes. *Adv. Mater.* **2015**, *27*, 1561–1566. [CrossRef]
83. Graz, I.; Krause, M.; Bauer-Gogonea, S.; Bauer, S.; Lacour, S.P.; Ploss, B.; Zirkl, M.; Stadlober, B.; Wagner, S. Flexible active-matrix cells with selectively poled bifunctional polymer-ceramic nanocomposite for pressure and temperature sensing skin. *J. Appl. Phys.* **2009**, *106*, 034503. [CrossRef]
84. Sekitani, T.; Yokota, T.; Zschieschang, U.; Klauk, H.; Bauer, S.; Takeuchi, K.; Takamiya, M.; Sakurai, T.; Someya, T. Organic Nonvolatile Memory Transistors for Flexible Sensor Arrays. *Science* **2009**, *326*, 1516–1519. [CrossRef] [PubMed]
85. Graz, I.; Kaltenbrunner, M.; Keplinger, C.; Schwödiauer, R.; Bauer, S.; Lacour, S.P.; Wagner, S. Flexible ferroelectret field-effect transistor for large-area sensor skins and microphones. *Appl. Phys. Lett.* **2006**, *89*, 073501. [CrossRef]
86. Chen, L.; Xue, F.; Li, X.; Huang, X.; Wang, L.; Kou, J.; Wang, Z.L. Strain-Gated Field Effect Transistor of a MoS $_2$ –ZnO 2D–1D Hybrid Structure. *ACS Nano* **2016**, *10*, 1546–1551. [CrossRef] [PubMed]
87. Yang, T.; Xie, D.; Li, Z.; Zhu, H. Recent advances in wearable tactile sensors: Materials, sensing mechanisms, and device performance. *Mater. Sci. Eng. R Rep.* **2017**, *115*, 1–37. [CrossRef]
88. Wang, L.; Liu, S.; Feng, X.; Xu, Q.; Bai, S.; Zhu, L.; Chen, L.; Qin, Y.; Wang, Z.L. Ultrasensitive Vertical Piezotronic Transistor Based on ZnO Twin Nanoplatelet. *ACS Nano* **2017**, *11*, 4859–4865. [CrossRef] [PubMed]
89. Yang, Z.W.; Pang, Y.; Zhang, L.; Lu, C.; Chen, J.; Zhou, T.; Zhang, C.; Wang, Z.L. Tribotronic Transistor Array as an Active Tactile Sensing System. *ACS Nano* **2016**, *10*, 10912–10920. [CrossRef]
90. Wang, Z.L. Progress in Piezotronics and Piezo-Phototronics. *Adv. Mater.* **2012**, *24*, 4632–4646. [CrossRef]
91. Liu, S.; Wang, L.; Feng, X.; Wang, Z.; Xu, Q.; Bai, S.; Qin, Y.; Wang, Z.L. Ultrasensitive 2D ZnO Piezotronic Transistor Array for High Resolution Tactile Imaging. *Adv. Mater.* **2017**, *29*, 1606346. [CrossRef]
92. Liu, S.; Wang, L.; Wang, Z.; Cai, Y.; Feng, X.; Qin, Y.; Wang, Z.L. Double-Channel Piezotronic Transistors for Highly Sensitive Pressure Sensing. *ACS Nano* **2018**, *12*, 1732–1738. [CrossRef]

93. Schwartz, G.; Tee, B.C.K.; Mei, J.; Appleton, A.L.; Kim, D.H.; Wang, H.; Bao, Z. Flexible polymer transistors with high pressure sensitivity for application in electronic skin and health monitoring. *Nat. Commun. Lond.* **2013**, *4*, 1859. [CrossRef] [PubMed]
94. Chen, S.; Zhuo, B.; Guo, X. Large Area One-Step Facile Processing of Microstructured Elastomeric Dielectric Film for High Sensitivity and Durable Sensing over Wide Pressure Range. *ACS Appl. Mater. Interfaces* **2016**, *8*, 20364–20370. [CrossRef]
95. Kwon, D.; Lee, T.I.; Shim, J.; Ryu, S.; Kim, M.S.; Kim, S.; Kim, T.S.; Park, I. Highly Sensitive, Flexible, and Wearable Pressure Sensor Based on a Giant Piezocapacitive Effect of Three-Dimensional Microporous Elastomeric Dielectric Layer. *ACS Appl. Mater. Interfaces* **2016**, *8*, 16922–16931. [CrossRef]
96. Zang, Y.; Zhang, F.; Huang, D.; Gao, X.; Di, C.; Zhu, D. Flexible suspended gate organic thin-film transistors for ultra-sensitive pressure detection. *Nat. Commun. Lond.* **2015**, *6*, 6269. [CrossRef]
97. Viry, L.; Levi, A.; Totaro, M.; Mondini, A.; Mattoli, V.; Mazzolai, B.; Beccai, L. Flexible Three-Axial Force Sensor for Soft and Highly Sensitive Artificial Touch. *Adv. Mater.* **2014**, *26*, 2659–2664. [CrossRef] [PubMed]
98. Someya, T.; Kato, Y.; Sekitani, T.; Iba, S.; Noguchi, Y.; Murase, Y.; Kawaguchi, H.; Sakurai, T. Conformable, flexible, large-area networks of pressure and thermal sensors with organic transistor active matrixes. *Proc. Natl. Acad. Sci. USA* **2005**, *102*, 12321–12325. [CrossRef] [PubMed]
99. Hua, Q.; Sun, J.; Liu, H.; Bao, R.; Yu, R.; Zhai, J.; Pan, C.; Wang, Z.L. Skin-inspired highly stretchable and conformable matrix networks for multifunctional sensing. *Nat. Commun.* **2018**, *9*, 1–11. [CrossRef] [PubMed]
100. Hwang, E.-S.; Seo, J.; Kim, Y.J. A Polymer-Based Flexible Tactile Sensor for Both Normal and Shear Load Detections and Its Application for Robotics. *J. Microelectromechanical Syst.* **2007**, *16*, 556–563. [CrossRef]
101. Choi, D.; Jang, S.; Kim, J.S.; Kim, H.-J.; Kim, D.H.; Kwon, J.-Y. A Highly Sensitive Tactile Sensor Using a Pyramid-Plug Structure for Detecting Pressure, Shear Force, and Torsion. *Adv. Mater. Technol.* **2019**, *4*, 1800284. [CrossRef]
102. Park, J.; Lee, Y.; Hong, J.; Lee, Y.; Ha, M.; Jung, Y.; Lim, H.; Kim, S.Y.; Ko, H. Tactile-Direction-Sensitive and Stretchable Electronic Skins Based on Human-Skin-Inspired Interlocked Microstructures. *ACS Nano* **2014**, *8*, 12020–12029. [CrossRef]
103. Kim, D.H.; Lu, N.; Ma, R.; Kim, Y.-S.; Kim, R.H.; Wang, S.; Wu, J.; Won, S.M.; Tao, H.; Islam, A.; et al. Epidermal Electronics. *Science* **2011**, *333*, 838–843. [CrossRef]
104. Yang, G.-Z.; Bellingham, J.; Dupont, P.E.; Fischer, P.; Floridi, L.; Full, R.; Jacobstein, N.; Kumar, V.; McNutt, M.; Merrifield, R.; et al. The grand challenges of *Science Robotics*. *Sci. Robot.* **2018**, *3*, eaar7650. [CrossRef]
105. Whitesides, G.M. Soft Robotics. *Angew. Chem. Int. Ed.* **2018**, *57*, 4258–4273. [CrossRef] [PubMed]
106. Laschi, C.; Mazzolai, B.; Cianchetti, M. Soft robotics: Technologies and systems pushing the boundaries of robot abilities. *Sci. Robot.* **2016**, *1*, eaah3690. [CrossRef]
107. Thuruthel, T.G.; Shih, B.; Laschi, C.; Tolley, M.T. Soft robot perception using embedded soft sensors and recurrent neural networks. *Sci. Robot.* **2019**, *4*, eaav1488. [CrossRef]
108. Rich, S.I.; Wood, R.J.; Majidi, C. Untethered soft robotics. *Nat. Electron.* **2018**, *1*, 102–112. [CrossRef]
109. Ji, S.; Jang, J.; Hwang, J.C.; Lee, Y.; Lee, J.H.; Park, J.U. Amorphous Oxide Semiconductor Transistors with Air Dielectrics for Transparent and Wearable Pressure Sensor Arrays. *Adv. Mater. Technol.* **2020**, *5*, 1900928. [CrossRef]
110. Wang, C.; Pan, C.; Wang, Z. Electronic Skin for Closed-Loop Systems. *ACS Nano* **2019**, *13*, 12287–12293. [CrossRef]
111. Lee, Y.; Ahn, J.H. Biomimetic Tactile Sensors Based on Nanomaterials. *ACS Nano* **2020**, *14*, 1220–1226. [CrossRef] [PubMed]
112. Hammock, M.L.; Chortos, A.; Tee, B.C.K.; Tok, J.B.H.; Bao, Z. 25th Anniversary Article: The Evolution of Electronic Skin (E-Skin): A Brief History, Design Considerations, and Recent Progress. *Adv. Mater.* **2013**, *25*, 5997–6038. [CrossRef]
113. Cheneler, D.; Ward, M.C.L.; Anthony, C.J. Bio-hybrid tactile sensor for the study of the role of mechanoreceptors in human tactile perception. *Microelectron. Eng.* **2012**, *97*, 297–300. [CrossRef]
114. Omerbašić, D.; Schuhmacher, L.N.; Bernal Sierra, Y.-A.; Smith, E.S.J.; Lewin, G.R. ASICs and mammalian mechanoreceptor function. *Neuropharmacology* **2015**, *94*, 80–86. [CrossRef] [PubMed]
115. Baik, S.; Lee, H.J.; Kim, D.W.; Kim, J.W.; Lee, Y.; Pang, C. Bioinspired Adhesive Architectures: From Skin Patch to Integrated Bioelectronics. *Adv. Mater.* **2019**, *31*, 1803309. [CrossRef] [PubMed]

116. Kim, S.J.; Song, W.; Yi, Y.; Min, B.K.; Mondal, S.; An, K.S.; Choi, C.G. High Durability and Waterproofing rGO/SWCNT-Fabric-Based Multifunctional Sensors for Human-Motion Detection. *ACS Appl. Mater. Interfaces* **2018**, *10*, 3921–3928. [CrossRef]
117. Park, Y.J.; Sharma, B.K.; Shinde, S.M.; Kim, M.S.; Jang, B.; Kim, J.H.; Ahn, J.H. All MoS$_2$-Based Large Area, Skin-Attachable Active-Matrix Tactile Sensor. *ACS Nano* **2019**, *13*, 3023–3030. [CrossRef]
118. Lou, Z.; Chen, S.; Wang, L.; Shi, R.; Li, L.; Jiang, K.; Chen, D.; Shen, G. Ultrasensitive and ultraflexible e-skins with dual functionalities for wearable electronics. *Nano Energy* **2017**, *38*, 28–35. [CrossRef]
119. Boutry, C.M.; Negre, M.; Jorda, M.; Vardoulis, O.; Chortos, A.; Khatib, O.; Bao, Z. A hierarchically patterned, bioinspired e-skin able to detect the direction of applied pressure for robotics. *Sci. Robot.* **2018**, *3*, eaau6914. [CrossRef]
120. You, I.; Choi, S.E.; Hwang, H.; Han, S.W.; Kim, J.W.; Jeong, U. E-Skin Tactile Sensor Matrix Pixelated by Position-Registered Conductive Microparticles Creating Pressure-Sensitive Selectors. *Adv. Funct. Mater.* **2018**, *28*, 1801858. [CrossRef]
121. Sundaram, S.; Kellnhofer, P.; Li, Y.; Zhu, J.-Y.; Torralba, A.; Matusik, W. Learning the signatures of the human grasp using a scalable tactile glove. *Nature* **2019**, *569*, 698–702. [CrossRef]
122. Spiers, A.J.; Liarokapis, M.V.; Calli, B.; Dollar, A.M. Single-Grasp Object Classification and Feature Extraction with Simple Robot Hands and Tactile Sensors. *IEEE Trans. Haptics* **2016**, *9*, 207–220. [CrossRef]
123. Liu, H.; Guo, D.; Sun, F. Object Recognition Using Tactile Measurements: Kernel Sparse Coding Methods. *IEEE Trans. Instrum. Meas.* **2016**, *65*, 656–665. [CrossRef]
124. Luo, S.; Mou, W.; Althoefer, K.; Liu, H. Novel Tactile-SIFT Descriptor for Object Shape Recognition. *IEEE Sens. J.* **2015**, *15*, 5001–5009. [CrossRef]
125. Kaboli, M.; Feng, D.; Yao, K.; Lanillos, P.; Cheng, G. A Tactile-Based Framework for Active Object Learning and Discrimination using Multimodal Robotic Skin. *IEEE Robot. Autom. Lett.* **2017**, *2*, 2143–2150. [CrossRef]
126. Cheong, W.H.; Oh, B.; Kim, S.H.; Jang, J.; Ji, S.; Lee, S.; Cheon, J.; Yoo, S.; Lee, S.Y.; Park, J.U. Platform for wireless pressure sensing with built-in battery and instant visualization. *Nano Energy* **2019**, *62*, 230–238. [CrossRef]
127. Park, Y.G.; Cha, E.; An, H.S.; Lee, K.P.; Song, M.H.; Kim, H.K.; Park, J.U. Wireless phototherapeutic contact lenses and glasses with red light-emitting diodes. *Nano Res.* **2020**, *13*, 1347–1353. [CrossRef]
128. Crowder, R. Toward Robots That Can Sense Texture by Touch. *Science* **2006**, *312*, 1478–1479. [CrossRef] [PubMed]
129. Kim, E.H.; Han, H.; Yu, S.; Park, C.; Kim, G.; Jeong, B.; Lee, S.W.; Kim, J.S.; Lee, S.; Kim, J.; et al. Interactive Skin Display with Epidermal Stimuli Electrode. *Adv. Sci.* **2019**, *6*, 1802351. [CrossRef] [PubMed]
130. Amoli, V.; Kim, J.S.; Kim, S.Y.; Koo, J.; Chung, Y.S.; Choi, H.; Kim, D.H. Ionic Tactile Sensors for Emerging Human-Interactive Technologies: A Review of Recent Progress. *Adv. Funct. Mater.* **2020**, *30*, 1904532. [CrossRef]
131. Jang, J.; Jang, J.; Kim, H.; Kim, H.; Song, Y.M.; Park, J.U.; Park, J.U. Implantation of electronic visual prosthesis for blindness restoration. *Opt. Mater. Express* **2019**, *9*, 3878–3894. [CrossRef]
132. Hong, M.-S.; Choi, G.M.; Kim, J.; Jang, J.; Choi, B.; Kim, J.K.; Jeong, S.; Leem, S.; Kwon, H.Y.; Hwang, H.B.; et al. Biomimetic Chitin–Silk Hybrids: An Optically Transparent Structural Platform for Wearable Devices and Advanced Electronics. *Adv. Funct. Mater.* **2018**, *28*, 1705480. [CrossRef]
133. Puangmali, P.; Althoefer, K.; Seneviratne, L.D.; Murphy, D.; Dasgupta, P. State-of-the-Art in Force and Tactile Sensing for Minimally Invasive Surgery. *IEEE Sens. J.* **2008**, *8*, 371–381. [CrossRef]
134. Wang, Y.; Wang, L.; Yang, T.; Li, X.; Zang, X.; Zhu, M.; Wang, K.; Wu, D.; Zhu, H. Wearable and highly sensitive graphene strain sensors for human motion monitoring. *Adv. Funct. Mater.* **2014**, *24*, 4666–4670. [CrossRef]
135. Kim, J.; Kim, M.; Lee, M.S.; Kim, K.; Ji, S.; Kim, Y.T.; Park, J.; Na, K.; Bae, K.H.; Kyun Kim, H.; et al. Wearable smart sensor systems integrated on soft contact lenses for wireless ocular diagnostics. *Nat. Commun.* **2017**, *8*, 14997. [CrossRef] [PubMed]
136. Park, J.; Kim, J.; Kim, S.Y.; Cheong, W.H.; Jang, J.; Park, Y.G.; Na, K.; Kim, Y.T.; Heo, J.H.; Lee, C.Y.; et al. Soft, smart contact lenses with integrations of wireless circuits, glucose sensors, and displays. *Sci. Adv.* **2018**, *4*, eaap9841. [CrossRef] [PubMed]

© 2020 by the authors. Licensee MDPI, Basel, Switzerland. This article is an open access article distributed under the terms and conditions of the Creative Commons Attribution (CC BY) license (http://creativecommons.org/licenses/by/4.0/).

Letter

A Hierarchical Learning Approach for Human Action Recognition

Nicolas Lemieux * and Rita Noumeir

Electrical Engineering Department, École de Technologies Supérieure, Montreal, QC H3C 1K3, Canada; Rita.Noumeir@etsmtl.ca
* Correspondence: nicolas.lemieux.1@etsmtl.net

Received: 28 July 2020; Accepted: 26 August 2020; Published: 1 September 2020

Abstract: In the domain of human action recognition, existing works mainly focus on using RGB, depth, skeleton and infrared data for analysis. While these methods have the benefit of being non-invasive, they can only be used within limited setups, are prone to issues such as occlusion and often need substantial computational resources. In this work, we address human action recognition through inertial sensor signals, which have a vast quantity of practical applications in fields such as sports analysis and human-machine interfaces. For that purpose, we propose a new learning framework built around a 1D-CNN architecture, which we validated by achieving very competitive results on the publicly available UTD-MHAD dataset. Moreover, the proposed method provides some answers to two of the greatest challenges currently faced by action recognition algorithms, which are (1) the recognition of high-level activities and (2) the reduction of their computational cost in order to make them accessible to embedded devices. Finally, this paper also investigates the tractability of the features throughout the proposed framework, both in time and duration, as we believe it could play an important role in future works in order to make the solution more intelligible, hardware-friendly and accurate.

Keywords: human action recognition; HAR; explainable deep-learning; 1D CNN; one-vs.-all; high-level activity recognition; intelligent sensors; modular method; light-weight method

1. Introduction

As human beings, part of our happiness or suffering depends on our interactions with our direct environment, which is governed by an implicit or explicit set of rules [1]. Meanwhile, a growing proportion of these interactions are now targeted towards connected devices such as smart phones, smart watches, intelligent home assistants and other IoT objects since their number and range of applications keep growing every year [2]. As a consequence of this phenomenon, efforts are made in order to improve the users' experience through the elaboration of some ever-more intuitive and comfortable human-machine interfaces [3]. With the relatively recent successes of artificial intelligence based algorithms and the emergence of a wide range of new sensors, human action recognition (HAR) has become one of the most popular problems in the field of pattern recognition currently and plays a key role in the development of such interfaces. In that context, RGB, depth, skeleton and infrared stream based approaches attracted most of the scientific community's attention as their non-invasive nature is well suited for applications such as surveillance and led to the creation of commonly accepted benchmarks such as NTU-RGB-D [4], which was recently enhanced as NTU-RGB-D 120 [5]. On the other hand, action recognition based on visual streams can only be used within limited setups, is prone to issues such as occlusion and often needs substantial computational resources.

Admittedly less popular, HAR based on inertial sensor signals is still a relevant subject of research. Despite the fact that with this approach, the users are required to wear some kind of device, thanks to the miniaturization of microelectromechanical systems (MEMS), inertial measurement units (IMU) are now seamlessly integrated with different day-to-day objects such as remote controls or smart-phones and wearable technologies such as smart watches or smart cloths. Furthermore, for applications such as sports analysis, fall detection or remote physiotherapy, it provides an interesting alternative, as it can be used anywhere, provides more privacy and is considerably less expensive.

Although many different datasets exist in that branch of HAR, none have really established themselves as a clear benchmark, as placement strategies of the IMUs, or the set of activities are mostly targeted towards specific applications. In this work, we opted for the University of Dallas, Texas, multimodal human action dataset (UTD-MHAD) in order to validate our approach, as we believed that it offered the most variability in terms of activities (27) and actors (eight). Not only did the proposed method achieve competitive results on the classification task using IMU signals, it was also designed in order to address two of the biggest challenges currently faced by HAR algorithms [6]. For that purpose, we propose a hierarchical representation of the different actions by sampling the maximum and minimum activation of each convolution kernel throughout the network, which could potentially help with (1) the recognition of high-level activities characterized by the large time variations in the sub-movements composing them. Moreover, as the proposed solution is built around a 1D-CNN architecture, it was also observed that it necessitated dramatically less operations or memory than the most popular architectures, thus greatly contributing to (2) the portability to limited resource electronics for HAR algorithms. Finally, in this paper, we also investigated the tractability of the features throughout the proposed framework, both in time and duration, as we believe it could play an important role in future works in order to make the solution more intelligible, hardware-friendly, robust and accurate. For the rest of the present article, the following structure will observed:

- Section 2 quickly reviews the literature.
- Section 3 provides a detailed explanation of the method.
- Section 4 details the temporal analysis, showing how feature elements can be localized in time and that they report the dynamics of different durations.
- Section 5 provides the results in order to validate both the performances and properties of the proposed method.
- Section 6 summarizes the important results and their implications and provides ideas for future work.

2. Related Works

2.1. Neural Network Based HAR

Originally based on conventional machine learning methods such as support vector machines (SVM), decision trees or k-nearest neighbour (k-NN), early methods for HAR relied on various time and/or frequency domain features extracted from the raw data. However, as for many other fields, inertial sensor based HAR benefited from gradient descent based methods. Besides improving the classification capabilities, these methods also alleviated the requirement of feature engineering as they learn the features and classifier simultaneously from the annotated data. As a matter of fact, Kwapisz et al. [7] observed that multi-layer-perceptrons (MLPs) were superior to decision trees and logistic regression for HAR. Similarly, Weiss et al. [8] observed that MLP outperformed decision trees, k-NN, naive Bayes and logistic regression when the training and evaluation was done on data gathered from the same user and also noted that these user-specific models performed dramatically better than impersonal models where training and evaluation users are different. Since then, models based on convolution neural networks (CNN) have been proposed for inertial sensor based HAR [9–12] and have also been proven superior to k-NN and SVM [11]. With these methods, the input signals usually go through multiple convolution and pooling layers before being fed to a classifier. Although 1D-CNN architectures are well suited for the time series type of data such as IMU signals, CNNs are more famous in their 2D form, considering the tremendous amount of success they have had in the field of image recognition. Consequently, Jiang et al. [13] proposed to construct an activity image, based on IMU signals, in order to proceed to HAR as an image recognition problem. Back to 1D-CNN, Ronao et al. [12] showed that wider kernels and a low pooling size resulted in better performances. More recently, Murad et al. [14] implemented a recurrent neural network (RNN) and demonstrated the prevalence of their method over SVM and k-NN. Moreover, employing the long short-term memory (LSTM) variation of RNN along with CNNs, Hammerla et al. [15] and Ordonez et al. [16] achieved better results than with some strictly CNN based methods. However, the CNN architectures they used in their comparative study had respectively a maximum of three and four convolution blocks. Meanwhile, Imran and Raman [9] conducted an analysis on the topology of the 1D-CNN, from which they concluded that five consecutive blocks of convolution and pooling layers were better than four. Furthermore, with their architecture and a data augmentation strategy, they also achieved state-of-the-art results on the UTD-MHAD dataset for both sensor based and multi-modal HAR. Yet, leaving data augmentation aside, the proposed method in this article slightly outperformed theirs for the sensor based HAR.

2.2. Temporal Normalization

As the popular machine learning frameworks require the inputs to be of a constant shape during the training process and as different actions usually have different durations, temporal normalization is mandatory. On that account, different strategies have been proposed. One way to do it is by randomly sampling a fixed number of frames from a longer sequence while keeping the chronological ordering [9,15]. It can also serve as a data augmentation technique, since the sampled frames can vary from one epoch to another. Another way to do it is to sample a fixed amount of consecutive frames from the action sequence [8]. In this case, the algorithms often have to learn from incomplete representations. Finally, a more conservative way to achieve temporal normalization is to extend, up to a fixed point, the signals with zeros. This technique is also known as zero-padding. It has the benefit of enabling the algorithms to learn features on complete and undistorted sequences. Therefore, it will be the preferred strategy in this work. Moreover, contrary to Imran and Raman [9], who reported that the performances of their CNN based method decayed with the augmentation of the amount of zero-padding, our method proved itself to be robust against it.

3. Proposed Method

Like the majority of HAR algorithms, the main objective of our method is to provide a way to successfully classify specific actions based on a multivariate time series input. In the sensor based variation of HAR addressed here, the input time series, X^0, consist of a fixed number of time steps, T_0, each reporting a dynamic occurring at a certain moment t, by providing, in a vector form, x_t, the speed and angular rate variations, γ and ω, with respect to a 3-dimensional (x,y,z) orthogonal coordinate system whose origin corresponds to the IMU sensor. This can be expressed mathematically as:

$$X^0 = [x_1^0, \ldots x_t^0, \ldots x_{T_0}^0] \quad \text{where} \quad x_t^0 = \begin{bmatrix} \gamma_t^x \\ \gamma_t^y \\ \gamma_t^z \\ \omega_t^x \\ \omega_t^y \\ \omega_t^z \end{bmatrix} \quad (1)$$

In order to train our algorithm, the original time series, X^0, is conveyed to a 1D-CNN constituted of multiple convolution blocks in cascade (i.e., the output of a specific block serves as the input for the next), each applying a certain set of convolution filters, batch normalisation and max pooling. From this process, L other time series are created, $\{X^l \in \mathbb{R}^{F_l \times T_l}\}_{l=1}^L$. Here, L is the number of convolution blocks; F_l is the number of filters in the lth convolution block's filter bank, $W^l \in \mathbb{R}^{F_l \times m_l \times F_{l-1}}$ (whose filters are of size m_l along the temporal axis); T_l is the number of corresponding time steps of the lth generated time series, $\mathbf{X}^l$. Hence, the lth time series is described as:

$$\mathbf{X}^l = [\mathbf{x}_1^l, \ldots \mathbf{x}_t^l, \ldots \mathbf{x}_{T_l}^l] \quad \text{where} \quad \mathbf{x}_t^l = [x_t^{l,1}, \ldots x_t^{l,k}, \ldots x_t^{l,F_l}]^\top \quad (2)$$

In these blocks, convolutions are carried without bias; thus, they can be described by the following equation:

$$\mathbf{z}_t^l = \phi\left(\mathbf{W}^l * \mathbf{X}_{[t, t+m_l-1]}^{l-1}\right) \quad (3)$$

where $\mathbf{z}_t^l$ is the vector resulting from the application of all the convolution filters of $\mathbf{W}^l$ to the portion of the previous time series whose vectors are between the tth and $(t + m_l - 1)$th time steps inclusively, $\mathbf{X}_{[t,t+m_l-1]}^{l-1}$; ϕ is the SeLU activation function [17], which demonstrated better experimental results; and $*$ is the convolution operator, which can be equivalently expressed as Equation (4) where $\mathbf{W}_i^{l,k}$ is the ith column of the kth filter of $\mathbf{W}^l$.

$$\mathbf{W}^{l,k} * \mathbf{X}_{[t,t+m_l-1]}^{l-1} \equiv \sum_{i=1}^{m_l} \langle (\mathbf{W}_i^{l,k})^\top, \mathbf{x}_{t+i-1}^{l-1} \rangle \quad (4)$$

Subsequently applying batch normalization and max pooling to the convolution output, the elements of the time step vector, $x_t^{l,k}$, of the different time series, $\{\mathbf{X}^l\}_{l=1}^L$, are calculated as:

$$x_t^{l,k} = \max\left\{BN_{\Gamma^k, \beta^k}(z_{2t}^{l,k}), BN_{\Gamma^k, \beta^k}(z_{2t+1}^{l,k})\right\} \quad (5)$$

where $BN_{\Gamma^k, \beta^k}(z_{2t}^{l,k})$ is the batch normalization operation, which is defined as:

$$BN_{\Gamma^k, \beta^k}(z_t^{l,k}) = \frac{z_t^{l,k} - \mu_B^k}{\sqrt{(\sigma_B^k)^2 + \epsilon}} \times \Gamma^k + \beta^k \quad (6)$$

where μ_B^k and $(\sigma_B^k)^2$ refer to the mean and variance of the elements of the kth dimension computed on the examples of the mini-batch, B; ϵ is an arbitrarily small constant used for numerical stability; and finally, Γ and β are parameters learned in the optimization process in order to restore the representation power of the network [18]. It can be deduced from Equation (5) that the width of the max pooling operator is 2; hence, the length of the time series is halved after each convolution block (i.e., $T_l = \frac{1}{2} T_{l-1}$).

Rather then connecting the output of the last convolution block to a classifier, as was done in previous 1D-CNN based works [9–12], the proposed method instead achieves high-level reasoning (inference and learning) by connecting to a classifier the maximum and minimum values of each dimension of each time series generated throughout the network. Equivalently, this concept can be regarded as generating a feature vector, $\mathcal{V}$, by sampling elements of the different time series as such:

$$\mathcal{V} = \bigcup_l \left\{ \max_t \{x_t^{l,k}\}, \quad \min_t \{x_t^{l,k}\} \right\}_{k=1}^{F_l} \quad (7)$$

and when doing so, it is important to keep a constant ordering of the elements of the feature vector. This way, the sampled values from a specific time series associated with a specific convolution filter always exploit the same connections to the classifier. For that purpose, Algorithm 1 was used in order to create the feature vectors:

As CNNs learn convolution filters that react to specific features, these maximum and minimum activation values are correlated with specific motions. To ensure that the convolution filters learn and capture discriminating dynamics for every action class, different sets of filter banks were independently learned through multiple binary classification problems and grouped convolutions. From this process, illustrated in Figure 1, N different feature vectors, $\{\mathcal{V}\}_{c=1}^{N}$, were created based on the discriminating filters learned for each of the N different actions. Additionally, this process also resulted in N different binary classifiers.

Algorithm 1: Feature vector harvesting method.

Input: *The set of time series generated by the L convolution blocks* $\mathbf{X} = [\mathbf{X}^1, \ldots \mathbf{X}^l, \ldots \mathbf{X}^L]$
Output: *Feature vector:* $\mathcal{V} = [\min_t\{x_t^{1,1}\}, \ldots, \max_t\{x_t^{L,F_L}\}]$

$\mathcal{V} \leftarrow$ new hash table;
for *each time series* $\mathbf{X}^l \in \mathbf{X}$ **do**
   min <- new hash table;
   Max <- new hash table;
   for *each dimension, k, of the lth time series vector* $x_t^l \in \mathbf{X}^l$ **do**
      insert $\min_t\{x_t^{l,k}\}$ into min;
      insert $\max_t\{x_t^{l,k}\}$ into Max;
   end
   insert min into $\mathcal{V}$;
   insert Max into $\mathcal{V}$;
end

As each classifier can be taken individually with their specific set of filters in order to recognize a specific action, our method is modular. Thus, it is possible to reduce the computation and memory requirements dramatically during inference if a single or a reduced set of actions is targeted.

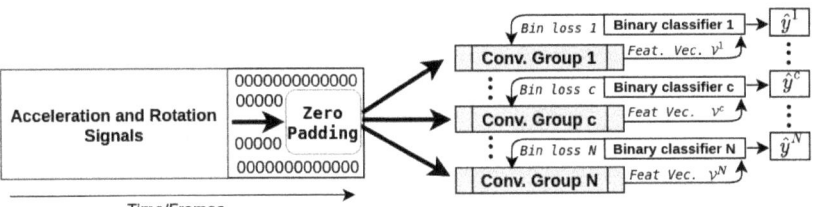

Figure 1. An high-level representation of the network architecture and learning mechanisms. Each class has its own convolution group that does the feature extraction and its own binary classifier.

Although it is probable that performances could be improved by tailoring a specific architecture for each class, this avenue was not explored in the present work. Instead, each convolution group has the same architecture that is provided by Figure 2.

As illustrated, it consists of five consecutive blocks that are defined by the following operations:

- A multi-channel 1D convolution layer
- Batch normalization
- Max pooling
- Feature sampling

According to the proposed architecture, it is also important to observe that in the first block, the convolution kernels' width (m_1) is set to 1; hence, instantaneous dynamics are sampled. As the information moves to subsequent blocks, longer discriminating dynamics are harvested by the coaction of both larger kernels and pooling layers compressing the temporal information while providing a certain degree of invariance towards translations and elastic distortions [19]. It is also possible to observe, in Figure 2, that each convolution layer has a total of 32 filters (f^l) from which it ensures that each feature vector (depicted at the bottom) has a total of 320 elements (32 min and 32 max for each of the 5 generated times series).

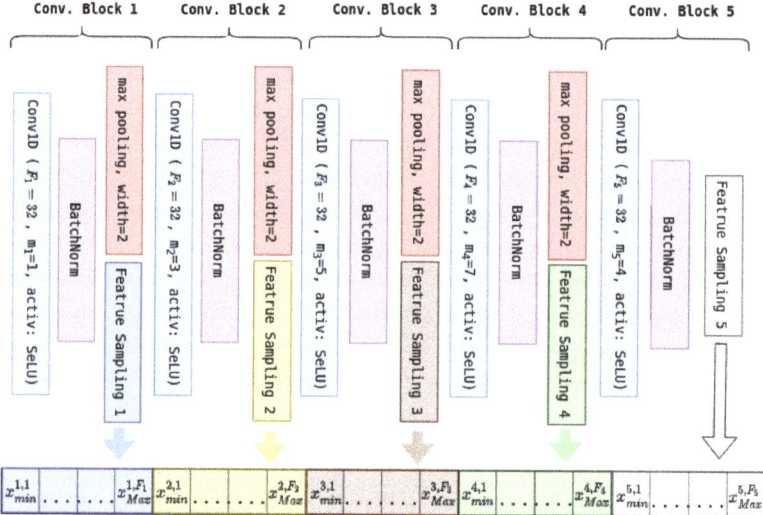

Figure 2. Architecture of a convolution group. For the convolution operation (in blue), F_l and m_l refer to the number of convolution filters (F_l) and their width along the temporal dimension (m_l) according to the conv. block to which they belong (l), and activ. refers to the activation function. The purple rectangle is there to illustrate the batch normalization operation applied to the convolutions' output. From this normalized output, max pooling is applied, resulting in a new time series X^l from which elements of the feature vector are sampled and serving as the next block's input.

In order to train binary classifiers (see Figure 1), some relabelling had to be done. Therefore, all the examples were relabelled with respect to the different groups as 1 if the group index, c, matched the original multi-class label and 0 otherwise.

$$y^c = \begin{cases} 1, & \text{if } y_c = 1 \\ 0, & \text{otherwise} \end{cases} \tag{8}$$

This process is thus described by Equation (8), where y^c refers to the label attributed to the examples going through the cth binary classifier and y_c is the cth element of the original multi-class label expressed as the vector $\mathbf{y} \in \{0,1\}^N$ such that the true class element is set to 1 and all others to 0 (one-hot-encoding).

$$\mathcal{P}_{rediction} = \arg\max_c \{\hat{y}^c\}_{c=1}^N, \tag{9}$$

In the proposed method, predictions were made based on a one-vs.-all approach, which is depicted by Equation (9), where $\hat{y}^c$ corresponds to the probability output for the positive class of the cth binary classifier.

As for the convolution groups, the architectures of the binary classifiers are identical. As shown on Figure 3, the feature vector (whose elements are in red) starts by going through a batch-normalization layer (in purple) before going through two fully connected layers (in blue). Unlike the convolution modules, bias was allowed, and the chosen activation function was ReLU. Additionally, dropout layers (in yellow) randomly dropping half of the connections after both fully connected layers were inserted in order to reduce overfitting. Lastly, as part of each learning process, the classifiers' outputs ($\hat{y}^c$ and $1 - \hat{y}^c$) were made "probabilistic" (positive and summing to one) using the softmax function (in green).

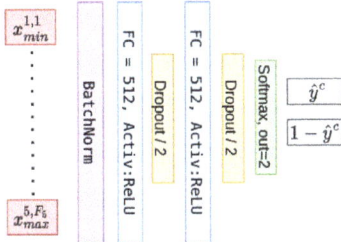

Figure 3. Binary classifier.

The cost function used during the training phase was the weighted cross-entropy, which is expressed by Equation (10). As it has been shown to be an effective way to deal with unbalanced data [20], the weights were set to be inversely proportional to the number of training examples of a specific class relative to the total number of training examples. Thus, by assigning a weight of 1 to the positive class' examples, the weight of the negative class' examples (label = 0) is $\frac{S_c}{M-S_c}$, where S_c is the number of training examples of the specific class c and M is the total number of training examples.

$$- y^c \log \left(\hat{y}^c \right) - \frac{S_c}{M - S_c} (1 - y^c) \log \left(1 - \hat{y}^c \right) \tag{10}$$

4. Temporal Analysis

With the proposed method, it is possible to localize in time each element of the feature vector used in order to make predictions and/or train the network. As a matter of fact, the functions torch.max and torch.min of the PyTorch library, used in order to create our feature vectors, return the index location of the maximum or minimum value of each row of the input tensor in a given dimension, k. Hence, this section will explain how the sampled elements of the feature vector can be associated with a confidence interval in the original time series (IMU signals) and that elements sampled from different convolution blocks report dynamics of different durations.

For the first convolution block output, this analysis is trivial. As the convolution kernels of the first block are of width one, if the returned index of the min and/or max function is t, Equation (5) indicates that this element is related to a specific dynamics that occurred either during the $(2t)$th or $(2t + 1)$th time frame of the original time series (IMU signals). Unfortunately, the exact occurrence cannot be determined as pooling is not a bijective operation. Furthermore, as information gets sampled from the elements generated by deeper blocks, this uncertainty grows, but remains bounded, making it possible to determine a confidence interval for the sampled features.

In order to illustrate this process, let us take a look at Figure 4, which takes the previous example one convolution block deeper. For both convolution blocks, the first line refers to the block's input; the following is the result of the convolution layer; and the third is the result of the pooling layer. In order to simplify the analysis, the time step vectors only have one dimension, and batch normalization is omitted as it has no influence on the temporal traceability. As the second block's convolution filter has a width of three (i.e., $m_2 = 3$), if a feature is sampled from the second time series, X^2, with a relative position index of t, the corresponding dynamic consequently occurred between the $(4t)$th and the $(4t + 7)$th time steps of the original signal.

Generally speaking, knowing that the stride of the convolutions are set to one and the max pooling width is two, it is possible to determine the length of a certain feature based on the convolution block from which it was sampled.

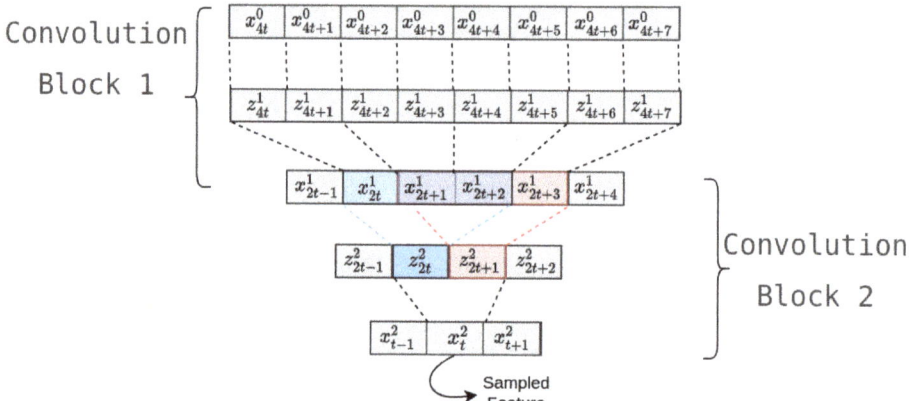

Figure 4. Temporal tracing of a feature of the second convolution block. The indexes correspond to those of Equation (10). The blue and red rectangles express the two different positions of the same convolution kernel of the second convolution block.

Defining D^l, m_l and E^l as the duration of the features, the width of the convolution filters and the temporal uncertainty caused by max pooling of the *l*th convolution block, it is possible to inductively calculate the duration of each convolution block feature using the following set of equations:

$$E^l = 2^{l-1}$$
$$D^1 = 1 \qquad (11)$$
$$D^l = D^{l-1} + E^{l-1} + (m_l - 1) \times 2^{l-1}$$

Consequently, the confidence interval, I, during which the dynamic of a certain feature occurred, can be expressed as:

$$I_t^l \in [t \times 2^l, t \times 2^l + D^l + E^l[\qquad (12)$$

Table 1 gives the relative duration, D, the relative uncertainty, E (both with respect to the original time step), and the real duration (knowing that the original signal was acquired at 30 Hz) based on the layer from which they were sampled and the width of the convolution filters specified by the proposed architecture.

Table 1. Characterisation of the uncertainty (E) and relative duration (D) of the sampled features based on the networks hyper-parameters (l) and (m).

Conv. Block (l)	Kernel Width (m)	Relative Duration (D)	Relative Uncertainty (E)	Feature Duration
1	1	1	1	0.033 s
2	3	6	2	0.2 s
3	5	22	4	0.73 s
4	7	70	8	2.33 s
5	4	118	16	3.93 s

5. Experiments

Using the publicly available UTD-MHAD dataset [21], which proposes a total of 27 different actions performed 4 times by eight different subjects (4 males and 4 females), this section will first demonstrate how our hierarchical framework makes our method robust towards zero-padding and that it is possible to train and infer on sequences of different lengths without impacting the performances. Then, we will assess the performances and compare them with state-of-the-art methods. Finally, we will conduct an analysis on the complexity of the method and see how it compares with some well-known CNN architectures.

Although it provides RGB, depth and skeleton streams, our experiments were conducted only on the inertial sensor signals, which were acquired from a single IMU worn on the right wrist for Actions 1 through 21 and on the right tight for Actions 22 through 27, as displayed in Figure 5. For all our experiments, the evaluation protocol suggested in the original UTD-MHAD paper [21] was followed, where odd subjects are for training and evens for evaluation, except in Section 5.2, which will additionally provide an assessment of the performances through a leave-one-out k-fold cross-validation protocol. In all cases, the experiments were performed using the PyTorch deep learning framework with stochastic gradient descent as the optimizer and a batch size of 16. The learning rate was initialized at 0.01 and decayed 1% per epoch. Weights were initialized using the Xavier method, and the bias of the classifier was initialized using a Gaussian distribution of mean 0 and variance 1.

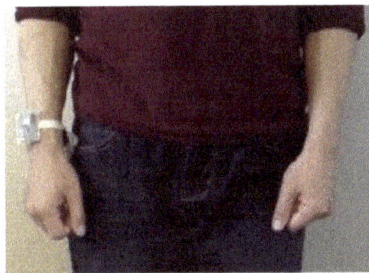
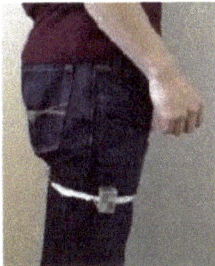

Figure 5. Wearable inertial sensor placements [21].

5.1. Robustness against Zero-Padding and Flexibility Towards the Input's Length

The idea behind our feature sampling method was to create a feature vector based on information sampled from multiple local signals instead of encoding the whole sequence into a feature vector. Hence, meaningless and/or redundant information such as zero-padding does not affect the feature vector, nor the classification performances. In order to validate this hypothesis, signals were extended up to various lengths with zero-padding. More precisely, training using sequences normalized up to 326, 700 and 1000 frames was conducted, for which the results are reported by Figure 6.

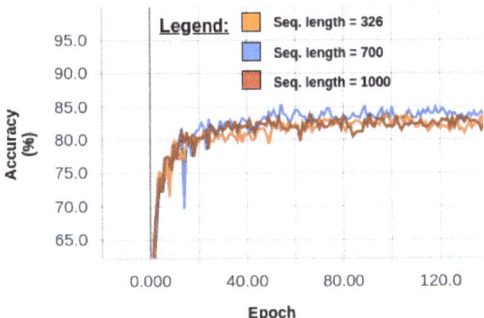

Figure 6. Learning curves assessing the accuracy obtained on the test set (Y axis) relative to the number of training epochs (X axis) for sequences (Seq.) zero-padded up to different extent.

As we can see, the performances are rather steady around 83% regardless of the amount of zero-padding added to the original sequence. This is an interesting result as Imran and Raman [9] previously conducted a 4-fold cross-validation analysis using only the subjects of the training set and observed that using the conventional CNN approach, where only the information encoded in the last layer is provided to the classifier, zero-padding the IMU signals of UTD-MHAD dataset caused the accuracy to decay by nearly 7%. More precisely, they transitioned from randomly sampled sequences of 107 time frames (which corresponded to the duration of the shortest action) to sequence zero-padded up to 326 time frames (which corresponded to the longest action). Intermediate lengths were also tested, where shorter sequences were zero-padded, while longer ones were randomly sampled. As observed on Table 2, their accuracy kept decreasing as the amount of zero-padding increased.

Table 2. Mean accuracy of the k-fold cross-validation analysis produced by Imran et al. [9] with respect to zero-padding on their 5 layer 1D-CNN.

Normalized Sequence Length	107	180	250	326
Max. Accuracy	83.99%	80.05%	78.42%	77.04%

Moreover, it was also observed that with our hierarchical method, it was possible to train the model using sequences of a certain length and proceed to classify sequences of a different length, which is impossible with the other CNN approaches. As a matter of fact, the parameters learned at the 100th epoch of the model trained with the sequence extended to 700 time frames (see Figure 6) resulted in an accuracy of 84.88%, which was also reproduced regardless of the testing examples being zero-padded up to 326 or 1000 time frames.

5.2. Performances

With our method, we obtained a maximal accuracy score of 85.35%, which resulted in the confusion matrix provided by Figure 7. As we can see, the performances were better on actions for which the inertial sensor was placed on the thigh rather than on the wrist.

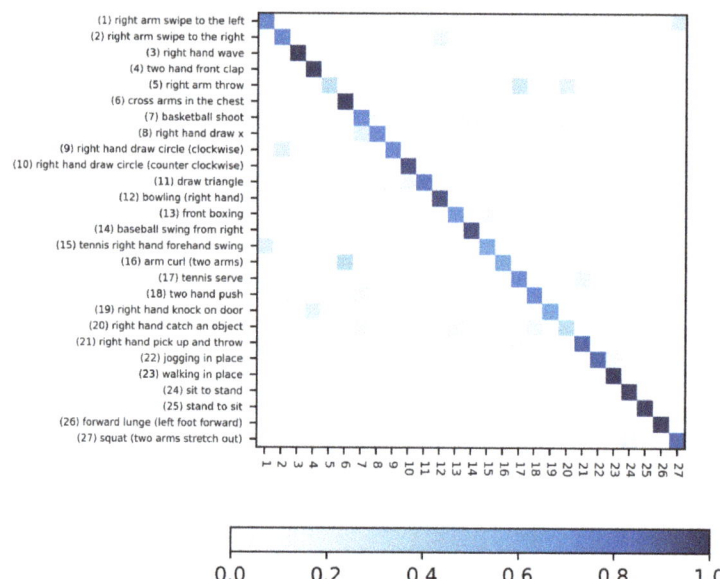

Figure 7. Confusion matrix obtained using the one-vs.-all discriminating approach.

In order to compare our result, we built Table 3, which indicates the accuracy of previous methods and the modality that they used in order to achieve it. Furthermore, we also report the performances on the NTU-RGB-D dataset for the methods that validated their approach on it using the cross-subject/cross-view evaluation protocol (CS/CV), as it is a well-established benchmark for HAR.

As we can see, our method is very competitive as it outperformed the current state-of-the-art using inertial data before it benefited from the data augmentation, which, in our case, was not implemented. Another important observation that can be made by taking a closer look at Table 3 is that the best overall performance was achieved by Imran and Raman [9] through a multi-stream fusion approach using inertial signals. Moreover, in the conclusion of their work, Imran and Raman argued that it was not only the complementarity between the different modalities that helped them achieve these results, but also the complementarity between the architecture treating the different data streams, thus further stressing the importance of 1D-CNN architectures.

Table 3. Comparison with the literature. CS/CV, cross-subject/cross-view.

Buffer Size	Modality	UTD-MHAD	NTU-RGB-D (CS/CV)
Chen et al. [21]	Inertial	67.20%	
Imran et al. [9] (w/o data augmentation)	Inertial	83.02%	
Imran et al. [9] (with data augmentation)	Inertial	86.51%	
Hussein et al. [22]	Skeleton	85.58%	
Wang et al. [23]	Skeleton	87.90%	76.32%/81.08%
Hou et al. [24]	Skeleton	86.97%	
Imran et al. [9]	Skeleton	93.48%	
Li et al. [25]	Skeleton	95.58%	82.96%/90.12%
Chen et al. [21]	Depth + inertial	79.10%	
Wang et al. [26]	Depth + skeleton	89.04%	
El Madany et al. [27]	Depth + Inertial + Skeleton	93.26%	
Imran et al. [9]	RGB + inertial + skeleton	97.91%	
Proposed method	Inertial	85.35%	

In order to compare the performances of our method against the one proposed by Wei et al. [28] that uses a 2D-CNN architecture applied to images generated from the IMU's signals, we also proceeded to the evaluation of the performances using a leave-one-out 8-fold cross-validation, for which the results are summarized by Table 4.

Table 4. k-fold validation on UTD-MHAD.

Test Subject	1	2	3	4	5	6	7	8
Accuracy	96.3%	89.8%	88.0%	90.7%	94.4%	91.6%	90.7%	85.1%

Computing the mean value of all these runs, we get a value of 90.8%, which is slightly better than the 90.3% obtained by Wei et al. [28].

5.3. Computational Complexity Analysis

As stated earlier, one of the greatest challenges currently faced by HAR algorithms is their portability to limited resource electronics; hence, we proceeded to do an analysis of the computational complexity and the number of parameters, which ended up demonstrating that our approach could be very easily integrated in limited resource electronics.

As a matter of fact, the number of operations needed by our model is directly correlated to the normalized length of the input sequence. As we can see in Figure 8, the relation is linear and is equal to 86.37 million multiply and accumulate (MAC) operations when the normalized length is equal to 326.

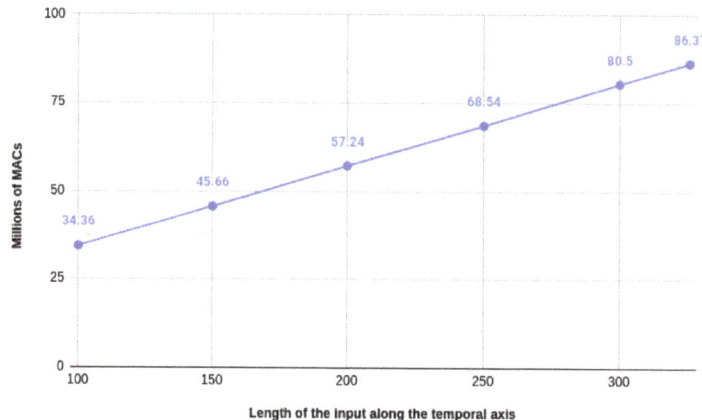

Figure 8. Learning curves assessing the accuracy obtained on the test set (Y axis) relative to the number of training epochs (X axis) for different amounts of zero-padding. MAC, multiply and accumulate.

Moreover, as our method is modular, the performance of each binary classifier can be studied independently. For that purpose, the precision and recall scores for each class are given by Figure 9.

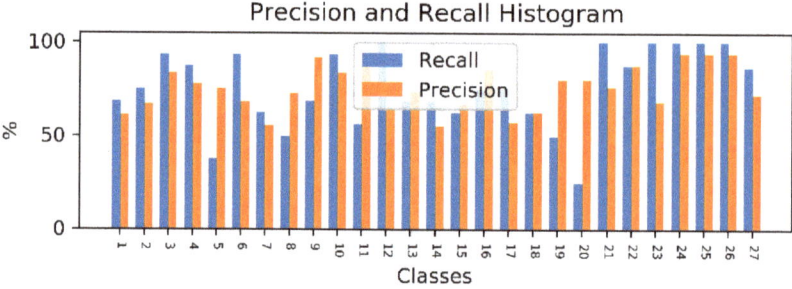

Figure 9. Histogram reporting the precision and recall score for each class.

Therefore, the number of operations and parameters can be divided by 27 in order to be integrated into a simple device only recognizing one action. In that case, the number of parameters would only be 343,830, which only takes about 1.4 MB of memory if the parameters are represented with single precision floating-point numbers, as was the case in our experiments. In the case of the number of operations, it comes down to about 3.2 million MACs. As MACs account for two floating point operations (one multiplication and one addition), if a processing unit has a throughput of 1 operation per clock cycle, a processing speed of only 3.2 MHz would be necessary in order to run our model under 1 s. As many inexpensive microcontrollers offer sufficient performances, this proves that our method could easily be embedded into smart devices. Finally, comparing our method with some of the most popular CNN architectures regarding the number of computations, on Figure 10 and the number of parameters on Figure 11, we can appreciate once more how hardware-friendly our method really is.

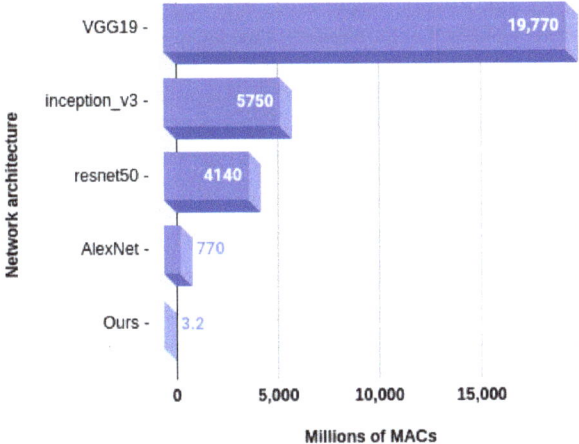

Figure 10. Number of computations needed by our model compared to popular CNN architectures.

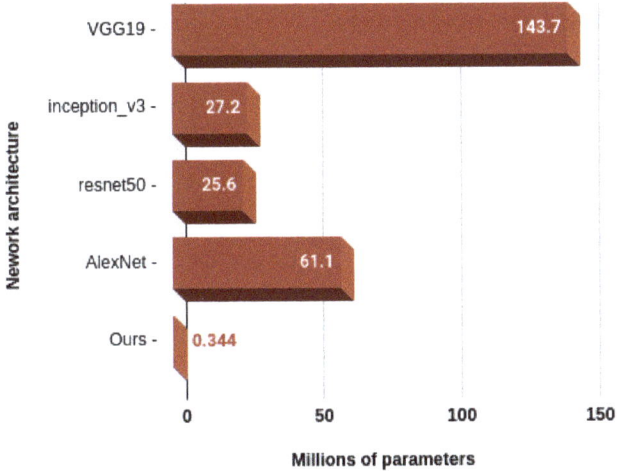

Figure 11. Number of parameters needed by our model compared to popular CNN architectures.

6. Discussion

In this paper, we presented a new framework based on a 1D-CNN architecture in order to perform action recognition on signals generated by IMUs. Although less accurate than methods using visual streams, this approach still has its advantages as it provides more privacy and can be used anywhere, as long as wearing the acquisition device does not become too inconvenient. Moreover, we demonstrated that our method is computationally inexpensive enough to be integrated into embedded devices. On another note, as the latent representation can be viewed as an organized set of elements assessing the presence of specific sub-events, the proposed method works in a hierarchical way. Yet, the temporal relationships between these sub-events are not captured implicitly or explicitly; thus, we believe that the proposed approach could help address the unsolved problem [29] of high-level action recognition with machine learning based methods as the difficulty that previous algorithms faced with this type of actions lies in the fact that they have important temporal variations between the sub-events composing them. This hierarchical approach also allowed us to infer on times series extended up to various lengths without compromising the accuracy.

Finally, we also demonstrated that the element of the latent representation can be traced in time, both in location and duration. In future work, we would like to investigate this ability further as we believe that it offers more transparency to the inner workings of the model by providing a way to interpret them. For example, this could be done by assessing if specific kernels are in fact reacting or not to discriminating movements based on the movements occurring in their confidence interval. On top of opening a window into the black-box of deep-learning algorithms, we believe that this approach could help reduce over-fitting and propose better architectures, tailored to specific actions, thus improving the overall performances.

Author Contributions: Conceptualization, N.L. and R.N.; methodology, N.L.; software, N.L.; validation, N.L. and R.N.; formal analysis, N.L.; data curation, N.L.; writing, original draft preparation, N.L.; supervision, R.N.; project administration, R.N.; funding acquisition, R.N. All authors read and agreed to the published version of the manuscript.

Funding: This research was funded by the Natural Sciences and Engineering Research Council of Canada, Aerosystems International Inc. and Prompt Quebec.

Conflicts of Interest: The authors declare no conflict of interest.

Abbreviations

The following abbreviations are used in this manuscript:

1D-CNN	One-dimensional convolution network
HAR	Human action recognition
IMU	Inertial measurement unit
IoT	Internet of Things
k-NN	k-nearest neighbour
LSTM	Long short-term memory
MLP	Multi-layer-perceptron
MAC	Multiply–Accumulate operation
ReLU	Rectified Linear Unit
RNN	Recurrent neural network
SeLU	Scaled exponential linear unit
SVM	Support vector machine
UTD-MHAD	University of Texas at Dallas-Multimodal Human Action Dataset

References

1. Nishida, T. Social intelligence design and human computing. In *Artifical Intelligence for Human Computing*; Springer: Berlin/Heidelberg, Germany, 2007; pp. 190–214.
2. Vermesan, O.; Friess, P. *Internet of Things-from Research and Innovation to Market Deployment*; River Publishers: Aalborg, Denmark, 2014; Volume 29.
3. Rautaray, S.S.; Agrawal, A. Vision based hand gesture recognition for human computer interaction: A survey. *Artif. Intell. Rev.* **2015**, *43*, 1–54. [CrossRef]
4. Shahroudy, A.; Liu, J.; Ng, T.T.; Wang, G. NTU RGB+D: A Large Scale Dataset for 3D Human Activity Analysis. In Proceedings of the IEEE Conference on Computer Vision and Pattern Recognition, Las Vegas, NV, USA, 27–30 June 2016.
5. Liu, J.; Shahroudy, A.; Perez, M.L.; Wang, G.; Duan, L.Y.; Kot Chichung, A. NTU RGB+D 120: A Large-Scale Benchmark for 3D Human Activity Understanding. *IEEE Trans. Pattern Anal. Mach. Intell.* **2019**. [CrossRef] [PubMed]
6. Wang, J.; Chen, Y.; Hao, S.; Peng, X.; Hu, L. Deep learning for sensor-based activity recognition: A survey. *Pattern Recognit. Lett.* **2019**, *119*, 3–11. [CrossRef]

7. Kwapisz, J.R.; Weiss, G.M.; Moore, S.A. Activity recognition using cell phone accelerometers. *Acm Sigkdd Explor. Newsl.* **2011**, *12*, 74–82. [CrossRef]
8. Weiss, G.M.; Lockhart, J. The Impact of Personalization on Smartphone-Based Activity Recognition. In Proceedings of the Workshops at the Twenty-Sixth AAAI Conference on Artificial Intelligence, Toronto, ON, Canada, 22–26 July 2012.
9. Imran, J.; Raman, B. Evaluating fusion of RGB-D and inertial sensors for multimodal human action recognition. *J. Ambient Intell. Humaniz. Comput.* **2020**, *11*, 189–208. [CrossRef]
10. Zeng, M.; Nguyen, L.T.; Yu, B.; Mengshoel, O.J.; Zhu, J.; Wu, P.; Zhang, J. Convolutional Neural Networks for human activity recognition using mobile sensors. In Proceedings of the 6th International Conference on Mobile Computing, Applications and Services, Austin, TX, USA, 6–7 November 2014; pp. 197–205.
11. Yang, J.; Nguyen, M.N.; San, P.P.; Li, X.L.; Krishnaswamy, S. Deep Convolutional Neural Networks on Multichannel Time Series for Human Activity Recognition. In Proceedings of the Twenty-Fourth International Joint Conference on Artificial Intelligence, Buenos Aires, Argentina, 25–31 July 2015.
12. Ronao, C.A.; Cho, S.B. Human activity recognition with smartphone sensors using deep learning neural networks. *Expert Syst. Appl.* **2016**, *59*, 235–244. [CrossRef]
13. Jiang, W.; Yin, Z. Human Activity Recognition Using Wearable Sensors by Deep Convolutional Neural Networks. In *Proceedings of the 23rd ACM International Conference on Multimedia*; Association for Computing Machinery: New York, NY, USA, 2015; pp. 1307–1310.
14. Murad, A.; Pyun, J.Y. Deep recurrent neural networks for human activity recognition. *Sensors* **2017**, *17*, 2556. [CrossRef] [PubMed]
15. Hammerla, N.Y.; Halloran, S.; Ploetz, T. Deep, Convolutional, and Recurrent Models for Human Activity Recognition using Wearables. *arXiv* **2016**, arXiv:cs.LG/1604.08880.
16. Ordóñez, F.J.; Roggen, D. Deep Convolutional and LSTM Recurrent Neural Networks for Multimodal Wearable Activity Recognition. *Sensors* **2016**, *16*, 115. [CrossRef] [PubMed]
17. Klambauer, G.; Unterthiner, T.; Mayr, A.; Hochreiter, S. Self-Normalizing Neural Networks. *arXiv* **2017**, arXiv:cs.LG/1706.02515.
18. Ioffe, S.; Szegedy, C. Batch Normalization: Accelerating Deep Network Training by Reducing Internal Covariate Shift. *arXiv* **2015**, arXiv:cs.LG/1502.03167.
19. Graham, B. Fractional Max-Pooling. *arXiv* **2014**, arXiv:cs.CV/1412.6071.
20. Aurelio, Y.S.; de Almeida, G.M.; de Castro, C.L.; Braga, A.P. Learning from Imbalanced Data Sets with Weighted Cross-Entropy Function. *Neural Process. Lett.* **2019**, *50*, 1937–1949. [CrossRef]
21. Chen, C.; Jafari, R.; Kehtarnavaz, N. UTD-MHAD: A multimodal dataset for human action recognition utilizing a depth camera and a wearable inertial sensor. In Proceedings of the 2015 IEEE International Conference on Image Processing (ICIP), Quebec City, QC, Canada, 27–30 September 2015; pp. 168–172.
22. Hussein, M.E.; Torki, M.; Gowayyed, M.A.; El-Saban, M. Human Action Recognition Using a Temporal Hierarchy of Covariance Descriptors on 3D Joint Locations. In Proceedings of the Twenty-Third International Joint Conference on Artificial Intelligence, Beijing, China, 3–9 August 2013.
23. Wang, P.; Li, W.; Li, C.; Hou, Y. Action Recognition Based on Joint Trajectory Maps with Convolutional Neural Networks. *arXiv* **2016**, arXiv:cs.CV/1612.09401.
24. Hou, Y.; Li, Z.; Wang, P.; Li, W. Skeleton Optical Spectra-Based Action Recognition Using Convolutional Neural Networks. *IEEE Trans. Circuits Syst. Video Technol.* **2018**, *28*, 807–811. [CrossRef]
25. Li, C.; Hou, Y.; Wang, P.; Li, W. Multiview-Based 3-D Action Recognition Using Deep Networks. *IEEE Trans. Hum. Mach. Syst.* **2019**, *49*, 95–104. [CrossRef]
26. Wang, P.; Wang, S.; Gao, Z.; Hou, Y.; Li, W. Structured images for RGB-D action recognition. In Proceedings of the IEEE International Conference on Computer Vision Workshops, Venice, Italy, 22–29 October 2017; pp. 1005–1014.
27. El Din El Madany, N.; He, Y.; Guan, L. Human action recognition via multiview discriminative analysis of canonical correlations. In Proceedings of the 2016 IEEE International Conference on Image Processing (ICIP), Phoenix, AZ, USA, 25–28 September 2016; pp. 4170–4174.

28. Wei, H.; Jafari, R.; Kehtarnavaz, N. Fusion of Video and Inertial Sensing for Deep Learning-Based Human Action Recognition. *Sensors* **2019**, *19*, 3680. [CrossRef] [PubMed]
29. Song, D.; Kim, C.; Park, S.K. A multi-temporal framework for high-level activity analysis: Violent event detection in visual surveillance. *Inf. Sci.* **2018**, *447*, 83–103. [CrossRef]

© 2020 by the authors. Licensee MDPI, Basel, Switzerland. This article is an open access article distributed under the terms and conditions of the Creative Commons Attribution (CC BY) license (http://creativecommons.org/licenses/by/4.0/).

MDPI
St. Alban-Anlage 66
4052 Basel
Switzerland
www.mdpi.com

Sensors Editorial Office
E-mail: sensors@mdpi.com
www.mdpi.com/journal/sensors

Disclaimer/Publisher's Note: The statements, opinions and data contained in all publications are solely those of the individual author(s) and contributor(s) and not of MDPI and/or the editor(s). MDPI and/or the editor(s) disclaim responsibility for any injury to people or property resulting from any ideas, methods, instructions or products referred to in the content.

www.ingramcontent.com/pod-product-compliance
Lightning Source LLC
LaVergne TN
LVHW070221100526
838202LV00015B/2069